The rough guide to FRANCE

KT-381-095

-The- rough guides

Other available Rough Guides include:
SPAIN, PORTUGAL, GREECE, YUGOSLAVIA, AMSTERDAM & HOLLAND, MOROCCO, TUNISIA, MEXICO and **PERU**

Forthcoming
PARIS, NEW YORK, CRETE, CHINA, KENYA, EASTERN EUROPE and **HALF THE EARTH: WOMEN'S EXPERIENCES OF TRAVEL**

Series Editor
MARK ELLINGHAM

Thanks for help, information and encouragement to Simon Schaffer, S D Saint Leger, J R E Hamilton-Baillie, Jean Llasera, Hossini Berrada, Oristelle Bonis, Rosi Braidotti, Willy Gaminara, Rosemary Bechler, Koral Island, Henri Yaouank, Paul and Paula Butler, Wendy Barker and Tony Stallard, Cathleen Griffin, Sue Dokins, Sarah Griffin, Daniel Coll and Sheila, Nicos Papadimitriou, Florica Kyriacopoulos, Peter Mills, John Fisher, Pauline Hallam, Gerry Dunham and all the many other people who helped along the way.

First published in 1986,
Reprinted 1986 & 1987
by Routledge & Kegan Paul Ltd.
11 New Fetter Lane, London EC4P 4EE
Published in the USA by
Routledge and Kegan Paul Inc.
in association with Methuen Inc.
29 West 35th Street, New York NY 10001

Phototypeset in Linotron Helvetica and Sabon
by Input Typesetting Ltd., London
Printed in Great Britain
by Cox & Wyman Ltd., Reading

Library of Congress Cataloging in Publication Data

Baillie, Kate

The rough guide to France
(The Rough guides)
Includes index.
1. France—Description and travel—1975—
Guide-books.   I. Salmon, Tim.   II. Sanger, Andrew.
III. Title.   IV. Series.
DC16.B195   1986   914.4′04927   85–25612
British Library CIP data also available

ISBN 0–7102–0438–8

The rough guide to
FRANCE

Written and researched by
KATE BAILLIE, TIM SALMON AND ANDREW SANGER

With additional research on Paris by
Richard Foltz

Maps by
CHRIS RICKETTS

Edited by

KATE BAILLIE AND TIM SALMON WITH MARK ELLINGHAM & MARTIN DUNFORD

Routledge & Kegan Paul
London and New York

CONTENTS

Part one BASICS

1

France: where to go and when / Getting there / Red tape and visas / Costs, money and banks / Health and insurance / Information and maps / Getting around / Sleeping / Food and drink / Communications – post, phones and media / Opening hours and holidays / Entertainment: music, cinema, theatre and festivals / Work and study / Police and thieves / Sexual and racial harassment / Other things / French and architectural terms: a glossary

Part two THE GUIDE

29

Part three CONTEXTS

471

Part one
BASICS

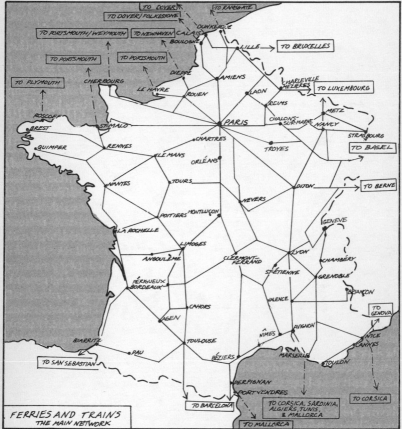

FERRIES AND TRAINS
THE MAIN NETWORK

FRANCE: WHERE TO GO AND WHEN

Chauvin was a Frenchman and no wonder. **France** is extraordinarily beautiful and diverse: its landscapes range from the fretted rocky coasts of Brittany to the limestone hills of Provence, the canyons of the Pyrenees to the Germanic picturesqueness of Alsace, the volcanic uplands of the Massif Central to the wide grain fields of Touraine, the wooded valleys of the Dordogne to the glacier-capped peaks of the Alps. Each region looks different, feels different, has its own style of architecture, its characteristic foods, often its own patois or dialect. And this strong sense of regional identity, sometimes expressed in the form of active separatist movements as in Brittany and Languedoc, has persisted for centuries in the teeth of centralised administrative control from Paris.

To the British eye the most striking feature of the French countryside is the space. There are huge tracts of woodland and undeveloped land without a house in sight. Industrialisation came late and the country remains very rural. Away from the main urban centres, hundreds of towns and villages have changed only slowly and organically, their old houses and streets intact, as much a part of the natural landscape as the rivers and hills and fields. Even if you confine your travelling to one particular region – which is the best way of getting to know the country – you get a powerful sense of the history and culture without having to seek out major sights. It is an ideal country for dawdling, and provides endless scope for all sorts of outdoor activities like walking, canoeing and cycling, to say nothing of the sophisticated fleshpots of the Mediterranean coast and the pleasures of eating and drinking exceptionally well, and for remarkably little.

Everywhere, there is an astonishing amount to see, from the Gothic cathedrals of the north (and south, for that matter), to the Romanesque churches of the centre and west, the châteaux of the Loire, the Roman monuments of the south, the ruined castles of the English and the Cathars and the prehistoric cave-paintings of the Dordogne. In the museums and galleries of Paris and numerous other cities unbeatable collections of paintings and objects illustrate every phase of French and European history and culture. Among the museums the French do best are those devoted to the rural arts and crafts of the regions, like the Basque museum in Bayonne and the Musée Dauphinois at Grenoble.

The people themselves are witty, humorous and sensual, with a great sense of style. One of the greatest pleasures of urban life, even in the north where the climate is similar to Britain's, is the outdoor life of the streets. In cafés, restaurants, markets and shopping centres people sit and talk and look and display.

As you go south, the **climate** becomes more and more Mediterranean, with short winters and long, hot, dry summers. In the west it is tempered by the nearness of the Atlantic. Though it is a great deal warmer than Britain, there are violent storms and thundery cloudy days in the summer months. The central and upland areas have a more extreme continental climate, with colder, snowy winters and hot summers. The Pyrenees and especially the Alps are snowbound from the end of October to May. It is a mistake to plan walking trips earlier than mid-June.

Another important factor to consider in deciding when to visit France is tourism itself. The main French **holiday period** is mid-July to the end of August, when almost the entire country except for those employed in tourism is on holiday. Since most French people – and what could be a better advertisement for the attractions of the country? – take their holidays in France, the resort areas get very crowded indeed. The seaside is worst, but mountains have become very popular too, especially the Alps. Hotels and campsites are full to bursting and prices are jacked up to take full advantage.

Average temperatures

	Jan	Mar	May	Jul	Sep	Nov
Lille (North)	5/0	10/3	15/9	23/12	19/12	9/3
Paris	6/1	12/4	18/12	25/14	20/13	10/4
Bordeaux (Aquitaine)	8/2	14/5	19/10	26/13	23/12	12/5
Montpellier (Languedoc)	11/2	15/5	20/12	28/17	24/15	14/6
Nice (Côte d'Azur)	12/4	15/7	20/13	26/19	25/17	16/8
Clermont-Ferrand (Massif Central)	7/−1	13/2	18/9	27/12	22/11	11/13
Dijon (Burgundy)	4/−1	12/2	16/10	26/13	20/12	9/3
Lyon	5/−1	12/3	18/11	27/14	22/13	11/3

Average sea temperatures

	May	June	July	Aug	Sep	Oct
Channel						
Calais to Le Havre	10	13	16	17	16	14
Cherbourg to Brest	11	13	15	17	16	14
Atlantic						
Brest to Bordeaux	13	15	17	18	17	15
Bordeaux to St-Jean-de-Luz	14	15	18	19	19	17
Mediterranean						
Montpellier to Toulon	15	19	19	20	20	17
Iles du Levant to Menton	17	19	20	22	22	19

All temperatures in **Centigrade** (C'); to convert to **Farenheit** multiply by 2 and add 30

For a recorded **weather forecast** you can phone the Paris forecasting office on 45.55.91.09 (45.55.95.02 for specific enquiries).

GETTING THERE

Train or coach
From London to Paris takes 5½–10 hours **by train** depending on the route you take and the type of Channel crossing you make. There are several Inter-City services every day. The **cheapest** – at £19 – is the night train, leaving Victoria at 8.40pm and arriving in Paris at 7.02 am.

If you're **under 26** you're entitled to buy the heavily discounted **B.I.G.E. tickets**, available in London from: *Euro-train* (operated by USIT, 52 Grosvenor Gdns, London SW1, 01-730 6525); *Transalpino* (71/75 Buckingham Palace Rd, London SW1, 01-834 9656; and offices all over Britain); or one of the larger student travel offices (see *Flights*, below). These can be booked from any station in Britain to any major station in Europe; they remain valid for two months and allow as many stopovers as you like along pre-specified routes (which can be different going out and coming home).

Again, if you're under 26 – or over 65 – you might consider an **Inter-Rail Card**, currently £119, and obtainable from British Rail and travel agents. This gives you a month's unlimited travel on all

European railways, plus half price discounts in Britain and on Channel ferries. Given the extensive and super-efficient nature of the French railways, this could be the best solution to your travel problems. The only restriction is, you need to have been resident in Europe for at least six months in order to be eligible. In theory this excludes most North Americans, though you'll find some travel firms don't stick too finely to the small print. The **EurRail Pass**, the official American alternative, is more expensive and does not cover travel in Britain. Although it is supposed to be bought outside Europe, you can get it in France at Paris airports and the Marseille, Nice and Paris-St-Lazare railway stations. Another pass to consider, which like these others has to be bought outside France, is **France Vacances Special**. Currently £94, it gives unlimited travel in France on any eight days during the course of one month, pluy two days' use of the Paris métro and buses.

Standard railway tickets – if you are over 26 and not a Senior Citizen – are bookable from most British Rail stations.

Paris is much the best first destination to head for, as it is the pivotal point of the rail network. The French Railways run an **Information Office** in Britain at 179 Piccadilly, London W1. 01-409 1224. There are British Rail offices in France at 12 bd de la Madeleine, 75009 Paris (266.90.53) and 33 rue de Tournai, 59043 Lille (06.29.44).

Coach services from London to Paris are operated by *Euroways* (01-730 8235), *Supabus* (01-730 0202 or any National Express depot) and *Hoverspeed* (01-554 7061). Journey time is 8 to 10 hours and the cost around £21. Euroways and Supabus serve other French destinations; for instance, Nice at £59 in 29 hours and Chamonix – via Geneva – at £43 in 22½ hours. These services are most frequent between 1 July and 15 Sept.

Driving or hitching

The best cross-Channel options for most drivers and hitch-hikers will be the **usual ferry links** between Dover and Calais (1¼ hrs) or Boulogne (1¾ hrs); Folkestone and Boulogne (1¾ hrs) and the Sally Line Ramsgate and Dunkerque (2½ hrs) – currently the cheapest. The much faster **Hoverspeed** crossings are worth considering for foot passengers,

as the difference in cost is only nominal. Driving time to Paris from any of these ports is about 3 hours by the Autoroute A1 or 4 hours on the toll-free N1.

If you come from the west of Britain or are heading for the west or south of France, by car or on foot, some of the **longer crossings** might be more convenient: from Newhaven to Dieppe (4 hrs); Portsmouth to Le Havre (5½ hrs), Cherbourg (4¾ hrs) or St-Malo (9 hrs); Weymouth to Cherbourg (4½ hrs); or, Plymouth to Roscoff (6 hrs) or Caen (5 hrs). There's a lot to be said for avoiding Paris, especially if you've got children, for you tend to arrive there about the time you want to be looking for a place for the night. And hitching from the Channel to Paris and then out again is a real headache nowadays – so much so that if you can possibly afford it you ought to get a train or coach ticket to somewhere beyond Paris. If you are coming **from Ireland**, *Brittany Ferries* operate services from Cork to Roscoff (13½–17 hrs) and *Irish Continental* from Cork to Le Havre (21½ hrs) and Rosslare to Cherbourg (17 hrs) and Le Havre (21 hrs).

Frequence of crossings vary enormously according to season. So too do **ticket prices**, which are also calculated by the size of car, number of passengers. Any travel agent will be able to provide up-to-date schedules and book you up in advance – definitely worth doing if you're driving.

For **coming back**, any major French travel agent will provide information about Channel crossings and handle bookings.

Going on from France, ferries leave Sète and Marseille for North Africa and various Mediterranean islands including Corsica (see p. 509).

Flights

Students – and anyone **under 26** – can take advantage of a range of special discount fares from London to France. The main destinations are Paris, Bordeaux, Toulouse, Montpellier, Marseille, Nice and Lyon, The best firms for these are mainly in London: *STA Travel* (at 74 Old Brompton Rd, SW7, 01-581 1022 and elsewhere) are particularly helpful and efficient; and there are always good deals at *USIT* (52 Grosvenor Gdns, SW1, 01-730 6525, and numerous branches in Britain and Ireland; see their *French Connection* leaflet), *WST* (39 Store St, WC1, 01-580 7733), and *Nouvelles Frontières* (1–2 Hanover St, W1, 01-629 7772).

There are few, cheap, ordinary charters, though Air France (London office: 158 New Bond St, W1, 01-499 9511) operates a wide range of **scheduled**

flights and run special offers from time to time.

From the United States or Canada you'll generally do better by flying first to London (on *Virgin Atlantic* or *People Express* from Newark for example) or perhaps to Luxembourg (cheap deals on *Icelandic Airways*) or Belgium (*Capitol* or *Metro*).

RED TAPE AND VISAS

At present, following 'temporary' legislation in 1986, everyone other than EEC nationals must have a **visa** to enter France. This position is liable to change, but check before leaving: last year dozens of Americans and Australasians were turned back at ferries and airports, without proper documentation. Visas can be obtained from any **French consulate.** Check their hours before turning up – and leave good time, since there are often queues.

If you are an **EEC national**, you need only your **passport** to enter France – and to stay for up to 90 days. The

British Visitor's Passport and the *Excursion Pass*, both obtainable over the counter at post offices, are valid. If you stay longer than three months, you are officially supposed to apply for a *Carte de Séjour*, for which you'll have to show proof of income at least equal to the current minimum wage. However, EEC passports are rarely stamped, so there is no evidence how long you've been in the country – and if your passport is stamped, cross the border, to Belgium or Germany for example, and re-enter for another 90 days legitimately.

COSTS, MONEY AND BANKS

France is not a cheap country to travel in, but nor is it wildly expensive. **Prices of food and accommodation** are slighly lower than in Britain. With the pound sterling at around 10F you can live well on £12–16; if you're into camping, walking and cycling, £10 is ample, including a restaurant meal a day, and if you buy your own food you could probably cut this in half. **Hotel rooms** can be found for 55–70F for a double, while the various types of **hostel** accommodation cost between 25 and 40F. Municipal **campsites** charge under 10F for one person and a small tent. **Eating out** is far cheaper and far better than in Britain or the US. Restaurants with three or four course menus between 55 and 65F are two a penny. Picnic and take-away food is cheap and excellent quality. Café eats and drinks are what make a hole in your pocket if you're not careful. Good ordinary table wine can be bought for well under £1 a litre, while at £2 you're getting something quite special. **Transport** will inevitably be a large item of expenditure if you move around a lot, which makes the Inter-Rail type of pass an attractive proposition for the restless. Local transport usually operates on a

flat rate, about 5F. Petrol costs around 25F a gallon – slightly less at autoroute self-service stations. Motorists should be wary of autoroutes: the tolls – at an average of 17 centimes per kilometre – soon mount up.

All of the above of course is affected by **where you are and when.** The big cities – Paris, especially – and popular tourist areas are invariably more expensive. Prices also directly reflect prime times, like July and August. And as always, if you're travelling alone you'll end up spending considerably more than you would in a group or couple – sharing rooms and food saves enormously. An **ISIC student card** is worth having; it'll get you into most museums and sites half price.

Banking hours are slightly unpredictable. In the main they are 8 or 9 am to 4 or 5 pm, Monday to Friday, with or without a lunch break from 12 until 2. Some open Saturday and close Monday. Nearly all close at noon on the eve of a public holiday. **Rates of exchange** and **commission** also vary from bank to bank. *BNP* (*Banque National de Paris* – not confined to Paris) offers the best exchange and takes the lowest commission.

Traveller's Cheques are the safest way of carrying your money. Some British banks issue special **'Eurocheques'** backed up with a card. With other banks, simply use your ordinary chequebook with a Eurocheque guarantee card (free). **Credit cards** are widely accepted. Just look out for the signs. The Visa/Barclaycard – known as the Carte Bleue in France – is almost universal. Access (Mastercard/Eurocard in France) comes a very poor second; only the *Crédit Agricole* and *Crédit Mutuel* banks will provide the cash advance facility for Access-holders. Also worth considering are post office **International Giro cheques**, which work in a similar way to ordinary bank cheques except that you can cash them through post offices – more common, especially out in the sticks, than banks and with longer hours.

HEALTH AND INSURANCE

Citizens of all **EEC countries** are entitled to take advantage of each other's **health services** under the same terms as residents of the country, if they have the correct documentation. So British citizens in France may expect to receive medical attention on the same terms as a French citizen, if they have with them Form E111. In theory you should apply for this on Form SA30 by post, one month in advance, to any DHSS office. In practice you can go along to any office with a Contributions counter – not a Supplementary Benefits counter – and have the counter clerk fill out a form for you on the spot.

According to DHSS explanatory leaflet SA36, you should post the whole lot plus your E111 to a local office of the *Caisse Primaire d'Assurance-Maladie* (sickness-insurance office). Be sure to keep a copy of everything . . . it's not unusual for the Caisse Primaire to 'lose' the papers of foreign applicants. A visit in person has no advantages. There are no on-the-spot payments – it can take a couple of months. There is a catch: parting with your E111 makes it impossible to visit a doctor again under the insurance scheme. The best thing is to make a note of the Caisse Primaire's address in that area, then hang on to the documents until the end of your visit.

Under the French Social Security system, every **hospital visit**, **doctor's consultation** and **prescribed medicine** is charged (though in emergency not upfront). Although all employed French people are entitled to a refund of 75–80 per cent of their medical expenses, this can still leave a hefty shortfall, especially after a stay in hospital. And getting your refund requires a complicated bureaucratic procedure which has to be followed to the letter.

A better idea is to take out ordinary **travel insurance**, which generally allows 100 per cent reimbursement, minus the first £5 or so of any claim. This is much more useful in the event of a serious accident. In France, accident victims have to pay even for the ambulance that takes them to hospital. North Americans and others will be well used to this and should ensure they have an insurance policy which covers health care abroad. Travel insurance also covers loss or theft of luggage, tickets, money etc., but remember that claims can only be dealt with if a report is made to local police within 24 hours and a copy of the report sent with the claim. Insurance **policies** can be taken out, on the spot, at just about any British bank or travel agent. *ISIS*, originally designed for students but now available to all, is a particularly good one – obtainable at any of the student-youth companies detailed under *Flights* (p. 5).

A **visit to a doctor** costs around 70F, if it is straightforward, and you will be given a *Feuille de Soins* (a signed statement of treatment). You should take any prescription to the *pharmacie*, where the medicines you buy will have little stickers (*vignettes*) attached to them, which you must remove and stick to your *Feuille de Soins*, together with the prescription itself. In **emergency**, the local hospital is usually the *Centre Hospitalier*; if desperate, and you know what's wrong, ignore the admissions and go straight to the relevant department to avoid bureaucratic delays. To call the **Police/Rescue service**, dial 17 or in Paris, *SAMU* (567.50.50) who offer urgent medical assistance. All **pharmacies**, too, are equipped, and obliged, to give first aid on request – though they'll make a charge.

INFORMATION AND MAPS

The French Government Tourist Office (in London at 178 Piccadilly, W1, 01-491 7622) gives away large quantities of glossily produced maps and pamphlets to do with every region of France, including lists of hotels and campsites. Don't cart the stuff with you; glossy paper is incredibly heavy. But use the handouts to supplement this guide during the planning stage.

Some principal FGTO offices abroad are:

AUSTRALIA	BWP House, 12 Castlereigh St, Sydney, NSW 2000 (612-231 5244).
CANADA	1840 Ouest rue Sherbrooke, Montreal, Quebec H3H 1E4 (514-931 3855); 1 Dundas St W, Suite 2405, (Box 8) Toronto, Ontario M5G 1Z3 (416-593 4717).
NETHERLANDS	Prinsengracht 670, 1017 KX Amsterdam (20-24 75 34).
SWEDEN	Nerrmalmstorg 1–511146, Stockholm (8-24.39-75).
USA	610 Fifth Avenue, New York, NY 10020 (212-757 1125); 646 N Michigan Avenue, Suite 630, Chicago, IL 60611 (312-337 6301); 9401 Wilshire Bvd, Beverley Hills, CA 90212 (213-272 2661); 360 Post St, San Francisco, CA 94108 (415-986461); World Trade Center no 103, 2050 Stemmons Freeway, (Box 58610) Dallas, TX 75258 (214-742 7011).

In France itself you'll find a **Synidcat d'Initiative (SI)** – or **office du Tourisme**, as they are sometimes called – in practically every town and many villages (addresses are detailed in the guide). From these you can get detailed local information, including listings of leisure activities, bike hire, laundrettes and countless other things. And always ask for the free town plan. Many SIs publish local car and walking itineraries for their areas. In mountain regions they often share premises with the local hiking and climbing organisers. They are often also willing to give advice about the best places to go in addition to just handing out paper. The regional tourist offices are administrative overseers rather than purveyors of useful practical information.

In addition to the various free leaflets – and this guide – the one extra you'll probably want is a reasonable **road map**. The *Michelin map no 989* is the best for the whole country. For more regional detail the Michelin yellow series (scale 1:200,000) is best for the motorist, but if you're not just driving check the *IGN maps* – their green (1:100,000), (1:50,000) and purple (1:25,000) series are unquestionably the best for cycling or walking. The IGN 1:100,000 is the smallest scale available with contours marked – essential for cyclists. Useful outlets, where you can obtain all these maps, include *Stanfords*, 12 Long Acre, London WC2, 01-836 1321; *McCarta*, 122 Kings Cross Rd, London WC1, 01-278 8278; *Roger Lascelles*, 47 York Rd, Brentford, Middx; *Map Shop*, 15 High St, Upton-on-Severn, Worcs; and *Heffers*, 3 Green St, Cambridge.

A useful free map for car-drivers, obtainable from filling stations and traffic information kiosks in France, is the *Bison Futé*, showing alternative back routes to avoid the congested main roads.

GETTING AROUND

With the most extensive railway network in western Europe, France is a country to travel by rail. The areas which are not well served are the mountains, both because of the ruggedness of the terrain and because there aren't many people, but often, where the train stops, an **SNCF** (the French rail company) bus carries on. The **private bus services** are confusing and uncoordinated. Where possible, it is very much simpler to use the SNCF. Approximate journey times and frequencies can be found in the **Travel Details** at the end of each chapter, and local peculiarities are also pointed out in the text of the guide.

Trains

SNCF trains are by and large clean, fast, stable and frequent, and their staff both courteous and helpful. All but the smallest stations have an information desk and *consignes automatiques* — coin-operated left-luggage lockers big enough to take a rucksack. Many (indicated in the text of the guide) hire out **bicycles**, often of rather doubtful reliability. **Fares** are reasonable, at an average — off-peak — of about 5p per kilometre. The ultra-fast *TGVs* (*Trains à Grande Vitesse*) require a supplement at peak times and compulsory reservation. The slowest trains are those marked *Autotrain* in the timetable, stopping at all stations. These are usually the only ones on which you can travel with a bike as free accompanied luggage — marked with a bicycle in the timetable. Otherwise you have to send your bike as registered luggage, which is quite safe and not expensive. Though it may well arrive in less time, the SNCF won't guarantee delivery in under five days.

While InterRail, EurRail and France Vacances **passes** are valid on all trains, the SNCF itself offers a whole range of **discount fares** on *Période Bleue* (blue period) days — in effect, most of the year. A leaflet showing the blue, white (smaller discount) and red (peak) periods is given out at *gares SNCF* (railway stations). **Under-26s** can buy a *Carte Jeune* for £10.50, allowing travel at half-fare on blue period days between 1 June and 30 September, including a free couchette on one journey. The *Carré Jeune* (same price) gives 50 per cent (blue) and 20 per cent (white) discounts on four journeys made during the year. **Married couples** can have a *Carte Couple*, at no cost, entitling one of them to a half-fare if they travel together off-peak. If you're **over 65**, there's a *Carte Vermeille*, for 57F, which gives you one year's half-price blue period travel. And any passenger buying a return ticket for a total distance of **over 1,000km**, and willing to start en periode bleue, can have a 25 per cent discount (*Billet Séjour*).

All tickets — but not passes — must be date-stamped in those orange machines that obstruct the entrance to station platforms. 'Compostez votre billet', they say, in French only. It is an offence not to. Rail journeys may be broken any time, anywhere, but after a break of 24 hours you must 'compost' your ticket again when you resume your journey. On night trains an extra 70F or so will buy you a **couchette** — well worth it if you're making a long haul and don't want to waste a day recovering from a sleepless night.

Regional **rail maps** and complete **timetables** are on sale at newsagents. Leaflet timetables for a particular line are available free at stations. *Autocar* at the top of a column means it's an SNCF bus service, on which rail tickets and passes are valid.

Buses

With the exception of SNCF services, **buses** play a generally minor role. They can, however, be useful for cross-country journeys. The most frustrating thing about them is that they never serve the regions no one else serves — which is precisely where you need them. Where they do exist in rural areas, the timetable is constructed to suit school kids and market days. They are cheaper and slower than trains.

Larger towns usually have a **gare routière** (bus station), often next to the gare SNCF. However, this is not always the case, for the private bus companies have difficulty coordinating their efforts. In some places not even the SI knows what they are up to.

Driving and hitching

Taking a car obviously gives you certain kinds of freedom you can't have otherwise, though it does have serious disadvantages, like isolating you from the country and its people. It'll cost more too, unless you camp, in which case it enables you to carry more equipment and be more self-sufficient. Car hire is not a sensible alternative, except on rare occasions, because of the cost — unless there are several of you to share it.

You'll need your driving licence; British, EEC or US are all acceptable. You should have your headlight dip adjusted to the right before you go — that's a legal requirement — and as a courtesy change (or paint) them to yellow. Garages are helpful, but not always familiar with British makes of car. If you have an accident or break-in, you should make a report to the local police (and keep a copy) in order to make an insurance claim.

Rules of the road are pretty much as in Britain, except for driving on the right. The one really important difference is that unless indicated to the contrary you must always give way to traffic coming from your right, even when it is coming from a minor road. This is the law of *Priorité à Droite*. In practice, except in town centres, there nearly always are 'indications to the contrary'. The main one is the yellow diamond roadsign, which tells drivers on main roads 'you have priority'. More crucial, a yellow diamond crossed out means you do not have priority. Signs saying *STOP* or *CÉDEZ LE PASSAGE* also mean you must give way.

For **Motorway** (autoroute) driving, call 1-705.90.01 (Mon–Fri 9–7) for up-to-the-minute information from the *Centre Renseignements Autoroutes*. Michelin's *Guide des Autoroutes* is also useful. Be wary of autoroute driving. It may be fast, but it is boring and the tolls are expensive. Use the *Bison Futé* free map (see p. 8), especially to avoid the tremendous jams that build up the first and last weekends of the August holiday and over the August 15 weekend.

Hitching, you'll have to rely almost exclusively on car drivers. Trucks very rarely give lifts. And it won't be easy. Unpalatable though you may find the idea, looking as clean, fresh, ordinary and respectable as possible makes a very big difference, as many a conversation with French drivers has made clear. Experience also suggests that hitching the less frequented D-roads paradoxically goes much quicker. In mountain areas a rucksack and hiking gear ensures an immediate lift from fellow aficionados. When leaving a city study the map to find a station on the road a few miles out and go there by train.

Autoroutes are a special case: hitching on the highway itself is strictly illegal, but you can make excellent speed going from one **service station** to another. If you get stuck at least there's food, drink, shelter. It again helps to have Michelin's *Guide des Autoroutes*, showing all the rest stops, service stations, tollbooths (péages),

exits, etc. All you need apart from that is a smattering of French and not too much luggage. Remember to get out at the service station before your driver leaves the autoroute. The tollbooths are a second best (it's legal). Ordinary slip-roads can be disastrous.

For **safer hitching** – and sexual harassment is as bad in France as Britain or the US – you could contact **Allostop**, a national organisation with offices in seventeen towns (Strasbourg, Bordeaux, Clermont-Ferrand, Rennes, Montpellier, Toulouse, Lille, Angers, Chôlet, Nantes, Angoulême, La Rochelle, Aix-en-Provence, Cannes, Paris, Grenoble, Lyon). You pay to register with them (150F per year or 40F for one trip) and they find a driver who's going your way and who'll take you along. You may be asked to contribute to petrol/autoroute expenses. The maximum is 16 centimes per km, say just over £10 for 500 miles. Allostop seems like a desperate measure and lacks spontaneity, but may be worth trying in some circumstances (local addresses are detailed in the guide). Similar organisations are: *Provoya* (47.70.28.59 in Paris); *Paris-Stop* (42.60.42.09 in Paris, 48.58.65.29 in Lyon); *Allauto* (20.54.15.27 in Lille); *SOS Depart* (42.27.52.18 in Aix, 91.62.70.46 in Marseille); *Télé-Stop* (61.52.21.37 in Toulouse); and *Auto-Contact* (55.44.33.68 in Bordeaux). There's a **free service** along the same lines in Le Havre (35.22.63.02), Limoges (55.77.53.53), and Poitiers (49.88.64.37).

Cycling and walking

Keen **cyclists** are much admired in France. The more professional you look, the warmer your welcome. Other traffic keeps at a respectful distance. Restaurants and hotels go out of their way to find a safe place for your bike, even letting you take it up to your room. Most large towns have well-stocked retail and repair shops, and bikes can be **hired** from most train stations and some tourist offices. Parts are cheaper than in Britain, but if you ride a British-made bike you should carry spare tyre and tubes, because French sizes are different. Equally, since most French cycling enthusiasm is directed to racing, you won't find parts for specialised low-gear machines.

Particular **regions** for cycle touring are the valleys of the Loire, Dordogne and Lot – not too hilly and full of interest, and from Strasbourg in Alsace southwest to Dijon and Beaune. Normandy and Brittany are ideal too, with an extensive network of minor roads to explore.

Many railway stations hire out bikes on a £20 deposit or more (detailed in the guide and a free SNCF leaflet – *Train et Vélo* – available from stations). But you'll be lucky to find a machine that is either completely reliable or the right size. Private bike shops – also detailed in the guide – are a better source and no more expensive.

Cross-Channel ferries take bikes free, as will British Air and Air France (unboxed, too), though you should contact them first. **Moving with your bike** on French trains is not as difficult as is sometimes reported (see *Trains* above). But since you can't just jump on any train, it is wise to keep long-distance train hops to a minimum.

The best **maps** are the contoured *IGN* 1:100,000 series. The *Cycle Touring Club*, Cotterell House, 68 Meadrow, Godalming GU7 3HS will suggest routes and supply advice for a small charge. *Cycle Touring in France* by Rob Hunter, (F. Muller Ltd, £4.95) is a useful handbook.

An alternative to setting up a cycling trip yourself is to try one of the **packaged cycling holidays**. *Susi Madron's Holidays with a Bicycle* (11 Norman Rd, Manchester M14 5LF, 061-224 7777) organise back-country rides in the Loire, Beaujolais, Jura, Camargue, etc. with accommodation and food included. The *Youth Hostel Association* also sell combined bike-hire and hostel packages: details from their main office at 14 Southampton St, London WC2 (01-836 8541).

Walkers are well served in France by a network of over 30,000km of waymarked long-distance paths, known as **sentiers de grande randonnée** – *GR* for short. Some are real marathons, like the GR5 from the coast of Holland to Nice, the trans-Pyrenean GR10 and the Grande Traversée des Alpes. The GR65 – the Chemin de St-Jacques – follows the ancient pilgrim route from Le Puy in the Auvergne to the Spanish frontier above St-Jean-Pied-de-Port and on to the shrine of Saint James (Santiago, St-Jacques) at Compostela. The GR3

traces the Loire from source to sea, and so on. Each path is described in a **Topoguide**, which gives a detailed account of the route, including maps, campsites, refuge huts, sources of provisions, etc. In addition many tourist offices can provide guides to their local footpaths, especially in popular hiking areas, where they often share premises with professional mountain guides and hike-leaders, who organise climbing and walking expeditions at all levels and open to all. The principal French walkers' organisation is the *Comité National des Sentiers de Grande Randonnée* (Paris office at 8 av Marceau).

Maps are listed under *Information and Maps*, but you might like to look at the specialised **walking maps** produced by *Didier et Richard* of Grenoble for the Alps. Hamlyn publish a general round-up of walking information in Rob Hunter's *Walking in France*, while Cicerone Press produce a number of English-language hiking and climbing guides: *Walks and Climbs in the Pyrenees* by Kev Reynolds, *The Tour of Mt Blanc* by Andrew Harper and *Walking the French Alps: GR5* by Martin Collins. Details of particular walks are given in the text of the guide.

Inland waterways

With some 7,500km of **navigable river and canal**, boating could be an unusually interesting way of exploring the French backwoods. Boats can be rented from British or French firms, if you don't have your own. There is no charge for use of the waterways, except on parts of the Moselle, and you can travel without a permit for up to six months a year. For details of permissible boat dimensions consult *Inland Waters of France* (Imray, 1984).

The principal **areas for boating** are Brittany, Burgundy, Picardy and Flanders, Alsace and Champagne. Brittany's canals don't really link up with the rest, but the others permit numerous permutations, including joining up via the Rhône and Saône, with the Canal du Midi in Languedoc. The 18C Canal de Bourgogne and 300-year-old Canal du Midi are fascinating examples of early canal engineering. The latter completely transformed the fortunes of coastal Languedoc, and in particular Sète, whose attractive harbour dates from that period. Together with its continuation, the Canal du Sète à Rhône, it passes within easy reach of several interesting areas.

The through-journey **from Channel to Mediterranean** requires some planning. The Canal de Bourgogne has an inordinate number of locks, while other waterways demand considerable skill and experience. The Rhône and Saône rivers, for instance, have difficult currents. The most direct route is from Le Havre to just beyond Paris, then south either on Canal du Loing et de Briare or Canal du Nivernais to the Canal Latéral de la Loire, which you follow as far as Digoin in southern Burgundy, where it crosses the river Loire and meets the Canal du Centre. You follow the latter as far as Chalon, where you continue south on the rivers Saône and Rhône until you reach the Mediterranean at Port St-Louis in the Camargue.

The French Government Tourist Office have plenty of **information** on river and canal boating, including a list of British rental companies. For a complete list of French companies, contact *Loueurs de Bâteaux de Plaisance*, Port de la Bourdonnais, 75007 Paris (45.55.10.49).

Skiing

Skiing – whether **downhill**, **cross-country**, or **mountaineering** – is enthusiastically pursued by the French. It can be an expensive sport to organise on your own, however, and the best deals are often to be had from package operators. These, you can arrange in France – most travel agents sell **all-in packages** – or before you leave. In Britain *Ski Magazine* is a good source of information and adverts. In France the umbrella organisation is the *Fédération Française de Ski*, 34 rue Eugène Flachat, Paris (47.64.99.39).

Broadly speaking, skiing is best in **the Alps**. The higher the resort the longer the season and the fewer anxieties you'll have about there being enough snow when you arrive. The highest are the purpose-built, modern ones: you put your skis on at the doors of the hotel lift. Great for full-time skiing, but they don't have the cachet, charm (not too much left, it has to be said) or the night-life of the older resorts like Megève and Courchevel. **The Pyrenees** are friendlier mountains, less developed – though that is not necessarily an advantage if you want to get in as many different runs as possible per day – and warmer, which means more problems with the snow.

Cross-country (*ski de fond*) is being promoted hard, especially in the smaller ranges like the Jura and Massif Central. At a basic level it's an easier sport for the less athletic and stiff-jointed, and, for the really experienced and fit, using snowbound GR routes you can substitute a fixed resort by relatively uncommercialised village stops. Alternatively, if you want to go for the real big time, the *Plas y Brenin Centre for Mountain Activities* (Capel Curig, Betws-y-Coed, Gwynedd, Wales) organise summertime **ski-mountaineering** courses in the Alps, including doing parts of the High Level Route.

Planes

The main **internal airline** is *Air Inter*, though there are lots of small provincial based companies. You could in theory fly to practically anywhere, but there is little point when you can travel about by train both more cheaply and, sometimes, quicker.

SLEEPING

We have incorporated suggestions about cheap places to stay under most of the destinations listed in this guide. The Paris chapter has particularly extensive listings, so you should look there for information about Paris.

Hotels, hostels, foyers and gîtes

There should be no difficulty **finding hotel rooms** outside the 15 July–30 August peak holiday period. There are thousands of simple, inexpensive hotels scattered all over the country. A good place to start looking in towns is around the railway station. The local SI will help with lists of accommodations, and may even make a booking for you, usually for a small fee. To book a hotel in France before you go, simply write or phone, if your French is good enough; or, ask the FGTO for their bilingual booking form and any assistance you need.

Since hotel **prices** go by the room, not the number of guests, double rooms (around 60–70F) work out much better value than singles (around 55F). A reliable chain of unpretentious provincial hotels are those run by the **Logis et Auberges de France** organisation, which puts out a handbook listing its establishments (around 4½ thousand) – free from FGTO. **Relais Routiers** – truck stops – often have low-priced rooms above their restaurants; their English-language handbook is sold (£4.95) by Routiers Ltd, 354 Fulham Rd, London SW10.

Hotels are **graded** by stars according to no very obvious criteria. Most of those with no star at all are perfectly adequate – particularly in country districts. Room prices must be displayed at reception and in the room itself – on the back of the door, usually. There is normally no need to take dinner in the hotel restaurant, though in resort areas in summer you may find you can't get anything without at least demi-pension. There is no need to take the hotel breakfast either.

The best cheap accommodation in towns is often the **youth hostel** (*Auberge de Jeunesse*). Though you are meant to be a member of the YHA (main office in Britain at 14 Southampton St, London WC2), you can often join on the spot. The cost is around 26F. Some have canteens and other facilities. All have kitchens where you can prepare your own meal. There are two Youth Hostel organisations and they are not on speaking terms with each other. Only one, the *Fédération Unie des Auberges de Jeunesse* (6 rue Mesnil, 75116 Paris), has its hostels listed in the International handbook. But YHA membership entitles you to use the rival hostels just as well, so get their leaflet of addresses: *Ligue Française pour les Auberges de Jeunesse*, 83 rue de Rennes, 75006 Paris.

A superior – indeed, sometimes luxurious – type of hostel accommodation available to YHA members in some larger towns are the **Foyers des Jeunes Travailleurs/Travailleuses**. These are residential hostels for young workers and students. The cost is around 35F, but for that you usually get an individual room. They nearly always have a good cafeteria canteen.

A third hostel-type alternative in country – especially hiking or cycling areas – are the very basic **gîtes d'étape**, providing bunk beds and primitive kitchen and washing facilities. They are marked on the large scale walkers' maps and listed in the GR *Topo-guides* – also in a booklet called *Accueil à la Campagne*, sold for £4 by the FGTO (though the list is not complete).

Mountain areas are also well supplied with **mountain refuge huts**, not normally open before the beginning of June. Though they mostly belong to the *Club Alpin Français*, you do not have to be a member of any club to use them. Cost is around 38F – less for members of affiliated climbing clubs.

A further possibility are the **chambres d'hôte** – country B & Bs in someone's house, but they cost almost as much as a cheap hotel. These too, along with gîtes d'étape and campings à la ferme, are listed in *Accueil à la Campagne*.

Camping

Practically every village and town in the country has at least one **campsite**, to cater for the thousands of French people who spend their summer holiday under canvas. The cheapest are the **Camping Municipal**, run by the local municipality: out of season many of them don't even bother to have someone around to collect the overnight charge – under 10F for one person and small tent. In season or when they are officially open, they are always clean with plenty of hot water. And they are often beautifully sited beside a river. There are **superior categories** of campsite, but with these you can pay a lot more money for facilities like swimming pools – of little interest to overnighters. In popular areas, however, remember that any campsite gets very full in summer; on the Côte d'Azur you need to reserve your emplacement a year ahead.

Camping à la ferme – on somebody's farm – is another possibility. It is usually more primitive, and not any cheaper. These sites too are listed in *Accueil à la Campagne*.

And, finally, a word of caution: you should never **camp rough** (*camping sauvage*) on anyone's land without asking permission first. Farmers have been known to shoot before asking questions.

FOOD AND DRINK

To eat **French food** is as good a reason for a visit to France as any other. Cooking has art status, the top chefs are stars and dining out is a national pastime, whether it's at the bistro on the corner or at a famed house of haute cuisine. Eating out doesn't have to cost much as long as you avoid tourist hotspots and treat the business of choosing a place as an interesting appetiser in itself.

Bars and cafés
Bars and cafés – there's no difference – commonly advertise *les snacks*, or *une cassecroute* (a bite), with pictures of omelettes, fried eggs, hot dogs or various sandwiches. And even when they don't they'll usually do you a half or third of a *baguette* (French bread stick), buttered (*tartine*) or filled with cheese or meat. This, or a croissant, with hot chocolate or coffee, is generally the best way to take **breakfast** – at a fraction of the cost charged by most hotels. In larger cities a further dimension is added by **salons de thé** – tea rooms – which often open mid morning and serve some kind of brunch. Currently trendy, however, they're on the whole pricier places to eat – and best later on in the day for fruit and China teas.

At **street stalls** you'll find many of the snacks available in bars, along with *crêpes*, *galettes* (fatter pancakes), *gaufres* (waffles), *frites* (chips) and *merguez* (North African spicy sausage); roving **vans** that stop by the roadside, in parks, main squares or alongside beaches, can also be depended on for *frites*, stuffed *baguettes*, sometimes omelettes. More inspired cold takeaways of prepared meats, salads, cheese and fully prepared main dishes are sold in **charcuteries** and large supermarkets. You buy by weight or you can ask for *une tranche* (a slice), *une barquette* (a carton) or *une part* (a portion).

Typical snacks, fillers and takeaways include:

Un sandwich/	a sandwich. . .
une baguette. . .	
. . . beurrée	buttered
. . . jambon	with ham
de Bayonne	smoked
. . . fromage	with cheese
. . . saucisson	with sausage
à l'ail/au poivre	garlic/pepper
. . . pâté, terrine	with pâté
de campagne	farmhouse
Croque-Monsieur	toasted cheese and ham sandwich
Croque-Madame	toasted cheese and bacon or sausage
Oeufs au plat	fried eggs
Oeufs à la coque	boiled eggs
Oeufs durs	hard-boiled eggs
Oeufs brouillés	scrambled eggs
Omelette . . .	omelette . . .
. . . nature	plain
. . . aux fines herbes	with herbs
. . . au fromage	with cheese
Crêpe . . .	pancake . . .
. . . au sucre	with sugar
. . . au citron	with lemon
. . . au miel	with honey
. . . à la confiture	with jam
. . . aux oeufs	with eggs
. . . à la crème de marrons	with chestnut purée
Carottes rapées	salad of grated carrots
Salade de tomates/ betteraves/ concombres . . .	tomato/ beetroot/ cucumber . . . salad

Other fillings/salads: *Anchois* – anchovy; *Andouillette* – tripe sausage; *Boudin* – black pudding; *Coeurs de palmiers* – palm hearts; *Epis de maïs* – sweetcorn; *Fonds d'artichauts* – artichoke hearts; *Hareng* – herring; *Langue* – tongue; *Poulet* – chicken; *Thon* – tuna fish. *AND SOME TERMS*: *Chauffé* – heated up; *Cuit* – cooked; *Cru* – raw; *Emballé* – wrapped up; *A Emporter* – takeaway; *Fumé* – smoked; *Salé* – salted/savoury; *Sucré* – sweet.

More serious business
Restaurants call themselves by a bewildering variety of terms: **auberges**, **brasseries**, **relais** or just plain **restaurants**. The main distinction is between brasseries – which do quick (but not necessarily cheap) meals at most hours of the day – and the rest, which stick to traditional **meal times** of around 12–2 and 7–9.30. Eating out at night it's wise not to go later than this or

you'll find what few places are open will serve meals only *à la carte* – invariably more expensive than eating the set *menu fixe*. And hunting out for places, don't forget **hotels** (always open to non-guests and sometimes the only option in small towns), **pizzerias** and **crêperies**. Self-service **cafeterias** exist too, and are useful at odd hours, but they're not exactly renowned for quality. On the road the chain of **Relais Routiers** 'truck-stops', all of them detailed in the Routiers handbook (see p. 13), are the best bet, cheap and reliable.

In theory all restaurants display their **menus** outside – if they don't they probably have a small local clientèle (generally a good sign). You are almost always offered a choice of one or more set meals – the **menus fixes** – and if you want the full works this is invariably a good deal. **Wine** (*vin*) or a drink (*boisson*) are often included in the price of a set meal, as sometimes is service: look for the word *compris* (inclusive); if you see *en sus*, *non compris* or no mention then you'll be paying extra. *TTC* means tax included. There is generally no minimum charge: if you decide to eat *à la carte* you can share a dish or just have starters, a useful strategy for vegetarians.

Restaurant dishes* vary enormously from region to region – the lists below are far from comprehensive – but there are certain standards like steak and chips (*steak frites*) or chicken and chips (*poulet frites*) that tend to dominate the set meals. Try not to get stuck with these: there's nearly always a *plat du jour*, the chef's daily special, and your first restaurant move should normally be to ask what it is and if it's still available. 'J'aimerais une comme ça' – I'd like one like that – can also be a rewarding phrase. In the French sequence of **courses** any salad (sometimes vegetables, too) comes separate from the main dish; cheese precedes dessert; and you will always be offered a coffee to finish (never *compris*). Ordering wine,

ask for *un quart* (¼), *un demi-litre* (½) or *une carafe* (a litre). You'll normally be given table wine unless you specify otherwise; if you're worried ask for *vin ordinaire*.

Soups (*Soupes*)

Bisque	Shellfish soup
Bouillabaisse	Marseillaise fish soup
Bouillon	Broth or stock
Bourride	Thick fish soup
Consommé	Clear soup
Pistou	Parmesan, basil and garlic paste sometimes added to soup
Potage	Thick soup, usually vegetable
Rouille	Red pepper, garlic and saffron mayonnaise served with fish soup
Velouté	Thick soup, usually fish or poultry

Starters (*Hors d'Oeúvres*)

Assiette anglaise	Plate of cold meats
Crudités	Raw vegetables with dressings
Hors d'oeuvres variés	Combination of the above plus smoked or marinated fish

Fish (*Poisson*), Seafood (*Fruits de mer*) and Shellfish (*Crustaces or Coquillages*)

Anchois	Anchovies
Anguilles	Eels
Araignée de Mer	Spider Crab
Barbue	Brill
Brème	Bream
Cabillaud	Fresh Cod
Calamares	Squid
Carrelet	Plaice
Congre	Conger Eel
Coques	Cockles

*The current gourmet trend in French cooking has abandoned rich creamy sauces and bloating helpings, concentrating instead on the intrinsic flavours of foods and new combinations where the mix of the colours and textures complements the tastes. The courses are no more than a few mouthfuls, presented with oriental artistry and finely judged to leave you at the end well-fed but not weighed down. Known as **nouvelle cuisine**, this at its best can induce gastronomic ecstasy from an ungarnished leek or carrot. What it does to salmon, lobster or a wild strawberry pastry elevates taste sensation to the power of sound and vision. But alas since this magical method of cooking requires absolutely prime and fresh ingredients and precision skills in every department, *nouvelle cuisine* meals are usually horrendously expensive.

Coquilles St-Jacques	Scallops	Boeuf	Beef
Crabe	Crab	Bifteck	Steak
Crevettes Grises	Shrimps	Caille	Quail
Crevettes Roses	Prawns	Canard	Duck
Daurade	Sea Bream	Caneton	Duckling
Ecrevisse	Freshwater Crayfish	Cervelle	Brains
Escargots	Snails	Châteaubriand	Porterhouse steak
Friture	Assorted small fried fish	Contrefilet	Sirloin roast
		Coquelet	Young coquerel
Gambas	King Prawns	Dinde, Dindon, Dindonneau	Turkey, different ages and genders
Grenouilles (cuisses de.)	Frogs (legs)	Entrecôte	Ribsteak
		Faux filet	Sirloin steak
Hareng	Herring	Foie	Liver
Homard	Lobster	Fraises de veau	Veal testicles
Huîtres	Oysters	Fricadelles	Meatballs
Langoustes	Sea Crayfish	Gigot (de)	Leg of lamb (leg of another meat)
Langoustines	Dublin Bay Prawns (what scampi comes from)	Grillade	Grilled meat
		Hâchis	Minced meat or Hamburger
Limande	Lemon sole	Langue	Tongue
Lotte	Burbot	Lapin, Lapereau	Rabbit, young rabbit
Lotte de Mer	Monkfish		
Loup de Mer	Sea Bass	Lard, Lardons	Bacon, diced bacon
Maquereau	Mackerel		
Merlan	Whiting	Lièvre	Hare
Morue	Salt Cod	Mouton	Mutton
Moules (marinières)	Mussels (with shallots in wine sauce)	Oie	Goose
		Os	Bone
		Porc, Pieds de Porc	Pork, pig trotters
Palourdes	Clams	Poulet, Poulette, Poussin	Chicken, young chicken, baby chicken
Praires	Small clams		
Raie	Skate		
Rouget	Red Mullet	Ris	Sweetbreads
Saumon	Salmon	Rognons	Kidneys
Sole	Sole	Rognons blancs	Testicles
Thon	Tuna	Sanglier	Wild Boar
Truite	Trout	Steack	Steak
Turbot	Turbot	Tortue	Turtle
		Tournedos	Fillet steak

Terms: Aïoli – garlic mayonnaise served with salt cod and other fish; Béarnaise – sauce made with egg yolks, white wine, shallots and vinegar; Beignets – fritters; La douzaine – the dozen; Frit – fried; Grillé – grilled; Hollandaise –, butter and vinegar sauce; À la meunière – in a butter, lemon and parsley sauce; Mousse/mousseline – mousse; Plateau de – plate of; Quenelles – light dumplings; Tourte – flan.

Tripes	Tripe
Veau, Tête de Veau	Veal, calf's head
Venaison	Venison

Boeuf bourguignon	Beef stew with Burgundy wine, bacon, onion and mushrooms
Canard à l'orange	Roast duck with an orange and wine sauce
Canard périgourdin	Roast duck with prunes, pâté de foie gras and truffles
Cassoulet	A casserole of beans and meat
Choucroute	Pickled cabbage with peppercorns,

Meat (Viande) and Poultry (Volaille)

Agneau	Lamb
Agneau de pré-salé	Lamb grazed on salt pastures

	sausages, bacon and salami
Coq au vin	Chicken cooked till it falls off the bone in a mixture similar to *Boeuf bourguignon*
Steack au poivres (verts/rouges)	Steak in a black (green/red) peppercorn sauce.
Steack tartare	Raw minced beef usually accompanied by a raw egg

Terms: *blanquette, daube, estouffade, hochepôt, navarin* and *ragoût* all mean stew
aile – wing; *blanc* – breast or white meat; *carré* – best end of neck chops or cutlets; *côte* – chop or cutlet; *cou* – neck; *épaule* – shoulder; *médaillon* – round piece; *pavé* – thick slice. For steaks: *bleu* – almost raw; *saignant* – rare; *à point* – medium; *bien cuit* – well done; *très bien cuit* – utterly cooked *brochette* – kebab; *en croûte* – in pastry; *farci* – stuffed; *au four* – baked; *garni* – with vegetables; *grillé* – grilled; *mijoté* – stewed; *quenelles* – light dumplings; *rôti* – roast; *sauté* – lightly cooked in butter; *tourte* – flan

Garnishes and sauces: *beurre blanc* – melted butter, vinegar and seasoning; *chasseur* – white wine, mushrooms and shallots; *diable* – strong mustard seasoning; *forestière* – with bacon and mushroom; *fricassée* – rich, creamy sauce; *mornay* – cheese sauce; *piquante* – gherkins or capers, vinegar and shallots; *provençale* – tomatoes, garlic, olive oil and herbs; *véronique* – grapes, wine and cream

Vegetables (Légumes), Herbs (Herbes) and Spices (Epices), etc.

Ail	Garlic
Aneth	Dill
Anis	Aniseed
Artichaut	Artichoke
Asperges	Asparagus
Aubergine	Aubergine, Eggplant
Avocat	Avocado pear
Basilic	Basil (almost always fresh)
Betterave	Beetroot
Cannelle	Cinnamon
Carottes	Carrots
Céleri-rave	Celeriac
Céleri	Celery
Champignons (de bois), (de Paris) cèpes, chanterelles, girolles, grisets, mousserons . . .	Mushrooms and some of the different kinds
Chou (rouge)	(Red) cabbage
Choufleur	Cauliflower
Ciboulettes	Chives
Citrouille	Pumpkin
Concombres	Cucumber
Courgettes	Courgettes, baby marrows
Cresson	Water cress
Echalotes	Shalots
Endive	Chicory
Epinards	Spinach
Epis de maïs	Sweet corn
Estragon	Tarragon
Fenouil	Fennel
Fèves	Broad beans
Flageolet	White beans
Frisée	A frizzy type of lettuce
Gingembre	Ginger
Haricots (verts, rouges, blancs, beurres)	(French, kidney, white, butter) beans
Lentilles	Lentils
Mangetout	An 'eat-all' bean
Marjolaine	Marjory
Menthe	Mint
Moutarde	Mustard
Oignon	Onion
Oseille	Sorrel
Persil	Parsley
Petits pois	Peas
Pignons	Pine nuts
Pissenlits	Dandelion leaves
Poireaux	Leeks
Poivrons	Sweet peppers
Pommes (de terre)	Potatoes
Radis	Radishes
Riz	Rice
Romarin	Rosemary
Safran	Saffron
Salade verte	Lettuce salad
Tomates	Tomatoes
Truffes	Truffles (underground fungi)

Gratin dauphinois Potatoes baked in cream and garlic
Pommes Château/fondantes Quartered potatoes fried in butter
Pommes lyonnaise Fried onions and potatoes
Ratatouille Mixture of aubergines, courgettes, tomatoes, garlic
Rémoulade A mustard mayonnaise
Salade niçoise Salad of tomatoes, radishes, cucumber, hard-boiled eggs, anchovies, onions, artichokes, green peppers, beans, basil and garlic (but rarely as generous, even in Nice).

Terms: *à l'anglaise* – boiled; *farci* – stuffed; *gratiné* – browned on top with cheese or butter; *jardinière* – with a mixture of diced vegetables; *parisienne* – with leeks and potatoes; *parmentier* – with potatoes; *primeurs* – early vegetables; *sauté* – lightly fried in butter; *tourte* – flan; *à la vapeur* – steamed

Je suis végétarien(ne). Il y a quelques plats sans viande? – I'm a vegetarian. Are there some non-meat dishes?

Fruits (*Fruits*)

Abricots	Apricots
Amandes	Almonds
Ananas	Pineapple
Banane	Banana
Brugnon, nectarine	Nectarine
Cantaloup	Round, green melon, orange inside
Cassis	Blackcurrant
Cerises	Cherries
Citron	Lemon
Citron Vert	Lime
Dattes	Dates
Figues	Figs
Fraises	Strawberries
Fraises de bois	Wild strawberries
Framboises	Raspberries
Fruit de la Passion	Passion fruit
Grenade	Pomegranite
Groseilles	Red currants and gooseberries
Marrons	Chestnuts
Melon	Melon
Mirabelles	Yellow plums
Myrtilles	Bilberries
Noix	Nuts

Oranges	Oranges
Pamplemousse	Grapefruit
Pastèque	Water melon
Pêche (blanche)	(White) peach
Poire	Pear
Pomme	Apple
Prune	Plum
Pruneau	Prune
Raisins	Grapes
Rhubarbe	Rhubarb

Terms: *beignets* – fritters; *compôte* – stewed; *corbeille de fruits* – fruit basket; *coulis* – sauce; *flambé* – set alight in alcohol; *frappé* – iced; *sorbet* – water ice.

Desserts (*Desserts* or *Entremets*) and Pastries (*Patisserie*)

Bombe	An ice cream dessert made in a round or conical mould
Bonbons	Sweets
Brioche	Sweet, high yeast bread
Clafoutis	Fruit flan, usually with berries
Crème Chantilly	Vanilla flavoured and sweetened whipped cream
Crème patissière	Thick cream made with eggs
Crêpes suzettes	Pancakes with orange juice and liqueur
Fromage blanc	Cream cheese more akin to strained yoghurt
Glace	Ice cream
Ile flottante or *Oeufs à la neige*	Soft meringues floating on custard
Macarons	Macaroons, not necessarily almond
Madeleine	Small sponge cake
Marrons Mont Blanc	Chestnut purée and cream on a rum soaked sponge cake
Palmiers	Caramelised puff pastries
Parfait	Frozen mousse, sometimes just ice cream
Paris-Brest	Pastry cakes filled with crème patissière

Pêche Melba	Cooked peaches, vanilla ice cream and a raspberry sauce
Petit Suisse	A smooth mixture of cream and curds
Petits fours	Mouth-sized cakes or pastries
Poires Belle Hélène	Pears and ice cream in chocolate sauce
Religieuse	Coffee or chocolate coated choux pastry puffs, supposedly in the shape of a nun
Yaourt	Yoghurt

and many, many more . . . .

Terms: *Bavarois* – refers to the mould, could be a mousse or custard cream; *biscuit* – a kind of cake; *chausson* – pastry turnover; *coupe* – a serving of ice cream; *crêpes* – pancakes; *galettes* – biscuits or pancakes; *génoise* – rich sponge cake; *quatre quarts* – type of sponge cake; *sablé* – sort of biscuit; *savarin* – in a ring-shaped mould; *tarte* – flan; *tartelette* – small flan; *barquette* – small, boat shaped flan; *truffes* – truffles, the chocolate or liqueur variety

Cheese (*Fromage*)

There are over 350 types of cheeses in France, most of them named after their place of origin. *Chèvre* is goats cheese, *le plateau de fromages* is the cheese-board and bread, but not butter, is served with it. Some useful phrases: *une petite tranche de celui-ci* (a small piece of this one); *Quels sont les fromages de la région?* (which are the local cheeses?) *Je peux le gouter?* (May I taste it?).

Basics

Bread	Pain
Butter	Beurre
Eggs	Oeufs
Milk	Lait
Oil	Huile
Pepper	Poivre
Salt	Sel
Sugar	Sucre
Vinegar	Vinaigre
Bottle	Bouteille

Glass	Verre
Fork	Fourchette
Knife	Couteau
Spoon	Cuillère
Table	Table
Bill	L'addition

And one final note: always call the waiter or waitress *Monsieur* or *Madame*, (*Mademoiselle*, if a girl)

Wine and drinks

Wine – *vin* – is the standard accompaniment to every meal and all social occasions. Red is *rouge*, white *blanc*, or there's *rosé*. **Vin de table** – plonk – is always good in wine-growing areas and is universally cheap. **A.C.** (Appellation d'Origine Contrôlée) wines are another matter. They can be excellent value at the lower end of the price scale, where favourable French taxes keep prices down to £1 or so a bottle (as opposed to, say, £4 in Britain), but move much above this and you're fast paying serious prices for serious bottles. In **restaurants**, of course, this is all the more so with A.C. mark-ups outrageous – as any visit to a supermarket will make clear.

Popular A.C. wines, which you'll find on most restaurant lists, include Côtes du Rhône (from the Rhône valley), St-Emilion and Médoc (from Bordeaux), Beaujolais and, well upmarket, Burgundy. Better on the whole to go for **local wines** – you'll find details in relevant chapters – and not to worry about any correct wine for a particular food. But to know what you're drinking, the **basic terms** are: *brut*, very very dry; *sec*, dry; *demi-sec*, sweet; *doux*, very sweet; *mousseux*, sparkling; *méthode champenoise*, mature and sparkling. There are grape types as well, but the complexities of the subject take up volumes . . .

In a bar, a glass of wine is simply *un rouge* or *un blanc*. If it's an A.C. wine you may have the choice of *un ballon* (round glass) or a smaller glass. *Un pichet* (a jug) is normally a ¼ litre. **Buying wine**, you'll do best at supermarkets or, better still, a *vigneron* (wine grower), who will let you taste some first and won't rip you off; to avoid misunderstanding, make it clear how much you want to buy (if it's only one or two bottles) right at the start.

Beer – *bière* – is invariably lager, with most of the familiar Belgian and German names available plus home-grown from Alsace. Draught (*à la pression*, usually Kronenbourg) is the cheapest drink you can have after coffee and wine – ask for *un demi* (¹/₃ litre).

Stronger alcohols are drunk from 5am, as pre-work fortifiers, right through the day though the national reputation for drunkenness has lost some of its truth. **Cognac** or **Armagnac** brandies and the dozens of **eaux de vie** (spirits) and **liqueurs** are distilled with the same perfectionism as in the cultivation of vines. Among less familiar names, try *Poire William* (pear liqueur), *marc* (distilled grape debris) or just point to the bottle with the most attractive colour. Measures are generous, but they don't come cheap; the same applies for imported spirits like whisky, always called *Scotch*. **Pastis**, aniseed drinks such as *Pernod* or *Ricard*, are served diluted with water and ice (*glaçons*) – very refreshing and not expensive. Two drinks designed to stimulate the appetite are **Pineau**, cognac and grape juice, and **Kir**, blackcurrant juice and white wine – or champagne for a *Kir Royale*.

On the **soft drink** front, bottled fruit juices include apricot (*jus d'abricot*) and blackcurrant juice (*cassis*), as well as the usual orange (*jus d'orange*), etc. You can also get fresh orange and lemon juice (*orange/citron pressé*), otherwise it's the standard fizzy cans, coke (*coca*) and so forth. Bottles of **spring water** (*eau de source*) and **mineral water** (*eau minérale*) – either sparkling (*pétillante*) or still (*eau plâte*) – abound, from the bestseller *Perrier* to the obscurest spa product. But there's not much wrong with the tap water, *l'eau du robinet*.

After overeating, **herb teas** (*infusions* or *tisanes*), served in every café, can be soothing. The commonest are *verveine* (verbena), and *tilleul* (lime blossom). Ordinary tea (*thé*) is Lipton's 9 times out of 10; to have milk with it, ask for *un peu de lait frais* (some fresh milk). **Chocolat chaud** – hot chocolate – unlike tea, lives up to the high standards of French food and drink and can be had in any café. **Coffee** is invariably espresso and very strong. *Un café* or *un express* is black; *un crème* is white; *un grand café* or *un grand crème* is a large cup. At breakfast you might also be offered *un café au lait* – espresso in a large cup or bowl filled up with hot milk. *Un déca* is decaff, widely available.

Every bar displays the full **price list**, usually without the 15 per cent service added, for drinks at the bar (*au comptoir*), sitting down (*la salle*) and on the terrace (*la terrasse*). Needless to say, these are progressively more expensive.

COMMUNICATIONS – POST, PHONES AND MEDIA

You can have letters sent to any post office; they should be addressed (preferably with the surname underlined and in capitals) **Poste Restante**, followed by the name of the town. Post offices are generally open 8–12am and 2.30–7pm, Monday to Saturday morning, and known either as a **PTT** or **Bureau de Poste**. To collect mail you'll need a passport or other convincing ID and there may be a small charge. You should ask for all your names to be checked – filing systems are not brilliant. For sending letters, remember that you can buy stamps (*timbres*), without queues or commissions, from *Tabacs*.

You can make **international phone calls** from any box (or **cabine**) and can receive calls where there's a blue logo of a ringing bell. Put the money (½F, 1F, 5F, occasionally now 10F, pieces) in first, dial 19, wait for a tone and then dial the country code (44 for Britain) and the number minus its initial O. For **calls within France** – local or long distance – dial all 8 digits of the number (which includes the former area code – displayed in every *cabine*). The exceptions are calling from Paris to anywhere else in France, when you must first dial 16, or when calling a Paris number from anywhere else, first dial 16–1. As an alternative to self-dialling, post offices often have a clerk who'll connect the call and you pay afterwards.

British **newspapers**, and the *International Herald Tribune*, are on sale in most large cities and resorts. Of the **French daily papers** *Le Monde* is the most intellectual and respected, with no concessions to entertainment (such as pictures) but a correctly styled French that is probably the easiest to understand. *Libération* (*Libé* for short) is moderately left-wing, independent and more colloquial with good, if choosy, coverage, while the best criticism from the left of the French government comes from *L'Humanité*, the Communist party paper. With the exception of *Le Matin*, all the other nationals are firmly on the right. So too are the majority of the regional newspapers, which enjoy much higher circulations than the Paris nationals. The most important of these is the Rennes-based *Ouest France* – though for travellers this, like the rest of the regionals, is mainly of interest for its listings. **Weeklies** on the Newsweek/Time model include the wide-ranging and obsessively pro-government *Le Nouvel Observateur* and its counterpoint, *L'Express*, property of James Goldsmith, who sacked the editor for an anti-Giscard article before the 1982 presidential election. The best investigative journalism is in the weekly satirical paper *Le Canard Enchaîné*, unfortu-

nately unintelligible to non-native speakers. And the foulest rag of the lot is *Minute*, the *Front National's* organ. 'Moral' censorship of the press is rare. As well as pornography of every shade you'll find on the news-stands covers featuring drugs, sex, blasphemy and bizarre forms of grossness alongside knitting patterns and DIY. French **comics**, which often indulge these interests, are wonderful. *Charlie-Hebdo* is one with political targets; and *Á Suivre*, which wouldn't cause problems at British Customs, has amazing graphic talents.

French **TV** in contrast, is prudish and lacking in any imagination – even if the 8 o'clock news on *Antenne 2* has upped its standards and popularity with star newscaster Christine Ockrent. If you've got a radio, you can tune into English news on the **BBC World Service** on 463m MW or on frequencies between 21m and 31m shortwave at intervals throughout the day and night.

OPENING HOURS AND HOLIDAYS

Almost everything in France – shops, museums, tourist offices, most banks – closes for a couple of hours at midday. There's some variation, and the lunch-break tends to be longer in the south, but the basic **working hours** are 8–12 and 2–6. Food shops often don't reopen till half way through the afternoon, closing just before suppertime, between 7.30 and 8. Sunday and Monday are the standard **closing days**, though you'll always find at least one *boulangerie* (baker's) open. The main thing to watch out for is getting picnic shopping done in time before the French shut their doors for lunch.

Museums are not on the whole generous with their opening times – 10–12 and 2–5 is normal, with an extra hour in the evening and midday hours added only at the most important in July and August. Individual hours are listed in the guide with the summer ones first: as 8.30/10–1/12 – Summer hours usually extend from mid-May or June to mid-September. Sometimes they apply only in July and August, occasionally from Palm Sunday to All Saints. Don't forget closing days – again usually Tuesday or Monday, sometimes both. **Admission charges** can be very off-putting – though most state-owned museums have one or two days of the week when

they're free, and you can get a big reduction at most places by showing a student card (or passport if you're under 18/over 60). **Churches and cathedrals** are almost always open all day, with charges only for the crypt, treasures or cloisters, and little fuss about how you're dressed. Where they are closed you may have to go during Mass, on Sunday morning or at other times which you'll see posted up on the door. In small towns and villages, however, getting the key is not difficult – ask anyone nearby or hunt out the priest, whose house is known as the *presbytère*.

One other factor can disrupt your plans – **holidays** (*jours fériés*). There are thirteen national holidays, on which everything apart from bars, restaurants and the odd *boulangerie*, locks its doors. When the holiday is a Thursday, the Friday tends to run at half power as most people *faire le pont* (bridge the holiday with the weekend). The national holidays are: 1 January, Easter Sunday, Easter Monday, Ascension Day (forty days after Easter), Pentecost (7th Sunday after Easter, plus the Monday), 1 May, 8 May (VE Day), 14 July (Bastille Day), 15 August (Assumption of the Virgin Mary), 1 November (All Saints), 11 November (1918 Armistice Day) and Christmas Day.

ENTERTAINMENT: MUSIC, CINEMA, THEATRE AND FESTIVALS

What follows is obviously a broad introduction. For specific venues and listings, consult relevant sections of the text – and particularly pp. 85–102 for all that's happening in Paris.

Music

The best contemporary music you'll hear in France is likely to be distinctly un-French – African, Salsa or jazz in Paris and other big cities, Celtic in Brittany – or classical.

Le Rock is not really a French idiom and what bands there are tend to find it difficult to find venues. Only Rennes, the Breton capital, has shown any interest in promotion; elsewhere, city councils are frequently obstructive, worried about their youth's morals and French-ness. The music, of course, does little to encourage people to depart from safe selections of British/US disco and mainstream chart hits. French rock often has a toytown sound about it – annoying even on a first listening – or else it's ponderous jazz-rock, influenced by the 1970s success of violinist Jean-Luc Ponty. There are a few exceptions – soul duo Rita Mitsouko are currently interesting, so are cult singers Charlelie Couture (rock funk and complex lyrics) and Bernard Lavilliers (rare political content) – but they seem unlikely to start any trends. If you like the sound of French being sung, there's greater wealth in the **Chansons**, a still active tradition that goes back to Edith Piaf and Georges Brassens, the 1960s star Françoise Hardy, and to Jacques Brel. Modern exponents include Alain Souchon and Serge Lama, both well worth seeing.

In Paris, above all, **jazz** is a different matter. You could listen to a different band every night for weeks in the capital's clubs, from trad, through be-bop and free jazz, to highly contemporary experimental. And there are many excellent **festivals**, particularly in the south: Juan-les-Pins, Nîmes and Nice (all in July), Paris (October/November), Nancy (every other year), and as part of general arts festivals in Billom (June/July) and Bordeaux (November). If you hear of *Urban Sax* playing at any of these – or

elsewhere – go along, if only for the drama of sixty-plus saxophonists performing together!

If your taste is for **classical music** and its descendents, you're also in for a treat. Pierre Boulez experiments with hi-tech sound beneath Beaubourg (see p. 74), Paris is to get a second opera house and in the provinces there are no less than twelve other companies (Strasbourg and Toulouse are said to be the best), and a further dozen orchestras. The places to check out for concerts are the *Maisons de la Culture* (in all the larger cities), churches (where chamber music is as much performed as sacred music, often for free) and festivals – of which there are hundreds, the most famous being at Aix in July.

Cinema and theatre

The French have treated **Cinema** as an art form, deserving of state subsidy, ever since its origination with the Lumière brothers in 1895. The medium has never had to bow down to TV, the seat of judgement stays in Cannes, and Paris is the cinema capital of the world. True, the country's high street *Gaumonts* screen the annual Belmondo gangster movie and dubbed Sci-Fi trash from the States, but there are *ciné-clubs* in almost every city, censorship is very slight, students get discounts, and foreign films are usually shown in their **original language** with subtitles (look for *version originale* or *v.o.* in the listings). Some British movie buffs actually go to Paris just for English-language films – classics and rarities are always playing.

The Cannes Film Festival where the prized *Palme d'Or* is handed out, is not, in any public sense, a **festival**. Those that are, where anyone can pay to see the films, happen at La Rochelle (*Rencontres Internationales d'Art Contemporain*; June to July); Sceaux (festival of women's films; see p. 96); La Ciotat (silent films; July); and Reims (thrillers, novels and films; October-November).

In **theatre**, directors not playwrights dominate. Scripts are there, if at all, to be shaken up or scrambled (*Richard II* in Japanese Noh style, for example). The earlier generation of Genet, Anouilh, Camus, joined by Beckett and Ionesco, hasn't really had successors. In the 1950s Roger Planchon set up a company in a suburb of Lyon, determined to play to working-class audiences and did so. It became the *Théâtre Nationale Populaire*, the no 2 state theatre after the *Comédie Française*, which does the classics with all due decorum. Another interesting group, *Théâtre de l'Action*, tours about the country staying in places before creating a show around local issues; while Ariane Mnouchkine organises militant improvisations with her workers' co-op in the *Cartoucherie* at Vincennes. Other big names come from novels and cinema into drama (Marguerite Duras) or involve themselves with opera as well as theatre (Patrice Chéreau). Peter Brook now works almost exclusively in France and Jean-Louis Barrault (of *Baptiste* fame) and Madeleine Renaud (one of the great stage actresses) are still around producing theatrical events in huge, bizarre spaces.

In all this, theatrical moments rather than speech, and the theatrical light on the subject rather than realism, are tantamount. If you find one of these shows on, it might be quite an experience even with language difficulties. **Café-Théâtre**, though far from avant-garde, is probably less accessible: satire, *chansons* and dirty jokes are the standard ingredients. But you could look out for **mime**. Marcel Marceau still performs and new talent keeps appearing from the *Jacques Le Coq*

school of mime in Paris. And finally, there are the classics and bourgeois favourites, staple fodder to keep municipal subsidies coming in.

For details of **Paris theatres** see p. 96. In **other cities** the theatres are often part of the *Maisons de la Culture* or *Centres d'Animation Culturelle*; local SIs should have programmes. The two major theatre **festivals** are the *Festival Mondial du Théâtre* in Nancy (June) and the *Festival d'Avignon* (July–August).

Fêtes and folk festivals

Folk festivals, wine and food binges and the like are two a penny in the summer season, but they are rarely more than just excuses to bring in the tourists (French or foreign) and their money. Agricultural shows and non-tourist events of that type are the most genuine community do's you are likely to see today.

There are, however, a few occasions that are fun and relatively un-phoney. The bonfire and **fireworks** parties on 24 June, the **night of St-Jean**, bring village and country towns into the streets with a pretext for the kids to let off squibs and bangers. The Flemish Fêtes des Géants and even the great gypsy gathering at Les-Saintes-Maries-de-la-Mer are commercialised now but still interesting. **Corridas** – bullfights – are held in the South, sometimes 'bloodless', sometimes along Spanish lines. But the real events that excite local interest are **boules championships**, **football** and Basque **pelota matches** and the **Tour de France** cycle race (in July).

WORK AND STUDY

For all its own employment problems, France remains a viable place to find work – at least on a **temporary basis**, on the grape harvests or in bars and restaurants at the big summer or Alpine resorts. More **permanent jobs** are a lot harder to come by, though EEC citizens now have no problems getting **work permits** and (if paper work is done in advance, see below) can sign on for up to three months' **benefit**. Best chances for a permanent post – unless you've some specific skill – remain, however, the old standards of **teaching English** in a language school or living with a family as an **au pair**.

Temporary work – harvests and resorts
If you're from an EEC country you can use the French **job centres** – the *ANPEs* (Agences Nationales pour l'Emploi) – to find work. There are ANPE offices in every town and after registering they will give you details of any available local jobs. Obviously you want to pick your town with a specific form of work in mind – which means either making for a resort area or, in the September harvest season, one of the **wine areas**. Among the most promising wine towns are Tours, Beaune, Angers, Mâcon, Dijon, Epernay, Perpignan, Bordeaux, Libourne and Villefranche-sur-Saône.

Make for one or two, rather than touring around, and ask at **youth hostels** as well as the ANPE. Champagne (see p. 359) usually has the best pay. Work often involves free accommodation, or at least wine and a place to camp, and sometimes meals. Arrange it only on the spot: ads in the UK or US are often very dodgy or lowly paid.

Other sources for finding temporary work are the *Offres d'Emploi* columns of local papers; the student organisation *CROUS* and youth centres of the *CIJ* (detailed, where relevant, in the guide). A useful gathering together of many of the options is to be found in the publication *Emplois d'Eté en France*, available from *Vac-Job* (4 rue d'Alésia, 75014 Paris) or in the UK from *Vac-Work* (9 Park End St, Oxford).

To **sign on for benefit** in France you must collect form E303 before leaving home, available in Britain from any DHSS office. The procedure is first to get registered at an ANPE office; you then take the form to the local *ASSEDIC* (benefits office) and give them an address, which can be a hostel or hotel, for the money to be sent. You sign on once a month at the ANPE and receive dole a month in arrears up to three months when officially you must leave the country or get a *carte de séjour* (see p. 6).

Teaching English or au-pairing
Much the simplest way of getting a job in a **French language school** is to apply from Britain. Check the ads in the *Guardian's* 'Educational Extra' (every Tuesday normally) or in the weekly *Times Educational Supplement* – late summer is usually the most fruitful time. You don't need fluent French to get a post, but a *TEFL* (Teaching English as a Foreign Language) qualification is a distinct advantage.

If you apply from home most schools will fix up the necessary papers for you. EEC nationals don't need a work permit, but getting a *carte de séjour* and social security (see p. 6) can still be tricky when employers refuse to help. It's quite feasible to find a teaching job when you're **already in France**, though you

may have to accept semi-official status and no job security. For the addresses of schools look under *Ecoles de Langues* in the *Professions* directories of city phone books. Offering **private lessons** (via university noticeboards, small ads) is a swamped market, and it's hard to reach the people who can afford it, but always worth a try.

Although working as an **au-pair** is easily fixed up through any number of agencies (lists available from the French Embassy), this sort of work can be a bit desperate unless you're using it to learn the language. Conditions, pay and treatment by your employers is likely to be little short of slavery. If you give it a go, best apply in France where you can at least meet the family first and check things out.

Another possibility, perhaps more remote, and definitely to be arranged before you leave, is to get a job as a **travel courier**. You'll need good French – German, too, would be an asset – and should write to as many tour operators as you can, preferably in early spring. Ads occasionally appear, too, in the *Guardian's* 'Creative and Media' pages (Mondays).

Studying in France
It's relatively easy to be a student in France. Foreigners pay no more than French nationals (around 400F a year) **to enrol** for a course and the only problem is supporting yourself through. Your *carte de séjour* and – within the EEC – social security will be assured and you'll be eligible for subsidised lodgings, meals and all the student reductions. Few people want to do first degrees abroad, but for higher degrees or other diplomas, the range of options is enormous. Strict entry requirements including an exam in French only apply for first degrees. Generally, French universities are much less formal than British ones and many people perfect the language while studying. For full **details and prospectuses**, go to the Cultural Service of any French Embassy: in London at 22 Wilton Crescent, SW1.

POLICE AND THIEVES

French **police** are barely polite at the best of times and can be extremely unpleasant if you get on the wrong side of them. There are three basic types – all of them armed. The **Police Nationale** and **Gendarmerie Nationale**, indistinguishable for all practical purposes, are the bulk of the force; they're occasionally helpful, but on the whole best avoided. Much more so, however, the **CRS*** (*Compagnies/Republicaines de Sécurité*), a mobile force of heavies, sporadically dressed in green combats and armed with riot equipment, whose brutality in the May 1968 battles turned public opinion and the left-wing trade unions to the side of the students. They still make demonstrations dangerous, arriving in huge van loads or lurking provocatively in favourite trouble spots, though even their activities are dwarfed by the separate **Paris police force**. Distinct from the other three, these are potentially more lethal, with a long history of unbelievable cock-ups in which they shoot people not suspected of any crime; their assaults on suspects are less newsworthy.

The most likely occasion when you may have to deal with the police is in **reporting a theft** in order to claim insurance. The *Police Nationale* or *Gendarmerie Nationale* are the ones to go to, but there's no guarantee they'll give you the requisite bit of paper. If you need **general assistance**, ordinary people are at least as likely to help as the police, and if you need someone in authority, best go to the town hall – the *Mairie /Hôtel de Ville*. In difficult circumstances, where the police are the only option, it's best to go with someone else – preferably French.

Petty theft, endemic along the Côte d'Azur, is also pretty bad in the crowded hang-outs of most big cities. But take normal precautions, don't be too flash with money and take out travel insurance, and you've little to worry about. If you should get attacked, hand over the money and start writing to your insurance company. **Drivers** face greater problems, most notoriously from break-ins. Vehicles are rarely stolen, but cassette players as well as luggage left in cars make a tempting target and foreign number plates are easy to spot. Again, good insurance is the only answer, but try not to leave any valuables in the car even so. If you have an accident while driving, you are officially supposed to fill in and sign a *constat à l'amaible*, which car insurers are supposed to give you with a policy; in practice, though, few seem to have heard of it.

For non-criminal **driving offences**, speeding etc., the police can impose an on-the-spot fine and be very unpleasant if you don't have immediate means of payment. Should you be arrested on any charge, you have the right to contact your Consulate (see p. 26). Although they're often reluctant to get involved, their duty is to assist you – likewise in the case of losing your passport or all your money.

Anyone caught bringing into the country or possessing any **drugs**, even a few grammes of marijuana, is liable to find themselves in jail and consulates will not be sympathetic. Which is not to say that hard drug-taking isn't a visible activity: in all the big cities kids are dealing in *poudre* (heroin) and the authorities are unable to do anything. As for dope, people are no more nor less paranoid about busts than they are in the UK.

On **less serious matters**, **camping rough** can bring you into contact with officialdom, though it's more likely to be the owner of the field who tells you to move off. Topless sunbathing is universally acceptable, but **nudity** in certain family resorts is not welcomed. Hostility is rare, however. You'll probably just be pointed in the direction of the nearest naturist beach. And, lastly, you're supposed to carry **identification** at all times in France, and the police are entitled to stop you in the streets and demand it. In practice they're rarely bothered, if you're clearly a foreigner, but if you go to them, 'Papiers!' will be the immediate first reaction.

---

*Honourable exception: the specialised **mountaineering sections**, who provide mountain rescue, guidance, etc. are extremely friendly and approachable.

SEXUAL AND RACIAL HARASSMENT

You're bound to come across **sexual harassment** in France. It is generally no worse nor more vicious than in the UK, but there are problems in judging men without the familiar linguistic and cultural signs. A 'Bonsoir' or 'Bonjour' on the street is the standard pick-up opening. If you so much as return the greeting, you've let yourself in for a stream of tenacious chat, and hard shaking-off work. On the other hand, topless bathing doesn't usually invite bother and it's quite common, if you're on your own, to be offered a drink in a bar and not to be pestered even if you accept. On the whole, Paris is far the most hassling place with constant observation and commentary as you walk down the street.

Very few French women **hitchhike**, except on the Côte d'Azur. If you want to hitch best use the agencies (see p. 10) and go for a mixed ride. Otherwise, take the same precautions as you would at home. **Camping rough** is not a good idea. You may have trouble at a campsite, but at least there will be people around for support. If things ever get desperate, don't go to the police. The Maitre/Hôtel de Ville will have addresses of women's organisations (Femmes Battues, Femmes en Détresse or SOS Femmes), though this won't be much help outside office hours. You'll find listings for Paris on p. 98. We've given contacts for other cities where possible, but there are very few permanent centres.

You may, as a woman, be warned against Les Arabes. This is simply **French racism.** If you are Arab or look as if you might be, your chances of avoiding unpleasantness are very low. Hotels claiming to be booked up, police demanding your papers and abusive treatment from ordinary people is horribly commonplace. In addition, being black, of whatever ethnic origin, can make entering the country difficult. Recent changes in passport regulations have put an end to incidents of outright refusal to let coloured British holidaymakers in, but customs and immigration officers can still, like their cross-channel counterparts, be obstructive and malicious.

OTHER THINGS

BEACHES are public property 5m above the high tide mark, so you can kick sand past private villas and arrive on islands but, under a different law, you can't camp.

BRING . . . Scotch, cassettes and painkillers are a bit more expensive in France; an alarm clock is useful for early trains.

CONSULATES British consulates in France have not yet been subjected to cuts, you'll find them in Paris, Bordeaux, Boulogne, Calais, Cherbourg, Dunkerque, Epernay, Le Havre, Lille, Lyon, Marseille, Nantes and Nice. Americans are represented in Bordeaux, Lyon, Marseille, Nice and Strasbourg. Principal addresses are detailed in the guide; for full details phone your consulate in Paris (see p. 104).

CONTRACEPTIVES Condoms (préservatifs) have always been available at pharmacies, though contraception was only legalised in 1967. You can also get spermicidal cream and jelly (dose contraceptive), plus the suppositories (ovules, suppositoires) and (with a prescription) the pill (la pilule), a diaphragm or IUD (le sterilet).

CUSTOMS If you bring in more than 5,000F worth of foreign cash, you need to sign a declaration at customs. There are also restrictions on taking francs out of the country, but the amounts are beyond the concern of most people.

DISABLED TRAVELLERS France has no special reputation for ease of access and facilities, but at least information is available. The tourist offices in most big towns and the head office in Paris have a free booklet, Touristes Quand Même, covering accommodation, transport and accessibility of public places as well as particular aids such as buzzer signals on pedestrian crossings. The ATH hotel reservation service in Paris (48. 74.88.51) has details of wheelchair access for 3 and 4 star hotels. Useful guides in English include Europe for the Handicapped Traveller (Vol no 3

France), from *Mobility International*, 2 Colombo Street, London SE1 or Rte 4, 1718 W 2525th Road, Ottawa, Illinois 61350; and the *Access Guides* to Paris, Brittany and the Loire Valley – from the Pauline Hephaistos Survey Project, 39 Bradley Gdns, London W13. Crossing the Channel, *Townsend Thoresen* allow registered disabled to take cars free of charge.

ELECTRICITY is 220V and most plugs are two round pins. In out-of-the-way rural districts you may still find 110V.

FEMINISM See p. 501.

FISHING You need to become a member of an authorised fishing club to get rights – this is not difficult, any tourist office will give you a local address.

GAY LIFE France is more liberal than most other European countries on homosexuality. There are thriving gay communities in Paris and many of the towns in the south. For contacts and publications see p. 99.

KIDS/BABIES pose few travel problems. They're allowed in all bars and restaurants, most of whom will cook simpler food if you ask. Hotels charge by the room – there's a small supplement for an additional bed or cot – and family-run places will usually babysit while you go out. You'll have no difficulty finding disposable nappies, baby foods and milk powders. The SNCF charge half-fare on trains and buses for kids aged 4–12, nothing for under 4s; with a *Carte Famille* one adult pays full fare and the other, and any children, half. As far as entertainment goes, most local tourist offices detail specific children's activities (we've included some of the more exciting), and wherever you go there's generally a good reception.

LANGUAGE COURSES can be taken at universities or colleges all over France, either for a whole year or just for the summer. You can get full lists from the Cultural Service of any French embassy.

LAUNDRIES Laundrettes are not the commonest sight along French high streets. Either carry travel-soap (or Dylon *Travel-Wash*) and wash your own or pay through the nose for a complete *blanchisserie* service.

LEFT LUGGAGE There are lockers at all train stations and *consigne* for bigger items or longer periods.

SWIMMING POOLS are well signposted in all French towns and reasonably priced. SIs also give addresses.

TAMPONS are available from all *pharmacies* but they are much cheaper in supermarkets.

TIME France is always 1 hour ahead of Britain, except between the end of September and the end of October (when it's the same).

TOILETTES are usually to be found downstairs in bars, along with the phone, but they're often hole-in-the-ground squats and paper is rare.

FRENCH AND ARCHITECTURAL TERMS: A GLOSSARY

These are either terms you'll come across in the guide, or come up against on signs, maps, etc. while travelling around. For food terms see p. 14, for straightforward language and phrases p. 511.

ABBAYE abbey

AMBULATORY covered passage around the outer edge of a choir of a church

APSE semi-circular termination at the east end of a church

ASSEMBLÉE NATIONALE the French parliament

ARRONDISSEMENT district of a city

AUBERGE DE JEUNESSE (AJ) youth hostel

BAROQUE High Renaissance period of art and architecture, distinguished by extreme ornateness

BASTIDE medieval military settlement, constructed on a grid plan

BEAUX ARTS fine arts museum (and school)

CAR coach, bus

CAROLINGIAN dynasty (and art, sculpture, etc.) founded by Charlemagne; late 8C–early 10C

CFDT Socialist trade union

CGT Communist trade union

CHASSE, CHASSE GARDÉE hunting grounds (beware)

CHÂTEAU mansion, country house or castle

CHÂTEAU FORT castle

CHEMIN DE ST-JACQUES medieval pilgrim route to the shrine of St James at Compostela in north-west Spain

CHEVET end wall of a church

CIJ (*Centre d'Informations Jeunesse*) youth information centre

CLASSICAL architectural style incorporating Greek and Roman elements – pillars, domes, colonnades etc. – at its height in France in the 17C and revived, as NEOCLASSICAL, in the 19C.

CLERESTORY upper story of a church, incorporating the windows

CLUNIAC monastic movement, and hence its architecture, derived from the Benedictine monastery at Cluny (see p. 349)

CODENE French CND (of sorts)

CONSIGNE left luggage

COUVENT convent, monastery

DÉGUSTATION tasting (wine or food)

DÉPARTEMENT county – more or less

DONJON castle keep

ÉGLISE church

ENTRÉE entrance

FERMETURE closing period

FLAMBOYANT florid form of Gothic (see below)

FN (Front National) fascist party led by Le Pen

FO Catholic trade union

FRESCO wall painting – durable through application to wet plaster

GALLO-ROMAIN period of Roman occupation of Gaul (1C–4C AD)

GARE station; **ROUTIÈRE** – bus station; **SNCF** – train station

GÎTE D'ÉTAPE basic hostel accommodation, from around Paris, primarily for walkers

GOBELINS best known of all tapestry manufacturers, from around Paris, its most renowned period being in the reign of Louis XIV (17C)

HALLES covered market

HLM council housing estate

HÔTEL a hotel, but also an aristocratic town house or mansion; **HÔTEL DE VILLE** – townhall

JOURS FÉRIÉS public holidays

MAIRIE townhall

MARCHÉ market

MEROVINGIAN dynasty (and art, etc.), ruling France and parts of Germany from 6C to mid 8C

NARTHEX entrance hall of church

NAVE main body of a church

PCF Communist party of France

PLACE square

PORTE gateway

PRESQU'ILE peninsula

PS Socialist party

PTT post office

QUARTIER district of a town

RELAIS ROUTIERS truckstop café-restaurants

RENAISSANCE art-architectural style developed in 15C Italy and imported to France in the early 16C by François I (see p. 495)

RETABLE altarpiece, retablo

REZ DE CHAUSSÉE (RC) ground floor

RN (*Route Nationale*) main road

ROMANESQUE (*ROMAN*) early medieval architecture distinguished by squat, rounded forms and naive sculpture

RPR Gaullist party led by Jacques Chirac

SI (*Syndicat d'Initiative*) tourist information office; also known as OT, OTSI and MAISON DU TOURISME

SNCF French railways

SORTIE exit

STUCCO plaster used to embellish ceilings, etc.

TABAC bar or shop selling stamps, cigarettes, etc.

TOUR tower

TRANSEPT cross arms of a church

TYMPANUM sculpted panel above a church door

UDF centre-right party headed by Giscard d'Estaing

VAUBAN 17C military architect – his fortresses still stand all over France

VOUSSOIR sculpted rings in arch over church door

ZONE BLEUE restricted parking zone

ZONE PIÉTONNE pedestrian precinct

Part two
THE GUIDE

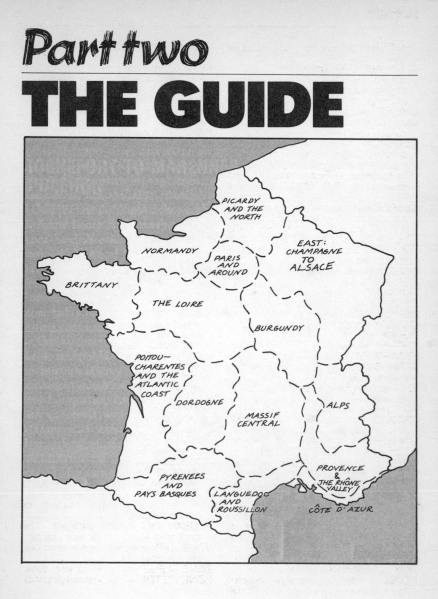

PICARDY AND THE NORTH

NORMANDY

PARIS AND AROUND

EAST: CHAMPAGNE TO ALSACE

BRITTANY

THE LOIRE

BURGUNDY

POITOU—CHARENTES AND THE ATLANTIC COAST

DORDOGNE

MASSIF CENTRAL

ALPS

PYRENEES AND PAYS BASQUES

LANGUEDOC AND ROUSSILLON

PROVENCE & THE RHÔNE VALLEY

CÔTE D'AZUR

Chapter one
PARIS AND AROUND

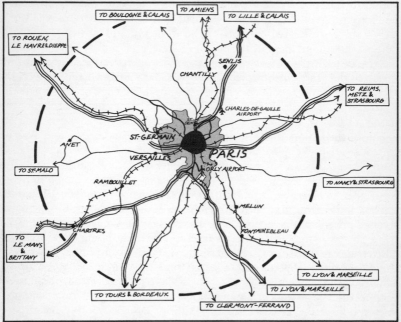

PARIS is a lot of things, many of them contradictory. It is the paragon of style, the most glamorous city in Europe, at least in popular imagination. But it is also dirty, noisy, dilapidated, aggressive and unfriendly. Even among their fellow-countrymen, its citizens have the reputation of being rude and arrogant. And you'll be lucky to get through your visit without catching the rough side of someone's tongue at least once, especially if you make no effort to speak French.

Paris creates its own myth, writes its history in capital letters. Sun King, Revolution, Terror, Empire, Commune, Popular Front, Resistance, May 1968, Impressionism, Surrealism, Existentialism, Structuralism. Piaf and Gabin, Chanel and Saint-Laurent, Sartre and Camus, Breton and Cocteau, Duchamp and Braque. Foreigners too: Miller, Stein, Hemingway and Anaïs Nin, Joyce and Beckett, Trotsky and Ho Chi Minh. People, places and events are invested with a peculiar glamour that elevates them and the city to an almost legendary realm. Perhaps it is not surprising that, finding themselves at the navel of the world, Parisians feel superior to ordinary mortals.

History has conspired to create this sense of being apart. From a shaky start the kings of France, whose seat was Paris, gradually extended their control over their feudal rivals, centralising administrative, legal, financial and political power as they did so, until anyone seeking influence, publicity or credibility in whatever field had to be in Paris. It was **Louis XIV** who consolidated this process. Supremely autocratic, considering himself the embodiment of the state – 'L'état, c'est moi' – he inaugurated the tradition of the city as symbol: the glorious reflection of the preeminence of the State, with projects like the Cour Carrée of the Louvre, the Observatoire and Invalides, and the triumphal arches of the Portes St-Martin and St-Denis. It is a tradition his successors have been only too happy to follow, be they emperor or president.

Napoleon I built the Arc de Triomphe, the Madeleine, and Arc du Carrousel. He extended the Louvre and instituted the Grandes Ecoles, those super-universities for super-competent administrators, engineers and teachers. He reorganised the *départements* and appointed a network of prefects answerable to himself to control them. **Napoleon III** had his Baron Haussmann, the **Third Republic** its World Fairs and Eiffel Tower. **Recent presidents** have built the skyscrapers at La Défense, the Tour Montparnasse, the Beaubourg centre and Halles shopping mall. **President Mitterrand** is promoting the space-age City of Science and Industry at the Porte de la Villette and a glass pyramid in the courtyard of the Louvre. All are prestige projects which have pushed far beyond current architectural taste and provoked shock-horror reactions from sentimentalists. Some, like La Défense, are chilling. Others, notably Beaubourg, are fun, uncharacteristically unpompous and highly successful in terms of their use. Porte de la Villette looks set to go one better.

In spite of these developments Paris remains compact and remarkably uniform, basically the city that **Haussmann** remodelled in the **mid-19C**. He laid out those long geometrical boulevards lined with rows of grey bourgeois residences, that are the hallmark of Paris. In doing so he cut great swathes through the stinking wen of medieval slums that housed the city's rebellious poor, already veterans of three revolutionary uprisings in half a century. If urban renewal and modernisation were part of the design, so was the intention of controlling this dangerous potential by opening up more effective fields of fire for artillery and facilitating the movement of troops. Not that it succeeded in preventing the Commune, the most determined insurrection since 1789.

But the effect of his demolitions, combined with the repression of the Commune, did put paid to several centuries of working-class revolt in the city. For they lost their leaders in the Commune and their homes to Haussmann.

The **tradition of conflict** between the citizenry and its rulers dates back well into the Middle Ages. Although in the meantime the nation prospered and Paris acquired an ever-increasing number of imposing monuments, nothing was ever done to alleviate the misery of the poor. And in a sense, although the traditional barricade-builders have long since been booted into the suburban factory-land, to be housed in depressing satellite towns, the old pattern still continues. Corporate business gets its way, the state invests in monumental building, the housing shortage remains acute, large areas of the city, especially in the east and north, fall into a state of decay that only the underprivileged immigrant communities are prepared to tolerate, and the unemployed beg on the streets in increasing numbers.

It is, though, the contradictions and contrasts that have made – and make – Paris such a lively, stimulating place. The glamour and wealth of the shop-windows in rue St-Honoré and the leafy residences of the 16ᵉ, against the urine-smelling squalor of rue de Flandre. The village atmosphere of Montmartre against the cold hard lines of La Défense. The multiplicity of markets and small shops against the giant precincts of Montparnasse and Les Halles. The devotion to *l'informatique* – minitel link-ups for all phone subscribers, micro-computer route-finders and videos installed in métro stations, against old ladies in black ironing sheets and shirts by hand in the laundries of Auteuil.

There are surprisingly few interesting **buildings** – **Notre-Dame**, the **Sainte-Chapelle** for its glass, the **Eiffel Tower**, **Beaubourg** and **La Villette**, some **Art Nouveau** and **Cubist** work in the 16ᵉ. The **monumental architecture** – Louvre, Arc de Triomphe, Concorde, Invalides, etc. – is grand and imposing, but best experienced as a theatrical backdrop glimpsed in passing behind a screen of trees.

There are some glorious **museums** you won't want to miss: the **Marmottan**, **Orangerie** and **Cluny**. But the greatest single pleasure is just strolling along, browsing visually, at the café-pâtisserie level of existence. The **Marais**, **Montmartre**, **Latin Quarter**, **Îles St-Louis** and **de la Cité** are, as ever, among the best areas for doing this. The big parks – Bois de Boulogne and Bois de Vincennes – are far enough out to require a special expedition, though the city's lack of open spaces is redeemed by unexpected bits of garden or churchyard like the **Mosque**, **Arènes de Lutèce** and the courtyard of the **Cluny museum**.

Getting around the city

Finding your way around is remarkably easy, for Paris proper, without its suburbs, is compact and relatively small, with a public transport system that is cheap, fast and meticulously signposted.

To help you get your bearings above ground, think of the **Louvre** as the centre. The Seine flows east to west, cutting the city in two horizontally. The **Eiffel Tower** is west, the white pimples of the **Sacré-Coeur** on

top of the hill of Montmartre north. These are the landmarks you most often catch glimpses of as you move about. The area north of the river is known as the **Right Bank** or *rive droite*, to the south is the **Left Bank** or *rive gauche*. Roughly speaking, west is smart and east is scruffy.

If you want a really clear picture of the layout of the city, the best **map** to buy is *Michelin no 10*, the 1:10,000 Plan de Paris. More convenient is the pocket-sized *Falkplan*, which folds out only as much as you want it to, or if you're staying any length of time the *Paris-Eclair*: an **A–Z**, with street index, bus route diagrams, useful addresses, car parks and one way streets. Various **free maps** – not so good, of course – are available from the **Office de Tourisme**, 127 av des Champs-Élysées, 8ᵉ (Mᵒ Charles-de-Gaulle-Etoile; 47.23.61.72; opens 9–10 every day in high season, 9–8 otherwise).

The number after Paris addresses – as 8ᵉ above – indicates the **arrondissement** or postal district. There are twenty *arrondissements* altogether, the first (written 1ᵉʳ) centred on the Louvre with the rest unfurling in a clockwise spiral from there. Their boundaries are clearly marked on all maps, and are an important aid to locating places.

The **métro** is the simplest way of moving around. Trains run from 5.30am to 12.30am. Stations (abbreviated: Mᵒ Concorde, etc.) are far more frequent than on the London Underground. **Free maps** are available at most stations. In addition, every station has a big plan of the network outside the entrance and several inside. The lines are colour-coded and numbered, although they are signposted within the system with the names of the stations at the ends of the lines. For instance, if you're travelling from Gare du Nord to Odéon, you follow the sign *Direction Porte d'Orléans*; from Gare d'Austerlitz to Grenelle you follow *Direction Pont de St-Cloud*. The numerous junctions (*correspondances*) make it possible to travel all over the city in a more or less straight line. For the latest in subway technology, use the express stations' computerised routefinders – at a touch of the button they'll give you four alternative routes to your selected destination, on foot or by public transport.

The most economical **ticket**, if you are staying more than a day or two, is the **Carte Orange**, obtainable at all métro stations (you need a passport photo), with a weekly (*hebdomadaire*) or monthly (*mensuel*) coupon. It entitles you to unlimited travel on bus or métro. On the métro you put the coupon through the turnstile slot, but make sure to return it to its plastic folder; it is re-usable throughout the period of its validity. On a bus you show the whole *Carte* to the driver as you board – don't put it into the punching machine. There is a tourist ticket, *billet de tourisme*, but it is overpriced. For a short stay in the city **single tickets** can be bought at reduced rate in *carnets* of ten (from any station). All tickets are available as first or second class (though class distinctions are only in force between 9am and 5pm) and there's a **flat rate** across the city –

one ticket per journey. Be sure to keep your ticket until the end of the journey; you'll be fined on the spot if you can't produce one.

The **same tickets** are valid for bus, métro and, within the city limits, the **RER** express lines. Some bus journeys 'cost' two tickets; if in doubt, ask the driver. The central zones 1 and 2 are quite sufficient for most *Carte Orange* holders.

Don't however use the métro to the exclusion of the *buses*. They are not difficult and of course you see much more. There are **free route maps** available at métro stations, bus terminals and the tourist office. Every bus stop displays the numbers of the buses which stop there, a map showing all the stops on the route and the times of the first and last buses. If that is not enough, each bus has a map of its own route inside. Generally speaking, they start around 6.30am and begin their last run around 9pm. **Night buses** run every hour from place du Châtelet near the Hôtel de Ville. There is a reduced service on Sundays. Further information from the transport board, *RATP* (43.46.14.14), which incidentally runs numerous excursions, including some to quite far-flung places, much cheaper than the commercial operators; their brochure is available at all railway and some métro stations.

If it's late at night or you feel like treating yourself, don't hesitate to use the **taxis**. Their charges are very reasonable.

Points of arrival

Arriving by train you'll find yourself at one of Paris's six mainline stations, all equipped with cafés, restaurants, *tabacs*, banks, *bureaux de change* (long waits in season) and connected with the métro system. The **Gare du Nord** (serving Boulogne, Calais, the UK, Belgium, Holland and Scandinavia; 42.80.03.03 for information, 48.78.87.54 for reservations) and **Gare de l'Est** (serving eastern France, Germany, Switzerland and Austria; 42.08.49.90 information, 42.06.49.38 reservations) are side by side in the north-east of the city, with the **Gare St-Lazare** (serving the UK, Dieppe and the Normandy coast; 45.38.52.29 information, 43.87.91.70 reservations) a little to the west of them. Still on the Right Bank but towards the south-west corner is the **Gare de Lyon** serving the Alps, the south, Italy and Greece (43.45.92.22 information, 43.45.93.33 reservations). Just across the river on the Left Bank the **Gare d'Austerlitz** serves the south-west, Spain and Portugal (45.84.16.16 information, 45.84.15.20 reservations), while **Gare Montparnasse** serves Versailles, Chartres, Brittany and the Atlantic coast (tel. 45.38.52.29).

Almost all **coaches** coming into Paris – whether international or domestic – use the main **gare routière** in **place Stalingrad**: there's a métro station here to get into the centre. It is just possible, with some operators, that you'll be dropped on **place de la Madeleine** right in the centre.

If you're **driving** in yourself, don't try to cross the city to your destination. Take the ring road – the *boulevard périphérique* – to the *Porte* nearest your destination: it's much quicker, except at rush hour, and easier to find your way. Once ensconced wherever you're staying, you'd be well advised to garage the car and do your moving about by other means, if for no other reason than parking is a terrible problem.

Arriving by air you'll land at one of three airports: **Roissy-Charles de Gaulle** (BA, British Caledonian and Air France, plus most transatlantic flights; 48.62.22.80) or **Le Bourget** (internal flights; 48.62.12.12), both north-east of the city; or, **Orly-Sud/Orly-Ouest** (Eastern Europe, Spain, Africa; 46.87.12.34 and 48.53.12.34) to the south.

Roissy is connected with the city centre by: *Roissy-Rail*, a combination of airport bus and RER Ligne B train to the Gare du Nord (every 15min from 5am to 11.15pm), where you can transfer to the ordinary métro; *Air France bus* to Porte Maillot (métro) on the north-west edge of the city beyond the Arc de Triomphe (every 15min from 5.45am to 11pm); *buses 350* to Gare du Nord and Gare de l'Est, and *351* to place de la Nation. Roissy Rail is cheapest and quickest (about 35mins).

Orly also has a bus-rail link, Orly Rail. RER Ligne C trains leave every 15mins from 5.30am to 11.30pm for the Gare d'Austerlitz and other Left Bank stops which connect with the métro. Alternatively, there are *Air France coaches* to the Gare des Invalides, in the 7ᵉ or *Orlybus* to Denfert-Rochereau métro in the 14ᵉ. Both leave every 10–15mins from 6am to 11pm. Journey time is about 35mins.

Roissy and Orly both have **bureaux de change** open every day from 7–11.

Finding a place to stay

The hotel situation in Paris is not promising at the best of times. The **worst periods** according to the hoteliers' own organisation are: 9–13 Jan, 2–13 Feb, 4–8 March, 5–8 and 17–22 April, 16–18 and 25–31 May, 1–11 June, 7–10 and 20–30 Sept, 14–18 Oct, 8–17 Nov. And in July and August you have to compete with all the other tourists. But there are various agencies to help, which we've detailed below.

Youth hostels, foyers and campsites
At the **cheapest end** of the scale there are **Youth Hostels** at 8 bd Jules Ferry, 11ᵉ (Mᵒ République; 43.57.55.60); 17 bd Kellermann, 13ᵉ (Mᵒ Porte d'Italie; 45.80.70.76); 151 av Ledru-Rollin, 11ᵉ (Mᵒ Ledru-Rollin; 43.79.53.86); and in the suburbs, at 4 rue des Marguerites, Rueil Malmaison (47.49.43.97; 15mins by train from Gare St-Lazare to Gare de Suresnes, plus 15mins' walk) and Centre de Séjour de Choisy-le-Roi, 125 av de Villeneuve St-Georges, Choisy-le-Roi (48.90.92.30; RER train

from St-Michel to Choisy-le-Roi, where you cross the Seine, turn right and follow the signs. Booking in advance is a good idea.

For a slightly classier **foyer bed**, the best thing is to go to the **Accueil des Jeunes (AJF)**, who have offices in the Gare du Nord (Mon–Fri 9.15–6.15, Oct–June; 9.15–9 every day, July–Sept; 42.85.86.19) and at: 119 rue St-Martin, 4ᵉ, opposite the Centre Beaubourg (Mᵒ Châtelet, Les Halles; Mon–Sat 9.30–7.30; 42.77.87.80); 16 rue du Pont Louis-Philippe, 4ᵉ, near the Hôtel de Ville (Mᵒ Hôtel de Ville; Mon–Fri 9.30–6.30; 42.78.04.82); 136 bd St-Michel, 5ᵉ, in the Quartier Latin (Mᵒ Pont-Royal; Mon–Sat 9.30–7; 43.54.95.86). They guarantee finding you 'decent and low-cost lodging with immediate reservation'; phone or call in when you arrive – there's no advance booking. The organisation runs five foyers of its own: *Fourcy*, 6 rue de Fourcy, 4ᵉ (42.74.23.45); *Le Fauconnier*, 11 rue du Fauconnier, 4ᵉ (42.74.23.45); *Maubuisson*, 12 rue des Barres, 4ᵉ (42.72.72.09); *François Miron*, 6 rue François Miron, 4ᵉ (42.72.72.09); and *Maurice Ravel*, 6 av Maurice Ravel, 12ᵉ (Mᵒ Porte de Vincennes; 43.43.19.01). The first four are very central, all in historic buildings near the Hôtel de Ville (Mᵒ St-Paul, Pont-Marie, Hôtel de Ville) – the best of the *foyers*. You could also try the **Centre International de Paris** (BVJ), 20 rue Jean-Jacques Rousseau, 1ᵉʳ (42.36.88.18, Mᵒ Louvre); and two other places run by the same outfit at 5 rue du Pélican, 1ᵉʳ (42.60.92.45; Mᵒ Palais-Royal) and 11 rue Thérèse, 1ᵉʳ (Mᵒ Pyramides; 42.60.77.23).

CIDJ (101, quai Branly, 15ᵉ; Mᵒ Bir Hakeim; 45.66.40.20; Mon–Fri 9–7) can provide further lists of youth centres. Another possibility for longer stays is **France Monde Etudiants**, 14 rue du Regard, 6ᵉ (45.44.47.52) who, from 1 June to 30 Sept, offer vacationing French students' rooms to foreigners. It is also worth trying the notice boards at the American and British churches.

There is a **campsite** – usually crowded and in theory reserved for French camping club members – by the Seine in the Bois de Boulogne (allée du Bord de l'Eau, 16ᵉ; Mᵒ Porte Maillot; 45.06.14.98) and three more just east of the city: *Camping du Tremblay*, quai de Polangis, Champigny-sur-Marne (RER: Champigny; 42.83.38.24); *Camping du Camp des Cicognes*, bord de Marne, Créteil (RER: Créteil l'Echat; 42.07.06.75).; *Camping de Paris-Est*, bd des Alliés, Champigny-sur-Marne (Mᵒ Joinville-le-Pont; 42.83.38.24). And one to the west at Versailles: *Camping Municipal de Versailles*, 31 rue Berthelot (RER: Porchefontaine; 49.51.23.61).

Hotels
Some of the *AJF foyers* – and the bd Jules Ferry youth hostel – offer double (or triple) rooms as well as dormitory beds. But for independence and choice of location there's obviously more scope in the city **hotels**,

and a few of them even work out cheaper for two or more people. Below is a list of places that we've checked out ourselves, divided into two broad categories – under 150F and between 150–250F a room. Some may have one or two cheaper rooms – but don't count on getting them. If you arrive late, or you don't feel like tramping the streets, make for one of the **bureaux d'accueil** operated by the tourist office who will find you a room for a small commission. This service is provided at the main office (127 Champs-Élysées, 9–10/8 daily) and at the principal railway stations: Austerlitz, Mon–Sat 9–8, 10 in summer; Est, Mon–Sat 8–1, 5–8, 10 in summer; Lyon, Mon–Sat 8–1, 5–8, 10 in summer; Nord, Mon–Sat 8–8, 10 in summer. If you don't like it you can always move on after one night.

UNDER 150F
Hôtel Henri IV, 25 place Dauphine, 1ᵉʳ. M° Pont-Neuf, Cité (43.54.44.53). Beautifully situated on Ile de la Cité. Very cheap and very booked up.
Hôtel Gay-Lussac, 29 rue Gay-Lussac, 5ᵉ. M° Luxembourg (43.54.23.96). Book a week ahead if possible.
Hôtel St-Michel, 17 rue Gît-le-Coeur, 6ᵉ. M° St-Michel (43.26.98.70). Very central – near place St-Michel.
Victoria Hotel, Cité Bergère, 6 rue du Fbg Montmartre, 9ᵉ. M° Montmartre (47.70.18.83). Situated in a quiet courtyard opposite Chartier's restaurant, along with several other reasonable hotels.
Hôtel du Ranelagh, 56 rue de l'Assomption, 16ᵉ. M° Ranelagh (42.88.31.63). Very pleasant and accessible cheapie near the Bois de Boulogne.
Hôtel du Théâtre, 5 rue de Chéroy, 17ᵉ. M° Rome (43.87.21.48). Near St-Lazare station. No beauty.
Idéal Hôtel, 3 rue des Trois-Frères, 18ᵉ. M° Abbesses (46.06.63.63). Very basic, but marvellous location. No reservations, so there is a good chance of finding space if you turn up before 11am.
Hôtel Tholozé, 24 rue Tholozé, 18ᵉ. M° Abbesses, Blanche (46.06.74.83). Basic but good location.

150–250F
Hôtel California, 32 rue des Ecoles, 5ᵉ. M° Maubert-Mutualité (46.34.12.90).
Hôtel des Carmes, 5 rue des Carmes, 5ᵉ. M° Maubert-Mutualité (43.29.78.40). Some much cheaper rooms.
Hôtel Esmeralda, 4 rue St-Julien-le-Pauvre, 5ᵉ. M° St-Michel, Maubert-Mutualité (43.54.19.20). Right on square Viviani with a superb view of Notre-Dame.

Le Latania, 22 rue de la Parcheminerie, 5ᵉ. Mᵒ St-Michel (43.54.32.17). Unprepossessing outside, but adequate.

Hôtel Mont-Blanc, 28 rue de la Huchette, 5ᵉ. Mᵒ St-Michel (43.54.49.44). Simple but adequate. Rooms are lighter higher up.

Hôtel Le Montana, 28 rue St-Benoît, 6ᵉ. Mᵒ St-Germain-des-Prés (45.48.62.15).

Ste-Eugénie Hôtel, 31 rue St-André-des-Arts, 6ᵉ. Mᵒ St-Michel (43.26.29.03). Rooms are adequate; great location.

Hôtel Récamier, 3bis place St-Sulpice, 6ᵉ. Mᵒ St-Sulpice, Mabillon (43.26.04.89). On a pretty square near Luxembourg gardens.

Hôtel du Palais Bourbon, 49 rue de Bourgogne, 7ᵉ. Mᵒ Varenne (45.51.63.32). Attractive 18C street near Musée Rodin.

Hôtel Chopin, 46 passage Jouffroy, 9ᵉ. Mᵒ Montmartre (47.70.58.10). Off one of the old-fashioned *passages*, near Chartier's.

Mondial Hôtel, 21 rue Notre-Dame-de-Lorette, 9ᵉ. Mᵒ. St-Georges (48.78.60.47).

Hôtel de Madrid, rue Geoffrey Marie, 9ᵉ. Mᵒ Le Pelletier, Cadet (47.70.85.87). Old-fashioned rooms with marble fireplaces and big, framed mirrors.

Grand Hôtel de l'Europe, 74 bd de Strasbourg, 10ᵉ. Mᵒ Gare de l'Est (46.07.76.27). Close to the station. Okay as a fall-back.

Hôtel Centre Est, 4 rue Sibour, 10ᵉ. Mᵒ Gare de l'Est (46.07.20.74). Near the station. Clean and friendly.

Plessis-Hôtel, 25 rue du Grand-Prieuré, 11ᵉ. Mᵒ République, Oberkampf (47.00.13.38). Better value than most.

Institut Hôtel, 23 bd Pasteur, 15ᵉ. Mᵒ Pasteur (45.67.10.48). Clean and adequate, on a leafy, animated street.

Hôtel Ini, 159 bd Lefebvre, 15ᵉ. Mᵒ Pte de Vanves (48.28.18.35). Decent hotel, but dull location.

Hôtel des Batignolles, 26–28 rue des Batignolles, 17ᵉ. Mᵒ Rome, place Clichy (43.87.70.40). Villagey area close to Montmartre with lots of small shops and restaurants.

Lévis-Hôtel, 16 rue Lebouteux, 17ᵉ. Mᵒ Villiers (47.63.86.38). Only ten rooms, but very nice, in small, quiet street off the colourful rue de Lévis market.

Modern Hôtel, 3 rue Forest, 18ᵉ. Mᵒ place Clichy (43.87.47.61). Adequate – next to monstrous modern tourist-grinder.

La Résidence Montmartre, 10 rue Burcq, 18ᵉ. Mᵒ Abbesses (46.06.45.28).

Hôtel André Gill, 4 rue André Gill, 18ᵉ – off rue des Martyrs. Mᵒ Abbesses, Pigalle (42.62.48.48). Cheap and friendly.

THE CITY

There are obviously numerous ways of approaching a city as big as Paris
– you don't have to start with the Eiffel Tower or Champs-Élysées. We've
structured our account in chunks of territory that seem to have a common
identity. Though they do not correspond exactly to the boundaries of the
twenty *arrondissements*, they are arranged in the same configuration,
starting in the centre of town and working outwards, south and west,
north and east. Apart from a couple of suggested walks – from the Parc
Monceau to the edge of Montmartre and along the bank of the St-Denis
canal – they are not itineraries to be followed slavishly.

Some cafés, markets, shops and museum buildings are mentioned here
in passing. For full respective details or listings see pp. 86, 100, 101 and
71.

The Champs-Élysées

La Voie Triomphale, or Triumphal Way, stretches in a dead straight line
from the eastern end of the **Louvre** to the modern complex of skyscrapers
at **La Défense** nine kilometres away, incorporating some of the world's
most famous urban landmarks – the Champs-Élysées, Arc de Triomphe
and Tuileries gardens. Its monumental constructions have been erected
over the centuries by kings and emperors, presidents and corporations,
to propagate French power and prestige. The tradition dies hard. Further
aggrandisement is planned for the end of the decade: an enormous white
marble arch at the head of La Défense – the 'Crossroads of International
Communication' – and a glass pyramid entrance in the central courtyard
of the Louvre. Work on the latter project has already begun, sealing off
the Cour Napoléon for the foreseeable future, while Louis XIV's Cour
Carrée has been given over to archaeologists hunting out traces of the
original medieval fortress.

The best view of this grandiose and simple geometry of kings to capital
is from the top of the **Arc de Triomphe**, Napoleon's homage to the armies
of France and himself (10–6/5 in winter; expensive). Your attention,
however, will be somewhat distracted by the mesmerising traffic movements in **place de l'Étoile**, the world's oldest organised roundabout,
directly below you. From here the broad **avenue des Champs-Élysées**
sweeps downhill to the east to end in the motorised maelstrom of **place
de la Concorde**, where the same anarchic vehicles make crossing to the
centre point a death-defying task.

As it happens, some 1,300 people did die here between 1793 and 1795,
beneath the Revolutionary guillotine: Louis XVI, Marie-Antoinette,
Danton and Robespierre among them. The centre-piece of the *place*,

chosen like its name to make no comment on these events, is an **obelisk** from the temple of Luxor, offered as a favour-currying gesture by the viceroy of Egypt in 1829. It serves merely to pivot more geometry: the alignment of the French parliament, the **Chambre des Deputés**, on the far side of the Seine with the church of the **Madeleine** to the north. Needless to say, it cuts the Voie Triomphale at a precise and predictable right-angle. And the symmetry continues beyond the *place* in the **Tuileries gardens**, disrupted only by the bodies sprawling on the grass, gays cruising the **Orangerie** at one end of the terrace and the queues for the **Jeu de Paume** Impressionist gallery at the other.

Back to the west, between Concorde and the Rond-Point roundabout, the Champs-Élysées is bordered by chestnut trees and municipal flower-beds, pleasant enough to stroll among but not sufficiently dense to muffle the discomforting squeal of accelerating tyres. The two massive buildings rising above the greenery to the south are the **Grand** and **Petit Palais** with their overloaded neoclassical exteriors and railway station roofs. On the north side, combat police guard the high walls round the presidential **Élysée palace** and the line of ministries and embassies ending with the US at the corner of place de la Concorde. On Sundays you can see a stranger manifestation of the self-images of states in the postage **stamp market** at the corner of avenues Gabriel and Marigny.

Though the glamour of the Champs-Élysées has long since dissipated, it is still the setting for major jamborees. On 31 December it's the Paris equivalent of Trafalgar Square with everyone happily jammed in their cars hooting the New Year in. On Bastille Day – 14 July – it turns into a parade ground for guns, tanks and President.

To reach **La Défense** at the extreme western end of the Voie Triomphale make one stop on the RER from Étoile – there you follow the signs for *Parvis*, avoiding at all costs the snare of the *Quatre Temps* hypermarket. Once on the *parvis*, you have before you and above you a perfect monument to the wastefulness and inhumanity of capital production. There is no formal pattern to the arrangement of towers. Token apartment blocks, offices of ELF, Esso, IBM, banks and other businesses compete for size, dazzle of surface and ability to make you dizzy. Mercifully, **bizarre art works** transform the nightmare into comic entertainment. Jean Miró's giant wobbly creatures despair at their misfit status beneath the biting edges and curveless heights of the buildings. Opposite, Alexander Calder's red iron offering is a *stabile* rather than a mobile and between them a black marble metronome shape without a beat releases a goal-less line across the *parvis*. A classic war memorial perches on a concrete plinth in front of a plastic coloured waterfall and nearer the river disembodied people clutch each other round endlessly repeated concrete flowerbeds. If the cubic arch comes into being, the wind-tunnel effect will be so great that any open window will tear off its hinges and plunge to the *parvis*.

The *passages*: Right Bank commerce

In the narrow streets of the 1er and 2e *arrondissements*, **between the Louvre and bd Montmartre**, the grand institutions of state are embedded in a welter of small business premises – the ragtrade, media, sex and old-fashioned shopping. The greatest contrast is provided by the crumbling and secretive **Passages**, shopping arcades with glass roofs, tiled floors and unobtrusive entrances, that predate the imposition of the *major boulevards*. Some are being done up and the shops leased to travel agents and beauty parlours, such as **Galerie Vivienne** (between rue Vivienne and rue des Petits-Champs) with its flamboyant décor of Grecian and marine motifs. The neighbouring **Galerie Colbert,**, said to be the most beautiful, is being converted into an extension of the Bibliothèque Nationale.

North of rue St-Marc the decline of the *passages* from their 19C chic is more noticeable. The grid of half-abandoned arcades round **passage des Panoramas** have a typical combination of bric-à-brac shops, bars, stamp dealers, and an upper-crust printer, established 1867, with intricately carved shop-fittings of the same period. In **passage Jouffroy** across bd Montmartre, a Monsieur Segas sells walking canes and theatrical antiques opposite a North African and Asian carpet emporium. Further on, beyond the next street, you can hunt for old comics and cameras in **passage Verdeau**.

The best stylistically are the dilapidated three-story **passage du Grand-Cerf** (Mo Etienne-Marcel) and **Galerie Véro-Dodat**, off rue Croix-des-Petits-Champs. This last is the most homogeneous and aristocratic, with painted ceilings and panelled shop-fronts divided by black marble columns. At no 26 Monsieur Capia keeps a collection of antique dolls in a shop piled high with miscellaneous curios.

Place du Caire is the centre of the ragtrade district, where frenetic trading and deliveries of cloth, the food market on rue des Petits-Carreaux, and general to-ing and fro-ing make a lively change from the office-bound quarters further west. Beneath an extraordinary pseudo-Egyptian façade of grotesque Pharaonic heads (a celebration of Napoleon's conquest of Egypt), an archway opens onto a series of arcades, the **Passage du Caire**. These, contrary to any visible evidence, are the oldest of them all, and entirely monopolised by wholesale clothes shops.

The garment business gets progressively more upmarket westwards from the trade area. Louis XIV's **place des Victoires**, adjoined to the north by the appealingly unsymmetrical **place des Petits-Pères**, is a centre for designer clothes, displayed in such a way as to deter all those without the necessary funds. Another autocratic square, **place Vendôme**, with Napoleon high on a column of recycled Austro-Russian canons, offers the fashionable accessories for haute couture – jewellery, perfumes, the Ritz, and a Rothschild office. The boutiques on **rue St-Honoré** and its

Faubourg extension reach the same class, paralleled across the Champs-Élysées by **rue François I**er where **Dior** has at least four blocks on the corner with av Montaigne. After clothes, bodies are the most evident commodity on sale in this area – on rue St-Denis, above all, where despite unionisation by the prostitutes the pimps reign supreme. Rue Ste-Anne is considerably more discreet, the reason being that the prostitutes are gay, transvestite and underage.

Nearby, the **Bourse** is the scene for dealing in stocks and shares, dollars and gold. The classical order of the façade utterly belies the scene within, like an unruly boys' public school, with creaking floors, tottering pigeon-holes and people scuttling about with bits of paper. There's hardly a computer in sight and the real financial sharks go elsewhere for their deals. The status of the City of London is the French no 2 grudge after the dominance of the English language, so plans to modernise the Bourse are always being promised.

There is another obese building on the Greek temple model in the neighbouring *quartier*, the **church of the Madeleine**, which serves for society weddings and the perspective across place de la Concorde. There's a **flower market** every day except Monday along the east side of the church and a luxurious Art Nouveau loo by the métro at the junction of place and bd Madeleine. In the north-east corner of the *place* are two

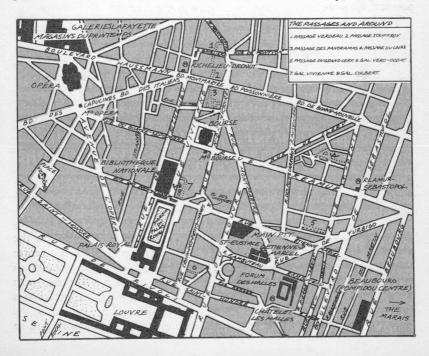

blocks of the best food display in Paris – at *Fauchon's* (see p. 102). If you want a cheap midday meal in this area, try rue des Capucines, off the boulevard half way between the Madeleine and **Opéra**, the most preposterous building in the city. Its architect, Charles Garnier, looks suitably foolish in a golden statue on the rue Auber side of his edifice, that so perfectly suited the court of Napoleon III. Excessively ornate and covering three acres in extent, it provided ample space for aristocratic preening, ceremonial pomp and the social intercourse of opera-goers, for whom the performance itself was a very secondary matter. Contemporary lovers of the art who can't afford a £30–60 ticket have to queue all night. You can visit the **interior** (11–5), including the auditorium, where the ceiling is the work of Chagall. The classic horror movie, *The Phantom of the Opera*, was set, though never filmed, here and underground there is a stream to lend credence to the tale.

At the other end of av de l'Opéra, the **Palais Royal**, originally Richelieu's residence, then royal property, now houses various government and constitutional bodies and the **Comédie Française** – where the classics of the French theatre are performed. The palace **gardens**, once a café hotspot and arena for public entertainment, are now no more than a useful shortcut from the Louvre to rue des Petits-Champs, though a certain charm lurks about rue Beaujolais bordering the northern end of the gardens with its corner café looking onto the Théâtre du Palais Royal and short arcades leading up to the main street. Across, just to the left, is the forbidding wall of the **Bibliothèque Nationale**, the French equivalent of the British Museum library. They have a public display of coins and ecclesiastical treasures (open 1–5), so you can at least enter the building should you feel so inclined.

Les Halles

In 1969 the main **Les Halles** market was moved out to the suburbs after more than 800 years in the heart of the city. There was widespread opposition to the destruction of Victor Baltard's 19C pavilions and considerable disquiet at what renovation of the area would mean. The authorities' excuse was the RER and métro interchange they had to have below. Digging began in 1971 and the hole has yet to be entirely filled. No trace remains of the working-class quarter with its night bars and bistros serving the market traders. Rents now rival the 16ᵉ and the all-night places serve and profit from the salaried and speed-popping classes.

From Châtelet-Les Halles RER, you surface only after ascending levels −4 to 0 of the **Forum des Halles** shopping centre. The aquarium-like arcades are enclosed by glass buttocks with white steel creases sliding down to an imprisoned patio. To cover up for all this commerce, a cultural centre tops two sides of the Forum in a simple construction –

save for the mirrors – that just manages to be out of sync with the curves and hollows below. From the terrace you can see an aimless sequence of metal arches, on which plants resolutely refuse to flourish, concrete trunks for water to dribble down and, at the edge of the endless worksite, the rotunda of the **Bourse du Commerce** and the Gothic monkeys' rock of **St-Eustache**. Visions of the ensemble completed with nine more major structures is too horrible to contemplate. Better to join the throng around the **Fontaine des Innocents** and watch and listen to water cascading down perfect Renaissance proportions. There are hundreds of people all around the Forum, filling in time, hustling or just loafing about. Pick-pocketing and sexual harassment are pretty routine and it can be very tense at night.

Retreating back towards the Louvre, streets like de l'**Arbre Sec** and **du Roule** revive the attractions of window shopping with displays of 1920s clothes, shop-fronts decorated to suit the wares inside and secluded *salons de thé* (see p. 87). Or you can shop in the Art Nouveau gold, green, and glass décor of the **Samaritaine** department store on the riverfront. **To the east** the area between place du Châtelet and Les Halles teems with jazz bars, night clubs and restaurants (see pp. 88/94) and is more crowded at 2am than 2pm.

In the daytime the main flow of feet is to and from Les Halles and **Beaubourg**, the **Georges Pompidou national art and culture centre**. At least, this much-discussed building with its external frame and coloured pipes, ducts and escalator has a powerful presence. And no matter what is going on inside it is permanently surrounded by mime, magic, fire and music buskers. The centre is open, free, every day except Tuesday, from 12–8 and until 10 at weekends; for galleries, cinema, kids, etc. see pp. 74/96/97. On the ground floor the postcard selection and art bookshop betters anything on the streets outside (and there are free loos). The escalator is usually one long queue, but you have to ride up this glass intestine once. As the circles of spectators on the plaza recede, a horizontal skyline appears: the Sacré-Coeur, St-Eustache, the Eiffel Tower, Notre-Dame, the Panthéon, the Tour St-Jacques with its solitary gargoyle and La Défense, menacing in the distance. From the platform at the top you can look down on the château-style chimneys of the Hôtel de Ville with their flowerpot offspring sprouting all over the lower rooftops.

Back on the ground, **visual entertainments** around Beaubourg don't appeal to every taste. There's the clanking gold *Défenseur du Temps* clock in the Quartier de l'Horloge, courtesy of Mayor Jacques Chirac; a *trompe l'oeil* as you look along rue Aubry-le-Boucher from Beaubourg; and sculptures and fountains by Tinguely and Nicky de St-Phalle in the pool between the centre and Eglise St-Merri, which pay homage to Stravinsky and show scant respect for passers by. The locality is much favoured by small commercial art galleries, St-Martin, Quincampoix and Beaubourg being the most popular streets. Rue Renard, the continuation of rue Beaubourg, meets the river at the **Hôtel de Ville**, the town hall. An illustrated history of the edifice, which has always been a prime target in riots and revolutions, is displayed along the platform of the Châtelet métro on the Neuilly-Vincennes line.

Le Marais and the Île St-Louis

Jack Kerouac translates **rue des Francs-Bourgeois** as 'street of the outspoken middle classes'., In fact, the name derives from the medieval residents of its almshouses. 'Street of the wealthy courtiers' would be more appropriate, for the 16C and 17C mansions that still make up more than half its length. At that period, the **Marais** – which occupies the area between Beaubourg and the Bastille, became the fashionable quarter for residences of the aristocracy. It was later abandoned to the masses, who, until some fifteen years ago, were living ten to a room on unserviced, squalid streets. Since then gentrification has proceeded apace and the middle classes are finally ensconced – not all outspoken, and mainly media, arty or gay. The renovated mansions, their grandeur mostly concealed by the narrow streets, have become museums, libraries, offices or chic flats. Though ringed by Haussmann's boulevards, the Marais itself was spared the Baron's heavy touch and very little has been pulled down in the recent upmarketing. It is Paris at its most desirable – old, secluded, as unthreatening by night as it is by day, and with as many little shops, *salons de thé* and places to eat as you could wish for. A few low-rent pockets still exist to the east and around **rue des Rosiers**, traditional Jewish quarter of the city. There have been several bomb attacks in the last few years on synagogues here and on Goldenburg's deli/restaurant, and NF spraycans periodically eject their obscenities on walls and shopfronts. Not surprisingly the reception given to strangers is rather stiff, but you can shrug off hostility in the **Hammam St-Paul** or in the deep armchairs of **Le Loir dans la Théière** salon de thé, both on rue des Rosiers. The peeling streets between **rues de Sévigné** and **Turenne** near rue St-Antoine are worth walking through just for contrast, if your destination is **place des Vosges**. This vast square of stone and brick symmetry was built for the majesty of Henri IV and Louis XIII, whose statue is hidden by trees in the middle of the grass and gravel gardens. Toddlers and octogenarians, lunch-break workers and schoolchildren come to sit or play here, in the only green space of any size in the Marais.

Below rue Rivoli/St-Antoine, many of the old houses have disappeared with the people, but a few medieval leftovers remain – **Hôtel Sens** on rues Hôtel-de-Ville and Figuier, and the tottering timbered dwellings on **rue François-Miron**. Mixed with smells of gardens, incense from St-

Gervais and food from a tiny restaurant, the steps of rue des Barres make a tranquil passage down to Pont Louis-Philippe and the Île St-Louis.

This island, unlike its larger neighbour, has no monuments or museums, just high houses on single-lane streets, a school, church and the best sorbets in the world chez *M Berthillon*. If you're the Pretender to the French throne or the Aga Khan, this is where you have your Paris home. If not, you can still seek seclusion on the *quais*, tightly clutching a triple cornet of sorbets as you descend the steps or climb over the low gate on the right of the garden across bd Henri IV to reach the best sunbathing spot in Paris. Nothing can rival the taste of iced passion or kiwi fruit, guava, melon or whichever flavour – a sensation that ripe, fresh-picked fruit can only aspire to. Nevertheless the island does have its own considerable charm, even when Berthillon and his six concessionaries are closed.

Île de la Cité

The Île de la Cité is where Paris began. The earliest settlements were sited here, as was the small Gallic town of Lutetia overrun by Julius Caesar's troops in 52BC. A natural defensive site commanding a major east-west river trade route, it was an obvious candidate for a bright future. The Romans garrisoned it and laid out one of their standard military town plans, overlapping onto the Left Bank. While it never achieved any great political importance, they endowed it with an administrative centre which became the palace of the Merovingian kings in 508, then of the counts of Paris, who in 987 became kings of France. So from the very beginning the Ile has been close to the administrative heart of France. Today the charm of the island lies in its tail-end – the **square du Vert-Galant**, its **quais**, the **place Dauphine** and the **cathedral of Notre-Dame** itself. The central section has been rather dulled by heavy-handed 19C demolition.

If you arrive by the **Pont-Neuf**, the city's oldest bridge, you will see some steps leading down to the *square*, a small tree-lined green enclosed within the triangular stern of the island. The prime spot to occupy is the extreme point beneath a weeping willow – haunt of lovers, sparrows and sunbathers.

On the other side of the bridge, opposite a statue of Henry IV who commissioned it, the sanded, chestnut-shaded **place Dauphine** remains one of the city's most charming squares, with a couple of restaurants, a *salon de thé* and much-sought-after cheap hotel, the *Henri IV*. Behind it the nondescript **Palais de Justice** has swallowed up the palace that was home to the French kings until 1360 and before them of the Roman governors. In a courtyard to the left of the main gate, stands the **Sainte-Chapelle**, built by Louis IX to house a collection of holy relics he had bought at extortionate rates from the bankrupt empire of Byzantium.

Though much restored, it remains one of the finest achievements of French Gothic (consecrated in 1248). Very tall in relation to its length it looks like a cathedral choir lopped off and transformed into an independent building. Its most radical feature is its fragility: the reduction of structural masonry to a minimum to make way for a huge expanse of stunning **stained glass**. The impression inside is of being enclosed within the wings of a myriad of butterflies – the predominant colours blue and red, and, in the later rose window, grass-green and blue. It pays to get there as early as possible (open 10–6/5 from 1 Oct–31 Mar; half price Sun & hols). It is a terrible tourist trap, and expensive: 30F with the ticket for the **Conciergerie**, the old prison where Marie-Antoinette and, in their turn, the leading figures of the Revolution were incarcerated before execution. The chief interest of the Conciergerie is the enormous late Gothic Salle des Gens d'Armes, canteen and recreation room of the royal household staff. You are missing little in not seeing Marie-Antoinette's cell and various other macabre mementoes of the guillotine's victims.

On the north side of the island, between here and Notre-Dame, there is a daily **flower and plant market** in place Lépine (birds on Sundays) by the Cité métro station. The **Cathédrale de Notre Dame** itself is so much photographed that even seeing it for the first time the edge of your response is somewhat dulled by familiarity. Yet it is truly impressive, that great H-shaped west front, with its strong vertical divisions counterbalanced by the horizontal emphasis of gallery and frieze, all centred by the rose window. It demands to be seen as a whole, though that can scarcely have been possible when the medieval houses clustered close about it. It is a solid, no-nonsense design, confessing its Romanesque ancestry. For the more fantastical kind of Gothic, look rather at the **north transept façade** with its crocketed gables and huge fretted window-space.

Notre-Dame was begun in 1160 under the auspices of Bishop de Sully and completed c1245. In the 19C, Viollet-le-Duc carried out extensive renovation work, including remaking most of the statuary – the entire frieze of kings, for instance – and adding the steeple and baleful-looking gargoyles, which you can see close-up if you brave the ascent of the towers (10–5.45/4.45; half price Sun & hols).

Inside the immediately striking feature, if you can ignore the noise and movement, is the dramatic contrast between the darkness of the nave and the light falling on the first great clustered pillars of the choir, emphasising the special nature of the sanctuary. It is the end walls of the transepts which admit all this light, nearly two-thirds glass, including two magnificent **rose windows** coloured in imperial purple. These, the vaulting, the soaring shafts reaching to the springs of the vaults, are all definite Gothic elements, yet, inside as out, there remains a strong sense of Romanesque in the stout round pillars of the nave and the general sense of four-squareness.

Before you leave, walk round to the public garden at the east end for a view of the **flying buttresses** supporting the choir, and then along the riverside under the south transept, where it is a delight to sit when the cherry blossom is out.

There is an interesting but expensive **museum** (10–6/5; half-price Sun) under the car-park-like space in front of the cathedral where are revealed the remains of walls, streets and houses of first millennium Paris.

The Left Bank

The term **Left Bank** (*rive gauche*) connotes Bohemian, dissident, intellectual – the radical student type, whether 18 years of age or 80. As a topographical term it refers particularly to their traditional haunts – the warren of medieval lanes round the **boulevards St-Michel** and **St-Germain**, known as the **Quartier Latin** because that was the language of the university sited there right up until 1789. In modern times its reputation for turbulence and innovation has been renewed by the activities of painters and writers like Picasso, Apollinaire, Breton, Henry Miller, Anaïs Nin and Hemingway after the First World War, Camus, Sartre, Juliette Greco and the Existentialists after the Second, and the political turmoil of 1968 which escalated from student demonstrations and barricades to factory occupations, massive strikes and the near-overthrow of de Gaulle's presidency. This is not to say that the whole of Paris south of the Seine is the exclusive territory of revolutionaries and avant-gardists. It does, however, have a different and distinct feel, and appearance, that you notice as soon as you cross the river.

St-Michel to rue Mouffetard

Bd St-Michel itself and the riverside streets to the east have become tawdry now and commercial, cashing in on the tourist appeal of the Latin Quarter. The narrow **rue de la Huchette**, once the mecca of avant-gardists, is entirely given over to Greek restaurants of indifferent quality and inflated prices. At its further end is **rue St-Jacques**, aligned on the main street of Roman Paris, in medieval times the road up which millions of pilgrims trudged at the start of their long march to St-Jacques-de-Compostelle in Spain (see p. 11). Just to the right, **St-Séverin** (largely 15C) is one of the more attractive Parisian churches with a very pretty Flamboyant choir (11–1 & 3.30–7.30).

Across the street **square Viviani** provides the most flattering of all views of Notre-Dame. The mutilated little church of **St-Julien-le-Pauvre** in one corner is as old as the cathedral, but nothing much to look at now. It used to be used for university assemblies until some rumbustious students tore it apart in the 1500s. Round to the left on rue de la Bûcherie the English bookshop, **Shakespeare and Co**, is haunted by the shades of Joyce and other great expatriate literati. The *quais* themselves, despite their romantic reputation, are not much fun to walk because of the traffic, unless you get right down by the water's edge.

The best strolling area this side of bd St-Michel is the slopes of the **Montagne Ste-Geneviève**, the hill on which the Panthéon stands. From the St-Germain-St-Michel crossroads, where the walls of the 3C **Roman baths** are visible in the gardens of the **Hôtel de Cluny**, go round through rue de Cluny to the entrance of the hôtel. It is a 16C mansion resembling an Oxbridge college, built by the abbots of the powerful Cluny monastery as their Paris pied-à-terre. It now houses a very beautiful **museum** of medieval art (see p. 75). There is no charge for entry to the quiet shady courtyard.

The grim-looking buildings on the other side of rue des Écoles are the **Sorbonne, Collège de France**, and **Lycée Louis le Grand**, all major constituents of the brilliant and mandarin world of French intellectual activity. You can put your nose in the Sorbonne courtyard without anyone objecting. The **Richelieu chapel**, dominating the uphill end, was the first Roman-influenced building in 17C Paris and set the trend for subsequent developments. Nearby the traffic-free **place de la Sorbonne** with its lime trees, cafés and student habitués is a lovely place to sit.

Further up the hill the broad rue Soufflot provides an appropriately grand perspective on the domed and porticoed **Panthéon**, Louis XIV's thankyou to Sainte Geneviève, patron saint of Paris, for curing him of illness. Imposing enough at a distance, it is cold and uninteresting close to – not a friendly detail for the eye to rest on. The Revolution transformed it into a mausoleum for great Frenchmen. It is deadly inside (10–6/4 cl. Tues). There are, however, several cafés to warm the heart's cockles down towards the Luxembourg gardens.

More interesting than the Panthéon is the mainly 16C church of **St-Etienne-du-Mont** on the corner of rue Clovis, with a façade combining Gothic, Renaissance and Baroque elements. The interior, if not exactly beautiful, is highly unexpected. The space is divided into three aisles by free-standing pillars connected by a narrow catwalk and flooded with light by an exceptionally tall clerestory. Again unusually – for they mainly fell victim to the destructive anti-clericalism of the Revolution – the church still possesses its rood screen, a broad low arch supporting a gallery reached by twining spiral stairs. There is some good 17C glass in the cloister. Further down rue Clovis a piece of Philippe Auguste's city walls survives.

Just a step to the south in the quiet rue des Fossés-St-Jacques is a small and very attractive wine bar, *Café de la Nouvelle Mairie*, whose kerb-side tables make an excellent lunch-stop. Continuing south down rue St-Jacques, you come to **Val-de-Grâce**, the city's most Baroque church, with a two-tiered pedimented front and ornate cupola copied from St Peter's in Rome – built in mid-17C for the long childless Anne of Austria in gratitude for the birth of her son, Louis XIV. But once you are over the Gay-Lussac intersection, the area is shabby and uninteresting, the animation of the Quarter Latin left well behind. Prices are cheaper as a result, though, if you're in need of a good fill.

If not, you'll find more enticing wandering in the little almost villagey streets **east of the Panthéon. Rue de la Montagne Ste-Geneviève** (a good restaurant street) climbs up from place Maubert across rue des Écoles to the gates of the **École Polytechnique**, one of the prestigious academies for entry to the top échelons of state power. There are cafés and restaurants outside the gates – sunny, peaceful spots. From here rue Descartes leads into the medieval **rue Mouffetard** a cobbled lane winding downhill to the church of **St-Médard**, once a country parish beside the now covered river Bièvre. The bottom half of the street with its fruit and veg stalls is still attractive. The upper half is all eating places, mostly Greek and little better than in rue de la Huchette. Like any place wholly devoted to the entertainment of tourists, it has lost its soul. The tiny **place de la Contrescarpe** half-way down was once an arty hangout; Hemingway wrote and Georges Brassens sang there. It is a dosser's rendez-vous now.

A little **further east**, across rue Monge, however, are some of the city's most agreeable surprises. Down rue Daubenton, past a delightful Arab shop selling sweets, spices, and gawdy tea-glasses you come to the crenellated walls of the Paris **mosque**, overtopped by greenery and a great square minaret. You can walk in the sunken garden and patios with their polychrome tiles and carved ceilings, but not the prayer room (9–12, 2–6; cl. Fri and Muslim hols). There is a **tearoom** too, open to all, and a **hammam** (see p. 104).

Opposite the mosque is an entrance to the **Jardin des Plantes**, with a small, cramped, expensive zoo, botanical gardens, hothouses and museums of paleontology and mineralogy – a pretty space of greenery to while away the middle of a day. By the rue Cuvier exit is a fine Cedar of Lebanon planted in 1734, raised from seed sent over from Oxford Botanical Gardens and a slice of an American sequoia more than 2,000 years old with Christ's birth and other historical events its life has encompassed marked on its rings. In the nearby physics labs Henri Becquerel discovered radioactivity in 1896, and two years later the Curies discovered radium – unwitting ancestors of the *force de frappe* (the French nuclear deterrent). Pierre ended his days under the wheels of a brewer's dray on rue Dauphine.

A short distance away, with an entrance in rue de Navarre and another through a passage on rue Monge, is Paris's other Roman remain, the **Arènes de Lutèce**, an unexpected backwater, quite hidden from the street. It is a partly restored amphitheatre, with a *boules* pitch in the centre, benches, gardens and a kids' playground behind.

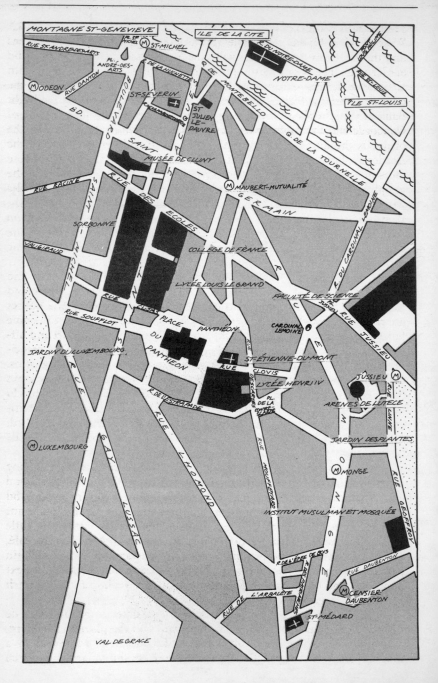

St-Germain

West of bd St-Michel the whole area between the Luxembourg gardens and the river is a delight, especially the **St-Germain quarter** north of bd St-Germain. The best way to approach it is over the **Pont des Arts**, with a lovely view upstream of the Ile de la Cité, the barges moored at the quai de Conti, the Tour St-Jacques and Hôtel de Ville breaking the Right Bank skyline, while downstream the eye is carried to the greenery of Concorde and the roofs of the Grand and Petit Palais. At the end of the bridge is the dome and pediment of the **Institut de France**, seat of the Académie Française, an august body of writers and scholars whose mission is to safeguard the purity of the French language. This is the grandiose bit of the Left Bank riverfront. To the left is the **Hôtel des Monnaies**, redesigned as the Mint in the late 18C. To the right is the **Beaux-Arts**, the school of Fine Art, whose students throng the *quais* on sunny days, sketch pads on knee. Further down in the ornate **Gare d'Orsay**, slowly being transformed into a museum as part of the long process of rationalising the distribution of the capital's art treasures.

The **riverside quarter** is cut lengthwise by **rue St-André-des-Arts** and **rue Jacob**. It is full of bookshops, galleries, antique shops, cafés and restaurants. Poke your nose into courtyards and sidestreets. The houses are four to six storeys high, 17C and 18C, some noble, some stiff, some bulging and skew, all painted in infinite gradations of grey, pearl and off-white. Broadly speaking, the further west the posher. Historical associations are legion. Picasso painted Guernica in rue des Grands Augustins. Molière started his career in rue Mazarine. Robespierre and co split ideological hairs at the *café Procope* in rue de l'Ancienne Comédie. In rue Visconti, Racine died, Delacroix painted and Balzac's printing business went bust. In the parallel rue des Beaux Arts, Oscar Wilde died, Corot and Ampère, father of amps, lived and the crazy poet, Gérard de Nerval, went walking with a lobster on a lead.

If you're looking for lunch, **place** and **rue St-André** offer a tempting concentration of places – from Tunisian sandwich joints to seafood extravagance – and a brilliant food market in rue Buci up towards bd St-Germain. Nearby rue Dauphine is pretty good, too: see the restaurant listings on p. 89. Before you get to Buci, there is an intriguing little passage on the left, **Cour du Commerce**, between a *crêperie* and the café, *Le Mazet*. Marat had his printing press in the passage, while Dr Guillotin perfected his namesake machine by lopping sheep's heads in the loft next door. A couple of smaller courtyards open off it, revealing another stretch of Philippe Auguste's wall.

An alternative corner for midday food or quiet is around rue de l'Abbaye (vegetarian meals here at *Guenmai*) and the **place Furstenburg**, a tiny square where **Delacroix's old studio** has been converted to a museum (at no 6; see p. 80). One street away are the square and church of **St-Germain-des-Prés**, with the *Deux Magots* café on the corner and *Flore* just down the street, both renowned for the number of philosophico-politico-poetico-literary backsides that have shined their seats. If you sit at the Deux Magots you are more than likely to be dragged embarrassingly into some street-clown's act. The square tower opposite announces the Romanesque origins of the **church of St-Germain**. There are Gothic elements inside, to say nothing of the dreadful 19C frescoes, but under the paint the nave and aisles are pure Romanesque. The oldest elements are the stubby columns in the triforium, which have been reused from a 6C church on the site.

South of bd St-Germain the streets round St-Sulpice are calm and classy. **Rue Mabillon** is pretty, with a row of old houses set back below the level of the modern street. There are two or three restaurants, including the old-fashioned *Aux Charpentiers*, decorated with models of rafters and roof-trees; it is the property of the Guild of Carpenters. On the left are the **halles St-Germain**, on the site of a 15C market. Rue St-Sulpice, with a delicious *pâtisserie* and a shop called *L'Estrelle* specialising in teas, coffees and jams, leads through to the front of the enormous church of **St-Sulpice**. The *Café de la Mairie*, on the sunny north side of the 18C square, is popular with the student crowd.

The church, erected either side of 1700, is austerely classical, with a Doric colonnade surmounted by an Ionic, and Corinthian pilasters in the towers, only one of which is finished. The interior (some Delacroix frescoes in the first chapel on the right) is not to my taste. But softened by the chestnut-trees and fountain of the square, the ensemble is peaceful and harmonious.

On the south side, rue Férou, where a gentleman called Pottier composed the Internationale in 1776, connects with **rue de Vaugirard**, Paris's longest street, going all the way out to Porte de Versailles, where the *Foires* (Ideal Home, Agricultural Show, etc.) take place, free. At 68 rue de Vaugirard *Le Pont Traversé* is just what a Parisian bookshop should be.

On the south side of the street are the **Luxembourg gardens** and **palace**, which Henri IV's widowed queen, Marie de Médicis, had built to remind her of the Palazzo Pitti and Giardino Boboli of her native Florence. Today it is the seat of the French Senate. The gardens, with formal chestnut *allées*, sunken pond and a more natural bit over to the south-west, are the chief lung and recreation ground of the Left Bank. The shady corner by the **Fontaine de Médicis** close to rue de Médicis is an ideal place to shelter on a hot summer's day. There are tennis courts, pony rides, playground, *boules* pitch, yachts to hire on the pond, and in the south-west corner a miniature orchard of pear trees. To the south the treelined gardens of avenue de l'Observatoire stretch down to the **Observatory**. Just before you get to it, on the corner of bd Montparnasse, in front of the *Closerie des Lilas* café, is a **statue of Marshal Ney**, one of Napoleon's most dashing generals, on the spot where he faced the firing squad in 1815.

Rue de Médicis has some handsome **bookshops**, though not for bargain-hunters. Albert Blanchard specialises in the very best antiquarian scientific books. No 3 goes for the occult. *L'Impensé Radical* deals exclusively in games. At the Vaugirard end, *Au Petit Suisse* is an attractive café. Right beside it is the back of the **Théâtre de l'Odéon**, whose pleasing Doric portico faces a semi-circular *place* and rue de l'Odéon, with more bookshops, leading back to bd St-Germain.

Montparnasse

Like other Left Bank *quartiers* **Montparnasse** still trades on its association with the inter-war artistic and literary boom, habitués of the *Select*, *Coupole*, *Dôme* and *Rotonde* cafés, all still going strong on the bd du Montparnasse east of the Gare. In the first years of the century it was also the stamping ground of outlawed Russian revolutionaries, so many of them that the Tsarist police ran a special Paris section to keep tabs. Trotsky and Lenin both lodged in the area, Trotsky in rue de la Gaité, now a seedy street of sex shops, dangerous undies and cinemas showing titles like *Etudiantes à sodomiser sans limites* (Girl students for buggery without limits) and *Tonnerre de Fesses* (Thunderclap of arses).

The boulevard teems with people, cinemas, restaurants, cafés, brasseries, bookshops. **Rue de Rennes** opposite the station is a major shopping street. Though the café clientèle is arty/bourgeois, the boulevard is far from smart. In fact it is a bit of a frontier, between the dull bourgeois streets to the north and the working-class, villagey, even slummy streets to the south, especially between av de Maine and the railway tracks which used to suck thousands of emigré Bretons into this part of the city. The station itself is the site of a huge modernistic redevelopment project, dominated by the **Tour de Montparnasse**, at 56 storeys Europe's tallest office block. You can go to the top more cheaply than the Tour Eiffel, but it certainly is not worth it except on a very clear day (9.30/10–11/ 10; 20F, children half-price).

On **bd Edgar-Quinet,** beyond the street **market**, is the main entrance to the **Montparnasse cemetery**, a gloomy city of the dead, with ranks of miniature temples, dreary and bizarre, and plenty of illustrious names for spotters, from Baudelaire to Sartre and André Citroën to Saint-Saens. In the south-west corner is an old windmill, one of the 17C taverns frequented by the carousing, versifying students who gave the district its name of Parnassus. If you are determined to spend your time among the dear departed, you can get down from here into the **catacombs** (Tues–Sun 10–12 & 2–5) in nearby place Denfert-Rochereau; they are abandoned quarries stacked with millions of bones cleared from overcrowded cemeteries in 1785 – claustrophobic in the extreme. Punks and art-radicals have recently developed a taste for this as a party location.

For an idea of an older, working-class, almost provincial Paris, wander the back streets between here and **Porte de Vanves**. Rue Didot, for instance, will take you to the Porte where, Saturdays and Sundays in av Lafenestre and Marc Sangnier, there is a **market** of old clothes, books, records and assorted bric-à-brac amid workers' housing estates.

The big 15ᵉ *arrondissement* to the west is of little interest, though there is a long food market in rue de la Convention and off it, in passage de Dantzig, a curious polygonal building known as **La Rûche**, where Modigliani, Léger and Chagall among others had their studios. It was designed by Eiffel as the wine pavilion for the 1900 trade fair.

Trocadéro, Eiffel Tower and Les Invalides

The vistas are splendid, from the terrace of the **Palais de Chaillot** (place du Trocadéro) across the river to the Tour Eiffel and Ecole Militaire, from the ornate 1900 Pont Alexandre III along the grassy Esplanade to the Hôtel des Invalides. But once you have said to yourself, 'How splendid!', there is little reason to get any closer. This is town-planning on the despotic scale, an assertion of power that takes no account of the small-scale interests and details of everyday lives.

The Palais de Chaillot, like a latterday Pharaoh's mausoleum (1937), is, however, home to several interesting **museums** (see p. 83) and a theatre used for diverse but usually radical productions. And the **Tour Eiffel**, though no beauty, is nonetheless an amazing structure. When completed in 1887 it was the tallest building in the world at 300m. Its 7,000 tons of steel, in terms of pressure, sit as lightly on the ground as a child in a chair. 'The first principle of architectural aesthetics,' said Eiffel, 'prescribes that the basic lines of a structure must correspond precisely to its specified use . . . . To a certain extent the tower was formed by the wind itself.' Though the tower served no purpose, its purely functional design was, and still is, a welcome and radical change from the stuffy monumentality of the buildings promoted by officialdom here and elsewhere in the world. Going to the top (10/10.30–11) costs 37F and certainly isn't worth it on a cloudy day.

Between the two bridges just downstream from the tower stretches a narrow artificial island with a walkway on top, known as the **Allée des Cygnes**. By the further bridge stands the original Statue of Liberty; model for the larger New York version.

The **Esplanade des Invalides**, striking due south from the river bank, is a more attractive uncluttered vista than the above. The wide façade of the **Hôtel des Invalides**, overtopped by its distinctive dome, fills the whole of the further end of the Esplanade. It was built as a home for invalided soldiers on the orders of Louis XIV. Under the dome are two churches, one for the soldiers, the other intended as a mausoleum for the king but now containing the mortal remains of Napoleon. The Hôtel (*son et lumière* in English from April to September) houses the vast **Musée de l'Armée** (see p. 82).

Both churches are cold and dreary inside. The **Église du Dôme**, in particular, is a supreme example of architectural pomposity. Corinthian columns and pilasters abound. The dome – pleasing enough from outside – is covered with paintings and flanked by four round chapels displaying the tombs of various luminaries. Napoleon himself lies in a hole in the floor in a cold smooth sarcophagus of red porphyry, enclosed within a gallery decorated with friezes of execrable taste and grovelling piety, captioned with quotations of awesome conceit from the great man: 'Cooperate with the plans I have laid for the welfare of peoples'; 'By its simplicity my code of law has done more good in France than all the laws which have preceded me'; 'Wherever the shadow of my rule has fallen, it has left lasting traces of its value.'

Immediately east of the Invalides is the **Musée Rodin** (see p. 79), on the corner of **rue de Varenne,** housed in a beautiful 18C mansion, which the sculptor leased from the state in return for the gift of all his work at his death. The garden, planted with sculptures, is quite as pretty as the house, with a pond and flowering shrubs and a superb view of the Invalides dome rising above the trees. The rest of the street, and the parallel **rue de Grenelle,** is full of aristocratic mansions, including the **Hôtel Matignon**, the Prime Minister's residence. At the end the attractive **rue du Bac** leads into **rue de Sèvres** by the city's oldest department store, *Au Bon Marché.*

Beaux Quartiers and Bois de Boulogne

The **Beaux Quartiers** are most of the 16ᵉ and 17ᵉ *arrondissements*. The 16ᵉ is aristocratic and rich, the 17ᵉ, or at least the southern part of it, bourgeois and rich, embodying the staid, cautious values of the 19C manufacturing and trading classes.

The northern half of the 16ᵉ towards place Victor Hugo and place de l'Étoile is leafy and attractive and distinctly metropolitan in feel, though more for the taxi-rider than the infantry. The southern part, round the old villages of **Auteuil** and **Passy**, has an almost provincial air, and is full of pleasant surprises for the walker. A good peg to hang a walk on is a visit to the **Musée Marmottan** (see p. 77) in av Raphaël, with its marvellous collection of late Monets. There are also several interesting pieces of **20C architecture** scattered through the district, especially by Hector Guimard, designer of the swirly green Art Nouveau métro stations, Le Corbusier and Mallet-Stevens, architects of the first 'cubist' buildings.

A good place to start is the **Église d'Auteuil** métro station. There are several **Guimard** buildings off rue Chardon-Lagache (34 rue Boileau, 8 av de la Villa-de-la-Réunion, 41 rue Chardon-Lagache, 192 av de Versailles and 39 bd Exelmans). From the métro exit, **rue d'Auteuil**, with a lingering village high-street air, leads to **place Lorrain** with a Saturday market. More Guimard houses are to be found at the further end of rue La Fontaine, which begins here; no 60 is perhaps the best in the city. In rue Poussin, just off the *place*, is the entrance to **Villa Montmorency**, a typical 16ᵉ 'villa', a sort of private village of leafy lanes and English-style gardens. Gide and the Goncourt brothers of Prix fame lived in this one. Behind it is rue du Dr-Blanche where, in a cul-de-sac on the right, are **Le Corbusier**'s first private houses (1923), one of them now the *Fondation Le Corbusier* (10–1 & 2–6; cl. weekends and Aug). Built in strictly cubistic style, very plain, with windows in bands, the only extravagance is the raising of one wing on piers and a curved frontage. They look commonplace enough now, but what a contrast to anything that had gone before. Further along Dr-Blanche, the tiny rue Mallet-Stevens was built entirely by **Mallet-Stevens** also in 'cubist' style. If you go through from there to the almost rural cutting of the disused Petite Ceinture railway, turn along to the right and under the subway, you come out by av Raphaël with the *Museé Marmottan* on the corner of rue Boilly.

The **Bois de Boulogne**, running all down the west side of the 16ᵉ, is supposedly modelled on Hyde Park, though it is a very French interpretation. It offers all sorts of facilities: the **Jardin d'Acclimatation** with lots of attractions for kids (see p. 97); the excellent **Musée National des Arts et Traditions Populaires** (p. 83); the **Parc de Bagatelle**, with beautiful displays of tulips, hyacinths and daffodils in the first half of April, irises in May, waterlilies and roses at the end of June; a riding school; **bike hire** at the entrance to the Jardin d'Acclimatation; **boating** on the Lac Inférieur; **race courses** at Longchamp and Auteuil. The best, and wildest, part for walking is towards the south-west corner. When it was opened to the public in the 18C, people said of it, '*Les mariages du Bois de Boulogne ne se font pas devant Monsieur le Curé*' – 'Unions cemented in the Bois de Boulogne do not take place in the presence of a priest.' Today's after-dark unions are no less disreputable, the speciality in particular of Brazilian transvestites.

Close by, overlooking the Seine from the west, the **Parc de St-Cloud** is also good for some fresh air and the visual order through pools and fountains down to the river and across to the city (Mᵒ Pont-de-Sèvres, Boulogne-Pont-de-St-Cloud, then walk across the river: or, take a train from St-Lazare to St-Cloud and head south).

The 17ᵉ *arrondissement* is most interesting in its eastern half. I would strongly recommend a walk from the lively **place des Ternes** with its cafés and flower market, through the stately wrought iron gates of avenue

Hoche into the small and formal **Parc Monceau,** surrounded by pompous bourgeois residences, and on to the 'village' of **Batignolles** on the wrong side of the St-Lazare railway tracks. By the av. Velasquez exit from the park the **Musée Cernuschi** (see p. 81) has a small collection of ancient Chinese art. From there, turn left on bd Malesherbes, then right along rue Legendre until you reach place de Lévis, already much more interesting than the sedate streets you have left behind. **Rue de Lévis** has one of the city's most strident, colourful and appetising food markets (some other stalls too) every day of the week except Monday. This is a good restaurant area, too, particularly up towards the railway around the rue des Dames, rue Cheroy (try the Moroccan *Zerda*) and the bottom-line rue Dulong.

Across the tracks, **rue des Batignolles** is the heart of Batignolles 'village', now sufficiently conscious of its uniqueness to have formed an association for the preservation of its '*caractère villageois*'. At the north end of the street is a semi-circular *place* with cafés and restaurants framing a small colonnaded church. Behind it is the tired and trampled greenery of square Batignolles, with the marshalling yards beyond. The long **rue des Moines** leads north-east towards Guy-Moquet. This is the working-class Paris of the movies, all small, animated, friendly shops, four- to five-storeyed houses in shades of peeling grey, brown-stained bars where men drink standing at the 'zinc'. If you come back on av de St-Ouen, go through **rue du Capitaine-Madon,** a cobbled alley with washing strung at the windows, leading to the wall of the **Montmartre cemetery,** on the off-chance that Hôtel Beau-Lieu still exists. Run by a 90-year-old, who has just died, it has remained unchanged for sixty years. Ramshackle, peeling, on a tiny courtyard full of plants . . . it epitomises the kind-hearted, no-nonsense, instinctively arty, sepia Paris that every romantic visitor secretly cherishes. Most of the guests have been there fifteen years or more! The new owner plans to refurbish it, so its days are probably numbered.

Montmartre and beyond

Montmartre lies in the middle of the largely petty-bourgeois and working-class 18e *arrondissement,* respectable round the slopes of the *Butte* (hill), distinctly less so towards the **Gare du Nord** and **Gare de l'Est.** Beyond the tracks of the Gare de l'Est you're into the slums, rotting and depressed.

The Butte itself is attractive, with a relaxed, sunny, countrified air. **Pigalle** though, at the foot of the hill, has lost its stuffing. You won't find the golden-hearted whores and Bohemian artists of popular male tradition. It's all sex shops and peep shows, the women tired and bored in the doorways. Like Soho, the tourists have to be shown it, or so their masters of ceremonies think; the natives keep away.

The Butte

Everyone goes up via the rue de Steinkerque and the steps below the Sacré-Coeur. If you approach from the west or south-west via **rue Lepic**, **place des Abbesses** or the **cemetery** in a quiet hollow below rue Caulaincourt (graves of Berlioz, Degas, Stendhal, Zola . . .), you can still have the streets to yourself.

Place des Abbesses is pretty, with one of the few complete surviving Guimard métro entrances: the glass porch as well as the railings and the slightly obscene orange-tongued lanterns. There is a nice bookshop in rue Yvonne-Le-Tac, the street where St-Denis, the first bishop of Paris, had his head chopped off by the Romans c250. Legend has it that he carried his head until he dropped, where the cathedral of St-Denis now stands, in a traditionally Communist suburb north of the city. **Place Dullin**, a bit further over, is also a beauty.

The **Bateau-Lavoir studios** in rue Ravignan (rebuilt now) are where Picasso, Braque and Juan Gris invented cubism, and Apollinaire and Max Jacob hauled poetry into the twentieth century. At the top of the rue Drevet stairs there is a lovely view back over the city from the tiny **place du Calvaire**. On the north side of the Butte, **rue des Saules** runs steeply down past the neat little terraces of the Montmartre **vineyard**, harvested at the beginning of October. On the right, rue Cortot leads past the **Musée de Montmartre** in a pretty old house with a view over the vineyard, rented at various times by Renoir, Dufy, Suzanne Valadon and her mad son, Utrillo. The actual exhibits are disappointingly uninteresting.

The heart of tourist Montmartre is **place du Tertre**, photogenic but totally bogus, jammed with overpriced restaurants and 'artists' doing quick portraits while you wait. Here, on 18 March 1871, Montmartre's most illustrious mayor, a future Prime Minister of France, Georges Clémenceau, flapped about trying to prevent the bloodshed that started that terrible and long-divisive civil war between the Commune and Thiers' Third Republic, between the radical, Communist, urban, muddled Left and the frightened, unwilling or reactionary Rest.

France had provoked a disastrous war with Bismarck's Germany. The emperor, Napoleon III, had been captured and Paris surrounded. The Germans would not accept surrender from any but a properly elected government. A cautious and reactionary government was duly elected and promptly capitulated, handing over Alsace and Lorraine. Frightened of Paris in arms, they tried to get hold of the artillery still in the hands of the National Guard. When, however, government troops went to fetch the guns parked at Montmartre, the people, fearing another restoration of empire or monarchy such as has happened after the 1848 revolution, persuaded them to take no action. Two of their generals were seized and shot against the wall, while the terrified government fled to Versailles, leaving the Commune master of Paris.

Divided among themselves and isolated from the rest of France, the *Communards* fought for their city street by street against government attack for a week between 21 and 28 May. No one knows how many died, certainly no fewer than 30,000 with another 10,000 executed or deported. A working-class revolt, as the particulars of those arrested clearly demonstrate, but it never had time to be socialist, as subsequent mythologising would have it. The terrible cost of repression had long-term effects on the French working-class movement, both in terms of numbers lost and psychologically. For after that, not being revolutionary could only appear a betrayal of the dead.

Between place du Tertre and the church of the Sacré-Coeur is the old church of **St-Pierre**, all that remains of the Benedictine convent that occupied the Butte Montmartre from the 12C on. Though much altered, it still retains its Romanesque and early Gothic feel. In it are four ancient columns, two by the door, two in the choir, leftovers from a Roman shrine that stood on the hill – 'mons mercurii', Mercury's Hill, the Romans called it.

As for the **Sacré-Coeur** itself, graceless and vulgar pastiche though it is, its white pimply domes are an essential part of the Paris skyline. Completed on the eve of the First War, its architect was Abadie, who made such a mess of restoring the Romanesque cathedral of St-Front in Périgueux. The irony is that St-Front was his model for this effort. The best thing about it is the **view from the dome** (9.30–12.30 & 1–5.30). It costs next to nothing, is almost as high as the Eiffel Tower, and you can see across virtually the whole city.

If you go down the north side of the Butte by the long **rue du Mont-Cenis**, where Berlioz lived, across the quiet and agreeable rue Caulaincourt, you come eventually to **Porte de Clignancourt**, where the main *marché aux puces*, or **flea-market**, is located under the boulevard périphérique. You won't find any bargains, but it is an entertaining trip to wander round the stalls and shacks selling jeans, bags, shirts, leather jackets, furniture and assorted junk (Sat, Sun and Mon, mornings mainly). *Chez Lisette*, a scruffy restaurant-buvette in the centre, is where the great gypsy jazz guitarist, Django Reinhardt, sometimes played. Just outside the market, at 126 av Michelet, *La Cigale*, a slightly seedy bar-restaurant, serves a decent meal (with affordable mussels) to the wheeze of an old accordeon.

East of the Butte, down towards the **Barbès-Rochechouart crossroads**, the crowds get thicker and thicker and you might be in any Levantine or North African souk. This is the district for cheap shopping. Just across bd Barbès, the **Goutte d'Or** and surrounding lanes make up the squalidest, smelliest corner of town, full of dingy bars and brothels. It is reputedly dangerous at night and its days are numbered. The Chirac administration have plans for wholesale demolition, shifting the North African community out to the suburbs, and have already earmarked a site for their new police station.

The canals, La Villette and St-Denis

The city gate of **La Villette** was for generations the site of the Paris abattoirs and meat market, capable, according to the 1884 Baedeker, of accommodating 22,000 sheep, 4,600 oxen and 7,000 calves and pigs. Opposite the entrance stood a row of restaurants famed for their meat, kosher butchers and shops selling heavy equipment for the trade, Some of the restaurants remain but for a very different clientele now that the whole site has been transformed with over £½ billion from the state coffers.

The number one extravagance has been the concrete hulk of the abandoned abattoirs metamorphosed into the **Cité des Sciences et de l'Industrie**, a cold, clinical but definitively high-tech building three times the size of Beaubourg, In front of it sits the **Géode**, a bubble of reflecting steel dropped from an intergalactic *boules* game in which half the sphere is a projection screen – one of the largest in existence – and half the space an arena for hologram and laser shows.

The largest of the market halls – an iron-frame structure designed by Baltard, the engineer of the vanished Les Halles pavilions – has become the **Grande Salle**, a vast and brilliant exhibition space. It is hard to imagine a better location for the contemporary art *Biénnale* than this glazed, cast-iron stucture with its mid-level walkways. Unfortunately it is hogged by trade shows for most of the year.

The surrounding recreation park with rock venue, cinema, theatre and the music conservatory to come, has had its first major implants – great, red, constructivist-style sculptures by Tschumi. Equally bizarre, though rather different, is the **Drgon Slide** for children made from recycled drums and pipes on the slope west of the Géode. The information centre for the Parc de la Villette is on your right as you approach the Grande Salle from the Porte de Pantin métro.

The whole Villette complex stands in the angle of intersection of the **Ourcq and St-Denis canals**. The first was built by Napoleon to bring fresh water into the city. The second is an extension of the Canal St-Martin. If you like decaying industrial townscapes, both the Canal St-Martin and the Canal St-Denis make interesting quayside walks.

For the **Canal St-Martin** you can either start from place de la République where the canal goes underground or quai de Valmy by the Gare de l'Est. The **west bank** is best for walking, with less rebuilding and demolition in progress. You pass old flats, workshops, cheap bar-restaurants, bits of garden by the locks. The canal is still in use, as a shortcut lopping off the great western loop of the Seine round Paris. You have to leave the quayside at the grubby, noisy **place de Stalingrad** (lots of socialist street names in working-class Paris and suburbs). In the middle, up against the overhead métro line, is one of **Ledoux**'s toll-houses, erected to collect taxes on all goods coming into the city through Louis XVI's tax wall, a major cause of resentment in the lead-up to the Revolution. The **international coach station** is also here.

North of the *place* begins the now defunct **Bassin de la Villette** dock – Paris used to be the first port of France. Along the cobbled quay the remaining warehouses await demolition. The people you pass are anglers, dog-walkers, lonelyhearts and the occasional glue-sniffer. At the further end, the run-down **rue de Crimée** crosses a unique hydraulic bridge (1885), operated by the canal water. From here on, the *quartier* to your left is as decrepit as you could find, full of close, decaying houses with burrowing, smelly passages into courtyards held together by improvised

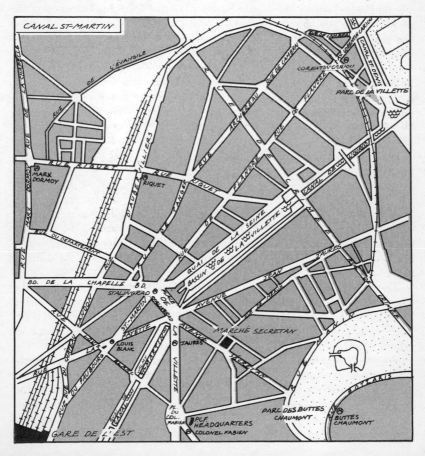

repairs. The film, *Diva*, was shot hereabouts. It is petty-crook, no-hope territory, both sides of **rue de Flandre**. And the high-rise estate on the west side of the street does not hold much promise of a brighter future either. Another immigrant ghetto, it is mainly North African this side of the rue de Tanger and place du Maroc, predominantly African round rue d'Aubervilliers. It is interesting, but you will feel an outsider and would do well to look as inconspicuous as possible.

With the **St-Denis** canal the best thing is to visit the town first, then walk the canal on the way home. The town's chief claim to fame – apart from being staunchly Communist – is its magnificent **Cathedral**. It was begun by Abbot Suger in the first half of the 12C and is generally regarded as the birthplace of the Gothic style.

Though its west front was the first ever to have a rose window, it is in the **choir** that you see the clear emergence of the new style, the slimness and lightness that comes with the use of the pointed arch, the ribbed vault and the long shafts of half-column rising from pillar to roof. It is a remarkably light church too, thanks to the clerestory (c1230) being almost 100 per cent glass – another first for St-Denis. And the **rose windows** in the transepts are so big they occupy the entire end-wall. Once the place where the kings of France were crowned, the cathedral has been since 1,000AD the place where they have all been buried. Their very fine **tombs** and **effigies** are deployed about the transepts and ambulatory – though there is a shocking charge for entry to this part of the church.

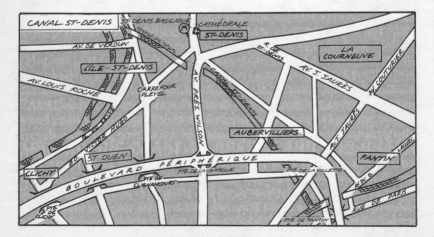

The **centre of St-Denis**, old-fashioned and provincial, is undergoing cheap-jack redevelopment, but still holds its thrice-weekly **market** in the shadow of the cranes round the place de l'Hôtel de Ville and the covered *halles*. It is a truly multi-ethnic affair these days, and the quantity of offal on the butchers' stalls – ears, feet, tails and bladders – shows it is no rich man's territory.

Returning to Porte de la Villette **by the canal bank** takes about 1½ hours. Go down rue de la République, past the church at the bottom and turn left when you hit the canal. You pass patches of greenery, country-style cottages butting directly on to the towpath, waste ground where larks sing, slums and improvised shacks as brightly painted as a Greek island house, derelict factories and a few warehouses still serving the barge traffic. Barge life appears romantic – probably more than it is. The old steel hulks slide by, gunwhales down, a dog at the prow, lace curtains at the window, a potted plant, a bike propped against the cabin sides, a couple of kids . . . . Not long after the start of the walk you come to a cobbled ramp on your left where there is a nice cheap restaurant called *La Péniche* ('barge', needless to say). If you turn in there, up rue Raspail, past another dirt-cheap café, you come to a dusty square, where the town council has named a street for Bobby Sands.

East: from Belleville to Chinatown

The **eastern districts** are no longer the revolutionary hotbeds of latterdays but it's still the cheapest side of town to live and the least frequented by tourists. Graced with the **Parc des Buttes Chaumont**, the **Bois de Vincennes** and the hills of **Belleville**, it offers a different, quieter Paris to explore.

Belleville and Père-Lachaise Cemetery
At the northern end of the Belleville heights is the **parc des Buttes Chaumont** (Mᵒ Buttes Chaumont or Botzaris) constructed under Haussmann in the 1860s to camouflage what until then had been a desolate warren of disused quarries and miserable shacks. The sculpted beak-shaped park stays open all night and unusually has no regulations about sitting on the grass. At its centre is a huge rock upholding a delicate Corinthian temple and surrounded by a lake which you cross via a suspension bridge on the shorter Pont des Suicides. Louis Aragon, the literary grand old man of the French Communist Party, wrote of this bridge as claiming victims among passers-by who had no intention of dying, but found themselves suddenly tempted by the abyss. Feeble metal grills erected along its sides put an end to such impulses.

The route from Buttes Chaumont to Père-Lachaise will take you through the one-time villages of **Belleville** and **Ménilmontant**, among the poorest quarters of the city. Each has large immigrant populations – Yugoslavs, Jews, Portuguese, Chinese, Arabs and Africans – and a consequent reputation for danger among western Parisians. But the first main street you'll cross, **rue de Belleville**, could be the main street of any French town, save for the Vietnamese and Chinese restaurants dominating the lower end. *Boulangeries* and *charcuteries* proliferate the length of the street and there's a market at the unfestive **place des Fêtes** half way up (on Tues, Fri and Sun). At the bottom end, just south-east of the cross-roads with bd de Belleville, one small sequence of streets and passages, doomed for demolition, is the nearest the area comes to living up to its slums-of-Tunis image. You are not more at risk here than in the centre of town (except perhaps from trigger-happy arms of the law) and in the daytime, the higher air and light is a positive relief from the hemmed-in centre. High rise development has, so far, been kept to the minimum and there are parts which still have a village-like feel. Half way down to the cemetery, just west of rue des Pyrénées, you get an unusual and spec-tacular view of the city, following the infinity lines of rue de Ménil-montant and focussing on the Beaubourg rooftop.

The **Père-Lachaise cemetery** is like a miniature city devastated by a neutron bomb, with a great number of dead, empty houses and temples of every size, style and date, and exhausted survivors – congregating aimlessly or searching with persistence. The former response manifests itself best around **Jim Morrison's tomb** in division six, where French hippies roll joints against a backdrop of Doors' lyrics and love declar-ations graffitied in every western language on every stone in sight. The second, the searchers, are everywhere, looking for their favourite famous dead in an arrangement of numbered divisions that is neither entirely haphazard nor strictly systematic. A safe bet for a high score is to head for the south-eastern corner (near the rue de la Réunion entrance and furthest from the main gate on bd de Ménilmontant). There you will find memorials to concentration camp victims and executed Resistance fighters of the last war, Communist Party general secretaries, Laura Marx and the **Mur des Fédérés**, where the last *communards* were shot in 1871. Defeat is everywhere. The oppressed and their oppressors interred with the same ritual, Abélard and Héloïse side by side in prayer, still chastely separate (division seven), the relative riches and fame as unequal among the tombs of the dead as in the lives of the living. The cemetery is open from 7.30–6 every day.

From the Bastille to Vincennes

The column with the 'Spirit of Liberty' on **place de la Bastille** was erected not to commemorate the surrender of the prison in 1789, but the July Revolution of 1830 which replaced the autocratic Charles X with the 'Citizen King', Louis Philippe. When Louis fled in the much more sig-nificant 1848 revolution, however, his throne was burnt beside the column and a new inscription added amid a climate as radical perhaps as any France had ever known. The provisional government that replaced the king – made up of liberal and socialist Republicans – gave to all

Frenchmen the right to vote, to free education and work. It fell within two months, unable to deal with famine and monetary collapse, but in May the workers took to the streets. Eastern Paris was barricaded and a revolution, with might have changed not just the regime but the very order of things, was set in motion.

It did not, of course, with the revolutionaries defeated amid massacres and deportations, and it is still the 1789 Bastille Day that the French celebrate. But the *place* remains the gathering point for the start of major demonstrations, with nearby **place d'Aligre** (with a cheap daily market) brought into the action for local political events. In the quieter backwaters to the north of rue du Faubourg-St-Antoine, above all on **rue de Lappe**, there are also the remnants of another very Parisian tradition – the **bals musettes**, or music halls of 1930s 'gai Paris', frequented between the wars by Piaf, Jean Gabin and Rita Hayworth. The most famous is *Balajo*, founded by one Jo de France, who introduced glitter and spectacle into what were then seedy gangster dives and brought Parisians from the other side of the city to the rue de Lappe low-life.

From Faubourg-St-Antoine, front line of the 1848 barricades, various buses will take you out **towards the Bois de Vincennes**. No. 86 crosses **place de la Nation**, another much barricaded junction, decorated with the bizarre ensemble of two medieval monarchs, looking very small and sheepish in pens on the top of two high columns and below, in bronze, the Triumph of the Republic. Bus 46, with the same destination, passes the **Musée des Arts Africains et Océaniens** (see p. 80) with its 1930s colonial façade of jungles, hard-working natives and the place names of the French Empire representing the 'overseas contribution to the capital'. The bus's next stop is the **Parc Zoologique**, which was one of the first zoos to replace cages with ditches and give the animals room to exercise themselves. It's far superior to its London equivalent, quite expensive and open from 9–6/5.30.

In the **Bois de Vincennes** itself, you can spend an afternoon **boating** on Lac Daumesnil (just by the zoo) or on Lac des Minimes across the other side of the wood. The fenced enclave on the southern side of Lac Daumesnil is a **Buddhist centre** with a Tibetan temple, Vietnamese chapel and international pagoda, all of which you can visit. As far as real woods go, the Bois opens out and flowers once you're east of av de St-Maurice, but the area is so overrun with roads that countryside sensations don't stand much of a chance. The largest road-free space, between routes de la Tourelle and Dauphine, is currently fenced off for tree planting, following demolition of the open **university of Vincennes**, a traditional centre of subversion razed to the ground in 1980 and incorporated in reduced form with Nanterre on the other side of La Défense. Between this absence and the Lac des Minimes, the **Parc Floral** testifies to the French lack of imagination in landscape gardening, but there are some fun things for kids. On the eastern side of the garden is the **Cartoucherie de Vincennes**, an old ammunitions factory, now home of the radical *Théâtre du Soleil* (see p. 96). On the northern edge of the Bois, the **Château de Vincennes**, royal medieval residence, then state prison, porcelain factory, weapons dump and military training school, is still undergoing restoration work started by Napoleon III. A real behemoth of a building, no amount of stone-scrubbing and removal of 19C gun positions is likely to greatly beautify it.

Chinatown and the south-east

The south-east quarter of Paris, **the 13ᵉ**, has similarities with the south-east boroughs of London. The tightly knit community around **rue Nationale** put up with their slum conditions because at least life could be lived on the street – in the shops, the cafés or with neighbours. Paris was another place, rarely ventured to. But come the 1950s and 1960s, the city planners, here as elsewhere, came up with their imagination-defying solution to housing problems and much of the region now resembles Lower East Side, Manhattan. The area between av d'Italie, rue Tolbiac and bd Masséna is the **Chinatown** of Paris, with every variety of Far Eastern cuisine, movies, tapes and publications on sale. A **market** between av de Choisy and d'Ivry (every day except Monday) makes even the French look censorious in their choice of food.

Nearer to the city centre, above bd Vincent Auriol, the buildings are ornate and bourgeois, dominated by the immense **Hôpital de la Sâlpe-trière**, built under Louis XIV to dispose of the dispossessed. It later became a psychiatric hospital, fulfilling the same function. Jean Charcot, who believed that susceptibility to hypnosis was proof of hysteria, staged his theatrical demonstrations here, with Freud one of his greatly interested witnesses. If you ask very nicely in the *Bibliothèque Charcot* (block 6, red route), the librarian may show you a book of photographs of the poor female victims of these experiments. For a more positive statement on women, take a look at the building at 5 rue Jules Breton which declares in large letters on its façade, 'In humanity, woman has the same duties as man. She must have the same rights in the family and in society.'

West of av d'Italie small houses with fancy brickwork or decorative timbers have remained intact and there's a rare taste of pre-tower block life. On **rue de la Butte aux Cailles** you'll find book and food shops, a community action centre, a workers' co-operative jazz bar (*La Merle Moqueur* at no 11), an excellent second-hand clothes and crockery shop (at no 58) and bars and bistros open till midnight. The *Bar des Sports* (no. 15) occasionally announces crocodile and turtle on the day's menu.

To the south-west, in the **14ᵉ**, several thousand students from over 100 different countries live in the curious array of buildings in the **Cité Universitaire** between bd Jourdan and the périphérique. The central

Maison Internationale resembles the Marlinspike of Tintin books. The other *Maisons* represent the unobvious selection of nations or people willing to subsidise foreign study. Armenia, Cuba, Indo-China and Monaco are neighbours at one end; Cambodia has been boarded up for years; Switzerland (designed by Le Corbusier in his stilts phase) and the US have the most applicants for their luxurious rooms; and extradition debate closed Spain; and the Collège Franco-Britannique is a red brick monster. The atmosphere is far from internationalist but you can eat very cheaply in the **cafeterias** if you have a student card.

Parc Montsouris, across the boulevard, looks a tempting place to collapse but you'll be up against more of the city's obsessionally whistling park police the moment you touch the grass. A beautiful reproduction of the Bardo palace in Tunis, built for the 1867 *exposition universelle*, is being allowed to decay. Lenin used to take strolls here when he was living nearby, as, no doubt, did Dali, Lurcat, Miller, Durrell and other artists who found homes in the tiny cobbled street of **Villa Seurat** off rue de la Tombe. Due north of the park – past Ste-Anne's psychiatric hospital where one of the greatest living political philosophers, Louis Althusser, is committed – lies the **Observatoire.** From the 1660s, when it was constructed, until 1884, all French maps had the zero meridian through the middle of this building. After that date, they reluctantly agreed that 0° longitude should run through a village in Brittany that is due south of Greenwich. Visiting the Observatoire is a complicated procedure and all you'll see are old maps and instruments, but you can sit in the **garden** on summer afternoons and admire the dome (entrance on bd Arago).

THE MUSEUMS

You may find there is sufficient visual simulation just wandering around Paris streets without exploring what's to be seen in **the museums**. It's certainly questionable whether the **Louvre**, for example, can compete in pleasure with the Marais, the *quais* or parts of the Latin quarter. But if established art appeals at all, the Paris collections are not to be missed.

The most popular are the various museums of modern art: in the **Beaubourg Pompidou** Centre, the **Palais de Tokyo** and new **Musée Picasso**, and, for the brilliantly represented opening stages, the **Orangerie, Marmottan** and **Gare d'Orsay** where the paintings from the **Jeu de Paume** are now displayed. Since Paris was the well-rocked cradle of Impressionism, Fauvism, Cubism, Surrealism and Symbolism, there's both justice

PARIS MUSEUMS

BOULEVARD BINEAU

AV. CHARLES-DE-GAULLE

AV. DE LA GRANDE ARMÉE

MUS. NAT. D'ARTS TRAD. POPULAIRES

AV. FOCH

PL. CHARLES DE GAULLE

AV. DES CHAMPS-ELYSÉES

MUS. CERNUSCHI

MUS. G. MOREA

BOULEVARD

HAUS.

ALLÉE DE LONGCHAMP

MUS. CONTREFAÇONS

AVENUE VICTOR HUGO

MUS. COSTUMES

MUS. GUIMET

PALAIS DE TOKYO

PALAIS DE CHAILLOT

GRAND PALAIS

PETIT PALAIS

JEU DE PAU

ORANGERIE

QUAI D'ORSAY

MUS. ARTS DÉCORAT

MUS. MARMOTTAN

AV. NEW YORK

MUS. S.E.I.T.A.

MUS. DE L'ARMÉE

MUS. LUNETTES

MAISON DE BALZAC

BD. DES INVALIDES

MUS. RODIN

BD. RASPAIL

BOULEVARD

AV. DE VERSAILLES

PTE DE ST CLOUD

BOULEVARD

PÉRIPHÉRIQUE

RUE DE VAUGIRARD

AV. DU MAINE

AV. CLICHY

AV. DE V MALESHERBES

P. DE

going back to earlier cultural roots, are some of the medieval works in the **Musée Cluny**, including the glorious *La Dame à la Licorne* tapestry.

Among the city's extaordinary number of technical, historical, social and applied art museums, the **Musée National des Arts et Traditions Populaires** is the most entertaining. Some of the smaller ones are dedicated to a single person – **Balzac, Hugo, Piaf** – and others to very particular subjects – **spectacles, counterfeits, tobacco,** even **bread.** We've detailed all we found interesting, though full lists (with their ever changing opening times, from any tourist office) will reveal others of appeal to the committed or specialist. There may, too, be **new ones** on the scene: the **Cité des Sciences et de l'Industrie** in the Parc de la Villette (imminent, see p. 64), the **Gare d'Orsay** across the river from the Louvre (dedicated to the artistic production of 1848–1914 and promised for 1987) and the **Musée Picasso** in the Hôtel Sale (5 rue de Thorigny), in the process of being rebuilt to display an enormous collection of works which the government craftily acquired in lieu of taxes after Picasso's death.

Admission prices vary: some, like the Marmottan, are pretty expensive though all offer student reductions if you've got a card. The Louvre and other state-owned museums **close** on Tuesdays (as throughout France) and have **free days** – usually Wednesdays or Sundays, and are usually crowded out. Keep an eye out for **temporary exhibitions** – some of which match any of Paris's regular museums – held in Beaubourg and the Grand Palais; these are usually well advertised by posters or there are full details in *Pariscope* and the other listings magazines.

Art and sculpture

Beaubourg (the Pompidou Centre)
Entrances from rue Beaubourg or the piazza on the west side; Mº Rambuteau/Hôtel de Ville. Open 12–10, wkends 10–10; cl. Tues; free Sun.

The **Musée National d'Art Moderne** on the 3rd and 4th floors of Beaubourg is second to none: a completely 20C collection which for once in a state gallery of modern art actually includes contemporaries – Jackson Pollock and Francis Bacon are especially well represented. Among highlights are Henri Rousseau's *La Charmeuse de Serpent* (1907), one of the earliest paintings here and well outside the major trends. Picasso's *Femme Assise* of 1909 introduces the reduced colours of Cubism, represented in its developed style by Braque's *L'Homme à la Guitare* (1914) and, later, in the perfect balancing act of Léger's *Les Acrobats en Gris* (1942–4). Among Abstracts, there's the sensuous rhythm of colour in Sonia Dalaunay's *Prismes Electriques* (1914) and a major collection of Kandinskys at their most harmonised and playful. In contrast, Dali disturbs or infuriates with *Hallucination Partielle, Six Images de Lénine sur un Piano* (1931) and there are more surrealist images by Magritte and de Chirico. One of the most compulsive pictures of 1920s female emancipation as viewed by a male contemporary is the portrait of *Sylvia von Harden* by Otto Dix. The sleeping woman in *Le Rêve* by Matisse is not focussed on gender but on the body at its most relaxed.

But these are only a very small selection of an array of pictures which encompass most movements in the art of this century. They have recently been rearranged for even better light and space, and really demand repeated visits. Alongside the permanent collection, too, there are imaginative theme-orientated displays of photography and drawing, while **young artists'** work gets a viewing on the ground floor and mezzanine. Right at the top of the centre is the **Grande Galerie** for big prestige expositions, often criticised for their blandness, but sometimes superb. And finally, below ground, you can wade through further temporary exhibitions – of architecture, urbanism and technology – in the **Centre de Création Industrielle**.

Much of the Beaubourg complex is free to walk around – including a kid's *atelier* (see p. 97) – but you have to pay **admission** for the modern art gallery except on Sundays. If you want to do any justice to the collection, and remain on your feet, a daypass is worth considering; least crowded times, in summer at least, are generally evenings.

Musée de Cluny
Place Paul-Painlevé, 5e (off rue des Ecoles); Mo Odéon, St-Michel. Open 9.45–12.30 & 2–5.15; cl. Mon.
If you have always found tapestries boring, this treasure house of medieval art may well provide the flash of enlightenment. There are numerous beauties: a marvellous depiction of the grape harvest; a Resurrection embroidered in gold and silver thread, with sleeping guards in medieval armour; a room of 16C Dutch tapestries, full of flowers and birds, a woman spinning while a cat plays with the end of the thread, a lover making advances, a pretty woman in her bath, overflowing into a duck pond. But the greatest wonder of all is *La Dame à la Licorne*, The Lady with the Unicorn: six enigmatic scenes featuring a beautiful woman flanked by a lion and a unicorn, late 15C, perhaps made in Brussels. Quite simply, it is the most stunning piece of art you are likely to see in many a long day. The ground of each panel is a delicate red worked with a thousand tiny flowers, birds and animals. In the centre is a green island, equally flowery, framed by stylised trees, and here the scene is enacted. The young woman plays a portable organ, takes a sweet from a proffered box, makes a necklace of carnations while a pet monkey, perched on the rim of a basket of flowers, holds one to his nose . . . .

Additional attractions include the original heads of the kings of Judah from the front of Notre-Dame, amusingly carved misericords, Limoges enamels, a Book of Hours sensibly arranged so that you can turn the leaves, and the original chapel of the Hôtel de Cluny with the most delicate and complicated ceiling held on a single column. Also incorporated in the museum is the frigidarium of the Roman baths, whose ruined brickwork you can see from bd St-Michel outside.

The Louvre
Palais du Louvre, 1ᵉ; Mᵒ Palais-Royal, Louvre. Open 9.45–6.30; cl. Tues; free Sun & Wed.

> You walked for a quarter of a mile through works of fine art; the very floors echoed the sounds of immortality . . . . It was the crowning and consecration of art . . . . These works instead of being taken from their respective countries were given to the world and to the mind and heart of man from whence they sprung . . . .

William Hazlitt, writing of the Louvre in 1802, goes on, in equally florid style, to claim for this museum the beginning of a new age when artistic masterpieces would be the inheritance of all, no longer the preserve of kings and nobility. Novel the Louvre certainly was. The palace, hung with the private collections of monarchs and their ministers, was first opened to the public in 1793, after the Revolution. Within a decade Napoleon had made it the largest art collection on earth with takings from his empire. However inspiring it might have been then, for most tourists these days going round the Louvre is an atonement for all the fun times in Paris. The museum is in fact in the process of being completely transformed. The final result, forecast for 1987, should diminish the need for heroic will power and stamina in the search for one work you like or are looking for amongst the 300,000. At present, with the alterations in progress, it's even worse than before with all the galleries switched about and virtually impossible to predict in a guide.

The collection has seven basic divisions: three lots of antiquities, sculpture, painting, applied and graphic arts. **Oriental Antiquities** cover the Sumerian, Babylonian, Assyrian and Phoenician civilisations, plus the art of ancient Persia. **Egyptian Antiquities** contains jewellery (of Ramses II, notable among others), domestic objects, sandals, sarcophagi – a thousand marvellously decorative pieces. Some of the major exhibits are: the pink granite *Mastaba sphinx*, the *Kneeling Scribe* statue, a wooden statue of *chancellor Nakhti*, the *god Amon*, protector of Tutankhamen, *Sethi* I and the *goddess Hathor*, a bust of *Amenophis IV*. The **Greek and Roman Antiquities** include the *Winged Victory of Samothrace* and the *Venus de Milo*, biggest crowd-pullers in the museum after the Mona Lisa. Venus, striking a classic model's pose, is one of the great sex-pots of all time.

She dates from the late 2C BC. Her antecedents are all on display too, from the delightful *Dame d'Auxerre* of 7C BC to the 5C BC bronze *Apollo of Piombino*, still looking straight ahead in the archaic manner, to the classical perfection of the Athlete of Benevento and the beautiful Ephebe of Agde. In the Roman section are some very pretty mosaics from Asia Minor and luminous frescoes from Pompeii and Herculanum, which already seem to foreshadow the decorative lightness of touch of a Botticelli still 1,000 years and more away.

The **Applied Arts** collection includes treasures from the Sainte-Chapelle, Limoges enamels, tapestries, jewellery, ceramics, furniture from the Renaissance to the 19C (Boulle's ornate pieces inlaid with copper and bronze) and Gobelin tapestries based on the designs of Boucher. The **Sculpture** section covers the entire development of the art in France from Romanesque to Rodin, including Michelangelo's *Slaves* commissioned for the tomb of Pope Julius II.

The largest and most indigestible section by far is the **paintings** – French from the year dot to mid-19C, with Italians, Dutch, Germans, Flemish and Spanish represented too. Among them are many paintings so familiar from reproduction in advertisements and on chocolate boxes that it is a surprise to see them on a wall in a frame. And unless you are an art historian, the parade of mythological scenes, classical ruins, piteous piety, acrobatic saints and sheer dry academicism is hard to make much sense of. A portrait, a domestic scene, a still life, is a real relief. Walking by with eyes selectively shut is probably the best advice. The early Italians are the most interesting part of the collection, at least up to Leonardo and the 16C. Giotto, Fra Angelico, Uccello's *Battle of San Romano*, Mantegna, Botticelli, Filippo Lippi, Raphael . . . all the big names are represented. It is partly their period, but there is still an innate classical restraint which is more appealing to modern taste than the exuberance and grandiloquence of the 18C and 19C. If you want to get near the *Mona Lisa*, go first or last thing in the day. No one, incidentally, pays the slightest bit of attention to the other Leonardos right alongside, including the *Virgin of the Rocks*.

If you're likely to be back in Paris in a few years, wait till the **glass pyramid** is in place and all the building works finished. Then you'll be able to glide down below the courtyard, consult computers, audio-visuals and multi-lingual 'hostesses' before taking ambulators and escalators to the relevant section, and sit down with a cup of coffee in between the galleries of a much enlarged museum.

Musée Marmottan
2 rue Louis-Boilly, 16ᵉ (off av Raphael); Mᵒ Muette. Open 10–6; cl. Mon; expensive admission.
The star of the show here is the collection of **Monet paintings** bequeathed

by the artists's son. Among them used to be a canvas entitled *Impression, Soleil Levant*, an 1872 rendering of a misty sunrise over le Havre, whose title the critics usurped to give the Impressionist movement its name. It was stolen from the gallery in October 1985, along with four other Monet's, two Renoirs, a Morisot and a Naruse. None of these extremely well-known paintings have come to light – they presumably decorate some private fortress for the pleasure of a single person. The Marmottan's best paintings, however, still hang on its walls: a dazzling collection of canvases from Monet's last years at Giverney (see p. 145). They include numerous *Nymphéas* (waterlilies), *Le Pont Japonais*, *L'Allée des Rosiers* and *Le Saule Pleureur*. Rich colours are laid on in thick, excited whorls and lines, signs on white canvas. Form dissolves. To all intents and purposes, these are abstractions and far more 'advanced' than work of say, Renoir, Monet's exact contemporary.

Though no rival to its pictures, the Marmottan house is in itself quite interesting, with some splendid pieces of First Empire pomposity – chairs with golden spinxes for armrests, candelabra of complicated headdresses and twining serpents – and a small and beautiful collection of 13–16C manuscript illuminations.

Musée d'Orsay
Quai Anatole France, 7ᵉ; Mᵒ Gare d'Orsay. Open 10.30–6; cl, Mon.
The huge vault of glass and steel of the disused 1900s railway station opposite the Louvre, so nearly demolished by a property developer, now houses the painting and sculpture of the immediately pre-modern period, 1848–1914. The fabulous collection of Impressionists from the Jeu de Paume at last has light and space – most of the landscapes and outdoor scenes by Renoir, Sisley, Pissarro and Monet are on the top floor. With them are the Cézannes, a step removed from the preoccupations of mainstream Impressionism, and various offsprings of the movement: pointilliste works by Suerat, Signac and others; Gaugin pre- and post-Tahiti; Toulouse-Lautrec at his caricatural night-clubbing best; and all the dazzling colours and disturbing rhythms of Van Gogh.

The middle level takes in Rodin and other late 19C sculptors, while Klimt and Matisse mark the transition to the moderns in the Beaubourg collection. On the ground floor Delacroix and Ingres link back to the Louvre, followed by the Symbolists and the realist school of Daumier, Corot and Millet. Manet's *Déjeuner sur l'Herbe*, which sent the critics into apoplexies of rage and disgust in 1863, introduces Impressionism.

The Gare d'Orsay probably has the most sensual collection of art in all of Europe. Its fabric and structure, so different in mood from when Orson Welles' filmed his *Kafka* in the building, is an extra source of pleasure.

The Orangerie
Place de la Concorde, 1ᵉ; Mᵒ Concorde. Open 9.45–5.15; cl. Tues; free Wed.

The **Orangerie**, on the south side of the Tuileries terrace overlooking place de la Concorde, has two oval rooms arranged by **Monet** as panoramas for his largest waterlily paintings. In addition there are southern landscapes by Cézanne, massive Picasso nudes, portraits by Van Dongen, Utrillo and Dérain, Monet's *Argenteuil* and Sisley's *Le Chemin de Mountbuisson*. Small, select and spaciously laid out, this is one of the least visited and most enjoyable of the Paris art museums.

Palais de Tokyo
Av de Président Wilson, 16ᵉ; Mᵒ Iéna, Alma-Marceay. Musée d'Art Moderne de la Ville de Paris, open 10–5.40; cl. Mon. Centre National de la Photographie, open 9.45–5.15; cl. Tues.

In the east wing of the **Musée d'Art Moderne de la Ville de Paris** hang works by Vlaminck, Zadkine, Picasso, Braque, Matisse, Gris, Valadon, Utrillo, Dufy, both Delauneys, Chagall, Léger, Modigliani an many others, including contemporary artists, Two enormous and contrasting murals – Matisse's *La Dance* and Dufy's *La Fée Electricité* – are the star pieces. The west wing of the Palais is dedicated to photography, past and present, in temporary exhibitions.

Musée Picasso
5, rue de Thorigny, 3ᵉ; Mᵒ St-Paul/Filles-du-Calvaire. Open 9.45–5.15; Wed late opening to 10; cl. Tues.

The largest single collection of Picasso's, beautifully arranged in the 17C mansion Hôtel Salé, became state property in lieu of tax after the artist's death. It includes all the different mediums he used, the paintings he bought or was given, his African masks and sculptures, photographs, letters and other personal memorabilia. You leave with a definite sense of the man and his life in conjunction with his production, partly because these were the works he wanted to keep. The paintings of his wives, lovers and children are some of the gentlest and most endearing. There are portraits during the period of the Spanish Civil War when Picasso was going through his worst personal and political crises. He is at his best when emotion and passion play hardest on his paintings, though for *Guernica* you have to go to Madrid. But taken as a whole, the Hôtel Salé does not represent his most enjoyable creations and can't compare with the Barcelona gallery. Temporary exhibitions, however, will bring the periods least represented: the Pink, Cubism, the immediate post-war and the 1950s and 1960s.

Musée Jacquemart-André
158 bd Haussmann, 8ᵉ; Mᵒ Miromesnil, St-Philippe-du-Roule. Open 1.30–5.30, cl. Mon, Tues & Aug.
The ceilings of the staircase and three of the rooms of this museum are decorated with **Tiepolo** frescoes. His French contemporaries of the 18C hang in the ground floor as well as his fellow Venetian, Canaletto. The collection contains several Rembrandts and, best of all, 15C and 16C Italian genius in the works of Botticelli, Donatello, Mantegna, Tintoretto, Titian and Uccello.

Musée Delacroix
6 place de Furstemburg, 6ᵉ; Mᵒ St-Germain-des-Prés. Open 9.45–5.15; cl. Tues.
Some attractive watercolours, illustrations from *Hamlet* and a couple of versions of a lion hunt hang in the painter's old studio, but there's nothing much in the way of major work.

Musée Gustave Moreau
14 rue de la Rochefoucauld, 9ᵉ; Mᵒ Trinité. Open 10–12.45 & 2–4.45; cl. Mon, Tues & holidays.
An out-of-the-way bizarre, overcrowded collection of cluttered, joyless paintings by the Symbolist, Gustave Moreau. If you know you like him, go along. Otherwise, give it a miss.

Ethnic, historical and literary

Musée des Arts Africains et Océaniens
283 av Daumesnil, 12ᵉ; Mᵒ Porte Dorée. Open 9.45–12 & 1.30–5.15; cl. Tues.
This strange museum – one of the cheapest and least crowded in the city – has an African gold brooch of curled up sleeping crocodiles on one floor and, in the basement, five live crocodiles in a tiny pit surrounded by tanks of tropical fishes. Imperialism is much in evidence in a gathering of culture and creatures from the old French colonies: hardly any of the black African artefacts are dated – the collection predates European acknowledgment of history on that continent – and the captions are a bit suspicious too. These masks and statues, furniture, adornments and tools should be exhibited with paintings by Expressionists, Cubists and Surrealists to see in which direction inspiration went.

Musée Guimet
6 place d'Iéna, 16ᵉ; Mᵒ Iéna. Open 9.45–12 & 1.30–5.15; cl. Tues.
Little visited, this features a huge and beautifully displayed collection of

Oriental art, from China, India, Japan, Tibet and south-east Asia. There is a particularly fine collection of Chinese porcelain on the top floor.

If Asian art appeals you may want also to take a look at the following:

Musée Kwok-On
41 rue des Francs-Bourgeois, 4e; Mo Rambuteau, St Paul. Open 12–6. Mon–Fri.
The exhibits here are all theatrical props and costumes from southern Asia: Peking opera outfits; masks from Japan; figures for shadow theatre from India, Cambodia and Indonesia; puppets and paintings of stage scenes – all fascinating and very beautiful.

Musée Cernuschi
7 av Velasquez, 17e (by east gate of Parc Monceau); Mo Monceau, Villiers. Open 10–5.40; cl. Mon.
A small collection of ancient Chinese art with some exquisite pieces, but of fairly specialised interest.

Musée de l'Histoire de France
Archives Nationales, 60 rue des Francs-Bourgeois, 3e; Mo. Rambuteau. Open 2–5, cl. Tues; Weds free.
The **Archives Nationales** have on show some of the authentic bits of paper that fill the vaults: edicts, wills and papal bulls; a medieval English monarch's challenge to his French counterpart to stake his kingdom on a duel; Henry VIII's RSVP to the Field of the Cloth of Gold invite; fragile cross-Channel treaties; Joan of Arc's trial proceedings with a doodled impression of her in the margin; and more recent legislation and constitutions. The Revolution section includes Marie-Antoinette's book of samples from which she chose her dress each morning and a Republican children's alphabet where J stands for Jean-Jacques Rousseau and L for labourer. It's scholastic stuff (and no English translations), but the early documents are very pretty, dangling seals and penned in a delicate and illegible hand.

Musée Carnavalet
23 rue de Sévigné, 3e; Mo St-Paul. Open 10–5.40; cl. Mon.
A Renaissance mansion in the Marais presents the **history of Paris** as viewed and lived in by royalty, aristocrats and the bourgeoisie – from François I to 1900. The rooms for 1789–95 are full of sacred mementoes: models of the Bastille, original Declarations of the Rights of Man and the Citizen, tricolours and liberty caps, sculpted allegories of Reason, crockery with revolutionary slogans, glorious models of the guillotine and execution orders to make you shed a tear for the royalists as well.

In the rest of the gilded rooms there are endless paintings of Paris at different dates, and overall it's not the most enticing of displays.

Musée de l'Armée
Hôtel des Invalides, 7e; Mo Invalides, Latour-Maubourg, Ecole-Militaire. Open 10–6/5.
France's national war museum is enormous. By far the largest part is devoted to the uniforms and weaponry of Napoleon's armies. There are numerous personal items of Napoleon's, including his campaign tent and bed, and even his dog – stuffed. Later French wars are illustrated, too, through paintings, maps and engravings. Sections on the two world wars are good, with deportation and resistance covered as well as battles. Some of the oddest exhibits are Secret Service sabotage devices, for instance, a rat and a lump of coal stuffed with explosives.

Individuals – and wax
Maison de Balzac *47 rue Raynouard, 16e; Mo Passy, La Muette. Open 10–5.40; cl. Mon; free Sun.*
Contains several portraits and caricatures of the writer and a library of works of his authorship, his contemporaries' and his critics'. Balzac lived here between 1840 and 1847, but literary grandees seem to share the common fate of not leaving ghosts.
Musée Edith Piaf *5 rue Crespin-du-Gast, 11e; Mo Ménilmontant, St-Maur. Admission by appointment only. (43.55.52.72).*
Fulsome displays of the possessions – clothes, letters – and pictures of the great cabaret singer.
Maison de Victor Hugo *6 place des Vosges, 4e; Mo Bastille. Open 10–5.40; cl. Mondays.*
This museum is saved by the fact that Hugo decorated and drew, as well as wrote. Many of his ink drawings are exhibited and there's an extraordinary Japanese dining room he put together for his lover's house. Otherwise the usual pictures, manuscripts and memorabilia shed sparse light on the man and his work.
Musée Grévin I *10 bd Montmartre, 9e; Mo rue Montmartre. Open 1–7, during school hols 10–7; no admissions after 6; very expensive.*
The main Paris waxworks are nothing like as extensive as London's and only worth it if you are desperate to do something with the kids. The ticket includes a 10-minute conjuring act.
Musée Grévin II *niveau 1, Forum des Halles, 1e; Mo Les Halles. Open 10.30–8; equally expensive.*
One up on the wax statue parade of the parent museum but typically didactic. It shows a series of wax model scenes of French brilliance at the turn of the century, with automatically opening and closing doors

around each montage to prevent you from skipping any part of the voice-over and animation.

Applied arts, science and quirks

Musée National des Arts et Traditions Populaires
6 rte du Mahatma Gandhi, Bois de Boulogne, 16ᵉ (beside main entrance to Jardin d'Acclimatation); Mᵒ Les Sablons, Porte-Maillot. Open 10–5.15; cl. Tues.
If you have any interest in the beautiful and highly specialised skills, techniques and artefacts developed in the long ages that preceded industrialisation, standardisation and mass-production, then you should find this museum fascinating. Boat-building, shepherding, farming, weaving, blacksmithing, pottery, stone-cutting, games, clairvoyance . . . all beautifully illustrated and displayed. Downstairs, there is a study section – cases and cases of implements of different kinds, with cubicles where you can call up explanatory slide shows at the touch of a switch.

Palais de Chaillot
Place du Trocadéro, 16ᵉ; Mᵒ Trocadéro. Musée de l'Homme: open 9.45–5; cl. Tues. Musée de la Marine: open 10–6; cl. Tues. Musée des Monuments Français: 9.45–12.30 & 2–5; cl. Tues. Musée du Cinéma: guided tours at 10, 11, 12, 2, 3 and 4; cl. Mon.
A row of four distinct museums. The first, the **Musée de l'Homme**, contains displays illustrating the way of life, costumes, characteristic occupations, etc. of numerous countries in all parts of the world and is beginning to look a little dilapidated. Next door, the **Musée de la Marine** has dozens of beautiful, large-scale models of French ships, ancient and modern, warlike and commercial. In the east wing of the Palais, the **Musée des Monuments Français** comprises full-scale reproductions of the most important church sculpture from Romanesque to Renaissance. Moissac, Saintes, Vézelay, Autun, Chartres, Strasbourg and Crusader castles are all represented. This is the place to come to familiarise yourself with the styles and periods of monumental sculpture in France. Also included are reproductions of all the major frescoes. Downstairs and visitable only in guided groups is the **Musée du Cinéma** with costumes, sets, cameras, projectors from the early days on.

Grand and Petit Palais
Av W-Churchill, 8ᵉ; Mᵒ Champs-Élysées, Clémenceau. Grand Palais open 10–8 (Wed till 10); cl. Tues. Petit Palais open 10–5.40; cl. Mon; free on Sun.

The **Grand Palais Galeries** hold major temporary art exhibitions, good ones being evident from the queues down av Churchill. In the **Petit Palais**, whose domed entrance is brazenly over the top, you'll find the Beaux Arts museum, which seems to be a collection of leftovers – from all periods – after the other main galleries had taken their pick. There's a certain interest in this – being able to compare the ugliness of an Art Nouveau dining room with the effete 18C furniture in the *Salles Tuck* – but this collection shouldn't be at the top of your list. Nor should the **Palais de la Découverte**, in the same block – the city's old science museum, dull and traditional, and about to be well and truly upstaged by the Cité des Sciences et de l'Industrie at La Villette (see p. 64).

Musée des Arts Décoratifs
107 rue de Rivoli, 1ᵉ; Mᵒ Palais-Royal. Open 12.30–6.30, cl. Mon & Tues.
This is an enormous museum, except by the standards of the building housing it – the Louvre – of which it takes up the end of the north wing. The contents are objects: beds, blankets, toys, tools and lampshades, in fact, almost anything that illustrates the decorative skills from the Middle Ages to the 1980s. A section on clothes and fashion should also be open by now.

Musée de la Publicité
18 rue du Paradis, 10ᵉ; Mᵒ Château-d'Eau. Open 12–6, cl. Tues.
Publicity posters, adverts and TV and radio commercials are presented in monthly exhibitions, concentrating either on the art, the product or the politics. There's an excellent selection of postcards for sale and very beautiful surroundings of Art Nouveau tiles and wrought iron.

Science and technology
Musée de l'Holographie *Niveau 1, Forum des Halles, 1ᵉ; Mᵒ Les Halles. Open 10.30–7; Sun/Mon 1–7.*
Like most holography museums to date, this one is less exciting than you expect, the fault lying with the state of the art. But there are a couple of holograms more inspired than women winking as you pass, and works where artists have combined holograms with painting. The most impressive technically are the reproductions of museum treasures and just like the originals you can't touch them.
Jardin des Plantes *5ᵉ; Mᵒ Austerlitz, Jussieu. Open 1.30–5, Sun 10.30–5; cl. Tues.*
There are three museums in the *jardin*: paleontology, botany and mineralogy of which the best is paleontology with a great collection of fossils, pickled bits and pieces and things dinosaurian.

Musée National des Techniques *270 rue St-Martin, 3ᵉ; Mᵒ Réamur-Sébastopol, Arts-et-Métiers. Open Tues–Sat 1–5.30; Sun (free) 10–5.15.* Utterly traditional and stuffy glass-case museum with thousands of technical things from fridges to flutes, clocks and trains. The only exceptional part is the entrance – an early Gothic church filled with engines, aeroplanes, cars and bikes.

Quirks and costume

SEITA *12 rue Surcrouf, 7ᵉ; Mᵒ Invalides, Latour-Maubourg. Open 11–6; cl. Sun; free.*
The state tobacco company has this small and delightful museum in its offices, presenting the pleasures of smoking with pipes and pouches from every continent – early Gauloise packets, painted *tabac* signs and, best of all, a slide show of tobacco in painting from the 17C to now.
Musée de la Contrefaçon *16 rue de la Faisanderie, 16ᵉ, Mᵒ Porte-Dauphine. Open 8.30–5; wkdays only.*
One of the odder ones – examples of imitation products, labels and brand marks trying to pass off as the 'genuine article'.
Musée des Lunettes et Lorgnettes de Jadis *2 av Mozart, 16ᵉ; Mᵒ La Muette. Open 9–1 & 2–7; cl. Sun/Mon.*
An optician hosts this huge collection of people's focussing aids: medieval lenses, Restoration monocles, and 20C flash specs.
Musée de la Mode et du Costume *10 av Pierre 1ᵉʳ de Serbie, 16ᵉ; Mᵒ Iéna, Alma-Marceau. Open 10–5.40; cl. Mon.*
Clothes and fashion accessories from the 18C to today exhibited in temporary thematic exhibitions. They last about six months and during changeovers (usually May–Nov) the museum is closed.

THE FACTS

Cafés, bars and cultural venues detailed below should give you an idea of Paris's potential for entertainment. For exhaustive **listings of what's on** in the city, there are three weekly guides, published on a Wednesday: *Pariscope, L'Officiel des Spectacles* and *7 à Paris*. Pariscope is probably the easiest to find your way around though since all three are just listings papers, with no critical articles, there is little to choose between them. The **English-language** magazine *Passion*, published monthly in Paris and written mainly by trend-seeking Americans, can sometimes be a worthwhile supplement.

Café life and drinking

You'll be happy in Paris if you're addicted to sitting around watching other people go about their business. **Cafés, bars** and **brasseries** beckon at every turn. All serve coffee, alcohol, sandwiches, ice creams and other snacks. In the morning you can get breakfast, of croissants, a *tartine* (baguette and butter, with jam sometimes), even eggs in the right place. And for the price of a coffee you can sit undisturbed for hours. Costs, inevitably, escalate in the posher neighbourhoods (beware the Champs-Élysées and rue de Rivoli) and anything consumed seated will be twice the price of standing at the counter. But prices are always posted outside, so there's no excuse for being ripped off.

The most enjoyable cafés are often ordinary, local places but there are **particular areas** which café-lizards head for. The most famous, perhaps is bd Montparnasse, where you'll find the *Select, Coupole, Dôme, Rotonde* and *Closerie des Lilas* – hangouts of Sartre and Apollinaire, Miller, Nin and Hemingway and most other **literary-intellectual** figures of the last six decades. Their reputation is now pretty skeletal though the sets are unchanged, if you're curious. *Flore* and *Deux Magots* on bd St-Germain are in similar vein. Less vicariously, **modern gathering points** include the attractive *La Palette* on the corner of rue Jacques-Callot, for students at the Beaux Arts; the cafés in place de la Sorbonne, off bd St-Michel, for Sorbonne students; and the rue Linne (opposite the rue Cuvier exit from the Jardin des Plantes) where the science faculties spill out. *Café de la Mairie* on place St-Sulpice (6ᵉ) and the *Café de la Nouvelle Mairie* wine bar at 19 rue des Fosses St-Jacques (5ᵉ) are two more relaxed, literary-youthful spots; *Au Bon Pêcheur* and *Au Père Tranquil* (both on rue Pierre-Lescot, (1ᵉʳ) are for the city's young poseurs, who sit scowling across the terrace tables at each other. *Village Voice* (6 rue Princesse, 6ᵉ) combines English-language bookshop and café; you can nibble while you read.

Elsewhere in the city you find particular identities in particular areas. **La Bastille** is a good place to tour – always lively at night. So too, though rather more upmarket, is **Les Halles**, home to the stylishly modernist *Café Costes* (4 rue Berger), *Au Père Tranquil* (16 rue Pierre-Lescot) and others incorporating designer café with designer client. Less affected, **the Marais** is thick with all kinds of places. *Ma Bourgogne* at 19 place des Vosges is well known; the *Centre Culturel du Marais* (20 rue des Francs-Bourgeois) is an art bookshop with salon de thé; and there are further **salons de thé** in *Le Loir dans la Théière* (3 rue des Rosiers; Tues–Sat 12–7, Sun 1–7) with deep armchairs and a mural of the Mad Hatter's Teaparty, *La Charlotte* (19 rue François Miron) and the rather self-conscious *Eurydice* (10 place des Vosges; 12–10, cl. Tues).

Tea-drinking places exist in other parts of the city too. *A Priori Thé* at 35–7 Galerie Vivienne (2ᵉ) is quiet and secluded. More interesting, on the Right Bank, are *Rose Thé*, full of antique bric-à-brac, opposite 68 rue St-Honoré (1ᵉʳ), and *Fanny Tea* in the very lovely place Dauphine on the Ile de la Cité. On the Left Bank, **the mosque** at 39 rue Geoffroy St-Hilaire (see p. 53) is one of the more unusual venues, as is *La Pagode* in the pagoda-cinema of the same name at 57bis rue de Babylone, 7ᵉ.

For **straight drinking**, any of the cafés and bars above are good bets. If you're particularly into **wine**, though, certain bars are known for their selections: *Aux Bons Crus* (7 rue des Petits Champs, 1ᵉʳ; provincial and pleasantly unchic; cl. weekends); *La Tartine* (24 rue de Rivoli, 4ᵉ; cl. Tues); *Au Sauvignon* (80 rue des Saints-Pères, 7ᵉ; cl. Suns); *L'Ecluse* (15 quai des Grands-Augustins, 5ᵉ; again cl. Suns); and the old-fashioned, cosy *Crocodile* in rue Royer-Collard (5ᵉ). **Beer** connoisseurs should try the *Académie de la Bière* (88bis bd de Port-Royal, 5ᵉ), with brews from twenty-two countries, including China, Mexico and Czechoslovakia, or *La Gueuse* (19 rue Soufflot, 5ᵉ), run by the same outfit. *Bar Belge de New Store* (63 av des Champs-Élysées, 8ᵉ), *Maison de l'Allemagne* (45 rue Pierre Charron, 8ᵉ) and *Au Général Lafayette* (52 rue Lafayette, 9ᵉ) specialise respectively in Belgian, German and French beers.

Finally, some chic **bars with music**: *Helium* (3 rue des Haudriettes, 3ᵉ with videos and occasional concerts), *Bleue Nuit* (11 rue des Vertus, 3ᵉ; smaller and usually fun) and *Piano Vache* (rue Laplace, 5ᵉ; new wave). *Harry's Bar* (5 rue Daunou, 2ᵉ), hardly chic any more, is the original **American bar** in Paris. *Polly Magoo* in rue St-Jacques in the 5ᵉ (no 11) is a scruffy **all-nighter**, frequented by chess addicts.

Eating

Far too many Parisian **restaurants** trade on tourists. To eat well, without spending an alarming amount, you need to know your way around. The lists below might look extensive but they're far outnumbered by the mediocre, especially, of course, in the central areas where there's no established clientele. Don't, however, be put off – just selective. And if you want to eat a *menu fixe*, go early: in the evenings it's often *à la carte* only after 9.30, and later than 10.30 it can be difficult to get a meal at all except in a few specific late night places.

Areas with the highest concentration of menus to consider include Les Halles, the Marais, the Latin quarter, Belleville, around métro Abbesses in Montmartre, and the Chinese quarter in the 13ᵉ. Beware that many restaurants **close** on Sundays or Mondays or both, and quite a number for the whole of July or August.

Snacks

Stalls along most **boulevards** sell *crêpes*, *croque monsieurs* and *baguette* sandwiches at unoutrageous prices: there's a particular concentration around the junction of bd St-Michel and St-Germain. For variety, **Tunisian** snacks like the *brik à l'oeuf* (a pastry envelope fried with an egg inside – hard to eat without getting egg on face) are common, as are **Greek** *souvlaki* (kebabs) and takeway fare. At the Les Halles end of rue St Honoré you'll also find an **Egyptian** *falafel* stall, and at the other end a **Japanese** snack-bar, *Ramen-Tei* at no 163.

Cafés – see the preceding section – will generally do you an omelette or fried eggs, as well as sandwiches. Some, like *Ma Bourgogne* (place des Vosges), *La Tartine* (at the seedier east end of rue Rivoli) and *Aux Bons Crus* (7 rue des Petits Champs) also have more gastronomic fare in the bread and meat line. And there are too the **drugstores** – pricier but good for salads, ice creams and *plats du jour* through till 1am. You will find them at 149 bd St-Germain (6e); 133 av des Champs-Élysées (8e); 1 av Mantignon (8e); and 6 bd Capucines (9e).

The best **ice creams and sorbets** in France are made and sold by *Berthillon* on the Ile St-Louis (31 rue St-Louis-en-l'Ile; open 10–8 Wed–Sun, cl. July–Aug). Their products are also available at *Lady Jane* and *Le Flore-en-l'Ile*, both on quai d'Orléans.

Meals from 50F to 80F

Note that this – and subsequent – price categories are based on the lowest available menu fixe. *Going* à la carte *will rocket the bill at almost all of them.*

Bistro de la Gare (30 rue St-Denis, 1er). Good quick standby from a limited French-Italian menu.

Drouot (103 rue de Richelieu, 2e). Admirably cheap and good food, served at frantic pace, in an Art Nouveau decor. Same management as the better known *Chartier* (in the 9e, see below).

L'Ebouillanté (rue des Barres, 4e; open 12–9, last order 8.30; cl. Mon). Small and unintimidating with tables outside and 'Parisian cuisine' of *blinis*, *brics* and gooey puddings.

Aux Savoyards, *Le Baptiste* (14 and 11 rue des Boulangers; both cl. Sun/Sat am). Noisy, friendly and full of students.

La Ferme Ste-Geneviève (40 rue de la Montagne St-Geneviève, 5e; cl. Mon/Tues midday). Good for hors d'oeuvres – which you can eat as much of as you want.

Bistro de la Gare (59 bd de Montparnasse, 6e). Same style (and management) as the *gare* in the 1er; sumptuous 1900 set.

Restaurant des Omelettes (29 rue St-André des Arts, 6e). A hundred different varieties.

La Table d'Italie, Brasserie Nesle (rue Dauphine, 6e). Good lunchtime places – eat at the counter in La Table – or try *Le Port Dauphine* further up.

Valentin (19 rue Marbeuf, 8e; open every day). A rare realistic option if you want to eat in the centre of monumental Paris.

Bistro de la Gare (38 bd des Italiens, 9e). Yet another one (see above).

Casa Miguel (48 rue St-Georges, 9e). Possibly the cheapest full meal anywhere in Inner Paris – and justly popular.

Chartier (7 rue Faubourg-Montmartre, 9e; open till 9.30). Another traditional cheapie with manic service and frogs and snails on the menu. Not for lingering but not to be missed.

Bar des Sports (15 rue de la Buttes aux Cailles, 13e). A local bistro with unusual and unecological fare (crocodiles, sometimes turtles).

Bergamote (1, rue Niepce, 14e). Good Normandy cooking. Drink cider.

Café-Restaurant à l'Observatoire (63 av Denfert-Rochereau, 14e; cl. Sun). A straightforward, quick eating place with *steack frites* and the like at their most basic and best. Very crowded at lunchtimes.

Le Commerce (51 rue de Commerce, 15e). Another in the Chartier/ Drouot line (see above).

Le Bistrot Champêtre (107 rue St-Charles, 15e open till 11). Unusually imaginative – and quality – *menu fixe*. Definitely recommended.

Au Bon Accueil (corner of rue Wilhelm and av de Versailles). Simple and pleasant *restaurant du quartier*.

Palais de Tokyo (av du Président Wilson). Snack bar between the museums – an excellent place for a midday meal.

Janot la Frite (place Clichy, 17e). No great excitement but edible and dead cheap.

Au Petit Moulin (17, rue Tholoze, 18e; cl. Weds). Tiny restaurant in a picturesque old house; excellent *plats du jour* and changing menus.

Le Maquis (69 rue Caulaincourt; open till 11; cl. Suns). A brilliant lunchtime menu which in summer you can eat outside.

More upmarket (around 120F)

Le Potiron (16 rue du Roule, 1e; cl. Sun/Mon). Run by women, with changing exhibitions of women artists' works as decoration and very imaginative dishes bordering on *nouvelle cuisine*.

La Petite Chaumière (41 rue des Blancs Manteaux, 4e; open till 10; cl. Sun/Mon). Tremendous seafood dishes. Relaxed place.

Brasserie Balzar (49 rue des Ecoles, 5e; open till 1.30 am.; cl. Tues). Classic, well-fed feeding place, near the top of the range.

Au Vieux Paris (2 rue de l'Abbaye, 6e; cl. Tues/Mon pm). Good value for money in an attractive cockeyed medieval house.

L'Oeillade (10 rue de Saint Simon, 7e; open till 9.45, cl. Sun). Home cooking in a nice atmosphere; run by two women.

Julien (16 rue du Faubourg St-Denis, 10ᵉ; open till 1.30am). The ambiance of the 1890s is still around in this swirling, mirrored interior and the plates of shellfish as good as they've probably always been.

Brasserie Flo (7 cour des Petites Ecuries, 10ᵉ; open till 1.30 am). The same outfit as Julien, similar decor and food plus specialities from Alsace. A great place to blow money but you'll need to book to do so – 47.70.13.59.

L'Éléphant Rose (7 rue Francis de Pressensé, 14ᵉ). Change of scene from the Art Nouveau brasseries: a co-op restaurant/*salon de thé*, good at any time of day.

Le Mouton Blanc (40 rue d'Auteuil, 16ᵉ). A haunt of Racine Molière and La Fontaine several hundred years ago, it now serves the well-heeled locals with an appealing choice of dishes.

Les Chants du Piano (3 rue Steinlen, 17ᵉ; open till 11; cl. Sun/Mon. Wonderful, visually and orally, with awesome desserts.

A La Pomponnette (42 rue Lepic, 18ᵉ). Regulars' diner-zinc counter, tobacco stains, and a friendly crowd feasting on culinary classics.

If you're feeling slightly crazed – or you happen on a 500F note or winning lottery ticket – Paris also, of course, has some really **spectacular restaurants**. For Nouvelle Cuisine at its best *Au Franc Pinot* (1 quai Bourbon, 4ᵉ; cl. Sun/Mon) and *L'Archestrate* (which really is obsessively expensive – at 84 rue de Varenne) are said to be the points of true experience. For philosophical nostalgia, matched by grand and vast choice of dishes, look in either at *La Coupole* (102 bd Montparnasse, 14ᵉ; open till 1.45 am) or the famed and intimidating *Le Train Bleu* (1st floor at the Gare de Lyon; open till 10pm) with its ludicrous fin-de-siècle murals of favoured train destinations.

Ethnic restaurants

Paris's **ethnic restaurants** offer some of the best and least expensive food in the city: North African, 'French' West African, Chinese, Arab, East European . . . often much better than you'd find it in its original environment. The selections below are only a tiny percentage of what's available. If you're after **North African** food you could just head for the 'Little Maghreb' area along bd de Belleville (though perhaps not alone, late) or rue Xavier-Privas in the 5ᵉ; for **Chinese** and **Indo-Chinese** there's a concentration around the av de la porte de Choisy in the 13ᵉ as well as the Belleville Chinatown; while the Latin quarter (now heavily commercialised) features limitless, if often limited, **Greek** restaurants.

West and Central African

Le Kinkeliba (5 rue des Déchargeurs, 1ᵉʳ. Wonderful smoked fish and yassa chicken – one of the best African restaurants in Paris.

L'Ajoupa (8 placc Ste-Opportune, 1ᵉʳ; cl. Sun/Mon am). Cheap and spicy.

La Savane (17 rue Marie-Stuart, 2ᵉ). Panther milk cocktails, tropical fruits, nut pâtés and other sun-soaked fare.

Kin Malebo (2 passage Louis-Philippe, 11ᵉ; open till 2am). Zairean meals at around 50F.

Le Fouta Toro (3 rue du Nord, 18ᵉ; evenings only; cl. Thurs). Inexpensive Senegalese dishes.

Le Port de Pidjiguiti (28 rue Etex, 18ᵉ; cl. Mons). Radical co-op with Guinea-Bissau the source of inspiration in the kitchen.

North American
What a Burger, Love Burger, Dallas Burger, Fun Burger, Burger King, Macdonalds, etc. Not yet as ubiquitous as the shit on the pavements but getting that way.

Arab/North African
Hassan (27 rue de Turbigo, 3ᵉ; open till midnight, cl. Mons). Ace Moroccan restaurant – North African food at its best and most beautiful. Slightly pricey.

Le Liban à la Mouff (18 rue Mouffetard, 5ᵉ). Very pleasant Lebanese fare. Unusually cheap.

Chez Nacef (26 rue de Bierre, 5ᵉ). Above average Algerian restaurant.

Chez Marcel (16–18 rue Lalande, 14ᵉ). Good value *menu fixe* until 9pm, very friendly and excellent couscous at all times.

Le Golestan de Perse (4 rue Sévero, 14ᵉ). Not Arab but Iranian with an excellent *menu fixe* around 50F.

Zerda (rue Cheroy, 17ᵉ). Good unpretentious Moroccan.

Oaj Djerba (110 rue de Belleville, 20ᵉ; open till midnight, cl. Fri/Sat midday). Basic Tunisian-Jewish food.

East European/Russian
Village Bulgare (8 rue de Nevers, 6ᵉ). Perhaps the only authentic Bulgarian restaurant in western Europe: try the *Cirene au Four* (baked ewe's cheese with vegetables) and *Gamza* wine.

Paprika (43 rue Polireau, 5ᵉ; cl. wkends). Affordable Hungarian cooking.

Kazatchok (7 rue Manuel, 9ᵉ). Most Parisian Russian restaurants are high-class establishments run by old aristos. This isn't: a small, friendly place with great smoked salmon *blinis*, *kotlet kievski* and other Slavic specials.

La Cracovia (10 rue Alexandre Dumas, 11ᵉ). Good solid Polish bistro.

Indo-Chinese
Orient Express (rue des Gravilliers, 3ᵉ). Chinese and Vietnamese with no frills, but good and reasonably priced.

L'Auberge des Temples (74 rue de Dunkerque, 10ᵉ; open till 10.30).

Choice of Chinese, Vietnamese, Thai, Cambodian and Japanese concoctions all under the one roof. Not expensive.

Éléphant Blanc (33 rue Trois-Frères, 18e). Best in Lao-Thai cuisine – rich in ginger, citronella and coconut milk. Middle range.

Réunion/Antillean

La Creole (122 bd Montparnasse, 14e). A bit gaudy, unpredictable but well located.

Ile de la Réunion (119 rue St-Honoré, 1er cl. Sat midday/Sun). Tropical island cuisine from one of France's remaining colonies. Cheap lunchtime menu, pricier at night. There are also a number of Antillean restaurants nearby in the 1er along rue de Montorgueil.

Vegetarian/macrobiotic

Larger than usual scope includes . . .

Restaurant Végétarien (2 place du Marché Ste-Catherine, 4e; open 11–6; cl. Sun). Small, quiet and inexpensive.

Piccolo Teatro (6 rue des Écouffes, 4e; open till 12.30am; cl. Tues). Delicious edibles with pedantic names. An extremely comfortable place – more of a late night *salon de thé* cum snackbar, really, than a restaurant.

Aux Abeilles d'Or (12 rue Royer-Collard, 5e). Vegetarian *nouvelle cuisine*.

L'Auberge In (34 rue du Cardinal-Lemoine, 5e; open till 10; cl. Sun). Wonderful *plats du jour*, home-made bread and a no-smoking room.

Mary's Restaurant (9 rue de Turenne, 9e; open till 10). As English as the name – reasonably priced gourmet flans and tarts.

Le Bol en Bois (35 rue Pascal, 13e; open till 10, cl. Sun). Japanese-inspired vegetarian.

Au Grain de Folie (24 rue La Vieuville, 18e; evenings only, open till 10.30; cl. Wed.). Good unpretentious cheapie.

Late night

Au Pied de Cochon (6 rue Coquillère, 1er; 24 hrs). The best known all-nighter with a *terrasse*, seafood specialities and cheaper eats at the bar.

Pub Saint-Germain-des-Prés (17 rue de l'Ancienne Comédie, 6e; 24 hrs). Seats 500 people and has an equally phenomenal range of beers. Food from omelettes and *steack frites* to a full meal at unshocking prices.

La Boulangerie (6 rue de l'Ancienne Comédie, 6e). Not a restaurant but a baker's – bread, brioche and croissants from 1am to 6am.

La Corossol Doudou (1 rue de la Ferrière, 9e; open till 7am.). Antillais restaurant.

Le Pigalle (22 bd de Clichy, 9e; 24 hrs). Bar, brasserie and *tabac*.

La Nouvelle Gare (49 bd Vincent Auriol, 13e; 24 hrs, cl. Sat midday and

Sun). For people coming off night shifts, the lowest late night prices and a great atmosphere.

See also p. 88 for addresses of late-night *drugstores*.

Music and nightlife

French rock has a – deservedly – miserable reputation, but in Paris there are plentiful musical alternatives. The **West African** link has spawned bands of its own in the city and brings others on tour; there are regular **salsa nights** and occasional bouts of **reggae**; and the French themselves take their **jazz** and **classical music** seriously.

Rock, African, Antillean and Salsa

Paris has very few venues for local rock bands to play – perhaps a quiet self-admission – and touring British or American bands tend to appear in the big **concert halls**: the *Forum des Halles* (15 rue de l'Equerre d'Argent, 1er; Mo Rambuteau), *Olympia* (28 bd des Capucines, 2e; Mo Opéra), *Palais des Sports* (Porte de Versailles), *Zenith* (211 av Jean-Jaurès, Porte de Pantin) or the new *Palais Omnisports de Bercy* (Porte de Bercy, 12e) The *FNAC* shops (see p. 102 for addresses) take bookings for most of these concerts without charging a commission. **Venues** detailed below are on the whole regular discos and clubs most days of the week, hosting live gigs on an occasional basis:

Phil-One (well-signposted in the La Défense). Big, with an excellent sound, a dancefloor of sorts and a quirky musical policy – some established rock bands but also African and Antillean festivals.

Rex Club (1 bd Poissonière, 2e), *Eldorado* (4 bd Strasbourg, 10e). Two discos with regular African sounds and bands from time to time.

Chappelle des Lombards (19 rue Lappe, 11e; Mo Bastille). Tango, salsa, African and Antillean music. Usually interesting.

Gibus (18 rue du Faubourg du Temple, 10e; Mo République). This is about the only place for Paris rock bands to play and most nights you'll need a twisted sense of humour. There's a listenable band, though, every alternate blue moon: *Rita Mitsouko* are perhaps the best with fresh sounds and complex electronic arrangements, *Indochine* are danceable, *Telephone* (the most famous French group) are stubborn if accomplished Stones disciples, and there's always a chance of catching a Belgian band – like *Minimal Compact* or *T.C. Matic*.

Les Trottoirs de Buenos Aires (37 rue des Lombards, 1er; Mo Châtelet). Argentinian and Chilean tango music – no dancing.

La Plantation (43 rue Montpensier, 1er; Mo Pyramides), *Le Malibou* (44 rue Tigetonne, 2e; Mo Etienne-Marcel), *Le Mambo Club* (20 rue Cujas, 5e; Mo Luxembourg). These all feature various types of African and Antillean sounds.

Discos

The more interesting are either private or among those listed above but if you're into **clubbing** to British and American sounds there's no shortage of other possibilities. Most are in the St-Germain or Champs-Élysées area. Entrance prices are slightly cheaper than London or New York equivalents, and your chances of being turned away are not quite so high, though the doormen, if anything, are more insulting and the clients more self-conscious.

Tango (11 rue au Maire, 3ᵉ; Mᵒ Arts-et-Métiers). Disco-bar with limited space but a lot of energy.

La Piscine (32 rue Tilsitt, 8ᵉ; Mᵒ Etoile). Dance on the tiles in a converted swimming pool. The cheapest Paris disco and one of the newest and most popular.

Les Bains (7 rue Bourg-L-Abbé, 3ᵉ; Mᵒ Etienne-Marcel). Another conversion, this time from an old bath-house. Entrance is free during the week but locals are snobbish and the waiters pester you constantly to buy expensive drinks and throw you out if you don't. Closed Monday.

Palace (8 rue du Fg Montmartre, 9ᵉ; Mᵒ Montmartre). Big, crowded venue where TV dance shows are often filmed. Afro night Thursday; cl. Mon and Tues.

La Scala (188bis rue de Rivoli, 1ᵉʳ; Mᵒ Palais Royal). Fancy place with three balconies and Italian decor. A bit mainstream.

Rock'n'Roll Circus (9 rue Caumartin, 9ᵉ; Mᵒ Harve-Caumartin). Last time Roxy Music played Paris, Ferry and Mackay were having a drink at the Helium and asked which nightclub they should try. 'Anywhere but the Rock'n'Roll Circus' came the reply – so this is where they went.

Jazz clubs

Jazz clubs are generally cheaper than their rock/disco equivalents, but like them no longer survive on an exclusive diet: several of the places below now regularly feature **Latin American** and **African** groups – in atmospheres often a lot more conducive.

Some **French jazzmen** to look out for are saxophonists François Jeanneau and Didier Malherbe, and violinist Didier Lockwood, all of whom still play small gigs in Paris in spite of having gained international reputations. Guitarist John McLauglin, too, lives in Paris and turns up from time to time in the clubs and, with most other Paris jazz and rock musicians, in the *Musicland* instrument shop on the bd Beaumarchais.

New Morning (7–9 rue des Petites-Ecuries, 10ᵉ; Mᵒ Château d'Eau). The best of the clubs and venue for most big foreign names. Plenty of room but a hefty admission charge.

Le Petit Journal (71 bd St-Michel, 5ᵉ; Mᵒ Luxembourg). Traditional and mainstream jazz with French musicians. A nice place.

Le Petit Opportun (15 rue des Lavandières-St-Opportune, 1er; Mo Châtelet). Good jazz in a cramped cellar – go early if you want to see as well as hear.

Le 28 Dunois (28 rue Dunois, 13e; Mo Chevaleret). Interesting venue in an out of the way warehouse. Cheap drinks, reasonable admission.

Caveau de la Huchette, (5 rue de la Huchette, 5e; Mo St-Michel). Again good value – though crowded.

The Slow Club (130 rue de Rivoli, 1er; Mo Châtelet). Miles Davis's old favourite. Still ranking high.

Le Furstemberg (25 rue de Buci, 6e; Mo Odéon). Small jazz combos.

Closerie des Lilas (171 bd Montparnasse, 14e; Mo Raspail). Good piano bar.

La Merle Moqueur (11 rue des Buttes-aux-Cailles; Mo Corvisart). Worker's co-operative bar where you'll find few other tourists – jazz on Monday nights, *chansons* on Thursdays.

Le Calvados (40 av Pierre Premier de Serbie, 8e; Mo Georges V). Latin American musicians, and the wonderful Joe Turner on piano around midnight – a spot he has occupied for twenty-five years.

Classical music

A strange but agreeable phenomenon for a big city: most of Paris's classical music **concerts** are held in **churches**. Keep your eye out for posters around town – or check *Pariscope*, etc. or the magazine *Le Monde de la Musique* – there are scores of possibilities, especially during the summer, from Vivaldi to Stockhausen and the new Systems composers. These concerts are either free or very cheap. Likely venues include St-Germain-des-Prés, St-Julien-le-Pauvre, les Invalides, St-Séverin, St-Thomas-d'Aquin. There are free organ recitals in Notre-Dame on Sundays at 5.45pm.

Other performances throughout the year are held at the *Salle Pleyel* (Mo Ternes), the *Théâtre Musical de Paris* (2 rue Edouard-Colonne, 1er), and of course the **Opéra** (place de l'Opéra, 2er; Mo Opéra; prohibitively expensive – though with occasional reductions for some performances).

The musical experiments creaming off the most state funds are **Pierre Boulez's** researches into electronic acoustics. His laboratory/concert hall is beneath Beaubourg (entrance beside the Stravinsky pool). There are frequent performances and you can listen to tapes of recent extracts at the reception (during office hours).

Movies and theatre

There are over 350 **films** showing in Paris in any one week – all of them detailed in the listings magazines. Most cinemas have low rates on Mondays and reductions for students Mon–Thurs, all are no-smoking and some still require you to tip the ushers. Almost all of the huge selection of foreign films get original version showings (*v.f.* in listings means it's dubbed) and most non UK and USA movies are screened here months before they get to London, if they ever do.

Of all the capital's **cinemas**, the most beautiful is the *Pagode* (57bis rue Babylone, 7ᵉ; Mᵒ François Xavier), originally transplanted from Japan at the turn of the century to be a rich Parisienne's party place. The wall panels of the Grande Salle are embroidered in silk, golden dragons and elephants hold the lights and a battle between Japanese and Chinese warriors rages on the ceiling. If you don't fancy the films being shown you can still come here for tea and cakes (see p. 87). *Kinopanorama* (60 av Motte Piquet, 15ᵉ; Mᵒ La Motte Piquet) has reintroduced organ interludes for some showings and has the widest screen in Paris. Or, for large scale kitsch, there's *Le Grand Rex* (1 bd Poissonnière, 2ᵉ; Mᵒ Bonne Nouvelle) with 2,800 seats, a ceiling with moving clouds and street scenery on either side of the screen; unfortunately it goes in for dubbed films.

More seriously, *cinémathèques* at Beaubourg and at the Palais de Chaillot show several different films daily from their library of international classics and obscurities, and seats are cheap. Several cinemas also run **festivals** so that you can pass an entire day or more watching your favourite actor/actress, director, genre or period. One such is *Le Studio 28* (10 rue de Tholozé, 18ᵉ; Mᵒ Blanche/Abbesses) which in its early days was done over by extreme right-wing catholics who destroyed the screen and the paintings by Dali and Ernst in the salle after one of the first showings of Bunuel's *L'Age d'Or*. The cinema still shows avant-garde premieres followed sometimes by discussions with the director. An **International Festival of Womens' Films** takes place in March at the suburb of Sceaux – details from the *Maison des Femmes* (8 Cité Prost, 11ᵉ; 43.48.29.91).

Parisian **theatre** – at least at the more **avant-garde** end of the spectrum – can be amazing simply as spectacle. A handful of directors (Antoine Vitez, Ariane Mnouchkine, Peter Brook) have superstar status and their productions are frequently epic. If you're interested, *Passion* magazine has regular coverage. Among the most promising **venues** are the *Théâtre du Soleil* (Mnouchkine's theatre, run as a workers' co-op at La Cartoucherie, Bois de Vincennes, Mᵒ Vincennes), the *Palais de Chaillot* (place du Trocadéro, 16ᵉ; Mᵒ Trocadéro) and the *Théâtre de l'Est Parisien* at Ménilmontant.

Café-théâtre, which all hip guide-writers feel obliged to recommend, relying heavily on contemporary allusions, slang and humour, it may be difficult to understand unless you actually live in the city. If you want to try, the *Café de la Gare* (41 rue de Temple, 4ᵉ; Mᵒ Hôtel de Ville), *Blancs-Manteaux* (15 rue des Blancs-Manteaux, 4ᵉ; Mᵒ Hôtel de Ville) and *Au Café d'Edgar* (58 bd Edgar-Quinet, 14ᵉ; Mᵒ Edgar-Quinet) are among the best known.

For serious straight theatre, check out the programmes of the **state-subsidised theatres**. The *Comédie Française* (2 rue de Richelieu, 1ᵉʳ; Mᵒ Palais-Royal) specialises in the 17C classics (left-over tickets sold off cheap on the night). More modern plays are performed at the *Théâtre de France* (at the Odéon, place Paul Claudel, 6ᵉ; Mᵒ Odéon), and at smaller houses spread about the city; the *Cité Internationale*, *Théâtre du Marais*, *Montparnasse*, and *Présent* are all names to look for in the listings. The *Huchette* (23 rue de la Huchette, 5ᵉ; Mᵒ St-Michel) has been playing the Absurd equivalent of The Mousetrap – Ionesco's *La Cantatrice Chauve* – for more than twenty-five years.

Kid's Paris

The star attraction for young children is the **Jardin d'Acclimatation** (Mᵒ Porte Maillot) in the Bois de Boulogne, open every day from 9–6.30 with special attractions Wed, Sat and Sun and during school holidays. There are puppets, bumper-cars, go-karts, pony and camel rides, sealions, a mini-train from Porte Maillot, a sort of magical mini-canal ride, and a superb collection of antique dolls at the *Grande Maison des Poupées*. For the older ones there is **mini-golf** and **bowling**, and at the entrance **bike hire** for roaming the park's cycle trails. Also, **boating** on the Lac Inférieur. The one drawback with the Jardin is that nearly every activity costs an additional fee.

Other places you can let kids off the leash are the **Jardin des Plantes** (Mᵒ Jussieu/Monge) with a small **zoo** (9–5.30) and **Natural History Musuem** (10–5.30; cl. Tues). The **best zoo** – and both are expensive – is the **Bois de Vincennes** (9–6/5.30 in winter; Mᵒ Porte Dorée). Numbers of squares and small public gardens have play areas with sand-pits and slides; square Viviani, for instance, opposite Notre-Dame could provide quick relief for a child with the screaming Gothic abdabs. **Parc Monceau** in the 17ᵉ has a roller-skating rink; the **Luxembourg gardens** have a larger playground, pony rides, toyboat hire on the pond and puppets.

Other **puppet-shows** take place Wed, Sat and Sun at the Champs-Élysées Rond-Point, and the Buttes-Chaumont park (Mᵒ Buttes-Chaumont). For these and the **circus**, check *Pariscope* and its peers.

Potential mountaineers can practise breaking their necks – no charge – on the **kid's climbing wall** at *Au Vieux Campeur* climbing-camping shop in rue des Ecoles, 5ᵉ.

The **children's workshop**, Atelier des Enfants, at the **Centre Beaubourg** could be fun (open daily except Tues and Sun); they organise games, painting, sculpture, etc. for over-5s. There is no language problem as the *animateurs* – organisers – speak English.

You could also try some **museums**: the **Aquarium** underneath the Palais Chaillot (10–5.30); the waxworks, **Musée Grévin**; **Musée de l'Armée, de la Marine, de l'Homme** – see pp. 82–3 for these. **Musée des Enfants** (12 av de New-York; M° Alma-Marceau; 10–5.30, cl. Mon; free Sun) purveys romantic sentimental images of childhood.

The ghoulish and horror-movie addicts should get a really satisfying shudder from the **Catacombs** (Tues–Sun 10–12 & 2–5; but read p. 57 first!) while the other pre-teen fixation might find fulfilment in the **sewers** – *Les Egouts* (boat tours Mon, Wed and the last Saturday of the month, 2–5).

Feminist Paris

With French feminism in its present doldrums places are closing rather than starting up, including the longstanding *Carabosses* bookshop-café haven. The one secure **feminist centre** for information, help, food, recreation and a meeting place for different organisations is the **Maison des Femmes** (8 Cité Prost, 11e; 43.48.24.91). They publish a fortnightly bulletin, *Paris Féministes*, run a cinema club and a radio station, *Les Nanas Radioteuses* (101.6 Mhz; Wed 6pm–midnight). The *Centre Audio-Visual Simone de Beauvoir* (32 rue Maurice Ripoche, 14e), named after its founder, is an **archive of audio-visual works** by or about women which you can look at for a small fee. For **books and reviews**, try the *Librairie Anima* (3 rue Ravignan, 18e) and *des Femmes Librairie-Galerie* (74 rue de Seine, 6e) which has foreign publications and exhibitions. The most comprehensive **library** is the *Bibliothèque Marguerite Durand* (Mairie du 5e, 21 place du Panthéon, 5e). *Elles Tournent La Page* (8 Impasse des Trois Soeurs, 11e) has a library along with **dance, fitness** and **writing workshops.**

There are all sorts of **courses and classes** from mime to plumbing organised by and for women, but what's lacking in Paris is more **eating and drinking places.** *Le Potiron* (see p. 89) is the only feminist restaurant in town.

Harassment on the streets is worse and more constant here than in the rest of France. If things get bad, you could turn to *SOS Femmes Alternatives* (54 av de Choisy, 13e; 45.85.11.37) or the *Foyer Flora Tristan* (7 rue du Landy, 92110, Clichy; 47.31.51.69). These organisations are primarily for battered women but since there's no rape crisis centre, they try to help all victims of male violence. If you feel that speaking on the phone would be too difficult, go to the nearest of the addresses above (and not to the police).

Gay Paris

Paris is fast becoming the San Francisco of Europe for **gay men**. New bars, clubs, restaurants, saunas and shops open all the time and in Les Halles and the Marais every other address is gay. The emphasis is on providing the requisites for a hedonistic life style rather than political campaigning. In 1984 the Minister of the Interior met a gay delegation – a coup certainly – but with homosexuality legal at 15 and discrimination/ harassment no great problem in the capital, protest is not a high priority. For **women**, it's a different matter. The politics are important and lesbian separatists are more active than their straight sisters in the women's movement. But a big problem is that too many gay women won't come out and places run by lesbians don't always publicise the fact for fear of reprisals. Nevertheless, the scene is still quite lively.

For a complete rundown of all the addresses – male and female – you need the **Gai Pied Guide**, which covers all of France. The gay **bookshop** *Les Mots à la Bouche* (35 rue Simart, 18ᵉ; 11–7; cl. Sun/Mon; and 6 rue Ste-Croix de la Bretonnerie, 4ᵉ; 11–8; cl. Sun) and the leftist *Parallèles* (47 rue St-Honoré; 1ᵉʳ; 10–7) stock this plus the monthly **Gay Pied magazine** and most French and foreign gay press. *L'Escargot* (40 rue Amelor, 11ᵉ), run by different gay organisations (male and female) offers a multitude of activities in the arts line and a **meeting place** – open 8–midnight wkdays, 5–2am Sats, 5–midnight Suns.

The principal **women only centre** is *L'Hydromel* at the Maison des Femmes (8 Cité Prost, 11ᵉ; Fri 6–10/Sat 4–midnight/Sun 4–10) with cheap eats; it's organised by *MIEL – Mouvement d'Information et d'Expression des Lesbiennes*. Two **mixed gay bars** with backrooms for women are *Le Champmeslé* (4 rue Chabannais, 2ᵉ) and *Le Tramway* (20 rue Mazargran, 10ᵉ).

Of the thousand and one **bars for men**, *Hôtel Central* (33 rue Veille du Temple, 4ᵉ) and *Broad Side* (13 rue de la Ferronnerie, 1ᵉʳ, have interesting reputations, as does the mixed *Le Duplex* (25 rue Michel Le Comte, 3ᵉ; open till 2am). A favourite gay male **dance spot** is *Le Piano Zinc* (49 rue des Blancs-Manteaux, 4ᵉ); another good one is *Le Manhattan* (8 rue des Anglais, 5ᵉ). For women there's the upmarket *Le Katmandou* (21 rue du Vieux Colombier, 6ᵉ); *Les Trois Fontaines* (196 rue de Grenelle, 7ᵉ), with Sunday afternoon tea dances; and the most crowded, *Le Lolita* (50 bd Edgar Quinet, 14ᵉ; mixed on Weds).

You can tune in to **Fréquence Gaie** on 97.2 Mhz, 24 hours, and if you need **help** call *SOS Gaies* (42.61.00.00) or *SOS Homosexualité* (46.27.49.36) or call in at *COPARH*, the *Comité Parisien Anti-Répression Homosexuelle*, (1 rue Keller, 11ᵉ; 48.06.09.39; open every afternoon and mixed).

If you're reading this before leaving for Paris, and your French is no great shakes, you might try to get hold of *Weaver's Gay paris* (Lithosphere, £2.95), a good insider's guide.

Consuming interests: markets and shops

You can buy practically anything in Paris – from any part of the world and down to the last detail. On the whole, though, you won't be getting a bargain: reasonable is the best deal available at the flea markets, and most of the more interesting shops come complete with prices to deter close inspection. Below you'll find a few of the exceptions: from second-hand fashions to Moroccan spice. For more **mundane needs** your best bets are the ordinary **local markets** (for food, see the following paragraph) and the **supermarkets**, of which the cheapest chain is *Ed-Discount*. **Drug-stores** (see p. 88 for addresses) are pricey but good for basics and open till 1am, or in the Quartier de l'Horloge, by Beaubourg, you'll find the **24 hour** Mon-Sat supermarket, *As Eco*. Most ordinary shops close on Sundays and Mondays and take long lunch hours during the week.

Markets

Street markets are always colourful centres of local activity in France, to say nothing of the mouth-watering displays on the food stalls. Three of the most enticing everyday ones are on **rue de Lévis** (in the 17e, cl. Mon), on the corner of **rue de Buci/rue de Seine** in the 6e and at the south end of **rue Mouffetard** (5e). There are much bigger markets in **rue de la Convention**, 15e (Tues, Thurs, Sun); **bd Port-Royal**, 5e (end of rue St-Jacques; Tues, Thurs, Sat); and **place Monge**, 5e (Wed, Fri, Sun). **Belleville** has a long, long market Tuesday and Friday (bd de Belleville, 20e), mainly North African and Chinese, and perfumed with the scent of spices and fresh herbs. There are **covered markets** (every day except Mon and Sun pm) in **St-Germain**, rue Mabillon (6e), in rue du Château-d'Eau, 10e and **av Secrétan**, 19e – the latter in a fine old iron-frame building.

The so-called **flea markets**, or *Marchés aux Puces*, are at **Porte de Clignancourt**, 18e (Sat, Sun, Mon 7–7); **Porte de Vanves**, 15e (Sat, Sun 7–7.30); **Porte des Lilas**, 19e (Sun 2–7); and **Porte de Montreuil**, 20e (Sat, Sun, Mon 7–7). Clignancourt is the biggest and also the most touristy, selling clothes, records, shoes, books, junk and expensive antiques – fun to visit despite its popularity and prices. Vanves (avenues Marc-Sangnier and Lefenestre) is best for bric-à-brac bargains. Porte de Montreuil has good rétro clothes. In **rue d'Aligre** (every day except Mon and Sun pm) in the 12e, the market occupies both a covered space and the surrounding streets, with barrels of olives, sacks of maize flour and more aromatic herbs. Its prices are among the lowest in town.

Only three Parisian **flower markets** survive: **place des Ternes** (daily) and the **Madeleine** (closed Mon), both in the 8e, and **place Lépine** on the Ile de la Cité, which becomes a **bird market** on Sundays. Another specialised gathering is the **stamp market** at the junction of avenues Marigny and Gabriel in the 8e (Thurs, Sat and Sun). And, lastly, the handsomest of the 19C iron and glass *halles*, the renovated **Carreau du Temple** on rue Perrée, 3e (cl. Mon and Sat and Sun pm) deals in mostly new clothes, but at wholesale prices.

Clothes
There's nothing to stop you trying on fabulously expensive creations by famous **couturiers** in rue du Faubourg St-Honoré and av François 1er, apart from the intimidating scorn of the assistants. Likewise you can treat the **younger designers** around places des Victoires as sight-seeing. But if you want **to buy**, the best area is the 6e: around rues de Rennes and de Sèvres, rue St-André-des-Arts, and rue St-Placide – the latter particularly good at the lower price range. Second best is **Le Halles** but beware the rip-offs in the Forum. More individual boutiques are to be found in the **Marais** – rue du Temple, rue Quincampoix – and for modern designer clothes, there's *Popy Moreni* (13 place des Vosges). This end of rue de Rivoli also has plenty of cheap chain stores, including a *Monoprix* supermarket for essentials, or you can get even better bargains on the boulevards between Richelieu-Drouot and République and in the **ragtrade district** round place du Caire.

Where Paris excels, however, is in the **secondhand gear**, from reject *fripe* to antique *rétro*. Some places to look for – or at – the latter are *Ragtime* (23 rue du Roule, 1er; afternoons only; 1900s to 1950s); *Hébé* (41 rue de l'Arbre Sec, 1er; great hats and stockings); *Duo 29* (29 rue du Roi de Sicile, 4e; very precious 1920s and 1930s dresses and shirts and jackets from latterday East Europe); and *Anouschka* (27 rue de la Grande Truanderie, 1er; 1950s speciality). For **more affordable** garments, try *Rétroactive* (38 rue du Vert Bois, 3e), *Réciproque* (95 rue de la Pompe, 16e) *Mise en Troc* (63 rue Notre Dame des Champs, 6e) and *Brocante* (58 rue de la Buttes aux Cailles, 13e), or do a round of the markets outlined above.

Books and records
With the reading public in Paris you'd think **books** would be cheap. They're not and that makes foreign publications extortionate. There are, however, a fair number of English-language bookshops. *Shakespeare and Co* (37 rue de la Bucherie, 5e) is a literary institution c/o Joyce and Sylvia Beach. Others include *Galignani's* (224 rue de Rivoli, 1er); *W H Smith* (248 rue de Rivoli, 1er); *Village Voice* (6 rue de Princesse, 6e; with café and committed Californians); and *Gilbert Jeune* (5 place St-Michel and 27 quai St-Michel, 5e; English sections include secondhand).

By far the pleasantest browsing, when the weather's good, is of the **quayside stalls** where you might come across anything. **Parallèles** (47 rue St-Honoré, 1er) is one place to go for **left-wing** literature. *Autrement Dit*

(73 bd St-Michel, 5ᵉ), *Lib '5* (5 rue Malebranche, 5ᵉ) and *Actualités* (38 rue Dauphine, 6ᵉ) all claim to be **avant-garde**. An old style haunt specialising in **French poetry** is *Le Pont Traversé* (64 rue de Vaugirard, 6ᵉ). For **literature in French from Africa, the Middle East and Antilles**, go to the excellent and very knowledgeable *L'Harmattan* (16 rue des Ecoles, 5ᵉ). For antiquated **travel books** try *Ulysses* (35 rue St-Louis-en-Ile, 4ᵉ). See p. 57, rue de Médicis, for antiquarian browsing.

The most reliably comprehensive and up-to-date **French bookshop** is *Fnac* (Forum des Halles, 1ᵉʳ/26 av de Wagram, 8ᵉ/136 rue de Rennes, 6ᵉ), who also have large English selections and massive stocks of **tapes and records** of every persuasion. Other bookshops that have music are *Gilbert Jeune* and *Parallèles* (see above). **Secondhand records** have a big market: *Le Crocodisc* (42 rue des Ecoles, 5ᵉ; for rock, jazz, reggae, Brazilian); *Disques B* (17 rue de Lappe, 11ᵉ; New Wave and Afro-Samba); *Dream-store* (4 place St-Michel, 6ᵉ; jazz, rock and folk). The city's main **jazz** specialist is *Le Monde du Jazz* (rue de la Petite Truanderie, 1ᵉʳ); for **classical** it's *Dave Music* (19 rue du Faubourg du Temple, 11ᵉ). And, finally, good arrays of **Arab music** are to be found at *Le Disque Arabe* (116bis bd de la Chapelle, 18ᵉ).

Foods

The street markets or their super/hyper replacements like place d'Italie's *Galaxie* (13ᵉ) are the most sensible places to buy food. But there are some **specials**. *Fauchon* (26 place de la Madeleine, 8ᵉ) is the Harrods of Paris groceries with a patisserie and coffee bar; *Ladurée* (16 rue Royale, 8ᵉ) features more cakes at great expense, with chocolate and coffee maca-roons out of this world, and, at the other end of the scale, there's the tiny chocolate shop *La Petite Fabrique* (19 rue Daval, 11ᵉ). *Goldenburg's* (7 rue des Rosiers) is a predominantly Jewish delicatessen; *Elombo* (29 rue Terre Neuve, 20ᵉ) is good for African specialities and at *Ferme St-Hubert* (21 rue Vignon, 8ᵉ) you'll find the city's most startling selection of cheeses, with expensive *dégustation*.

Toys, trivia and miscellaneous

The most entertaining and tempting Paris window-shopping is those small cluttered shops which reflect the owner's particular interest, obsession or taste. Perhaps the strangest collections are in the *Passages* – sculpted canes in Passage Jouffroy, old comics in Passage Verdeau, pipes in Passage des Princes . . . (see p. 44) but you'll find traders in off-beat merchandise all over the place.

Among the more wonderful are *Carambol* (20 rue des Francs-Bour-geois, 4ᵉ), with wonderful wooden toys and kaleidoscopes; *Pierre Sieur* (3 rue de l'Université, 5ᵉ) – playing cards from all over the world; *L'Impense*

Radical (1 rue de Médicis, 6ᵉ) – games familiar and obscure plus reading matter; *Les Cousins d'Alice* (on the corner of rues Lalande and Daguerre, 14ᵉ) – Alice in Wonderland decorations and reasonably-priced wooden toys; *Bandes Dessinées* (2 rue des Tournelles, 4ᵉ – back copies of all the bizarre French comics; *A l'Image du Grenier sur l'Eau* (45 rue des Francs-Bourgeois, 4ᵉ) – 1900s postcards; *Jadis et Naguère* (57 rue Daguere, 14ᵉ) – jewellery, clothes, gadgets and silly souvenirs like Eiffel Tower candles; *Atelier des Brikezolces* (21 rue Liancourt, 14ᵉ) – ceramics; *Chic et Choc* (by rue Rambuteau exit of Les Halles RER station) – the owner being the Paris transport authority – towels, wallets, lighters, etc. all with a métro ticket emblem.

Listings

Airlines *Air France* are at 2 rue Scribe; *Air-Inter* at 228 rue de Rivoli; full lists of the rest from any Tourist Office. For details of **transport to the airports**, see p. 38.

American Express 11 rue Scribe, 9ᵉ (42.66.09.99; Mᵒ Opéra). Banking service open Mon–Fri 9–5. Office and poste-restante, till 5.30.

Babysitting There are two main agencies. *Ababa Une Maman en Plus* (43.22.22.11, seven days a week; includes English speakers) and *Allo Maman Poule* (47.47.78.78). Apart from these, you could try the American College in Paris (103 bd de l'Hôpital, 13ᵉ; 45.86.19.42), or if you know someone with their own phone dial up Babysitting on 'Elletel' via their *minitel*.

Banks Standard banking hours are Mon–Fri 8.30–5. Branches open on Sats include *Crédit Commercial de France*, 115 Champs-Élysées, 8ᵉ – all day; *BNP* 49 av des Champs-Élysées/2 place de l'Opéra (2ᵉ) – mornings; and *UBP* at 125 av des Champs-Élysées – open Sat and Sun 10.30–1 & 2–6. The **Bureaux de Change** at the railway stations are open all day until 9 or 10 at night: at Gare de Lyon and Gare du Nord every day; St-Lazare and Austerlitz every day except Sunday. *Crédit Agricole* (for **Access** cash advances) have branches at 166bis bd Sébastopol, 4ᵉ; 31 rue de Constantine, 7ᵉ; 14 rue de la Boétie, 8ᵉ; and 91/93 bd Pasteur, 15ᵉ. *Barclays* are at 157 bd St-Germain (8ᵉ), and elsewhere.

Bike hire *Autotheque*, 16 rue Berger, 1ᵉʳ (42.36.39.36) and 80 rue Montmartre, 2ᵉ (42.36.50.93) – the latter has Solex and motorbikes as well; *Paris-Vélo*, 2 rue de Fer-à-Moulin, 5ᵉ (43.37.59.22); and *Loca-cycles*, 3 rue du Vieux-Colombier, 6ᵉ. Take care!

Car pound If your car is towed away you should find it at 39 rue de Dantzig, 15ᵉ (45.31.82.10).

Car rental Good French firms include *Mattei*, 205 rue de Bercy, 12ᵉ (43.46.11.50), 102 rue Ordener, 18ᵉ (42.64.32.90) and *Autorent*, 11 rue

Casimir-Perier, 11e (45.55.53.49), 98 rue de la Convention, 15e (45.54.22.45) and 196 rue St-Jacques, 5e (43.25.88.10). In addition there's Avis, Hertz and the rest – the tourist office will have all the bumf. **Car repairs** 42.57.33.44 is the emergency number if you're stuck – but only between 7am–10pm.

Consulates American – 2 av Gabriel, 8e (42.96.12.02; Mo Concorde); Australian – 4 rue Jean-Rey, 15e (45.75.62.00; Mo Bir-Hakeim); British – 109 rue du Faubourg St-Honoré, 8e (42.60.14.88; Mo Miromesnil); Canadian – 4 rue Ventadour, 1er (42.96.87.19; Mo Pyramides); Dutch – 7–9 rue Eble, 7e (43.06.61.88; Mo St-François-Xavier); Irish – 12 av Foch, 16e (45.00.20.87; Mo Étoile); New Zealand – 7 rue Léonard-de-Vinci, 16e (45.00.24.11; Mo Victor-Hugo) Swedish – 17 rue Barbet-de-Jouy, 7e (45.55.92.15; Mo Varenne).

Dental treatment *Urgences dentaires* emergency service – phone 42.61.12.00. *SOS-Dentaire*, 85–87 bd de Port-Royal, 14e (43.37.51.00; 8pm–12am).

Emergencies *SOS-Médecins* (43.77.77.77 and 47.07.77.77) for 24-hour medical help. Phone 43.78.26.26 for **24-hour ambulance service**. American Hospitals: 63 bd Victor-Hugo, Neuilly (47.47.53.00; Mo Porte-Maillot, bus 82 to end of line).

Festivals There's not much in the carnival line, though kids armed with bags of flour to make a total fool of you appear on the streets during **Mardi Gras** (in February). There are marching bands and buskers for the **Summer Solstice** (21 June) and **14 July** (Bastille Day) is celebrated with official pomp in parades of tanks down the Champs-Élysées, firework displays and concerts. But it's events like Mitterrand's election that really get people out on the streets. This, of course, may not happen again. If you're into the politics of the European Left, however, the French Communist Party host a **Fête de la Humanité** each year at La Courneuve, just north of Paris, with representatives of just about every CP in the world and stalls, bands and eats that bring in Parisians of most persuasions to the left of Le Pen.

Hammams Turkish baths – an unexpected Parisian delight. The Jewish *Hammam St-Paul* (4 rue des Rosiers, 4e; women: Weds & Fris 5pm–11; men: Thurs 10–2 & Sats 9–8) has sauna, massage, etc. – and a restaurant. At *Hammam de la Mosquée de Paris* (39 rue Geoffrey-St-Hilaire, 5e; women: Mons 11–6; Thurs 11–9 & Sats 11–6; men: Fris 11–8 & Suns 11–7. You can take steam baths in the Mosque complex with mint tea to follow.

Language schools French lessons from the *Alliance Française* (101 bd Raspail, 6e) or Ecole *France Langue* (2 rue Sfax, 16e), amongst numerous others.

Laundrettes Self-service places have multiplied in Paris over the last few years and you'll probably find one close by where you're staying. Central locations include: 24 place Marchais-St-Honoré, 1er; 1 rue de la Montaigne-Ste-Geneviève, 5e; 91 rue de Seine, 6e; 108 rue du Bac, 7e; 5 rue de la Tour-de-Auvergne, 9e; and 96 rue de la Roquette, 11e.

Left luggage Lockers and longer term *consigne* at all the stations.

Libraries Foreign Cultural Institutes (Britain: 9 rue de Constantin; US: 10 rue du Général Camou) have free access libraries, with newspapers, etc. Interesting Parisian collections include the *BPI* at Beaubourg (vast – and with all the foreign press, too), *Forney* (books being a good excuse if you want to visit the medieval bishop's palace at 1 rue du Figuier in the 4e), and the *Historique de la Ville de Paris*, a 16C mansion housing centuries of texts and picture books on the city (24 rue Pavée, 4e).

Lost property 36 rue des Morillons, 5e (Mo Convention).

Pharmacies 24-hr service at Dhery (84 av des Champs-Élysées, 8e).

Police Dial 17 for emergencies. The main Préfecture, if you need to report a theft, is at 7 bd du Palais, 4e (42.60.33.22).

Post office Main office at 52 rue du Louvre, Paris 75001: open 24 hours for **telephones** and **poste restante**.

Swimming pools *Butte aux Cailles* (5 place Paul Verlaine, 13e; bizarre brick building and little harassment); *Pontoise* (19 rue de Pontoise, 5e, reserved for school children most of the time but nude swimming two evenings a week – check Pariscope, etc.); *Deligny* (opposite 25 quai d'Anatole France, 7e; open-air, crowded and an amusing if expensive spectacle).

Taxis Impossible at meal times but otherwise you'll find stands throughout the city, often by métro stations. Alternatively, phone one of these numbers: 42.00.67.89, 47.39.33.33, 47.35.22.22 or 42.03.99.99.

Telephones Nine out of ten phone boxes are defunct – best phone from a post office or a café, where you may need *jetons* rather than coins and you may be forced to consume something.

Tourist information Main office at 127 av des Champs-Élysées, 8e (47.23.61.72); open 9–8/10, Sun 9–6/8. Other offices at the four main stations: Austerlitz, Nord, Lyon and Est. For info in English phone 47.20.88.98.

Train information Phone 42.61.50.50, or individual stations.

Travel firms *USIT Voyages* (6 rue de Vaugirard, 15e; Mo Odéon) is an excellent and dependable **student-youth agency** – good for buses to London, Dublin, Amsterdam, etc. as well as discount flights. *Nouvelles Frontières* (66 bd St-Michel, 6e) have some of the cheapest charters going, and **flights** just about anywhere in the world. For national and international **coaches** you can get information and tickets at the main terminus in place Stalingrad (Mo Stalingrad). **Hitching out** of Paris can be a nightmare but for a small fee you can join *Allostop* who will arrange you a ride where you merely make a small contribution towards petrol: they're at 65 passage Brady, 10e (42.46.00.66; open Mon–Fri 9–7.30, Sat 9–1 & 2–6).

VD clinic *Institute Prophylactique* (36 rue d'Assas, 6e; free).

Work Not easy: look for ads in *Libération*, *Le Figaro* or *Passion* magazine, or try the youth organisation *CIDJ* (101 quai Branly, 7e) or the French job agency *ANE* (53 rue du Généreal Leclerc, Issy Les Moulineaux; Mo Marie d'Issy; 46.45.21.26).

OUT FROM THE CITY

The region around the capital – known as the **Ile de France**, and the borders of all neighbouring provinces, are studded with large scale **châteaux**. Many were once royal or noble retreats for hunting and other leisured pursuits, some like Versailles were for more serious state show. The actual mansions and palaces – and **Versailles** above all – can be tedious in the extreme. But **Vaux-le-Vicomte**, at least, is magnificent; **Fontainebleau** is pleasantly Italian; and at any you can get a taste of country air in the forests and parks around and get back to Paris comfortably in a day.

If you've limited time, though, and even a slight curiosity about church buildings, forget the châteaux and make for the **cathedral of Chartres** – all it is cracked up to be. From here too you can easily enough return to Paris, or heading out you're well poised for Le Mans (see p. 204) and Brittany. Other points to leave Paris by, detailed in this section, include **Anet** (a short detour on the road to western Normandy), and **Chantilly** and **Senlis** off the routes north to Lille and Calais. These again are enjoyable enough stopovers but perhaps more realistic and rewarding if you're rambling out by car rather than as special excursions in themselves.

VERSAILLES, ST-GERMAIN AND MALMAISON

The **Palace of Versailles** is foul from every aspect, a mutated building gene allowed to run like a pounding fist for lengths no feet or eyes were made for, its décor a grotesque homage to two of the greatest of all self-propagandists – Louis XIV and Napoleon. The mirrors, in the famous Hall of, are smeared, scratched and not the originals – for these a Breton boy is currently serving fifteen years for breaking glass with explosives. In the park, big enough for three Monacos, the fountains only gush on selected days. The rest of the time the statues on the empty pools look as bad as gargoyles taken down from cathedral walls.

It is hard to know why so many tourists come out here – in preference to all except the most obvious sights of Paris. yet they do, and the **château** (9.45–5, except Mons) is always a crush of bodies. If you are curious, you'll pay for the experience and have a choice of two endurance-testing itineraries. If you just feel like taking a look, and a walk, **the park** (open dawn to dusk) is free and the scenery better the further you go from the palace – there are even informal groups of trees near the lesser outcrops of royal mania, the Grand and Petit Palais. There is, too, a very wonderful and genteel place to have **tea** – the *Hôtel Palais Trianon* (near the park entrance at the end of bd de la Reine), much more worthwhile than shelling out for admission, with trayfuls of patisseries to the limits of your desire for about 50F.

To get to Versailles, take the *RER line CS* to VERSAILLES-RIVE GAUCHE (40mins), turn left out of the station and immediately right to approach the palace. Maps of the park can be had from the SI on rue des Réservoirs to the right of the palace.

Louis XIV, the monarch who neutered aristocratic dissent by forcing the nobles to play elaborate rituals in the court of Versailles, was himself born in the Château of **ST-GERMAIN-EN-LAYE**. This had been a royal residence since the Middle Ages and once Versailles was completed, Louis lent it to the exiled James II of England, who died here in 1701. The château now houses a collection of Celtic, pre-historic, and Roman things from all round France in the **Musée des Antiquités Nationales** (open 9.45–12 & 1.30–5.15; cl. Tues). You may not be very excited by this but there's a great walk from the gardens of the château, along a terrace high above the Seine, designed by Le Nôtre. The Fôret de St-Germain covers the loop made by the river but it's too riddled with roads to be much of a forest. St-Germain-en-Laye is the end stop of *RER line A1* and the château is right by the station.

Half way between St-Germain and Paris is the Château of **MALMAISON**, the home of Empress Josephine and, during the 1800–4 Consulate, of Napoleon too. According to his secretary, 'it was the only place next to the battlefield where he was truly himself'. After their divorce, Josephine stayed on here, occasionally receiving visits from the Emperor, until her death in 1814. The **château** (10–12 & 1.30–4.30; cl. Tues; guided tours only) is set in the beautiful grounds of the Bois-Préau. It's relatively small and surprisingly enjoyable. The visit includes private and official apartments, in part with original furnishings though complemented with pieces imported from other imperial residences. There are further Napoleonic bits and pieces in the **Bois-Préau museum** (same hours as above). Getting there is, again, simple enough: take the *RER* to La Défense, then bus 158 to MALMAISON-CHÂTEAU, the nearest bus-stop. Alternatively, take bus 431 to place de l'Eglise in the attractive town centre – it is ten minutes' walk thence to the Bois-Préau, and a further ten minutes through the park to the château.

VAUX-LE-VICOMTE AND FONTAINEBLEAU

VAUX-LE-VICOMTE, near Melun 46km south-east of Paris, is one of the great classical châteaux. Louis XIV's finance superintendent, Nicholas Fouquet, had it built at colossal expense using the top designers of the day – the royal architect Le Vau, the painter Le Brun and Le Nôtre, the landscape gardener. The result was magnificence and precision in perfect proportion and a bill that could only be paid by someone who occasionally confused the state's account with his own. The housewarming party to which the king was invited was more extravagant than any royal event – a comparison that other finance ministers ensured that Louis took to heart. Within two months Fouquet was jailed for life on trumped up charges and Louis carted Le Vau, Le Brun and Le Nôtre off to Versailles to work on a gaudy and gross piece of one-upmanship. The château is **open** April–October 10–6 (winter: weekend afternoons only; and cl. Jan); **trains** from the Gare de Lyon leave for MELUN (25mins) and there are direct **buses** from Melun SNCF to the château.

Energetically, you could spend the morning at Vaux-le-Vicomte and continue by train from MELUN to **FONTAINEBLEAU** – an instructive and remarkably pleasant exercise in rapid châteaux touring. A hunting lodge from as early as the 12C, the **château** here began its transformation into a palace under the 16C François I. A vast, rambling place, unpretentious despite its size, it owes its distinction to a colony of Italian artists imported for the decoration – above all Rosso Il Fiorentino, who completed the celebrated **Galerie François I**, vital to the evolution of French aristocratic art and design. The gardens are equally luscious but if you want to escape to the wilds, the surrounding **forest of Fontainebleau** is full of walking and cycling trails and its rocks are a favourite training-ground for French climbers. Paths and tracks are all marked on Michelin map 196 (*Environs de Paris*).

The château, rarely overcrowded, is **open** 10–12.30 & 2–6 (cl. Tues). **Trains** take around 45mins from Gare de Lyon (25mins from Melun) and there's a local bus to the gates from the SNCF.

CHARTRES AND ANET

The mysticisms of medieval thought on life, death and deity expressed materially in the masonry of the **Cathedral** at **CHARTRES**, should best be experienced on a cloudfree winter's day. The low sun transmits the stained glass colours to the interior stone, the quiet scattering of people leaves the acoustics unconfused and the exterior is unmasked for miles around. The masterwork is flawed only by changes in Roman Catholic worship. The immense distance from the door to the altar, through mists of incense and drawn-out harmonies, emphasised the doctrine of priests as sole mediators of the distance between worshipped and worshippers. The current central altar, from a secular point of view, undermines the theatrical dogma of the building and puts cloth and boards where the coloured lights should play.

A less recent change, of allowing the congregation chairs, also covers up the **labyrinth** on the floor of the nave – an original 13C arrangement and a great rarity since the authorities at other cathedrals had them pulled up as distracting frivolities. The Chartres labyrinth traces a path over 200m long enclosed within a diameter of 13m, the same size as the rose window above the main doors. The centre used to have a bronze relief of Theseus and the Minotaur and the pattern of the maze was copied from classical texts, the idea of the path of life to eternity being fairly similar in Greek myth and medieval Catholicism. During pilgrimages the chairs are removed so you may be lucky and see the full pattern. But the geometry of the building, the details of the stonework – the Renaissance choir screen and host of sculpted figures above each door – and the shining circular symmetries of the transept windows are in any case more than enough wonders to enthrall. Among paying extras the *crypt* and *treasures* can be ignored without much loss but, crowds permitting, it's worth climbing the **north tower**. Admission hours for the main building are 7.30–7.30/7. There are gardens beyond the chevet from where you can contemplate the terrestial stress factors balanced by the flying buttresses.

The **Beaux Arts museum** in the former episcopal palace just north of the cathedral has some beautiful tapestries, a room full of Vlaminck and Zurbaran's **Ste Lucie**, as well as good temporary exhibitions (10–12 & 2–5; cl. Tues). Behind it, rue Chantault leads past old town houses to the **river Eure** and Pont des Massacres. You can follow this reedy river lined with ancient wash-houses upstream via rue des Massacres on the right bank. The cathedral appears from time to time through the trees and, closer at hand, on the left bank is the Romanesque church of **St-André** now used for art exhibitions, jazz concerts, etc. Crossing back over at the end of rue de la Tannerie into rue du Bourg takes you back to the cathedral through the medieval town, decorated with details such as the carved salmon on a house on place de la Poissonerie. Further south, around **rue du Cygne** is the place to look for bars and restaurants. The **SI** is on the cathedral *parvis*, at 7 Cloître Notre-Dame, and can supply **free maps** and help with **rooms** if you want to stay.

Arriving at the **Gare SNCF** (frequent trains from Paris-Montparnasse in 50–65mins), av J-de-Beauce leads straight up to place Châtelet. Past all the coaches on the other side of the *place*, rue Ste-Mesme crosses place Jean-Moulin – the cathedral is down to the left. Rue d'Harleville goes to the right to bd de la Résistance, a section of the main road ring around the old town: the memorial on the corner of the street and the boulevard is to **Jean Moulin**, Prefect of Chartres until he was sacked by the Vichy government in 1942. When the Germans occupied Chartres in 1940, he had refused under torture to sign a document to the effect that black soldiers in the French army were responsible for Nazi atrocities. He later became de Gaulle's number one man on the ground, coordinating all the Resistance groups. He died while being deported to Germany in 1943.

If you're heading up towards Rouen from Chartres or driving towards western Normandy from Paris, you might like to stop at **ANET**, 20km or so north of Dreux, and dominated by another semi-royal **château**. Diane de Poitiers, respected widower in the court of François I and powerful lover of the king's son Henri, decided that her marital home at Anet needed to be bigger and more comfortable. Work started with Philibert Delorme as the architect in charge and the designs as delicate and polished as the Renaissance could produce. Within a year Henri inherited the throne and immediately gave Diane the château of Chenonceau. But the Anet project continued, luckily for Diane since Henri's reign was brought to an untimely end and his wife demanded Chenonceau back. Diane retired to Anet where she died. Her grandson built a chapel for her tomb alongside the château which has remained intact. The château would have been completely destroyed by the first owner after the Revolution had it not been for a protest riot by the townspeople that sent him packing. As it is, only the front entrance, one wing and the château chapel remain, now restored to its former glorification of hunting and feminine eroticism with the swirling floor and domed ceiling of the chapel its climax. The château is open March–Nov 2.30–6.30 except Tues; Sun all year 10–11.30 & 2–6.30/5.

Between Chartres and Paris you cross the **forest of Rambouillet** – large enough for real walks though you must take the *Chasse* (hunting) signs seriously. GR1 goes through RAMBOUILLET (30mins by train from Gare Montparnasse) north to MONTFORT-l'AMAURY (35mins) and south to ST-ARNOULT-EN-YVELINES; there's a cycle track between Rambouillet and Montfort-l'Amaury. The **château of Rambouillet**, another former royal residence, is now a presidential one.

CHANTILLY

The **château** at **CHANTILLY**, about 40km north of Paris, was once the home of the Grand Condé, cousin and general to Louis XIV. It now contains, in the **Musée Condé** (10.30–6; cl. Tues), one of the finest museums in the Paris region. Particularly rich in French painting and illuminated manuscripts, its great treasure is the most celebrated and reproduced of all the medieval Books of Hours, *Les Très Riches Heures du Duc de Berry*. Sadly, but understandably, only facsimiles of the original are on display.

Chantilly is also a Mecca for the horsey. It is the French Newmarket and holds two of the season's classiest flat races in June. The vast Condé stables, the **Grandes Ecuries** (2–6, Easter–Nov, Thurs, Sun & hols only), have been made into a living **Museum of the Horse** (10.30–5.30; cl. Tues; expensive) complete with daily displays of horse prowess.

The attractive old town of **SENLIS** nearby (reached like Chantilly by train from the Gare du Nord) has a **cathedral** contemporary with Notre-Dame and all the trappings of medieval ramparts, Roman towers and royal palace remnants to entice hordes of daytrippers and weekenders from the capital.

TRAVEL DETAILS

Trains
From Gare du Nord through services to Britain via Calais and Boulogne (frequent) and Dunkerque (less so), and to Belgium, Holland and Amsterdam; also to Amiens (at least hourly; 1¾ hrs), Arras (1 hr40) and Lille (2–2½hrs).
From Gare de l'Est frequent trains to Nancy (2½–3hrs), Reims (1¼hrs), Strasbourg (4hrs), Besançon (3hrs) and Metz (2½hrs).
From Gare St-Lazare 2 to Dieppe (2¼hrs); frequent service to Le Havre (2–2½hrs), Cherbourg (3–3½hrs), Rouen (1¼hrs).
From Gare Montparnasse frequent service to Brest (5½–6hrs), Nantes (3½hrs) and Rennes (2½hrs).
From Gare d'Austerlitz numerous trains to Tours (2hrs), Poitiers (3hrs) and Bordeaux (5hrs); about 6 each to Bayonne (6–8hrs) and Toulouse (7–8hrs).
From Gare de Lyon almost hourly TGVs to Dijon (1hr40) and Lyon (2¼hrs); 7 or 8 regular trains to Dijon (2½hrs) and Lyon (5–6 hrs); almost hourly service to Grenoble, changing at Lyon (3 hrs45 by TGV); 10 or more to Marseille (5hrs by TGV) and Nice (10½hrs).

Buses
Regular connections to just about all points in France – and Britain, Belgium, Holland, Scandinavia, Spain, Morocco, Italy, etc. – from the terminal in **place Stalingrad** (Mº Stalingrad).

Hitching
Hitching out of Paris isn't easy, especially in high summer when you are likely to face very long delays. It's much better to spend a few extra francs taking a train or bus 50km clear of the city down your planned route. If, however, you are determined to try, place yourself at one of these points:
Heading south: Mº to Porte d'Italie then walk 300m south to the motorway slip roads – A6 for Lyon, Marseille, Nice or Perpignan, A10 for Tours, Bordeaux and Le Mans.
Heading east: Mº to Porte de Charenton then walk 500m south to the A4 slip road (for Reims, Metz, Strasbourg, Nancy) just north of the Pont National.
Heading north: Mº to St-Denis-Porte de Paris and look for the blue motorway signs – N1 for Boulogne, Calais and Amiens, N14 for Rowen, Dieppe and Le Havre.
Alternatively, for a small outlay, you can register with the hitching organisation Allostop; they will find you a ride and you just make a small contribution towards petrol (see p. 105 (Travel firms) for their address and opening hours).

Flights
Inter-Air and *Air-France* connect Paris with all major **French cities**: see p. 103 for their addresses. For **International Flights** see p. 105 (*Travel Firms*).
Transport connections with the three Paris airports – Roissy-Charles de Gaulle, Le Bourget and Orly – are detailed on p. 38.

Chapter two
PICARDY AND
THE NORTH

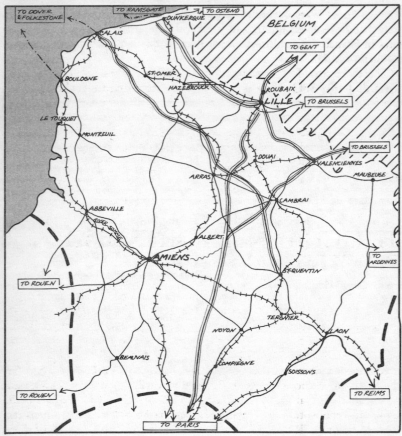

Even among the French, the most assiduous tourists of their own country, **Picardy and the north** has few adherents. It's a region most people tend to travel through, rather than about, with little more than a passing glimpse for the looming Gothic cathedrals of Amiens, Laon and Beauvais. All of which, in its way, seems fair enough.

It is likely, however, that you'll both arrive and leave France in this region — at **Calais**, **Boulogne** or **Dunkerque** — and there are curiosities only a short distance from the familiar Channel ports and main routes to Paris. The obvious invaders' path into the country, from northern Europe as well as from Britain, the towns here have shaped a great deal of French history. There are innumerable defensive **citadels**, many designed by Vauban in the 17C at the end of a long period of conquests by English kings and Burgundian dukes. And from a more recent age the region around Flanders and the Somme is imprinted with the battles of the two Great Wars. At **Vimy Ridge** near Arras, First World War trenches have been preserved intact, one of the most extraordinary and poignant sites in France, while almost every village between Arras and Amiens has its memorial.

There are, too, less sombre concerns, particularly as you press south towards Paris. **St-Quentin** is a lively and interesting university town to break up a journey. So too is **Compiègne**, with its magnificent forest, long a royal retreat from the capital. But above all, perhaps, there is the obvious: the **cathedrals**. **Amiens** is arguably the grandest in France, and if you see this and its neighbours en route to Paris, you are well on the way to understanding – and most likely enthusing over – the development of French Gothic.

THE CHANNEL PORTS AND ROUTES TO PARIS

The **ports** in this section – **Boulogne**, **Calais** and **Dunkerque** – offer the cheapest and most efficient access between Britain and France; you'll find details of frequency and duration of sailings in the *Travel Details* at the end of this chapter (see p. 113).

Moving on, there are frequent trains and buses to **Lille and Arras** (see the following sections, pp. 128–32) and **towards Paris**. From Dunkerque or Calais the usual preferred routes are via St-Omer and Amiens or St-Omer and the motorway; from Boulogne via Montreuil and Amiens (the Route Nationale, RN1). For schedules of trains and buses on all of these, again see the *Travel Details* on p. 113.

DUNKERQUE (DUNKIRK)

Overhung by chemical smog and military history, **DUNKERQUE** is about as unappealing an introduction to France as could be imagined. It is a vast port, and a considerable industrial centre in its own right, at the edge of the grim heartlands of the north. If you arrive here by car there are clinical rewards in an efficient ferry-to-autoroute access. By public transport things are a little slower with the ferry terminal some 15km from the town and SNCF station. There is, however, a free shuttle service, *Sally Line* buses dropping you in the central **place E. Bollaert**, close by a distinctive brick medieval **belfry** – the old town's principal local land-mark and home of the SI.

Arriving with time to spare the only real local sight is the **Musée des Beaux Arts**, at the opposite end of rue Clemenceau (the main drag) from the SI 'tower'. Amid the paintings here is a fascinating *galerie ornithologique* and, perhaps, inevitably, a display on the infamous Allied withdrawal from the beaches of May 1940. This, the much-filmed 'Victory in defeat', has a very different slant on this side of the Channel. A French version has France, the maiden in distress, abandoned by the fleeing British – who of course return to sip tea on their isolated island from 1940–4 with only their bad weather to contend with. The museum (cl. Tues) tells the story fairly straight. If you want to see the actual beaches from which the 340,000 troops embarked you'll need a local bus to neighbouring MALO-DES-BAINS, now a popular resort with French weekenders.

Save for a ferry strike there seems little reason to stay. If you're committed, though, you'll find inexpensive **hotels** around the gare SNCF in the somewhat squalid place de la Gare and a **youth hostel** 3km out in place Paul Asseman (bus 3 to the adjoining *piscine*). You can **eat** well, for relatively little, at the *Auberge du Flamand* (11 place Charles Valentin, near the museum and townhall), *La Crêperie* (place Roger Salengro) and self-service *Cafétéria Forum* (rue de l'Amiral Ronarc'h). *Fruits de mer*, those plates of well-defended crustaceans, are as elsewhere on this coast, a speciality.

CALAIS

CALAIS is just 24 miles from England – the Channel's narrowest crossing – and comfortably established as the most popular or at least the busiest, French passenger port. It's a function which in every way dominates the town. Easily so perhaps, for there's not much else. In the last war the British destroyed the town to prevent, or at least slow, its use in what seemed an imminent German invasion. Ironically, the French still refer to it as 'the most English town in France' – a reference to two centuries of occupation (from Edward III to Mary Tudor) and the 19C presence of Nottingham lace factories. Today the dominant image, for Brits at least, is a daytrip to the hypermarket.

If all this suggests that you can do a lot worse than buying a through ticket from Dover – to Amiens if not to Paris – it's hard to argue. Calais *is* uninspiring. Even its municipal statue by **Rodin**, the 'Six Burghers' fronting the **townhall**, is pretty wretched. Its subject can't have helped the artist. The Burghers in question were 14C local heroes who offered their lives in sacrifice if Edward III agreed to spare the rest of the population; he actually took them up on this, though was eventually persuaded to remit sentence.

The townhall, or Hôtel de Ville, is itself easily spotted – one of the few surviving buildings of old Calais, 20C but rising in extravagant Flemish style. If you're very into Rodin you might backtrack a couple of blocks from here to the **Musée de Calais** (10–12 & 2–5.30), unremarkable for the most part but with two interesting minor works. Wandering in the other direction you'll enter **Calais Nord**, looped by canals. It's quieter and with a little more character. Off to the right, as you cross the bridge, an old German blockhouse in the **Parc St-Pierre** has been converted to a **Musée de la Guerre**, a chilling record of the Nazi occupation.

These though all seem peripheral pursuits if you happen to have time to fill. The real business of Calais is arriving and leaving – and consuming. On the latter front the best places to stock up on quality French **food** for the ferry (and beyond) are the covered market just off place d'Armes (Weds/Sats) or the open air one in Calais Sud just off bd Lafayette. On Sundays place d'Armes – the nearest Calais comes to a focus – hosts bric-à-brac stalls. Among the numerous restaurants, many of the best

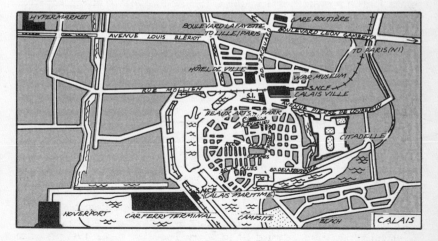

value places are, too, in and around place d'Armes. One which comes highly recommended is *Touquet's* on rue Royale. **Rooms**, if needs be, shouldn't be hard to find. Two good, inexpensive places are *Le Folkestone* (28 rue Royale) and *Hôtel de Boulogne* (41 quai du Rhin); others flank the two parks, or there's a campsite beside the sandy and relatively functional beach. If you need full lists, or bookings, the **SI** can help: they're at 12 bd Clémenceau (open daily in season, cl. Suns in winter). Almost directly opposite is the town **railway station**, *Calais Ville*, with reasonable services to Amiens/Paris and to Lille; arriving on the ferry, however, you can just go straight on from the *Calais Maritime* station The town's **gare routière**, of limited use, is tucked away behind the theatre in Calais Sud.

INLAND FROM CALAIS OR DUNKERQUE: ST-OMER AND CASSEL

First step inland for many visitors to France is **ST-OMER**, and surprisingly quite a few take a liking to this cold, rather seedy little town. True, it establishes an immediately distinct – and very un-English – character. The landscape seems to expand and the town itself has flights of Flemish magnificence: the townhall, especially, and some of the mansions on rue Gambetta. But it's hard to get exactly excited over the place, nor to credit the SI's wild claims for its cathedral as 'the most beautiful religious edifice in Northern France after Amiens'. It is certainly some way after Amiens.

On the positive side, you can eat and sleep well and for little. A couple of options are *Hôtel du Commerce* (3 rue St-Adegonde), and *Hôtel de l'Industrie* (a nice place, with an active bar, in pedestrianised rue Louis Martel). There are pleasant public gardens. And there are, too, some very Flemish-seeming waterways, cut between plots of land on reclaimed marsh, just outside of town along the river Aa. If you're feeling run-down these have a certain spell, and you can go out by boat from the *Taverne Flamande* at 60 route de Clairmarais.

Perhaps more interesting than anything at St-Omer, however, is **CASSEL**, 20km out on route D933. A tiny place, this has a very much more pronounced Flemish character: a fine Gothic church, a lovely, broad Grande Place, a public garden and mill, and some magnificent old mansions, *hotels* and alleyways. You'll need your own transport to justify the trip but, if you have, it's well worth it.

BOULOGNE, LE TOUQUET AND MONTREUIL

BOULOGNE is quite distinct from Dunkerque and Calais: recommendation in itself. Rising above the port is a medieval centre, the **Haute Ville**, flanked by grassy ramparts and a grand black-domed cathedral.

Below, amid the newer shopping streets of the **Ville Basse**, are some of the best *charcuteries* and *pâtisseries* in the north, and an impressive array of fish restaurants. Alone among the north-east Channel ports it is a place which might tempt you to stay.

It is also an important harbour – largest fishing base in Europe, so it is claimed – and long established. Julius Caesar crossed to conquer Britannia from here in 53BC, and, but for a last minute change of heart, Napoleon would have done the same in 1803. Just north of the town on the N1 stands the **Colonne de la Grande Armée**, where the latter Emperor is said to have turned his troops east towards Austria. Symbolically, the column was originally capped by a bronze statue of Napoleon in Roman garb – though its head, equally symbolically, was shot off by the British navy in the last war. It is now displayed, along with items donated by a local born Egyptologist, in the **town museum** (Wed–Sun 9–12 & 2–6).

Ferries dock within a few minutes walk of the town centre, **place Dalton**; arriving by hovercraft, a little further out, you'll be met by a free shuttlebus. If you intend to stay, stop off at the <u>SI (in the covered walkway)</u> who can supply a mass of information and advise on availability of rooms, which in summer fill early. The **youth hostel**, up by the ramparts at 36 rue Porte Gayole, is probably your best bet; phone 21.31.48.22 to check space. Most of the other cheap **hotels** enclose the

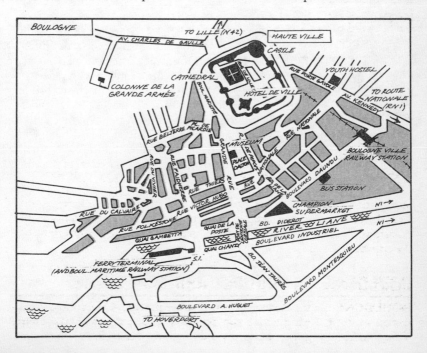

port area. **Eating**, there are dozens of possibilities around place Dalton (*Chez Jules* serves meals all day: a rarity in France) and around the cathedral but bear in mind the day-tripper trade and be selective. Buying your own food, Boulogne has an outstanding **cheese** shop, *Olivier* in rue Thiers, and *pâtisserie*, *Derrien's* in Grande rue and two weekly **markets** in place Dalton (Weds and Sats). The *Champion Supermarket*, bang in the centre, is useful too for last minute supplies, if you're headed back for Britain.

The **Cathédrale de Notre-Dame**, dominating the town from its site in the Haute Ville, is worth making time for. It's an odd building, raised in the 19C, without any architectural knowledge or advice, by the town's vicar. Against all the odds it seems to work. In the crypt (open 2–5, cl. Mons) you can see frescoed remains of the earlier building and relics of a previous Roman temple to Diana. Above, a curiosity is a white statue of the Virgin and Child on a boat-chariot, drawn here, on its own wheels, from Lourdes. Opposite, the **townhall** can be visited, largely for the view from its belfry and ramparts. Other buildings in the **Haute Ville** are currently under restoration, though if you're really interested there are sporadic guided tours run by the *Renaissance de Vieux Boulogne* (details from the SI).

Le Touquet

Thirty-eight km from Boulogne, **LE TOUQUET** is one of those peculiarly northern French resorts – once the height of fashion, now essentially suburban. In the 1920s and 1930s, and for a spell after the war too, the town, with its broad sands and huge luxury villas, ranked with places on the Côte d'Azur. At one time, so it is said, it saw flights from Britain every 10min. The opening up of long-distance air travel put an end to this, though not completely and forever. The British rich, sniffing a fresh chance of elitism, are now back in some force. The airport is busy with private planes, over from the shires for the weekend, and the older hotels, many of which look like filmsets anyway, are repopulated with budding young Bridesheads.

It is an extraordinary set-up really and not one I'd personally recommend without an anarchic sense of humour and a Super-8 camera. For anyone interested, though, **access** is quite simple. You take the train from Boulogne to ETAPLES and from there – where signs in English almost take over – a local bus. For somewhere reasonable to **spend the night** try *L'Union* (71 rue de Metz), *L'Auberge* (42 rue d'Etaples) or *Hotel Armide* (56 rue Léon Garet: full board for a good price). There's also a campsite, on the waterfront of the Canche estuary, but this demands three nights minimum stay, which is almost certainly too long. If you're mobile, and have come here with strict **sociological intent**, take a glimpse (and a jug) at the *Hôtel le Manoir*.

Heading inland: Montreuil

It is usually a good sign if a French town features in Victor Hugo. MONTREUIL-SUR-MER, long stranded inland, is the setting for *Les Misérables*. It is a place of character and, as a first stop in France en route to Amiens and Paris, deserves more attention than it usually gets.

From the road below it is certainly striking: a hilltop fort enclosed by a huge set of Vauban **ramparts**, rebuilt after an early bout of destruction by Charles V. The 'new' town lies outside these, cobbled for the most part as it runs up from the river and railway station (on a little country line to Arras and Lille). There are inexpensive **rooms** and meals here at the *Hôtel Central* (7 rue du Change) but unless you're after privacy you might as well stay up at the **youth hostel**, in the citadel itself. This offers the additional advantage of gaining free access to the *enceinte*, which is otherwise open only from 9–12 & 2–6 and for a small fee.

Entered through a gate between sturdy 13C towers, the **Citadelle**, like the ramparts, was reconstructed by Vauban. It is overgrown, and after dark quite atmospheric. There are subterranean casemates and a 14C tower which records the arms of thousands of noblemen killed at Agincourt in 1415. The site of the battle, at present day AZINCOURT, is just 38km distant, turning south along the D71 at HESDIN. Nearby, on towards Abbeville, is another great battle site of the Middle Ages, CRÉCY.

AMIENS

Except to visit its cathedral, few travellers would probably stop at AMIENS. Beaten about during both world wars, and with heavy traffic pounding along the through-roads built over the old ramparts, it is not an obviously likeable city. Yet it is not uninteresting. There's a major university here and it makes its presence felt in the run-down medieval **quartier St-Leu**, just north of the cathedral towards the river Somme. So too, amid the decaying canalside cottages, does the city's Arab population. Graffiti can be lively.

It is, however, the **Cathédrale Notre-Dame** which provides the city's focus, whatever your interests. Built over the first half of the 13C its style is pure Gothic, the ornamentation heavy and elaborate but – for once – altogether graceful. Even the two unusual towers, the only later additions, seem to enhance the building with their irregularity.

The cathedral statuary, above all on the main (west) façade, demands individual attention – its culmination a hierarchy of 150 figures grouped around Christ in Majesty. Inside, this sense of wild ambition, and flamboyance of scale, is continued. Ruskin reckoned the apse 'not only the best but the very first thing done perfectly in its manner by northern Christendom'. Which is probably right. As far as details go, take a good look at the choirstalls (another incredible assembly of Old Testament figures, this time 16C), the extravagantly traced rose windows, and the superb frieze on the choir-screen depicting the life of St Firmin. This, for all the Gothic statement of the church, still seems rooted in the Romanesque in its wry humour. St Firmin, the martyr said to have brought Christianity to Amiens, is shown preaching to the town, the women listening to his sermon, the men talking amongst themselves. (The cathedral is open to visitors from 7.30–12 & 2–5.30, 6 or 7.)

If you're spending time in Picardy, you might take a look at Amiens' two **regional museums**. Close by the cathedral in the 17C Hôtel de Berny there are *local history collections*, and another mansion, three blocks south of the townhall, houses a *Musée de Picardy* – archaeology, ceramics and local paintings. A third museum-cum-documentation centre is devoted to *Jules Verne*, who spent most of his life in this city. If you're a devotee it's in his old house at 2 rue C Dubois. (All three are open standard hours, cl. Mons.)

This, aside from strictly consuming interests, is about the extent of curiosities – except for the **hortillonages**, on the edge of town. These are a series of cultivated plots, intercut by small waterways, amid reclaimed river marshland. Farmers travel about them by punt and a few still take their produce into the city by boat for the Saturday morning Marché sur l'Eau on the bank of the Somme in place Parmientier. If you want to see them you can take an inexpensive boat trip from the riverside offices of the *Association pour la Sauvegarde des Hortillonages* (57 chemin de Halage; again cl. Mons). Or you can walk – about 40mins each way along the Somme river path.

Arriving by train or bus in Amiens you will find yourself facing a large concrete tower block, the **Tour Perret**. The cathedral rears up behind this, about 5mins' walk. In summer there are **SI** offices (free maps) in front of both the cathedral and station. Other times you'd need to go to the main office in the *Maison de la Culture* (1 rue Jean Catelas), 15mins' walk from the station, leaving the tower on your right, along rue Noyen and its continuations. All three offices will book you a **room** but there's nowhere very cheap. Choose between *Hotel Central* (rue Alexandra Fatton: opposite the station) or two by the cathedral: *Hôtel les Touristes* (22bis place Notre Dame) and *La Renaissance* (8bis rue André; cl. Suns and 2nd half of August). The **youth hostel** and **campsite** are a lot less pricey but a fair slog. Turn right out of the station along bd d'Alsace Lorraine, over the Somme bridge and keep going . . . they're side by side, a little over 1km, on the left by a bleak-looking lake.

Good places to eat include a number of cheap **brasseries** and restaurants in front of Tour Perret and towards the centre of town around place Gambetta, a small square surrounded by snackbars and foodshops. Other specific places worth seeking out are the crêperie *La Mangeoire* (3 rue des Sergeants; cl. Sun/Mon), *Valentin* (52 rue des Jacobins; cl. Sat pm/ Sun & Aug) and *Pizzeria Richard* (54 rue Jean-Jaurès; cl. Mon).

Finally, some details on **getting out.** For Paris or beyond, choose between train, bus or the rides-sharing agency *Allostop* (45 rue des Otages; Mon–Fri 9.30–12.30 & 1.30–6.30; Sat am only). For St-Quentin or Beauvais you're best off by bus. Albert (at the heart of the battlefields region, see p. 127) is about 40mins by bus or train, either of which continues on to Arras and the extraordinary trenches at nearby Vimy Ridge.

BEAUVAIS

Heading south from Amiens towards Paris the countryside becomes broad and flat – agricultural but not rustic. BEAUVAIS seems to fit into this landscape. Rebuilt, like Amiens, after the last war it's a drab, neutral place, again redeemed for tourists only by its enormous 'radiating Gothic' **Cathedral**. This rises crablike above the town, its roof unadorned by any tower or spire and seeming squat for all its height. It is a building which perhaps more than any other in northern France demonstrates the religious materialism of the Middle Ages – its sole intention and function to be taller and larger than its rivals.

The cathedral choir, completed in 1272, was once in fact 16ft higher than that of Amiens, though only briefly; it collapsed in 1284. Its replacement, completed three centuries later, was raised by the sale of indulgences – a right granted to the local bishops by Pope Leo X. This too, however, fell within a few years and the church, as it was left, has a forlorn, mutilated air. The appeal of the building, and its real beauty, is in its glass, its sculpted doorways, and the remnants of the so-called **Basse Oeuvre**, a 9C Carolingian church incorporated into the structure.

Stopping at Beauvais to break the journey you'll probably want to give the rest of the town no more than a passing look. If you're between buses, however, there's a **museum of tapestry** (*Galerie National de Tapisserie*; 9.30–12.30 & 1.30–5.30/6.30, cl. Mon) behind the cathedral and another, devoted to local history and archaeology, in the sharp, black-towered building opposite (*Musée Départemental*; 10–12 & 2–6, cl. Tues). The rousing statue in the central square is local heroine Jean Hachette, a fighter and inspiration in the defence of the town against the Duke of Burgundy in 1472. Just off the square, in place Clémenceau, the SI can provide exhaustive further information. If you want to stay, two moderately cheap **hotels** are *de la Poste* (near the cathedral at 19–21 rue Gambetta) and *Le Brazza* (22 rue de la Madeleine), and there's a **campsite** just out of town on the Paris road. The **gare SNCF**, however, is only an hour away from Paris: the station, a short walk from the centre and cathedral, is on bd Général de Gaulle.

SOUTH-EAST PICARDY

As Picardy reaches to the south-east, away from the coast and the main through routes to Paris, it becomes considerably more inviting. In the *département* of Aisne, particularly, where the region merges with neighbouring Champagne, there are some very real attractions in their own right – handsome cathedral towns set amid lush, wooded hills. All are in easy reach of the main routes, with a network of bus connections from Amiens and good train and bus links to Paris.

ST-QUENTIN

A lively and expanding town with a stylish Gothic centre, **ST-QUENTIN** is good to make for after a flying visit to Amiens. It is large enough, and far enough from Paris, to have a considerable life of its own, and there is nearly always some event going on . . . a jazz festival, art exhibitions, dance programmes. For a full run-down make on arrival for the **SI**, adjoining the townhall in the central **place Hôtel de Ville**, and pick up a map and the free monthly broadsheet *Regards et Passions*. To get into the centre from the **gare**, cross the river Somme and follow rue Général Leclerc and its continuation, rue d'Isle. **Accommodation** is plentiful. *Hôtel du Deoart* (place Monument des Morts) is a bargain for both rooms and meals; there's a cheaper than usual **youth hostel** (bd Jean Bouin; 2km from the station – bus 3 to rue H Dunant) and, by the river, a campsite. For good **eating** you might also check the menus at *Maxime's* in place Hôtel de Ville: though a three-star restaurant there's usually one inexpensive option.

The **Hôtel de Ville** is itself an extraordinary sight. Provincial in the grandest possible sense of the word, its 16C Gothic façade seems an almost pure exercise in stonecarving and elaboration. It is certainly an unhumbled response to the town's **Basilica**, another of Picardy's tremendous achievements in medieval Gothic, which in turn must have been a response to the great neighbouring cathedrals of Amiens and Laon. Built over the 13–15C, and staking out the whole centre of the town, this is a strong, elegant church, specious and powerful within, and preserving some unusual murals. In its crypt, logically enough, is a tomb said to be that of the 4C Saint Quentin.

Nearby in the centre are two specialist **museums**, each surprisingly impressive. **Musée Antoine Lecuyer** (reached from the Basilica at the end of rue Raspail) is devoted almost exclusively to the portraits of **Maurice Quentin de la Tour** – eighty-seven paintings in all, mostly of the court of his day, but including 18C contemporaries such as Jean-Jacques Rousseau. It's open wkdays (except Tues) 10–12 & 2–5, Sat 10–12 & 2–6,

Sun 2–6 only. The other museum, at 11 rue des Cannoniers (away from the basilica, south of place Hôtel de Ville), contains what must be one of the world's largest collections of **insects**, 600,000 in all, of which there are at least 10,000 on display. The *Musée d'Entomologie*, it is open in summer 2.30–6.30, cl. Mons/Thurs; Oct–March 2.30–5.30, cl. Suns-Mons.

LAON AND SOISSONS

High on a narrow ridge, lofty by Picardy standards, **LAON**'s Ville Haute is a striking and monumental sight. It is enclosed, more or less completely, by ramparts and at its highest point is one of France's earliest and loveliest cathedrals. Seen together with those of Amiens and St-Quentin – and then Reims and Chartres or Rouen – this will give you a really good feeling for the development of French Gothic. Though you could equally come here for the feel of the town and the countryside alone: it's another active cultural centre, and in fine walking country.

From St-Quentin buses to Laon are relatively sparse and trains circuitous, changing at Tergnier. You may find it easier to hitch. Arriving, you're likely to be dropped in the lower town, the **Basse Ville**, connected to 'Old Laon' by a regular stream of taxis and buses, or a steep climb. Once up, you'll find the **SI** next to the cathedral, and nearby two of the best value **places to stay**: *Hôtel-Restaurant de la Paix* (52 rue St-Jean, cl. Aug) and the *Maison des Jeunes* (20 rue du Cloître, behind the cathedral: a residential foyer with some short-stay rooms and cheap, if unspec-tacular, meals). If these are full – as is quite possible in summer – the SI can advise on alternatives, or you could as easily go on to Soissons or Noyon. **Camping** is on the edge of the Basse Ville, 600m off route N44.

Laon **Cathedral**, lightly and beautifully proportioned, was a highly experimental design and one which had great influence on the burgeoning, full-blown, Gothic style. It was begun around 1155 and substantially completed by the early decades of the 13C. It's lost two of its seven towers but those that remain, with their animal statuary, give an idea of the scale of the architect's ambitions. And the building is full of novelties beyond this. It has one of the first attempts at rib-vaulting, a new concept of depth in the entrance porches, and, most influential of all, introduced above them, the rose window.

Towards the southern ramparts, a couple of blocks back from the cathedral in rue G Ermant, you come upon a church in almost complete contrast. This is **Chapelle des Templiers**, a tiny 12C sanctuary built in circular form in recollection of the Holy Sepulchre in Jerusalem by the Order of Knights Templar. A resonant place, though bare of decoration, it is now set in a quiet little garden by the local museum (10–12 & 2–5/6; cl. Tues).

The rest of the Ville Haute – which rambles off to the right into the

Bourg quarter around Eglise St-Martin – is good to wander, with universally grand views from the **ramparts**. If you want information on the villages around, and suggestions on possible walks, call in at the **Comité Dep. du Tourisme**, located in a spectacular 16C *hôtel* at 1 rue St-Martin. They can rent you **bikes**, if you ask, and will steer you to any **events** that are on. There's usually something happening at the *Maison des Arts* in place Aubrey, and a concentration during the Heures Médiévales festival during the second and third weeks of September. If you feel like trying pétanque, the town also has an impressive **sports centre** (in the Basse Ville) along with a tremendous heated **swimming pool** (8–1 & 3–8; cl. Sun pm/Mon am).

Going **on from Laon** keep in mind that last trains leave early: to Amiens around 7.30pm, to Paris, via Soissons, shortly after 8pm.

Soissons

Half an hour by train from Laon, **SOISSONS** can lay claim to a long and highly strategic history. Before the Romans arrived it was already a town, its kings controlling parts of Britain as well as Picardy. And in the 5C it was here that the Romans suffered one of their most decisive defeats to the Franks, making Soissons one of the first real centres of the Frankish kingdom. Napoleon, too, considered it a crucial military base: a judgement perhaps borne out this century in extensive war damage.

Exploring this part of the country, the town is a useful and quite attractive place to stay. There are several moderately-priced **hotels**: *de la Gare* (by the station), *du Nord* (left out from the station in rue de Belleu: a cheaper option) and *La Marina* (2 rue St-Quentin in the centre). Rooms are sometimes available as well at the two youth *foyers* (for women at 8 rue de Bauton; men at 20 rue Malieu). Or again there's a **campsite** – 1km from the gare on av du Mail.

As far as its own interest goes, Soissons has a fine, if little sung, **Cathedral** – 13C with majestic glass and vaulting – but it is the ruined **Abbaye de St-Jean des Vignes** that is the highlight. The façade of this tremendous Gothic building rises sheer and grand, impervious to the lack of anything behind its shell. The monastery, save for remnants of a cloister and refectory, was dismantled in 1804.

Soissons is relatively compact. From the **gare** SNCF (with good services to Laon and Paris) the town is a short walk along av Gen. de Gaulle. The **halte routière** is near the townhall in av du Mail; infrequent buses leave for Noyon and Compiègne as well as Laon.

COMPIÈGNE AND NOYON

COMPIÈGNE is a university town: elegant, cultural and worth a day or two of anyone's time. It is best known, at least among the French, for its forest and for its royal palace, a retreat of French monarchs from the 14C on, and magnificently rebuilt under Louis XV and XVI. Neither of which should put you off. You could have an interesting time in Compiègne without so much as setting foot in a state apartment.

Not that the **Palais de Compiègne** is dull, for all its forbidding exterior and size. The lavishness of Marie Antoinette's rooms is almost compelling, and there's a fascination, too, in imagining Napoleon living among the splendour. All so soon after the Revolution. It has to be said, though, that the palace guided tours (9.30–11.45 & 1.30–4.45; cl. Tues) are expensive and the included Museums of Vehicles and the Second Empire not unmissable. The palace gardens – the **petit parc** – are probably enough. Serene and formal, with a long avenue extending away into the forest, they are open daily from 7.30–8/6.30.

In the town the most striking building is, as so often in Picardy, the **Hôtel de Ville** – Louis XII Gothic with a riot of 19C statuary including, inevitably, Joan of Arc, captured in this town by the Burgundians before being handed over to the English. The **SI** has its offices here and will provide you with a plan of the town, an exhaustive visitors' route handily etched on. In good Michelin fashion they suggest half an hour to get around the lot, which would really mean jogging. Best to be more selective. If you've an interest in Greek vases **Musée Vivenel** (rue d'Austerlitz; 9–12 & 2–6/5) has one of the best collections around.

Alternatively, and above all if you're here in spring or autumn, head out to the **forest**, whose 60 or more square miles touch the edge of the town. Very ancient, and cut by a succession of hills, streams and valleys, this is grand rambling country – on foot or by car. The SI can again provide routes. There are a couple of villages right at the heart – VIEUX MOULIN and ST-JEAN AUX BOIS – and on beyond at PIERREFONDS a classic medieval romance castle. Up in the north of the forest, 8km from Compiègne, is a stranger sight in a railway siding known as the **Clairière de l'Armistice**. It was here, in a train carriage, that the First World War was brought to an end on 11 November 1918. The *actual* carriage, somewhat ironically, was destroyed in 1945 but its replacement is no doubt much the same and the objects within are the originals. (It is open 8/9–1.30/12 & 1.30/2–6.30/5.30.)

Compiègne can have a lot going on – with more fringe-type events than its neighbours in Picardy – and there's no shortage either of **brasseries**. Rock bottom prices at *Cafétéria Le Lys* ((37 rue Solferoin; cl. Sun/ Mon & July/Aug), *Crêperie l'Igloo* (31 rue de Paris) and *A la Dernière Minute* (in place de la Gare, with a few rooms, too). Slightly more expensive are *La Pizza* (10 rue des Boucheries) and an excellent Vietnamese place, *Le Phnom Penh* (13 rue des Lombards). **Pâtisseries** are also rewarding, with liqueur-laced cream pastries, and there's a big all day Saturday market in the square by place Hôtel de Ville. As for **rooms**, the

youth hostel is 1km from the station at 6 rue Pasteur (40.26.00; served by bus 3 to rue des Fosses), and there are lowish prices at the *Hôtel Biguet* (off place St-Clement in rue des Bouvines). **Bus** and **railway stations** are adjacent. Coming into town, cross over the wide river Oise and walk up rue Solferino to place Hôtel de Ville. Services are both a bit sketchy in this area but they do complement each other so you can usually get where you want.

Noyon

Rowing along the Oise on his *Inland Journey* of 1876, Robert Louis Stevenson stopped briefly at Compiègne and at neighbouring **NOYON**, which he reckoned 'a stack of brown roofs at the best, where I believe people live very respectably in a quiet way'. It *is* a bit like that, though the **Cathedral**, to which Stevenson warmed – 'my favourite kind of mountain scenery' – is impressive at least in passing. Spacious and a little stark, it blends Romanesque and Gothic with easy success, and is flanked by the ruins of 13C cloisters and a strange, exquisitely-shaped **Renaissance library**. Close by, signs direct you to **Musée Calvin**, ostensibly on the site of the reformer's birthplace. The house here, though, is entirely a reconstruction, hoping to up the town's tourist potential. The respectable citizens of Noyon were never among their local boy's adherents and long ago tore down the original.

   Hotels here are pricier than at Soissons. Cheapest, if you're stuck, are *Le Balto* in place Hôtel de Ville and, for doubles, *Hôtel-Restaurant Le Grillon* (rue St-Eloi). The local **campsite** is 4km out of town along the Compiègne road, towards the roofless abbey of CHIRY-OURSCAMP. **Buses**, mainly for Compiègne, leave from outside the gare SNCF. **Bikes** are for rent there, too. Big days in Noyon are Saturday morning, when a colourful produce **market** spills out across place Hôtel de Ville, and the first Tuesday of the month, which sees a cattle market taking over virtually the entire town centre.

THE BATTLEFIELDS AND INDUSTRIAL NORTH

Normandy, Picardy and Flanders are all littered with the monuments, battlefields and cemeteries of the two World Wars. Nowhere though with the intensity of the region north of Amiens – around Albert and Arras. It was here, among the fields and villages of **the Somme**, that the main battlelines of the First World War were drawn. These can be visited most spectacularly at **Vimy Ridge**, 8km north of Arras. Lesser sites, often more poignant, are dotted around the **Circuit de Souvenir**, signposted from Albert and detailed on a local tourist pamphlet, somewhat kitschily translated into English as 'Down Memory Lane'. By train you can reach Vimy from Arras and another impressive battlefield, **Beaumont-Hamel**, from the station of Beaucourt-Hamel on the line between Amiens and Arras.

ALBERT AND THE *CIRCUIT DE SOUVENIR*

The church at **ALBERT** – now, with the rest of the town, completely rebuilt – was one of the minor landmarks of the First World War. Hit by German bombing, its tall tower suspended at a precarious angle a statue of the Madonna. The British, entrenched over three years in the region, came to know it as 'the leaning Virgin'.

Arriving – by train from Amiens or Arras – the town's new tower is the first thing that catches your eye, now capped by an equally improbably-posed statue. There is an **SI** office close by in rue Gambetta (open June–mid-Sept only, 2–5pm) and a couple of good inexpensive **hotels**: *Basilique*, in the same street, and *de la Paix* in rue Victor Hugo. Modern Albert does not, however, invite much of a stay unless you've a really strong battlefield interest – in which case you could spend weeks in the region. Virtually every village around, whether on the *Circuit* or not, seems to have one or more battle monuments or military graveyards, and the parish cemeteries too almost always shelter a few soldiers from the Great War. Two that I visited, very much at random, were LA BOISELLE, a village just north of Albert, where the first confrontation in the Battle of the Somme took place on 1 July 1916, and FORCEVILLE, very typical with its British and parish cemetery next to each other down a tiny country track.

More deliberately, you could head for the battlefield at **BEAUMONT-HAMEL**, 2km walk up a lane from Beaucort Hamel SNCF. This, like Vimy Ridge, was defended by Canadian troops – a regiment of Newfoundlanders who suffered massive losses during the summer of 1916 – and has been made over by the French to their government. It is though a much less well known site, with hardly a dozen or so tourists a week to judge by the visitors' book, and its trenches are being allowed to weather away. Which doesn't mean they have lost impact. Behind the monument, with its caribou emblem and biblical quotation, a deep main line twists its way about, its walls punctuated by poky little dugouts, other more eroded trenches leading off to either side. The memory of war still seems shockingly contemporary.

ARRAS AND VIMY RIDGE

ARRAS has been rebuilt perhaps more times than any other town in France. Its history of conflict dates back to the early 15C – a temporary truce was signed here before Agincourt – and in addition to the destructions of this century it has seen capture and bombardment by Austrians, Spanish, British and Germans.

Oddly enough it bears few obvious marks. Reconstruction here, particularly after the last war, has been careful and stylish, and two grand squares in the centre – **Grande place** and **place des Héros** – preserve a historic character. Around both are restored Renaissance mansions, built in relatively restrained Flemish style, and on the latter a grand and ornate **townhall**, its entrance hall sheltering a pair of *géants* (festival giants) awaiting the city's next annual fete. By a slightly unsettling quirk of architectural development the townhall actually looks very like a cathedral, with its tremendous and flamboyant belfry, and the **Cathedral** – originally 17C – looks not unlike a townhall. More striking in itself, again in this historic centre, is the former Benedictine Abbey of **Palais St-Vaast** – revived from its ruins after wars in the 18C *and* present century. It now houses a city museum with unexciting collections of paintings (one reasonable Corot), fragments of sculpture and local ceramics; hours are 10–12 & 2–5.30 (cl. Tues) if you need somewhere to escape the (frequent) rain.

The most fascinating sight in Arras though is, perhaps logically, underground: **les Souterrains** (or *les Boves*), dank passageways and spacious vaults tunnelled below the centre of the city. Their entrance (Tues–Sat 2.30–6; Suns 10.30–12.30 & 3–6.30; pricey) is actually inside the townhall. Once down you are escorted round an impressive physical area and given an interesting survey of local history. During the Great War the rooms, which often have fine tiled floors and lovely pillars and stairways, were used as a British barracks and hospital.

On the edge of town, extending this memory, is Arras's **Memorial to the Missing**, its walls recording the names of a staggering 36,000 men whose bodies were not recovered after First World War battles in this area alone. Nearby, an equally grim reminder of the last war, is the **Mur des Fusillées**, on which spot 200 French Resistance members were executed by firing squad. Perhaps because Arras is still a military town – the modern barracks are close by – these sites seem particularly powerful.

If you are staying in the town – as you'll probably need to do, visiting Vimy without your own transport – there's a **youth hostel** in Grande place (at no 59), a **campsite** 1km out from the station on the Baupame road, and two good value **hotels** (*Les Grandes Arcades* in Grande place, and *Le Rallye* at 9 rue Gambetta near the station). The *Arcades* also does good food, in a fine setting, or there are several **crêperies** around place des Héros. Other Arras restaurants tend to the expensive, often featuring local speciality *andouillet* (tripe-sausage – beware!). The **SI**, who are worth consulting on transport to (and tours of) local battlefield sites, are at 7 place du Maréchal Foch, opposite the station.

Vimy Ridge

Eight km north of Arras (on route D49), **VIMY RIDGE** was the scene of some of the most exhaustive fighting of the Great War: almost two full years of battle, culminating in its capture by the Canadians in April 1917. It is a vast site, given in perpetuity to the Canadian government in respect for the sacrifice, and has been preserved in part as it was during the conflict. There are long muddy networks of trenches and tunnels, sometimes half-hidden by mounds of earth and often pockmarked by shells and craters. There are underground clearings, hideous places, where men used to shelter during heavy bombardments and where makeshift hospitals used to operate. And apparently, below the ground, there are still some 11,280 undiscovered corpses – and countless rounds of unexploded ammunition. It is a place that still needs signs to warn against straying from the directed paths.

The experience of a visit evokes with few parallels the insanity of that First World War, fought in numbers that can still shock today and in ways which even then belonged to a distant age. The Canadian and German lines are amazingly close – the 'whites of their eyes' takes on a real meaning – and the trenches are somehow much lower and more primitive than you expect; you'd have to keep your head down at all times. For the record, the battles here claimed over 60,000 Canadian lives, and presumably an equivalent number of Germans. The Canadian's memorial monument is on top of the ridge – on what was, and still is, known as 'hill 145' – surveying most of the battlefield area.

Visits – April–Sept, 10–6 daily – around the site are supervised by Québecois students, who will give you more sobering statistics. You can just wander about on your own though and, bizarrely, you won't be alone, even among tourists. Local French youth come here to mill about, adults simply to stroll. Weirdest of all, during the summer afternoon I spent at the site, a wedding party actually drove out to picnic and have their photos taken. Among the great death . . .

LILLE

It was the Mayor of **LILLE**, Pierre Mauroy, whom the newly elected President Mitterrand appointed as Prime Minister in 1981. The city – way the largest in these northern regions – is the very symbol of French industry and working-class politics. It spreads far into the countryside in every direction, a mass of dark suburbs and traditional heavy plant, and it contains, on a significant scale, most of the problems and assets of contemporary France. There is some of the worst poverty and racial conflict in the country here, and a crime rate rivalled only in Paris and Marseille. There is regionalism – Lillois sprinkle their speech with a French-Flemish patois and to an extent assert a Flemish identity, holding joint anti-nuclear demonstrations with Belgian groups, for example. And there is classic French affluence. The city has a lovely central heart – **Vieux Lille**, vibrant and obviously prosperous commercial areas and modern residential squares, and it's a place which takes its culture and its restaurants very seriously.

All of which is to say that, though you may not consider Lille a prime French destination, if you're travelling through this region it's at least worth a night. **Arriving**, the encroaching suburbs look pretty grim, but from the **gare SNCF** (or adjoining **gare routière**) you're only a few minutes' walk from Vieux Lille and the central pedestrianised area around it. The point to make for is **place Ribour**, an airy, modern-looking square with an old palace that now houses the **SI**. Vieux Lille begins immediately to the north. Off to the west (three or four blocks left on our plan) stylish rue de Béthune leads into **place Béthune**, another fine square, with some excellent cafés, and beyond to the city's **Musée des Beaux Arts** in place de la République. The museum (open 9.30–12.30 & 2–6; cl. Tues; free Wed/Sat pm) is like so many of those in major French cities in its studious collections of each art genre – paintings, ceramics, tapestries . . . . Here, the emphasis is very much on the Flemish painters – from 'primitives' like Dirk Bouts, through the Northern Renaissance, to Ruysdael, De Hooch and 17C schools. It's an instructive display, helped by a small library of art books provided for browsing in the entrance hall, and boasts too an additional scattering of Impressionists – including works by Monet and Corot.

It's in **Vieux Lille** though, that you're likely to spend most time. Just up from place Ribour in its traditional centre, the old exchange building, or **Bourse** – lavishly ornate, and as perfect a representative of its age as could be imagined. To the merchants of 17C Lille, as prominent then as now, all things Flemish were the very epitome of wealth and taste, and they were not men to stint on detail, here or on the imposing mansions around. The building today, long pre-empted, has been converted to an organised fleamarket, with stalls selling books, junk and flowers.

Turning the corner from the Bourse, you can see how the Flemish Renaissance architecture developed, becoming distinctly French, and combining brick with stone in grand flights of Baroque extravagance. The superlative example of this style, the **Théâtre de l'Opéra**, has a façade so strident it's almost ridiculous. It was built only at the turn of this century, along with the equally inflated **belfry** and **chamber of commerce** opposite.

Beyond, there's a similar fascination in many of the streets, added to by the fact that many of the buildings here still see similar use to their original intent. The **Hospice Comtesse**, for example, 12C in origin though much reconstructed in the 18C, served as a hospital right through to the Second World War. Its old ward, the Salle des Malades, can be visited; it's more or less opposite the Cathedral in rue de la Monnaie. The **Cathedral** itself, built only in the last century, is undistinguished – and particularly so in comparison with Lille's earlier principal church, Gothic **St-Maurice** towards the station.

The **Citadelle**, towering above the old city, was constructed in familiar star-shaped fashion by Vauban. Still in military hands it can be visited only on Sunday by guided tour (details from SI for enthusiasts). Wandering through the old city, however, it is interesting to walk up this way. Turning a corner at rue de la Monnaie on to rue d'Angleterre you enter a completely **Arab quarter** of town, a sudden and unexpected change from the refined neighbouring streets. Conditions here, as in most of the big city Arab districts, are poor and overcrowded: a straight reflection of French attitudes towards what many still regard as a 'migrant' work force.

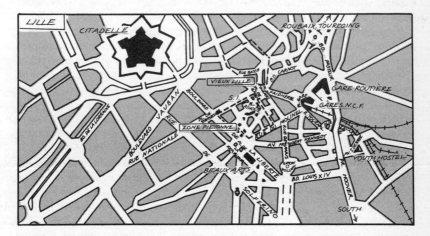

Rooms and details

For a good room and a good location in Lille you'll need to pay. Most of the inexpensive **hotels** are gathered around the railway station and are pretty uninviting, in addition to the quarter converting evenings to a red light area. One of the best places is *Floréal* (21 rue Ste-Anne: one block from the station). Moving away, *Hôtel Constantin* (5 rue des Fosses, in the pedestrianised centre) is a step upmarket in all respects. A good fallback, despite an unpromising approach, is the **youth hostel** at 1 ave

Julien-Destrée. This isn't too far from the station: to get there walk south-east along rue Tournal, cross the pedestrian subway under the autoroute and you'll find it across the car park opposite the Foire Commerciale. It looks like a Swiss chalet.

The main area for **brasseries** – in all price categories – is around place Rihour and place Béthune. Rue St-Etienne, too, just across rue Nationale, has a good selection. Among more specific places to recommend, outside this area, there's ambitious and reasonably-priced food at *L'Idéal* (8 rue Vieux Fauborg), a nice crêperie at 4 place Louise de Bettignies (*La Gala-tière*) and an all night brasserie (*Jean's*) in place du Théâtre. In rue Royale, below the **Citadelle**, you'll find a cluster of **ethnic places**: Tunisian, Cambodian and Vietnamese. But Arab restaurants around here tend to be overpriced, at least to outsiders. For **drinking**, Lille students with money hang around Le Pubstore at 44 rue de la Halle. Rather cheaper is La Petite Cour (rue du Curé St-Etienne: almost opposite rue St-Etienne across rue Esquermoise).

Art and music **events** are always worth checking up on, either at the SI (who publish a monthly guide called *Chtimi*) or in the local paper. The major **fair** of the year is the *Grande Braderie*, a vast market-place filling miles of the city streets over the Whitsun weekend. A big street parade, and festival of the giants, is held at this time.

Getting around Lille you may want to make use of the city's métro – the totally automatic *VAL* (map and info at all stations). **Getting out**, trains and buses complement each other's services. The *Allostop* agency for hitchers shares an office with the SI.

TRAVEL DETAILS

Trains

London to Paris through services run direct from the port stations at Calais or Boulogne, stopping en route only at Amiens.

From Calais-Ville 6 daily to Paris (3½hrs), via Amiens (1¾hrs); 9 or 10 daily to Boulogne-Ville (½hr) and Etaple-Le Touquet (1hr); frequently to Lille and stops en route (1–1½hrs; some with change at Hazebrouck).
From Boulogne Ville 8 daily to Paris (3hrs), via Amiens (1¼hrs); 9 or 10 to Calais-Ville (½hr) and Etaple-Le Touquet (20mins), Montreuil (½hr) and Arras (2hrs).
From Dunkerque 7 or 8 daily to Paris (3hrs10), via Arras (1hr20); 3 or 4 daily, not Suns, to Calais-Ville (1hr).

From Amiens very frequently to Paris (1¾–2hrs); several daily to Compiègne (1¼hrs) and Laon (2hrs).
From Beauvais 6 or 7 daily to Paris (1hr10).
From St-Quentin frequent service (7am–midnight) to Paris (1¾hrs), some via Compiègne (50mins), a few at all stations including Noyon and Tergnier (change for Laon); additional stopping trains run between Compiègne and Tergnier, and 4 daily from Tergnier to Laon (25mins).
From Laon erratic service (mornings/evenings) to Paris (2hrs20), via Soissons (1hr40); more frequent between Laon and Soissons.
From Lille very frequently to Paris (2–2½hrs); *TGV* daily around 7am to Arras (40mins), Longeau (1hr10) and

Lyon (4hrs40); regularly to Brussels (2hrs).

Buses
From Dunkerque several daily to Calais.
From Calais 5 daily to Boulogne (1hr) and Le Touquet (2hrs).
From Boulogne 5 daily to Calais (1hr) and Le Touquet (1hr).
From Amiens buses in all directions, including Beauvais (1¾hrs), St-Quentin (2½hrs) and Albert (40mins).
South Picardy sporadic buses link most of the towns – Compiègne, Beauvais, Soissons, Chantilly, St-Quentin, Noyon – with each other and with Amiens and Paris.

Ferries
From Dunkerque *Sally Line* (28.68.43.44) to Ramsgate: 4 daily most of the year in 2½hrs.
From Calais *Townsend Thoresen* (21.97.21.21) to Dover: every 1–2hrs from 7.30am–10.45pm, some night crossings, in 1¼hrs. *Sealink* (21.96.70.70) to Dover: 10–18 daily, round the clock in 1½hrs. *Hoverspeed* (21.96.67.10) to Dover: 6–30 daily in 35mins (daytime only; longer journey in bad weather).
From Boulogne *Townsend Thoresen* (21.31.78.00) to Dover: every 3hrs (1–2hrs in Sept/Oct) in 1hr40. *Sealink* (21.30.25.11) to Dover: currently 2 daily on Weds/Sats only in 1¾hrs (service may be reduced or even withdrawn in 1986); and to Folkestone: 4–12 daily, some at night, in 1hr50. *Hoverspeed* (21.30.27.26) to Dover: variable service in around 40mins.

Note that all phone numbers above are for agents in the respective local ports, preceded by the port's departmental area code. If you don't have a car you'll probably save both money and time buying rail or coach and ferry through tickets from Paris or other main cities.

Flights
From Le Touquet *Air-UK* services to London-Gatwick, Southampton and Southend.

Chapter three
NORMANDY

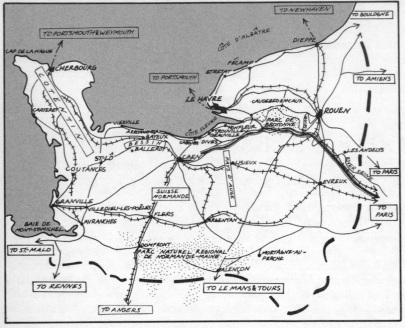

To the French, at least, the essence of **Normandy** is its produce. This is the land of butter and cream cuisine, famous cheeses and seafood, cider and calvados – and the countryside, with its rich orchards and dappled dairy cows, follows suit. In this perhaps is there most to appreciate: there does seem something unique about a French region where the lack of wines is almost a virtue. But the province is hardly short on conventional sights either. There are churches here – **Rouen, Caen, Mont St-Michel** – as impressive as any in the country, and travelling about it's incredible quite how much has survived, or been restored since, the 1944 Battle of Normandy. You could spend months without exhausting the province's **Romanesque** and **Gothic architecture, let alone all the châteaux and medieval manorhouses.** And there are more recent creations too – **Monet's garden at Giverny** and at **Le Havre** a fabulous collection of paintings by **Dufy, Boudin** and other **Impressionists.**

   Politically, Normans tend to agree with the French stereotype of themselves as mistrustful, closed and conservative, with an avid love of taking each other to court. The rural population identifies with the age-old *pays,* mistrusting people in neighbouring *pays* and using the phrase 'gone east' with equal disapproval for a move 10km away or a move to Alsace. None of which bodes well for the region's new, miniscule and somewhat bizarre separatist lobby, the **Normandy Nationalist Party**. These neo-Norse people use English as the next best language after Saxon and talk about Sinn Fein and the Duchess of Normandy (the British Queen) in equally glowing terms. The only sentiment of their compatriots they can hope to play on is a shared hatred of the Parisians, who use the Seine valley for their country homes and the Côte Fleurie for their seaside weekends.

CÔTE D'ALBÂTRE

There's no doubt that Normandy's Channel ports, **Dieppe** and **Le Havre**, provide a better introduction to France than their counterparts to the north in Picardy. The white cliffs put on an impressive show, almost justifying the 'Alabaster coast' epithet, and if you've wheels there are occasional surprises beyond the windswept and tide-chased walks – a wonderful Lutyens fantasy at **Varengeville**, the Hammer Horror Benedictine distillery at **Fécamp**. Without transport there's still the **Beaux Arts** in **Le Havre** although beyond this you may want to move on swiftly. There are livelier, warmer coasts to the west, and it's only a short train or bus ride to Rouen.

DIEPPE

Crowded between high cliff headlands, **DIEPPE** is a rather attractive port to arrive at. It's industrious, with the commercial docks unloading half the bananas of the Antilles among other things and markets selling fish straight off the boats with the usual French flair for displaying edibles. In fact it's likely to be the sole, scallops and turbot served up in most of the restaurants that tempt you to stay here. If you're looking for a **room**, make for *Au Grand Duquesne* (in the centre at 15 place St-Jacques), *La Providence* (157 av de la République in the suburb of Neuville to the west of the ports) or the **youth hostel**, 2km south of the centre on rue Louis Fromager (*Janval bus* from the gare routière). The nearest **campsite**, *du Près St Nicholas* is 3km down the coastal road to Pourville; the **gares SNCF** and **routière** are about 150m south of the fishing port. The **SI**, in the modern Hôtel de Ville on bd Général de Gaulle (west from the fishing port), can supply maps and plans.

Before Parisians had fast enough cars to drive further west they used to take the sea air at Dieppe, promenading along the front while the 19C English colony indulged in the peculiar pastime of bathing. Hence the extravagant space allotted to the seafront and 'salt water therapy centre' now hemmed in with car parks. In the centre the streets are rundown and in continual shadow – little advertisement for the 18C town planning to which they are supposed to be a monument. Livelier, particularly for its **Saturday market,** is the pedestrianised **Grande Rue** which has efficiently got its act together for English day trip shoppers and last minute ferry departers.

As far as actual monuments go, the obvious place to head for, the medieval **castle** overlooking the seafront from the west, is the home of the **Musée de Dieppe** and two showpiece collections. The first is a group of *Dieppe carved ivories* – virtuoso pieces of sawing, filing and chipping of the plundered riches of Africa, shipped back to the town by early Dieppe 'explorers'. The other, a hundred or so prints by the co-founder of cubism, *Georges Braque*, who went to school in Le Havre, spent summers in Dieppe and is buried just west of the town at Varangeville-sur-Mer (see below). Only a small number of prints are displayed at any one time but in theory you can see the rest if you ask. One side exit from the castle takes you out onto a path up to the **cliffs** while on the other side steps lead down to **square du Canada** – basically a commemoration of the colonisation of Canada by Dieppe sailors but also dedicating a small plaque to the Canadian soldiers who died in the disastrous 1942 raid, justified later as a trial run for the 1944 Normandy landings.

Varengeville: Lutyens and Braque
Braque's grave is in the clifftop church of **VARANGEVILLE** (a 25min bus ride, nos 311/312 from Dieppe, afternoons only). The tombstone is monstrous and the view along the cliffs more appealing than the artist's stained glass windows. But the main point of the excursion and something un-French in almost every respect, is the **Bois des Moutiers**, one of the architect Edwin Lutyens's first commissions. Back along the road from the church, you can visit its gardens from 15 March to 15 Nov (9–12 & 2–7; cl. Sat am) and the house in July to August (cl. Sun am and Tues). Admission is expensive but you'll be guided with genuine enthusiasm round the quirks and games as well as highly innovative engineering of the house. The colours of the Burne Jones tapestry hanging in the stairwell were copied from Renaissance cloth in William Morris's studio – the rhododendrons were chosen from similar samples. Paths lead through vistas based on paintings by Poussin, Lorrain and other 18C artists and no modern roses are allowed to update the colours.

EASTWARDS: ST-VALÉRY, FÉCAMP AND ETRETAT

From Dieppe to Le Havre the coast is eroding at a ferocious rate, and it's conceivable that the small resorts here, tucked in among the cliffs at the ends of a succession of valleys, may not last more than another century or so. For the moment, however, they are quietly prospering, with casinos, sports centres and yacht marinas ensuring a modest but steady summer trade. The first of any size is **ST-VALÉRY-EN-CAUX**, a rebuilt town which is the clearest reminder of the fighting here – and massive destruction – in 1940. There's a monument on the western cliffs to the French cavalry division who faced Rommel's tanks on horseback, brandishing their sabres in hopeless heroics. On the opposite cliffs, beside the ruins of a German gun position, is another monument, this time to a Scots division, rounded up while fighting their way back to Le Havre and boats home.

Further along you reach **FÉCAMP**, a serious fishing port like Dieppe, with a seafront promenade and little other animation. The reason, though, to pay a brief visit here is to take a look at the **Benedictine Distillery** in rue Alexandre le Grand, in the narrow strip of streets running parallel to the ports towards the town centre. For this a taste for 19C operatic horror sets is more important than a liking for the liqueur in question. Tours (9.30–11.30 & 2–5.30) start with a small *museum*, set firmly in the Middle Ages beneath a nightmarish mock-Gothic roof with props of manuscripts, locks, testaments, lamps and religious paintings. The first whiff of Benedictine comes in the grim rust and grey coloured *Salle des Abbés*, and at this point the script abruptly changes – from mysterious monks to exclusive product and commodity. The boxes of ingredients are a rare treat for the nose (be wary with the myrrh) and theatre returns down in the old distillery (now forsaken for new commercial premises out of town) with boxes of herbs being thrown in to great copper vats. Finally you are offered a *dégustation* in their bar across the road – neat, in a cocktail, or on crêpes.

If your aesthetic sensibilities need soothing after this, the genuinely medieval nave and Renaissance carved screens of the **Eglise de la Trinité** in the town centre may do the trick. Alternatively, you could feast your eyes on a Renaissance chancel on a grass floor with the open sky above and an intact Gothic lady chapel: the remains of the **Abbaye de Valmont**, 11km east from the coast (bus 261 or 311 from Fécamp). This is open 10–12 & 2–6, except Weds (and, from Oct–April, Suns).

Further still, and splashed across most of the *département's* tourist brochures, are the cliff formations of **ETRETAT**. Without the prior publicity, these could be quite thrilling as you first catch sight of the arches and needles from the beach or clifftop. You'll need transport though – Etretat is not on the bus and train routes – and to explore them you've got just 3 hours either side of low tide. The standard high vantage point on the eastern side has a lifesized aeroplane in concrete relief and an elongated arch inclining to the sky, a moving commemoration of two pilots last seen over Etretat attempting a Paris-New York flight in 1927.

Well sheltered from the elements, the town itself is a pleasant enough little resort and has a rather nice idiosyncrasy of beached boats converted with thatched roofs into sheds, or these days, beach bars. **If you want to stay**, two hotels to try are *Normandie* (place Foch) and *de la Poste* (6 av George V). The campsite is 1km from the centre on rue Guy de Maupassant, the SI is on place de la Mairie. In terms of accommodation, however, FÉCAMP offers more possibilities: a youth hostel on rue du Commandant Rocquigny, east of the port (35.72.06.45; open July–15 Sept), a hostel in the centre (13 rue de l'Inondation), hotels *de la Plage* (87 rue de la Plage), *au Petit Bar* (rue des Prés), *Moderne* (3 av Gambetta), and a campsite superbly located on the western heights. Fécamp's SI is just behind the seafront next to the yacht harbour and its *gares SNCF* and *routière* between the port and the town centre on av Gambetta. There's also a youth hostel in ST-VALÉRY (35.97.03.98).

LE HAVRE

Even more so than Dieppe, ferry passengers at **LE HAVRE** rush to leave this port, the second largest in France, after Marseille. It's usually dismissed as dismal, disastrous and gargantuan even though there's not much in the way of tower blocks and it's a lot more human than some of the new Paris developments. You may not like it, but an immense city conclusively destroyed in the last war and rebuilt along new lines from the plans of a single architect between 1944–64 is a rather rare entity. Le Havre has had a Communist mayor for decades and its two twin towns, wonderfully, are Leningrad and Southampton. Thanks to the politics of the town hall, the museums are free or have a minimal token charge.

The port, taking up half the Seine estuary, extends far further than the town. Av Foch, the central street, runs east-west, looking on to the sea between the beach and the yacht harbour at one end, and at the other the **SI** alongside the Hôtel de Ville and a kiosk where you can get a bus map. The **gares SNCF** and **routière** are 1km further west along rue Lecesne and the transport system includes a funicular and giant escalator to get up north. If you're looking for **accommodation**, try *Jeanne d'Arc* and *Séjour Fleuri* on rue Emile Zola or *St-Michel*, 36 rue d'Ingouville and the municipal **hostel**, 27 rue de la Mailleraye. The **campsite** is in the Forêt de Montgeon (bus 12 from Hôtel de Ville, direction Rouelles, stop Hallates and a bit of a walk through the woods).

The finest buildings in Le Havre surround the **Bassin de Commerce**, with tinted glass at the eastern end, a slender white footbridge and, at the other end, the equally gleaming truncated cooling tower of the **Espace Oscar Niemayer** framed by the bridge spire and St Joseph's lighthouse-like belfry in the distance. The tower holds a theatre and cinema and an ever-hopeful socialist sentiment by the fountain at its base. A plaza for busking, strolling and idling, slopes down to bars and shops as well as exhibition and concert space (what's on details from SI).

On bd J. F. Kennedy, overlooking the port entrance, is the **Beaux Arts**, one of the best designed art galleries in the country and with one of the loveliest collections of its 19C and 20C paintings – fifty canvases by Eugène Boudin and works by Corot, Courbet, Pissaro, Sisley, Gaugin, Léger, Braque and Lurcat. Raoul Dufy, a native of Le Havre, has a whole room for his drawings and paintings in which the windows at the base of the walls show waterlilies in a shallow moat outside. Waterlilies in oil appear along with Westminster and a sunrise snowscape by Monet. Even if you're determined to rush off straight after, allow yourself to be delayed just long enough to visit; it's open 10–12 & 2–6, cl. Tues. With more time to spare, you might like to see what the **old Havre** looked like in the pre-war days when Sartre wrote *La Nausée* here: there are pictures and bits gathered from the rubble in one of the very few buildings that escaped, the **Musée de l'Ancien Havre** at 1 rue Jérome Bellarmato, just south of the Bassin du Commerce (open 10–12 & 2–6, cl. Mon and Tues).

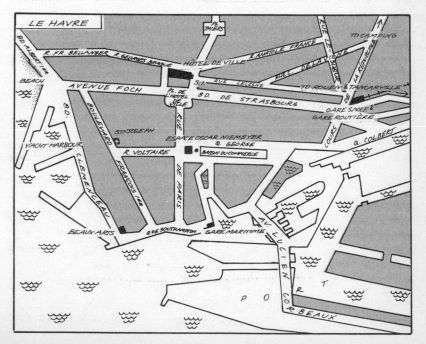

THE SEINE VALLEY

The days of the Seine's tidal bore and treacherous sandbanks are over. Heavy ships serenely make their way up the looping river to the provincial capital of Rouen, the largest city of Normandy and the only one worth a longish stay. Further upstream, Monet's wonderful house and garden at Giverny and the English frontier stronghold, the Château Gaillard, also justify taking a slow route into Paris. Driving this way, the immense Tancarville suspension bridge spans the opening of the estuary, while at Caudebec, the yellow stays of Pont de Brotonne produce artistic optics as well as a bridge; for unhurried river crossings there are *bacs* (ferries: cheaper for cars than the bridge tolls).

TOWARDS ROUEN: JUMIÈGES ABBEY AND THE BROTONNE PARK

La Havre and Rouen are such vast industrial conglomerates that the countryside around them wouldn't appear to have obvious promise. In fact, though not entirely rural, it's a surprisingly beautiful area, designated the Parc Naturel Régional de Brotonne with imaginative projects run by local people to preserve the environment and traditional activities. Its highlight, to outsiders, is the majestic Abbaye de Jumièges but if you've time – and wheels – there are less frequented attractions south of the river. Details on all aspects of the park can be obtained from the very helpful *Maison de Parc* (2 Rond Point Marbec, Le Trait). Bikes can be hired from M Jaubert, rue de la Vicomté, Caudebec. Buses 191/192 between Le Havre and Rouen run north of the river ignoring the loops though you can pick up a connection (or hitch) towards Jumièges at YAINVILLE or DUCLAIR on the main road.

Moving away from Le Havre, across the river from the last of its refineries, the *parc* comes as quite a shock. Camargue horses and Scottish highland cattle graze in the Vernier marshes and upstream the scenery on both sides of the Seine is soft and lush like a giant green cat asleep. If you're making for Jumièges – by bike or car – you might first take a look at another medieval abbey, L'ABBAYE DE ST-WANDRILLE, founded, so legend has it, by a 7C count who, with his wife, renounced all earthly pleasures on the day of their wedding. The abbey's buildings are an attractive if curious collection: part ruin, part restoration and, in the case of the main buildings, part transplant – a 15C barn brought in here just a few years back from another Normandy village miles away. Monks will show you around every afternoon at 3 and 4, and at 11.30 on Sundays.

The **Abbaye de Jumièges**, in the next loop of the Seine, 12km upstream, is an extraordinary ruin – definitely one of the sights of Normandy. It dates, at least in its present appearance, from the 11C and was consecrated in the presence of William the Conqueror. The towers, over 170ft tall, still stand. So too does part of the nave, roofless now but all the more impressive for that. Visits unescorted, are from 9/10–12 & 2–6/4, and, across the river near **HAUVILLE** (off the road to GUÉRANDE), you can also look round a **windmill**, one of six owned by the Jumièges monks, who farmed and forested all this area. Its outline – based on contemporary castle towers – looks peculiarly like a six-year-old's drawing; restored by the *parc*, it is open at weekends, from 2.30–7. If you've time, move on from here to the neighbouring village of **LA HAYE DE ROUTOT**. The churchyard here is a novelty – a pair of millennia-old yew trees shaped into a chapel and grotto – but the feature for which the village is best known (at least in Normandy) is its annual **Fête de Ste-Claire**. This is held on 16 July – a date worth coinciding with – though a video scene of the goings on is shown in a local reconstructed boulangerie (July–Aug 2.30–6.30 daily except Tues; April–June & Sept–Oct wkends only). The chief feature of the festival is a towering, conical bonfire, topped by a cross which must survive to ensure a good year while the smouldering logs are taken home as protection against lightning.

For **accommodation** in the *Parc* south of the river, there's a *gîte d'étape* at ROUTOT (c/o M Verhaeghe, 32.57.31.09) and a few rooms available at the *Maison des Métiers* (32.57.40.41) in BOURNEVILLE which is also a beautifully presented museum of traditional farming and building techniques (open 2–7, April–Dec, cl. Mon). The most practical places to stay, however, are on the north bank at CAUDEBEC-EN-CAUX (with a campsite, good restaurants and one cheap hotel, *Le Cheval Blanc* at 4 place Réné Coty) or in DUCLAIR (hotels *L'Aigle d'Or* at 75 rue Jules Ferry or *Le Tartarin* at 125 place du Général de Gaulle).

ROUEN

You could spend a day wandering around **ROUEN** without realising that the Seine ran through the city. The war destroyed all the bridges, the area between the cathedral and the *quais* and much of the left bank industrial quarter. After repairing the damage, enormous sums were spent on an upmarketing restoration job that has turned the centre into the closest idea of a medieval city that our ignorant imaginations can come up with. So it looks authentic and probably isn't in the slightest. Historians consulted on the project suggested that the houses would have been painted in bright, clashing colours – an idea not considered sufficiently evocative or picturesque by the city authorities. Still, the churches are extremely impressive and the whole place faintly seductive.

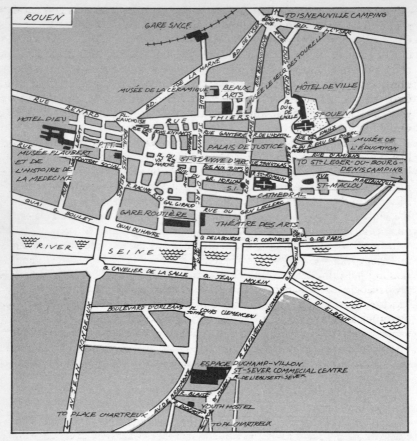

Socially, rather like London, the north of the city dominates, with south-of-the-river presented (falsely) as culturally barren. Politically, Rouen's docks and industries stretch out so far that many workers live outside the municipal boundaries which might explain why the Left is not in power. A tour of Rouen's politicians would, in fact, be even more interesting than its churches: the mayor is secretary-general of the UDF (the Giscard centrist conglomerate); Laurent Fabius was *député* for the area before being parachuted to Paris for premiership grooming, and the director of the Communist daily, *L'Humanité*, belongs to Rouen PCF.

The town

Rouen spends a bigger slice of its budget on **monuments** than any other provincial town, which maddens many a Rouennais – but as a tourist you'll probably not object. In fact your one complaint may be the lack of time to visit them all. The obvious buildings to look in at as you stroll round the centre are the Cathedral (Gothic perfection), the church of St-Ouen (ditto), the church of St-Maclou (Gothic-Flamboyant near perfection) and Joan of Arc's modern memorial church on the burning site at place du Vieux-Marché, and the Palais de Justice (Renaissance perfection). From the top of the belfry alongside the clock spanning rue du Gros Horloge, towers and spires array themselves in startling density: you can climb up to see them, 10–12.15 & 2.30–5.30; cl. Tues and Oct–March.

The west façade of the **Cathédrale-de-Notre-Dame**, sculpted intricately like the rest of the exterior, was Monet's subject for a study of changing light (the paintings are in Paris, see p. 78). Inside, the carvings of the misericords in the choir provide a study of 15C life – in secular scenes of work and habits as well as the usual mythical beasts. Unfortunately the ambulatory, with recumbent English royals and Diane de Poitier's husband's tomb, are only accessible via guided tour.

St-Ouen is larger than the Cathedral and has far less decoration, with the result that the Gothic proportions have that instant hard hit which nothing built since the Middle Ages can compete with. The world which produced it, and nearer the end of the era, the light and grace of St-Maclou, was one of mass death from the plague. The **Âitre St-Maclou** (entrance between 184 and 186 rue Martainville) was a cemetery for the victims, now the tranquil garden courtyard of the Beaux Arts school. If you examine the once open lower storey of the surrounding buildings you'll discover the original deathly decorations.

The **museums** – pick up a full list of addresses and times from the SI, 25 place de la Cathédrale – are, like the monuments, well up to standard: **Antiquities**, particularly good on tapestries; **Ceramics**, a speciality of Rouen; and the **Beaux Arts**, containing amongst the dominant 17C French contents, works by the Rouennais Géricault, Sisley and Monet in the Impressionist section, Dadaist pictures by Marcel Duchamp, and a collection of portraits by Jacques Emile Blanche (1861–1942) of his contemporaries – Cocteau, Stravinsky, Gide, Valéry, Mallarmé and others. Next door, on rue Jacques Villon, the **Musée Le Secq des Tourelles** has a brilliant collection of every sort and date of wrought iron object displayed in an old church. Opening hours for this, the *Beaux Arts* and *Musée de Céramique* are 10–12 & 2–6 (cl. Tues/Weds am); the *Musée des Antiquités* is open 10–12 & 2–5.30 (cl. Thurs); none is expensive.

On the corner of rue Eau de Robec and rue Ruissel there is, too, one of a new breed of intellectually self-conscious French museums – the **Musée de l'Éducation** (Tues–Sat 1–6), covering the upbringing, education and general influences on children. If you're interested in establishment French ideology it's illuminating. If not, **rue Eau de Robec** is itself a good example of Rouen restoration: a pure, shallow stream makes aesthetic appearances between paved crossings to the front doors of neatly quaint houses, now inhabited by successful antique dealers. In an earlier age these were described by one of Flaubert's characters as a 'degraded little Venice'. But to seek out the Rouen of the city's great novelist you now have to look in at another museum. This is not the *Pavillon Flaubert* at Croisset-Canteleu – which with the other literary museums (the two homes of Pierre Corneille) only prove the pointlessness of the genre – but the **Musée Flaubert et de l'Histoire de la Médicine,** at the Hôtel Dieu Hospital. It's on the corner of rue de Lecat and rue du Contrat Social in walkable distance from the centre (or bus 2a) and it's infinitely more relevant to Flaubert's writings than the manuscript copies and personal mementoes in the Pavillon museum. Flaubert's father was chief surgeon and director of the medical school, living with his family in this house within the hospital. Even during the cholera epidemic when Gustav was 11, he and his sister were not stopped from running around the wards or climbing along the garden wall to look into the autopsy lab. Some of the medical exhibits would certainly have been familiar objects to him – a phrenology model, a childbirth demonstrator like a giant ragdoll, and the sets of encyclopedias. Hours are 10–12 & 2–6 (cl. Mon); ring several times.

Practicalities

A 5min bus ride (nos 12/15/20) from the **gare SNCF** will bring you to the **centre** and it doesn't matter much whether you get off at the 3rd, 4th or 5th stop, the last being the Théâtre des Arts backing on to the river and one block east from the **gare routière.**

Cheap and central **hotel accommodation** is no problem: try hotels *Régent* (128 rue Beauvoisine), *des Flandres* (5 rue des Bons Enfants), *Saint Ouen* (43 rue des Faulx) or *Moderne* (59 rue St-Nicholas). The **youth hostel,** south of the river at 17 rue Diderot (35.72.06.45) is 10mins from the Théâtre des Arts on the bus lines to Grand Quevilly: stop *Diderot* on 5 or *Barcelone* on 6. The **campsites** are all out of town, the two closest are *L'Aubette* at 23 rue du Vert Buisson, Leger du Bourg Denis (bus 180 from gare routière, stop *Carville*); and *Le Cheval Rouge* at Isneauville (buses 15/151/150 from gare routière, stop *Cheval Rouge*).

Pâtisserie shops on almost every street gloat at being in the capital of the cream and butter province and a daily **food market** graces place Vieux Marché. For some good traditional cuisine, expensive but not outrageous, try *Le Vieux Carné* (34 rue Ganterie). A good, cheap midday **meal** can be had at *Le Green Park*, (9 rue Grand Pont) and for functional, and unpoisonous, eating there's *Matussière* (97 rue Ecuyère).

Rouen is said to be the capital of French **rock**, no great title perhaps. The place to check out bands is *Exo 7*, place Chartreux south of the river (buses 5/170/120) with live gigs at no 44 and disco Friday and

Saturday nights at no 13. Nearer the river, tucked into the St-Sever hypermarket, the *Espace Duchamp Villon* is the venue for (fairly) **alternative events** – theatre, cinema, dance and jazz (programmes from SI or newspapers). And for modern **visual arts**, there's the *Centre d'Art Contemporain* on the right bank (11 place Général de Gaulle). If you're planning to stay for more than a week or so, the annual handbook sold in all the newsagents, *Le P'tit Normand*, is very helpful, specially with restaurant addresses.

UPSTREAM: CHÂTEAU GAILLARD AND MONET'S GARDENS

Upstream from Rouen high cliffs on the north bank imitate the coast while looking down onto waves of green and scattered islands in the Seine. But the most dramatic sight, high above **LES ANDELYS,** is Richard the Lionheart's **Château Gaillard.** Constructed in a position of indubitable power, this looked down over any movement on the river at the frontier of the English king's domains. It was built in under a year (1196–7) and might well have survived intact into this century had Henry IV not ordered its destruction in 1603. It would, however, have taken more recent devices to reduce Château Gaillard to rubble: the dominant outline remains and, for once, there's free access at all times. The best route up is the path off rue Richard Coeur-de-Lion in LE PETIT ANDELYS.

For a strange and complete shift of mood you could, with a car or a lucky hitch, leave the ancient fortifications and be within half an hour in **Monet's gardens** with the waterlily pond at **GIVERNY**. Monet lived in this house from 1883 till his death in 1926 and the gardens that he laid out were considered by many of his friends his masterpiece. Each month is reflected in a dominant colour, as are each of the rooms, hung as he left them with his Japanese print collection. May and June, when the rhododendrons flower round the lily pond and the wisteria winds over the Japanese bridge in bloom are the best of all times to visit. But any month, from spring to autumn, is overwhelming in the beauty of this arrangement of living shades and shapes. You'll have to contend with crowds and little black boxes snapping up images of the waterlilies far removed from Monet's rendering – and admission is expensive – but there's no place like it. The gardens are open 10–6; the house 10–12 & 2–6, April–Oct only. If you want to see the real painted lilies, the best collections are in Paris – the Marmottan, Jeu de Paume and Orangerie.

Neither Giverny nor the Château Gaillard are easy to get to **by public transport**. Your best bet **for Giverny** from Rouen would be a train to VERNON and then a 10min ride on the *Gisor* bus from the station. **For Les Andelys** there's an infrequent bus from Rouen or, a bit more expensive but scenic, a tourist boat from by the POSES DAM (bus 130 from Rouen); the boat goes to Les Anderlys and Vernon – ask at Rouen SI for details. **Accommodation**, with just one cheap hotel at Les Andelys, *Au Soleil Levant* (2 rue Général de Gaulle) and a youth hostel in Vernon (28 av de l'Ile de France; 32.51.55.23) is not much easier. In such agreeable countryside so close to the capital where large country estates abound – empty half the time – and whole villages have turned into Parisian weekend colonies, it's assumed any visitor has a car.

BASSE NORMANDIE

Self-satisfied resorts for the capital's rich followed by the beaches of the Allied armies landings in 1944 and then the wilder, and in parts deserted, shore around the Cotentin peninsula make up the coast of Lower Normandy. Getting to see the top two favourite sights – Mont St-Michel and the Bayeux tapestry – is easy. What's more difficult, without wheels, is exploring inland – the constantly changing countryside, its edibles and intoxicants, the most famous taking its name from the *département* of Calvados.

EASTERN CALVADOS COAST: HONFLEUR TO CABOURG

Strong contender for cutest town in Normandy, **HONFLEUR** was a turn-of-the-century hangout of painters and poets. The municipal gallery has kept some of the paintings, the favourite views and buildings of the town got through the war without a scratch, but unfortunately the Bohemian life is no longer catered for. Meals, apart from crêpes and snacks, are expensive and so too are **rooms**: there are only two remotely moderate hotels, *des Pèlerins* west from the centre at 6 rue des Capucins (31.89.19.61) and, to the south, *de la Clair*, 77 cours Albert Manuel (31.89.05.95). For help, the **SI** is just outside the **gare routière** at 33 cours des Fosses or there's a campsite at the west end of bd Charles V on place Jean de Vienne. Transport connections for getting to Honfleur are sparse. The nearest train station is at PONT L'EVEQUE (20mins by bus on line 50, *Lisieux*). Otherwise you're dependent on buses – regular enough but only if you're coming from Caen or Le Havre (eight a day in each direction, line 20).

The painter Boudin, forerunner of Impressionism, was a native of Honfleur and there's a fair selection of his works in the **Musée Eugène Boudin** – west of the port on place Erik Satie. They have a certain appeal here in context, particularly the crayon seascapes, but it's the Dufys, Marquets, Friesz' and above all the Monets that most impress. Admission to the museum – cl. Jan–mid-Feb and Tues, otherwise summer 10–12 & 2–6, winter 2.30–5 (wkends also 10–12) – gives you access as well to one of Monet's subjects, the **Clocher Ste-Catherine**, built almost entirely of wood – supposedly due to economic restraints after the Hundred Years War. It makes a change from the great stone churches of Normandy and has an added peculiarity of a double nave. From the street behind you can see yacht masts through the windows of the houses that drop three storeys to quai Ste-Catherine below. These ill-matched, tottering, quayside houses harmonise in the most unlikely fashion to form a beautiful back-drop to the **Vieux Bassin**, once the walled city. This is good to wander in, and if you want direction has a few minor **museums**; the best of them, with diverse collections, is the *Musée d'Art Populaire* though visits – an hour's guided tour – aren't exactly casual.

Heading **west along the corniche** from Honfleur, green fields and fruit trees lull the land's edge and cliffs rise from sandy beaches all the way to TROUVILLE (15km). The **resorts** aren't exactly cheap but they're relatively undeveloped and if you want to stop by the seaside this is the place to do it. The next stretch, from Trouville to Cabourg, is the **Riviera of Normandy** with Trouville playing at Nice to Deauville's Cannes, except that they are hardly a stone's throw away from each other.

TROUVILLE retains some semblance of a real town, with a constant population and industries other than tourism. But it is still a resort – and has been ever since the imperial jackass, Napoleon III, started bringing his court here every summer in the 1860s. One of his dukes, looking across the river, saw, instead of marshlands, money, lots of it, in the form of a racecourse. His vision materialised and villas appeared between the racecourse and the sea to become **DEAUVILLE**. Now you can lose money on the horses, cross five streets and lose more in the casino, then lose yourself across 200m of sports and 'cure' facilities and private bathing huts before reaching the *planches*, ½km of duckwalk, beyond which rows of primary coloured parasols obscure the view of the sea. French exclusiveness and self-esteem oozes from every suntanned pore and a visit to the **SI** on place de la Mairie in Deauville – or by the casino in Trouville – is repaid with some spectacularly revolting brochures (in English). As you might expect, **hotels** are either upmarket or overpriced. If desperate, try *Le Lutrin* (48 rue Gambetta) in Deauville, *La Paix* (4 place F Moureaux) and *Charmettes* (22 rue de la Chapelle) in Trouville, or one of the three **campsites** (two in Trouville, one in Deauville). The **gares SNCF** and **routière** are between the two towns just south of the marina.

The smaller **resorts west towards Cabourg** are equally crowded and equally short on the inexpensive hotels. But they're less snobbish, and there are plenty of campsites and with an eye on the tides you can also escape the built-up promenades, walking beneath the **Vaches Noires** cliffs from VILLERS to HOULGATE (4½km). At **CABOURG**, however, you'll come face to face with a pure creation for a certain aged class. The town centre fans out in perfect symmetry fronted by the straightest promenade in France. The resort, contemporary with Deauville, seems to have stuck entirely in the 19C, immobilised by Proust perhaps, who wrote for a while in the **Grand Hôtel** – one of an outrageous ensemble of buildings around the **Jardins du Casino**. There's an **SI** here with full details on **rooms** (try hotels *Le Crible* on place du 8 Mai, on *Le Rally* at 5 av Général Leclerc). Arriving by **bus** you'll be dropped off at the gardens on av Pasteur. Walking through them and turning right on av de la Mer will take you down to the Jardins du Casino. By **train** you'll come in at Cabourg's much older neighbour, **DIVES**, which is just across the river. It has nothing in common with the aristocratic resort except for its significance to Proust. The land's end church of Balbec in *Du Côté de Chez Swann* is Proust's dream version of **Notre Dame** in Dives. There's a reasonable **hotel** here, *de la Gare*, and a lively **Saturday market** around the ancient timbered *halles*. If you want to **camp**, there's a site off the road between the two towns and a couple of others out from Cabourg on the road to Lisieux.

THE BESSIN: CAEN AND BAYEUX

From the air, **CAEN**, capital of Basse Normandie, must appear like a vast array of scattered crates and boxes interrupted by the spires and buttresses of the two abbeys and eight old churches, and the wide spaces inbetween taken up by roads and roundabouts. The central feature is the ring of ramparts that no longer has a castle to protect. Caen was substantially destroyed in two months of fighting in 1944 and some of the churches are still in ruins or mid-restoration. Unemployment is now salting the scars and the newest construction, a dangerous toy, Europe's largest particle accelerator for nuclear physics research, doesn't shorten the dole queues. Caen is the sort of town where the discos let women in free and where the annual listings guide gives a detailed rundown of the city's prostitutes. It's pretty dead in summer and the only people guaranteed to find any satisfaction here are church enthusiasts. The two great Romanesque constructions, **St-Étienne** and **Abbaye de la Trinité**, were built under the orders of William the Conqueror and his wife Matilda. For richness and grace they can't compete with the, recent by comparison, Renaissance stonework of **St-Pierre** church, but the exterior of St-Étienne with its monastic (now municipal) buildings alongside take some beating. As do, too, the stone pictures on the capitals in Matilda's abbey.

If you're going to stay, **accommodation** is no problem. There's *Zeralda*

(20 av de la Libération), *Demolombe* (36 rue Demolombe), *Cordeliers* (4 rue des Cordeliers) and *Centre* (98 rue St-Jean) to name but a few cheap hotels. Rue de Geole, a good restaurant street, runs parallel to the ramparts on the west side down to the central place St-Pierre where you'll find the **SI**. The **gare routière** is a few blocks west on rue des Bras and there are frequent buses between place St-Pierre and the **gare SNCF** south of the river. The town **campsite** is further upstream on route de Louvigny (bus 13, stop *Camping*), facing the desolate vast patch of green known as the Prairie.

BAYEUX – 15mins by train – is no great improvement on Caen, though redeemed for any half-interested visitor by its tapestry (and, at least in passing by its massive cathedral). **The Bayeux Tapestry** is housed in the **Centre Guillaume le Conquérant** (rue de Nesmond), signposted from all directions (open June–Sept 9–7, winter 9 or 9.30–12 & 2–6). Visits are well planned if slightly tortuous. You start off with a strip of canvas (almost the length of the original) with photographic extracts and detailed commentary, move on to slide projections on canvas hung as sails, then upstairs and into a plush cinema for a film on the general context, craft and yet another run through of the story (French and English versions alternate). Only after this – and the souvenirs desk – do you finally approach the real thing, a 70m strip of linen embroidered nine centuries ago with coloured wools. By this stage though, however annoying the build-up, you can race along reading the tapestries as you would a cartoon, which is really what its style resembles.

From the *centre* it is a short and very obvious walk to the **Cathédrale Notre-Dame**, Romanesque in part though rather losing its edge beneath the fungoid 18C baldequin that flanks the pulpit. Its crypt, however, is a beauty – the columns graced with frescoes of angels playing trumpets and bagpipes and looking tired for eternity.

If you want to stay in Bayeux, the street going north from the cathedral leads to the **SI** on the corner of rue Cuisiniers. Parallel, on rue Larcher, is a reasonable **hotel**, *La Tour d'Argent*. Another, *de la Gare*, is down by the railway station; or there's a **youth hostel** (July–Aug only; by the – very ordinary – war museum on rue des Cordelias) and **campsite** (alongside the northern bypass, bd d'Eindhoven). The **gare routière** is on the central place St-Patrice; following the main street in from here you'll arrive at the SI.

Heading **south-west from Bayeux**, just off the road to ST-LÔ, are two remarkable buildings: the **Abbaye de Cerisy-la-Forêt** (5km north, midway along) and the **Château de Balleroy** (3km south-east at the same junction). Neither are easy to get to without transport but with a bike or car you'd be foolish to miss them. Romanesque CERISY, with its triple tiers of windows and arches, laps light into its cream stone and makes you sigh in wonder at the skills of medieval Norman masons; it is open 9–6 (free visit). At BALLEROY, you switch to an era when architects ruled over craftsmen. The main street of the village leads straight to the Château, masterpiece of the celebrated 17C architect François Mansard and standing like a faultlessly reasoned and dogmatic argument for the power of its owners and their class. The present owner is the American press magnate Malcolm Forbes, pal of the likes of Nixon and Nancy Reagan; his is the enlarged colour photograph sharing the stairwell with Dutch still lifes and he's made a mark on most other aspects of the house, too – only the *salon* has been left in its original state of glory with brilliant portraits of the then royal family by Mignard. Admission (expensive) includes a *hot air balloon museum*, one of Mr Forbe's hobbies; hours are 9–12 & 2–6, cl. Weds.

THE D DAY BEACHES

Over 100,000 soldiers are buried in the cemeteries along the beaches from the mouth of the Orne to Les Dunes de Varneville on the Cotentin peninsula – the opening scenes of the Allied offensive of June–August 1944. The ensuing **Battle of Normandy** also killed thousands of civilians and reduced nearly 600 towns and villages to piles of rubble but, within a week of its conclusion, Paris was liberated.

Bits of shrapnel could still be found, and sold, along with packets of sand, in the recent junketings of the 40th anniversary celebrations. And every other coastal village has its **War museum** – peculiar places since they would be unbearable if they really represented their subject. Instead they're full of Boys Own fodder – weapons, models, uniforms and a superabundance of authentic trinkets – and tell the story of the great altruistic USA descending like an avenging angel (with the other armies in tow) to end the Second World War. The simultaneous breakthrough on the eastern front by the Russian allies goes unmentioned. Nor is there any recollection of the British civilians being blitzed by doodlebugs while building the invasion material, or by V2s well after August 1944, and as for events in Japan 1945, they rarely feature in the French conception of the last war.

Of large scale debris left in situ, the most remarkable are the remains of the prefab **Port Mulberry** lying on the seabed and on the beach at ARROMANCHES-LES-BAINS. And if you can forget D Day, this is also great **seaside**: sand and seafood (best oysters at Courseulles), plenty of campsites and no Deauville chic. From Bayeux the *coastal buses* are 74 for Arromanches and Courseulles; 70 for Port-en-Bessin and Vierville and 7/30 for Isigny. Reasonable priced **places to stay** include at ARRO-MANCHES, *Hôtel de Normandie* (place du 6 Juin); at PORT-EN-BESSIN, *de la Place* (quai Letourner); at ISIGNY-SUR-MER, *du Commerce* (5 rue E. Demagny) and a youth hostel (in the Stade Munici-pale; June–Sept; 31.22.00.33) at VIERVILLE-SUR-MER.

CHERBOURG TO MONT ST-MICHEL

If the murky metropolis of **CHERBOURG** is your port of arrival, best head straight for the **gares** SNCF and **routière** on either side of av Millet behind the inner dock. Travelling by bus is not easy in northern Cotentin. Nor is hitching: the local *patois* has a special pejorative word for 'stranger' used for foreigners, Parisians and southern Cotentins alike. But if you can make your way west to **LA HAGUE**, the northern tip of the peninsula, you'll find wild and isolated countryside where you can lean against the wind, watch waves smashing against rocks or sunbathe in a spring profusion of wild flowers. With a bit of luck you will miss the plutonium production plant near Jobourg and its discharge released 5km off Cap de la Hague. Bracken-covered hills and narrow valleys lead up to the west coast and the Nez de Jobourg cliffs, claimed in wild local optimism to be the highest in Europe but dramatic enough nonetheless. On the other side, facing north, PORT RACINE is known as the smallest port in France and probably is. **Accommodation**, however, is distinctly lacking in these half tumbled down villages. There are **campsites** at OMONVILLE-LA-ROGUE, VAUVILLE and further afield at URVILLE-NACQUERVILLE (which also has the hotel *Beaurivage*).

South of La Hague a great curve of sand – some of it military training ground – takes the land's edge to FLAMANVILLE and another nuclear installation. But the next two sweeps of beach down to CARTARET, with sand dunes like mini mountain ranges, are probably the best beaches in Normandy if you want solitude. There are no resorts, no hotels and just two **campsites** – at LE ROZEL and SURTAINVILLE.

ST-LÔ, the chief town of the Manche *département*, was completely devastated in the 1944 Battle of Normandy. In its new form it is in parts very ugly, sometimes curious, and, in the case of the **Cathedral**, astonishingly brilliant. The main body of this building has been repaired and rebuilt with its strange southward veering nave, but the shattered west front and the stump of the collapsed north tower have been joined by a startling sheer wall of icy green stone. Close by, in the central **place Hôtel de Ville**, are the curiosities: a Resistance monument at an ivy hung door (all that is left of the old prison), and, a few metres away, a lighthouse-like 1950s folly – which you can climb; ask at the Mairie. Worth time too is the **Musée des Beaux Arts**, cramped at the back of the Mairie and full of treasures: a Boudin sunset; a Lurcat tapestry of his dog Nadir and the Pirates; works by Corot, Van Loo, Moreau; a Léger watercolour; a series of extraordinarily unfaded 16C Flemish tapestries on the lives of two peasants, and sad bombardment relics from the town. It is open 10.30–12 2.30–6/5; cl. Tues & Sun am, and it is free. St-Lô is not really a place to base yourself but if you need somewhere to stay *La Laiterie Normande* (1 av de Verdun), *Régence* (18 rue St-Thomas), *Les Ramparts* (3 rue des Prés) and *de la Piscine* (13 promenade des Alluvions) should all have **cheap rooms**. The **SI** is just off the central square at 2 rue Havin; the **gare routière** south of place Hôtel de Ville on rue Octave Feuillet, the **gare SNCF** is just across the river to the east.

Trains from St-Lô go to **COUTANCES** on the west coast then down to Mont St-Michel. If you're remotely interested in church architecture take it in two steps. The famous **cathédrale de Notre-Dame** of Coutances holds forth in Gothic glory from the summit of the town and the hard walk up from the station is well rewarded. Further south the crowded towns and small resorts all compete for views and proximity to that hard act to follow, the island across the bay, **MONT ST-MICHEL.**

> I reached the huge pile of rocks which bears the little city dominated by the great church. Climbing the steep narrow street, I entered the most wonderful Gothic dwelling ever made for God on this earth, a building as vast as a town, full of low rooms under oppressive ceilings and lofty galleries supported by frail pillars. I entered that gigantic granite jewel, which is as delicate as a piece of lacework, thronged with towers and slender belfries which thrust into the blue sky of day and the black sky of night their strange heads bristling with chimeras, devils, fantastic beasts and monstrous flowers, and which are linked together by carved arches of intricate design.

Maupassant's description, and as accurate today. But a warning: this is, after Versailles, the most visited monument in France; there are rip-off shops, bars and hotels and wafts of gastronomic delights – the fluffy omelette speciality – that are way overpriced. Guided **tours of the abbey** are from 9.30–5.30 (10–12 & 1.30–4 in winter). The nearest **gare SNCF** is at Pontorson (6km south) where you can hire a bike from the station or take an expensive bus to the Mont. As far as **accommodation** goes, you could try *Le Normandie* hotel (82 rue St-Michel) but don't bank on rooms being available. There is, however, a campsite. Other hotel possibilities, all on bus 12 from the Mont (though this has only one service daily) include *Le Pommery* in CEAUX (11km east); *La Grillade* (*Chez Arsene*) in PONTAUBAULT; *Le Select* (11 rue de Montain) in AVRANCHES or a number of places in St-MALO (see p. 160 in the following chapter). Pontaubault and Avranches also have campsites.

INLAND: BOCAGE NORMANDE TO PAYS D'AUGE

The wooded country of southern, **inland Contentin** – and above all the **Bocage Normande** – is Normandy's cider and calvados country. Both are much in evidence, along with more durable specialities, at **VILLEDIEU-LES-POÊLES**, literally 'City of God the frying pans'. A touristified place, kitchen utensils and copper souvenirs gleam from all its shops and the **SI** on place des Costils has lists of *ateliers* to visit and details of the copper work museum. There are though other interests – including one of the twelve bell foundries left in Europe, the **Fonderie Cornille Havard** at 13 rue du Pont Chignon. Work here is part time due to limited demand but it's always open during the week (8–12 & 2/1.30–6/5.30) and you may find the forge lit. If this small town charms you into staying, there's a **campsite** by the river and a reasonable **hotel**, *de Paris*, on the route de Paris. The gare SNCF, on the Paris-Granville line, is just south of the town. Going anywhere off the railway line is more problematic. There is a bus connection to PONTORSON, but only once a week – a pattern repeated elsewhere inland, where there are hardly any big towns. If you have got wheels though you can buzz down south and sample some **calvados**, the great Norman apple brandy, at the Co-*Opérative Fermiclava* ISIGNY-LE-BUAT (wkdays 10–5; on grand Chemin) or *Gilbert* (Manoir du Coquerel, MILLY; Mon–Fri 8–12 & 2–5, Sat 8–12) and walk it off in the park of **St-Symphorien-des-Monts** (7km south-east of St-Hilaire). The park – open from 9–8 mid-March to mid-November – is expensive but tranquility is assured, particularly towards evening. It's a wonderful place: contented-looking beasts like yaks and bisons, and threatened domestic animals, graze in semi-liberty in fields and woods around a lake inhabited by swans and flamingos.

To the east cider and calvados are joined by **poiré**, a less known and uncommercialised fermented pear drink – sometimes very good. This region, stretching from MORTAIN to within a few kilometres of MORTAGNE-AU-PERCHE is part of the Parc Naturel Régional Normandie-Maine, covered in forest and orchards and dotted with the odd châteaux and abbey. It is well outside the mainstream of tourism and is not very rich – the *parc* encourages small-scale production of cider, honey, even rabbits, as long as the *paysans* can continue to make ends meet. If such low key endeavours sound interesting make your way to the *Maison du Parc* at CARROUGES (between the village and the château). They're an excellent source of information for accommodation, bike hire, *dégustations*, ruined castles and canoeing.

To the north, between CAEN and FLERS, you enter an area known as the **SUISSE NORMANDE**. This is a little far-fetched – there are no actual mountains – but it is nevertheless quite distinctive. The river Orne has cut a deep valley through the rocks, leaving cliffs and crags amidst wooded hills at every turn. A 35min bus ride from Caen (line 34) brings you into the region at **THURY HARCOURT** where the SI in place St-Sauveur can suggest walks, rides, *gîtes d'étape*, etc. and *SIVOM* at 15 rue de Condé hires out canoes. The central town – on the same bus line – is **CLECY** (SI at Mairie) where tourists well outnumber residents in summer. Children might like the model railway here at the **Musée du Chemin de Fer Miniature** in the Parc des Loisirs (open June–mid-Sept 10–12 & 2–7), but there's not much to keep you in these towns and certainly no cheap accommodation.

Finally, there's the **Pays d'Auge**, extending inland from the Côte Fleurie to the department of Orne along the Touques and Vie rivers. This embraces such places as PONT l'EVÊQUE and CAMEMBERT and, as you might expect, dairy cows munch on the lushest Norman pastures for the good of best selling cheeses. The old farmhouses and manors in crisscross soft red stonework are as pretty as the orchards and cows. But it's really the food that's of most interest. As well as cheese, the dish to go for is *Poulet Vallée d'Auge*, chicken cooked in cream, calvados and cider.

The largest town of the d'Auge, LISIEUX, is 35mins by train from Caen – another war-damaged city though the bombs spared its Gothic cathedral. It's not the pleasantest place in Normandy but if you're travelling through it is good on cheap **accommodation**: *Condorcet* (26 rue Condorcet), *Lourdes* (4 rue au Char), *Maris Stella* (56bis rue d'Orbec). The **SI** at 11 rue d'Alençon (left out of the station, then right) can provide the details for the rural area. Some hotels to try further south are *La Couronne* (7 rue du 8 Mai) and *Le Soleil d'Or* (16 place Mackau) in VIMOUTIERS and *de l'Ouest* and *de l'Etoile* in GACE. Both towns also have **campsites**.

TRAVEL DETAILS

Trains
Through services to Paris connect with all ferries at Dieppe, Le Havre and Cherbourg: if you're doing this it's easiest to buy a combined rail-ferry-rail ticket from your point of departure.

From Dieppe 5 daily to Rouen (¾hr); 5 daily to Paris-St-Lazare (2¼hrs).
From Le Havre at least hourly to Rouen (¾hr) and Paris (2hrs).
From Rouen 8 daily to Caen (2¼hrs); at least hourly to Fécamp (1hr) and to Paris-St-Lazare (1¼hrs).
From Caen at least hourly to Paris-St-Lazare (2¼hrs); 2 daily to Rennes (2hrs) via St-Lô (1hr), Coutances (1¼hrs) and Mont St-Michel (1½hrs); 9 daily to Le Mans (2hrs) and Tours (2½hrs); hourly to Cherbourg (1–1½hrs).
From Cherbourg frequently to Caen (1¼hrs) and Paris (3¼hrs).
From Granville 13 daily to Paris-Montparnasse (3½hrs).

Buses
From Dieppe 5 daily to Paris (2¼hrs);

1 daily to Fécamp (1½hrs).
From Rouen hourly to Le Havre (2¾hrs); 2 daily to Dieppe (1¾hrs), Fécamp (2½hrs) and Lisieux (2½hrs).
From Caen 3 daily to Le Havre (3hrs), via Cabourg, Deauville and Honfleur; 4 daily to Fécamp (1½hrs).
From Lisieux 5 daily to Honfleur (¾hrs).

Ferries
From Dieppe *Sealink* (35-84.22.60) to Newhaven (4 daily in 4hrs).
From Le Havre *Townsend Thoresen* (35-21.36.50) to Portsmouth (2 daily in 5½hrs). *Irish Continental Line* (35-26.57.26) daily to Cork (21½hrs) and to Rosslare (21hrs). *P & O Normandy Ferries* (35-26.57.26) to Southampton (2 daily in 5½hrs).
From Cherbourg *Sealink* (33-96.70.70) to Portsmouth (1 daytime crossing; 4¾hrs) and to Weymouth (1 daytime crossing; 4½hrs). *Townsend Thoresen* (33-44.20.13) to Portsmouth (3 daily; 4¾hrs). *Irish Continental Line* (33-44.28.96) to Rosslare (17hrs).

Chapter four
BRITTANY

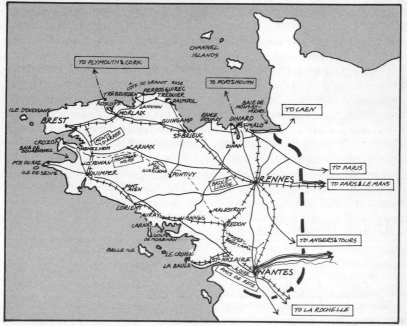

There's no one area – and certainly no one city – in **Brittany** that typifies the province's character. It lies in the people more than the places. For generations Bretons risked their lives fishing and trading on the violent seas or struggled with the arid soil of the interior. And this toughness and resilience is touched by the Celtic culture: mystical, musical, sometimes morbid and defeatist, sometimes vital and inspired.

The last independent ruler of Brittany, the Duchess Anne, succeeded in protecting Breton **autonomy** only through marriage to two successive French monarchs. After her death, in 1532, François I moved in, taking her daughter and lands, and sealing the union with an act supposedly enshrining certain privileges. These included a veto over taxes by the local *parlement* and the people's right to be tried, or conscripted to fight, only in their province. The successive violations of this treaty by Paris, and subsequent revolts, form the core of Breton history since the Middle Ages. Maintained often as a near colony, Bretons have seen their language steadily eradicated, and the interior severely depopulated through lack of centralised aid. Today, the people still tend to treat France as a separate country, even if few of them actively support Breton **nationalism** (which it's a criminal offence to advocate). The recent economic resurgence, helped partly by summer tourism, has largely been due to local initiatives. Ignoring Paris pressures, **Brittany Ferries** have re-established an old trading link, carrying Breton produce as well as passengers across to Britain and Ireland. At the same time a Celtic artistic identity has consciously been revived. At local festivals, and above all the **Interceltic festival** at Lorient in August, traditional Breton music, poetry and dance are given great prominence; while if you're actually a fellow Celt (Welsh speakers will be understood) you'll everywhere be treated as a comrade.

For most visitors to this province, though, it is **the Breton coast** that is the dominant feature. After the Côte d'Azur, this is now the most popular summer resort area in France – for both French and foreign tourists. The attractions are obvious and real enough: warm white sand beaches, towering cliffs, rock formations and offshore islands and islets, and everywhere the stone *dolmen* and *menhir* monuments of a prehistoric past. The most frequented areas are the **Côte d'Emeraude**, around **St-Malo**, and the **Morbihan coast** below **Auray** and **Vannes**. Accommodation and campsites here are plentiful, if pushed to their limits through from mid-June to the end of August, and for all the crowds there are resorts as enticing as any in the country. Over in **southern Finistère** ('land's end') and along the **Côte de Granit Rose** in the north you may have to do more planning. As, too, if you come to Brittany well out of season, when many of the coastal resorts close up completely.

But whenever you come, and wherever you're headed, don't leave Brittany without having visited at least one of its scores of **islands** (the **Île de Bréhat** is one of the best and most accessible), nor without taking in cities like **Quimper** and **Morlaix**, testimony (like the parish *enclos* of Finistère) to the riches of the medieval duchy. And take time out, too, from the coast to explore **the interior**, particularly the western countryside around the **Monts d'Arées** and the **Montagne Noire**. Here you pay for the solitude with very sketchy transport and few hotels. But Brittany is one of the few areas of France where *camping sauvage* (outside sites) is tolerated, there are sporadic *gîtes*, boats for rent on the **Nantes-Brest canal**, and hitching is very possible so long as you're happy to travel relatively small distances.

Finally, a note on the **Pardons**, pilgrimage-festivals organised around local saints, which guidebooks (even local tourist offices) tend to try to promote as spectacles. They are not, unlike most French festivals, phoney affairs kept alive for the tourists, but instead deeply serious and rather gloomy affairs. If you're looking for traditional Breton fun, and you can't make the Lorient festival (or the smaller *Quinzaine Celtique* at Nantes in June/July), the events to look out for are gatherings organised by the numerous local **Celtic folklore groups** – *Cirlces* or *Bagadou*.

RENNES, THE CÔTE D'EMERAUDE AND ÎLE DE BRÉHAT

If you're coming from Paris, **Rennes** is probably your best initial target. The administrative centre of Brittany, it's well connected with the capital (3 hours by train from the Gare Montparnasse) and has sources of information for just about anything you might care to do in the province. To the west is one of the mythic regions of the country – Merlin's forest of **Brocéliande**. North, you'll find good transport access to the port of **St-Malo**, medieval **Dinan** and, beyond, the **Côte de Granit Rose** and the **Île de Bréhat** – arguably most beautiful of the Breton islands.

RENNES AND BROCÉLIANDE

Capital and power centre of Brittany since the 1532 union with France, **RENNES** seems, outwardly at least, uncharacteristic of the province, with its neoclassical layout and the pompous scale of its buildings. It was burnt, very severely, in a fire of 1720 and the remodelling was handed out to Parisian architects – not in deference to the capital but to rival it.

Arriving here at the **gare SNCF/gare routière**, you may feel like moving straight on. But there's interest enough in and around the city if you're not exclusively committed to the picturesque. Buses 1/20/21/22 will take you into the central **place de la République** (the 4th stop). Nearby, at the Pont du Nemours, is the main **Tourist Office** for the province (Mon–Sat 9–7.30; cl. lunchtimes and Mons out of season) where you can pick up full lists of Breton campsites, hostels and hotels. Further info on bikes, riding, hiking-routes, waterways and boat or canoe can be obtained at the **Association Bretonne** (*ABRI*) office at 3 rue des Portes Mordelaise (Mon–Sat 9–12 & 2–6), the last gatehouse left of the ramparts in the city's one surviving medieval quarter. Among **central hotels**, try *de Léon* (15 rue de Léon), *Le Magenta* (35 bd Magenta), *St-Malo* (8 rue Dupont-les-Loges) and *Le Riaval* (9 rue de Riaval). The **youth hostel** is a couple of kilometres out at 40 rue Montaigne (on bus route 1 towards Torigne: stop Léon Bourgeois). Bus 3 takes you north-east to Gayeulles (direction St-Laurent) where there's a bit of a walk down a lane to the city's **campsite**.

The city's one central building to survive the great fire was symbolically enough, the **Palais de Justice**, home of the old Rennes *parlement* – a mixture of high court and council with unelected members. You can see round this building where the *parlement* fought battles with the French

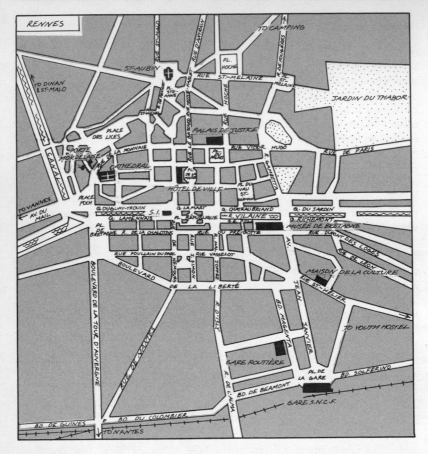

governor from Louis XIV's reign up until the Revolution. Tours are at 9.45, 10.30, 11.15, 2.15, 3, 4, 4.45 daily in season, cl. Tues and start from the far right-hand corner of the courtyard. The series of 17C chambers are each more opulently gilded and adorned than the one before, culminating in the debating hall hung with Gobelin tapestry scenes in the history of the duchy and the province. Every centimetre of the walls and ceilings is decorated – the Sun King style but on a relatively small scale.

On the other side of the sordidly channelled Vilaine river, at 3 quai Emile Zola, the **Musée de Bretagne** gives one of the best possible introductions to the culture and history of Brittany. Its presentation is impressively accessible with a startling section dealing with the transition from the 19C to the present century – an ongoing process which you'll experience in peculiar jolts of time lag as you travel around Brittany. The building also contains an outstanding collection of pictures, from Leonardo drawings to 1960s abstracts in a **Musée des Beaux Arts**. One room is dedicated to Brittany with mythical scenes – the Ile d'Ys legend by Luminais – and real life – a woman waiting for the fishermen to come back through stormy seas. Both museums are open 10–12, 2–6, cl. Tues, with a cheap combined ticket.

The main **medieval quarter** that escaped destruction is bordered by the canal to the west and the river to the south. This is the liveliest part of town and stays up late, particularly around St-Aubin church. Good cheap **food** is to be had at *La Ship Shop*, 30 rue St-Malo; there's an excellent *crêperie* at 5 place Ste-Anne and round the back, through an archway off rue Motte Fablet, you can get a wonderful view of medieval high-rise housing. More **restaurants** (including the vegetarian *Le Verseau*, 8 rue St-Melaine) and an interesting selection of **bars** are congregated around place St-Michel and rue de Penhoet. A mixed gay bar, run by Lesbians, is at 21 rue St-Malo, *Le Galago*: another nearby, *La Tringuette*, is more male-orientated.

Lastly, a few **incidentals**: If you're interested in talking to Breton campaigners, the place to go is the *Centre Rennais d'informations Bretonnes* (30 place des Lices). For cassettes of Breton-Celtic music, books, posters and postcards take a look at *Co-op Breizh* (17 rue Penhoet). The *L'Arvor* **cinema** (29 rue d'Antrain) shows v.o. (original language) films. And if you plan on reasonably long-distance **hitching**, the *Allostop* number is 99.30.98.87.

Brocéliande – the Forêt de Paimpont

Thirty km to the west of Rennes, the **Forêt de Paimpont**, known also by its ancient name of *BROCÉLIANDE*, is Merlin's forest. Medieval Breton minstrels, like their Welsh counterparts from whom or with whom the stories originated, set the tales of King Arthur and the Holy Grail both in *Grande Bretagne* and here in *Petite Bretagne*. For all the magic of these shared legends, however, and a succession of likely-seeming sites, few people come out here. If you like the idea of a day's roaming about it isn't difficult. The bus from Rennes to Guer runs twice a day past the southern edge of the forest, stopping at FORGES-LES-PAIMPONT, and another, around the north corner, to MAURON.

MAURON is a good point to start. From the hamlet of FOLLE PENSÉE, just south of the village, it's a circuitous but enjoyable 20 min walk to **La Fontaine de Barenton** – Merlin's spring. The path leads off from the end of the read at FOLLE PENSÉE, turning to the right, it runs through pines and gorse to a junction of forest tracks: here take the track straight ahead for about 100m and an unobvious path to the left goes into the woods and turns back north to the spring – walled and filled by the most delicious water imaginable, as you might expect from the elxir of eternal youth. After drinking, stroke the great stone slab beside the spring to call up a storm, roaring lions and a horseman in black armour. This is where Merlin first set eyes on Vivianne who bound him willingly in a prison of air.

Another forest walk, more scenic but without a goal, is the **Val sans Retour** (the Valley of no Return), off the GR37 from Tréhorenteuc to La Guette. The path to follow leads out from the D141 just south of TRÉHORENTEUC to a steep valley from which exits are barred by thickets of gorse and giant furze on the rocks above; it at one point skirts an overgrown table of rock, from which the seductress Morgane enticed unwary boys.

If you feel like **staying** in these parts, there is a *gîte d'étape* at FORGES-LES-PAIMPONT (on the GR37, past the Val), c/o Mme Farcy (99.06.93.46), and another at the larger village of **PAIMPONT**, c/o M & Mme Grosset (99.07.81.40). Paimpont, which is probably the best place to stay, also has two **campsites** – and an **SI** in the abbey on the edge of its lake. Or, alternatively, you could make slightly further afield to **CONCORET**, with a **youth hostel** and, a couple of kilometres east, another lake, the **Etang du Comper**, flanked by the one-time château of the enchantress Vivianne.

THE RANCE ESTUARY: ST-MALO, DINARD AND DINAN

West of Norman MONT ST-MICHEL (see p. 152), the first Breton town of any real consequence is **ST-MALO**, one of the more pleasant (if also more costly) French ports to arrive by ferry from England. A walled city, built with the same grey granite as the Mont, it presents itself only to the sea and to the Rance estuary. If you're approaching from Rennes, and feeling leisurely you can appreciate this best by making the last stretch **by boat** – either from DINARD, just across the estuary, or, a little extravagantly, from DINAN. For details of both, see below. Otherwise, coming in by bus or train, you'll find the old city concealed by modern suburbs right until you're in it: the **buses**, however, do take you to the main city gate, the **Porte St-Vincent;** **trains** stop at the docks, 10mins walk away.

Once within the old ramparts, St-Malo can seem slightly grim and squat, and over-run by summer tourists – it is the most visited place in the province. But once you leave the popular thoroughfares of this tiny **citadelle**, with its high, late 17C stone houses, random exploration is fun and you can surface to the light on the ramparts or pass through them to the beaches. The **town museum**, in the castle to the right as you enter Porte St-Vincent, glorifies, on several exhausting floors, St-Malo's sources of wealth and fame – colonialism, slave trading and privateering amongst them. In the 1530s a St-Malo sea captain disembarked from the

St Lawrence river and declared Canada to be the possession of the King of France; the early free market economist, originator of the term *laissez-faire*, was a *Malouin* and, the town's proudest possession, buried on the *Ile de Grand* (which you can walk to from the citadelle at low tide) is the poet Chateaubriand. Chateaubriand's French fame, as one of his contemporaries, Marx, explained is 'because he is the most classic incarnation of French *vanité* in every regard . . . the false profundity, Byzantine exaggeration, emotional coquetry . . . in form and content a never-before-seen mishmash of lies'. Suitably enough, he features heavily on all the tourist brochures – as does his rather dull childhood mansion at nearby COMBOURG.

Some **hotels** to try in the old city are *Fougères* (4 rue Groult St-Georges), *Annick* (13 rue du Boyer) and *Marguerite* (2 rue St-Benoît). There's a **campsite** in Paramé, the eastern suburb, at 13 rue des Ecoles, and a **youth hostel** at 37 av Père Umbricht (99.56.15.52). If you have problems, the **SI** is just in front of the Porte St-Vincent.

The road **from St-Malo to Dinard** crosses the estuary along the top of the world's first **power dam** which, alas, failed to set a non-nuclear example to the rest of the province. You can see how it works in a half-hour visit (8.30–9) from the entrance on the west bank, just downstream from the lock. If you're catching the bus between St-Malo (St-Vincent gate) and Dinard, get off at LE RICHARDAIS for the dam, and at *Gallic* for the centre of Dinard.

DINARD with casino, spacious shaded villas and a social calendar of regattas and ballet, owes its metamorphosis from a fishing village, like the Côte d'Azur resorts it resembles, to the tastes of the affluent 19C English. It's an expensive and not especially welcoming place to stay – the only reasonably-priced hotels are *de l'Arrivée* (5 place de la Gare) and *Petit Auberge* (64 av George V) – though pleasant enough to while away the odd hour. If you do so, you'll find an enjoyable coastal path, Promenade du Clair du Lune: this goes up from the estuary beach, *plage du Prieuré*, over the tiny port, and up to Pointe du Moulinet for views over to St-Malo. You can continue round the point to another beach, by the casino, and on round more rocky outcrops to a more secluded strand at neighbouring ST-ENOGAT.

The **boats from Dinard** (tickets at 27 av George V, regular departures) to St-Malo are fun; down the Rance to Dinan they become real pleasure trips. Approached by a steep and cobbled street with fields and bramble thickets on either side, up to the 600-year-old ramparts partly hidden in the trees, **DINAN** itself is rather wonderful. Its citadel has preserved almost intact its 3km circuit, and inside are street upon street of late medieval houses. It's a bit too good to be true, in brochure terms, but surprisingly not excessively deluged with tourists. There are no very vital museums: the monument is the town, and time is easiest spent in rambling from crêperie to café, admiring the houses on the way. Unfortunately there's only one small stretch of the **ramparts** that you can walk along – from the gardens behind St-Saveur to just short of the Tour Sillon – but you get a good general overview from the **Tour de l'Horloge** (open July–Aug only 10–12 & 2–6; cl. Sun) on rue de l'Horloge or from the top of the keep guarding the town from the south. The latter, known as the Château Duchesse Anne is open 9–12 & 2–7 (earlier Tues and out of season) and includes admission to the nearby **Tour Coëtgen** where stone 15C nobles have been grouped together like some kind of medieval time capsule, about to depetrify at any moment. In the valley just beyond the château there's an animal park and playground – good for kids bored with the Middle Ages.

St-Saveur church, which seems an inevitable target of any Dinan wanderings, is a real mix-up of ages, with a Romanesque porch and 18C steeple. Even its nine Gothic chapels have numerous and asymmetrical vaulting; the most complex pair, in the centre, are wonderful and would make any spider proud. North of the church rue du Jerzual leads down to the gate of the same name and on down (as rue du Petit Fort) to a majestic old bridge over the Rance, lined with artisans' shops and restaurants.

Modern Dinan does exist, though rather gloomily, excluded from the *enclos*. In it you'll find the **gares SNCF** and **routière** a short walk away from place Duclos and the Grande Rue entrance to the citadel (left along rue Carnot and right at place du G Leclerc). Two **hotels** near the station are *de France* (7 place du 11 Novembre) and *de la Consigne* (40 rue Carnot). Within the walls there's *du Théâtre* (2 rue Ste-Claire) and *La Duchesse Anne* (10 place Duguesclin). The **SI** is opposite the Tour de l'Horloge in the Hôtel Kératry; the closest **campsite** is at 103 rue Chateaubriand which runs parallel to the western ramparts. Dinan's **youth hostel** (39.10.83), in the Moulin de Méen at TADEN is not on any bus route; if you follow the *quai* seawards from the port on the town side you'll see a small sign to the left after 2 km.

AROUND THE COAST TO BRÉHAT AND THE *GRANIT ROSE*

West from Dinard rocky points and huge, ruddy-coloured cliffs dominate the coast. There are small resorts between them – some like ST-CAST undeniably attractive – but for the most part this is an overdeveloped and expensive stretch, and its beaches, for all their prettiness, overexposed. If you want a place to stop en route to the Ile de Bréhat and the more enticing Côte de Granit Rose, there's a primitive, summer-only **youth hostel** at PLEVENON, 4 km back from the dramatic (and touristed) Cap Frehel, and another, if this is full, at the otherwise dour **ST-BRIEUC**.

Best, if you're heading for Plevenon, to confirm a place in advance (96.61.29.33; July–Aug). If you're driving, or cycling, the church at KEKMARIA NISQUIT is worth a detour, with medieval frescoes of Ankou – death's labourer – in his usual skeletal guise enticing the rich, the religious and the poor to join him in a dance of death.

Île de Bréhat

The ÎLE DE BRÉHAT – in reality two islands joined by a tiny bridge – gives the appearance of spanning great latitudes. On the north side it's windswept meadows of hemlock and yarrow, sloping down to chaotic erosions of rock; on the south, you're in the midst of palm trees, mimosa and eucalyptus; and all around are a multitude of little islets – some walkable at high tide, others *propriété privée* and most just pink-orange rocks. Connected regularly by **ferry** (10mins) from POINTE DE L'ARCOUEST (a short bus ride or hitch from the fishing port of PAMPOL) it has to be one of the most beautiful places in Brittany, or for that matter France.

As you might suspect, this island paradise has attracted Parisians and the like looking for holiday homes. Over half the houses now have temporary residents and young *Bréhatins* leave in ever increasing numbers for want of a place of their own – or work. In winter the remaining 300 or so natives have the place to themselves, without even a *gendarme*; summer sees two imported from the mainland, along with upwards of 3,000 tourists. As one of their number, though, you should find the *Bréhatins* friendly enough – it's the second home owners they can't stand.

Inevitably the island's three **hotels** are permanently booked in summer (and expensive); in winter only *Aux Pêcheurs* stays open. But for **campers** Bréhat has a wonderful site in the woods high above the sea west of the port and when it's closed you can pitch your tent almost anywhere. From the port the right hand track leads past the island's only *bike hire* outlet and then turns north towards **Le Bourg** – Bréhat village – where the square is the centre of all activity. An *SI* is in the old Mairie on the right and most days there's a small market; restaurants are neither numerous nor cheap so picnic fare is the best bet. The beach that's swimmable at low tide is the **Grève de Guerzido** on the east side facing the mainland. Up nearer the town the water is a bit murky and the east coast generally is less accessible because of private estates. But in the north, even when Le Bourg is blocked up with visitors, you can walk and laze about in near solitude. Bréhat no longer has a castle, (blown up twice by the English) but it does have a 19C **fort** (in the woods before the campsite) with outer defences and inner courtyard planted with flowers and vegetables by a dozen squatters who don't have to worry about eviction threats from the sympathetic island council.

The Côte de Granit Rose

Named, logically enough, after its pink-tinged granite rock, this most northern reach of the Breton coast is, like Bréhat, littered with hundreds of islets and rocks, making appearance with the tides. It runs, flanked a little inland by the GR34, between PAIMPOL and TRÉGASTEL. **Bus services** are virtually non-existent, other than between these two towns and LANNION, so if you plan to explore in any real way, wheels of some kind are essential. So too, unless you're highly organised, is a tent. There are **campsites** dotted all along the coast but little other accommodation: a **youth hostel** at LANNION (6 rue du 73ᵉ Territorial; 96.37.91.28) and a couple of **gîtes d'étape**, at LOUANNEC (c/o Mme Kremer, *Villa Stelle*; 96.23.15.62), east of PERROS GUIREC, and south of TRÉGUIER near LA ROCHE DERRIEN (*Château de la Roche Jagu*; 96.95.62.35).

In passing, take a look at **TRÉGUIER**, an ancient diocese with a fine cathedral, and **LANNION**, with its Église de Brelevenez. Neither town, however, holds much joy. Nor, really, do the resorts between PERROS GUIREC and TRÉBEURDEN, where the water-carved rocks have been given the names of legendary figures, skulls, rabbits, even pancakes. **TRÉGASTEL**, with a campsite, and **TRÉBEURDEN**, with a youth hostel (96.23.52.22), are functional stopovers. At PERROS GUIREC, the big resort, you can take a **boat trip** out to the seabird reserve of the **Sept Îles** (June–Aug, usually at 2pm, sometimes also 9am). Strangest sight along this coast, however, outdoing anything the erosions can manage, is just south of TRÉGASTEL-BOURG, on the route de Calvaire, where an old stone saint halfway up a high calvary raises his arm to bless or harangue the gleaming white discs and dome of the Lannion telecommunications research centre.

FINISTÈRE – THE LAND'S END

It's hard to resist the lure of the **Finistère coast** – with its dramatic cliffs and headlands – but in summer at least you'll do well to steer clear of the brochure sights of **Crozon** and the **Pointe de Raz**. Instead, try basing yourself at either **Morlaix** or **Quimper** (each good for a long stay), climb the **Menez Hom** to admire the anarchic limits of western France, or, with a tent and transport, make for the near wilderness of the **northern stretches** beyond Brest. And explore **inland**: the best part of the Breton interior for cycling or walking, scattered with a grand series of medieval churches.

Making for Finistère **from Paris**, Quimper is just 6hrs distant and reasonably well connected.

MORLAIX, ROSCOFF AND SOME BRETON CHURCHES

MORLAIX, one of the great old Breton ports, thrived off trade with England, in between wars, during the 'Golden Period' of the late Middle Ages. Built up the slopes of a steep valley with sober stone houses, its present grandeur comes from the pink granite viaduct carrying trains from Paris to Brest way above the town centre. Though there's not a great deal to do here, save exploring the paths and stairways up the valley, Morlaix is a lot livelier than most Breton towns and a good base for visiting the grand *enclos*, or parish churches (see below), dotted about the countryside towards Brest.

Orientation is quite straightforward. The central square, with the local SI and Hôtel de Ville, is **place des Otages**. To its south extends the **old town**, once a walled and moated *citadelle*, and still with plenty of medieval houses to remember its existence. If you arrive at the **gare routière** you'll find yourself a couple of blocks from the main *place*, towards the port on **place Cornic**; from the **gare SNCF** the quickest route down to the centre is along the Venelle de la Roche, which also brings you out at place Cornic. Inexpensive and central **hotels** to try include *du Roy d'Ys* (8 place des Jacobins); *des Halles* (23 rue du Mur); *Ste-Melaine* (77 rue Ange de Guernisac) and *des Arcades* (11 place Cornic). For the **youth hostel** (3 route de Paris; 98.88.13.63) take the KERNÉGUES bus from the Hôtel de Ville as far as rue de Paris — the route de Paris is just beyond if you turn left at place Traoulen. The same bus in the opposite direction takes you to LA VIERGE NOIRE and its **campsite** (on the right about 250m walk further north). The streets between Église St-Melaine (above the SI) and place des Jacobins in the old town are the best **restaurant** hunting grounds. You can also get a good value basic meal at *Hôtel des Halles* and guinness at a bar on the south side of place des Halles. For late evening **drinking**, *La Père Ubu* (37 rue de Callac, near the youth hostel) has good taped music, darts and boisterous Bretons till 1am (midnight in winter cl. Sun/Mon) and occasional café-théâtre and live jazz.

North of MORLAIX, and connected by SNCF trains and buses, **ROSCOFF** has taken over now as local port, with regular **ferry services** to Plymouth (see p. 181) and to the nearby Île de Batz. A small resort in its own right, sheltering a nice enough beach, Roscoff can be a pricey place to stay — if you plan to do so, pick up a list of phone numbers at Morlaix and call ahead. The **ÎLE DE BATZ**, served several times daily during summer months (sporadically in winter), is a different matter. Arrive at the quay and old island town and you can walk uphill to a **youth hostel** (98.61.77.69) or **campsite**. There are fewer attractions than on Bréhat but also fewer tourists and finding an albeit windswept stretch of coast to yourself is little problem.

Inland to Brest – the Breton *enclos*

Breton Catholicism has a very distinctive character, closer to the celtic past than to Rome. There are hundreds of saints who've never been approved by the Vatican but whose brightly painted wooden figures adorn every Breton church. Their stories merge with the tales of moving *menhirs*, ghosts and sorcery; visions and miracles are still assumed; and death's workmate, Ankou, is a familiar figure, even if no one now would dread his manifestation.

Many of the churchyards – **enclos** – in this part of Brittany have outside the porch stone calvaries sculpted with detailed scenes of the Crucifixion above a crowd of saints, gospel stories and legends. In the richer parishes a high stone arch leads into the churchyard adjoining an equally majestic ossuary, where the old bones would be taken when the tiny cemeteries filled up. Most of them date from the two centuries on either side of the union with France in 1532 – Brittany's wealthiest period – and nothing is more telling of the decline in the province's fortunes. Everywhere you'll find magnificence in the *enclos paroisseau* (parish), often decorated inside as richly as the architectural ensemble out, while their villages are now often close to the breadline.

The three most famous *enclos* are the neighbouring parishes of **GUIM-ILIAU, ST-THÉGONNEC** and **LAMPAUL-GUIMILIAU**, south-west from Morlaix on the SNCF bus route. At Guimiliau poor **Katel Gollet** (Katherine the Damned) is depicted tormented in hell – for the crime of hedonism rather than manslaughter. In the legend she danced all her suitors to death until the reaper-figure **Ankou** stepped in to whirl her to eternal damnation but at **LA ROCHE** (15km or so on towards Brest), where the ruined castle above the Elhorn estuary is said to have been her home, it is Ankou who appears on the ossuary with the inscription 'I kill you all'. If you've wheels, a 5km detour south-east of La Roche brings further variations at **LA MARTYRE** (where Ankou clutches his disem-bodied head) and its adjoining parish PLOUDIRY, the sculpting of its ossuary affirming the equality of social classes – in the eyes of Ankou. Best of all the Ankou representations, however, is at **PLOUMILLIAU**, between Lannion and Morlaix (and again on the bus route) where he stands in the church, a wooden skeleton 1m high with scythe and spade; this used to travel with every coffin to the local cemetery, the familiarity of his figure perhaps making death less sinister.

If these *enclos* spark your interest, and you've time or ideally a car, **other calvaries** to take a look at include PLEYBEN, south of the Monts d'Arées; LANRIVIAN, in the centre of Brittany; and GUEHENNO, south-west of Josselin. Another Breton church speciality is the intricate carving and paintwork of **rood screens**: exceptional examples are the St-Fiacre chapel outside LE FAOUET (between Lorient and the Montagne Noire) and the chapel at KERFONS (south of Lannion), though both wonderful works of art are kept locked up save for one *pardon* and for visitors in July and August.

OUT FROM BREST: THE CROZON PENINSULA AND MONTS D'ARÉES

You may need to change buses in the monstrous port of **BREST** but there's little to entice you to stay. If by some chance you're stuck for a night, there's a reasonable **youth hostel** 2km from the gare SNCF at LE MOULIN BLANC (98.41.90.41; take the *Autobus Rouge* from the station). Otherwise head out fast.

Stretching southwards from BREST, the central **coast of Finistère** is a torn chaos of estuaries and promontories, easing into more conventional sands only at the Bay of Douarnenez. The most dramatic feature is the **Presqu'île de Crozon** – the Crozon peninsula, a craggy outcrop of land shaped like a long-robed giant, arms outstretched to defend bay and roadstead. With wheels (see below for bike hire details) make for **MENEZ HOM**, at the giant's feet, where you can climb up for a really grandiose view of the land and water alternating out to the ocean. Getting down to the coastal headlands themselves can be a bit of a disappointment after this vision: CAP DE LA CHEVRE (the southern point), POINTE DU TOULINGUET (east of CAMARET) and the northern arm all have military installations, and the other extremities are overvisited. But it is the cliffs that tourists make for here and some of the **beaches**, like **LA PALUE** on the southern arm, are almost deserted. The more crowded resorts of **CAMARET** and **MORGAT** are attractive enough, too, though accommodation at these can be expensive. But there are **campsites** all around the peninsula and its hinterland, and a fair number of reasonable **hotel possibilities**: at CAMARET, *du Styvel* (quai Styvel); at MORGAT, *des Grottes* (102 bd de la France Libre); at TAL AR GROAS, *de l'Aber*; at ROSCANVEL, *Kreis Ar Mor*; or at PLOMODIERN, *La Crémaillère*. There's also a **gîte d'étape** at KERDILÈS, 1km from Landevennec (c/o M & Mme Gall. 98.27.31.49) and another at POLÉBRET PLAGE near Plomodiern, (c/o M Kervella; 98.26.50.14). **Bikes** can be hired at FAILLER (34 rue de Poulpatré) or in the main town of CROZON where the SI is on place de l'Église. Morgat also has an *SI* just before the beach on bd de la France. There are three **buses** a day from LANDEVENNEC along the peninsula to CAMARAT via CROZON and ROSCANVEL; and five from CHÂTEAULIN SNCF to PLOMODIERN, CROZON and CAMARAT.

Inland, this reach of Brittany is still more rewarding, with the Breton landscape rising to a rare but convincing impression of mountains – the Monts d'Arées. First though a quick excursion, if you've transport, east from the Menez Hom; the village of **TRÉGARVEN**. This has one of those small, quirky museums of France, ludicrous enough on paper but with a definite fascination on the spot. The **Musée de l'École Rurale**, it is housed in the village's old secondary school, closed down due to lack of numbers in 1974 and re-opened recently as a re-creation of a Breton classroom around 1920. Its interest, as the caretaker – one of the school's last five pupils – will explain, lies in the fact that at this date all the kids would have spoken Breton at home and been forbidden to speak it here. The teacher gave a little wooden cow to the first child to utter a word and they could get rid of the *vache* only by squealing on the next offender. The lesson, to parents and pupils alike, was obvious enough: that Breton was backward and a handicap. It was taught, with considerable success, throughout the province, and only recently have things begun to change. Breton language primary schools do now exist; a sixth former, after battles with Paris, was allowed to pass all his *Baccalauréat* papers which he'd written in Breton; and the SNCF had to back down after refusing a cheque made out in Breton. If such matters hold interest, the museum is open from May–Sept from 2.30–7; it stands at the crossroads of the ARGOL-DINEAULT and TRÉGARVEN-MENEZ HOM routes, unconnected by bus.

The **Monts d'Arées** seem even higher than they are – rising only to 380m at the wild-looking ridge encircling the Lac de Brennilis. But, forming part of the **Parc Naturel Régional d'Amorique**, they provide grand backdrop to some attractive hiking country. Going up to the ridge itself, you should be wary of peat bogs round the lake (and the Brennilis nuclear power station and its military antennae neighbours). But there is lovely countryside amid the **Forêt de Huelgoat**, a fabulous arrangement of rocks, waterfalls, grottoes and a gurgling stream. To explore this, the best base to make for is **HUELGOAT** itself: **stay** either at the *Hôtel l'Armorique* (1 place Aristide Briand; 98.99.71.24) or the campsite (a short walk towards the lake along the Brest road). The **SI** here will show you maps of the region, and try to sell you a plan of the woods though you don't really need it – every rock and path is signposted and most tracks rewarding. Alternative places to stay in this region include a good smattering of **campsites**; **hotels** at BRASSPARTS (Auberge de Terroir, route du Faou), BERRIEN (Hôtel des Monts d'Arées), LOCMARIA BERRIEN (Auberge de la Truite) and SIZUN (des Voyageurs, 2 rue de l'Argoat); and a couple of **gîtes** at LE FAOU. Bikes can be rented at Huelgoat (from the garage at 1 rue du Lac) and several of the other villages.

To the south, Brittany's other 'mountain range', the **Montagne Noire**, lacks credibility, despite a spiky rise to the stark slate landmark of the **Roc de Toullaëron**. Over to the west, nearer the sea, is the fantasy village of **LOCRANON** – on the minor road from the Crozon peninsula to Quimper. Locranon's merchants of unreality are a sequence of film directors, most notably and most recently Roman Polanski, who used this as the setting for Tess. For its filming every visible porch had to be changed, and new windows inserted on the Renaissance houses of the main square, to make the place more English. All because of Roman's passion for youth, and France's lenience on extradition. The town's main source of income is in fact highbudget tourists, who buy, indiscriminately, carved wooden statues by local artisans, pottery from the Midi or leather jackets, provenance unknown. Every sort of craft artefact is sold in this village, some of it produced in open **ateliers**, others through the hands of third parties whose sleek cars are parked beside the shops. One of the artisans suggested converting the loft above his studio to a *gîte d'étape* for young people but the idea was rejected out of hand by the powers that be. If you stop, count on moving on: Quimper, more welcoming and exciting, is only a few stops beyond on the bus.

QUIMPER AND THE LAND'S END *POINTES*

QUIMPER, capital of the ancient diocese, kingdom and later duchy of Cornouailles, is the oldest Breton city. According to the only source – legends – the original bishop of Quimper, St Corentin came with the first Bretons across the channel to the place they named Little Britain, some time between the 4C and 7C. He lived off half a regenerating and immortal fish all his life and was made bishop by one King Gradlon, whose life he later saved when the seabed city of Ys was destroyed. According to one version, Gradlon built Ys in the Baie de Douarnenez protected from the water by gates and locks to which only he and his daughter had keys. She sounds like a pleasant sort, giving pet sea dragons to all the citizens to do their errands but St Corentin saw decadence and suspected evil. He was proved right: the princess's keys unlocked the gates, the city flooded and Gradlon escaped only by obeying Corentin and throwing his daughter into the sea. Back on dry land and in need of a new capital, Gradlon founded Quimper.

Modern Quimper is very laid back, the sort of place you could do a lone night's café crawl without paranoia. And it's not bad-looking either, with old granite buildings, two rivers and the rising woods of Mont Frugy overlooking the centre of town. There's no pressure to rush round monuments or museums and you can get to the sea in unhurried fashion on a boat down the Odet.

A short walk along the Odet brings you from the **gare SNCF** and main **gare routière** to the centre of the city around the enormous **Cathédrale St-Corentin**. A construction problem faced this, back in the 15C, when the nave was being added to the older chancel: the extension would either have hit existing buildings or the swampy edge of the then unchannelled river. The masons eventually hit on a solution and placed the nave at a slight angle – a peculiarity which, once noticed, makes it hard to concentrate on the Gothic splendours within. The exterior, however, gives no hint of the deviation, with King Gradlon mounted in perfect symmetry between the spires – though whether he would have advised a riverbed nave is another question. Alongside is the **Bishop's Palace**, also slightly quirky in its construction with a wonderful spiral staircase.

The Bishop's Palace houses a small, very forgettable museum of Breton bits and pieces. Much more compelling is the **Beaux Arts** in the Hôtel de Ville (9.30/10–12 & 1.30/2–7/6; cl. Tues) with its amazing collections of drawings by Cocteau, Max Jacob and Gustav Doré (shown in rotation) and 19C and 20C paintings of the Pont-Aven school and Breton scenes by the likes of Eugène Boudin. If you're interested in seeing pottery made on an industrial scale, and an exhibition of the changing styles since the first Quimper ateliers of the late 17C, the **Faïenceries de Quimper** is another worthwhile visit. It's on Place Berardier, downstream from the centre on the south bank of the Odet (half-hour guided visits, Mon–Fri 9.30–11.30 & 1.30–5).

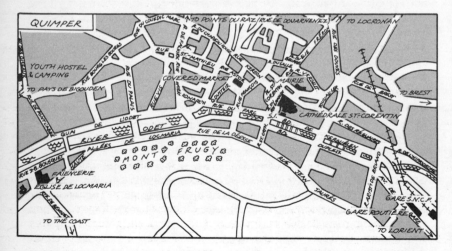

The liveliest corner of Quimper, with good crêpes and ice creams while you mull around in the cafés, is usually **place du Beurre**. Around the church of **St-Mathieu** can be fun, too, and across the river there are a couple of good **bars** on rue St-Catherine – draught guinness at no 15. The **covered market** is quite a delight, not just for the food, but for the view past the upturned boat rafters through the roof to the cathedral's spires.

As for **details**, the **SI** (by the cathedral at 3 rue Gradlon) can supply lists of just about anything you might have in mind. If you're leaving **by bus** check with them where to make for – departure points for different companies and destinations are spread all over town. Best value of the **hotels** are the *de Cornouaille* (46 rue A Briand, by the *gares*), *de l'Odet* (83 rue de Douarnenez) and *Sapinière* (286 route da Benedot). The **campsite** and **youth hostel** are downstream at 6 av des Oiseaux in the Bois du Seminaire (Bus 1, direction Penhars; stop *Chaptal*). **Bikes** can be hired at *M Hénaff*, (107 av de Ty Bos). During the week preceding the last Sunday in July there's the **Festival Cornouailles**: a jamboree of Breton music, costumes and dances: and every room in the town taken.

Down the Odet – and out to the headlands

Boats down the Odet to the coast leave from the end of quai de l'Odet, opposite the Faïenceries; times vary with the tides so check with the SI (who also sell tickets). Once out of its city channel the Odet takes on the anarchic shape of most Breton inlets, spreading out to lake proportions then turning narrow corners between gorges. The upmarket resort of **BENEDOT**, the boat's destination, has little appeal but you can always head east for more of the Breton speciality – alluring beaches. This bottom corner of Brittany, the **Pays de Bigouden**, is also the place you're most likely to see women wearing coiffes for non-promotional reasons. The local variety is fairly startling – 30cm high tubes of lace that stay on defying gravity in the strong gusts of wind. World **windsurfing championships** are held at **POINTE DE LA TORCHE**, at the southern end of the Baie d'Audierne, and there are usually some afficionados of the sport twirling about with effortless ease. But warning signs about swimming should not be ignored. For safer seas framed by white sand beaches there's the coast from PENMARCH to LOCTUDY and beyond. It's about an hour on the bus from Quimper to this southern tip and it's one of the more frequent services.

An hour and a half's bus ride east of Quimper takes you to the land's end of France, the **POINTE DU RAZ**. As you approach, the vision of the ocean is blocked by a hypermarket of souvenir shops and then military installations but once past these you reach plummeting fissures, filling and draining with deafening force, and can walk on precarious paths above them (shoes that can grip are not a bad idea). Two stops back on the bus back to AUDIERNE, the odd graffiti on walls and boardings is the only reminder that this is **PLOGOFF** where ecologists, autonomists and, principally, the local people fought riot police and paratroopers for six weeks in 1980 to stop the opening move in a nuclear power station project. The plans have not officially been dropped though they are 'shelved' by the present government.

For details on the southwards continuation of the Breton coast – towards Lorient and Vannes – you'll need to treat the following section (Nantes and Southern Brittany) in reverse. Heading inland, see p. 180 for PONT-AVEN and QUIMPERLÉ, p. 173 for the NANTES–BREST CANAL.

NANTES AND SOUTHERN BRITTANY

Nantes, the original medieval capital of Brittany, is another obvious approach to the province: like Rennes, it is well served by trains from Paris (3½hrs), and a principal transport hub for the region. **Inland** from here the main interest lies along the **Nantes-Brest canal**. Towards the sea the Loire estuary with its dying industries is redeemed by the magnificent bridge at St Nazaire. **The coast**, with the warmest Breton beaches, is another matter – crowded to the gills through July and August with both French and foreign tourists.

NANTES, THE CANAL AND THE ESTUARY RESORTS

The medieval associations of **NANTES** are dwarfed by the later dominance of its port and the wealth gained from colonial expeditions, slave trading and shipbuilding and the recent, but now declining, industrial growth. It's enormous, exhausting to get round and claustrophobic, with tower blocks masking the Loire and dual carriageways tearing the city. Very much a gateway to Brittany – of which it is no longer officially a part – rather than any end in itself.

The city's **Castle**, however, is one of the most historic points in all Brittany – witness to the Act of Union and to the 1598 Edict of Nantes, which enshrined certain Protestant privileges and lasted almost a century. It is moated today by traffic rather than water, but, within easy reach of the **gare SNCF** (to the west) and **gare routière** (on av Carnot, due south) is a good place to make for with time to spare between buses or trains. There's free admission to the courtyard and ramparts (10–12 & 2–6) while an additional ticket buys entry to three small and interestingly laid out **museums**. The *Musée des Salorges* covers the economic activity of the city over the last 200 years; *des Arts Populaires* has a good collection of furniture, costumes, tools and musical instruments (which you see still in everyday use in parts of Finistère); and the more unusual *Musée des Arts Décoratifs* is of contemporary textile work.

To the west and north of the castle spreads the **medieval extent** of the city, with plenty of places to eat and drink (and the **SI**) grouped about place du Change. If you're stuck here, the cheapest place for **rooms** is *Centre Jean Macé*, 90 rue du Préfet Bonnefoy, north of the castle. Otherwise try the hotels *Ste-Reine* (1 rue Anatole le Braz), *Trianon* (43 bd Victor Hugo) or *Sanitat* (18 rue d'Alger).

The Nantes-Brest canal

The **Nantes-Brest canal** is one of the pleasantest routes through the Breton interior – whether on the water or walking or riding along the tow paths. It is cut halfway by the barrage of LAC DE GUERLEDAN making the stretch from Pontivy to Carhaix unnavigable except for canoes. But the eastern part through MALESTROIT and JOSSELIN is a substantial trip in itself. And if you can get together a group of four or six people, hiring a boat works out little more expensive than hotel rooms; though the price jump in July and August is considerable. The best **boat hire** near Nantes is *Flotte Vacances*, Base Nautique, Suce-sur-Erdre (40.25.18.87), 35mins by train on the Chateaubriant line. For information about **canoe hire** go to the Nantes *Centre Régional d'Information Jeunesse* (10 rue La Fayette).

If you just want to take in one stretch of the canal, on or off the water, **MALESTROIT** is undoubtedly the best place to make for. Secluded inland, it is little bothered by the frenetic summer resorts around Quiberon and in addition to its own medieval charms boast one of the most interesting museums around – dedicated to the activities of the Breton Resistance during the last war. To reach the town there are **buses** (sporadically) from Nantes, more regularly from Vannes (see p. 181). There's just one **hotel**, *Aigle d'Or* (1 rue des Ecoles), which isn't cheap but has a reasonable restaurant and there are alternatives in a **gîte d'étape** up at the canal lock (c/o M Halier; 97.75.11.66) and a **campsite**, below the main bridge. The **gare routière** is on the main bd du Pont Neuf; the **SI**, further down the road towards the bridge, can provide details of **canoe and boat hire**; and the Aigle d'Or rents out **bikes**.

The centre of Malestroit, a short walk from any of these points, is **place du Bouffay**, by the church. As you come into the square you'll see the leaning, half-timbered house on the corner with, on different beams, an anxious bagpipe-playing hare looking over its shoulder at a dragon's head, and an oblivious sow in a blue buckled belt threading her distaff. Throughout the town medieval monsters, twisted faces and beasts of all descriptions peer from the buildings. The only ancient walls without adornment are the ruins of the **Chapelle de la Madeleine**, east of the river before it joins the canal, where one of the many temporary truces were signed during the Hundred Years War.

The **Musée de la Résistance Bretonne** is beyond ST-MARCEL, a small village off the Vannes road, 2km from Malestroit (no bus). The museum is on the site of a battle in June 1944 in which the Breton *maquis*, joined by Free French Forces parachuted in from England, successfully diverted the local German troops. The strongest feature in the presentation is the illustration of the pressures that made the majority collaborate: the reconstructed street corner in which all life has been jerked out by the occupiers; the big colourful propaganda posters offering work in

Germany, advertising executions of *maquis*, equating resistance with aiding US and British big business; and against these, the low budget, flimsily printed Resistance pamphlets. (It's open 10–7 June–Sept, otherwise 10–12 & 2–6.)

If you're heading north along the canal you'll soon come to the three Rapunzel towers embedded in a vast sheet of stone of the **château** of **JOSSELIN**. The family in possession of this used to own a 'third of Brittany, though the present proprietor contents himself with the position of local mayor. Tours of the pompous apartments of the ducal residence are not very interesting but the Duchesses' collection of dolls from all parts of the world, housed in *Musée des Poupées* behind the castle, is rather special. Hours for both are May–Sept 10–12 & 2–6 (cl. Mon); the rest of the year 2–6 only on Weds, wkends and holidays. There's another **gîte d'étape** and **canoe hire** by the lock.

The Loire estuary and nearby resorts

In summer Nantes and its fellow port and shipbuilding city of St-Nazaire empty for seaside weekends: at LA BAULE, the chicest resort in Brittany; at LE CROISIC or BATZ-SUR-MER, less refined to the west; or to the almost unbroken line of holiday flats, *Pepsi* and *frites* stands of the PAYS DE RETZ coast, south of the Loire estuary. But none of these options compete with the Gulf of Morbihan (covered in the following section) nor with most of Finistère, but if you're looking for a quick dash to the sea and a beach there are functional possibilities. And if you're making for the mouth of the Loire there is also an inspiring piece of engineering – the Pont de St-Nazaire, a great elongated S-curve of a suspension bridge, its lines only visible at an acute angle at either end. Driving across it inflicts a hefty toll, but bikes go over for free.

The best sandy coves in the region, bizarrely enough, are to be found on the outskirts of **ST-NAZAIRE**: just off to the west, they are linked by wooded paths and near deserted. But it's a gloomy city, bombed near to extinction in the last war, and with its shipyards, once the most important in France, closing all around it. The one reason you might want to stay here, though, is relative ease of finding accommodation – elsewhere in short summer demand. Among the least expensive options are **hotels** *Normandy* (35 rue de la Paix), *Touraine* and *Windsor* (at 4 and 53 av de la République) and a **hostel**, the *Foyer du Travailleur* at 30 rue Soleil Levant. Frequent **trains** run through Nantes to St-Nazaire (in 40mins) and on westwards to the resorts – PORNICHET, LA BAULE-ESCOUBLAC (20mins), BATZ and LE CROISIC.

Approaching **LA BAULE** on the train from Nantes makes for a startling contrast of economics and social patterns. All the little estuary towns en route have been struck hard by unemployment, along with the cities at either end but when you reach the seaside the affluence seems almost ludicrous. Around La Baule's crab-shaped bay bronzed nymphettes and would-be Clint Eastwoods ride across the sands into the sunset – a scene completed by cruising lifeguards, horse dung removers and fantastically priced cocktails. Everything, in fact, is expensive at La Baule, with even the campsites charging hotel prices. But the beach, undeniably, is impressive and there is, too, a brilliant ice-cream shop, *A Manuel*, on the corner of the promenade.

Cheaper campsites, sporadically available rooms and above average beaches can be found at **PORNICHET** (just east of LA BAULE if you want to commute in) and at **BATZ–SUR-MER**.

To the north, for another total switch, are the semi-deserted peat bogs of **LA BRIÈRE**, whose remaining inhabitants still cut the peat, fish for eels in the streams and gather reeds. Tourism, recently, has arrived and is resented. The touted attraction is hiring a punt, which will get you lost for a few hours with your pole tangled in the rushes. Not recommended.

VANNES AND THE GOLFE DE MORBIHAN

It was from **VANNES** that the great Breton hero Nominöe set out to unify Brittany, beat the hell out of the Francs and push the borders past Nantes and Rennes to where they were to remain up until the French Revolution nearly a millenium later. Here too the Breton *Etats* assembled to ratify the Act of Union in the building known as *La Cohue*. So, **Vieux Vannes**, the old centre of chaotic streets, crammed around the cathedral, ramparted and enclosed by gardens and a tiny stream, has reason to feel smug.

From the **gare SNCF** and main **gare routière** it's about 10mins' walk, to the right then left down rue Olivier de Clisson, to the new **centre** of town – shifted outside the medieval city in the 19C craze for urbanization. The grandest of the public buildings here, guarded by a pair of sleek and dignified bronze lions, is the **Hôtel de Ville** at the top of rue Thiers. Walk a couple of blocks down from it and you'll find the SI (with free maps and usual bundles of information) at no 29. In peak season Vannes can become quite claustrophobic but it still offers a better choice of **hotels** than anywhere else around the Golfe. Two central ones are *La Bretagne* (34 rue du Méné) and *Le Moderne* (2 rue de la Boucherie). There are cheaper places on rue Olivier de Clisson, and on that east side of town there's *Au Relais Nantais* (38 av A Briand) and *La Marée Bleue* (8 place de Bir Hakeim). For food, Vieux Vannes is nothing but restaurants, *crêperies*, ice-cream parlours and *pâtisseries*. But for brasseries and café watching go to place Gambetta overlooking the port below the southern gate of the ramparts.

A late night bar (open till 1am) with a friendly atmosphere and Irish folk bands is *Le Pandemonium* on rue de la Boucherie. By day, even if you're set on heading coastwards, Vieux Vannes demands some exploration. **La Cohue**, stretching between rue des Halles and the Cathedral Square, has reverted after 750 odd years to its original use as a marketplace (for crafts now), having served in the meantime as high court and assembly room, prison, revolutionary tribunal and theatre. The local *Beaux Arts* has taken over its top floor while the stalls below offer a short cut through to the cathedral: the latter a waste of time, aesthetically speaking, save for an early medieval box, beautifully painted with somewhat bizarre scenes, in the *Sacristy* (10–12 & 2–5 in summer, cl. Suns). Nearby in rue Noë is the **Château Gaillard**, its archaeological finds from 400,000BC to the Roman occupation laid out with great precision, and round the corner in **Hôtel de Roscannec** (19 rue des Halles) there's an equally efficient display of stones, fossils, shells and stuffed birds. Both museums are open June–Sept 9.30–12 & 2–6, though it seems a pity you can't just stumble on their exhibits lying about on the beaches or strewn around the dolmens and tumuli.

Morbihan – and its islands

Vannes is on the sea since its harbour is a channelled inlet of the ragged-edged **Golfe de Morbihan**, which lets in the tides through a narrow gap between the peninsulas of Rhys and Locmariquer. By popular tradition the **islands** scattered about this enclosure used to number the days of the year, though for centuries the waters have been rising and there are now just under one for each week. Of these, thirty are owned by film stars and the like, while two – the ÎLE AUX MOINES and ÎLE D'ARZ – have regular populations and ferry services. The rest are the best, and a boat tour, about them, or at least a trip out to GAVRINIS, is one of the most compelling attractions of southern Brittany.

There are dozens of different **gulf tours** available in season (all of them detailed by the Vannes SI) but the best value is probably from PORT NAVALO (four buses daily from Vannes) where the *TCVP* ferries run from mid-March to mid-September or, if you just want to visit Gavrinis, the *VBA* ferry from LAMOR BADEN (every ½hr from 9–11 & 1.30–5.30 late March–late Sept; on demand the rest of the year). Trips direct from VANNES itself cost a bit more.

The **islands of the gulf** – and indeed this whole region – are dotted with prehistoric **stoneworks**: *dolmens* (flat stones) and *menhirs* (long stones) as they are known from the local language. The ÎLE DE GAVRINIS has the most interesting – a tremendous dolmen where the stones of the chamber are all carved with curving lines, slightly Aztec in style, which the archaeologists, for want of imagination, say are purely decorative. Another dramatic group of menhirs, arranged in a figure of eight, are to be seen on the tiny barren island of **ER LANNIC** – though only at low tide when the water gives these smaller islets the appearance of stranded hovercrafts, skirted with mud.

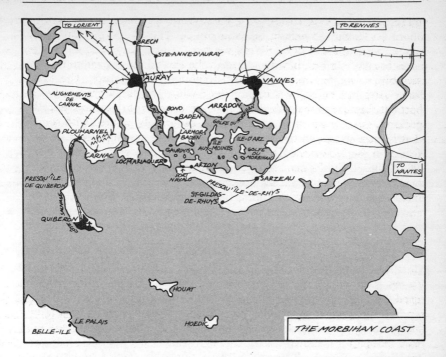

THE MORBIHAN COAST

Despite the attractions of the southern edge of the gulf – the warmer side, where pomegranates, fig trees and camelias flourish as well as the cultivated oysters on the mud – the currents of the gulf make this no place for swimming. The ocean beaches on the Presqu'île de Rhuys are the places to head for: east from **ST-GILDAS-DE-RHUYS** is the most enticing and least crowded stretch with glittering gold and silver coloured rocks. There's a campsite at St-Gildas as well as at **SARZEAU, PORT NAVALO** and **ARZON** – all on the bus from Vannes. Over to the north bus services are more restricted with just one daily connection to LAMOR BADEN and BADEN, and one to the village of **LOCMARIQUER** (with a change at AURAY) where you'll find more campsites and remains of the largest known menhir.

AURAY AND THE PRESQU'ÎLE DE QUIBERON

Blocking the ocean to the west of the Golfe de Morbihan, the **Quiberon peninsula** is a long established resort area – very crowded and very expensive through July and August. On its periphery, however, is the most famous and spectacular of prehistoric Breton sites, the 2,000-menhir alignments of **Carnac**; while, if you're into islands, there is good access to **Belle Île** or the smaller, hardier **Îles de Houat** and **Hoëdic**.

Auray

There's something slightly dull about **AURAY** – with its twee, over-restored old quarter – but it's a lot less crowded than Vannes, a lot cheaper than Quiberon town, and usefully poised for exploring Carnac, the peninsula or even the gulf. Paris-Quimper **trains** make a stop here (there's a summer-only connection on down to Quiberon) and you can hire **bikes** at the station – worth doing, whatever your plans, since it's a good 20mins walk in to the centre, place de la République. **Hotels** to try, at pretty much average prices, are *Moderne* (in the *place*), *L'Armoric* (St-Goustan), *Belvédère* (2 rue du Belvédère) and *Ty Guen* (93 av de Gaulle). The **SI**, also in the *place*, have various local maps; or if you're making for the islands, you can pick up comprehensive details at the *Îles du Ponant promotional association* at 11 place du Joffre. The town's most remarkable building – by far – is close by here, a vast Gothic church, dissolved by Louis XIV and now let out to clubs, with stray cats and the odd wrecked car keeping an eye on the gargoyles.

But it is the **St-Goustan quarter** that the town showpieces – a brief freewheel along rue du Château and across its highly picturesque bridge. On foot you can make your way down through Promenade du Loch to the river. The quarter, tarted up with expensive restaurants, has a fine enough setting, though beyond that it's a little empty in feel and interest. Its **quay**, downstream, is named, surprisingly, after Benjamin Franklin – who landed here, blown off course from Nantes, on his way to sign the first ever US-French alliance in 1776.

More rewarding, if you're rented wheels, is to head out to CARNAC (see below); to the evocative **Abbaye de Chartreuse** (on the left, north of the station), with its sculpted reliefs by David d'Angers of the 18C Royalist rebellion, in part an independence struggle, and piles of bones (10–12 & 2–5.30); or to the **Ecomusée St-Degan** (July–mid-Sept only, 2–6), 2km towards BRECH off the road from AURAY to STE-ANNE. This last is a group of reconstructed farm buildings, representing the local peasant life at the beginning of this century. It's all a bit too rustically charming, but a nice attempt to break out of the glass cases and wax models of most folk museums.

And finally, before the peninsula proper, if you find yourself in Brittany around 26 July one of the largest of the Breton **pardons** takes place at **STE-ANNE D'AURAY**. Some 25,000 pilgrims gather for the occasion to hear mass in the church, mount the *scala sancta* on their knees and buy trinkets and snacks from the street stalls. The origin of this *pardon*, typical of many, lies in the discovery in 1623 of a statue of Ste-Anne by a local peasant, one Nicolazic. He claimed to have been directed to the spot by visionary appearances of the saint (the Virgin's mother) and to have been instructed by her to build a church. Twenty years later, on his deathbed, the church authorities were still interrogating him as to the truth of his story, but the church was constructed and already a place of pilgrimage. Both church and statue were later destroyed in the Revolution; the present basilica, though not exactly moving, does its best to make up through size.

Carnac and Quiberon

According to one theory – local legend – the alignments at **CARNAC**, rows of 2,000 or so **menhirs** stretching for over 4km to the north of the village, are Roman soldiers turned to stone by the pope, St Cornely, whom they were pursuing. Another, with mathematical backing, says the giant menhir of Locmariaquer and the alignments were an observatory for the motions of the moon – a nice kick in the teeth for the civilised progress of science. But history has seen them used for centuries as ready quarried stone and then, when prehistoric archaeology became fashionable, dug up by the peasants to prevent an influx of academics and tourists disturbing precious crops. It's impossible to say how many have disappeared, nor really to prove anything from what's left; perhaps they were just the meaningless task ordered by some bigshot to occupy his slaves or jobless.

Carnac is itself a popular and very crowded resort, with expensive hotels but plenty of *campsites*. Its **SI** is on place de l'Église and you can **hire bikes** to roam about the site at *Lorcy*, 6 rue du Courdiec. However, it's clear that by far the best way to see the alignments would be from the air. This you can in fact do, and splitting costs three or four ways it's not much more costly than a meal. At the **Aérodrome de Quiberon** near the tip of the peninsula, there are currently two companies operating short flights over the peninsula and Morbihan: the *Quiberon Air Club* (year round except Jan) and *Thalass Air* (to the left of the Air Club building; July–Sept with a reservation the same day, phone 97.30.40.00).

This is beyond doubt the best reason for pressing on down to **QUIBERON**, the resort, which seems otherwise nondescript, in an upmarket sort of way. Two other possible reasons would be to walk along the **Côte Sauvage** (a wild and highly unswimmable stretch, where the stormy seas look like flashing scenes of snowy mountain tops) or to get out to one of the **islands**. BELLE ÎLE, the largest, is served quite regularly by ferries from PORT MARIA (30min crossing) though, like the mainland Côte Sauvage, it's more hiking or biking territory than a place to swim. HOUAT and HOËDIC (1½hr crossings from Quiberon, daily except Tues) are both tiny, making their few islanders' livings from fish. Both have blustering, cliff-top walks. For Hoëdic, the least frequented, check there's a return boat if you don't plan to camp. All three islands have campsites.

Boat timetables are available from the SI in QUIBERON at 7 rue de Verdun, just on the left as you leave the gare SNCF. PORT MARIA has bus connections, fitting in fairly well with ferry departures, with the Quiberon station, Carnac and Auray; these are also operated by the SNCF.

ON WEST: LORIENT, LOCHRIST AND PONT-AVEN

Looking for a beachside stop, you'll do best by picking around the Golfe de Morbihan or heading straight on to the coast around QUIMPER. The **seaside** between them is developed and often none too enticing, dogged by thick drifts of seaweed steered in by the tides. Prices, too, can be offputting: coastal Brittany is not often cheap but resorts here seem especially exorbitant. If it's only a bed that you need, then there are **youth hostels** at LORIENT (phone 97.37.11.65 and check it's open: the address is 41 rue Schoelcher, 3km from the gare SNCF on busline C), at the ÎLE DE CROIX (summer only: again check with LORIENT, which is where the island's ferries leave from) and at the tunny-fishing port and smart resort of CONCARNEAU (positioned near the main beach; 97.97.03.47 for wise reservations). **LORIENT**, fourth largest Breton city and a considerable port, is only really worth making for in its own right over the first weekend of August and the **InterCeltic Festival**. Representatives of all seven 'Celtic' nations turn up for this, five languages mingle and Scotch and guinness flow with the French and Spanish wines and ciders. Most of the activities take place around the central place Jules Ferry, which is where most people end up sleeping, too – the hotels, hostel and campsite proving totally unable to cope with the influx.

Any other time of year and you're best off inland, at least if you're mobile. At **LOCHRIST**, a few kilometres north of Lorient, the great Hennebont ironworks look down on the Blavet river, chimneys still standing but smokeless and silent. Strikes and demonstrations failed to prevent its closure in 1966 and the only work since has been to set up a museum, the **Musée Forges d'Hennebont**, which documents the works' 100-year history from the workers' point of view. Some of the men put out on the dole in 1966 have contributed their memories and tools; for others the museum is the lid on the coffin. It's an excellent museum in its contents and presentation but after seeing the joyful pictures of successful strikes in the 1930s, this museum's existence is a sad defeat. But if it's on your route it's worth a stop: the bus station is just opposite, across the river; hours are Tues–Thurs 9–12 & 2–6, Fri 9–12 & wkends 2–6.

Beyond, towards QUIMPER, the hillside town of **QUIMPERLÉ** has a Romanesque church – rare in Brittany – with an original and rather wonderful apse. And at **PONT-AVEN** there are attractive river walkways, woods and a handful of galleries. This town was actually Gauguin's last residence before he went off to exoticism in Haiti but for all the local hype it has no permanent collection of his works. The so called **Musée**

Gauguin in the townhall goes so far as hosting annual exhibitions on the numerous painters who preceded or followed the painter here – but don't count on works by the man himself; it's open Easter–Sept 10–12.30 & 2–7. Still, the town is excessively pretty, every other building seems to be a gallery or studio, and it's easy enough to while away an afternoon. If you need to stay be warned that the three **hotels** are all expensive and the nearest campsite is 4km distant at Roz Pin on the road to Névez.

TRAVEL DETAILS

Transport in Brittany can be a tricky and time-consuming business. Most of the main towns have train links with Rennes and/or Nantes and there's a rough loop of the coast. These apart, getting between towns is often a matter of fitting in with a web of independent private bus lines – their services, especially inland, often geared to schools and markets. The timetables supplied at stations are a help – there's one for each of fourteen sectors detailing both buses and trains – but this is one part of France where you may find it more rewarding to pick a couple of main bases and hire a bike.

Trains
From Rennes frequently to Paris-Montparnasse (3¼hrs) via Le Mans (2hrs), to St-Malo (1hr), to Vannes/Lorient/Quimper (1hr/1½hrs/2¼hrs) and to Morlaix/Brest (2hrs/2¾hrs); 5 daily to Roscoff (2¾hrs); 4 daily to Quiberon (2¾hrs; via Vannes – summer only) and Mont St-Michel (¾hr).
From Roscoff 5 daily to Morlaix (½hr) and Rennes (2¾hrs).
From Brest 6 daily to Quimper (1½hrs).
From Nantes very frequently to Paris-Montparnasse (3½hrs); slightly less so to Angers (¾hr), La Baule/Croisic (1hr/1¼hrs) and Vannes/Quimper (1¾hrs/3½hrs).

Buses
From Rennes more or less hourly to Dinan (1½hrs); 8 daily to Dinard (1¾hrs); 3 daily to Nantes (2½hrs) and Josselin (1¼hrs).
From Quimper 4 daily to Brest (1½hrs); daily to Morlaix (1¾hrs).
From Lannion 9 daily to St-Brieuc (1hr); 6 daily to Trégastel (1hr); daily to Morlaix (1¼hrs).
From St-Brieuc 7 daily to Pampol (1½hrs); 4 daily to Dinan (1hr).

From Vannes daily to Malestroit (¾hr).
From Carnac 2 daily to Lorient (1¼hrs).

Ferries
From St-Malo *Brittany Ferries* (99-56.68.40) to Portsmouth: 9hr overnight crossing.
From Roscoff *Brittany Ferries* (98-69.76.22) to Plymouth (2 daily in 6hrs) and to Cork (daily; 13½-17hrs). Also to the Île de Batz (several times daily in season, irregularly out; 15mins).
From Dinan daily boat up the estuary to Dinard (2½hrs) and to St-Malo (3hrs); May–Sept only.
Dinard–St-Malo Regular boats (10mins).
From Pointe de l'Arcouest Regular ferry to the Île de Bréhat (10mins).
From Quimper Daily boat down the Odet to Benedot (1¼hrs); May–Sept only.
From Nantes boats can be hired for the Nantes-Brest canal (see p. 173). Also at Malestroit, Josselin, Quimper and elsewhere.
From Vannes/Port-Navalo/Lamor Baden (and other ports) ferries to Île de Gavrinis and boat trips to other islands in the gulf of Morbihan (see p. 176).
From Quiberon regular ferry to Belle Ile (1hr), less frequently to Houat and Hoëdic.
From Lorient regular summer ferry to the Ile de Groix (45mins).

More details and ferry schedules for the Breton islands can be obtained from A.P.I.T. (11 place Joffre, Auray; 97.56.52.57) or principal tourist offices in the province, or Maison de la Bretagne, Centre Commercial, Maine-Montparnasse, 17 rue de l'Arrivée, 15ᵉ, Paris (45.38.73.15).

Chapter five
THE LOIRE

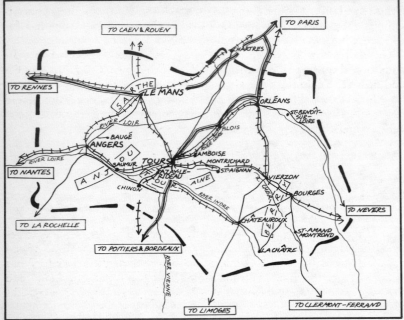

Intimidated by the density of châteaux – and all their great Renaissance intrigues and associations – people tend to make bad use of time spent in **the Loire**. Which is a pity, for if you pick your castles selectively, stamp out all sense of duty from the awaiting guided tours, and spend days on river banks supplied with cheese, fruit and white Loire wines, then this can be about the most enjoyable province of them all.

The central region of **Touraine** – 'the heart of France' – has the best wines, the most scented flowers and delicious fruit, the top **châteaux** (**Cheanonceaux, Azay-le-Rideau** and **Loches**), and, without any class overtones, the purest accent in the land. It takes in three tributaries, as well as a section of the main river: the **Cher, Vienne** and **Indre**, each of which have their seductions, when you can gain access to their banks. If you've just a week or so to devote, this is the part to make for and explore. **Orléanais**, along the northern stretches, does its best to compete but it is too close to Paris for its own good.

As for the **Loire** itself, its most salient features are whirlpools, banks of quicksand, vicious currents and a propensity to flood. No one swims in it or boats on it, no goods are carried along it – it's just there, the longest French river. As well as the select handful of châteaux, it has a few additional sights that can stand comparison with the pleasures of drunken river picnics: most unmissably, the tapestries in **Angers**, the gardens at **Villandry** (outside Tours) and the Romanesque abbey at **St-Benoît-sur-Loire**. Of the cities, **Le Mans** is the least touristy, **Tours** is tedious but good on museums, **Orléans** has charm, **Saumur** is perfect for indolence but not hot on entertainment.

Generally, this is a rich, right-wing, laid back region where air-conditioned car or coach tourism is the norm and people tend to be polite and passive. **Exploring** on your own, it's a good idea to rent wheels, at least for occasional forays. Buses can be sparse (their times are not geared to outsiders' use), trains limiting, and in any case this is wonderful and easy **cycling** country.

ANJOU AND TOURAINE

This is the first — and best — stretch of the Loire, as the river emerges from its gorged course from Nantes. Progress upstream, or down if you approach from Paris and **Tours**, is reasonably straightforward by bus and train over the main châteaux circuit. But you'll quite probably find the greatest rewards by picking a few bases and exploring the riverbanks or lesser local sights.

ANGERS

'Black' **ANGERS**, Anjou's capital, takes its epithet from the gloomy coloured slate and stone quarried here since the 9C. It is a depressing town — not a place to spend a holiday — but go there all the same, just for a day. For Angers possesses two works of art more stirring and stunning than all the châteaux and their contents put together: both are **tapestries**, the 14C **Apocalypse** and the 20C **Chant du Monde**.

The Tapestry of the Apocalypse is to be found in **Angers Castle** a formidable early medieval fortress with seventeen circular towers — splayed out like elephants' legs to grip the rock below the kilometre long curtain wall. Inside there are a few miscellaneous remains of the counts' royal lodgings and chapels, but the immediate and obvious focus is the tapestry, whose 100m length (of an original 168m) is well displayed in a modern gallery. Woven between 1375 and 1378, it takes as its text **St John's Vision of the Apocalypse**, as described in the Book of Revelations. If you happen to have a bible with you, so much the better since, though the French biblical quotations are given, the English 'translation' is just explanations. The vision is of the run up to the Day of Judgement signalled by the seven angels blowing their trumpets after which 'hail and fire mingled with blood . . . were cast upon the earth and the third part of trees was burnt up and all green grass . . . and as it were a great mountain burning with fire was cast into the sea and the third part of the sea became blood . . .' (Ch 8, vs 7, 8). A burning star poisons a third of the waters, locusts like scorpions are let loose from the bowels of the earth. The battle of Armageddon rages with Satan, 'the great red dragon' and his minions of composite animals marking their earthly followers and the holy forces retaliating by breaking the seven vials of plagues. The vision ends with the sacred city of the blessed, the heavenly Jerusalem, and Satan buried for a thousand years. The slightly flattened medieval perspective in the design becomes a hallucinatory quality – they are extraordinarily beautiful and terrifying, possessing an alarming power to evoke the end of the world either in accordance with their 1C text or as a secular holocaust.

If you can take anything else in, there are more tapestries, of a gentler nature, in the sporadically open **Royal lodgings** and **Governor's Lodge**. The castle itself is open 9.30/10–12 & 2–6/5. Admission is reasonable.

The city's modern tapestry – **Le Chant du Monde** was designed, in response to the Apocalypse, by Jean Lurcat. Physically it is almost as large and it is also incomplete – Lurcat began the project in 1957 but died, nine years later, before its completion. In a way its subject is vaster, because humankind is itself responsible for its destruction or creation. The first four tapestries deal with *La Grande Menace*, the threat of nuclear war: the bomb itself, the Hiroshima Man, flayed and burnt with the broken symbols of belief dropping from him, the collective massacre of the *Great Charnel House* and the last dying rose falling with the post holocaust ash through black space – *the End of Everything*. From then on, the tapestries celebrate the joy and glory of life and the interdependence of its myriad manifestations: fire, water, champagne, the conquest of space, poetry and symbolic language. The artist's own commentary is available in English.

Modern tapestry is an unfamiliar art, the colours are so bright and Lurcat's style so unlike anything else that your initial reaction may be just of visual assault. In which case, enjoy the building, the Hôpital St-Jean, which from 1174 to 1854 was a hospital for the poor. It's on bd Arago, upstream from the castle – about ¼hr's walk – across Pont de la Haute Chaine and second left; hours are 10–12 & 2–6, cl. Mon.

This side of the Maine, known as **La Doutre** (the other side, literally) has quite a few old buildings and a very odd slaughterhouse clock by the Pont de la Basse Chaine. If you want to do the full sightseeing bit, Christine, who's English, at the SI does good tours of this area and the centre and gets you into buildings you otherwise can't visit like the

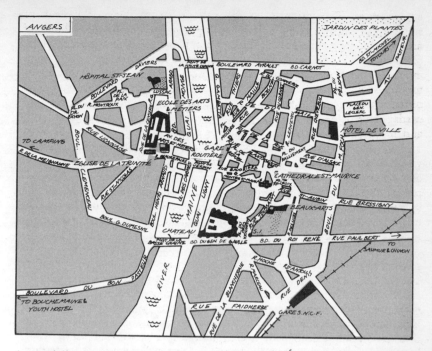

beautifully muralled Romanesque galleries of the **Église de Ronceray**. The abbey to which this church belonged, now the *École des Arts et Métiers*, juts into the 12C **Église de la Trinité**, where an exquisite Renaissance wooden spiral staircase fails to mask this bizarre piece of medieval building joinery. If you cross the central Port de Verdun back to the centre, just to the right after the quayside road, a long flight of steps leads up to the **Cathédrale St-Maurice** – inspiring in this approach, and the early medieval façade, though for little else. Behind it, on place Ste-Croix, the town's favourite carpentry detail is the unlikely genitals of one of the carved characters on the medieval **Maison d'Adam**. Old Angers does not extend much further: in place du Ralliement a giant turkey made of aeroplane wings is the central sculpture.

The best sculptures elsewhere in the town are those of **David d'Angers** (1788–1856), exhibited in a brilliant gallery built by glassing over the ruins of a 13C church, the **Église Toussaint**. The main **Beaux Arts** collection next door has delightfully purposeful babies as creative cupids in Boucher's *Génie des Arts*, the beautiful *La Femme au Masque* by Lorenzo Lippi and representative works from the 13C to the 20C. The **Musée Pince** exhibits antiquities and treasures from the Far East with an excellent Japanese collection. All the museums are open 10–12 & 2–6 (cl. Mon) and a single ticket can be bought which includes the tapestries.

Some practical details

For a room, the most central **hotels** are *Saint Julien*, 9 place du Ralliement, *Les Négociants*, 2 rue de la Roë and *La Tour*, 66 rue Baudrière. There are cheap places too around the **gare SNCF** – south of the centre, about 5mins' walk from the castle; the gare routière is up by the Pont de Verdun, between the place de la République and the river. The best **camping site** is north-east of the city at Parc de la Haye, AVRILLÉ: bus 3 to RONCEVAUX (change at Clinique from buses gong to Avrillé); a **youth hostel**, open only in summer, is at the *Centre d'Accueil du Lac du Maine* (bus 6 to Bouchemaine, stop Lac du Maine, Accueil). Downstream, between La Pointe and Bouchemaine, you can **hire canoes** at the *Base Nautique*.

The streets around **place du Ralliement** are the best for **restaurants** and there is a **market** every day in place Sainte Croix. The **SI** (which runs an accommodation service) is on place Kennedy, facing the castle, with, just up the road, the *Conseil Interprofessionel des Vins d'Anjou et de Saumur* where you can taste wine and get information about all the Anjou vineyards.

The Allostop phone number for lifts is 41.87.21.21 (5–7 wkdays).

VINEYARDS AND CHÂTEAUX AROUND ANGERS

Lazing about the Loire and its tributaries between visits to vineyards could fill a good summer week around Angers, as long as you are mobile. Otherwise it is a two bus a day problem, or no buses at all, with the exception of the Savonnières vineyards (which you can reach by train), and some easy hitching routes, such as Brissac-Quincé, 20km south of Angers (also on the 9 bus). Best plan, obviously enough, is to rent a bike: there's a rental in ANGERS, *Manceau*, at 8 rue du Maréchal Juin, or various outlets (including the gare SNCF) at SAUMUR if you approach from the other direction.

For your châteaux duty in these parts **BRISSAC** (at Brissac-Quincé), owned from 1502 to this day by the same line of dukes, has a 17C addition arrogantly outreaching the 15C fortified towers and some beautiful painted ceilings. It is otherwise a riot of aristocratic bad taste, though with one interesting portrait in the Gallery of Ancestors – of Madame Cliquot, the first woman to run a champagne business, if not any business, and her grand-daughter, the present duke's gran, who was, apparently, one of the first women to get her driving licence. The château is open 9.30–11.20 & 2.15–4.15 (later in summer), cl. Tues and from 16 Nov to 6 Feb. To the north (17km on from Angers) five years' work at the end of the 15C produced the fortress **LE PLESSIS BOURRÉ**, looking as if it still awaited attack from across its vast moat. But the Treasurer of France who commissioned it had it luxuriously fitted out inside – best of all are the secular and allegorical scenes painted on the guardroom ceiling. Admission here is 10–12 & 2–5 (7 in summer), cl. 15 Nov–15 Dec and Tues in winter; it is, however, impossible to get to without your own wheels. For a more accessible glimpse of a real monster of a mansion, see what you make of the **CHÂTEAU SERRANT**, just outside ST-GEORGES-SUR-LOIRE on bus route 18 from ANGERS.

Nearby, along the north bank of the Loire, BOUCHEMAINE, SAVENNIÈRES and LA POSSONNIÈRE are the **communes** for the dry white *appellation Savennières* – one of the few white wines that can live a century. The most famous is *Coulée de Serrant* to be tasted and bought at the **CHÂTEAU DE LA ROCHE AUX MOINES,** just upstream from Savennières. **ROCHEFORT-SUR-LOIRE,** on the south bank, is the first of the appellation *Coteaux du Layon Villages*, a golden sweet white wine, and following this wine along the river Layon, winding below vine covered hills as far as Faye d'Anjou, is a hedonist dream. The road is free of *Dégustation* signs but the *vignerons* are not hard to find. In the summer at **ST-AUBIN-DE-LUIGNÉ** (no 6 bus after Rochefort) you can hire **rowing boats** at the SI, next to the **campsite**.

SAUMUR AND AROUND

Angers to Saumur is the loveliest stretch of the Loire. The land on the south, planted with vines and sunflowers, gradually rises away from the river with long since deceased windmills still standing and no vast châteaux eagling on rocks. Across the water cows graze in wooded pastures. For **transport** you have a choice of train or one of three buses – 5 along the south bank, no 11 that crosses half way and no 10 that stays north of the river.

Saumur

Exceptionally for small Loire towns **SAUMUR** is not dominated by its fairy-tale style castle, omnivisible though it is. Nor is it dominated by the military which it might well be as the home of the French Cavalry and Armoured Corps Academy since 1763. Even the local sparkling wines are based in the suburb of St-Hilaire-St-Florent. Saumur is just peaceful and pretty, to the dissatisfaction of the Town Hall who decided in 1984 to enliven the place with an annual *International Festival of Videos* (the first week of July). With Angers, Chinon and plenty of vineyards in easy reach you may want to stay here a while. Some inexpensive **hotels** to try are *La Bascule*, 1 place Kléber; *Central*, 23 rue Daillé and *La Croix de Guerre*, 9 rue de la Petite Bilange, all in the centre on the south bank. Alternatively, on the Île d'Offard, connected by bridges to both banks of the town, there's a very good **youth hostel** (with boat and bike hire) and on the eastern tip a **campsite**. Due to a barrage you can even swim here, in the north stream.

Orientation is straightforward. Arrive at the **gare SNCF** and you'll find yourself on the north bank proper: turn right and you cross a first bridge to the island, a second, the old **Pont Cessart,** to the main part of the town on the south bank. The **gare routière** is pretty much in the centre – a couple of blocks back from the Pont Cessart by the church of St-Nicholas. Saumur's main street, **rue d'Orléans,** cuts back through the south bank sector: the **SI** is off to its right (coming from the river) along rue Beaurepaire (no 25), the old quarter, around St-Pierre and the castle, to the left. Around **place St-Pierre** is the best **eating** area: *Auberge St-Pierre*, actually on the square, sometimes has langoustines on a cheapish menu, or there are good *crêperies* and other places on the streets heading back to rue d'Orléans.

But before hunting for restaurants, you should go dragon hunting in the **Église St-Pierre.** There are at least seven, one in stone, one carved in wood and more woven into the 16C tapestries that tell the legend of St-Florent, an early scourge of these beautiful beasts who symbolise sin. Medieval fantasy creatures would not be out of place either romping round the ramparts of the **Castle:** you can visit its dungeons and watchtower on your own, with relaxed guides taking over for the two museums. The **Musée des Arts Décoratifs** has a huge collection of European china, amongst other things but it's the **Musée de Cheval** that's really a treat. Progressing from a horse skeleton, through the evolution of bridles and stirrups over the centuries, this eventually reaches an amazing collection of saddles from all over the world; the difference between the art of California and Iran, Japan and Tibet, the Sudan and China is as well manifested in riding seats as it is in poetry or music. Both museums, and the castle, open in July–Aug 9–7 & 8.30–10pm, otherwise 9–11.30 & 2–6. (cl. Tues and at 5pm Nov–March).

By knocking at the guarded gate on av Maréchal Foch, west of rue d'Orléans, you can also visit, escorted by a soldier, a **Musée de la Cavalerie** (2–5; Sun 9–11.30; cl. Fri & Aug). Amongst the uniforms, weapons and battle scenes (including very recent engagements), there is one moving room, dedicated to the cavalry cadets who held the Loire bridges between Gennes and Montsoreau against the Germans for three days in 1940, after the French government had surrendered. The **Riding School,** demilitarised in 1972, has moved to St-Hilaire-St-Florent. Horse fanatics can apply to the SI for details of visits and displays of anachronistic battle manoeuvres by the crackshot Cadre Noir. The metal mounts of the 20C, if you like that sort of thing, can be seen at the **Musée des Blindés,** northeast of place du Chardonnet.

Lastly, the **Maison du Vin** next door to the SI, has information on local wines and addresses of wine growers. A good red is the *Saumur Champigny* from around the village of CHAMPIGNY. The *Caves Coopérative* at ST-CYR EN BOURG (near the gare SNCF) have miles of cellars and you can taste different wines without being obliged to buy.

Baugé and Fontévraud

In **BAUGÉ** a short trainride north of Saumur towards Le Mans, the nuns at the **Chapelle des Incurables** claim to have a cross made from the True Cross. The wood is certainly Palestinian though the story of its origin prior to its donation to an Angevin crusader is somewhat dubious. But anyway it's the double armed cross that became the emblem of the Dukes of Anjou and Lorraine, and, in this century, of the Free French Forces. To see it, ring at no 8 in rue de la Girouardière (10–12 & 2.30–5; Sun 3–4 & 6–7). The **SI** in Baugé is worth visiting merely for the sake of walking freely into a 15C **castle**. And take a look, too, at the **Hospice St-Joseph** (east of the château up rue Anne de Melun) for its 17C dispensary, with beautiful woodwork shelves, floor and ceiling and the vials, flacons and contents as they were in 1874; it's open, for free, 10–12 & 3–5.30/4.30. Suns 10.30–12 – the hospital receptionist will direct you. For the church-curious, three parishes around Baugé have strange twisting towers – PONTIGNÉ, FONTAINE GUÉRIN and VIEIL BAUGÉ (this last leaning as well).

The big site touted around SAUMUR, however, is the **ABBAYE DE FONTÉVRAUD**, 13km to the south-east on bus route 16. The guided tour here is one of the longest and most exhausting in this chapter and its highpoints are the tombstone effigies of Henry II, Eleanor of Aquitaine, Richard the Lionheart and Isabelle of Angoulême (King John's missus). This may not excite, over much, though the abbey does have a straight historical interest. It was founded in 1099 as both a nunnery and a monastery with an abbess in charge – a radical move even if the post was filled only by queens and princesses. The premises had to be immense to house and keep separate not only the nuns and monks but also the sick, the lepers and repentent prostitutes. Visits are from 9–12 & 2–6.30/ 4 Oct–March; cl. Tues.

INTO TOURAINE: CHINON AND AZAY-LE-RIDEAU

A fortress of one kind or another has existed at **CHINON** since the Stone Age and the ruins of the last one since the age of Louis XIV. A favourite Plantagenet residence, it was, much later, one of the few places Charles VII could stay while Henry V of England held Paris and the title to the French throne. Charles's situation changed with the arrival here in 1429 of Joan of Arc who recognised him, disguised in a crowd of courtiers, and persuaded him to get his act together and give her an army. All that remains of the scene of this encounter, the *Grande Salle*, is a wall and first-floor fireplace. Visits to this and to the restored *Royal Lodgings* – both guided – are not very worthwhile. More interesting is the *Tour Coudray*, over to the west, covered with intricate 13C graffiti carved by imprisoned and doomed Templar knights; Joan is said to have stayed here too. Like the rest of the château complex, it is open 9–12 & 2–6 (9–6 in July–Aug. cl. Dec, Jan & Weds from Oct–mid-March).

Below, the town continues this celebration of the long dead, and in sterile fashion: medieval streets, a wine and barrel making museum with gross animated models and free tasting of the worst wine, no cheap hotels and everything closed up well before midnight. There is a **youth hostel** close to the **gare** SNCF on rue Descartes (the continuation of quai Jeanne d'Arc eastwards) and at the **campsite**, across the river, you can hire **canoes** in summer. The SI at 12 rue Voltaire has bikes for hire. The most reasonable restaurant is *Le Panurge* on place de l'Hôtel de Ville.

The man who vies with Joan of Arc for snackbars, shops and streets named in their honour in Chinon is **Rabelais** (1494–1553) who wrote approvingly of wine, food and laughter in deeply serious and difficult humanist texts, and was born at nearby **LA DEVINIÈRE** (requisite author's room on show). Another Touraine birthplace-plus-museum, its subject obvious enough, is over to the south-west at DESCARTES. The town of **RICHELIEU**, however, did not see the cardinal until he was grown up, bought the place, had an enormous château built, and rearranged the village into an enclosed town of model classical planning. The château has disappeared without trace; the town survives to please square and right-angled minds.

If the château was removed from **AZAY-LE-RIDEAU**, you'd still have the serene setting of the island in the Indre, the old mill by the bridge, the Carolingian statues embedded in the façade of St-Symphorien church, and a quiet village. But the **Château** is one of the loveliest, pure Renaissance and required viewing – which you can do for free from the surrounding park. Guided tours of the interior, furnished in Renaissance style, don't add much to this experience, concentrating on sexist jokes at the expense of the wife of the financier who had it built in the 1520s. The portrait gallery has the whole 16C crew – François I, Catherine de Médicis, the de Guises, etc. – and, single highlight, a semi-nude painting of Gabrielle d'Estrée, Henri IV's lover. If you're committed, hours are 9.15–12 & 2–6.30/4.45. There is a large **campsite** upstream from the château and trains and buses to Chinon and Tours.

For something rather strange and totally off the tourist track, make your way to **CHEILLÉ** a small village 6km west of Azay and linked by some (not all) of the Chinon trains. In the church here is a life sized wooden crucifix that differs from almost every other representation of Christ in that he has no beard. The effect is astounding: Christ no longer a hippy but someone whose face could be contemporary to any time. It is the work of a very passionate artist, but who or when is not documented. If the church is locked, ask for the key at the house next door.

TOURS

'TOURS has an immense air of good breeding . . . you have visions of portentiously dull entertainments in lofty gilded saloons where everything is rather icily magnificent' – an English travel writer in 1913. The magnificence might be more diluted now but you get a similar impression: it is a very bourgeois city dulled by being well within evening's out distance of Paris. If you decide to stay it's likely to be for the museums – of wine, crafts and a well above average *Beaux Arts* – and for the pleasures (and *dégustations*) of the vineyards around.

Accommodation shouldn't be a problem. There's a **youth hostel** at Parc de Grandmont (bus 6 or 2, stop *Auberge de Jeunesse*; 47.28.15.67), a municipal **campsite** on the north bank of the Loire (bus 6, stop *St-Radegonde*) and a wide range of **hotels.** You'll find cheap ones in the unpleasant area around the station (*L'Olympic*, 74 rue B Palissy; *Family*, 2 rue Traversière); *Mons Hôtel*, nearer the cathedral at 40 rue de la Préfecture; and up by the old town, *Le Sully* (7 rue Néricault-Destouches) and *Breton* (13 place des Halles). The *Foyer* at 16 rue B Palissy may also have rooms available.

At the head of **rue Nationale** – Tours' main street – statues of Descartes looking suitably doubtful and Rabelais gleefully certain, over-

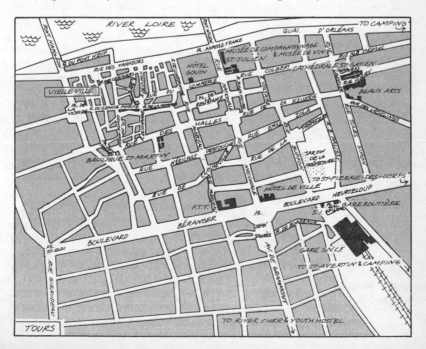

look the Loire. A short walk back from the river and you come to the church of St-Julien, with, alongside, two of the town's most compelling museums. In the **Musée de Campagnonnage** it is for once the people who built rather than ordered the châteaux and cathedrals who are celebrated. As well as documents of the origins and militant activity of the 'guilds', there are masterpieces, in the original sense of the term, of crafts from cake-making and carpentry to locksmithery and slatelaying, the relevant tools exhibited alongside. The **Musée du Vin** next door, has some great quotations on the subject: Virgil on planting vines as you'd arrange cohorts in battle; the grape being born from the blood of vanquished giants (anon. Egypt); Victor Hugo – 'God only created water, man made wine' and Colette going over the top with 'the barren chalk weeps in wine tears of gold'. The exhibits make up a pretty comprehensive treatment of the history, mythology, related industries and production of the wondrous liquid, though there is nothing on recent technical innovations. Behind the museum, a Gallo-Roman wine press from Cheillé sits in the former cloisters of St-Julien's church. Both museums are open 9–12 & 2–6 (cl. Tues); admission is cheap.

Over towards the **Cathédrale St-Gatien** – with its crumbling, flamboyant Gothic front – you'll find the city's third museum, the **Beaux Arts**, shadowed by a huge and aged Lebanon cedar. This has some beauties amidst its rambling collection: *Christ in the Garden of Olives* and the *Resurrection* by Mantegna; Franz Hal's portrait of Descartes looking like the second Dr Who; Balzac painted by Boulanger; prints of *The Five Senses* by the *Tourainais* Abraham Bosse; a sombre Monet; and a cheering tapestry by Caldor. Rembrandt's *Flight into Egypt* is difficult to see through the security glass. Open 8–12.45 & 2–6; it is again good value.

Old Tours crowds about the place St-Pierre-le-Puellier, over to the west of rue National and past the *Hôtel Gouin* – a small archaeological museum with a Renaissance façade that will stop you in your tracks. It is the medieval half-timbered houses and bulging stairway towers of the 12C, 13C and 15C and 1970s restoration, however, that are the city's showpiece. They look like cut-out models – to confuse further a landing Tardis place St-Pierre has an excavated Gallo-Roman cemetery – though the Renaissance stone and brick buildings have firmer grip on reality, particularly the **Écoles des Langues Vivantes** in rue Briconnet with sculpted dogs, drunks, frogs and monsters. West of rue Bretonneau modern artisans' workshops slot smoothly between anarchic medieval dwellings. The pre-restoration inhabitants of the quarter were Portuguese (some of whom remain) and Algerians (whom the council, predictably, kicked out of residence). But it's trendies who dominate this surreal district with their English *peurbs*, night *cleurbs* and life till late. The unflashy *Le Petit Faucheux* (23 rue des Cerisiers) has music and shows at weekends and darts, cards and chess the rest of the week.

Rue du Grand Marché and rue de la Rôtisserie, on the periphery of old Tours, and rue Colbert (which runs down to the cathedral), are the most promising **restaurant** streets; *Les Lionceaux* (at 17 rue Jules Favre, off rue Colbert) has the cheapest *menu fixe*. The regional speciality is greasy potted pork – *rillettes*, or pieces of cold pork – *rillons*. But for sugar and chocolate pigs, Tours also has some excellent **pâtisseries**: *La Marotte* (3 rue du Change), *La Chocolatière* (6 rue de la Scellerie) and others along rue Nationale. *Les Studios* on rue des Urselines shows eight good **films** a week (v.o.'s) at reasonable cost. And lastly, if you want to **hire bikes** for one of the excursions below the place to try is *Au Col de Cygne*, near the station at 46 rue du Dr Fournier, and if you've kids to entertain, there's a real treat in a gleaming SNCF **steam engine**, clamberable and placed in a square by the crossroads of boulevards des Deportés and Paul Langevin in the suburb of St-Pierre-des-Corps (bus 3, stop *Deportés*).

Around Tours: gardens and vineyards

Even if you imagine you'll have no interest in them, take time to get out to the **gardens** at VILLANDRY. No ordinary patterns of opposing primary colours, this recreated Renaissance garden is more like a tapestry of that age, but one that changes with the months and only fades in winter. Carrots, cabbages and eggplant are exalted to coloured threads woven beneath rose bowers. Herbs and ornamental box hedges are part of the same artwork, divided by vine-shaded paths. From a terrace above, you can see the Cher meeting the Loire and châteaux on the northern bank. The gardens are open from 9 until sunset; for an extra few francs you can see the Spanish paintings and medieval Moorish ceiling from Toledo in the château (guided tour, Palm Sunday–12 Nov, 9–6). No buses go from Tours to Villandry but the 13km along the Cher is an idyllic bike ride.

VOUVRAY, 10km east of Tours on the north bank, is the *appellation* for the most delicious white wine of the Loire. A good year lives to be 100, can be *sec*, *demi-sec* or *pétillant* (sparkling) and is best from the grape of a single vineyard. The **SI** at the Hôtel de Ville can provide addresses of **vignerons** but all the roads leading up the steep valleys are lined with *caves*. The view of the vines from the top of the hill is an outrageous inducement to drunkenness. Vouvray has a **campsite** between the Loire and the Cisse and bus 61 runs from place St-Vincent just south of the SI to place Jean-Jaurès in Tours.

To go with the wine, Touraine produces **chèvre** (goat's cheese) and the best of those cylindrical and speckled miniature building blocks you see on market stalls come from around the small town of STE-MAURE. The SI here in rue du Château can provide addresses for *dégustations* and the medieval covered market will be well stocked. One producer is M Raguin, by the Château d'Eau in NOYANT-DE-TOURAINE on the Chinon road. Ste-Maure is on the DESCARTES bus route from Tours.

ALONG THE TRIBUTARIES

The **Vienne**, **Indre** and **Cher** rivers share none of the Loire's dangerous habits, but they're difficult to get at unless you're prepared to hunt out the paths through the farmlands on their banks. Officious notices you see are more often to do with fishing restrictions than telling you to keep away. Trains and roads follow the Cher from **Tours** and the Indre from **Loches**: for the Vienne, best hire a canoe at **Chinon**.

The Indre: Loches
The walled citadel of **LOCHES** is by far the most impressive of Loire valley fortresses with unbreached ramparts and Renaissance houses below still partly enclosed by the outer wall of the medieval town. It is an hour's train journey away from Tours and hotel accommodation is expensive, but there is a good **campsite** across the Indre. From the station av de la Gare leads to place de la Marne and the **SI**.

The southern end of the **Citadelle** is taken up by dungeons and a keep initiated by Foulques the Black, 11C Count of Anjou, with cells and a torture chamber added in the 15C. Cl'mbing, unescorted, to the top of the keep is fun even if the surrounding countryside is no more exciting than the English Home Counties. There is not a lot in the 15C extension, grateful thanks to the people of Loches who destroyed most of the equipment in the Revolution. The very professional guides make up for the lack of exhibits by their spiel but the English text can't capture the goriness.

At the other end are the **royal lodgings** of Charles VII and his three successors. The medieval half of the palace witnessed two women of some importance to Charles, though they probably wouldn't have got on had they been contemporaries. Joan of Arc, victorious from Orléans, came here to give the defeatist Dauphin another pep talk about coronations. While some time after the Maid's death, the less significant and much sexier Agnes Sorel, Charles' lover, resided here. Even the Pope fancied her, which allowed Charles to be the first French king to have an officially recognised 'mistress'. Her tomb now lies in the 15C wing with her portrait by Fouquet and a painting of the Virgin in her likeness. Hours are 9–6 in July–Aug, otherwise 9–12 & 2–6/5 winter, cl. Wed and Dec–Jan; guides are optional.

Just across the Indre from Loches is the village of **BEAULIEU-LÈS-LOCHES** – an extraordinary, unvisited place, thoroughly medieval in appearance and with its parish church built into the spectacular ruins of an **abbey** contemporary with the Loches keep. Its other church, **St-Pierre**, holds the bones of Foulques the Black.

If you follow the Indre into Berry, the river itself will be the only source of interest, save, perhaps, for the Romanesque church in CHÂTILLON-SUR-INDRE on the borders of Touraine and Berry. CHÂTEAUROUX, the largest town on its banks, is grey and bureaucratic, but further south, it flows past NOHANT and LA CHÂTRE (see p. 203).

The Cher: Chenonceaux and beyond

The waters of **the Cher** must get a shock when they merge with the Loire. This reasonable river keeps to its depth and flows so slowly and passively between the arches of CHENONCEAUX that two châteaux appear. The reflected mansion is hands down winner of all Loire châteaux for architecture, site, contents and organisation.

The building of **CHENONCEAUX** was always controlled by women. Catherine Briconnet, whose husband bought the site, hired the first architects in the 1520s. Diane de Poitiers (lover of Henry II), Catherine de Médici (wife of Henry II) and her daughter-in-law Louise de Lorraine successively owned and adapted the château during the rest of the 16C. After a long period of disuse, Mme Dupin brought 18C life to this gorgeous residence along with her guests Voltaire, Montesquieu and Rousseau, whom she hired here as tutor to her son. Restoration back to the 16C designs was completed by another woman in the late 19C; it is now a profitable business owned and run by the Menier chocolate family firm.

In summer it is teeming but, luxuriously, visits are unguided. There is an exhausting amount of eye-seducing tapestries, paintings, ceilings, floors and furniture, and the gallery across the Cher could capture you for hours despite the potted plastic plants. One exceptional picture, even in this collection, is Zurbaran's *Archimedes* (in the Salle Fançois I) clothes inside out and falling off, and a working man's face that suspects no one will believe his invention.

Admission, not surprisingly, is expensive. It is open through the summer from 9–7, closing at 6.30 in Sept, 6 in Oct and March and at 4.30 (and 12–2) from mid-Nov–mid-Feb. The easiest connection is with TOURS, half an hour by train from the station of CHENONCEAUX-CHISSEAUX (five departures daily in either direction).

A few km east of Chenonceaux, on the main road, the **Fraise d'Or**, an old-fashioned distillery, complete with shiny copper stills, specialises in strawberry, raspberry and cherry liqueurs that taste as if the fruit got drunk of its own accord. The visit round the distillery includes *a dégustation* of three of their eighteen liqueurs and eaux-de-vie, of herb, spice, fruit, nut, and, most divinely, rose petal, bases. (Open Easter–Sept 9–11.30, 2–6).

The best **places to stay on the Cher** are MONTRICHARD with its full complement of medieval houses and ruined castle or the market town of ST-AIGNAN with no visitable château but a wonderful church. Two possibilities for rooms in **MONTRICHARD** are **hotels** *du Courrier* (4 rte de Blois) and *Gare* (20 av de la Gare); an *SI* is by the castle and there is a **campsite** on the river. At **ST-AIGNAN**, try the **hotel** *du Moulin* (7 rue Nouilliers) or the riverside **campsite**; hire **boats** for an afternoon at the island; and treat yourself – the **food** market and shops are excellent, and not too expensive dishes using local wines are served at the *Relais de la Poste* (3 rue de l'Ormeau). The capitals in the **Église St-Aignan**, the local sight, are adorned with mermaids, a multi-bodied snake biting its own necks, a man's head tunnelled by an eagle, doleful dragons and other wonders of 12C imagination; in the crypt, if you can find the lightswitch, there are superb, brightly coloured, medieval frescoes.

For the town of BOURGES, upstream along the Cher in Berry, see p. 202.

AMBOISE

Returning to the Loire, the **wine** reaches considerable heights in the **Touraine-Amboise appellation**. If you're mobile, take the road from CHENONCEAUX to AMBOISE and stop by the petrol station and crossroads (4½km to Amboise) where M Delecheneau sells his *sec* and *demi-sec* white and sublime *demi-sec rosé* and will show you his barrels named after cows and his grandfather's old press.

You will need some wine to deal with **AMBOISE**, a prissy little town wallowing in long past splendours. It is the home power base of Michel Debré, de Gaulle's first prime minister, who keeps his master's flame alive and pure, and also one of Mick Jagger's favourite residences where he can go quite unrecognised. There is a good island **campsite** – but over-priced hotels and restaurants and nothing open after 10pm. The **Centre Charles Péguy**, on the west end of the lle d'Or, may have rooms and hires out **canoes**. For **bikes**, go to the snackbar in the campsite; for information the *SI* is on the waterfront east of the bridge. Arriving, the **gare SNCF** is a fair walk away from all this on the north side of the river.

The best thing in Amboise is **Max Ernst's** prototype ET/toybear and turtle **fountain**, with the Friday and Sunday market behind it on the riverside. What is left of the **Château** might qualify for second best if you could go round it at a slower pace. The *Tour des Minimes*, the original entrance and 15C forerunner of the multi-storey car park ramp, is architecturally the most exciting part. The Loire presents one of its most panoramic poses to the viewpoint from the top, but blood and guts of rebellious Huguenots are the reference for the hooks along the battlements. Caught plotting to get rid of the Catholic de Guise family, the power behind young François II, they were summarily tried in the *Salle des Conseils* and the whole town hung with their corpses. The last French king of all stayed in this château, hence the abrupt switch from solid Gothic furnishings to Empire style. It is open 9–12 & 2–6.30, closing at sunset in winter.

One man of far greater renown than any of the French kings, who died in Amboise in 1519, was **Leonardo da Vinci**, invited here by François I. **Clos Lucé**, where he stayed, at the end of rue Victor Hugo, does not contain a single original work. But it does have models of Leonardo's inventions, recently constructed according to his detailed plans. It is great to see materialised the incredible leaps over the technology barrier that Leonardo made but I bet he'd wish that they had put motors in. Even the best model, the wooden tank, does not have the same effect as Leonardo's sketch, beetling along with manic velocity, kicking up dust. But then he did know how to draw. Hours are June–Sept 9–7, otherwise 9–12 & 2–6 (cl. Jan); admission is more expensive than it should be.

ORLÉANAIS, BERRY AND SARTHE

Orléanais is in many ways a countryside suburb of Paris, and its principal châteaux (see below) demand more than usual motivation. The city of **Orléans**, however, has enough in itself (and nearby) to merit a stop between Touraine and Paris.

To the south, **Berry**, centred on **Bourges**, has medieval links and more modern literary connections: an obvious route if you are heading down towards the Massif Central and Roussillon. **Le Mans**, heart of the **Sarthe** region, is much less explored, save as a transit point en route to Brittany. But unpackaged and untouristed, it's an unexpected pleasure.

BLOIS, CHEVERNY AND CHAMBORD: THE MONSTER CHÂTEAUX

Catherine de Médicis forced Diane de Poitiers to hand over Chenonceaux in return for the château of **CHAUMONT**, upstream from Amboise towards Orléans. Diane got a very bad deal and so does any tourist doing the guided tour. This is one to avoid.

Another of Catherine's residences, just to the north of the unwanted Chambord, was the château at **BLOIS**, where she died in 1589. All six kings of the 16C spent time here and it was later given to Louis XIII's brother to keep him away from Paris. Hence the courtiers' mansions that fill the town, and, what with earlier non-regal ownerships, the **Château**'s building montage of distinct, unmatching wings: Feudal, Gothic, Renaissance and Classical. But for all its furnishings and portraits, not a flicker of a ghost excites the atmosphere. The Blois horror story is Henri III's murder of the Duc de Guise and his brother, the ones who had had the Huguenots executed at Amboise. The king panicked after the *Etats Généraux* assembled here in the glossy medieval *Grande Salle* in 1588, with an overwhelming majority supporting de Guise, the stringing up of protestants, and aristocratic rather than regal power. He did the deed himself and was then knocked off by a monk the following year. In a later century, revolutionaries were tried in this hall for conspiring to assassinate Napoleon III, a year before the Paris commune. One good thing about Blois: you can go round without a guide (except in winter); it's open June–Aug 9–6.30, the rest of the year 9–12 & 2–6.30/5 from Oct–March.

Some inexpensive **hotels** in Blois are *St-Nicholas*, 2 rue du Sermon, *Etoile d'Or*, 7 rue du Bourg Neuf and *du Bellay*, 12 rue des Minimes. The **campsite**, with **bike** and **boat hire**, is across the river on the Lac de Loire at Vineuil. There is one **youth hostel** (March to mid-Nov) at LES GROUETS, 5km downstream (bus 70, stop *Église des Grouets*) and another 10km upstream at MONTLIVAULT (mid-June–mid-Sept; Orléans bus, stop *Auberge de Jeunesse*). The Blois **SI** is at 3 av Jean Laiguet which runs from place Victor Hugo just behind the château, to the **gare SNCF**, which also does *bike hire*. Next to the **bus** office (at 6 place Victor Hugo) there's a bar that stays open late, but this is not a town for guarantees of exciting times. By day, if you like your France 18C, it's a pleasant enough place to wander.

Seventeenth-century purists have their treat at the château of **CHEVERNY** built between 1604 and 1634 and never altered. It belongs to a descendant of the original owner, his entrance charges are the highest in the Loire and in winter he exercises his hounds and horses to the accompaniment of hunting horns and tourist coachloads. Much more interesting, if you feel like taking in another château around Blois, is **BEAUREGARD** – closer, too, at a cyclable 9km. Highlight of the Castle, most of it the same date as Cheverny, is a portrait gallery of 363 paintings of kings and their contemporaries. Admission, at standard Loire charges, is 9.30–12 & 2–6.30/5 Oct–March and Weds.

CHAMBORD, François I's little hunting lodge, is the ugliest construction in the Loire valley, save for the nuclear power stations which it could probably house without stretching. It is though entertaining to circle on foot or by bike and to run about inside, up and down the double spiral staircase, around the chimneys and through miles of mostly unfurnished rooms and corridors. There is free access to the grounds and visits are unguided; 9.30–12 & 2–7 (mid-June–Aug)/6/5 (Nov–March). To get there on public transport you'll have to use the expensive château tour buses from Blois.

ORLÉANS AND UPSTREAM

Directly below the turned up nostrils of the capital, poor **ORLÉANS** feels compelled to recuperate its faded *gloire* from 1429, when Paris was infested by disease and the English, and the Loire valley was the capital of France. The city's deliverer on that date is honoured everywhere, though nothing contradicts the overriding feeling that Jeanne d'Arc was and is a myth. In earlier times still, Orléans was Clovis's capital and in the days of Asterix it was the chief city for a powerful Gallic group. But now, not only do Orléanais go to Paris for their evenings out, they commute to work there as well.

The **gare SNCF** (with **bikes** to hire), **gare routière, urban bus office** and **SI** are grouped together at **place Albert I** on the semi-circle of dual carriageway running round the town centre. Rue de la République leads down from here to central **place du Martroi** and a 19C statue of the Maid. To the east and down to the river are the scattered vestiges of several older Orléans, all the nicer for not being in one stage set block. Rue de Bourgogne, parallel to the river and erstwhile Gallo-Roman high street, has a good choice of **restaurants** of varying nationalities. **Accommodation** is easy with the usual cheap hotels near the station and, in the centre, *Carmes* (57 rue des Carmes), *Charles Sanglier* (8 rue Charles Sanglier) and *L'Univers* (70 rue d'Illiers). The **youth hostel** is at 14 rue du Faubourg Madeleine, across the dual carriageway to the west; the nearest **campsite** is at OLIVET (rue du Pont Bouchet) between the Loiret river and the Loire.

The **Cathédrale Ste-Croix**, built, battered and carried on for five and a half centuries, is wonderful. And full of Joan, who celebrated her victory here. In the north transept, her pedestal is supported by two jagged and golden leopards (the English) on an altar carved with the battle scene. The late 19C stained glass windows in the nave relate Joan's life (starting from the north transept) with caricatural faces for the snoutish, loutish anglo-saxons and snooty French nobles She appears again in pensive mood, her skirt riddled with 20C bullets outside the red brick Renaissance **Hôtel de Ville** across place d'Étape from the cathedral. The best escape from the Middle Ages is the modern art collection in the basement of the **Musée des Beaux Arts**, opposite the Hôtel de Ville, with canvasses by Picasso, Miró, Braque, Dufy, Renoir and Monet all, alas, in horribly heavy frames. But if you want to go back much earlier in time, drop in at the modern **Préfecture** on rue du Bourgogne (door no 9) and ask the receptionist if you can look in the basement, where a low budget reception

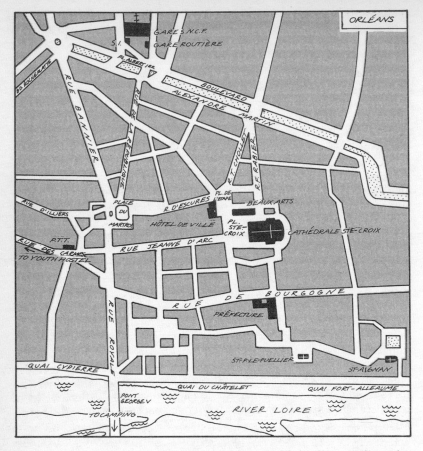

room provides odd surroundings for an excavated dwelling, or bits of it, from the end of the 1C and the walls of a 9C church.

Between the Préfecture and the river, narrow streets surround the **Dassaux vinegar works**, a long established concern whose buildings encircle the house Isabelle Romée moved to, a few years after her daughter was burnt at the stake in Rouen. The factory is in imminent danger of liquidation, and such are the priorities of this culturally beleaguered city that the authorities have already bought the relevant bit and plan to turn it into a museum. Down the road, a plaque marks the house of Joan's brother and companion-in-arms, on the corner of rue des Africains and **rue de la Folie**. The latter street has provided surfaces for some Kandinskyish murals, signed Daridan '84, whose continued existence can't, unfortunately, be guaranteed. Though deserted most of the time, this old quarter is a very pleasant area and spared the postcard stalls and trendy shops and bars. Two churches are on the precious monuments list: the remains of **St-Aignan** and its 11C crypt and the Romanesque **St-Pierre-le-Puellier**, the old university church, now used for concerts and exhibitions.

The inevitable **Maison de Jeanne d'Arc**, on place Général de Gaulle, is fun for children, with good models and dioramas of the breaking of the Orléans siege. Copies of artists' rendering of Ste Jeanne show that the page-boy cut and demure little face are part of the myth – there is no contemporary portrait and alas no death mask. (Open 10–12 & 2–6, Nov–April 2–6 only; cl. Mons; cheap entrance.)

The **Centre Charles Péguy**, down the road in another Renaissance mansion, is a thankful reminder that Joan of Arc's history is not the only one. The late 19C and early 20C is the period presented, around the life and work of Charles Péguy (1873–1914), Christian socialist writer who came from Orléans. Though there are cartoons and drawings, the main exhibits are texts (and no translation): Zola's front page '*J'accuse*' letter to the President and the broadsheets by both sides in the Dreyfus affair; front covers of opposition journals; documentation of the CGT's general strike call in 1907 for the 40-hour week (which it took till 1936 to win) and various books and pamphlets. (Open 1.30–6, cl. Sun; free.)

Upstream – St-Benoît

Along the Loire **upstream from Orléans,** single track roads run along the top of the flood banks, ideal for bicycling. There are plenty of riverside campsites but the countryside is miserably dull, with the marsh-ridden Sologne to the south and the north bank gearing itself up for the treeless wheat plain to Paris. There is no more good wine either, until SANCERRE and POUILLY on the Burgundy border. The river itself is like a richman's son pretending to be a pauper. A paddling pool on pram wheels could look more treacherous, yet it can inflate within 24 hours and deluge the valley.

An afternoon's bikeride crossing over to the north bank at Château-neuf-sur-Loire would bring you to **ST-BENOÎT-SUR-LOIRE** (and buses or hitching might take as long). In the **Abbaye de Fleury** at this village, a marble mosaic of Roman origin covers the chancel floor of one of the most awe-inspiring Romanesque churches in France, built in pale yellow to cream coloured stone between 1020 and 1218. The oldest part, the porch, illustrates the *Vision of the Apocalypse* by the fantastically sculpted capitals and by the layout which follows the description of the New Jerusalem in *Revelations*; foursquare, with twelve foundations and three open gates on each side.

BOURGES

There's a terminal frustration in a city parading more than enough starred sights to fill a day and then turning into a lifeless, provincial backwater come nightfall. Such is **BOURGES**. The problem is analogous to its one-time status in the 15C – capital of France but what France?

So, first priority, a fairly comprehensive list of **late evening places**: *Le Guillotin*, bar, restaurant and café-théâtre upstairs (15 rue Edouard Vaillant); *Crêperie des Jacobins*, bar and restaurant (rue des Armuriers); *Bar Mirabeau*, brasserie, comedian barman but junkie clientele (59 rue Mirabeau). As for other practicalities, there is a **youth hostel** at 22 rue Henri Sellier (48.24.58.09; cl. Sat and not on a bus route), and a **campsite** across the stream from the hostel (entrance on bd de l'Industrie: bus to JUSTICES from place Cujas, stop Joffre and walk down boulevard). Cheap **hotels** in the centre are *de Tours* (5 rue Calvin); *L'Étape* (rue Casanova); *de l'Agriculture* (15 rue du Prinal). The **SI** is by the cathedral, place E Dolet. The **gare routière**, place Parmentier, is half way between the cathedral and the **gare SNCF**, ½km to the north. **Bikes** can be hired from *LocaBourges*, rue Edouard Vaillant.

From the outside, Bourges' **Cathédrale St-Etienne** looks like a doomed medieval space programme. Encircled by stone rockets, the flying buttresses were ready to swing open, releasing the vast coffin-like top storey of the nave to be projected into space. But not long after the control towers were completed, a major technical hitch appeared in the form of a west front door squatting on the launch pad, followed by the collapse of the north tower. By the early 16C, the rebuilding of the latter had grounded the cathedral for ever. Which is a great pity, except for the interior which bears no resemblance to a space craft, and whose best feature, the stained glass windows wouldn't have worked in outer space.

All the other old buildings and streets of Bourges are on a loop round this centre. On rue Jacques Coeur stands the head office, stock exchange, dealing rooms, banksafes and home of Charles VII's finance minister, **Jacques Coeur** (1400–56). This medieval shipping magnate, moneylender and arms dealer dominates Bourges as the Maid does Orléans – the 'King of Bourges' as the English called Charles VII, doesn't get a look in. Jacques Coeur's career provides an early example of the profitability of war for some. Until just a few years before his death, the English were still in control above the Loire yet his business interests stretched from Paris to Damascus. The visit to his palace is quite fun. There are hardly any furnishings, but the man may have left his mark in the stonework (restored in the 19C) and it's the only mansion where you are shown the original toilets. (Guided visits from 9/10–11.15 & 2–5.15/4.15 Nov–March.) The nearby pâtisserie shop, on the corner of rue d'Auron and rue des Armuriers, which claims to be Jacques Coeur's birthplace, isn't, but you can eat good cakes there in a partly medieval room. The

SI will lovingly detail the city's **other mansions, ancient halls** and **museums** for you, but none of them match Jacques Coeur's palace and the cathedral.

LITERARY ASSOCIATIONS IN BERRY

Alain Fournier, author of *Le Grand Meaulnes*, was born near Bourges in 1886. Some scenes of the novel are set in the city, but the lost domaine of 'la fête étrange' is somewhere near **EPINEUIL-LE-FLEURIAL** (the Ste-Agathe of the novel), 25km south of ST-ARMAND MONTROND. Just before Meaulnes first sees the château, the location is described only by: 'In the whole of the Sologne it would have been hard to find a more desolate spot than the region in which he now found himself.' Albicoco's excellent film of the book was shot around Epineuil and is much more rewarding to see than searching for an actual château that fits all the details. Fournier spent his childhood in Epineuil and the elementary school, the one described in the book, can be visited out of class hours.

NOHANT, just north of La Châtre, is where **George Sand** (1808–76) spent half her life. After the publication of a novel set locally which received great attention, she wrote: 'this unknown Vallée Noire, this quiet and unpretentious landscape . . . All this had charms for me alone and did not deserve to be revealed to idle curiosity'. She went on to say that she was compelled to write and had not given a thought to potential notoriety. What the critics jumped on in this novel (*Valentine*) and her others were 'anti-matrimonial doctrines', in fact no more than that ill-matched couples should be able to separate. Simone de Beauvoir described her as a 'sentimental feminist' – George Sand was certainly no activist except for the brief period of the 1848 revolution. Her male friends called her a man eater and present day anglo-saxons too often refer to her as Chopin's mistress. Her literary output was enormous and the French recognise her as one of their great writers. But her significance now is more for her life than her works.

The **Château de Nohant** is open 9–11.45 & 2–6 (mid April–Oct only) for rather hasty guided tours. You are shown the dining room laid for guests: Flaubert, Turgenev, Dumas, to which could be added Delacroix, Balzac and Liszt. The piano that George Sand gave Chopin, her guest for ten years, sits in the living-room with the family portraits. The writer's son Maurice built the puppet theatre with Chopin, jealousy fits allowing, and made the puppets with his mum.

In **LA CHÂTRE** itself, where every other place name is George Sand, the **Musée de la Vallée Noire** (71 rue Venose) dedicates one floor to the writer. There are plenty of pictures as well as words: George Sand's caricatures of her friends, a photograph of Chopin, drawings of other Nohant guests, Maurice's illustrations for his mother's work and the doodles on her manuscripts.

LE MANS

Half way between Normandy and the Loire, **LE MANS** is the capital of Sarthe, a department that contains more châteaux than both banks of the Loir, most privately owned and closed to the public. The pastimes of wine tasting, château spying and water gazing are best done on the Loir river. Sarthe as a whole is France at its most *douce* – a bit boring perhaps, if less overrun by tourists than neighbouring regions.

Le Mans itself is taken over by motor fanatics in the middle of June for the famous 24-Hour race. But the rest of the year it is still lively – and with good public services and free museums (courtesy of the Communist townhall) and one of the most beautiful old quarters of any city in France. This, the **Vieille Ville**, floats on a hill above the Sarthe river, partly enclosed by 3C–4C Gallo-Roman walls and with the immense Gothic apse of **St-Julien's cathedral** ascending the hill from the south-east to its Romanesque nave on place du Château. Some of the stained glass windows here were in place when the first Plantagenet was buried in the church but the brightest colours in the otherwise austere interior come from the tapestries.

Elsewhere, in the old town, intricate Renaissance stonework, medieval half-timbering, sculpted pillars and beams and grand classical façades make up the street fronts. In the 1850s a road was tunnelled under the quarter, then a slum, so it preserves a self-contained unity above the modern town: steep walled steps lead up from the river and longer flights descend the southern side using the old Gallo-Roman entrances. The transformation, for once, has not been a total upmarketing job: a new HLM council block manages not to clash with the 3C **Tour Madeleine** behind it; there are cafés and restaurants, a Friday/Saturday market on place du Château, a good cinema, *Ciné Poche* at 97 Grande rue, and a pleasing absence of souvenir shops. The tunnel comes out on the south side, by an impressive monument to Wilbur Wright, into place des Jacobins, the vantage point for St-Julien's flying buttresses. From here, you can walk east through the park to the **Musée Tessé**, a mixed bunch of pics and statues including George de la Tour's light at its most extraordinary in the *Extase de St François* and copies of brilliant medieval populist murals in Sarthe churches. (Open 9–12 & 2–6.)

The modern centre of Le Mans is **place de la République**, lined by a Pythonesque mixture of belle époque and Americana office blocks. The cafés and brasseries on the square stay open till late and restaurants are easy to find in the streets around. The SI is on the north side with the roads on either side leading to the Vieille Ville and the urban bus office in the underground shopping centre. Buses 16, 5, 31, 3 and 41 go from the **gare SNCF** up av Général Leclerc, near the top of which is the **gare routière**, to the *place*. Off av Général Leclerc, there are two cheap **hotels** on rue du P Mersenne, *Au Vin d'Anjou* (no 15) and *Select* (13) and at 15 bd de la Gare, *Hôtel de la Terrasse*. There is no youth hostel and no nearby campsites but there are some *Foyers* and *Centres d'Hébergement* – ask at the SI for addresses. The **ALLOSTOP** number is 43.24.70.69.

In 1908, Wilbur Wright took off, alongside what is now the fastest stretch of the **24 Hours circuit** and stayed in the air for a record breaking 1hr 31.5 mins. The invitation to use the grounds came from two brothers, busy manufacturing some of the first internal combustion engine cars. The **Musée de l'Automobile**, in the middle of the Bugatti and 24 Hours circuits, documents these early transport successes and has a superb collection of cars from 1885 to recent winners of the great race, almost all in working order. It is open 9–12, 2–7/6 (cl. Tues in winter). Motor-bikes, go-karts and even lorries race on the Bugatti circuit and some practising vehicle is bound to provide the appropriate soundtrack for this Steve McQueen starred scene. Not surprisingly, the tracks are not on the bus routes – the nearest are the termini of 6 and 7 (*Raineries* and *Guette Loup*) – but you might get a fast lift.

TRAVEL DETAILS

Trains
From Angers frequently to Paris (3¼hrs) via Le Mans (1hr) to Nantes (¾hr) and to Tours (1½hrs) via Saumur (¾hr); 8 daily to Savennières-Béhuard (¼hr).

From Tours at least hourly to Paris-Austerlitz (2½hrs) via Blois (½hr) and Les Aubrais-Orléans (1¼hrs); at least 10 daily to Angers (1½hrs) via Saumur (¾hr) and to Le Mans (1¼hrs); 8 daily to Azay-le-Rideau/Chinon (½hr/1hr); 6 daily to Loches (1hr); 5 daily to Chenonceaux-Chisseux/St-Aignan (½hr/1hr) and to Bourges (2hrs).

From Orléans every 5mins to Les Aubrais-Orléans (4mins).

From Les Aubrais-Orléans 1 every half-hour to Paris (1¼hrs); 4 daily to Bourges (1¼hrs).

From Le Mans frequently to Paris (1¾hrs), to Nantes (1¾hrs) via Angers (1hr) and to Rennes (2hrs).

Buses
From Angers 6 daily to Saumur (1½hrs); 2 daily to Rennes (2¾hrs); 5 daily to Baugé (1¾hrs).

From Saumur 3 daily to Fontévraud (½hr); daily to Chinon (¾hr).

From Tours 7 daily to Amboise (½hr); 4 daily to Loches (¾hr); 3 daily to Azay-le-Rideau/Chinon (½hr/1¼hrs); 2 daily to Chenonceaux (1hr) and Ste-Maure (¾hr); daily to Montrichard (1¼hrs) and Richelieu (1½hrs).

From Blois 4 daily to Orléans (1½hrs); 1 or 2 daily to Cheverney.

Chapter six
POITOU-CHARENTES AND THE ATLANTIC COAST

Newsstands selling the *Sud-Ouest* paper at Poitiers announce that this is the beginning of the **South-West**. Not the Mediterranean, certainly, but in summer from here on, in the light, in the warm air, in the fields of sunflowers and the shuttered siesta-silent air of the farmhouses, you get that first exciting promise of the South.

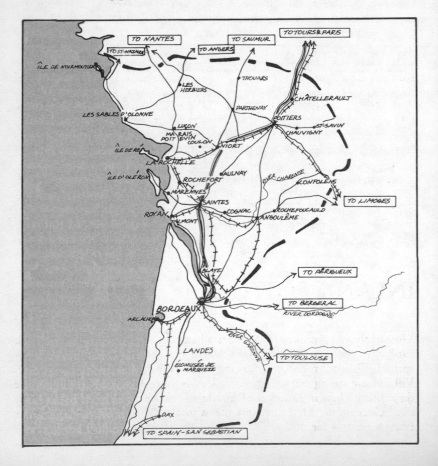

The coast, on the other hand, remains distinctly Atlantic – dunes, pine forest, reclaimed marshland, and misty mud flats. It has great charm in places, particularly the islands of **Noirmoutier, Ré** and **Oléron** and particularly out of season. But it is family, camper, caravanner seaside; it lacks the glamour and excitement of the Côte d'Azur; the sandy beaches are beautiful but not too good for keen swimmers; the water murky and often shallow for a long way out. Of its two long-established ports, **Bordeaux**, for all its size and past, seems drab on a casual visit. **La Rochelle**, however, is one of the prettiest and most distinctive towns in France.

Inland, the **valley of the Charente** river, slow and green, epitomises the blue-overalled, Gauloise-smoking, shrewd-eyed, bottom-fishing peasant France. The towpath is walkable for long stretches, or mountain-bikable. And there are boat trips from Saintes and Cognac. The **Marais Poitevin** marshes, too, with their poplar groves and island fields reticulated by countless canals and ditches, are both unusual landscape and good, easy-going walking or cycling country.

But perhaps the most memorable aspect of the countryside – and indeed of towns like Poitiers too – are the exquisite and innumerable **Romanesque churches**. This was a significant stretch of the medieval pilgrim routes – across France and from Britain and northern Europe – to the shrine of **Saint Jacques** (St James, or Santiago as the Spanish know him) at Compostela in north-west Spain, and was well endowed by its followers. The finest of the churches, perhaps in all of France, dot the countryside around **Saintes** and **Poitiers**: informal, highly individual and so integrated with their landscape they often seem as rooted as the trees.

And lastly, of course, remember that this is a region of **seafood** – fresh and cheap in every market for miles inland, with oysters adding a touch of the fleshpots to any picnic – and, with the regions of **Bordeaux** (Claret) and **Cognac**, of distinguished local wines.

INLAND POITOU

Most of the old **province of Poitou** is a huge expanse of rolling wheatland, sunflower and maize plantations where the combines crawl and giant sprinklers shoot great arcs of white water over the fields in summertime. Villages are strung out along the valley bottoms. It's the heartland of the domains of Eleanor, Duchess of Aquitaine, whose marriage to the English king Henry II in 1152 brought the whole south-west of France under English control for 300 years. It is also the northern limit of the langue-d'oc speaking part of the country, whose **Occitan** dialect survives in the speech of the old-timers even today.

Hitching is the easiest way of **moving around** within the area, though the main destinations are all easily accessible by mainline train from Paris. POITIERS is just 3 hours, with frequent connections on to LA ROCHELLE, BORDEAUX and the Atlantic coast.

POITIERS AND AROUND

It was at **POITIERS**, in 732, that Charles Martel defeated the Moors of Spain and reversed, or at least halted, the spread of Islam through Europe. Viewed in retrospect his battle seems one of the most significant events of the Middle Ages, and it is not surprising to find that this is a town of very great church riches. Whether you've an interest in holy buildings or not, stop long enough to take a look at Romanesque **Notre-Dame-la-Grande**. If you like it, or if this is what you have come to Poitiers to see, you may find the town and its surroundings keep you for some days.

Arriving by **train**, it's a short walk in to the centre and the main square at place Leclerc. The **gare routière** is only slightly further out, on place Thézard below the Parc de Bloissac. There are several cheap **hotels** opposite the gare SNCF: the *Cyrano* is basic, but clean, with a cafeteria underneath. *Alsace-Lorraine* (2 rue Alsace-Lorraine), just south of place Leclerc, is good, and more central. Best of all is *Plat d'Étain* on the north side of the *place* though it is graded two-star and a bit more expensive. The **youth hostel** is at 17 rue de la Jeunesse (bus 9 from the station to the *Bellejouanne* stop about 3km away); **Camping Municipal** is on rue du Porteau, north of the town. If you have any difficulty with accommodation, ask the SI, who in summer run an additional annexe outside the station.

The town centre occupies the top of the hill with the pedestrian rue Gambetta running through the middle. A little way along on the right you come to one of Poitiers' principal buildings of medieval and modern times, **the Palais de Justice**, its 19C façade hiding a magnificent example of medieval secular architecture – the great hall of the palace of the dukes of Aquitaine, first erected in the 12C. It is a vast room nearly 50m long with wide tie-beams supporting its wooden roof. Here, Jean, Duc de Berry, held his court, while stairs in the corner give access to the old castle keep, where Joan of Arc was put through her ideological paces by a committee of bishops worried no doubt about endangering their own immortal souls and worldly positions by approving someone who might prove to be a charlatan or a heretic. They also, incidentally, had her virginity checked out by a posse of respectable matrons.

But all this is delaying the moment of truth. Back up the hill, past the Faculty of Science, and down rue de la Régatterie, and you come upon

the great church of **Notre-Dame-La-Grande**. Begun in the reign of
Eleanor, you cannot call it elegant; the proporations are squat and loaded
with sculptural detail to a degree that the modern eye finds fussy. But
look at the detail, for it is this which is fun in Romanesque art, ranging
from the domestic to the disturbingly anarchic. In the blind arch right of
the door, a woman sits in the keystone with hair blowing out from her
head. In the frieze above, Mary places her hand familiarly on Elizabeth's
pregnant belly. You see the newborn Jesus admired by a couple of daft-
looking sheep and gurgling in his bath-tub. Higher still are portraits of
the apostles, and right at the top, where the eye is carried deliberately and
inevitably, Christ in Majesty in an almond-shaped inset. Such elaborated
sculpted façades and domes like pinecones on turret and belfry are the
hallmarks of the Poitou brand of Romanesque.

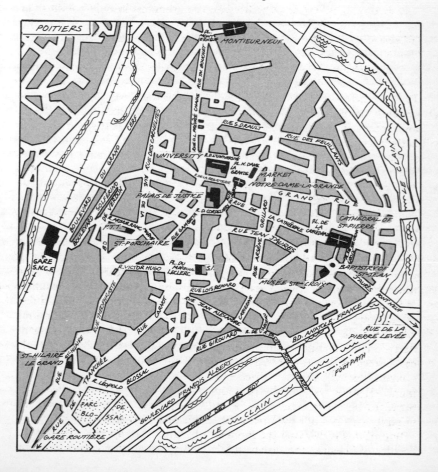

Smack opposite, as you come out of the church, is the original **university building**, where Descartes was a student. On the left, rue du Marché and rue de la Cathédrale lead to the 13–14C **Cathédrale St-Pierre**, which lies well down the east slope of Poitiers' hill. Its broad façade of pale stone is broken by three doorways and a rose window surmounted by a gallery. Pigeons roost and plants root in the tightly clustered figures adorning the voussoirs of the doorways. Inside is a vast, bare space flooded with pale light. Some of the glass is 12C, notably the Crucifixion in the centre window of the apse, in which the features of Henry II and Eleanor are supposedly discernible. The choir stalls are full of characteristic medieval detail: a coquettish Mary and child, a peasant killing a boar, the architect at work with his dividers, a baker with a basket of loaves.

Behind the cathedral towards the river Clain you come to another church, the much-altered **Ste-Radegonde**, founded in the 6C by the wife of the Frankish king, Lothair I, and beyond it to rue Jean-Jaurès, where, on an island in the middle of the roadway, is one of the oldest Christian buildings in the country, the **Bapistry of St-Jean** (10.30–12.30 & 3–4). No beauty – it looks like a second-rate Roman temple: its great age gives it venerability. It dates from the mid-4C. Initiates were baptised at the octagonal *piscine* sunk into the floor. The existence of water conduits in the bottom shows that it was served by running water, but their position relative to the bottom shows that the water could not have been more than 30–40cm deep, which gives the lie to the received belief that early Christian baptism was by total immersion.

In the side-street opposite is Poitiers' museum, **the Musée Ste-Croix** (10–12 & 2–6; cl. Tues; free). Downstairs is an interesting collection of local farming implements, among them an 'alambic ambulant' or itinerant still, of a kind in use until surprisingly recently. There is also a good Gallo-Roman section with some handsome glass, pottery and sculpture, notably a pretty marble Minerva (1C).

At the bottom of rue Jean-Jaurès, the Pont Neuf crosses the Clain. Further on, in rue de la Pierre Levée, are more relics of Poitiers' remotest past: the **Hypogée martyrium**, a 7C subterranean chapel, and the **Pierre Levée** itself, a dolmen, where in Rabelais' time, as he says, students used to come to meet and carry on and scratch their names. There is a riverside walk from the Pont Neuf to Pont St-Cyprien just upstream. On the further bank, neat *potagers* – vegetable gardens – come down to the water's edge with a little mud quay at the end where a punt is moored by a chain, where 'monsieur' spends many a weekend hour patiently waiting for a fat carp. Such carefully tended, well-manured *potagers* are a feature of every French provincial town. Sometimes they are to be found right in the heart of the town, as if some atavistic refusal to become completely urban.

If you cross Pont St-Cyprien and climb uphill bearing left in rue Girouard, you come to the **Parc de Blossac**, a pretty, formal garden with clipped limes and gravelled alleys, *boules* pitches, a café and a view. From the park gate, rue Léopold and rue de Doyenné, where Rabelais lived, bring you to the church of **St-Hilaire-le-Grand**, with the roofs of its six radiating chapels, ambulatory and apse mounting in harmonious symmetry to the gable end of the nave and the chopped off remains of the bell-tower. Despite 19C alterations, including a new façade and demolition of part of the nave, St-Hilaire still has features which make it one of the most interesting buildings of its time. The original wooden roof, burnt in the 12C, was replaced by a series of octagonal cupolas on squinches – an arrangement shared by only one other aisled church in France. To support the weight of this new vault, the architects added a forest of auxiliary columns, creating three aisles either side in place of the original one.

So much, then, for the city's churches. If they don't inspire, head straight for the coast (there are good connections by train and bus to La Rochelle and Bordeaux) or try some local walks. The SI sell a guide to **walking possibilities** in the region, and the GR364 starts out from here, reaching the Vendée coast via Parthenay (see p. 213). **Eating,** there's a good salon de thé/restaurant opposite Notre-Dame and a cheap simple Pizzeria (*Capuccino*) outside the Faculty of Science in rue de l'Université. Other places in rue Carnot. **Culturally,** despite the university, there's not a great deal going on, though you might check out the Montierneuf area for **bars** (*L'Arlequin*, on the *place*, can be fun) and the CIJ (64 rue Gambetta) for information.

More Romanesque – St-Savin and Chauvigny
Close by and just visitable in the day, ST-SAVIN and CHAUVIGNY have exceptionally fine churches, particularly St-Savin, whose abbey preserves very good Romanesque frescoes. You need to make an early start if you are to do both in one day using public transport. The first bus leaves at 6.15am and gets you to St-Savin at 7.13. There is a bus back to Chauvigny at 10. Then you have a choice of two buses to return to Poitiers. The timetable may seem brutal, but there is no other way of doing it, unless you hitch. Alternatively, both places have two or three reasonable **hotels** and Chauvigny has a **campsite**.

ST-SAVIN, on the bank of the river Gartempe, is tiny. The bus puts you down beside the abbey near the modern bridge. There is a **medieval bridge** a little way downstream with stone prows parting the current round its piers, a nice walk and vantage point if the bus has deposited you with time to fill before opening. Looking back at **the abbey** from here – built in the 11C, possibly on the site of a church founded by Charlemagne – it seems very permanent and severe, in contrast to the softer lines of the domestic dwellings at its feet. It is a powerful building, its belltower crouched over the crossing of transept and nave, yet it is saved from heaviness by the sense of upward thrust generated by the lines of the plain buttresses on the gable wall of the transept, the vertical ribs of the apse and the cluster of reinforcing pilasters at the corner of the tower itself. And nothing could be lighter and more graceful than the harmonious proportions and relations of apse and radiating chapels, transept and tower together. The soaring crocketed spire on the west tower, which first catches the eye today, is a Gothic addition.

Once **inside** (hours are 9–12.30/11 Suns & hols & 2.30–7/5 Oct–June) you descend a flight of steps to the narthex and thence to the floor of the nave, which stretches away from you to the raised choir, high, narrow, barrel-vaulted and flanked by bare, round columns. Their capitals are deeply carved with interlacing foliage. Light floods in from the aisles. There has been some tinkering by restorers, but even without its frescoes the church is a model – indeed, served as a model – of Romanesque architecture.

The whole of the vault of the nave, undisturbed except at the beginning by transverse arches, is covered with paintings, the right side rather better preserved than the left. The colours used are few – red and yellow ochre, and green, mixed with white and black. Yet the paintings are full of light and grace. The scenes depicted are taken from the stories of Genesis and Exodus. Some are instantly recognisable: Noah's three-decked ark, Pharoah's horses rearing at the engulfing waves of the Red Sea, graceful workers constructing the Tower of Babel.

CHAUVIGNY is a busy market town on the banks of the Vienne. Its half-dozen factories – porcelain and timber – provide work for the surrounding area. The **market** is held on Saturdays between the church of Notre Dame and the river: clothes, records, radios, but above all a mouthwatering selection of food – pâtés encased in pristine aspic (one beauty, decorated with the yellow segments of scallop flesh, called 'amandes'), oysters, prawns, crayfish, cheeses galore. The cafés are fun, too, bursting with noisy wine-flushed farmers combining business and society.

What you must not miss is the **church of St-Pierre** (11C) with its grotesque sculptures. There is nothing refined about them. Here you feel was an artist who came from the same peasant stock as his audience, prey to the same superstitions, the same fears of things that went bump in the night and lurked in the wet woods. Rue du Château opposite the church of Notre-Dame on the main road winds right-handed up the rocky spur on which the old town stands. Past the ruins of a castle that belonged to the Bishops of Poitiers and the better preserved château d'Harcourt, you come to St-Pierre with its most attractive and unusual east end. Inside, it is damp and in a poor state of repair. The choir capitals are the things to look at. There is no symmetry or logic; each one is quite different. And what a terrifying world they evoke. Graphically illustrated monsters, bearded, moustachioed, winged, scaled, human-headed with manes of flame, grab hapless mortals, naked, upside down and puny, and rip their bowels, and crunch their heads. The only escape offered is in the naively serene events of Christ's birth: on the second capital on the south side of the choir, the angel announces Christ's birth to the shepherds, their flock represented by four sheep that look like Pooh's companion, Eyore, while just round the corner the archangel Michael weighs souls in hand-held scales and a scaly devil tries to grab one for his dinner. The oddest scene is on the north side: a Siamese-twin dancer grips the hindlegs of two horse-like monsters which are gnawing his upper arms.

PARTHENAY AND NIORT

Forty-nine km west of Poitiers, **PARTHENAY** (regular SNCF buses) was once an important staging post on the pilgrim routes to Compostela. As you approach, the open landscape of the Poitou plain is replaced by *bocages* – small fields enclosed by hedges and trees. As in England, the fashion for grubbing up woodland and creating vast windswept acreages in the name of efficiency and productivity is dying out. And not just for aesthetic reasons: wind erosion has left scarcely 10–15cm of top soil on the plain of Poitou. The adviser to a farmers' collective told me Parthenay's colourful Wednesday livestock market is one of the biggest in France.

From the station, **av de Gaulle** leads to a large square (**SI** on the corner). From the west side, rue Jean-Jaurès crosses the shopping precinct. A right turn in **rue de la Saunerie** brings you to the **Tour de l'Horloge**, the fortified gateway to the old citadel on a steep-sided spur sticking out into a loop of the river Thouet. Just along on the right the *mairie* faces the church of Ste-Croix (12C) across a small garden with a view over the ramparts and the gully of St-Jacques with its medieval houses and vegetable plots climbing the further slope. Further along is a house where Richelieu used to visit his grandfather, then a handsome but badly damaged Romanesque portal, all that remains of the castle chapel of Notre-Dame-de-la-Couldre. Practically nothing is left of the castle. From the end of the street you look down on the **Pont St-Jacques**, with its twin-towered gateway, through which flocks of pilgrims poured into the town for a night's shelter. You get to it by turning left out of the Tour de l'Horloge and down the Vaux St-Jacques, as this medieval lane is called. It is still highly evocative with its crooked half-timbered dwellings crowding up to the bridge. They are only now beginning to be restored. Some look as if they have received little attention since the last pilgrim shuffled up the street.

If you want to stay, there are two reasonable **hotels** in bd Meilleraye by the main square, *Grand Hôtel* and *Hôtel de la Meilleraye* and *Hôtel du Nord* (Logis de France) in Av de Gaulle. The **campsite** is at Le Tallud, about 3km west on the D949.

There are three extremely fine **Romanesque churches** within easy reach of Parthenay. One – with an equestrian statue of a knight hawking on the façade – is only about 20mins' walk on the Niort road, at PARTHENAY-LE-VIEUX. The others are at AIRVAULT, easily accessible on the Parthenay-Thouars SNCF bus route, and ST-JOUIN-DE-MARNES, 9km north-east (have to hitch or walk that). Or, you could go on to THOUARS (cheap hotels and Camping Municipal), and combine a visit to the 16C Château d'Oiron with St-Jouin (only 8.5km).

NIORT on the way to LA ROCHELLE and the MARAIS POITEVIN, is bigger and prettier. If you are in a car, it could be the best base for exploring the *marais*, and whatever your mode of travel, it is the last place before the marshes to get a really wide choice of provisions to stock up with. In itself it is worth a morning's stroll.

The most interesting part of the town is round **rue Victor-Hugo** and **rue St-Jean**, mostly a pedestrian area, full of medieval houses, some stone, some half-timbered. Coming from the station, you take rue de la Gare as far as av de Verdun (**SI** and the main **Post Office** on the corner), where you turn right into place de la Brèche. Rue Victor-Hugo is the continuation of rue Ricard on the left of the square. It follows the line of the medieval market in a gully separating the two small hills on which Niort is built. Up to the right, opposite the end of rue St-Jean, is an oddly-shaped – triangular – Renaissance mansion of 1535, very narrow, with lantern, belfry, and machicolations, capable perhaps of repelling drunken revellers, but no match for catapult or sledgehammer.

Niort's river is the **Sèvre Niortaise**, not to be confused with the Sèvre Nantaise which flows northwards to join the Loire at Nantes. There are gardens and trees along the bank. Over the bridge is a ruined glove factory, vestige of Niort's once thriving leather industry. At the time of the Revolution it kept more than thirty cavalry regiments in leather breeches. Today the biggest industry is insurance. The 'most bourgeois town in France', someone commented, because of the prosperity brought by the huge number of major insurance companies making their HQ here.

Just downstream, opposite a riverside car park, is the **market hall**, with a café doing a good cheap lunch, and beyond, vast and unmistakable on a slight rise, the keep of a castle begun by Henry II of England. This is now a museum (open 9–12 & 2–6/5 in winter; cl. Tues) mainly of local furniture and costumes; it is interesting to see how only 100 years ago each village had its distinctive style of dress.

There are several **hotels** close to the station: *Bordeaux, l'Europe, Modern, Terminus* – all in rue de la Gare. *Bordeaux* and *Modern* are the cheapest. **Camping Municipal** is in the Parc des Expositions, the **gare routière** in rue Viala, off place de la Brèche. **Bike hire** is available from the station: maximum period of rental three days. If you found a trustworthy machine, you could hire here and make a bike tour of the *marais* – the best way to see it; it is completely flat and small enough to be seen in two to three days. Before setting out, pick up the sheaf of walking itineraries available from the SI.

THE MARAIS

The **Marais Poitevin** is a strange, lazy landscape of fens and meadows, shielded by great poplar trees and crossed by an elaborate system of canals, dykes and slow-flowing rivers. Recently declared a National Park, the French know it as *La Venise Verte* – the Green Venice – and a tourist industry of sorts has been developing around the villages, where you can hire punts for jaunts on the waterways. This, sadly, seems doomed to be the region's future. But the marshes are not yet dead, or completely phoney, and the flat-bottomed punts remain the principal means of transport for many farmers – inevitably, for there is no dry land access to many of the fields. Just avoid weekends, when the coming transformation seems all too clear.

Access is easiest at the village of **COULON**, on the Sèvre, at the east edge of the marsh; it is just 10½km from NIORT, by bike or occasional bus. As you would expect in a marshland village, Coulon's houses are small, low and obviously poor. **Punts**, with or without a guide, can be hired here by the half day – touristy perhaps but fun on a sunny day with a picnic. There are two **hotels** in the village, both Logis de France – the *Central* and (cheaper) *Au Marais* – and an attractive, unfussy **campsite**, in a meadow about 2km downstream (25mins' walk).

Getting about the Marais as a whole, a **bike** is ideal. If you **walk**, best stick to the lanes since cross-country tracks tend to end in fields surrounded by water. Once off the riverside COULON-ARCAIS road there is practically no traffic. At the seaward end of the marsh, **south of Luçon**, the landscape is quite different, all straight lines and open fields of wheat and sunflower. The little mounds that were once islands are now villages. Further north up the coast at LA DAVIAUD, in the **Marais Breton**, there is an **écomusée** illustrating the social and environmental history of the marshes – the Centre de découverte du Marais Breton-Vendéen (10.30–12.30 & 3–6; cl. Mons; Nov–March wkends only).

LA ROCHELLE AND THE ISLANDS

This is great stretch of coast for young families, especially the **islands**, with miles of safe sandy beaches and shallow water. But unless you're camping or have booked something in advance, accommodation will be a near-insuperable problem in August. Out of season you can't rely on sunny weather, but that should not deter you if you like the slightly melancholy romance of quiet misty seascapes and working fishing ports. **Nantes** (see p. 172) in the north, **La Rochelle** and **Royan** in the south – all well served by rail – are the best bases. Away from these centres you'll have to take pot-luck with the rather quirky bus routes.

NORTH: LES SABLES AND THE ÎLE DE NOIRMOUTIER

The area round **LES SABLES D'OLONNE** and northwards has been heavily developed with costa-style apartment blocks. If you are passing through, there's a surprisingly good modern art section in the Musée de l'Abbaye Ste-Croix on rue Verdun (10.30–12 & 2.30–6.30) but there seems little reason to stay. If you need to, there's a youth hostel (July–Aug only) in rue des Roses and a campsite in rue Maréchal Leclerc, both east of the centre and *gares*.

There are two possible attractions, however, which might make you want to linger in this part of the country. The Île de Noirmoutier, one of the more desirable locations on this coast, can be reached in 3 hrs by bus from LES SABLES: though an island, it's connected to the shore by a tollbridge. And inland, at the ruined **Château of Le Puy** in LES ÉPESSES, a remarkable **lakeside extravaganza** is enacted, most nights from June to August. This is a weird affair: the enactment of the life of a local peasant from the Middle Ages to the last war, complete with fireworks, lasers, dances on the lake and *Comédie Française* voice-overs. The story, précised in a brief English text, is interesting but incidental – the spectacle is the thing. For details ask at the SI in LES SABLES (rue Maréchal Leclerc) or, nearer to the event, at LES HERBIERS. To get to LES ÉPESSES you'll need to take a train to CHOLET and a bus from there; Puy de Fou itself is 2½km from Les Épesses, on the D27 to CHAMBRETARD. There is one reasonably-priced **hotel** in LES ÉPESSES (*Le Lion d'Or*, 2 rue de la Libération) and a wider choice (*Relais*, *du Centre* or *Chez Camille*) at nearby LES HERBIERS.

The **ÎLE DE NOIRMOUTIER**, spared the high-rise development of its adjoining coast, was an early monastic settlement. It is now very much a tourist resort, and a relatively upmarket one: villas here are in great demand. But though this is the island's main economy, it doesn't dominate everything. Salt marshes here are still worked, spring potatoes sown and fishes fished.

The island town, NOIRMOUTIER EN L'ÎLE boasts a 12C castle (with a couple of museums), a church with a Romanesque crypt, an excellent market (Tues/Fri) and most of the life – piano bars extending normal café hours. There are campsites dotted about the island – maps from the SI on the main road from the bridge at MARMATRE, bike hire from *Vel-hop* (55 av Joseph Pineau) or *Fabre* (rue du Centre, Marmatre). Among hotels to try in the town are *Le Bois de la Chaize* (23 av de la Victoire), *La Marée* (2bis Grande Rue) and *Chez Bébert*, 37 av Joseph Pineau, or at BARBATRE; *La Fosse* (57 rue de la Pointe) or *Le Marina* (1 route du Gois).

Exploring **around the Island,** the western coast resembles the mainland with great curves of sand while the northern side dips in and out of little bays with rocky promontories inbetween. Inland, were it not for the salt water dykes, the horizon would say that you were miles from the sea. It is a strange place with only one hostile element apart from the storms in spring, a powerful community of mosquitoes. The more southerly resorts, though built up, have not been main targets for the developers. In the village centres there are still the one-storey houses, whitewashed and ochre-tiled with decorative brickwork round the windows and S or Z shaped coloured bars on the shutters that you see throughout La Vendée and southern Brittany.

LA ROCHELLE AND THE ÎLE DE RÉ

LA ROCHELLE is unusually elegant: its centre immaculately preserved in 17–18C arcades, its waterfront guarded by twin medieval towers, its markets and street stalls supercharged with the exotic delights of Atlantic shellfish. It has always been an independent, adventurous place. Eleanor gave the town a charter of freedom from feudal obligations in 1199 and it rapidly became a port of major importance, trading in salt and wine, and skilfully exploiting the quarrel between the English and French to its own advantage. After the disasters of the Wars of Religion it became the principal port for trade with the French colonies in the West Indies and Canada. Indeed, many of the settlers, especially in Canada, came from this part of France.

Finding your way around is straightforward. Everything of interest is to be found in the area behind the waterfront, in effect, between the **harbour** and the **place de Verdun**, about 10mins' walk away. There is no need to bother about public transport, except for getting to the campsite or youth hostel. To reach the harbour area from the **station**, you simply walk straight down the street in front of you, **av de Gaulle.**

The quayside is dominated by the **Porte de la Grosse Horloge,** an originally Gothic gateway into the old town, remodelled in the 18C. In front, towards the Tour de la Chaine, are the more upmarket seaview cafés and restaurants, overlooking the affluent ebb of a yacht-filled **harbour**. If you linger, best remain standing, or move on, up to the **Tour de la Canterne** and beyond onto the **ramparts** where a stretch of park and gardens leads down to the **town beach**, very crowded in season, but fun and backed by hot-dog stalls, amusements and (for the yachties) a casino.

Over towards the centre, **rue du Palais** and **rue de l'Escale** are full of lovely houses, some stone, some half-timbered, with the timbers protected from the weather by slates overlapping like fish-scales. Towards the end of rue de l'Escale at the corner of rue Fromentin, is a magnificent 17C house, adorned with statues of famous medical men, like Hippocrates and Galien. In rue des Augustins, off rue du Palais, the regional tourist board has its offices in a courtyard (at 11bis), the back of which is formed by the so-called **Maison Henri II**, a fine 16C loggia and gallery flanked by slated turrets. Two streets further along on the right is rue Fleuriau with the **SI**. Then you debouch into **place de Verdun** with the town's unattractive, hump-backed classical cathedral on one corner, on the right a splendid Edwardian-style café – *Café de la Paix* – all mirrors, gilt and plush, where bourgeois ladies come to sip lemon tea and nibble daintily

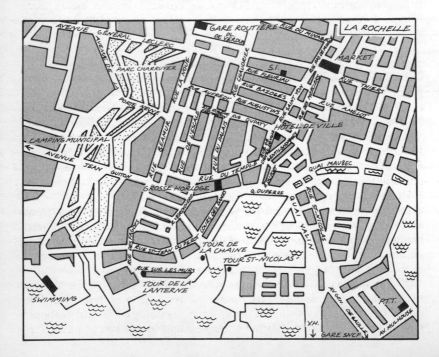

at sticky cakes. Just beyond is a shop selling pâtés, shellfish and ready-made *plats*, so beautiful they bring tears to the palate. But for cheaper eats – from stalls or in cafés – keep going to the **market**, with its covered hall and outside clothes and flower sellers. Another lively café, *de la Poste*, is down in the small secluded square by the 16C **Hôtel de Ville**.

Among a cluster of museums in La Rochelle, the **Musée du Nouveau Monde**, next to the SI in rue Fleuriau, is out of the ordinary. It occupies the former residence of the Fleuriau family, rich shipowners and traders, who, like many of their fellow-Rochelais, made fortunes out of the slave trade and West Indian sugar, spices, coffee and so on. Its elegant, panelled interior, painted that very French grey, is pleasingly discreet. There is a fine collection of prints, paintings and photos of the old West Indian plantations; 17C and 18C maps of America; photogravures of Red Indians from around 1900, with incredible names like Piopio Maksmaks Wallawalla and Lawyer Nez Percé; and an interesting display of aquatint illustrations for Marmontel's novel *Les Incas*. They are an amazing mixture of sentimentality and coy lubricity, permissible, no doubt, because of the exotic setting and 'primitive' native actors. The captions might have been lifted from Tintin: 'Alonzo dans le royaume de Tumbès', 'Naufrage de Telasco et d'Amazili'. Flimsily clad maidens abound. (Admission is 10–6 daily, cl. Tues.)

Lesser museums include the **Musée d'Orbigny** and a *Beaux Arts* (10–12 & 2–6/5, cl. Sun am & Tues, same ticket for both); the former with a good collection of porcelain and bits to do with the city's history, the latter not terribly exciting.

Staying in La Rochelle, there's a reasonable range of possibilities: a **youth hostel** (left of the gare SNCF in Port des Minimes, or bus 10 from place Verdun), two **campsites** (*Soleil* by the hostel; *municipal* on the other, western side of town – bus 6) and a good number of **hotels**. The *François Premier* in rue Bazoges off rue Chaudrier is a nice two-star, in the middle price range. *Atlantic* in rue Verdidière behind Cours des Dames is central and cheapish. So are *L'Océan* in Cours des Dames, and *Le Perthuis* (15 rue Gambetta) and *Le Centre* (3 rue Thiers) close by the market. Several others dot the streets leading to the station: *Bordeaux* (45 rue St-Nicolas) is inexpensive and old-fashioned.

Eating, try the rue du Port/rue St-Sauveur area, just off the waterfront and rue St-Nicolas. *Pub Lutèce* in rue St-Sauveur is a reasonably priced brasserie. *Café-Resto à la Villette* behind the market hall has good *plats du jour*, as does *L'Ouvreboîte* in rue Verdidière. The seafood restaurants in rue de la Chaine and rue St-Jean are excellent, but pricey.

As for other practicalities, there's bike hire at the gare SNCF and from **M Salaun**, 3 place de la Solette on the left bank of the canal. Also, **free municipal bikes** on quai du Carénage on the east side of the old harbour, for use within the town. **CDIJ**, 14 rue des Gentilshommes, behind Hôtel de Ville, has an information service, including Allostop, for young people. For summer **boat trips** round La Rochelle and to neighbouring islands, ask at the SI. For walkers, the regional tourist board produce a pamphlet called *Promenades à Pied en Charente-Maritime*, covering Île de Ré, Île d'Oléron, Brouage, Rochefort and Saintonge. Getting out, the main **gare routière** is on place Verdun though for certain destinations you'll need to use other terminals. *Citram* (30 cours des Dames) run to Angoulême, Saintes, Cognac, St-Jean d'Angely and Rochefort; *Océcars* (44 cours des Dames) is more local, serving the coastal towns and villages.

The Île de Ré and Île d'Aix

Very close to La Rochelle, the ÎLE DE RÉ is a low, narrow island some 30km in length, surrounded by long sandy beaches. The north-west is salt marshes and oysterbeds, the central part small-scale cultivation of vines, asparagus and wheat. Out of season it has a slow, misty charm, life in its little ports revolving exclusively round the cultivation of oysters and mussels. In season, though, it is incredibly crowded, with upwards of 400,000 visitors passing through.

It is easy to get to, with or without your own transport: Régie Départementale d'Aunis et Saintonge run **buses** from La Rochelle (SNCF, Grosse Horloge and place de Verdun). It is possible to juggle the timetable so as to spend time in, say, St-Martin and Ars-en-Ré or Les Portes and still get back the same day. **Ferries** cross from LA PALLICE, La Rochelle's deep water port, to SABLONCEAUX every half hour – 20mins in season. **Hotels** and **campsites** are plentiful in all the island villages, though obviously packed to their limits through July–August.

LA PALLICE was a big commercial port, before the recession, and its shipyards were important. But now, like British yards, times have changed. In mid-1984 the last ship was on the stocks; and everyone was wondering whether there would be any more orders. It is a naval base, too. As you ride by you notice some colossal weather-stained concrete sheds. They are submarine pens built by the Germans to service their Atlantic U-boat fleet during the war. Too difficult to demolish, they are still in use.

I went as far as ST-MARTIN, the capital, an attractive little fishing port. Its whitewashed houses cluster round the stone quays of a well-protected harbour. Trawlers and flat-bottomed oyster boats, piled high with cage-like devices used for 'growing' oysters, slip out every morning on the muddy tide. The quayside café 'Boucqingam' (sic) recalls the military adventures of the said Duke.

To the east of the harbour, you can walk along the almost perfectly preserved fortifications – redesigned by Vauban, after Buckingham's attentions – to the citadel, long used as a prison. It was from here that the *bagnards* – prisoners sentenced to hard labour on Devil's Island in

Guyana or New Caledonia – set out: not to return. The notorious Papillon himself left from the little prison harbour.

The tiny ÎLE D'AIX, just south of La Rochelle, where Napoleon spent his last days in Europe, makes a good trip too. Less frequented than the bigger islands, it is small enough to be walked round in about 3 hours. **Access** is by *Océcars* bus to FOURAS (about 45mins from La Rochelle), thence to POINTE DE LA FUMÉE for the ferry.

ROCHEFORT TO MARENNES – AND THE ÎLE D'OLÉRON

ROCHEFORT (30mins by train from La Rochelle) was created by Colbert, Louis XIII's navy minister, as a naval base to protect the coast from English raids. It is a dull place, built on a grid plan with regular ranks of identical houses – a joy to the military mind. If, however, you have a taste for the bizarre, then there is one powerful reason for visiting – the house of the novelist Julien Viaud, alias **Pierre Loti**. Son of an impecunious townhall clerk, he joined the navy like many another Rochefort lad, and stayed there forty years an officer, writing numerous best-selling romances with exotic oriental settings and characters.

The **house** (10–12 & 2–5; cl. Sun–Mon am, Oct–March cl. Tues as well) is at 141 rue Pierre Loti. It is part of a terrace of modestly proportioned grey stone houses, outwardly a model of petty bourgeois conformity and respectability. Inside, surprise follows surprise: a medieval banqueting hall complete with Gothic fireplace and Gobelin tapestries, a monastery refectory with windows pinched from a ruined abbey, a Damascus mosque, where in honour of guests, a man-servant was despatched to play the muezzin from a miniature minaret; a Turkish room, with kilim wall-hangings and a ceiling made from an Alhambra mould. To suit the mood of the place, Loti used to throw extravagant parties: a medieval banquet with swan's meat and hedgehog, a *fête chinoise* with the guests got up in costumes he had brought back from China where he took part in the suppression of the Boxer revolt.

There is a cheap **hotel**, the *Hippocampe*, rue Duvivier near place Colbert, and the two-star *Hôtel de France* at 55 rue du Dr Pelletier also has some inexpensive rooms. **Camping Municipal** is on the southern edge of town. A good place to **eat** is the *Self-Service* by the Arsenal in rue Toufaire or *l'Étalon*, in the same street. The SI and **bus station** are all just off rue du Dr Pelletier.

Eighteen km south-west, **BROUAGE** is a perfect little 17C *bastide*, its fortifications intact, created by Richelieu during the siege of La Rochelle in 1626. You reach it by the D733 which crosses the Charente by the old **Pont Transbordeur**, no longer in use. It is a great iron gantry with a raft-like platform suspended on hawsers, on which a dozen cars were loaded and floated across the river. Either turn right for Soubise and Moëze, or go on to St-Agnant. Either way you cross the lovely dead-flat salt marshes, reclaimed and transformed into meadows grazed by white Charolais cows and intersected by dozens of reed-filled drainage ditches where herons watch and yellow flags bloom. The skies are huge, specked with wheeling buzzards and kestrels. Good country for biking or walking.

You enter the town by the Porte Royale in the north wall. Outside, where the harbour once was, are oyster *claires*, the partly fresh-water pools where oysters are fattened in the last stage of their rearing. Within the walls, the streets, laid out on a grid pattern, are lined with low, two-storey houses. It is utterly quiet and rural.

A few kilometres further south, past the pretty, unfussy **Château de la Gataudière** built in the 18C by the man who first introduced rubber to France, you come to the village of **MARENNES**, the real centre of oyster production in this area which supplies over 60 per cent of France's consumption. If you want to visit the oysterbeds, and see how the business works, you can do so here; just ask any of the local SIs to phone ahead for you. If you want to stay in Marennes there's a youth hostel (July–Aug) and, in the middle of the village, the inexpensive *Hôtel-Restaurant du Commerce*.

The **ÎLE D'OLÉRON**, France's largest island after Corsica, is just up the road from Marennes, joined to the mainland by another toll bridge. Flat and more wooded than the Île de Ré, with extensive pine woods at Boyardville and St-Trojan, it has long sandy beaches, but rather shallow water. The little towns, too, have been spoilt by the development of hundreds of holiday homes – and it can be a real battle in the summer season to find a place to stay.

The interior is pretty and distinctive. Waterways wind right into the land, their gleaming muddy banks overhung by round fishing nets suspended from ranks of little piers. There are so many oyster *claires* the island must look like an Afghan mirrored cushion from above. With its pines, tamarisks, and woods of evergreen oak, the stretch from Boyardville to St-Pierre is the prettiest and most distinctive. BOYARDVILLE itself is completely without interest. There are ranks of *bouchots*, the stakes they grow mussels on, all along the shore, but while it is tempting to help yourself you should know that you are stealing: these are not natural mussels. ST-PIERRE is the prettiest town.

Travelling along this whole **section of coast** you may find hitching the simplest option. Many of the towns, however, are also served by the **Aunis and Saintonge buses**. The Saintes-St-Denis-d'Oléron line serves all the towns of Oléron, Marennes, St-Sornin, and Balanza between one and three times a day. Other lines serve Marennes, Ronce-les-Bains, La Tremblade, Saujon and Royan. Check all these routes locally, because times and itineraries can vary on different days of the week.

TOWARDS BORDEAUX: ROYAN AND THE GIRONDE

Pre-war **ROYAN** was a fashionable resort patronised by the well-heeled. It is still popular, but the modern town is a dreary illustration of the rationalism of 1950s town planning: broad boulevards, car parks, shopping precincts, planned greenery. Its **beaches**, however, are beautiful, of a fine pale sand, meticulously harrowed and raked, and, to the north, backed by the pine forest of la Coubre. They're still dogged by rather shallow, murky water but you can swim happily enough.

There is also one sight worth seeing in Royan – the 1950s **Cathedral** designed by Gillet and Hébrard, in a tatty square behind the main waterfront. Though the concrete has weathered badly, the overall effect is dramatic and surprising. Tall V-sectioned columns give the outside the appearance of massive fluting and a 'stepped' roof-line rises dramatically overhead to culminate in a 65m bell-tower. The interior is even more striking. Using uncompromisingly modern materials and designs, the architects have succeeded in out-Gothicking Gothic. The stained glass panels, in each of which a different tone predominates, borrow their colours from the local seascapes – oyster colours, sea, mist and murk – before a sudden explosion of colour with Christ above the altar. **Staying** in the town is expensive and, in season, short in supply. Your best bet would be to camp up the coast to the north or visit for the day from Saintes or Rochefort. The most interesting way to arrive would be on foot: two days from Saintes on the **GR4**, via Brouage. The **SI** and **PTT** are close to the Rond Point de la Poste at the east end of the seafront; **gares routière and SNCF** in nearby cours de l'Europe. **Bike hire** from SNCF or bike shop in cours de l'Europe near SI. Various **cruises** are organised from Royan in season, including one to the Cordouan lighthouse commanding the entrance to the Gironde, first erected by the Black Prince. A **ferry** crosses to the Pointe de Grave in 20mins, whence there is a **cycle trail** (and the GR8) down the coast to the bay of Arcachon.

An ideal bike-picnic excursion – just over an hour's ride – is to **TALMONT** (on GR360), 16km south on the shore of the Gironde. Apart from a few ups and downs through beautiful pine woods outside Royan, it is all level pegging. **Talmont church** (12C), clustered about by its low-crouching village, stands at the tip of a small promontory ending in a cliff above the Gironde. Gabled transepts, a squat square tower, an apse simply but elegantly decorated with blind arcading, the stone a tawny, warm colour, weathered and pocked like a sponge. In sun or cloud it stands magnificently against the forlorn brown or grey seascapes typical of the Gironde. Entrance is through the north transept, where the voussoirs in the doorway are carved with acrobats standing on each other's shoulders and, in the outer braid, two tug-of-war teams hauling roped lions up the arch. Inside, it is as beautiful as out.

Heading on in this direction to BORDEAUX (see p. 231) an interesting approach is to take the ferry across the Gironde estuary from **BLAYE** (another Vauban fortress) to LAMARQUE on the edge of the Médoc vineyards (about eight crossings daily: take cars). The Gironde shore road is pretty, with the wide, brown, melancholy estuary to the west and vineyards to the east. SNCF buses run into Bordeaux from MOULIS-LISTRAC, or you can hitch.

THE CHARENTE – AND THE SOUTH

It is hard to believe that the peaceful fertile valley of the **river Charente** which has given its name to the two modern *départements* that cover much of this chapter, was once a busy industrial waterway, bringing armaments from **Angoulême** to the naval shipyards at **Rochefort**. The turrets of minor **châteaux** belonging to wealthy cognac-producers rise above the woods and the valley slopes, crowned with low ochre-coloured farms, are green with vines. The towns and villages may look old-fashioned, but the prosperous shops and smart new villas on the outskirts are proof that where the grape grows money and modernity are not far behind.

The valley itself is easy to travel as the main road and railway to Limoges run this way. North and south, Poitiers, Périgueux (for the Dordogne) and Bordeaux are also easily reached by train. **South of Bordeaux,** apart from the through line to Spain, the great flat stretch of the Landes is extremely difficult to get around. But you won't be missing much if you just head on down to the Basque country, for there are few places to see inland and the coast, though beautifully sandy, is only accessible at a handful of dull modern resorts.

SAINTES

Capital of the old province of Saintonge, **SAINTES** is a lively market town on the banks of the river Charente. It was an important centre under the Romans and still preserves some interesting remains from that period. It has two particularly fine Romanesque churches and an attractive centre of narrow lanes and medieval houses. It also has the doubtful distinction of being the birthplace of Dr Guillotin, who advocated execution by decapitation, although he did not personally invent the machine that bore his name.

The modern town is bisected by av Gambetta and the cours National. The **railway station** is in av de la Marne at the east end of av Gambetta, with several cheap **hotels** in the vicinity. **Camping Municipal** is in rue de Courbiac – right at the start of cours National along the bank of the river. There is a friendly **youth hostel** in rue du Pont Amilion, just behind the Abbaye-aux-Dames church, to the left of av Gambetta as you come from the station, with space for tents.

On the riverbank just upstream from the road bridge is a Roman votive arch, known as the **Arc de Germanicus**. Erected in AD19 in honour of Tiberius, Germanicus and Drusus, it stood on the Roman bridge until this was demolished in mid-19C to make way for the modern one. The **SI** is right beside it, and next door an **archaeological museum** housing a goodly collection of Roman bits and pieces mostly rescued from the 5C city walls, into which they had been incorporated.

Up rue Arc de Triomphe, you come to the church of St-Pallais (12C) and, through an arch into a gravelly courtyard to the **Abbaye-aux-Dames** itself. Consecrated in the 11C and later used by Benedictine nuns specialising in the education of aristocratic young ladies, it is considered one of the best examples of the Saintonge school of Romanesque architecture. The best feature is the tower: square with pinnacles at each corner at the first level, then an octagonal storey, surmounted by a beautiful rotunda pierced by twelve bays separated by slender pillars, and capped, like Notre-Dame in Poitiers, by a pinecone. Inside is a single broad space undivided by aisles, and roofed with two big domes – very plain and evocative of a barefoot, vigorous faith.

A footbridge crosses the Charente beside the Arch of Germanicus. The street beyond leads past the covered **market** (full of mouthwatering goodies) to place du Marché at the foot of the cathedral of St-Pierre, which again began life as a Romanesque church, though it has been much altered, particularly subsequent to damage inflicted during the Wars of Religion – Saintonge, like La Rochelle, being a Huguenot stronghold. Its enormous, heavily buttressed tower, capped by a hat-like dome instead of the intended spire, is the town's chief landmark. The largely 16C interior, much stained by damp, is not very interesting.

Outside, place du Synode, lined with lime trees, leads to the handsome municipal buildings. Just up to the right is rue des Jacobins with the municipal library in the Hôtel Martineau, with an exquisite central courtyard full of trees and shrubs. This is the heart of the old quarter. A 17C mansion in rue Victor Hugo houses the **Musée des Beaux-Arts** (10–12 & 2–6; cl. Tues), containing a collection of local pottery and some not very exciting paintings.

If you continue along rue des Jacobins, past the library and up the hill to the Capitol, with a fine view back over the cathedral tower, you come eventually to the broad cours Reverseaux. Downhill to the left you pass through an avenue of trees with a steep little valley on your right. Two signs advise you to see the concierge if you want to visit **Les Arènes**, the Roman arena, whose ruins you can see at the head of this valley. The conventional approach is from rue St-Eutrope, past the church and right in rue Lacurie. Much more interesting, but it does involve an illicit scramble over the fence, is straight down a path into the valley bottom, where there is a grassy walk between lovely sloping gardens, with the tower of St-Eutrope dominating the skyline on your left.

The arena – in fact, an amphitheatre – is dug into the end of the valley. It dates from the early 1C and is one of the oldest surviving. Most of the seats are grassed over, but it is an evocative little place. It is not hard to hear the echoes of that alien but civilising tongue mingling with some local Gaulish patois all those centuries ago, when Saintes had twice its present population.

St-Eutrope, in its namesake *rue*, dedicated to Saintes' first bishop and martyr in the 3C, consists of two 11C churches. The upper one, which lost its nave in 1803, has some fine capitals in the old choir, which are best seen by putting 1F in the slot and shinning up to the gallery, whence you get an excellent view of two beauties: the souls of the dead being weighed on the left and Daniel on the right with lions licking his feet. But the best thing by far is the lower church, entered from the street. Daylight scarcely filters in. Massive pillars support the vaulting, with capitals superbly carved wih stylised vegetation. There is a massive font and the 4C sarcophagus of St-Eutrope himself.

There are two good **restaurants** on the riverside place Blair, and, if you're a cyclist, an excellent **bike shop** whose owner, an ex-pro and unquenchable enthusiast, would go well out of his way to help you. There is a **crêperie** in rue Victor Hugo and a couple of good cheap places in the transverse rue St-Michel. **PTT** in cours National by the bridge. The **SI** run **river trips** to Cognac in the summer – much the nicest way of getting there; at CHANIERS, on the river about 10km east, the *Restaurant de la Charente* is very good, packed out for Sunday lunch with prosperous local farmers (best phone to book if you want to join them: 46—1.00.73).

Churches around Saintes

If you have a car there are several marvellous Romanesque churches within easy reach, notably FENIOUX to the north towards St-Jean-d'Angely and RIOUX to the south. There is also the fine château of ROCHE-COURBON off the Rochefort road. But car or no car, there is one place worth any amount of trouble to get to if you are into Romanesque, and that is the 12C pilgrim church of **St-Pierre** at AULNAY. It stands all on its own outside the town in a cemetery full of cypress trees and strange sarcophagus-like tombs. Its beauty lies in its combination of simple lines, perfect proportion and a wealth of delightful and exceptionally skilful and lively sculptural detail.

Without your own transport, the simplest way to get there is by train from Saintes to ST-JEAN-D'ANGELY, a journey of 25mins. St-Jean has some pretty old houses, but is not worth a stop in its own right. Thereafter you have to hitch. After 3km on the Poitiers-Angoulême road, you take the left fork for Aulnay on the D950: St-Pierre is off to the right before you reach the town.

The church's finest sculpture is on the west front, south transept and apse. On the former two blind arches flank the central portal: the tympanum of the right depicts Christ in Majesty, the left St Peter crucified upside down with two extraordinarily lithe and graceful soldiers balancing on the arms of his cross to get a better swing at the nails in his feet. The pure round arch above the south door is decorated with four curving bands of even more intricate carving, while the apse is a beauty, framed by five slender columns and lit by three perfectly arched windows. The centre one is flanked by figures wrapped in the finest twining foliage – to say nothing of the corbels and capitals. The interior capitals are delightful too: Delilah cutting Samson's hair, human-eared elephants bearing the Latin inscription 'Hi sunt elephantes' – presumably for the edification of the ignorant locals, devils pulling a man's beard and so on. Outside, in the cemetery at the west end, the 'monument' is a *croix hosannière*, so-called because on Palm Sunday the priest and congregation would re-enact Christ's entry into Jerusalem, the priest reading the story while the congregation filed past laying branches by the cross and crying 'Hosanna'.

NUAILLE-SUR-BOUTONNE, 9km west of Aulnay, has another remarkable church. ST-MANDÉ and SELLES-LES-ÀULNAY – tiny rural villages even closer – have simpler but, in their way, equally charming churches of the same period.

COGNAC

Even if the name didn't give it away, it wouldn't take long to discover what the town of **COGNAC** is about. For its smell is everywhere in the air as you stroll around the crooked medieval lanes of the riverside quarter, and the buildings dominated by great warehouses, or *chais*, their outside walls blackened by colonies of a tiny fungus which thrives on the fumes from the precious, maturing liquid. Cognac is cognac, from the tractor-driver and pruning-knife-wielder to the manufacturer of corks, bottles and cardboard boxes. Untouched by the recession (80 per cent of production is exported), it will thrive, it seems, as long as the world has sorrows – a sunny, prosperous, respectable, self-satisfied little place.

The simplest way of getting there is by train – 20mins from Saintes,

45 from Angoulême. From the station, you go down rue Mousnier, then right in rue Bayard, past the PTT, up rue du 14 Juillet, with a good supermarket and the reasonably priced *Sens Unique* restaurant, to the central place François I, dominated by an equestrian statue of the king rising from a bed of begonias. There are a couple of **cafés** and a **brasserie** on the square. The SI is close by. Ask there about visiting the various *chais*, the St-Gobain glass works (second biggest bottle-maker in Europe) and river trips – upstream through the locks to Jarnac is particularly beautiful.

From the north side of the square, **rue d'Angoulême** leads past shops specialising in those archetypal French frivolities – pastries and *lingerie* – to the market square overlooked by the tower of St-Léger (entrance in rue Aristide Briand). Straight on down you come to **Grande Rue** winding through the old quarter to the *chais*. On the right is all that remains of the château where king François I was born in 1494.

To the left are the *chais* and offices of the **Hennessy cognac** company. Like the other main **warehouses** they are open, free, from 9–11 and 2–5 except weekends (only *Polignac* and *Otard* open wkends, and then only in July–Aug). The consensus is that Hennessy are the best to visit – a seventh generation Irish family firm or at least Irish in origin. The first Hennessy, an officer in the Irish brigade serving with the French army, hailed from Ballymacnoy in County Cork, gave up soldiering in 1765 to set up a little business here.

The **Hennessy visit** (free) begins with a film explaining what's what in the world of cognac. Only an *eau de vie* distilled from grapes grown in a strictly defined area can be called cognac – and this stretches only from the coast at La Rochelle and Royan to Angoulême. It is all carefully graded according to soil properties – chalky, essentially. The inner circle, from which the finest cognac comes – Grande Champagne and Petite Champagne (not to be confused with the bubbly) – lies mainly south of the Charente.

Hennessy alone keep 180,000 barrels in stock. All are regularly checked and various 'coupages' or blendings made from barrel to barrel. Only the best is kept. And what is the best? That – and, in effect, the whole enterprise – depends on the tastebuds of the *maître du chais*. For six generations that job has been in the same family – an interesting genetic refinement for the Darwinian. The present heir apparent has already been twelve years under his father's tutelage and is not yet fully qualified.

Upstream from the bridge, **Parc François I**, a lovely quiet wood of evergreen oaks stretches along the riverbanks to the Pont Chatenay, where there's swimming – in the river or a pool – and the town campsite. As for rooms, there's a Logis de France hotel, *d'Etape* on the Angoulême road and *La Résidence* at 25 av Victor Hugo, both of them reasonable. *Tourist* at 166 av Victor Hugo and *Cheval Blanc* in place Bayard are cheap and okay. **Bike hire** from *Demontier*'s in av Victor Hugo.

There are some attractive **walks** around Cognac. You can follow the towpath – *le chemin de hâlage* – all the way upstream on the left bank of the Charente to Pont de la Trâche, then on along a track to Bourg-Charente, with an excellent restaurant called *La Ribaudière* by the bridge and a pretty Romanesque church – about 3 hours all in all. A byroad leads back to ST-BRICE on the other bank, past sleepy farms and acres of shoulder-high vines. From there another lane winds up the hill and over to the ruined abbey of CHÂTRES, abandoned amid brambles and fields about 3km distant. Or, alternatively, at the hamlet of RICHE-MONT, 5km north-west of Cognac, you can bathe in the pools of the tiny river Antenne below an ancient church on a steep bluff lost lost in the woods.

ANGOULÊME AND THE ROAD TO LIMOGES

ANGOULÊME was evangelised in the 3C by the cultivated saint, Ausonius, a Gallo-Roman landed gent, poet and cleric. It was much fought over in the Anglo-French squabbles and again in the Wars of Religion – another Protestant stronghold. After the revocation of the Edict of Nantes, a good proportion of its citizens – among them many of its skilled papermakers – emigrated to Holland, never to return. Marguerite de Valois, sister of François I, was born here. One of the 'characters' of French royal history, she became queen of Navarre, was a strong Protestant sympathiser (grandmother of Henri IV) and wrote a collection of Boccaccio-like tales, which hold a respectable place in the canon of French literature.

The **old town** occupies a steep-sided plateau overlooking a bend in the Charente. Its scruffy labyrinthine streets, only just beginning to undergo gentrification, fit every foreigner's stereotype of what a French working-class neighbourhood should look like. The papermills which made its prosperity are now almost completely defunct. On the southern edge of the plateau stands the **Cathedral**, whose west front, like Notre-Dame at Poitiers, is a fascinating display board for some very expressive and lively medieval sculpture, most of it 12C, and culminating, as ever, in a Risen Christ with angels and clouds about his head, framed in the habitual mandorla. The frieze beneath the tympanum to the right of the west door is interesting. It commemorates the recapture of Spanish Zaragoza from the Moors and shows on the left a bishop transfixing a Moorish giant with his lance, and, on the right, Roland killing the Moorish king who, having invited Charlemagne to his aid, refused to let him into his city, thus forcing him to make the retreat that led to the massacre of his rearguard by the Basques above St-Jean-Pied-de-Port. Unfortunately much of the rest of the building has suffered from the attentions of the once admired and now reviled Abadie and his desire to rediscover the pure Romanesque by destroying wholesale all that followed it.

From the front of the cathedral, you can walk all round the ramparts encircling the plateau with long views over the surrounding country, largely filled with urban sprawl now. There are public gardens below the parapet at the west end and a gravelly esplanade by the lycée where locals gather to play *boules*.

Angoulême is easily accessible by rail: 45mins from Cognac, 50 from Limoges and an hour from Poitiers. There is a branch office of the SI outside the station, from which av Gambetta, with the gare routière and several cheap if unprepossessing hotels, leads uphill to the town centre through place Pérot (*Hôtel de la Bourse* – Logis de France). Other hotels include *du Palais*, place Louvel (bit pricier); *Le Crab*, 27 rue Kléber (Logis de France) and *de la Paix*, place Hôtel de Ville – both cheap. To get to the youth hostel on an island in the Charente, turn right at the first lights on av Gambetta, over the railway bridge and right again to the river – you cross by the footbridge and the hostel is just to the left; it serves meals – **Camping Municipal** is nearby, beyond the Pont de Bourgines. The SI (in the Hôtel de Ville) are very helpful; they provide, among other things, route details for walks in the area – *circuits pédestres*. Angoulême **festivals** include a brief jazz blow at the beginning of June and – unique and rather wonderful – the *Bande Dessinée* (in February), a good convention of comics, high art in France, from politics to pornography.

There are two interesting places west of Angoulême on the way to Limoges – LA ROCHEFOUCAULD and CONFOLENS.

LA ROCHEFOUCAULD (15km) is on bus and train routes – 20mins by train. By road you pass through RUELLE, now a missile-manufacturing centre (Exocet, reputedly), formerly a major naval armaments foundry, specialising in casting gun-barrels, which were shipped down the Charente to the yards at Rochefort.

La Rochefoucauld itself is the site of a huge Renaissance **château** on the banks of the river Tardoire, which still belongs to the family that gave its name to the town. It is only open in August, when there is a brigade-sized cast for the son et lumière. Unfortunately, you cannot quite see the courtyard from outside, which is the château's best architectural feature. Two hotels, if you need them: the *Gare* (Logis de France; av de la Gare) and *Vieille Auberge* (two star; Grand-Rue). **Camping Municipal** is in rue des Flots.

CONFOLENS is about 40km further (buses from Angoulême). If you are travelling by train, best to go to ST-JUNIEN on the Limoges line and hitch back. The country changes west of Angoulême, becoming hillier and more wooded, with buttercup pastures grazed by liver-coloured Limousin cows. You enter the valley of the river Vienne and Confolens is on the left bank, a quiet town of ancient houses climbing a hill above the river (**hotels** and **Camping municipal**). Its chief claim to fame today is an

International Folklore Festival, held every year in the second and third weeks of August.

BORDEAUX

BORDEAUX is prosperous and populous – pushing a quarter of a million inhabitants – and it's a city which ought to be interesting. There's a big city-port mix of peoples; a very long history, bound up with the English (whose base this was during their 300-year involvement in Aquitaine), the local claret wine, and the Girondin movement of the Revolutionary period; and a grand enough riverside site. Yet spending time here never seems very rewarding. If you lived in the city maybe it would be different: as a casual visitor you may as well plan on a quick transit.

First, then, some basic **practicalities**. If you need to stay, you'll find the rock-bottom **hotels**, in a rock-bottom area, around the St-Jean railway station. Rue Charles Domecq is probably the best bet, with lots of one and two-star places, and, in cours de la Marne opposite, inexpensive places to eat, including a good clutch of Vietnamese restaurants. The **youth hostel** is in cours Barbey, off cours de la Marne on the left, with a **laundrette** not far away, in rue Begles. The **market**, Marché des Capucins, is also in cours de la Marne, and there are numerous other food

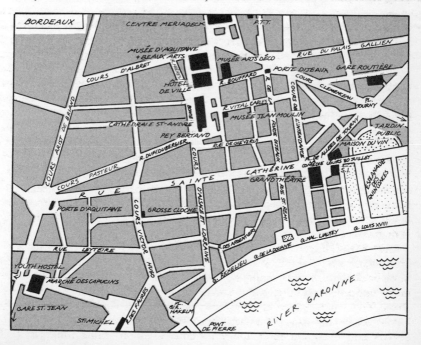

shops in the neighbourhood, which is poor, working-class and, above all, immigrant.

Bus 7/8 from the station will take you in to place Gambetta, a convenient stop for the museums, cathedral and town centre. But it is more interesting to walk, through the seedy quarter behind the market to **cours V Hugo**, where on Sundays an African-Algerian market takes over the street, and thence under the heavy Gothic tower (Grosse Cloche), down rue St-James (Vietnamese and Algerian restaurants) to **place Laffargue**. A left turn there takes you into **rue Ste-Catherine**, one of the city's main shopping streets, and on to place de la Comédie, at its end, dominated by the unsurpassably elegant classical façade of the **Grand Théâtre** (1780) with an immense colonnaded portico topped by statues of Muses and Graces. Built by the architect Victor Louis, it was the first purpose-built theatre in France, certainly the finest building in the city. This is the heart of smart Bordeaux. **Place Gambetta**, nearby, is the city's pivot – a once majestic square, conceived as an architectural whole in the time of Louis XV. Its house fronts, arcaded at street level, are decorated with rows of carved masks. The guillotine lopped 300 heads here at the time of the Revolution.

West of place Gambetta you come to the **Cathédrale St-André**. Its west front is a blank wall, and much of the building's exterior detail is lost under inches of grime. But what catches the eye first and saves the building from dismissal is the great upward, airy lift of the twin steeples over the north transept – an effect of lofty extravagance reinforced by the adjacent but separate campanile, the **Tour Pey Berland**. The interior is strange. The first impression, in the transepts, is of squeezed, narrow height. The nave, broad and aisleless, with Gothic vaulting on a Romanesque base, is wider and lower than the choir, so that as you look down the length of the church the roof of the nave cuts off your view of the full height of the choir

The square outside is attractive, with trees and a café on the north side by the classical Hôtel de Ville. *Le Musée*, on the south side, is an atmospheric old-fashioned café, as is *Le Pey Berland* round the corner in rue Duffour-Dubergier, next to the **Centre Informations Jeunesse Aquitaine** – a friendly crew, who claim to be able to cope with most questions and problems. Rue Frères-Bonie, in the south-west corner of the cathedral square, has several cheap Vietnamese and Algerian restaurants.

Among the city's half dozen museums, the **Musée d'Aquitaine** is worthwhile if you've visited – or intend to – the prehistoric caves around Les Eyzies. Its prehistoric and Gallo-Roman archaeological collections include the famed *Venus à la Corne* from Laussel. Hours are 2–6 daily (cl. Suns & Tues). The **Musée des Beaux Arts**, next door (10–12 & 2–6, cl. Tues), musters a fair roster of names – Perugino, Delacroix, Matisse, Rodin – but no great excitement.

Some practicalities

The **SI** (12 cours du 30 Juillet) change money Sat & Sun, 9–12 & 2–6; they also run daily bus tours of the surrounding **vineyards**, including Graves, Sauterne, Médoc and St-Emilion, with commentary in English and French (departure 1.45pm from the SI). The Entre-Deux-Mers tour includes a visit to the very lovely ruined abbey of **La Sauve Majeure** with some of the finest extant Romanesque capitals. For detailed information about the region's wines, consult the **Maison du Vin**, opposite the SI.

Getting out, the **gare routière** (Citram) is in rue Fondaudège, near place Tourny; **Allostop** are at 59 rue des Ayres (56.81.24.59); or you could try the following vantage points: **hitching** for Bergerac, bus 5, from just across the Pont de Pierre to the corner of av Clémenceau; for Paris, no 92, from Porte Cailhau to Ambares; for Toulouse, no B, from place de la Victoire to terminus; for Bayonne-Biarritz, no G, from place de la Victoire to terminus.

Consulates in Bordeaux include Britain (15 cours de Verdun; 56.52.28.35), Canada (8 rue Claude Bonnier; 56.96.15.61); and the USA (22 Cours du Maréchal Foch; 56.52.65.95).

ARCACHON AND ROUTES SOUTH

Summer weekends, the Bordelais repair en masse to **ARCACHON**, a seaside resort 40mins by train across the flat sandy forest of the *landes*. The beaches of white sand are magnificent, but crowded. The town, a sprawl of villas great and small, is expensive, though there are a fair number of campsites. If you're stuck, there's an SI to the left of the station in place Roosevelt. For the waterfront, go straight ahead, past an aquarium run by Bordeaux university (9.30–8, 1 June–10 Sept; cl. in winter).

Arcachon's chief curiosity is the **dune de Pilat**, at 114m – the highest sand dune in Europe – a veritable mountain of wind-carved sand, about 8km down the coast. Buses from the railway station (**bike hire**), every half hour in July and August, about five a day at other times. From the end of the line, by a hotel with an unpronounceable Basque name, the road continues straight on, uphill, for about 15 mins. There is the inevitable clutch of stalls selling ice-creams, *galettes* and junk, and from the top a superb view of the bay of Arcachon and the forest of the *landes* stretching away to the south. There is also a great slide down to the sea (but a long haul back up!).

At **LE TEICH** (SNCF), about 12km east of Arcachon in the south-east corner of the bassin d'Arcachon, one of the most important expanses of wet-lands remaining in France has been converted into a **bird sanctuary** (information from the *mairie* in Le Teich; admission normally 10–6 daily from 1 March–30 Sept).

The Landes today support nearly 2¼ million acres of forest, but until the 19C this was a vast infertile swamp, badly drained because of the impermeable layer of grit deposited by the glaciers of the quaternary age and steadily encroached upon by the shifting sand dunes of the coast. At MARQUÈZE, about 15km east of Labouheyre on the N10 from Bordeaux to Bayonne, the *Parc Naturel Régional des Landes de Gascogne* has created an *écomusée* (open daily mid-June–9 Sept; Suns only otherwise). A resuscitated steam train runs between Labouheyre and Sabres, stopping at the *écomusée* (several in the day, from June to Sept; check for other times of year). SNCF trains stop at Labouheyre on the Facture to Bayonne run; connections from Bordeaux to Facture.

And lastly, Romanesque buffs travelling south to Toulouse should make a stop at the otherwise dull little town of MOISSAC, where the church of St-Pierre contains some of the great masterpieces of Romanesque sculpture in its cloister and south portal. The same aficionados travelling south-west towards Biarritz might like to hop off the main line train at DAX to see the frieze on the apse of the church of St-Paul-les-Dax (11C) (Right out of the station, across the railway bridge, then second left.) A good picnic spot too.

TRAVEL DETAILS

Trains

From Poitiers frequent service to Châtellerault (20mins) and Paris-Austerlitz (2hrs50min); also frequently – same line – to Niort (1hr), Surgères (1hr25) and La Rochelle (1hr45); several daily to Angoulême (1hr), Bordeaux (2hrs10), Dax (3½hrs), Bayonne (4hrs), Biarritz (4¼hrs), St-Jean-de-Luz (4hrs40), Hendaye (4hrs55) and Irun (5hrs5); several daily to Limoges (2¼hrs).
From Les Sables d'Olonne several to Nantes (1½hrs) and Paris-Montparnasse (4hrs45).
From La Rochelle several daily to Nantes (1hr50); and to Bordeaux (4hrs) via Rochefort and Saintes.
From Royan frequent service to Angoulême (2hrs) via Saintes (40mins) and Cognac (1hr).
From Bordeaux frequent service to Paris-Austerlitz (4–5hrs), stopping at Angoulême (1hr) and Poitiers (2hrs); also regularly to Bayonne/Biarritz (1hr40) and St-Jean-de-Luz (2¼hrs), and to Toulouse (2hrs20); 5 daily to Périgueux (1hr20) and Brive (2½hrs).
From Angoulême 4 daily to Limoges (1½–2hrs).

Buses

From Poitiers several SNCF to Parthenay (1–1½hrs); 3 daily to Châteauroux (3¼hrs) via Chauvigny (35mins), St-Savin (1hr), Le Blanc (1hr25); 1 daily to Ruffec (2¼hrs); 1 daily to Limoges (3hrs).
From Parthenay several SNCF to Thouars (1hr) via Airvault (25mins) and to Niort (50mins).
From Les Sables d'Olonne 4 SNCF to Luçon (2hrs) and Nantes (5½hrs), both via the coast road.
From Saintes 2 to St-Denis-d'Oléron (2hrs).

Chapter seven
THE DORDOGNE

Most interesting and beautiful in the hilly wooded east, **the Dordogne** has unfortunately begun to capitalise heavily on the tourist attractions of its caves, castles and food. In season crowds at the sights can be oppressive, but even so nothing should deter you from getting to see the **prehistoric paintings** in the caves round **Les Eyzies** and at the much quieter **Pech-Merle** on the river Lot to the south.

Heavily contested by the English and the French during the Hundred Years War, the whole area is scattered with more or less **ruinous castles** like **Bourdeilles**, **Beynac** and **Bonaguil**, and **bastides** – the small military settlements built by both sides to secure their own patches. **Monpazier**, the best preserved of these, lies like the castles mentioned above on the cross-country route of the GR36.

Several other **GRs** bisect the central and eastern parts of the region and, if you're into walking, these – or a bike – make much the most appropriate way of getting about. The landscape is small-scale and detailed, just right for slow travelling. And the hills are not too strenuous either, until you get up into the north-east beyond Brive and Limoges where the wilder foothills of the Massif Central begin.

Though not themselves interesting enough to merit more than a brief stay, the towns of **Limoges**, **Cahors**, **Périgueux** and **Brive** are the best bases to work out from. Strategically placed at top, bottom and middle of the region, they are well connected by train with each other and places beyond.

PÉRIGORD

This central part of the Dordogne, divided into **Périgord Blanc** and **Périgord Noir**, is where most of the tourism is. The Blanc, named for the colour of its chalky soil, is the more fertile open country round the regional capital of **Périgueux**. The Noir is the more southerly bit round the banks of the **river Dordogne**, where the oak woods give the landscape a darker hue. It's the gourmet centre too, where the food buffs come – though you'll need to watch the pennies if you get into the restaurant round. Pâtés, truffles, foie gras, duck and potted everything are what the connoisseurs are after.

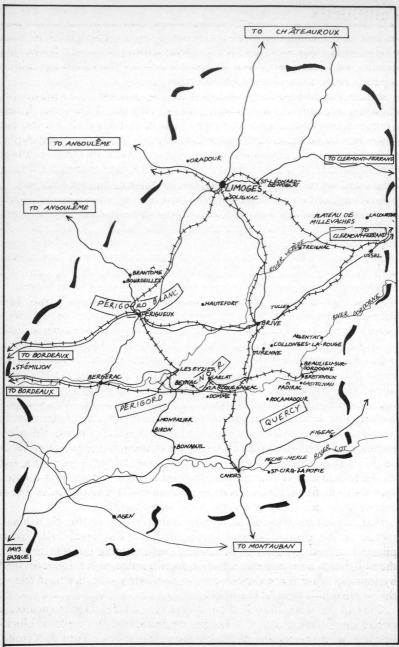

PÉRIGUEUX

Almost at the exact centre of the Périgord region, **PÉRIGUEUX** is an obvious and enjoyable base. It's a market centre, open and lively, and like the rest of its *département* grown rich on the proceeds of agriculture – pâtés, wines, nuts, sheep – and tourism.

Rooms are easily enough found, with the greatest concentration of cheapies, as usual, opposite the railway station. Pick from **hotels** *Terminus*, *du Midi*, *des Voyageurs* or the one-star Logis de France, *des Charentes* (with an inexpensive restaurant): all are in rue Dénis-Papin. Closest **campsite** is *Barnabé-Plage* on the east bank of the river l'Isle; there's another, *de l'Isle*, 3km out on the Brive road. From the station it's a short walk into the old quarter of town beyond **place Bugeaud**.

First stop, as far as Périgueux's own interest goes, should be the **Musée du Périgord** (10–12 & 2–5, cl. Tues), built on the site of an old monastery – from which it retains a star-vaulted chapel, filled with medieval tools and domestic objects. The museum's best collection is its Gallo-Roman section – Périgueux was one of the major towns of Roman Aquitaine – with some particularly beautiful mosaics. Upstairs, poorly displayed, is a prehistoric section, worth a glimpse before tramping off to the caves.

Below the museum follow **rue du Plantier** – with its grand 16C Gamenson mansion – and you arrive at the west front of the city's cathedral, the **Basilique St-Front**. Twelfth-century Romanesque, at least in origin, this ought to be a treat but, like the cathedral at Angoulême, it was got at in the last century by that industrious architect, Abadie. As Freda White pointed out, in her *Three Rivers of France*, it's probably 'the supreme example of how not to restore': too white, too new, too regular, with breast-shaped domes littered all over the roof. Abadie added seventeen of these, and almost totally demolished the rest of the church, 'correcting' all that was irregular or unsymmetrical, altering the elevations, rounding the (pointed) arches, and refashioning the sculpture. A pity: it was an interesting church, modelled on St Mark's in Venice and the Holy Apostles in Constantinople. You can still see the vast interior space with its five huge domes supported on massive square piles, but it neither looks nor feels right anymore, inside or out.

Walk round to **place de la Clautre** and you can see the plain blank façade of the church St-Front superseded, an enormous belfry with pilasters capped by Corinthian columns surmounting the join between the old church and the new. Below, a small garden with a fountain held by four girls in Empire dresses gives a good view over the river Isle to the wooded hills beyond the town.

Over to the west, outside the old centre, – **bd des Arènes** encloses a public garden and ruins of a Roman **amphitheatre**. A couple of blocks below is another reminder of the Roman past, the brick **Tour de Vésone**, part of a temple dedicated to the local patroness, and beyond it the **Porte de Normandie** and **Maison Romane** — bits and pieces of columns and statues hastily cobbled together to make a defensive wall against the Visigoth invasions of the 4C.

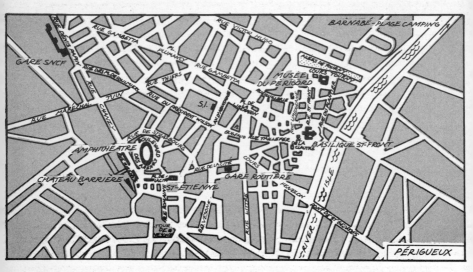

Specifics: food, info and GRs

There's no shortage of good **restaurants** in Périgueux, though they tend to the expensive. Exceptions, and good standbys, include *Lou Chabrol* (22 rue Eguillerie) and *Pizzeria Les Coupoles* (rue de la Clarté), both near the cathedral and cl. Sun/Mon.

Among useful **sources of information**, both for the Périgord and the Dordogne as a whole, are the **SI** and **CIJ** (alongside each other in rue d'Aquitaine) and the **Office Départemental de Tourisme** in rue Wilson. The latter, from mid-June–mid-Sept, organise **coach trips** to various sights in the province — worth considering since some can be time-consuming and tricky to reach without your own transport.

If you're into walking, look in at the **GR office** at 15 av de Lattre-de-Tassigny and ask for their booklet, Randonnées Pédestres en Périgord. Several **GRs** cross the area, among them: GR36, south to Les Eyzies and Biron, north towards Angoulême; GR461, the old packhorse trail from Montignac to Terrasson (20km); GR36, a 68km haul from La Capelle-Biron to Monbazillac; GR6, Ste-Foy-la Grande to Souillac (75km), via Monbazillac, Tremolat, Sarlat and Carlux; GR64 from Les Eyzies to Grolejac (65km), via St-Cyprien and Domme; and GR436 from Brantôme to Pensol (65km). There are too a number of local, short-haul walks.

CLOSE BY PÉRIGUEUX: HAUTEFORT, BRANTÔME AND BOURDEILLES

East of Périgueux on the D704 to Limoges, the château of **HAUTEFORT**, its 17C elegance in marked contrast to most of the rough stone fortresses of Périgord, stands proudly on a wooded ridge overlooking the surrounding farmland. The 12C fortress which originally stood on this site belonged to the troubadour, Bertrans de Born, who was known in particular for his *sirväntes* or political songs. Dante in the *Inferno* places him in the lowest circle of Hell, though Bertrans and his fellow troubadours with their Provençal songs were the immediate artistic ancestors of Dante himself, Petrarch and the poets of northern Italy, who were in turn to have so much influence on the beginnings of English poetry. The castle was later home to Marie de Hautefort, the young beauty Louis XIII fell in love with.

You enter the **château** (9.15–11.30 & 2.15–6.30, Palm Sun–1 Nov; rest of year, Sun only, 2–5) by way of a drawbridge across a moat, surrounded by formal gardens. Its residential quarters face south across a wide courtyard, flanked by wings that terminate in round, domed towers – the south-east a small chapel. Down in the village below is a large domed hospice, now a church, of the same period as the château.

There is a morning bus from Périgueux to Hautefort via Cubjac on Wed and Sat, otherwise only in the evening. In either case it is not possible to get there and back in the day. You stand a fair chance hitching, or you could get a Brive train as far as La Bachellerie near the turn-off for Hautefort. The most attractive road is the D5 along the river Auvézère via Cubjac, passing through TOURTOIRAC, where Antoine-Orélie I, King of Araucania, died in 1878. This bizarre character was a Périgueux lawyer who, deciding he was born for higher things, borrowed money and set sail for Patagonia, where he proclaimed himself king of the Araucanian Indians.

BRANTÔME, 27km north of Périgueux on the Angoulême road, is a lovely but touristy village on a curve of the river Dronne. An unusual 16C bridge with a 90-degree bend joins the public gardens to the right bank of the river, where the SI is housed in a Renaissance pavilion at the end of an *allée* of limes. There's an attractive but pricey restaurant in an old mill just below the bridge. On the left is the pale stone façade of the 18C **Hôtel de Ville**, formerly part of a monastery, where in the 16C Pierre de Bourdeilles, scurrilous author of scandalous tales of court life, was once lay abbot. Next door the abbey church has a very fine Romanesque belfry. **Getting to Brantôme** is simplest by hitching; there are buses, but only for school and the Wednesday market. Hotels here, be warned, are expensive, though there is a **campsite** to the right over the bridge on the Angoulême side of the village.

BOURDEILLES, 16km downstream by a beautiful road on the right bank of the Dronne (8km if you turn left on the D106 before Brantôme), is a sleepy backwater: an ancient rural village clustering round its castle on a rocky spur above the river. Its **castle** (9–11.30 & 2–6; cl. 15 Dec–1 Feb, first week in Oct & Tues from 15 Sept–15 June) consists of two buildings, one a 13C fortress, the other an elegant Renaissance residence begun by the lady of the house as a piece of unsuccessful favour-currying with Catherine de Médicis. Unsuccessful, because Catherine never came to stay, and the château was left unfinished. From the top of the octagonal keep there is a lovely view of wooded hills, cornfields, and the river below pouring over a weir and down to an ancient bridge.

The **house** is now home to a particularly good collection of furniture bequeathed to the state by its former owners. There are some splendid Spanish dowry chests; a 16C Rhenish Entombment with life-sized statues, the very image of the serious, self-satisfied medieval burgher; a 15C primitive Catalan triptych of an exorcism, with a bull-headed devil shooting skywards out of a kneeling princess; and a pair of elaborately carved French buffets with the *cache-serrure* sliding up between the thighs of a buxom maid.

LES EYZIES AND THE PREHISTORIC CAVES

Half an hour or so by train from PÉRIGUEUX lies **LES EYZIES**, centre of a luxuriant cliff-cut region riddled with caves and subterranean streams. It was here that skeletons of Cro-Magnon man were first unearthed in 1868 by labourers digging out the Périgueux-Agen railway line, and here too that an incredible wealth of archaeological and artistic evidence of the life of late Stone-Age man has since been found. The cave paintings alone are not only remarkable for their great age, but also, far from being unintelligible scratches, for their colour and the exquisite way they are drawn. Some say it was here the story of western art began . . . .

Les Eyzies itself is a rambling, unattractive little village wholly, and perhaps not surprisingly, given over to tourism. There's a riverside **campsite**, *La Rivière*, but otherwise, its central location apart, it doesn't make the best place to stay. Hotels are pricey and likely to ask for demi-pension. Better to try **LE BUGUE**, 10km down the Vézère river, where there's an excellent and inexpensive **hotel** and **restaurant** by the station on the road into town. Four **trains** a day run to Les Eyzies from Périgueux, and the Périgueux SI issue a sheet detailing how to get there and back in a day. If you're coming from the other direction, there are two trains daily from Bordeaux to LE BUISSON, where you can either change or hitch.

The most spectacular cave of all is the one at **LASCAUX**, a little way up the Vézère near MONTIGNAC. It was only discovered in 1940, and quite by chance when four boys who had lost their dog fell upon a deep cavern decorated with hundreds of marvellously preserved paintings of animals in yellow, red and black. Sadly, because of deterioration from the body heat and breath of visitors, the cave has been closed since 1963, and all you can see now is a tantalising replica.

Though not so big, the lovely **FONT-DE-GAUME** cave on the D47 15mins' walk from Les Eyzies is open (9–11.15 & 2–5.15 1 May–30 Sept; rest of the year 9–10.15 & 2–3.15; cl. Tues; expensive admission). A word of warning, however: the cave can only be visited in groups of twenty or fewer, and tickets sell out fast. To be sure of a ticket in season (and especially on a Sunday, when they're half price) get to the ticket office as soon as possible – at least an hour before morning opening time, preferably more in July and August. It is in any case nicer to be in the first group of the day – it's quieter then and you have a greater sense of exploring.

The setting is utterly sylvan. The cave mouth, a fissure from which a resurgent stream once issued, is well concealed by rocks, oak and hazel; below is a lush little valley. But it wasn't always like this. When Stone Age man first settled here – about 25,000BC – the Ice Age was still on and the Dordogne was tundra, the domain of roaming bison, reindeer, and mammoth.

Inside, the cave is a narrow twisting passage of irregular height with pock-marked uneven walls. There's no lighting, and you quickly lose your bearings in the dark. When the guide finally halts and focusses her torch, you see the first **paintings**, a frieze of bison, at about eye level, reddish-brown in colour, massive and full of movement, and very far from the primitive representations you expect. Further on, in a side passage, two horses stand one behind the other, forelegs outstretched as if, as the guide suggests with some relish, to attempt *un début d'accouplement* ('the beginning of copulation'). But most miraculous of all is a frieze of five bison discovered in 1966 during cleaning operations. The colour, remarkably sharp and vivid, is preserved by a protective layer of calcite. Shading under the belly and down the thighs is used to give three-dimensionality with a sophistication that seems utterly modern. Another panel consists of superimposed drawings, a fairly common phenomenon in cave painting, sometimes the result of work by succeeding generations, but here an obviously deliberate technique. A reindeer in the foreground shares legs with a large bison behind to indicate perspective.

Stocks of artists' materials have also been found: several kilos of prepared pigments; palettes – stones stained with the ground-up earth pigments; crayons – sort of painting sticks made of wood. Clearly painting was a specialised, perhaps a professional act, reproduced in dozens and dozens of caves in this area, in the central Pyrenees and northern Spain in the Upper Paleolithic era.

The sheer beauty and skill of the paintings is impressive at one level, but what does it all mean? For a start, people never lived down here: Font de Gaume is only 130m long, but many caves are far longer, with terrifyingly difficult access through twisting slippery passages only passable on your belly. Cave people had only the most primitive lamps to light their way and paint by. So what moved them to choose these inaccessible spots?

There are various **theories**. Most agree that the caves were sanctuaries: if not actually places of worship, they at least had religious significance – you can sense that. One theory is that making images of animals that were commonly hunted, like reindeer and bison, or feared, like bears and mammoths, was a kind of sympathetic magic intended to help men either catch or evade these animals. Another is that they were part of a fertility cult: sexual images of women with pendulous breasts and protuberant rumps are common, and it seems too that certain animals were associated with the feminine principle and are found in association with various symbols that may represent femininity. Others argue, from parallels with the Australian aborigines who use similar images to teach their young vital survival information and about the history and mythological origins of their race, that these cave paintings served a similar purpose in a world without literature, when there was no other way of passing on vital knowledge. But there remain all sorts of unexplained things, like the numerous abstract signs that appear in many caves – for instance, and the arrows which clearly cannot be arrows, because Stone Age flint arrowheads look totally different from ours.

Further up the same road from FONT-DE-GAUME, the **GROTTE DES COMBARELLES** (same hours) has hundreds of engraved drawings of animals. Close by, at the **Château de Laussel**, one of the great pieces of prehistoric art was found – a small bas-relief of an exaggeratedly female figure holding what looks like a slice of water-melon, known as Vénus à la Corne (Venus with the Horn of Plenty). She dates from the Aurignacian period – earlier than the cave paintings by a millennium or two – and now resides in the museum in Bordeaux (see p. 232). There is a copy in the **Musée National de Préhistoire** in Les Eyzies (9.30–12 & 2–6/5; cl. Tues) along with numerous prehistoric artefacts and art objects ranging from the earliest scratchings to a reproduction of one of the most beautiful pieces of Stone Age art, two clay bisons from the Tuc d'Audoubert cave in the Pyrenees.

There are several other prehistoric sites further up the Vézère valley.

SARLAT AND PÉRIGORD NOIR

SARLAT, capital of Périgord Noir, is, like Périgueux, a pretty market town. But it is also a major tourist attraction, of the kind that goes in for phoney medievalism and jousting in the streets: something no doubt inspired by the pristine preservation of its 16C centre, stacked high with honey-coloured houses.

Though not actually fortified, many of these **houses** were clearly built with an eye to defence, with lots of towers and turrets and steeply pitched roofs, weighed down by heavy stone tiles (or *lauzes*) stacked up horizontally on the rafters. One of the finest is next to the cathedral. But this is basically a town to wander about – and around. The **Dordogne valley** is lovely here, dotted with ruinous castles from the Hundred Years War. If you decide to make this a base, there's a **youth hostel** in av Selves, on the north edge of town just off the Périgueux road, two **campsites** (*Les Acacias* is simple, in a fine setting, 2km beyond the railway viaduct) and a handful of **hotels** – *Marcel* (down the road from the hostel, reasonable and with a decent restaurant), *de la Mairie* (place Liberté) or the *Lion d'Or* (av Gambetta – at the north end of rue de la République). **Getting here**, there are trains and buses from Périgueux, and a rail link on to Bergerac and Bordeaux. The road along the banks of the Dordogne, from Bergerac, is quite hitchable too, or you can walk here from Les Eyzies along a leg of the GR6.

Exploring the valley from Sarlat, **LA ROQUE-GAGEAC**, tucked under a cliff on the right bank, is almost too perfect – so much so that it keeps winning prettiest village competitions, and pulling in the inevitable coachtours. But the river on this stretch, with fish rising to the May fly and acacias dripping the banks, makes a glorious stop. There are four campsites. High on the opposite bank, **DOMME** is also a spectacle – a classic *bastide* town. And **BEYNAC**, just downstream is another river-bank eye-catcher, with a 13C castle on the edge of a 150m drop, built to command the river traffic in the days when the river was the only route open to traders and invaders. By road it is 3km to the **castle** (9.30/10–12 & 2/2.30 – 7/6) but a steep lane leads up through the top of the village in 15mins. It is protected on the landwards side by a double wall; elsewhere air does the job. The flat terrace at the base of the keep, which was added by the English, conceals the remains of the houses where the beleaguered villagers lived, one of which has been partly excavated. England's cut-throat king, Richard Coeur-de-Lion, held the place for a time, until a gangrenous wound received while besieging the castle of Châlus north of Périgueux put paid to his term of bloodletting.

Originally, to facilitate defence, the rooms inside the keep only communicated via a narrow spiral staircase – in stone, not wood, as in the reconstruction, because of the danger of fire. The division of domestic space into dining-rooms and so forth only came about when the advent of artillery made these old *châteaux forts* militarily obsolete. From the roof, there is a stupendous – and vertiginous – view up-river to the châteaux of **Marqueyssac, Fayrac** and **Castelnaud**. Fayrac, all pepperpots and slated towers now, was an English forward position in the Hundred Years War when the Dordogne river was a frontier.

DOWNSTREAM: TOWARDS BORDEAUX

Downstream from Sarlat, past Bergerac, the Dordogne is wide and fertile, planted with vines, maize and tobacco. It is not the most exciting stretch, but pleasant enough travel, and if you're interested in wine there are plenty of visiting/tasting possibilities.

BERGERAC itself, a traditional heartland of French Protestantism, is an attractive and prosperous farming centre, with a small **Musée du Tabac** (suitably in place du Feu, in the 'old town'; 9–12 & 2–6, cl. Mons). Though as ancient as anywhere on the Dordogne, it is essentially a modern place, for it was devastated several times over in the Wars of Religion, and most of its population emigrated overseas after the evocation of the Edict of Nantes lost Protestants their guaranteed privileges. There are numerous **hotels**.

STE-FOY-LA-GRANDE, next town to the west, also a bastion of Protestantism, still retains some of its original *bastide* features. Beyond it, the **vine** takes over more and more, covering the valley bottom and gently sloping flanks. Past CASTILLON-LA-BATAILLE, where a memorial commemorates the final defeat of the English in 1453, and you arrive at this region's most famous wine town, **ST-ÉMILION**. Entirely surrounded by vineyards, its old grey houses straggle down the south-facing slopes of a low hill. If you are interested in visiting the vineyards, ask at the **Maison du Vin** on top of the hill near the prominent belfry, which belongs to the so-called **Église Monolithe**, a church hewn from the rock beneath it. Tickets to visit the church are obtainable from the **SI** (by the belfry).

Entry to the church is off a small square with a large locust tree in the middle, below the cliff on which the belfry is built. The visit starts in a dark hole in someone's back yard – the cave where Saint Émilion is said to have come as a hermit in the 8C. A rough-hewn ledge served as his bed and a carved seat his chair, where, so you're told, barren women still come to sit in the hope of getting pregnant. Above it is a half-ruinous Benedictine chapel, that the Revolution converted into a barn. Fragments of frescoes include one of St-Valérie, patron saint of wine-growers.

On the other side of the yard, a passage tunnels into the rock beneath the belfry. Inside are three chambers dug out of the soft limestone, used as ossuary and cemetery during the 8C–11C. In the innermost chamber, discovered by a neighbour enlarging his cellar some fifty years ago, a large tombstone bears the inscription: 'Aulius is buried between saints Valérie, Émilion and Avic.'

The **church** itself (9–12C) is an incredible place. Simple and huge, the entire structure, barrel-vaulting, great square piers and all, has been hacked out of the rock. The windows of Chartres cathedral were stored here for safekeeping during the war. The whole interior was painted once, but only faint traces remain. The paintings were scraped off in the Revolution, and a gunpowder factory installed in the church. These days, every June, the wine council – *La Jurade* – assembles in the church to evaluate the previous season's wine and decide whether each producer's produce deserves the 'appellation contrôlée' accolade.

The town comes to an abrupt end behind the **SI** with a grand view of the moat and old walls. To the right, the Collegiate church of the Cordeliers has a handsome but badly mutilated doorway and pretty 14C cloisters (ask at SI).

CAHORS AND THE LOT

Travelling **south from the Dordogne** takes you into the drier, poorer and more sparsely populated province of **Haut Quercy**, where there are few facilities for tourists and you don't get much help from public transport. So it's an ideal area to hike, bike and camp, and once you're away from the few sights you will have most of it to yourself. In addition to the GRs, some thoughtful authority has marked out a **circuit des bastides**, which makes an excellent cycling itinerary.

MONPAZIER AND THE CHÂTEAU DE BIRON

MONPAZIER, midway between the Dordogne and the Lot, is the best of all the *bastides*. Built in 1284 by Edward I of England, who was also Duke of Aquitaine, it can scarcely have spread beyond its original limits. Picturesque though it all is, however, the village's history – as so often in this region – is a hard one. Twice, in 1594 and again in 1637, it was the centre of peasant rebellions, provoked by the misery that followed the Wars of Religion* and, as usual, brutally suppressed: the peasants' leader being broken on the wheel in Monpazier square.

---

* Sully, the Protestant general, describes a rare moment of light relief in the terrible wars, when the men of the Catholic **bastide**, VILLEFRANCHE-DE-PÉRIGORD (pretty

It is sleepy today, and depopulated. At the street ends the fields begin and you look out over the surrounding country. There is an ancient *lavoir*, where the women used to wash their clothes, a church, much mucked about, and a gem of a central square – sunny, still and slightly menacing, like a Sicilian piazza at siesta time. Deep, shady arcades pass under all the houses, which are separated from each other by a small gap to reduce fire risk. At the corners the buttresses are cut away to allow the passage of laden pack animals.

Coming here, there is a bus (*Transports Fauchier*, 2¼ hrs; daily except Suns) from Périgueux, or you can take a train to BELVÈS (17½km) or LE GOT (13km) on the Périgueux–Agen line, and walk or hitch from there. **Staying**, there is a choice of **campsites**: the *municipal*, 2km northwest, or a *Camping à la ferme*, 5km along a country lane at La Bouyssou – signposted as you enter Monpazier. It is a great spot. If there are not many people, the old couple who run the farm let you camp on the grass under the pines by the house and provide meals. They still speak Occitan together, the old language of the south and west of France. They found it easier than French, they said. It was, after all, their first language – they did not learn French until they went to school. It was the same on all the farms in their youth. Their children understand Occitan still, but do not use it, while their grandchildren knew only a few words.

A short distance to the south the vast **CHÂTEAU DE BIRON** dominates the countryside for miles around. It is open for guided tours only (9/10–11.30 & 2.30 – 6/5; cl. Tues for most of the year) and while these are in progress you are booted unceremoniously even from the grassy courtyards within its walls, where there is a Renaissance chapel and guardhouse and tremendous views over the roofs of the lord's village down below.

A single street runs through the **village**, past a covered market on timber supports iron-hard with age, past a pretty bourgeois residence with a *cour* in front, and out under an arched gateway. Well-manured vegetable plots interspersed with iris, lily and Iceland poppies lie under the tumbledown walls. At the bottom of the hill, another group of houses stand on a small *place* with a broken well in front of a half-ruinous church, its Romanesque origins covered by all sorts of subsequent alterations, and with a massive old home-made ladder leading to the belfry.

much closer to the railway than Monpazier – only 2½km) planned to capture Monpazier on the same night as the men of Monpazier planned to capture Villefranche. By chance both sides took different routes, met no resistance, looted to their hearts' content, returned home congratulating themselves on their luck and skill, only to find in the morning that things were rather different. The peace terms were that everyone should return everything to its proper place.

The road carries on south up hill and down dale, past a few poor farms and miles of oak woods to LACAPELLE-BIRON, where there is a monument to the wartime *déportés*, and on to **St-Front-Sur-Lémance**, with a fortified church. St-Front is back on the railway line and the best point of access for BONAGUIL CASTLE, at the end of a wooden spur commanding two valleys, about 8km to the south-east. Built during the 15C–16C, with a double ring of walls, five huge towers and a narrow-pointed boat-shaped keep, it was the last of the really medieval castles to be constructed, albeit designed to resist artillery. The site is superb. Admission is expensive and only by guided tours (hourly between 10–12 & 3–6; more sporadically at other times), so if you plan to visit, don't, as I did, turn up at 11.10.

CAHORS

At **CAHORS**, capital of the old province of Quercy, you finally reach the Lot, which flows roughly parallel to the Dordogne to join the great river Garonne, south-west of Bordeaux. In its time, Gallic settlement and Roman town; held briefly by the Moors; governed by the English; bastion of Catholicism in the Wars of Religion; sacked in consequence by Henry IV; 400 years the possessor of a university; birthplace of Gambetta, after whom so many French streets are named – modern Cahors is a sunny southern backwater. Its two most interesting sights are the **cathedral** church of St-Étienne and the remarkable 14C **Pont Valentré**.

The **Pont**, with its three powerful towers, originally closed by portcullises and gates that turned it into an independent fortress, guards the river crossing on the west side of town. It is one of the most photographed monuments in France and rightly so, for it is one of the finest surviving bridges of its time.

Just upstream a resurgent river issues from the valleyside, known as the *Fontaine des Chartreux*. The Roman town was named after it, Divona Carducorum. It still supplies the town with drinking water.

The town is sited on a peninsula formed by a tight loop in the river. The layout is easily mastered. **Rue de la Barre** and **bd Gambetta** bisect north to south from the old town walls that cut off the peninsula to the more modern bridge, Pont Louis-Philippe, and beyond it the ragged **camping municipal**. The bus and railway station (with bike rental) is a short hop from all this – which soon becomes clear as you walk in. If you want a map, make for the **SI** near the cathedral in the centre of town on rue Joffre. **Hotels** include *Mon Auberge*, in rue Jean-Jaurès, to the right of the station, *l'Escargot* (5 bd Gambetta) and *de la Paix* (in place des Halles, by the cathedral).

Consecrated in 1119 Cahor's **Cathedral** is the oldest and simplest in plan of the Périgord-style churches. Like St-Étienne at Périgueux, it has a nave without aisles or transepts, roofed with two big domes. In the first are 14C frescoes of the stoning of St Stephen. The Gothic choir and apse are extensively but crudely painted, to their right a door opens into a Gothic cloister, which, though damaged, still retains some intricate carving. On the north-west corner pillar a graceful girl with broad brow, good figure and ringlets to her waist serves as a model for the Virgin. From the cloister an arch opens on to a courtyard by the Renaissance archdeacon's house.

The exterior of the church is not exciting. A heavy square tower dominates the plain west front. The best feature is the elaborately decorated portal in the street on the north side. Christ in Majesty dominates the tympanum, surrounded by angels and apostles. Cherubim fly out of the clouds to relieve him of his halo. Side panels show scenes from the life of St Stephen. On the outer ring of voussoirs a line of naked figures are being stabbed in the arse and hacked at with axes.

North and south of the cathedral, towards the river bank, there is a warren of narrow lanes and scruffy alleys. Many of the houses, turreted and built of flat, thin southern brick, date from the 14C, 15C and 16C. On the south side, place Jean-Jacques Chapou ('créateur et animateur du maquis du Lot, mort pour la France le 17 juillet 1944') is bordered with lime-trees. The *halles* are nearby. To the right in rue du Docteur Bergonniaux is a nice little restaurant – *La Brasserade*.

THE PECH-MERLE CAVE

East of CAHORS, SNCF buses follow the beautiful, deep-cut, twisting valley of the Lot to **CONDUCHÉ** (good value *Hôtel-Restaurant des Grottes*). From here it's a further 4½km up the valley to the village of **CABRERETS** (another good Hôtel-Restaurant, *de la Sagne*) and another 1½km to the cave at PECH-MERLE. You'll need to hitch or walk – no hardship along this minor road through thick-wooded limestone hills. If you want to camp there are limitless spots between Cabrerets and Pech-Merle.

PECH-MERLE (Palm Sun–30 Sept & Suns 9–12 & 2.30–6; Oct wkdays only at 10, 11 & 4.30; expensive admission), bigger and less accessible than Les Eyzies, does not suffer from the same problems of overcrowding and consequent dangers of deterioration. Normally there should be no difficulty in getting tickets. The admission charge includes a film and excellent **museum**, where the history of prehistory is illustrated by colourful and intelligible charts, a selection of objects (rather than the usual 10,000 flints), and beautiful slides displayed in wall panels. It is interesting, too, to see the skulls of Neanderthal man and Homo sapiens side by side – the former's jaw muscles much cruder, to chomp junks of raw meat and crush heads, like the cave bear illustrated alongside him.

The **cave** itself is far more beautiful than those at Padirac or Les Eyzies, with galleries full of the most spectacular stalactites and mites, structures tiered like wedding cakes, drapes and shapes like whale baffles, discs and cave pearls. Yet, the visit is less awe-inspiring than, say, Font de Gaume. The cave is wired for electric light, and the guide, who talks, like a recorded message, rushes you through in order to cover the ground in the scheduled time.

The first drawings you come to are in the so-called *Chapelle des Mammouths*. They are done on a white calcite panel that looks as if it had been specially prepared for the purpose. There are horses; bison charging head down, with tiny rumps and arched tails; tusked and whiskery mammoths. Then you pass into a vast, magical chamber where the famous *horse panel* is visible on a lower level. Here is another remarkable example of the way in which the artist uses the contour and relief of the rock to do the work for him. An utterly convincing mammoth is suggested by just two strokes of black. The cave ceiling is covered with finger marks, preserved in the soft clay, sketches of a mammoth, a female figure. You pass the skeleton of a cave hyena that has been lying there for 20,000 years – wild animals used these caves for shelter and sometimes, unable to find their way out, starved to death in them. And finally, the most moving and spine-tingling experience at Pech-Merle – the footprints of a Stone Age man and child preserved in a muddy pool.

Not far away from Pech-Merle, perched high on the south bank of the Lot valley, is the cliff-edge village of **ST-CIRQ-LAPOPIE**: with its cobbled lanes, half-timbered houses, gardens and greenery and fantastic site an obvious candidate for art-and-craftiness. You won't regret the steep pull up from the river (**SNCF bus** from Cahors stops at gare St-Cirq), but the knell of the place as a real village has already sounded. (*Hôtel du Causse* and **camping** at La Truffière 3km south-east over the rim of the valley.)

THE EAST

The eastern part of the region butts up against the foothills of the Massif Central. Moving north-south is easy enough, for the Limoges-Brive-Toulouse railway skirts the hills all the way – the **Brive-Limoges** section is worth riding just for the spectacular scenery in the Vézère river gorge. Brive and Limoges are the best starting points, but once you get away from them transport and accommodation can be tricky. Traffic is too thin on the ground to count on reaching a destination in a fixed time if you're hitching, so it's best to carry a tent as well.

BRIVE AND THE UPPER DORDOGNE

BRIVE is a good base for the Upper Dordogne: an easygoing town, and attractive enough, but with no particular sights of its own to bring in (or hold) the tourists. It's a useful railway junction and has good bus links from the gare routière on av Général Leclerc on the south side of the boulevard that rings the town centre. There is also a youth hostel – rare in this part of France, on av Maréchal-Bugeaud – and a campsite, just across the river.

Turennes, Collonges and Beaulieu

Very occasional local trains run south from Brive in 30 mins to TURENNES, a distinctive village of steep-roofed, turreted houses and a castle on a high projecting rock. Several centuries ago this formed the capital of a powerful viscounty, but it has long since faded into rustic insignificance. You can visit the **castle** (9–12 & 2–7 mid-March–Oct; rest of the year Suns only 10–12 & 2–5), one tower of which forms part of a house that is still lived in. From the other, the *Tour de César*, there is a view as far as the mountains of Cantal on a clear day.

The administrative capital of the Turennes viscounty was at COLLON-GES-LA-ROUGE, a little way to the east. You can get to it on the D38 which forks left off the Brive-Turennes road, or directly from Turennes on the D150 which turns left by the station and goes through the village of NOAILHAC – about 7km. Or you could go via SAILLAC, about 3 hours' walk, which has an interesting Romanesque church with an elaborately carved tympanum concealed inside the porch, supported by a column with spiralling motifs of animals twisting up it.

Collonges itself is a gem – its houses, festooned with wistaria and pepperpot towers, built entirely in warm, red sandstone. It is grand, but on a small scale: minor noblemen aping, within their means, the grandiloquent gestures of their superiors. The church (11C–12C), fortified in the Wars of Religion, fronts a square and a covered market with its old-fashioned baker's oven still in position. Inside, a curiosity are the two naves, side by side, where Protestant and Catholic services were conducted simultaneously.

There is a **campsite**, a few minutes walk down the road at MEYSSAC, and in Collonges, an unpretentious **hôtel-restaurant** the *Relais de St-Jacques de Compostelle*, reason in itself for stopping here, with excellent and vast portions.

Down in the valley, on the right bank of the river, BEAULIEU-SUR-

DORDOGNE boasts one of the most prized pieces of all French Romanesque sculpture in the south doorway of its **abbey church of St-Pierre**. The doorway is unusually deep-set, with a tympanum dominated by a Christ in Glory with a face like a Chinaman, extending his right arm in welcome to the chosen. All around is sculpted a complicated pattern of angels and apostles executed in that curious dancing style, with the dead raising the lids of their graves. Underneath is a frieze of monsters crunching heads.

There is a **youth hostel** in Beaulieu, and **SNCF buses** connect with the stations at BIARS-BRETENOUX, ARGENTAT and TULLE.

ARGENTAT is another pretty village, just below the first of the dams that now control – and mar – the upper reaches of the river, from here on more and more a mountain river in its narrow wooded gorges. At **BRETENOUX**, a 13C *bastide* with a cobbled square surrounded by arcaded houses, there is an attractive **campsite** by the river Cère. Close by, on a high spur, is the superb 11C **Château de Castelnau** (9/10–11.45 & 2–5.45/4.45. cl. Tues), furnished with fine Beauvois and Aubusson tapestries and sheltering its village beneath the castle walls.

Padirac, Rocamadour and Millevaches

The high ground to the west is the edge of the **Causse de Gramat**, one of the high limestone plateaux characteristic of the old province of Quercy, which begins hereabouts. There is a marked changed of vegetation as you climb out of the valleys. The soil is poor, the grass yellowy, the ground littered with stones and patches of rock breaking through. Scrub oak and juniper abound; caves and underground rivers riddle the rock.

Two of the Dordogne's most famous tourist attractions are to be found on the *causse*: one a cave, at PADIRAC, the other, ROCAMADOUR, a pilgrim shrine. Neither is easy to get to, without your own transport or taking a coach tour, and unless you've a really specific interest, I'd advise giving both a miss. Mass tourism can be an unattractive sight – and not something you need fall upon in this, or indeed most other parts of France.

For the record, though, **PADIRAC**'s dimensions are impressive – an enormous limestone sink-hole, about 100m deep. But it is just a cave – without paintings; it is expensive and you'll queue some time for the **boat tours** on its underground river (8/9–12 & 2–7/6; 8–7 in Aug). Outside hundreds of school parties zip round the zoo and souvenir shops.

The village of **ROCAMADOUR** must have once been beautiful: tucked under a cliff in the deep and abrupt canyon of the ALZOU stream, and visited for centuries for the shrine of its miracle-working **Black Virgin**. But the coach tours are here in even greater force, the church and castle have been restored beyond all reality, and every house is selling hideous junk to the tourists.

If you must visit, Brive-Capdenac **trains** stop at ROCAMADOUR-PADIRAC station about 40mins' walk away. Padirac is a good 2½ hours' walk.

North-east of Brive the country gets progressively wilder and hillier, full of streams and woods of beech, birch, chestnut and conifers, good only for grazing sheep. Places are few and far between – isolated hamlets and grey stone farms with a few weathered old peasants inured to the hardships of upland life. Hard to get lifts round here although, surprisingly, the area is well served by the SNCF. **Trains** run from USSEL and MEYMAC via EYMOUTIERS, across the edge of the **Plateau of Millevaches** – with high ground up to 900m – to Limoges. From USSEL (**youth hostel**), an SNCF bus goes to **LA COURTINE**, a good walking centre on the plateau. Ussel is also on the main road and railway from Bordeaux to Clermont-Ferrand. Just east of the road, near Egletons, are the romantic ruins of the castle of VENTADOUR – no more than a few blocks of masonry rising above the woods.

LIMOGES

LIMOGES has been around since Roman times. St Martial converted it to Christianity in the 3C. The Black Prince butchered a goodly number of its citizens in 1370 for daring to resent his overlordship. It is the capital of the province of Limousin, whence comes the term 'limousine' from the local shepherds' cloaks that wrapped round the whole body. But its great fame is due to its **craft industries: enamel** in the Middle Ages and since the 18C, some of the finest **china** ever produced. If these appeal, then the city's unique museum collections – and its Gothic cathedral – will reward a visit. But it has to be said that the industry today seems a spent tradition. It has been hit hard by the recession (or at least has fallen from fashion among the new rich); the local *kaolin* (China clay) mines are now exhausted; and the workshops survive mainly on the tourist trade – most of its junk beggaring description.

The best of the museums – with its showpiece collections of enamel ware from the 12C on – is the **Musée Municipal** (10.11.45 & 2–6/5; cl. Tues except in July/Aug). There's an interesting progression to be observed here, though to my taste the best stuff is the earliest, the *champlevé*. Done on copper plate, with the enamel filling hollowed-out designs, this is simple, sober and Byzantine in influence. The later work, especially the 17C and 18C, is much more exuberant, the range of colours far greater, the portraiture amazing. In the 19C it seems to have lost all style, however, and though there are contemporary artisans in the city working in the medium their work, too, judging from this display, is not a lot more successful.

For collections of the porcelain, along with extensive representative china displays from around the world, continue to the **Musée Adrien Dubouché** (10–12 & 1.30–5; cl. Tues & hols), just off place Winston Churchill. Again, explanatory panels describe the processes for making the various different wares. If sufficiently interested it is possible to visit a number of active workshops (lists and details from the SI).

The municipal museum occupies the old Bishop's palace. The **Cathédrale St-Étienne**, inevitably, is right opposite. Begun in 1273, it was planned on the model of the cathedral of Amiens, though only the choir, completed in the early 13C, is pure Gothic. The rest of the building was added in dribs and drabs over the centuries, the western part of the nave not until 1876. The most striking external feature is the 16C façade of the north transept, built in full flamboyant style with elongated arches, clusters of pinnacles and delicate tracery in windows and galleries. The doors are carved with scenes from the lives of St-Étienne (Stephen) and St-Martial.

At the west end of the nave the tower, which is built on a Romanesque

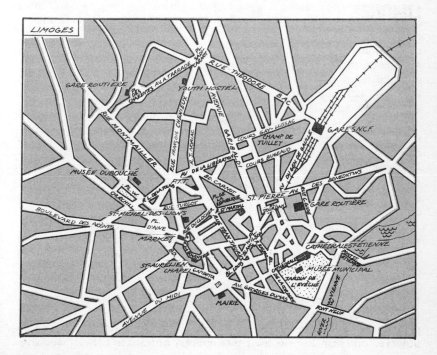

base massively reinforced to take the weight, has octagonal upper storeys in the manner characteristic of most churches in the region. It once stood as a separate campanile and probably looked the better for it. **Inside** the effects are much more pleasing. The pinky stone looks warmer than on the weathered exterior. The sense of soaring height is accentuated by all the upward-reaching lines of the pillars, the net of vaulting ribs, the curling, flame-like lines repeated in the arcading of the side chapels, the rose window and so on, and particularly, as you look down the nave, by the narrower and more pointed arches of the choir.

Over to the west of the cathedral is the old quarter of the town, partly renovated. Make your way through to **rue de la Boucherie**, for 1,000 years the domain of the Butchers' Guild (and with several nice-looking restaurants). The dark, cluttered chapel of **St-Aurélien** with a 14C butter cross outside belongs to them. At the top of the street is the **market** (place de la Motte) and to the right, partly hidden by adjoining houses, the church of **St-Michel-des-Lions** (14–15C), named after the two badly weathered Celtic lions guarding the south door. It has a particularly fine octagonal tower and spire, one of the best in the region, and inside is dark and atmospheric, basically a large rectangular 'hall' with three divisions of equal height. There are two extremely pretty 15C windows either side of the choir, with lovely dense colouring, especially the one in the south aisle depicting the Tree of Jesse.

From place de la Motte, rue du Clocher leads to rue Jean-Jaurès, with the Post Office a couple of blocks up to the left. Straight across, rue St-Martial leads past the car park in place de la République where the 4C crypt of the long-vanished **abbey of St-Martial** (July–30 Sept, only 9.30–12 & 2.30–5) was discovered during building operations in 1960, to the church of **St-Pierre-du-Queyroix**. Very plain outside, this has an attractive, though shortish, belfry, which served as a model for the cathedral and St-Michel. The interior, partly 12C (the exterior was remodelled in 16C), has a sombre strength from the massive round pillars which still support the roof. Like St-Etienne it has that slightly pink granite glow. There is a fine window at the end of the south aisle depicting the Dormition of the Virgin, signed by Jean Pénicault in 1510 – one of the great enamel artists.

Limoges has numerous **hotels** in the streets either side of Champs de Juillet in front of the railway station. There is a very nice **youth hostel** at the *Foyer des Jeunes Travailleuses* (single rooms, canteen) in the tiny rue Encombe-Vineuse to the right off rue Chenieux south of place Carnot, with a useful **laundrette** close by in av Labussière. Rue Chenieux has a couple of good brasseries.

The **gare SNCF** has good rail connections to almost anywhere you might think of going on to. **Departmental buses** leave from place des Charentes in av Adrien-Tarrade (also off place Carnot); private buses from the **gare routière** in rue Gide near the railway station. There is a biennial international exhibition of enamel work in July and August.

AROUND LIMOGES: ORADOUR AND LIMOUSIN VILLAGES

The villages below are all within an easy day's reach of Limoges. Solignac is walkable – if you've got tough feet. And you'll need the walk from Oradour to the train station to recover from the macabre shock of the ruined village.

Oradour-sur-Glane

Twenty-five km north-west of LIMOGES, the village of **ORADOUR-SUR-GLANE** stands just as the soldiers of the SS das Reich Division left it on 10 June 1944, after killing all the inhabitants in reprisal for attacks by French *maquisards*. It seems irreverent to approach it as a 'sight'; perhaps it should be seen more as a shrine. There are **buses** from place des Charentes in Limoges, but the timetable is pretty inconvenient. The best thing is to take a **train** to St-Victurnien on the Angoulême line, about 25mins; you can get there and back in a day. Then walk the 7km to Oradour, 1½–2 hours.

ST-VICTURNIEN is a tiny village on the Vienne, with a **hotel** and **campsite** (open only in season). Turn right out of the station, through the village and up a wooded hill past meadow and hedge to the N141, 2km. Cross straight over and continue 5km through quiet, woody country with orchids and Lady's Smock in the verges, buttercups and asphodels in the pasture. You might get a lift; there is hardly any traffic. Then turn left at the next main road, and ORADOUR is in front of you, a modern village built beside the old with a 1950s concrete church, which tries, but fails, to be impressive – and it would be difficult to devise an architectural space commensurate with the task of commemorating, forgiving and transcending that dreadful act.

A gate into **the old village** admonishes: 'Souviens-toi,' – remember. The village street leads past roofless houses gutted by fire. Telegraph poles, tram cables, gutters are fixed in tormented attitudes where the fire's heat left them. Pre-war cars rust in the garages. A yucca, grown into an enormous clump, still blooms in the notary's garden. Last year's grapes hang wizened on a vine whose trellis has long rotted away.

Behind the square is a memorial garden, a plain rectangle of lawn hedged with beech. A dolmen-like slab on a shallow plinth covers a crypt containing relics of the dead, and the awful list of names. Beyond, by the stream, stands the church where the women and children – 500 of them – were burnt to death.

St-Léonard-de-Noblat

ST-LÉONARD-DE-NOBLAT, 25mins by train from Limoges on a branch line, is a small market town of narrow streets and medieval houses with jutting eaves and corbelled turrets and a very lovely **church** (11–12C). Its six-storeyed tower is a beauty. The bottom two storeys are solid and square. The next two decrease in height and recede slightly. The top two are octagonal with a short stone spire. The transition from square to octagonal is cunningly concealed by producing long pointed gables above the arcades of the fourth storey. The west front, surmounted by a plain gable and with a very wide portal flanked by multiple miniature pillars, is a 13C addition. The interior is strong and simple: barrel vaults on big, square piles, a high dome on an octagonal drum above the crossing, transepts also domed – the whole in grey granite.

To **hitch** out of Limoges in this direction, take bus no 1 from place Carnot, across Pont Neuf to the terminus on the St-Léonard-Bourganeuf-Aubusson road.

Chalusset and Solignac

South of Limoges, infrequent trains down to Brive stop at the station of SOLIGNAC-LE-VIGET: closest point of access to the ruined castle of Chalusset and abbey of Solignac, in the wooded valley of the Briance. This is perhaps the most attractive daytrip you could make from Limoges – and, if you're feeling energetic, you could even forget the trains and walk the whole way (13km to Solignac; 19km if you hike to Chalusset, too, and back). If you decide to do this, cross the Vienne in Limoges by the Pont St-Martial and take the back road to Solignac. If hitching, leave by Pont-Neuf on the Brive-Toulouse road. Turn right after a few 100m and continue uphill out of town. After 6km take the St-Yrieix turn-off on the right. It is 6km from there down into the green valley of the Briance at Le Viget.

The 12C **CHÂTEAU DE CHALUSSET**, which the English held during the Hundred Years War, is 4km on from here, up a lane to the left. At the highest point of the climb, about 40mins from Le Viget, an iron belvedere in the wood on the right of the road gives a dramatic view across the valley to where the ruined *donjon* rises above the trees. To get there you turn downhill to the right for 1km until you cross the Briance. Opposite the end of the bridge a path climbs up to the castle. About an hour from Le Viget and an hour back.

SOLIGNAC is 15mins' walk the other side of Le Viget. You can see the **abbey** ahead of you with the tiled roofs of its octagonal apse and neat little brood of radiating chapels. The 12C façade is plain with just a little sculpture; the granite it is built of does not permit the intricate carving of limestone. Inside it is beautiful. A flight of steps leads down into the nave with a dramatic view down the length of the church.

There are no aisles, just a single space roofed with two big domes. No ambulatory either: an absolutely plain Latin cross in design. It is a simple, sturdy church, with the same sort of feel of plain robust Christianity as the crypt of St-Eutrope in Saintes.

TRAVEL DETAILS

Trains

From Périgueux 5 to Le Buisson (50mins); 5 or 6 to Bordeaux (1½–2hrs); 5 to Brive (1–1¼hrs); 5 to Les Eyzies (½hr); 3 to St-Front-sur-Lémance (1½hrs); 4 to Agen (2½hrs); about 10 to Limoges (1–1½hrs); for Paris-Austerlitz, change at Limoges.

From Le Buisson 4 to Sarlat (½hr); 5 to Bergerac (40mins); 3 to Bordeaux (2hrs).

From Bergerac 3 to Sarlat (1½hrs); 1 to Périgueux (1hr50); 7 to Bordeaux (1¼–3hrs).

From Brive 1 to Turennes (¼hr), plus one morning train on Sundays; 3 to Roc-amadour-Padirac (40mins); about 10 to Cahors (1¼–1½hrs); 6 or 7 to Toulouse (2½hrs); 5 to Meymac (1½hrs), Ussel (1hr45); 3 to Clermont-Ferrand (3hrs 40); 6 to Aurillac (1hr45–2hrs); 2 or 3 to Bordeaux (2½hrs).

From Limoges frequent service to Paris-Austerlitz (3½–4hrs); 3 to Angou-lême (2hrs); 4 to Poitiers (2–2¼hrs); 5 to St-Léonard-de-Noblat (25mins); 5 to Eymoutiers (50 mins); 3 to Meymac (hr 50); 3 to Ussel (2 hrs); about 10 to Brive (1hr10).

SNCF bus

From Cahors infrequent to Figeac and Capdenac via Conduché and St-Cirq (2hrs), also east along the Lot to Montsempron (1hr20) via Fumel (for Bonaguil castle).

Chapter eight
THE PYRENEES AND PAYS BASQUE

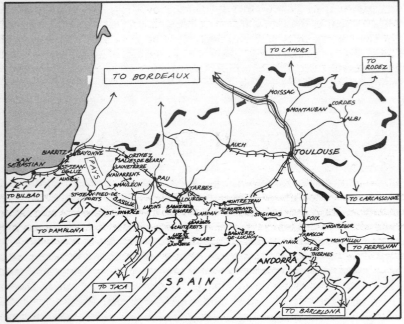

Basque-speaking and wet in the west; craggy, snowy, patois-speaking in the middle; and dry and Catalan to the east: **the Pyrenees** are individual-istic mountains. The whole range is marvellous walkers' country, especially the central region around the **Parc National des Pyrénées**, with its 3,000m peaks, streams, forests, flowers and wildlife. If you're a serious and committed hiker it's possible to go right across, from Atlantic to Mediterranean, along the **GR10** trail and the **Haute Route des Pyrénées**. But there are numerous local walking centres as well – **Cauterets, Luz-St-Sauveur, Barèges, Ax** – all of them far less commercially developed than their equivalents in the Alps. The **hiking season** (see p. 268) is mid-June through to September: earlier in the year few refuges are open and you will run into snow even on parts of the GR10. The routes don't need to be difficult or demanding, though they can be if that's what you're after. Whatever you intend, however, bear in mind that these are big mountains and treat them with respect: to cover any of the proper walks you'll need proper boots and, despite the southerly latitude, warm sweaters and wind-proof clothing.

As for more conventional tourist attractions in this region, the **Basque coast** is beautiful but very popular, suffering from seaside sprawl and a massive surfeit of campsites. **St-Jean-de-Luz** is by far the prettiest of the resorts; **Bayonne** the most attractive town (with an excellent Basque museum and art gallery); **Biarritz** the most over-rated. The foothill towns of the Pyrenees are on the whole rather dull, though **Pau** is worth a day or two and **Lourdes** so awful it needs to be seen. To the north, where the rivers Ariège and Garonne run clear of the mountains, the great city of **Toulouse** and neighbouring **Albi** boast impressive medieval connections – and architecture.

EUSKAL-HERRI: THE PAYS BASQUE

The three **Basque provinces** – Labourd, Basse-Navarre and Soule – share with their Spanish neighbours a common language, *Euskara*, and a strong sense of separate identity. They use their language – young as well as old – and they refer to their country as a land in itself, **Euskal-herri** or, across the border in Spain, *Euskadi*. Unlike the Spanish, however, few French Basques favour an independent state or secession from France. There is no equivalent of ETA here, and there are signs that the old sympathy, which allowed refuge to Spanish Basques wanted on terrorist charges, is waning. It was Franco, dead now for a decade, who had kept up the political momentum.

Administratively, the three Basque provinces are organised together in a single *département* – the result of French centralising zeal after the Revolution, when the Basques' thousand-year-old *fors* (rights) were abolished. Ironically, this move has probably been responsible for preserving French Basque unity.

THE BASQUE HINTERLAND: ORTHEZ TO ST-JEAN-PIED-DE-PORT

If you've a car and a tent – or a bike and a lot of energy – the Basque country offers a whole network of remote upland and valley lanes, all beautiful country and scattered with the distinctively built and coloured Basque villages. I came in on foot at ORTHEZ, intending to follow the **GR65**, the pilgrim route to Compostela for the two or three days to the

Spanish frontier. Finding no one could tell me where it was, I gave up the idea and hitched down to SALIES-DE-BÉARN: which seemed as good a way as any into the province. If you do want to follow the GR65, the path in fact crosses the main Pau road at ARAGNON about 8km east of Orthez.

The route from ORTHEZ, with the remains of a towered medieval bridge spanning the rocky Gave de Pau, starts on the main road, but from PUYÔO to SALIES and onwards it is the kind of road where hitching seems a luxury: idling territory, which it would be a shame to pass through too quickly or easily. There are, though, SNCF buses over the whole stretch, and a train connection at **PUYÔO** on the main BAYONNE-PAU road.

SALIES is a typical Béarnais village of winding lanes and flower-decked houses with brightly painted woodwork. The river Saleys, hardly more than a stream, runs through the middle separating the old village from the 19C development which sprang up to exploit the saline waters for which it has long been famous. It is a charming, if unremarkable, little place, good for an overnight stop, with a **Camping Municipal** and tiny **youth hostel**, both on the rugby pitch.

Going south again, the D933 winds over hilly farming country to **SAUVETERRE-DE-BÉARN**, another pretty country town beautifully sited on a scarp high above the Gave d'Oloron. From the terrace by the church you look down over the river and the remains of a fortified bridge. At the end of the terrace the ruins of a castle stand atop the steep slope, its empty joist sockets making perfect pigeon-holes. The church itself, 13C with a square tower and tall apse, is attractive from the outside, but of no interest in.

There are two or three reasonably priced and attractive **hotels** in the street past the church. Across the river (**campsite** by the bridge) the D933 continues to a crossroads with the D936 – about 2km. A left turn here takes you along the flat bottom of the valley to NAVARRENX (18km).

NAVARRENX is an old-fashioned market town, built as a *bastide* in 1316 and still surrounded by its ancient walls. You enter by the fortified Porte-St-Antoine. There is again nothing to do except enjoy the sleepy rural atmosphere. The Mayor's office in the townhall dispenses what tourist information there is in a cheerful, unsystematic way. The whole place could have come off a film-set for a movie about the French: it confirms every Anglo-Saxon's stereotype image of rural France, the back country, or arrière-pays. *Hôtel du Commerce* by the Porte St-Antoine is reasonably priced.

The **GR65** passes through the town. You pick up the waymarks on the telegraph poles in SUSMIOU at the western end of the bridge. Turn left over the bridge on the Mauléon road, then right on a byroad shortly after. The path meanders westward following byroads, farm tracks and footpaths to the vicinity of ST-PALAIS, where it turns south-west to follow the main St-Palais to St-Jean-Pied-de-Port road. To hitch to MAULÉON, keep on to the crossroads with the Sauveterre-Oloron road and cross straight over. It is wooded, hilly country all the way. It looks fertile, but there is little depth of soil and precious little level ground. You are now on Basque territory.

MAULÉON was the ancient capital of the viscounty of Soule. It lies in the bottom of the flat hot valley of the river Saison. In the centre is the sombre Renaissance Hôtel d'Andurain, built around 1600 by a bishop of Oloron. Its chief claim to fame today is as the world capital of *espadrille* manufacture. I was given a lift to the town by the owner of one of these factories, who showed me round his works, the fourth largest in volume of production. It was surprisingly rudimentary: a simple shed in which forty-three employees, working round the clock in shifts, produce 4,000 pairs a day. Nearly all the work is done by hand, stitching, forming the soles, gluing. The machinery is very basic. Most of the manual operations are terribly repetitive; some requiring almost contortionist agility and incredible speed.

There is nothing to keep you in Mauléon, but potential enough roundabout. A route I didn't do is up the Saison river to STE-ENGRÂCE, with a very fine Romanesque church, one of the remotest corners of the Pays Basque and a major centre for sheep, cows, and *pottoks*, a breed of miniature horses raised for their meat. Nearby are the **Gorges de Kakouetta**, impressively deep and narrow but already something of a tourist trap, I was told. The trans-Pyrenean footpath, the **GR10**, passes through.

It is a twisty, hilly ride from Mauléon over the Col d'Osquich to the St-Palais/St-Jean-Pied-de-Port road (24km), then 16km south-west to St-Jean.

ST-JEAN-PIED-DE-PORT

The old capital of Basse Navarre, **ST-JEAN-PIED-DE-PORT** lies in a circle of hills at the foot of the Roncevaux pass into Spain. It owes its name to its position, 'at the foot of the *port*' – a Pyrenean word for pass. It has only been part of France since the Treaty of the Pyrenees in 1659. In the Middle Ages it was an important pilgrim centre, for numerous routes through Europe converged here. It was the pilgrims' last halt before struggling over the pass to the Spanish monastery of Roncesvalles, where Roland, Charlemagne's general celebrated in medieval romance, wound his horn in vain and the pilgrims planted their palm-branch crosses so thick there were often thousands at a time.

The town lies on the river Nive, enclosed by walls of pinky-red sandstone. Above it rises a wooded hill crowned by the inevitable Vauban fortress, while to the east a further defensive system guards the road to Spain. The more recent overspill, pleasant but unremarkable, spreads down across the main road on to lower ground.

The old town consists of a single cobbled street, **rue de la Citadelle**, which runs downhill from the **Porte St-Jacques**, so nàmed because it was the gate by which the pilgrims entered, to the **Porte d'Espagne** commanding the bridge over the Nive. A plain red church stands beside the Porte d'Espagne and, opposite, a short street leads through the **Porte de Navarre** to the modern road. From the Porte d'Espagne, with its view of balconied houses overlooking the stream, rue d'Espagne leads uphill to the so-called Route Napoléon. Off to the left is the town *fronton*, the pelota court which you'll find in just about every Basque town. Just beyond, the **Camping Municipal** – best bet if you want to stay, since St-Jean's quaintness brings in the tourists, and its hotels are pricey and require half-board in July and August.

Numerous tracks lead from St-Jean up **into the mountains** towards the Spanish border. It is all sheep country, and if you are interested in getting an idea of what the old transhumant pastoral life was like, this is the place to do it. The SI (on the main road) can provide ideas for drivers. If you are a walker, the last leg of the **GR65** starts from St-Jean and follows the line of the Roman road across to Spanish Asturia.

Go up rue d'Espagne and out through the city walls. The first waymarks are on the first telegraph pole on the left. A little further on you turn up a lane to the right; the GR10 and GR65 run together here. Keep up the lane, between grassy banks, past fields and isolated farms. The farmhouses have immensely broad roofs, one side short, and the other long enough to cover space for stalls, tools and so on: it is very quiet and rural, with long views out across the valleys. The climb becomes steeper above a little group of houses known as HOUNTO. It is no good asking the way, even if you can find someone to ask. Though everyone speaks French, the Basque names are impossible to pronounce correctly and no one understands what you are talking about. Above Hounto you come out on top of a grassy spur. The GR65 turns left up what looks like an old drove road and rejoins the tarmac lane higher up by two small sheds at the edge of beech woods. It is about 2 hours fairly brisk going to these sheds. You get your first glimpse of the higher Pyrenean peaks to the east. Above the trees you come out on the bare grassy uplands dotted with sheepfolds. Where the lane bends round the head of a stream gully there is a sheepfold – *cayolar* – right beside the road, where a shepherd lives with his dog and flocks through the summer months, milking his sheep twice a day and making his cheese.

Much of the **grazing** throughout the mountains is owned in common by various communes, and from time immemorial they have made elaborate agreements to ensure a fair share-out of the best pasture and avoid disputes. One of the oldest of these *faceries*, as they are called, concluded by the inhabitants of Roncal and Baretous in 1375, is still in force, renewed each year on payment of three white heifers. A measure of the predominance of sheep in the Basque economy: *aberats* – the Basque for rich – means 'he who owns large flocks'.

The route continues along the track to a fork (3½ hours) with a small white statue of the Virgin. Here, the GR65 goes right towards Spain (another 1½ hours) and the GR10 turns down left. The left fork is steep and bumpy but passable for cars. After a twisty descent it brings you out at the tiny hamlet of ESTÉRENÇUBY, then down along the Nive and back to ST-JEAN.

THE ROAD TO THE SEA: ST-JEAN-DE-LUZ

The D918, the main road to BAYONNE, follows the twisting valley of the Nive to CAMBO, unfortunately bypassing the villages. Here, however, it turns sharply west for ST-JEAN-DE-LUZ, running along the way through a succession of small foothill communities.

ESPELETTE, the first, is a typical Basque village of gaily painted half-timbered houses. Take a look at the church with its heavy square tower and slated steeple. Stairs climb to the men's galleries, while you enter the body of the building through carved doors beneath. Inside is an aisleless nave with three tiers of galleries, the usual heavy gilt altarpiece and a painted wooden ceiling. In the churchyard are a number of the peculiarly Basque, disc-shaped gravestones.

About 15mins' walk beyond Espelette, a minor road forks left to the exceptionally pretty village of AINHÖA, well-preserved and undisturbed by any modern development. Most of the houses have their timbers painted red, in contrast to the dark blue *Hôtel Ohantzea*, a reasonably-priced two-star *Logis de France*, patronised in the past by the Duke of Windsor. It would be a good place to give yourself a treat. The local church is of characteristic Basque design with a fine plain timber ceiling and altarpiece of gilded prophets and apostles with the air of modern bankers. The GR10 leaves the village just below the church.

The Spanish frontier is 3km away at DANCHERIA. There is a back road through the woods, which ends at a stream crossed by a plank bridge with a *venta* on the Spanish side, selling booze, butter and numerous other products of French manufacture very much cheaper than in France. Pernod, for instance, is something like a quarter the price. Needless to say, they do a roaring trade. Hordes of French come to shop at these *ventas* all along the border at weekends. A certain amount of smuggling is tolerated, but you have to watch out for the *douane volante*, the flying customs, who lie in wait on back roads.

Frontier people always do a good line in illicit cross-border trading, but I was told that some sizeable fortunes had been made in Ainhöa, one gentleman managing to leave each of nine children £100,000. Wartime was particularly profitable, with an almost money-no-object trade in refugees. A nasty business: French fugitives were charged a 'reasonable' rate, while Jews had to pay £1,000 a head whether they were alone or in a group. And then there was the Spanish Civil War and the Franco regime . . . If it was not trafficking in people, it was blackmarket coffee or any other commodity in short supply one side of the border or the other.

Try the GR10 for the AINHÖA-SARE stage – about 3 hours. From Sare there are buses to ST-JEAN-DE-LUZ on the sea.

St-Jean-de-Luz

ST-JEAN-DE-LUZ is by far the most attractive resort on the Basque coast. Sure, it gets crowded, and, yes, its main seafront is undistinguished, though there is a long curving beach of beautiful fine sand. It is a small place, with a population of only about 12,000, but with a tough, resilient identity of its own that has much to do with the fact that despite the importance of its tourist revenues it remains a thriving fishing port, the most important in France for catches of tuna and anchovy. The old houses round the harbour, both in St-Jean and Ciboure on the far side (they are really one town), are very picturesque, but not in vapid picture-book manner. St-Jean keeps its feet on the ground. It is still a real place.

Being the only natural harbour on the coast between the Spanish frontier and Arcachon it has been an important port for centuries. Whale and cod have been its special preoccupations. Its sailors voyaged as far afield as Newfoundland, which the Basques claim to have discovered 100 years before Columbus reached America. In the 17C, Dutch and English whalers, who had learnt their trade from Basque harpooners, drove them from their traditional ports of call in Arctic waters, so an enterprising Basque devised a method of boiling down the blubber on board, enabling the ships to stay at sea much longer. In the 18C, under the provisions of the Treaty of Utrecht, they lost their Newfoundland cod-fishing grounds and were only saved from ruin, like their brothers in Bayonne, by turning privateer and seizing other nations' shipping.

The major event in the schoolbook history of St-Jean was the wedding of Louis XIV and Maria Teresa, Infanta of Spain. The couple were married in the church of St-Jean-Baptiste, and the door through which they left the church has been walled up ever since. The extravagance of the event is beyond belief. Cardinal Mazarin alone presented the queen with 12,000 pounds of pearls and diamonds, a gold dinner service and a pair of sumptuous carriages drawn by teams of six horses each – all money made in the service of France.

The focus of life for visitors is **place Louis XIV** near the harbour, with its cafés, bandstand (free concerts) and plane trees. Leading through to the beach is the short **rue de la République**, full of restaurants, and ranging through most price categories. The 17C house with turrets (10.30–12 & 3–6, 6 June–15 Sept) on the harbour side of the *place* is where Louis XIV stayed at the time of his marriage. It was built by a shipowner, Lohobiague, in 1635 and still belongs to the same family. Maria Teresa lodged just along the quay in an Italianate mansion of faded pink brick. In the corner house on rue Mazarin, just back from the waterfront, Wellington made his HQ during the 1813–14 winter campaign against Marshal Soult.

A short distance up **rue Gambetta** on the town side of the *place* you come to the church of **St-Jean-Baptiste**, the largest of the Basque churches. It is a plain fortress-like building from the outside. Inside, the barn-like nave is roofed in wood and lined on three sides with tiers of dark, oak galleries. These are a distinctive feature of Basque churches, and were reserved for the men, while the women sat in the floor of the nave. The walled-up door through which Louis and his bride passed is on the right of the main entrance. The ex-voto model of a paddle-steamer hanging from the ceiling is Empress Eugénie's 'Eagle', which narrowly escaped shipwreck on the rocks outside St-Jean in 1867.

The best view of old St-Jean is from the bridge to **Ciboure**, whose own waterfront, where Ravel was born, is even prettier.

There are several reasonable **hotels** near the station: *Hôtel Toki-Ona*, rue Marian Garay; *Elizabeth*, rue Labrouche; *Verdun*, opposite the station; *Continental* and *Hôtel de Paris*, both on the corner of rue Labrouche. *Camping de la Rade* is the nearest **campsite**, about 15mins' walk from the **SI** in place du Maréchel Foch (left of the station); go along Ciboure waterfront for about 300m and turn left in rue du Dr Micé, then left again – the camp is on the flank of the hill. **Bike rental** at the station or *ADO* in rue Labrouche. **Pelota** matches take place every Saturday at the *fronton* at the far end of rue Gambetta. You can arrange with the SI to visit the Irouléguy wine *caves*. Also there are buses up from the station to SARE for the La Rhune railway, 900m up and smack on the Spanish frontier.

BAYONNE AND BIARRITZ

BAYONNE and BIARRITZ are virtual continuations of each other, filling in all available space behind the coast. Their characters, however, are entirely different. Bayonne, a clean, sunny, southern town, workaday and very Basque; Biarritz, upmarket and tight-assed, and redeemed only by its waves – some of the best surfing territory anywhere in Europe.

Bayonne

BAYONNE actually stands back – some 6km – from the Atlantic: a position that's protected it from any real exploitation by tourism. Which is fortunate. For, with its half-timbered houses, their shutters and woodwork painted in the peculiarly Basque tones of green and red, this is one of the most distinctive, and enjoyable, towns in France. Most travellers treat it merely as a transit point between resorts but if you want to spend time by the sea this is as good a base as any from which to make forays. And it is good for a spell in its own right, too.

You arrive, by train or bus, at the **SNCF station**, in the shabby quarter of **St-Esprit** on the bank of the Adour. Just upstream is a massive fortress built by Vauban in 1680 to defend the town against Spanish attack, though it did not see much action until the Napoleonic wars, the garrison here holding out against Wellington for four months in 1813. Immediately opposite the station, past the St-Esprit church, a long **bridge** spans the Adour to reach the old city centre, cut through by a second river, the Nive.

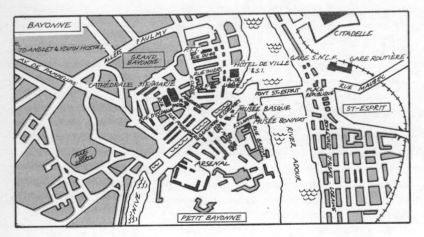

The Nive quays are fun to wander, and at the corner of the second bridge is a **Musée Basque**, worth visiting if you have any curiosity for the province and its people. Its exhibits are superb, illustrating Basque life through the centuries. There are reconstructed farm buildings and house interiors; various implements and tools of a kind used by pastoral people throughout Europe; *makhilas* – a peculiarly Basque kind of offensive walking-stick (father to son returning from market: 'Was there a makhila fight then?' 'No, father.' 'Bah, that wasn't much of a market!'); a section on Basque seagoing activities (Columbus' skipper was a Basque and another Basque, Sebastian de Caro, made the first round-the-world voyage in 1519–22); *pelota*; and famous Basques, among them Simon

Bolivar, de Lesseps of Suez canal fame, and Mr Laxalt, senator for Nevada. (Hours are 9.30/10–12.30/12 & 2.30–6.30/5.30, cl. Suns.)

The city's second museum, **Musée Bonnat** (June-Sept 10–12 & 4–8; otherwise wkdays 1–7, wkends 10–12 & 3–7; cl. Tues), is nearby on rue Jacques Lafitte, with another excellent collection – this time of works left to Bayonne by the painter. It's an unexpected treasury, and a refreshing change from the run-of-the-mill stuff of most provincial galleries.

The **Cathedral** looks its best from a distance, its twin towers and steeple rising with airy grace above the houses. Close to, the yellowish stone shows bad weathering, with most of the decorative detail lost. The interior is more impressive thanks to the height of the nave and some 16C glass well set-off by the prevailing gloom. Like other southern Gothic cathedrals of the period (about 1260) it was based on more famous northern models, in this case Soissons and Rheims. On the south side is a 14C cloister with a lawn, cypress trees and beds of begonias – a quiet spot, hidden from the city, and with a rather flattering view of the church.

From the cathedral square rue de la Monnaie and rue du Pont-Neuf lead downhill to the main square, **place de la Liberté**, full of *pâtisseries* and *confiseries* with a good strong odour of chocolate, a business introduced to Bayonne by Jews expelled from Spain in 1611. For Biarritz and the **beaches** you can hop on a bus in the square, by the large Hôtel de Ville. The **SI** are inside here, and can give information about cruises on the Adour, visiting the Izarra liqueur distillery, and the various local **festivals**. Bayonne's own principal event is the *Fêtes traditionelles*, held with a *Corrida* at the beginning of August.

There are several **cheap hotels** within sight of the station, and places to eat. The **campsite**, *de la Chêneraie* is in the St-Frédéric quarter on the north bank of the Adour; the **youth hostel** at Anglet between Bayonne and Biarritz (*Ligne Bleue* bus, direction Biarritz-La Négresse, from Hôtel de Ville to Cinq Cantons: there turn left down Promenade de la Barre, then fifth left along Promenade des Sables and finally right onto the Route des Vignes – about 25mins' walk).

Biarritz

BIARRITZ developed as a watering place for the rich in the mid-19C, with the English, as on the Côte d'Azur, to the fore. The Empress Eugénie, wife of Napoleon III, spent her childhood summers here and in 1854 persuaded her husband to accompany her, which launched the place as a resort for Europe's aristocracy. The vast, barrack-like Hôtel du Palais above the Grande Plage was originally their holiday home. Queen Victoria visited once, and Edward VII and the Duke of Windsor, trendsetter for British blades, were regulars. In season it is full of people, rich and un-rich, yet it is not a relaxed place. Its pompous, ponderous architecture, too, gives it an unfriendly air.

West of the **Grande Plage**, which is overlooked by two massive casinos, is a series of sea-girt rocks and promontories, and beyond, first, the sheltered **Plage du Port-Vieux**, then the immense **Plage de la Côte des Basques** backed by grey-white cliffs. The Atlantic weather of course is not as reliable as the Mediterranean. A clammy, though romantic, sea mist is not uncommon in the mornings. But if conditions are right, you can certainly get some marvellous swimming and surfing.

On the Plateau de l'Atalaye above the rocky promontory of the Rocher de la Vierge is the **Musée de la Mer** (9–7, July–Aug; rest of year, 9–12 & 2–7; expensive), hardly a must, but with interesting exhibits to do with the fishing industry, the region's birds, and an aquarium of North Atlantic fish.

Hotels are pricey and booked up in summer. Some cheaper ones are near the station in La Négresse. There are three city **campsites** – *Splendid* (rue d'Harcet), *Biarritz* (28 rte d'Harcet) and *Municipal* (Bois de Boulogne) – and others dotted up and down the coast. But for a bed I'd choose Bayonne or the Anglet youth hostel (*Ligne Bleue* bus *Direction Bayonne* to Cinq Cantons from the Hôtel de Ville: then see Bayonne, above, for directions).

THE CENTRAL PYRENEES

This is where the **high peaks** are and the best part for anyone who likes the great outdoors. Getting there is simple enough as far as the foothill towns – by train on the Bayonne-Toulouse line. It's inside the range that **moving about** is slow. The few buses, and most traffic, keep to the north-south valleys, which is a bore when you want to switch from one valley system to the next without having to come all the way out of the mountains each time. The GR10 provides a good link if you are ready to walk all the way. Otherwise it is possible to hitch. The main passes at **Col d'Aubisque** and **Col du Tourmalet** have spectacular scenery – though you will find you invariably get left on the top by someone just coming up for the view and going back the same way.

As for less hearty interests, there is a highly unusual fortified church at **Luz-St-Sauveur**, which you are likely to be going through anyway. And at **St-Bertrand-de-Comminges** a bit further east, the whole package – village, church, surrounding countryside – definitely merits the short detour from the Luchon road.

For **ideas and information** (in French) about walking and other activities in the Pyrenees (canoeing, riding, cycling), contact c.i.m.e.s.-pyrénées, 3 square Balagué, 09200 Saint-Girons and ask for the booklet, *Randon-*

nées Pyrénéennes. The French walkers' guides are *Pyrénées Occidentales* by Ollivier; *Haute Randonnée Pyrénéenne* (the High Level Route HRP) by Georges Veron, published by the Club Alpin Français; and the GR10 Topo-Guide. An excellent **English guide** is Kev Reynolds' *Walks and Climbs in the Pyrenees* (Cicerone Press). There are also three small ones done by Arthur Battagel for West Col, which include the Spanish side of the range. The best **maps** are the IGN 1:25000 series; Nos 273, 274 and 275 cover the Parc National.

PAU

Capital of the ancient viscounty of Béarn, **PAU** has a more than usually powerful history. In the 16C it was at the centre of the Wars of Religion, provoked here by Béarn's tough Protestant ruler Jeanne d'Albret, and leading to equally ruthless reprisals by the Catholic king Charles X. Later, when Jeanne's son Henri himself became king of France, switching faiths in the process, he found it necessary to accommodate the regional sensibilities of his Béarnais subjects by announcing that he was giving France to Béarn rather than Béarn to France. Like the Basque and other Pyrenean provinces which came into existence as counties and viscounties in feudal times, it held onto its separatist leanings well into the 17C. Even today many of the Béarnais are still speaking Occitan rather than French.

The town is good-looking and lively, with a university, and due in part to tourism, in part to discovery of a gas field at Lacq, a fairly buoyant prosperity. It occupies a grand natural situation on a steep scarp overlooking the Gave (river) de Pau and from its **boulevard des Pyrénées**, the promenade which runs along the rim of the scarp, there are superb views of the Pic du Midi d'Ossau, Vignemale and other high peaks. Not surprisingly, it has become the most popular jumping-off point for the Parc National des Pyrénées, and it's well equipped for the purpose. The SI (at the end of place Royale) supply all kinds of walking information and a useful pamphlet, *Randonnées Pyrénéennes*. More specialist knowledge can be gleaned from either the *Club Alpin Français* (rue René Fournets; 59.27.71.81) or the *Pyrénéa sports* (12 rue des Bains; 59.27.23.11). There's an excellent climbing shop, *Romano-Sports*, knowledgeable, English-speaking and with good equipment to hire. And various organisations run guided hikes: among them *Randonneurs Pyrénéens* (9 rue Latapic; 6.45–7.45pm daily) and *Les Amis du PNP Occidentales* (24 rue Samonzet; 59.27.15.30).

As for its own sights, Pau's **Château**, at the west end of bd des Pyrénées, was done up by Louis Philippe in the 19C after standing empty for 200 years, and then tinkered with by Napoleon III and Eugénie – it was another of their country places. Not much remains of the original appearance except the keep but two museums are housed there. The *Musée*

National (9/9.30–11.45 & 2–5.45/4.45) consists mainly of Napoleon III and Eugénie's pompous weekend apartments and Henri IV memorabilia (the sea-turtle's shell that served as his cradle, and so on); *Musée Béarnais* (9.30–12.30 & 2.30–6.30), on the top floor, has a very good collection of costumes, Pyrenean animals, birds, butterflies and objects illustrative of the pastoral life.

Rooms are reasonably plentiful. There's a **youth hostel** (with a canteen) on rue Michel Houneau and several reasonable **hotels** in and around rue du Maréchal-Joffre; **restaurants** too, especially towards the château. *Au bon coin* is a good locals' place – west end of place Forail, off rue Carnot; you eat in the back room of a café, over the evening's TV. Among more interesting **bars** are *de la Poste* (along from the PTT on cours Basquet) and *Le Béarnais*, the latter a big student hangout at the eastend of rue Emile-Guichenne. Two **campsites**: *Municipal* on bd du Cami Salie (off av Sallenave towards the autoroute on the northern edge of town) and *Camping 'Le Coy'* behind the station at the Base Plein Air, Bizanos.

Arriving, the **SNCF station** is down by the river: a free funicular shuttles you up to-bd des Pyrénées. The **gare routière** (for non-SNCF buses) is near the youth hostel on rue Michel Houneau. For long-distance **hitching**, check *Allostop* on 59.82.97.10. And lastly, but pretty essential if you're hiking about the region, you'll find a 24-hr service *laundrette* at 11 rue Castelnau.

THE PARC NATIONAL DES PYRÉNÉES OCCIDENTALES

You really need to carry a **tent** to make the most of the park, unless you stick completely to the trails and hop from one refuge to the next for your accommodation – more expensive, of course, than camping. The hotels in the trailhead towns like CAUTERETS, LARUNS, GAVARNIE and BARÈGES tend to be booked from very early in the year.

As for the difficulty of **the walks** actually described here, there are not any which require special expertise. And none is beyond the capabilities of someone reasonably fit. The **Pic du Midi d'Ossau** is the most strenuous, and the best, because it is more off the beaten track.

This applies to good weather conditions. Obviously if you see frozen snow and don't know how to cope with it, turn back. The HRP and the climbs to the **top** of many peaks are another matter. Basically, if you have never seen the likes of it before, don't do it!

Pau to Laruns and the Pic du Midi d'Ossau

Access **to the trailhead** for the **Pic du Midi** is not difficult. On Saturdays and Sundays in summer an SNCF bus goes the whole way from PAU to

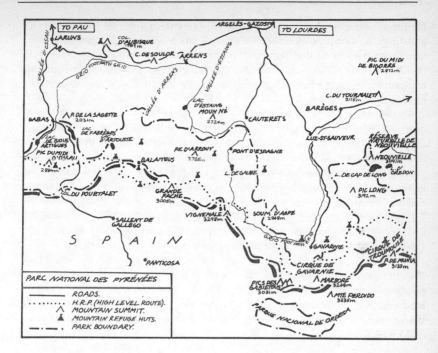

GABAS and on to the start of the *téléférique* for the Artouste railway; it leaves at 9.50am and returns to Pau at 5.25pm. At other times there are *Citram* buses (from Palais des Pyrénées or the railway station in Pau) as far as LARUNS; or you can take a train as far as the station of BUZY and then an SNCF bus to LARUNS; or you could hitch – fellow hikers/climbers are always setting out.

The road runs due south up the valley of the Gave d'Ossau. If you're driving be careful not to take the right fork for Oloron in Gan. **LARUNS** is enclosed in a narrow valley bottom, surrounded by steep grassy and wooded heights. There are some fine old houses in the back streets, especially down towards the river in the quarter known as Le Pont – old farms with mullioned windows and wide roofs spanning living quarters and farm space – and there are **hotels**, **restaurants** and an **SI** round the main square. Several campsites, too. If you are planning to hike or camp it is best to stock up with provisions in Laruns. There is nothing in Gabas, though *Camping Bious-Oumettes*, close to the start of the Pic du Midi path, has a shop which opens around 15 June.

To get to GABAS take the right fork over the bridge south of Laruns, where the road winds steeply into the upper reaches of the Gave d'Ossau valley. It is 13km and there is not a lot of traffic, but you should get a lift without much difficulty from other walkers or employees of the various National Park installations, especially early in the morning.

From the old spa of EAUX CHAUDES a tiny lane climbs the west flank of the valley to GOUST, a hamlet of two or three isolated farms high on the valley side. It is a bit of a slog on foot, but worth it if you are interested in seeing what rural life in these remote parts must have been like. Just below the hamlet a path leads off left of the lane under the pylons to the **Pic de Bouerzy**, about 3½ hours. It is not very clear higher in the woods; you'd need the local guidebook, but there are fantastic views of the Pic du Midi from the summit.

GABAS is only a hamlet, with a CAF refuge, a National Park office and a minuscule 9C chapel by the road, now restored. The 'main' road continues left past the **Lac de Fabrèges** to the **Col du Pourtalet** on the Spanish frontier. From the *lac* a *téléférique* goes to the Pic de la Sagette (2,032m) above Gabas, where it connects with the **miniature railway** that runs for 10km through the mountains to the **Lac d'Artouste**. It was built in the 1920s to service a hydro-electric scheme and then converted for tourist purposes. There was too much snow and the weather was foul when I was in the area, but normally the train runs from early June to mid- or late September. It is a very beautiful and spectacular trip – about 4 hours, including time to walk down to the lake. The first train leaves at 10am, but you need to allow half an hour on the *téléférique*. Don't forget to take warm clothes as you will be at an altitude of 2,000m.

The Pic du Midi
For the **PIC DU MIDI** take the lane to the right out of GABAS (it is also the route of the GR10). It is 4½km steep climb up a wooded ravine to the dammed-up LAC DE BIOUS-ARTIGUES, so named because it flooded the *artigue* – a Pyrenean word for mountain pasture – that formerly existed beside the infant *gave*. Just below the dam you pass the stony terraces of **Camping Bious-Oumettes**. Beside the lake at the end of the track is the **Refuge Pyrénéa Sports**, open to all (meals): manned 1 June–31 Oct.

The twin-pointed summit of the Pic (2,487m), sticking up out of the forest, is a distinctive landmark for miles around. I did the circuit in snow and thick cloud, with my nose in compass and map all day in conditions of near white-out. The round trip takes about 7 hours, excluding the summit: It can be broken by a stay at the CAF *Refuge de Pombie* (manned 15 June–15 Oct) below the vast southern walls of the mountain.

From the Bious-Artigues lake, follow the GR10 round, up the left bank of the *gave* and past the turning to the LACS D'AYOUS (another fine walk: *Refuge d'Ayous*, open 15 June–1 Oct). Cross the Pont de Bious and continue upstream across an expanse of flat wet meadow to a signpost saying **Lac de Peyreget** to the left. There follows a steepish zigzagging climb to the timberline and a long traverse right to the junction with the HRP path (1 hour from *Pyrénéa Sports*). Keep left, with the ground falling away on your right. At the Lac de Peyreget, either follow the HRP steeply up left towards the **Col de Peyreget**, or keep right – due south – to the **Col d'Iou**. From the latter, traverse leftwards following the contour to the **Col de Soum**, where you turn north-west, then north to the **Refuge de Pombie** (about 4 hours). The path must be very clear in dry weather. From the refuge it continues north beneath the Pic and the long Arête de Moundelhs back to *Pyrénéa Sports* (about 3 hours).

There is a path **off the mountain** from the Col du Soum, and another **from the Pombie refuge**, which I took. The latter leads due east down the valley of the Pombie stream, through meadows full of flowers – daffodils, orchids, violets, fritillaries. I saw a herd of izards on the slopes to my left. At the **Cabane de Puchéou** – a shepherd's hut – you cross to the left bank of the stream and carry on down to the next bridge. The HRP continues on the left bank past the Cabane d'Arrégatiou and comes out at the southern end of the Lac de Fabrèges. The right-hand path crosses the bridge and descends through the woods to a big expanse of meadow by the Gave de Brousset at **SOQUES** (about 2 hours from Pombie), where you join the Col de Pourtalet road and can hitch back to GABAS.

I met a couple of young shepherds in the valley below Pombie who told me that some young people were taking to the pastoral life again. They had sheep, which they raised mainly for the milk which was sold for making Roquefort cheese, and some horses which they sold for meat. They brought their flocks up to the mountains in May and took them down in late September before the first snow, in time for their ewes to lamb in October. They rented their pastures from the local communes; a whole mountain might cost up to £300.

The Col d'Aubisque, Cauterets and around

From LARUNS there is one daily bus **to the Col d'Aubisque**; if you miss it another couple go as far as EAUX-BONNES and one to GOURETTE, or again you could probably hitch. Alternatively, the GR10 runs from GABAS to GOURETTE over the Col de Tortes and on to the Col d'Aubisque – and thence beyond to ARRENS and, via the Vallée d'Estaing, to CAUTERETS.

The only other approach to CAUTERETS is by bus from LOURDES (daily but infrequent service).

The Col d'Aubisque and the route to Cauterets
The **Col d'Aubisque** (1,709m) is a grassy rounded ridge, an important

grazing ground, with tremendous views over the valleys below and the rocky precipices of the snowy Pic de Ger (2,613m) to the south. Along the crest of the ridge are a number of shooting butts used in autumn for the massacre of the migrating ring-doves (*palombes*), a favourite sport along the Pyrenees. In choosing the cols to save labour, the poor birds present a sitting target. In some places they are caught in huge nets strung across their habitual routes. In others, the hunters construct wooden towers like forest fire-watch posts.

The Col is part of the Tour de France route, an irresistible challenge to any French cyclist worth his salt. You see swarms of them toiling up, making it a matter of pride to find the breath for a cheery *bonjour*. There is a café at the top. If you are hitching, stay close to the café. The next place is 18km away.

Down in the valley you pass through ARGELÈS, then PIERREFITTE-NESTALAS, where you fork left for **CAUTERETS**, a pleasant though unexciting little spa in a magnificent situation, tightly enclosed by immense wooded hillsides and peaks. Its only interest is as a base for exploring the surrounding mountains. The **Parc National** has an office next to the **bus station**, which looks as if it came off the set of a Swiss western. The **SI**, in the main square, houses a *Bureau des Guides* (open 6–7 daily in July and Aug; services include organised walks and climbs, and in summertime they run a *crèche* – from 8–12.30 and 1.30–6, with meal provided). The cheapest **place to stay** is the *gîte d'étape*, *Le Cluquet* in av Dr Donner (open 6 June–9 Sept) past the *télésiège du Lys* and the tennis courts; you can put up your own tent or use one of the dormitories. The hotels, *du Béarn* in av Général Leclerc, *Bigorre* and *Centre Poste* in rue de Belfort aren't expensive but they are likely to require *demi-pension* in summer. The nearest **campsite** is *Les Glères* at the entrance to Cauterets. For **eating**: the *crêperie* in rue Richelieu has a cheap, four-course menu which includes wine; *Brasserie Le Centre*, at the corner of rue de Belfort and place Foch (by the SI), serves a *plat du jour* generously garnished with *frites* and salad – and quite interesting too: *agneau montagne*, quails, etc. *La Hutte Boyrie Sport*, a sports shop on place Foch, hires **hiking and climbing gear**.

Hikes around Cauterets

The classic and consequently very trippery excursion from Cauterets is up the Val de Jéret to the **Pont d'Espagne**, where the Gave de Gaube and the Gave du Marcadau hurtle together in a boiling spume of spray and go rushing down to Cauterets over one spectacular waterfall after another. The best way to avoid the tourists is to take the **Parc National path** from LA RAILLÈRE, 3km from Cauterets (regular buses). It starts on the right by the bridge and runs all the way beside the stream through beautiful woods of beech and pine. It comes out by the café-bar at Pont d'Espagne: about 2 hours up and 1½ down.

From Pont d'Espagne you can fork right up the **Vallée du Marcadau** to the **Refuge Wallon** (about 5 hours return) or left up into the hanging valley of the Gave de Gaube with the very lovely little **Lac de Gaube** backed by the high snowy wall and glaciers of **Vignemale** (3,298m). There is even a *télésiège* to save you the first part of the ascent to the *lac*. Beyond the lake the path continues due south to the CAF **Refuge des Oulettes** below the north face of Vignemale (about 3 hours from Pont d'Espagne), whence you can return to La Raillère via the beautiful and quieter **Vallée de Lutour** (about 2½ hours). The HRP and various Parc National paths crisscross the area, and any of the refuges can be used as a base for further day walks.

Another much less frequented walk from Cauterets is to the **Lac d'Ilhéou along the GR10**, which starts at the western edge of the town. To avoid the initial steep climb you can take the *télécabine du Lys*, near the Cauterets station, to the **gare intermédiaire de Cambasque**. Cross the stream and continue up the right bank to the end of the tarmac at the **Cabane de Courbet**. Thence up a track, first, on the left bank, then on the right. After a short distance – keep a good lookout – the GR10 leaves the track and climbs up the slope to the left, steadily gaining height to cross a chute of boulders beside the long white thread of the **Cascade d'Ilhéou** waterfall. Over the rim of the chute you come to a small tarn with the **Refuge d'Ilhéou** in sight ahead. A few more minutes on the track bring you to the refuge on the shore of the lake – very pretty in June with snow still on the surrounding peaks and ice floes drifting on its still surface (3–3½ hours).

Luz and the Cirque de Gavarnie

The usual approach to **Gavarnie**, best known of the Pyrenean cirques, is via LUZ-ST-SAUVEUR, also served by buses direct from LOURDES, at least daily.

Apart from its convenience for the car-borne – with plentiful hotels and campsites around – **LUZ** boasts an interesting fortified church, built in the late 12C by the Knights of St John and flanked by two stout towers. You enter the church under one of them, through an original doorway with a Christ in Majesty carved in fine-grained local stone. In the lanes around the church a regular market is held. On the uphill side is a good cheap **Logis**, the *Hôtel des Ramparts*, and beyond it a **gîte d'étape, youth hostel** and **campsite** (*Les Cascades*). Another campsite, slightly nearer, is *Le Toy*, by the crossroads for Gavarnie along with a helpful local **SI**.

GAVARNIE – the village – is a further 20km up the ravine, connected by two daily buses from LUZ. If you're really into hiking you could walk this, along a variant of the GR10. The track leads through GÈDRE (with two campsites and a fork, left, to the less touristed Cirque de Troumousse).

The *Cirque de Gavarnie*, carved out by a glacier of which barely the roots of the tongue remain, is an awe-inspiring natural amphitheatre, nearly 1,700m deep. It consists of three sheer bands of rock discoloured by the striations of seepage and waterfalls, and separated by sloping ledges covered with snow. To the east it is dominated by the jagged peaks of Astazou and Marboré, all over 3,000m. In the middle, a corniced ridge sweeps round almost level to Le Taillon, hidden behind the Pic des Sarradets which stands slightly forward of the rim of the cirque, obscuring the *Brèche de Roland*, a curious vertical slash, 100m deep and about 60 wide, said to have been hewn from the ridge by Roland's sword.

In sad contrast to these natural beauties, the village is an untidy straggle of souvenir shops, car parks and refreshment joints. And it stinks of horse-shit from the dozens of mules, donkeys and horses used to ferry the idle and gullible up to the foot of the cirque. It is an easy 50min walk on your own flat feet. Luckily, the scale of **the cirque** is sufficient to dwarf any number of tourists and their noise, but it is best to go up to the cirque before 10 in the morning or after 5, when the grandeur and silence are almost alarming and the dung less overpowering. The track ends at the *Hôtellerie du Cirque*, basically now a snack bar. To get to the foot of the cirque walls you have to clamber over slopes of frozen snow. Take care not to stand too close, especially in the afternoon, because of falling stones. To the left a 400m waterfall, the **Grande Cascade**, pours wavering and pluming down the rock faces. It is a fine sight in the morning when it appears to pour right out of the eye of the sun.

To the right of the first rock band a section of the HRP climbs steeply up behind the Pic des Sarradets to the CAF **Refuge des Sarradets**. An easier path goes up the Pouey Aspé valley and round the west side of the Pic (3–3½ hours). Several 3,000m peaks are easily accessible from the hut.

A good, not too demanding day's outing would be to visit the Cirque, then take the clear path from the Hôtellerie du Cirque up the east flank of the Gavarnie valley to the **Refuge des Espuguettes**. It is a pretty path cut into steep rocky slopes. At the top you emerge into open meadows with the Cabane de Pailla in a hollow and the Refuge des Espuguettes on a grassy bluff some 45mins' climb above you. The bare peak ahead is **Piméné** (2,801m), an easy, if tedious, climb of about 2 hours, offering superb views of the Cirque, Monte Perdido and away into Spain. It is certainly worth climbing as far as the refuge. To return to Gavarnie, turn right at the signpost below the refuge.

Of **hotels in Gavarnie,** *des Voyageurs* is the best bet with *L'Astazou* a poor second. A good place to **eat** is *La Ruade*, opposite the *Voyageurs*, – very friendly and pretty cheap if you are two or more and share a *raclette* or *fondue*. The *La Bergerie* **campsite** on the Cirque side of the village has the best view of the Cirque, and its bar provides a breakfast of sorts; the other campsite, *Le Pain de Sucre*, is 2km north of the village. CAF's **refuge,** *Les Granges de Holle*, 1km up the track to the Port de Gavarnie, is open all year round. *La Cordée*, opposite *La Ruade*, hires axes and crampons. The CRS **mountain rescue post** opposite the Bergerie campsite provides the latest in weather reports, and snow conditions. And lastly, be warned that the village has just one *alimentation* and you'll need to get there early in the day to buy bread or fresh fruit.

East to Barèges and Bagnères

At the eastern edge of the Parc National, **BARÈGES** is just 7½km on from LUZ (buses from LOURDES). It has been popular as a spa – its waters renowned for the treatment of gunshot wounds – since 1677 when it was visited by Mme de Maintenon with her infant charge the seven-year-old Duc de Maine, son of Louis XIV. Today it is a skiing and mountaineering centre. The **GR10** passes through and numerous other paths lead off into the **Néouvielle massif,** full of lakes and (by friends) highly recommended as a walking area.

Above Barèges, the left side of the valley is a vast expanse of pasture completely denuded of trees, with clusters of stone *bergeries* dug into the slope, looking just as they do in 19C prints. The **Pic du Midi de Bigorre** (2,872m) comes into view at the head of the valley. Jagged precipitous ridges hang over the road to the right. The **Col du Tourmalet** itself, at 2,115m the highest road pass in the Pyrenees, is a desolate windy spot with a track leading off left to the Pic.

Once over the col you drop down past the monstrously ugly ski resort of LA MONGIE into woods of spruce and pine which continue down to the broad green valley of **CAMPAN,** whose flowery meadows are dotted with farms. The village has an interesting 16C covered market, old houses and another curious looking fortified church. School buses go from here to Bagnères.

BAGNÈRES DE BIGORRE, also a spa, and with a certain faded elegance, drew the attention of Hilaire Belloc in his book on the Pyrenees. 'The rule holds here', he wrote, 'as everywhere, that where rich people, especially cosmopolitans, colonials, nomads, and the rest, come into a little place, they destroy most things except the things that they themselves desire. And the things that they themselves desire are execrable to the rest of mankind.' That's a little harsh as a description of Bagnères, but it is not a place to make a special stop. If you need to, there are reasonable rooms at **hotels,** *Nice* and *des Américains* in rue de l'Horloge, *Hôtel des*

Petites Vosges (old-fashioned and quaint) and *Hôtel de France* in bd Carnot. **SNCF buses** leave for Tarbes from the railway station on av de Belgique just north of the town centre.

LOURDES

What can you say about **LOURDES**? Its *raison d'être* is clear the moment you arrive. Signs at the station direct the faithful, whole and halt: Secours Catholique, Accueil des Pèlerins, Sortie des Pèlerins, Trains de Pèlerinage. (A *pèlerin* is a pilgrim.)

Prior to 1858 Lourdes was nothing. In that year Bernadette Soubirous, the 14-year-old daughter of an ex-miller, had the first of eighteen visions of the Virgin Mary in a clammy rock overhang called the Grotte de Massabielle by the Gave de Pau. Since then, Lourdes (population 18,000) has become a Mecca for Catholics – over 4 million of them each year, many hoping for a miraculous cure for scientifically intractable ailments.

The thing which strikes you first is the incredible concentration of cheap **hotels** – over 150 one-star hotels alone – and the equally startling number, and variety, of nuns. And after that it is hard to be charitable. Practically every shop is given over to the sale of indescribable religious kitsch: Bernadette in every shape and size, adorning barometers, thermometers, plastic tree-trunks, key-rings, toilet-water bottles, bellows, candles, sweets, plastic grottoes illuminated by coloured lights . . . Woody Allen, who joked he'd come here when he'd completed psychoanalysis, would be impressed. And the scenes – and crowds – as you press on to the Gave de Pau and the **Cité Religieuse** that has grown up around it stay in this element, the architecture of the basilica seeming actually to reflect and compete with the souvenirs.

The **Grotto** itself is a moisture-blackened overhang by the riverside with a statue of the Virgin in waxwork white and Mothercare blue. Her expression is not inspiring, but it seems to work. Hanging in front are a number of rusty crutches, evidence of the miracle.

Lourdes' only secular attraction is its **castle**, poised on a rocky bluff guarding the approaches to the valleys and passes of the central Pyrenees. Briefly an English stronghold in the late 14C, it later became a state prison. Lord Elgin, of Marbles fame, was briefly an inmate in 1804. Within, these days, is a surprisingly excellent **Musée Pyrénéen** (9–11 & 2–6; a little pricey – and go at opening time if you want to enjoy an hour's relative calm). Its collections include Pyrenean fauna, all sorts of fascinating pastoral and farming gear. In the rock garden outside are some beautiful models of various Pyrenean styles of house, as well as of the churches of St-Bertrand-de-Comminges and Luz. There is also a section on the history of Pyrenean mountaineering.

The **SI** in **place du Champ Commun** will help you find a place to stay.

The nearest **campsite** is in **rue de Langelle** off the principal north-south street. **Hostel-style** accommodation can be had at the *Centre Pax Christi* (route de la Forêt) and *Camp des Jeunes*, Ferme Milhas (av de Monseigneur Rodhain), both on the western edge of town. The **bus station** is in place Capdevielle.

Tarbes

There is nothing to draw anyone to TARBES **except,** for those interested in military history, the **Musée International des Hussards** (10–12, 2–6; cl. Mon & Tues) in the very attractive **Jardin Massey** near the station. It houses an extensive collection of cavalry uniforms, principally 19C and 20C hussars, but including samples of other European and US cavalry regiments. They are splendidly extravagant, the epitome of that old-fashioned quality of 'dash', which made the hearts of ladies flutter at glittering balls. There's a **youth hostel** on quai de l'Adour at the eastern edge of town (open daily July-Sept; cl. wkends the rest of the year), and the usual group of **hotels** around the gare SNCF.

ST-BERTRAND AND BAGNÈRES-DE-LUCHON

If you are on your way south to walk at BAGNÈRES-DE-LUCHON, there is a very attractive stop to be made en route – at the cathedral village of ST-BERTRAND, just a short distance from the railway station at MONTRÉJEAU (youth hostel).

To reach it, take an SNCF bus for LUCHON from the station and get off in the hamlet of LABROQUÈRE by the bridge over the Garonne (about 5km). Turn right over the bridge: St-Bertrand is a pleasant 2km walk along a quiet country lane between fields of wheat, barley and hay, with the poplar-lined river on your right, and its cathedral on a neatly defined knoll commanding the plain, grey and fortress-like against the wooded slopes behind. Midway you pass the village of VALCABRÈRE with rough stone barns with open lofts for hay-drying abutting the lane, and just off to the left, the exquisite Romanesque church (11C) of **St-Just-St-Pasteur**, long and low, with a square tower and a cemetery of cypress trees. A little further is a crossroads with the foundations of various Roman buildings either side, the remains of **Lugdunum Convenarum**, founded in 72BC. It was once a town of some 60,000 inhabitants. The Jewish historian Josephus says it was the place of exile of Herod Antipas and his wife Herodias, who beheaded John the Baptist. It was destroyed by Vandals in the 5C and again by the Burgundians in the 6C, after which it remained deserted until Bishop Bertrand began to build his cathedral around 1120.

The village of **ST-BERTRAND,** many of its houses 15C and 16C, clusters tightly round the church, protected by ramparts. The white-veined façade of the **Cathedral** (closed for lunch; pricey admission) seems vaguely austere as you approach, elevated above a small square. Off to its right is a cloister, mostly Romanesque, open on the south side with a view over a narrow green valley to the hills beyond where, a sign by the public WC says, a local *maquis* unit had its lair in wartime.

In the aisleless interior, the small area at the west end reserved for the laity has a superbly carved 16C oak organ loft, a pulpit and spiral stair. But the church's great attraction – and if you are at all interested in Renaissance art this alone merits a visit – is its **Choir**, built by Toulousain journeymen and installed in 1535. The elaborately carved stalls – sixty-six in all – are a feast of virtuosity, mingling piety, irony and malicious satire, each one the work of a different journeyman. It is in the misericords and partitions separating them that the ingenuity and humour of their creators is best seen. Each of the gangways dividing the sections of misericords has a representation of a cardinal sin freestanding on top of the end partition. In the middle gangway on the south side, for example, Envy is represented by two monks, faces contorted with hate, fighting over the abbot's baton of office, pushing against each other foot to foot in a furious tug-of-war. The armrest on the left of the roodscreen entrance depicts the abbot birching a monk. The Bishop's throne has a particularly lovely back panel in marquetry, depicting St-Bertrand himself and St John. In the ambulatory a 15C shrine depicts scenes from St-Bertrand's life; the church and village are visible in the background of the top right panel.

Thirty-eight km south of MONTRÉJEAU (and again on the SNCF bus routes), **BAGNÈRES-DE-LUCHON** – Luchon, for short – is another excellent, though, in season, very crowded walking centre. The area to the south is particularly good: **Lac d'Oô**, **Lac d'Espingo**, **Lac Saussat** and the **Pic du Céciré** on the GR10.

TOULOUSE AND THE EAST

In addition to its own sunny, cosmopolitan charms **Toulouse** is a very accessible kick-off point for any destination in the south and west of France. Of immediately adjacent places **Albi** is the number one priority, with its highly original cathedral and unique collection of Toulouse-Lautrec paintings. The southern **road to Andorra** and Spain may tempt you too. If it does you'll find this end of the Pyrenees very different from the west. It is drier, more eroded and much less touristed. Plus, there is a crop of ruined **Cathar castles** with tales of brutality and heroism to stir the imagination of the most committed history-hater.

TOULOUSE

A big city with a compact historic centre, **TOULOUSE** is a lively place – the more so if you reach it after a week or more in the mountains. It owes its present fame, and economic activity, to the **aerospace industry** – the first Concorde was built here and in the early days of flying the first French overseas flights set out from the city, piloted by such as Saint-Exupéry. Its **past** – reflected in two glorious and important **churches**, and a tremendous **museum of medieval sculpture** – finds roots in the feudalism that developed out of the breakdown of Charlemagne's empire, when the counts of Toulouse extended their power across the whole of southern France. For a while they maintained the greatest court in the land but in the early 13C Count Raymond VI fell foul of Pope Innocent III over the spread of the **Cathar heresy** through his ill-regulated dominions. When the Pope's envoy was assassinated, Raymond was excommunicated and the Albigensian crusade launched against his lands. Simon de Montfort, the brutal leader of the crusade, besieged Toulouse twice, unsuccessfully, and was killed in the course of the second attempt (1218). Worn down by a generation of warfare and intrigue, Raymond VII negotiated the highly disadvantageous Treaty of Paris in 1229, under the terms of which his daughter was to marry the king's brother, Alphonse of Poitiers, and on her death the county of Toulouse was to revert to the crown. Which duly happened in 1271: a major step in the expansion of the central power of the kings.

    Arriving by bus or train you'll find yourself at the **gare Matabiau** – a little over 10mins walk from the old centre. There's an **SI** here (the main one is in the central place du Capitole), a **city bus terminus** (with the **gare routière** to the right) and, opposite, numerous **hotels**. *L'Europe, Le*

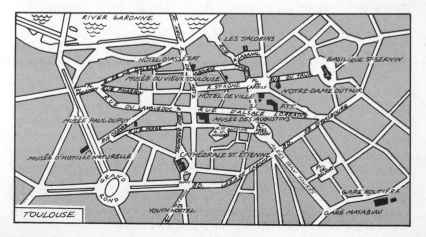

Perpignanais, Séverin and *Toulouse* look the more salubrious: be wary of the back streets towards place Belfort, a seedy area big on prostitution. To get to the **youth hostel** take bus 14 from the station to place Dupuy (not far – just across a canal bridge) and from there a 22 going back towards the canal and up av Jean-Rieux (the hostel is at no 125).

Simplest way into the centre is down the broad **Allées Jean-Jaurès**, with numerous bars. At the bd Strasbourg intersection there are several good brasseries, reasonably priced and with pavement tables. The quarter has a high proportion of West and North Africans, and a lot of big city hustle. **Place Président-Wilson** is a lively square, with some attractive little streets leading left to the smaller **place St-Georges**, always fun, with someone drumming or playing guitar, and the city's trendier bars.

The **Musée des Augustins**, which incorporates the two surviving cloisters of an Augustinian priory, is just below place St-Georges and if you're only staying for a day it should be your first priority. Its collections are of unusually fine Romanesque and medieval sculpture, much of it saved from now-vanished city churches. As always, regardless of the ostensible theme, what is interesting is the highly naturalistic representation of contemporary manners, fashions and so on. Merchants with forked beards, one touching another's arm in a gesture of familiarity and collusion that says, 'We understand each other. We're men of business. We belong to the same class.' Notre-Dame-de-Grâce: a pretty, bored young mother looking away from her child which strains to escape her hold. A headless Saint Barbara in that characteristic pose, found in painting too: weight on one leg, hips and tummy thrust slightly forward, slenderwaisted, bodice framed by long tresses. A lot of beautiful work. (Admission is 10–12 & 2–6, cl. Tues & Weds am.)

Rue Alsace-Lorraine, the main shopping street, always thronged with people, runs north-south past the museum. The whole area between here and the wide **place du Capitole** and on up to place **St-Sernin** is a labyrinth of sunny, elegant streets, many lined with Renaissance houses (see, especially, rue des Changes, St-Rome, rue de la Bourse; and, south of rue de Metz, rues Pharaon, Mage, de la Dalbade). There is something special about the flat, narrow Toulousain brick; besides its rosy, cheerful colour, it gives a pleasingly small-scale, detailed finish to façades and sets off any wood or stone. The acme of Toulousain bricklaying skills is to be seen in works like the belfry-wall of **Notre-Dame-du-Taur** (rue du Taur) with its diamond-pointed arches and openings, and in the superb belfries of Les Jacobins and St-Sernin, the city's two big churches. Oddly enough little of their accomplishment spreads to the **Cathédrale St-Etienne**, a peculiar-looking building near the museum, put together over four centuries.

St-Sernin, at the north end of rue du Taur, is the largest Romanesque church in France – an enormous hall begun in 1080 to accommodate the hordes of passing St-Jacques pilgrims. The most striking external feature is its octagonal brick belfry and the apse with stone-roofed chapels, five radiating from the apse itself, four from the transepts. The sculptures of the *Porte Miègeville* (early 12C) on the south side of the nave established a Toulousain style of carving whose influence can be seen on many southern churches. Inside, the long high nave is supported on square brick piers with half-round pillars reaching to the base of the vaulting ribs. Double aisles of diminishing height are surmounted by a gallery running right round the church. There is a charge for going into the ambulatory – worth paying for the beautiful 11C reliefs on the end wall of the choir.

Les Jacobins (10–12 & 3–6.30) in rue Lakanal, a few blocks west of place du Capitole, is one of the supreme examples of southern Gothic. Building was started in 1230 by the Dominicans, who set up here in the wake of their founding father, St Dominic, who had come to the region to preach against the rampant Cathar heresy. Like Albi, the church is a huge fortress-like rectangle of unadorned brick buttressed by plain brick piles – quite unlike the architecture you normally associate with Gothic. The interior is a single space divided into two by a central row of pillars capped by minimal capitals from which spring an elegant splay of vaulting ribs. Thomas Aquinas's bones lie beneath the altar.

Other Toulouse museums, if you have time on your hands, include the **Musée du Vieux Toulouse** (7 rue du May; 2.30–5.30), concerned primarily with the history of the city and local popular art, and the **Musée Labit** (43 rue des Martyrs de la Libération; 10–12 & 2–5, cl. Tues) with respectable if not especially memorable collections of Middle and Far Eastern art.

And last, **a few details**: the **CROUS** office at 7 rue des Salenques publishes a booklet detailing services for students; **Allostop** have an office at 2 rue Malbec (61.22.68.13; 3.30–6.30 Tues–Fri; Sat 10.30–12.30); there's a **laundrette** at 20 rue Coujas; and in mid-June the city holds a three-day **fair**, *La Fête du Grand Fenêtra*.

ALBI

Though not itself an important centre of Catharism, **ALBI** gave its name to both the heresy and the crusade to suppress it. Today it is a small industrial town an hour's train ride north-east of Toulouse, with two unique sights: a **museum** containing the most comprehensive collection of **Toulouse-Lautrec**'s work (Albi was his birthplace) and the most remarkable Gothic Cathedral you ever saw.

You see the **Cathedral** the moment you arrive at the train station, dwarfing the town like some vast bulk carrier run aground, the belfry its massive 13-14C superstructure. If the comparison sounds unflattering, perhaps it is not amiss, for this is not a conventionally beautiful building – it's about size and boldness of conception. The sheer plainness of the exterior is impressive on this scale, and it is not without interest: arcading, buttressing, the contrast of stone against brick – every differentiation of detail becomes significant. Entrance is through the south portal, by contrast the most extravagant piece of Flamboyant 16C frippery. The interior, a hall-like nave of colossal proportions, is covered in richly colourful paintings of Italian workmanship (16C also). A good screen, delicate as lace, shuts off the choir; Adam makes a show of covering his privates, Eve strikes a flaunting model's pose beside the central doorway. The choir screen is itself decorated with countless statuary.

Next to the cathedral, a powerful red-brick castle, the 13C *Palais de la Berbie* (SI in one corner), houses the **Musée Toulouse-Lautrec** (10–12 & 2–6, cl. Tues). It contains paintings, drawings, lithographs, all his posters, from the earliest work to the very last – an absolute must for anyone interested in Belle Epoque seediness and – given the predominant Impressionism of the time – the rather offbeat painting style of T-L. The artist's house in rue Toulouse-Lautrec (9–12 & 3–7), July–Aug; expensive) is also visitable.

Opposite the east end of the cathedral, *rue Maries* leads into the shopping streets of the old town. The little square and covered passages by the church of St-Salvy on the right are interesting. If you keep going east you come to the broad **Lices Pompidou** leading down to the river and the road to Cordes. On the right is rue de la République, with a very scruffy **youth hostel** at no 13. As for other places to stay: *Hôtel St-Clair* in rue St-Clair off rue Ste-Cécile is comfortable and central, or there are several **hotels** in **av Joffre** outside the railway station. **Camping** *Parc de Caussels* is about 2km east on the D999. The **gare routière** is on place Jean-Jaurès*; bikes can be hired from *M Rey* at 41 bd Soult.

For **eats**, try *La Dariole* or *Auberge Saint-Loup*, both in rue Castelviel at the west end of the cathedral, or *La Crêperie* in rue Toulouse-Lautrec. The café on the cathedral square, *La Tartine*, does salads and desserts.

Cordes

Twenty-four km north-west of Albi, an easy hitch or brief train ride (as far as Vindrac 3km away with bike hire from the station), is the town of CORDES, founded in 1222 by Raymond VII, Count of Toulouse, and pretty much intact, covering the top of a markedly conical hill. The

---

* Much is made hereabouts of the Socialist leader and pacifist, Jean Jaurès. He was born in nearby Castres, and came to prominence as the leader of a glassworkers' strike in 1896. They set up a cooperative, the *Verrerie Ouvrière*, which still functions today, albeit all automated and monitored by computer. The **Musée Jean-Jaurès** in av Dembourg (named for the Parisian woman who financed the first cooperative) contains documents to do with the strike and Jaurès' life – not of much interest for most visitors.

ground beneath the town is riddled with tunnels, used for storage and refuge in time of trouble, for Cordes was a Cathar stronghold. It is worth seeing because it is such a perfect example of a medieval town. It has become, however, a major tourist attraction: medieval banners flutter in the streets, and artisans practise their crafts – unfortunately, the kiss of death. The youth hostel, in considerable contrast, is in such a state of disrepair that it is unusable. There is **camping** 1km down the Gaillac road.

AUCH

AUCH, about 80km due east of Toulouse, is an attractive old town on the river Gers, worth visiting primarily for the exceptionally beautiful stained glass and wood-carving (both 16C) of its cathedral church of Ste-Marie, and its Armagnac brandy! The best approach from the **gare SNCF** is straight down rue Voltaire to the river. You get a fine view of the east end of the cathedral as you cross the bridge, turn left and climb the stone steps on the right to the tree-filled place Salinis abutting the south side of the cathedral. The fortified tower on your right is the 14C Tour d'Armagnac.

The **Cathedral** is basically late Gothic, almost expiring Gothic in fact, with a classical west front. The wood-carving is in the **choir stalls**. Very similar to that at St-Bertrand-de-Comminges, it is believed to have been executed by the same craftsmen. Magnificent stuff, quite unsurpassable. The **windows**, equally lovely and attributed to Arnaud de Moles, parallel the scenes and personages depicted in the stalls.

South of the cathedral, rue d'Espagne leads to the **Pousterles** a number of scarcely shoulder-wide medieval stairs leading steeply downhill to rue Caumont. At the beginning of rue d'Espagne is the modest *Hôtel des Trois Mousquetaires* (this is d'Artagnan country), with a restaurant, and just beyond it the *Belle Époque* restaurant, with good, cheap *plats du jour*. On the opposite side of the cathedral square the **SI** is located in a half-timbered 15C house on the corner of rue Dessolles (ask them for ideas and information about travelling in this backward and little visited corner of France). Beyond is place de la Libération, with cafés and restaurants, and off right, below the Allées d'Etigny, the **gare routière**.

Other hotels to try are: *Moderne*, opposite the station; *Le Relais de Gascogne* and *Hôtel de Paris*, both with restaurants, in av de la Marne, at the end of av de la Gare, which passes in front of the station. The **youth hostel** (*Foyer des Jeunes Travailleurs*; with canteen) is on a housing estate at LE GARROS, about 25mins' walk from the station; aim for rue Augusta and keep going until you reach the Nervol petrol station, where you turn left, then right into rue du Bourget. **Camping Municipal** is also off the continuation of rue Augusta.

SOUTHERN PYRENEES: AX-LES-THERMES

Buses and trains go **south from Toulouse** via FOIX and AX-LES-THERMES. The landscape at this end of the Pyrenees is markedly different, much drier and more southern in feel. The hills up the Ariège valley, where the road runs, are jagged and eroded, with outcrops of limestone breaking through the scrubby Mediterranean-type vegetation.

FOIX looks well, tightly enclosed by steep hills and dominated by the three towers of its ruined castle, but is not worth a special stop. It was deeply embroiled in the Cathar struggles of the 13C. In 1290, its Counts married into the house of Béarn and moved their seat to Orthez. It became part of France only in the reign of Henri IV. For walkers, the Ariège *Comité Départemental de Randonnée Pédestre* is at 14 rue Lazéma (61.65.29.00).

Sixteen km further south, **TARASCON-SUR-ARIÈGE** is prettily situated and a convenient stop-over for visiting the prehistoric cave at NIAUX. There are a number of **hotels** and **restaurants** in the centre of town by the bridge and a campsite, *du Pré Lombard* (turn left over the bridge and walk along the river bank for about 10mins). **NIAUX** is 5km away up the road to Vicdessos, a tiny village strung out along the road in the bottom of a green mountain valley. The **cave** entrance is under an enormous rock overhang high on the south flank. The approach road is on the left opposite the church – about 20mins' walk, and very pretty. Visits take place 8.30–11.30 & 1.30–5.15 1 July-30 Sept, and at 11, 3 and 4.30 the rest of the year. Only twenty people are allowed in at a time. You need to book, preferably 48 hours in advance. The guide's telephone at the cave is 61.05.85.10; otherwise, ring 61.05.88.37 between 7 and 8pm.

There are about 4½km of galleries in all, mostly closed to the public, with **prehistoric paintings** of the Magdalenian period (c20,000BC) widely scattered throughout. The paintings you can see are in a vast chamber about 800m slippery walk from the entrance of the cave along a subterranean river-bed. The subjects are horses, wild goat, stags and bison. No colour is used, just a dark outline and shading to give body to the drawings, which have been executed with a 'crayon' made of bison fat and manganese oxide. It is an extraordinary mix of bold impressionistic strokes and delicate attention to detail – the bison with their nostrils, and eyes with the pupils drawn in, their hooves and heels and the tendons marked on their inner thighs.

Another 10km up the valley, VICDESSOS and AUZAT are good walking centres. The **SI** in both places organise hikes and will provide information for the independent walker.

AX-LES-THERMES is another ancient spa. Its chief interest is as a centre for exploring the surrounding mountains and staging-post on the way to Andorra or on down the N20 to Font-Romeu and, ultimately, Perpignan and the Mediterranean. The SI here are next to the Hôtel de Ville on the main street, and can provide comprehensive **hiking info**. They also run a variety of **guided walks**, ranging in cost from about £45 for a weekend to about £100, all in, for a five-day hike. The footsore can take advantage of the *Bassin des Ladres*, a public pool of hot water where people sit to bathe their feet; it is all that remains of a hospital founded in 1260 by St-Louis for soldiers wounded in the Crusades.

There are numerous **hotels**. *La Terrasse* in rue Marcaillou, over the bridge from the SI is very cheap. *Hôtel des Pyrénées*, a one-star Logis de France with restaurant, opposite the SI, is good value, and there is an attractive old café on the corner just uphill. *Terminus* opposite the **gare SNCF** on the way into the town is also reasonable and has a good restaurant. The nearest **campsite** is *Le Malazéou*, on the riverbank below the station. There is a *gîte d'étape* on the GR10 at MERENS 8½km on the Andorra side of town.

Barely 20km north-east is the tiny (population: 10) village of **MONTAILLOU**, subject of a learned and very readable study by the French historian, Le Roy Ladurie. The book covers the years around 1300 when the Inquisition was trying to extirpate the Cathar heresy from its last strongholds in the remote communities of the Pyrenees. It is based on Inquisition records of submissions of local people under interrogation. What they revealed to their interrogators is incredible – details down to the most intimate minutiae of their lives. Much of the book reads like a really good gossip: who is sleeping with who, where the sheep are being pastured this year, which paths you take to cross into Spain . . . a fascinating recreation of life in a medieval village.

There is not much traffic on the road, but it is hitchable. You take the D613 from Ax over the steep Col de Chioula (1,400m). Montaillou lies to the right of the road in the valley below the col. The whole area is very depopulated. Montaillou's inhabitants still bear the names of their Cathar ancestors – the churchyard is full of them. There is nothing left to see, but it is pretty and highly atmospheric if you have read the book. A stump of tower remains of the castle. It was once 45m high to facilitate visual communication with Montségur, the noblest of the Cathar fortresses, about 11km north-west as the crow flies. It should be walkable – about 5 hours, I reckon. There appears to be a track from Comus just below Montaillou down the Gorges de la Frau. (BELCAIRE, 7km down the road, has an inexpensive and very good restaurant, *Hôtel Bayle*.)

TRAVEL DETAILS

Trains
From Bayonne several daily to Bordeaux (1hr50) via Dax; several to St-Jean-de-Luz (30mins); several to Irun (1hr); 4 to St-Jean-Pied-de-Port (1hr10); 4 to Toulouse (4hrs) via Puyôo (30mins), Orthez (50mins), Pau (1½hrs), Lourdes (1hr40), Tarbes (2hrs), Lannemazan (2hrs40), Montréjeau (2hrs50), St-Gaudens (3hrs), Boussens (3¼hrs) — more frequent over short streches of the route.

From Toulouse regular to Luchon (2¼hrs), and to Barcelona (7¼hrs) via Pamiers (50mins), Foix (1hr5), Tarascon (1hr20), Ax-les-Thermes (1hr45) and La-Tour-de-Carol (2hrs55); several to Auch (1hr); several to Albi (1hr).

Buses (SNCF)
From Puyôo 2 or 3 most days to Mauléon (1½hrs) via Salies-de-Béarn (¼hr) and Sauveterre (50mins).

From Pau: 1 daily in summer to Artouste (1¼hrs) via Laruns and Gabas.

From Lourdes regular but infrequent to Cauterets (1hr) via Pierrefitte (35mins): and to Barèges (1hr25) via Luz-St-Sauveur (1hr5).

From Tarbes regular to Bagnères-de-Bigorre (35mins).

From Lannemazan regular but infrequent to St-Lary (1hr) via Arreau.

From Montréjeau regular but infrequent to Luchon (1hr) via Labroquère (5mins — for St-Bertrand-de-Comminges).

From Boussens: regular but infrequent to St-Girons (45mins).

Buses (private)
From St-Jean-de-Luz very frequent to Hendaye; 4 to San Sebastian; 6 to Sare-la-Rhune; also to Espelette (35mins), Cambo-les-Bains (45mins) and Hasparren (1hr5).

From Bayonne 7 to Cambo-les-Bains; 2 to Mauléon; almost hourly to St-Jean-de-Luz; 4 to San Sebastian.

From Biarritz 4 to Hendaye; 3 to Pau (2hrs10) via Orthez and 3 via Salies-de-Béarn (2½hrs); very frequent to St-Jean-de-Luz.

From Pau to Lourdes (1½hrs); Mauléon (1hr50); Orthez (1hr10); 4 to Eaux-Bonnes (1hr25) via Laruns (1hr10); 3 go on to La Gourette (1hr45) and 1 to Col d'Aubisque (2 hrs).

From Lourdes to Barèges (1hr) via Luz-St-Sauveur (45mins); 2 to Gavarnie (1hr25) via Luz.

From Toulouse Several daily to Ax-les-Thermes (3hrs10) via Pamiers (1hr25), Foix (2hrs) and Tarascon (2hrs25); also to Auch.

From Auch services to Tarbes, Lourdes, Montauban, Agen, Mont-de-Marsan and Lannemazan.

Chapter nine
LANGUEDOC AND ROUSSILLON

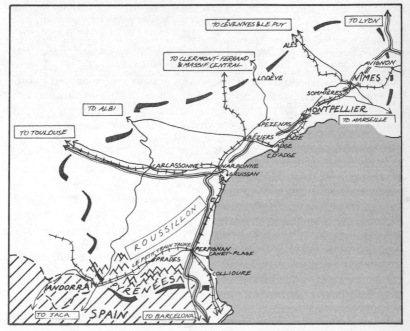

One of France's most distinct regions and, culturally speaking at least, one of the most interesting, **Languedoc** has a sense of individual identity you'd be pushed to find anywhere in France outside Corsica. This far south, you can feel the sway of Spain growing stronger – in the look of the people, their accent, and in language too. The local tongue, the ancient *langue d'oc* or *Occitan*, is still spoken (albeit as a patois, and in rural areas), while down the coast, in the **Roussillon** area, Catalan is spoken as much as French. Perhaps not surprisingly, a strong tradition of separatism shines through all this, rooted in the work of local trade unions and socialists like Jean Jaurès (see p. 482), and manifest today in determined attempts to put the local dialect on a par with French, and widespread suspicion of central government from Paris.

Occitan, an old Provençal language, was in fact once spoken across the whole of southern France, from Bordeaux to Lyon, and not until centuries later did the south break into its different principalities and counties. The greatest of these was Languedoc itself, which held much of the land west of the Rhône and where people were perfectly aware of their differences from the barbarian Frankish kingdoms further north. In an age with no politics as we understand it, when the only ideas were religious, a wave of **Catharism** (see p. 301) in southern Languedoc in the Middle Ages, and then **Protestantism** in the northern part of the province a couple of centuries later, was the southerners' only way of stating their independence from Catholic France. Despite the undoubted religious fervour they inspired, both were in modern terms separatist movements, and as such gave the Crown and Church excuse for some bloodthirsty military excursions; the Occitan language was outlawed, and the population depleted by slaughter and emigration. It was a period which may have strengthened – even shaped – the region's sense of itself, but politically it was an end. Languedoc's capital, and ancient university city, of **Montpellier** today covers only the Mediterranean *départements* west of the Rhône. And though the last century has seen a partial recognition of *Occitan*, the young who study it do not speak it.

Economically, Languedoc and Roussillon are **wine and agricultural** regions – Languedoc, with considerable success, as producer of much of the nation's cheap table wines. On **the coast** the vast sandy beaches are well on their way to development – promoted as an alternative to the more famous Mediterranean stretches of the Côte d'Azur. But as long as you avoid brash new resorts like **Cap d'Agde** or **La Grande Motte**, it's easy enough to find a mile or two to yourself. And **inland,** tourists are few, the countryside scattered with traditional stone villages, small market towns and a handful of superb antiquities, best of all at Roman **Nîmes** and medieval **Carcassonne**.

NORTHERN LANGUEDOC

Heading south form Paris, via Lyon and the Rhône corridor, you can go one of two ways: east into Provence and the Côte d'Azur, which is what most people do, or west to Nîmes, Montpellier and the comparatively untouched northern Languedoc coast. Nîmes itself, while not technically part of Languedoc, makes for a good introduction to the region, a hectic modern town worth a stop both for its impressive Roman remains and some scattered attractions – the **Pont du Gard** for one – nearby. **Montpellier**, too, repays a day or two, not so much for any historical attractions as for a heady vibrancy and its proximity to **Sète** – much the best springboard for this part of the coast.

NÎMES

An animated modern city, and the 19C textile town that manufactured and lent its name to the most all-pervasive and perennially fashionable fabric ever (*de Nîmes* – denim), **NÎMES** is a likeable place to hole up for a day or two. And as well as making a good base for excursions out to the Pont du Gard and around, its array of Roman buildings counts as one of the finest still standing in the world.

You don't have to be here long before you notice the emblem of the city – a chained crocodile – symbol since Caesar Augustus's victory over Antony and Cleopatra at Actium, when he gave the city to his troops in reward for their valour. In those days Nîmes was an important post on the trading routes between France and Spain; later sacked by Vandals, and settled by a succession of warlike tribes, it became part of the French kingdom in 1299; centuries on, as a Protestant strongpoint, it was the scene of one of the most ruthless events in the Wars of Religion, when Catholic troops executed hundreds of Camisards in the city.

To see the remnants of Nîmes' **Roman past**, buy a single ticket for admission to all the sites. Largest and most immediately impressive is the **Arènes** or amphitheatre, a neat stone oval capable of seating 20,000 spectators. Though only the 20th largest theatre built in the Roman

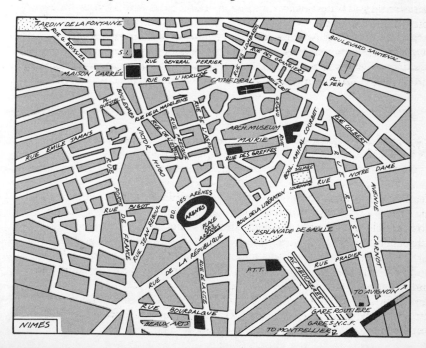

world, it is today by far the most complete. Dating to the 1C AD, it was in medieval times, taken over and adapted as a quarter of the city – one of the poorest Languedoc slums by all accounts but long since cleared out and laid open to the public. Summer Sundays echo its original use with some latterday bloodsports, Spanish-style *Corridas*, or bullfights.

Standing quietly in a small square on its own (in rue Perrier), the **Maison Carrée** offers a rather less awesome glimpse of Roman France: a small temple, possibly to Youth, built of white stone and so pretty that Stendhal declared that an exact copy should be built in Paris; Colbert thought the original should be transported stone by stone to Versailles; and even Henry James was moved to describe it as 'perfectly felicitous'. Scattered around are numerous bits and pieces of Roman masonry, and inside there's a **Museum of Antiquities**, with some good sculpture and a frieze of Nemausus, goddess of the local spring after which the town was named.

The spring itself, **La Fontaine**, together with the rather forlorn ruins of a nymphaeum, the so-called **Temple of Diana** (9–12 & 2–5), forms part of the **Jardins de la Fontaine**. Laid out around the Roman baths, this is slightly west of the town centre – follow the canal from Square Antonin to place Pablo Picasso. A grand park, all broad steps, gravelled open spaces and benches with people talking, 'a mixture', as Henry James described it, 'of old Rome and 18C France', the Jardins rise to the park of Mont Cavalier, topped by the **Tour Magne**, an uninspiring Roman watchtower offering amazing views over the city and countryside beyond.

Beyond these there's little to see in Nîmes, though the very southern energy of its streets make it a nice place just to hang out. Boulevards lined with shops and cafés follow the course of the ancient ramparts, ascribed to their builder, Augustus, on the **Porte d'Arles** at the end of bd Courbet; and the medieval and Renaissance city clusters around the **Cathedral**, a dim-lit, fortress-like structure, Romanesque but totally rebuilt and mucked about with in the last century. Alphonse Daudet was born in its shadows, as was one Jean Nicot – a doctor, no less! – who introduced tobacco to France from Portugal in 1560, and gave his name to the world's most popular drug. Lastly; three museums in the city: **Musée de Vieux Nîmes** (9–12 & 2–5), in the Bishop's Palace beside the cathedral, has surprisingly interesting displays of Renaissance furnishings and Languedoc bullfighting, the **Beaux Arts**, in rue Cité Foulc (9–12 & 2–6; cl. Tues), prides itself on a huge Gallo-Roman mosaic showing the *Marriage of Admetus*, and in a 17C Jesuit chapel on bd Courbet the **Musée d'Archéologie et Histoire Naturelle** (same hours as Vieux Nîmes) gives further background on Roman Nîmes. Nearby, in Square de la Bouqerie, in 1705, stood the gibbet, wheel and stake erected for the public torture and execution of the unfortunate Camisards. And above the square towers the **Castellum**, distribution point for the waters brought to the town across the Pont du Gard.

The Pont du Gard

Perhaps more interesting – and certainly more elegant – than any of the Roman monuments in Nîmes itself is the **Pont du Gard**, west of the city towards Montpellier. A slim, high net of golden masonry, raised by the Romans to supply Nîmes with fresh water, it marches off, still triple-tiered, into the valley around the river Gard. It was built in 19BC, stayed in use 500 years without maintenance, and another 500 thereafter, and supplied, so it's estimated, some 44 million gallons daily. If you've a good head for heights – and a certain craziness – you can still walk down it today, though there's a 50ft drop on either side. The slope, in best traditions of Roman engineering, is imperceptible.

To **get out to the Pont**, you can take an organised excursion through the SI in Nîmes, or, a better approach, make your own way by bus (or fairly promising hitch) to the village of REMOULINS on the D981, just a kilometre distant. En route there's not a lot to delay you, though just outside LUNEL, the first town west of Nîmes, notice one of the largest bottling and processing plants you're likely to confront. This is the home of **Perrier** (who if you're really curious, or just want to check out how natural all the sparkles are, run tours at various points in the day).

Events, rooms and eats

There's always a lot going on in Nîmes – a cheap Sunday **fleamarket,** a Monday **produce market** under the plane trees on bd Gambetta – and from May through to October dozens of **other events**, exhibitions, bullfights, concerts, drama and **festivals**. The *Foire de Nîmes* is held in May; in mid-July the city hosts a brilliant week-long *Jazz Festival* in the Arènes, which attracts plenty of big names; and the *Autumn Music Festival* runs from the end of September to the end of November – two months of great music, much of it to be heard at *Musique en Stock*, 28 rue Jean Reboul, a club with plenty of jazz, blues, soul, funk and rock & roll. You can pick up infomation on these and other happenings from the **SI** (open daily, except Suns in winter) near the Maison Carrée, which, if you're stuck, also changes money.

As regards a room, middle-range **hotels** gather round Square de la Couronne, and there's an enticing two-star, good value in its own court-yard, on the corner of av Feuchères, opposite the SNCF station. A no 6 bus from bd Libération (top of av Feuchères) takes you the 3km or so to the **youth hostel** on chemin de la Cigale (66.23.25.04) and a small **campsite**; or there's a larger and better-equipped **campsite** on Route de Generac, 4km out of town.

There are certainly no shortage of eating places; boulevards Courbet and Libération harbour a stock of reasonably-priced **brasseries** and pizzerias, and bd Victor Hugo several popular cafés and a restaurant, *La Feria*, with a cheap four-course menu. *À L'Escargot* and *Auberge Lou Gardianne*, in the pedestrian zone on rue Fresque, both do inexpensive three-course meals, as do a couple more budget places in rue Grizot. And, if your French is up to it, it may be worth checking out what's on at the **café-théâtre**, Le Titoit de Titus (6 rue Titus).

MONTPELLIER

MONTPELLIER has a thriving, youthful air. An ancient trading centre, it has been a cosmopolitan and intellectual city for a thousand years – since the 10C when a group of Jewish physicians living in the town founded its university. In 1204 it became part of the kingdom of Aragon, fifty odd years later it joined the kingdom of Majorca, and in 1349 was sold for cash to the French crown. Fiercely Protestant, however, it was gutted by Royal troops in the 17C, like so many Languedoc towns. But the mansions, at its centre, and newer pedestrian developments, reflect a city well able to come back into its own.

At its hub is **place de la Comédie** – *L'Oeuf* to the initiated – a spacious square paved with cream-coloured marble, stylish cafés and a bulky 19C Opera House. At the outer end to this it gives onto the long tree-studded Esplanade and ivy-clothed **Musée des Beaux-Arts** (or *Musée Fabre* after the founder of the collection), an unusually good collection of Impression-

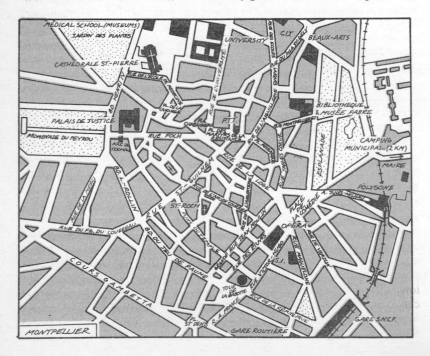

ists. For this it owes much to local patron Alfred Bruyas, friend and confidant to, apparently, most of the 19C French painters, in whose pictures he often figured prominently. There are a number of portraits of him here by Gustave Courbet, among them *The Meeting*, depicting a well-turned out Bruyas running into the artist on a country road; interesting Courbet, a marvellously arrogant and handsome self-portrait, alone casts a shadow on the ground. Other items in the Bruyas bequest include canvases by Manet, Matisse Delacroix and Gericault. Though it's the 19C stuff for which the museum is most famous, take a look at some of the further rooms before you leave. Best are works by the Venetians – Veronese, Palma Giovane, and an early Zuburan, *St Agatha*, amputated breasts in hand.

More or less adjacent to *l'Oeuf* is the **Polygone**, a vast indoor shopping centre (with some cheap eating places inside) and behind it, extending down towards the river, one of the most ambitious municipal housing projects to be seen – Richard Boffil's ambitious, neoclassical **Antigone** complex. In the other direction spreads Montpellier's older quarter, a tangle of lanes fanning out either side of rue de la Loge, and known inventively as *Lou Clapas* (the rubble). It is an odd mix of chic restoration and squalid disorder: squares with playing fountains, buildings of pale stone and courtyards falling into quiet, peeling decay. Two museums here may have mild appeal if you're at all interested in the local history of the area – the **Musée Régional**, housed in the Hôtel de la Varenne on place Petrarque (Tues-Fri 2–6), and **Musée Fougau** (Wed/Thurs 3–6) with displays on Occitan life and customs.

But it's the **University** which dominates the town, and gives its overriding character, both physically, in the sheer number of people studying here – 40,000 at the last count – and in the influence it wields over Montpellier's cultural and intellectual life. Some of the university buildings are open to the public, in the shape of the **Musée Atger**, which has a distinguished collection of French and Italian drawings, and the strange and macabre **Musée d'Anatomie**, both housed in the medical school on bd Henri IV. Behind stands Montpellier's **Cathedral**, a bizarre blend of styles concocted over five centuries, and though not as hideous as is sometimes made out to be, certainly not a beautiful building, with a large, plain interior broken only by sporadic flurries of decoration. Across the street is the **Jardin des Plantes**, the oldest botanical garden in France, and, rising above that, the 18C **Promenade de Payrou**, a broad and high-paved esplanade with a neoclassical water tower and views out to the low, rolling Cévennes in the far distance. If you're here on a Saturday check out the huge **fleamarket** which sprawls under the arches of the nearby aqueduct, called *Les Arceaux*, and then shifts itself over to Nimes for the following day.

Practicalities

The *Occitan* movement is at its most fervent in Montpellier, and the original Provençal streetnames have been reinstated on many of the street signs, despite the efforts of anti-Occitan, French nationalist enthusiasts to paint them out. Rue de l' Université – or *Carrierie de la Blancaria* – holds a number of inexpensive **cafés and restaurants** – *Chez Jules*, *La Saladière* and *Fac'Burger Cafétéria* – and in rue Jacques Coeur are *Crêperie des 2 Provinces* (with 140 different types of crêpe) and *Auberge Inn*, part of a cheap and trusty vegetarian chain. More centrally, *Ya Bon* and *Le Yam's*, on place de la Comédie, are cheap and vibrant cafés that do simple meals.

For **accommodation**, the *Majestic Hotel* (4 rue Cheval Blanc) and *Hôtel des Touristes* (10 rue Baudin) are both clean, central and don't cost the earth; and *Hôtel Rouergue* is handy for the university at 18 rue J J Rousseau. *CIJ* (Centre Internationale des Jeunes), in Impasse de la Petite Corraterie, is a **foyer** that lets out rooms in July and August (67.79.61.66), and *CROUS* offers lodging assistance specifically for foreign students – find them at 11 rue Baudin. *Camping*, make for the municipal site, a couple of kilometres out of town on route de Mauguic (bus no 15).

The main **SI office** at 6 rue Maguelone (there's also an annexe at the SNCF station, should you arrive that way) have full listings of just about everything in and around Montpellier. For up to the minute info on what's happening – and there's always plenty – check their noticeboards and ask for copies of *Le Mois à Montpellier* and *Montpellier Votre Ville*. Riotous **solstice fairs** take place all over town at midsummer (*Fêtes de St-Jean*); there's a superb month-long **dance festival** in June and July, and an international **Festival of Music** (classical) from early July to the first week of August. Montpellier has excellent bus and train connections, and a free bus – no 16, marked *Le Guilhelm* – runs between both stations and Promenade le Peyrou in the centre of town. There's an *Allostop* office in rue du Plan d'Olivier and a *discount travel service* in the gare SNCF. There you can also hire a **bike**, or wait until you get into town and go to *Le Vélo*, 6 rue des Ecoles Laïques. Should you need one, the main regional **hospital** is St Charles, 300 rue Brousonnet (67.63.91.64).

HEADING INLAND

N109 (easy hitching), known as Route de Lodève, cuts west from Montpellier into rolling vineyard country and a string of isolated towns and villages – none of them greatly visited. **GIGNAC**, where an 18C bridge crosses the Hérault, is small and medieval, another old Protestant stronghold, now a viable stopover with one small **hotel** and a **campsite**. Push north from here on D32 and you reach **ST-MARTIN-DE-LONDRES** (from the Occitan *Loundres* – otters), a lovely old town of arcaded houses set around a triangular main square, and with a decent **campsite** out on the Sommières road. Further on through dramatic river gorges, you reach the **GROTTE DES DEMOISELLES**, most spectacular of the many caves of the region, a set of vast cathedral-like caverns hung with stalactites, eerie pools and dark, dripping tunnels. Deep inside the mountain, it is reached by funicular (regular departures).

The **GROTTE DE CLAMOUSE**, in the Hérault gorge north of ANIANE, is less exciting. But the village of **ST-GUILHELM-LE-DÉSERT**, once virtually inaccessible, beyond, gives purpose to the route. Beautiful, if no longer remote, it rambles along the banks of the rushing Verdus – everywhere channelled into carefully tended gardens. Grand focus of the village is the magnificent 10–11C **Abbey Church**, still active if architecturally impoverished. The order allowed their cloister to be pillaged by the Cloisters Museum in New York – a considerable loss judging by the fragments left on display. Sadly, tourism has hit St-Guilhelm in a big way; but out of season it still feels a close religious community.

CLERMONT-L'HÉRAULT, on the other side of the Route de Lodève, is a pleasant and bustling provincial town, an important local centre with a big weekly market (Weds), an impressive fortified church and a realistically priced **hotel** – the *Terminus*. Forging on to Lodève itself, the road hits country already much cut about by uranium mining and threatened with further development. The fact that the area around the village of **ST-MARTIN-DU-BOSC** has soil with the highest concentration of radioactivity in the world gives some indication of just how much things are going to be changing here in the future. **LODÈVE**, at the confluence of the Lergues and Soulondres rivers, and almost in the shadow of Larzac (see p. 326), is a raucous sort of place with a huge Saturday market, another interesting fortified cathedral and, in Allée de la Résistance beside the park, a daring and unusual *Monuments des Morts* by the local artist Darde – more of whose work is on display at the Hôtel Fleury, along with variable exhibitions of painting. If you're staying any length of time the **SI** is at 7 place de la République, next door to the **gare routière**,

PÉZENAS

Market centre of the vine-smothered coastal plain, **PÉZENAS** looks across to rice fields and shallow lagoons or *étangs*, hazy with heat and dotted with pink flamingos. A small country town, local tourist pamphlets have rather grandly dubbed it the Versailles of Languedoc – reference to its long association with the *États Généraux* of the province and its time as an elegant, aristocratic watering hole. It has, however, retained perfectly the air of a gentrified resort, with a 17C centre, the Vieille Ville, carefully protected from development.

As well as this rather dubious past, the town makes much of its brief connection with **Molière,** who with his theatre company visited Pézenas several times, once staying for a productive period of months and putting on his plays at the *hôtel Alphonse* in rue Conti, which now has an ice-cream parlour in its coach-house. When here he lodged in the *Maison du Barbier Gely,* in the stagily unspoilt **place Gambetta,** today occupied by the **SI,** and he figures prominently in the **Musée Vulliod St-Germain,** housed in an 18C palace just off the square but not exerting any particular pull with its recreated interiors and 17–18C paintings. The SI tout (and sell) a guide to all the sites – mansions and former palaces – though you can just as easily follow the explanatory plaques fixed up all over the centre. Not included in the route is a former Jewish ghetto of two streets, Litania and Juiverie, unaltered, they say, since the 14C.

Place de la République is the venue for an enormous Saturday **market,** and it's also the place to take a bus to MONTPELLIER, BÉZIERS or AGDE – they stop outside *Café Alran.* For **brasseries, hotels** and the services of a **post office** go to place due 14 Juillet, 5mins' walk away.

TO THE COAST: SÈTE, AGDE AND AROUND

On the face of it **Languedoc beaches** aren't particularly enticing – bleak strands, often irritatingly windswept and cut off from their hinterland by marshy *étangs.* But what they do have is long hours of sunshine, 125 miles of sand still only sporadically populated, and relatively unpolluted water. This could change, as for the last couple of decades the French government has poured money into this area at a terrific rate, building seven new resorts in twice as many years. But for the moment, as long as you steer well clear of these new towns – ugly, soulless places for the most part anyway – deserted beaches are still there for the walking.

First-built of the new resorts, on the fringes of the Camargue, was **LA GRANDE MOTTE,** an extravagant futuristic vision of concrete and glass pyamids and cones ranged around a broad sandy beach. In summer its waterside and streets are chocked tight with semi-naked bodies; wintertime it's a depressing, wind-battered ghetto with a few permanent residents. A little way east are **PORT CAMARGUE** boasting a sparkling new marina, and **GRAU DU ROI,** older and until recently a slightly tatty fishing port, but now well on its way into the 21C. Inland a few kilometres lurks appealingly named **AIGUES MORTES,** a 13C town built by Louis IX on a grid plan, with impressive sturdy town ramparts that remain virtually intact. Outside the walls amid drab modern development, flat salt plains lend a certain other-worldly appeal, but inside all is now geared for tourists. If you come, climb up the **Tour de Constance** on the north-west corner and walk the ramparts, gazing over the wierd mist-ridden flats of the Parc de Camargue. And beat a hasty retreat.

Sète

Further down the coast, and perched around a steep outcrop of land on the corner of the Bassin de Thau, SÈTE has been an important harbour for 300 years. A scrubby port, cut with water and lined with tall terraces and seafood restaurants, it's a lively place, particularly during its furious summer *joustes nautiques*. As a base for exploring this part of the coast, or just a night's stopover, you'd be pushed to beat it.

From a distance, Mont St-Clair, the hill round which Sète groups, is thought to resemble a dolphin, which is why a hopelessly unlifelike black dolphin pops up everywhere as the emblem of the town. Part is pedestrianised, crowded and vibrant, with café tables scattered about outside. Climb up from the vieux port to the **Cimetière Marin**, the sailors' cemetery, where the poet Paul Valéry is buried. A native of the town, he called Sète his 'singular island', and the **Musée Valéry** above the cemetery has a room devoted to him, as well as a small but strong collection of modern French paintings. Georges Brassens has a room to himself too: singer-songwriter, associate of Sartre, and the radical voice of a whole generation in France, he was also born and raised in Sète and is buried in the Cimetière le Py on the other side of the hill – despite his song 'Plea to be buried on the beach at Sète'. Below the sailors' cemetery, couched neatly above the water, is Vauban's **Fort St-Pierre**, which houses a *Festival of Open Air Theatre* in August, and a *film festival* in June. And, on the subject of **festivals**, the aforementioned **joustes nautiques** are always worth seeing – water jousting contests, and highly virile events, unchanged for 300 years, in which young men in rival boats try to knock each other into the canal with 3m-long lances, to the accompaniment of music and much drinking, they take place throughout the summer but especially on the Sunday nearest 29 June, 14 July, Monday nearest 25 August and first Sunday in September.

The **SI** have a central annex on place A Briand - best bet for summer information; their main office is way out on Quai d'Alger, opposite the ferry port for **boats to Morocco and the Balearic islands**. The **gare routière** is even more awkwardly placed in Quai de la République, and the **gare SNCF** further out still on Quai Midi Nord – though it's on the main bus route which encircles Mont St-Clair. Other than a frequently full **youth hostel** (67.53.46.68) with **campsite**, high up in the town at rue Général Revest, your chances of a **cheap room** are limited. But try *Hotel le Midi*, 13 rue Semard, or *Hôtel le Tramontane*, at 5 rue Mistral. For full details of (and information on vacancies at) the numerous campsites scattered about the Sète coast phone the *Mairie Service des Campings* (67.74.88.30) or consult the SI. Two of the largest are *Les Régales* and *Le Pont Levis*, both on the circular bus route (which you can pick up at the town centre or gare SNCF) and conveniently near a beach. Leaving, bear in mind that **hitching out** is supremely difficult – better to take a train or bus to the nearest town and try from there. Just 7km north-east lies FRONTIGNAN, highly industrial, but noted for a Muscat wine so delicious it was described by Colette as 'like a sun stroke, or love at first sight, or the sudden realisation of a nervous system'.

Agde and nudism

At the other end of the Bassin de Thau, **AGDE** is historically most interesting of the coastal towns. Originally Greek, and maintained by the Romans, it thrived for centuries trading with the Near East and was for well over 1,000 years the seat of the local bishop. Outrun as a seaport by Sète though, it later degenerated into a sleazy fishing harbour. It is today a major tourist centre, however, and boasts few remains of its long history. Apart from the odd fragment of town wall there's precious little to see. The grim, heavily battlemented **cathedral** is worth the very briefest of stops: like the rest of the town, it is built of the distinctive dark stone quarried from the nearby extinct volcano, Mont St-Loup, a fortified and unbeautiful structure. Likewise the museums. If you've time to fill between buses, the *GRASPA* diving club display antiquities they've dug up locally, though the best have found their way to Paris. The Musée Agathois shows further exhibits of local history.

Places to eat are in good supply, but tend to be poor quality and overpriced. **Hotel rooms**, too, go for rip-off rates, and only a few offer affordable rates for full or half board – *Chez Rosette* in rue Gohin is one. If you're **camping** there are around twenty-five sites in the vicinity, all vast, zealously-equipped and usually packed to the gills. Should none of this put you off Agde totally, and you want more information on the place, the **SI** is under the town hall arcade at the bottom of av de Vias.

CAP D'AGDE, reachable by bus from Agde, sits at the south of the Hérault, largest and by far the most successful of the new resorts, sprawling laterally from the large volcanic mound of the Cap in an excess of pseudo-traditional modern buildings that offer every type of facility and entertainment – all expensive. It's perhaps best known for its colossal **Quartier Naturiste**, one of the largest in France, with the best of the beaches, space for 20,000 visitors and its own (nude) restaurants, banks, post offices and shops. Access is possible, though expensive, if you're not actually staying there. But if you want to get inside for free you can simply walk along the beach from neighbouring Marseillan-Plage, and remove tell-tale fabrics en route.

SOUTHERN LANGUEDOC

The southern portion of Languedoc cuts a slender triangle west, its watery coastal flats rising to low undulating hills as you forge inland. **Carcass-onne**, with its immaculately preserved medieval *cité*, has to be a major target, and though the coast is for the most part worth missing out entirely, **Béziers** and **Narbonne** make for worthwhile diversions on the way.

This is the real heartland of the province, still with separatist leanings, and it was here in the 12C that the heretical medieval creed of **Catharism** filtered through from the Balkans, taking root amidst peasants and nobility alike. Cathars held there to be two equal forces in the universe: one, the physical world, inherently evil, and the other, the spiritual, basically good. Though they believed themselves good Christians, they despised the materialism of the Catholic church, the brazen corruption of its priests, and the conjunction of church and state. Instead of an organised priesthood they had *parfaits*, who lived ascetically on charity and renounced the physical world through their own esoteric rites. Characteristic of Cathar rites was the consolamentum, administered by the parfait to the sick or dying, who would then proceed to starve themselves to death.

The crushing of the Cathars, under the papal-sponsored **Albigensian Crusade**, took place in the early 13C. Led by Simon de Montfort and Arnald-Amaury Abbot of Citeaux, the northern barons and their troops were granted forty days remission in advance and given rights to any lands they seized. Eventually Simon de Montfort took possession of almost the whole county of Languedoc, though it was over twenty years before the last communities gave themselves up, or starved themselves to death, in the mountain fortresses they had built as refuge.

BÉZIERS

The first place the **anti-Cathar crusade** reached, on 22 July 1209, was BÉZIERS, an ancient city with a large population that included a couple of hundred Cathars. The local people refused to hand them over, and Arnald-Amaury, never one to mince his words, uttered his most famous pronouncement: 'Kill them all. The Lord will know His own' – an order which was zestfully carried out. Close to 60,000 inhabitants, it has been estimated, were slain although the Abbot himself, in a report to the Pope stated with regret that 'We were only able to slay 20,000'. Many took sanctuary in the old cathedral of St-Nazaire, which was set on fire and destroyed along with its occupants. As further humiliation, the new

Cathedral was erected soon after in Gothic style, the latest fashion from the north of France – huge, opulent and ludicrously ornate.

These events, though they took place over 700 years ago, still taint the atmosphere of the town, which is staunchly pro-Occitan and anti-French – a uniquely southern combination of sleazy elegance and abundant energy, and with street signs that are largely bilingual. Best introduction to the Cathar and subsequent past is to look in on the **Musée du Vieux Bitterrois** on rue Massol and the jumbled **Beaux-Arts**, behind the cathedral in place de la Révolution where in 1851 the army shot and killed demonstrators opposed to the new monarchy of Napoleon III. For the rest Béziers has a mainly Renaissance appearance, nowhere more so than in **Allées Paul Riquet**, a magnificent broad and shady central esplanade, with a florid theatre at one end and shops, bars and restaurants along its side. At its end is the gorgeous park of **Plateau des Poètes**.

Béziers is centre of Languedoc's huge wine industry, and a good starting point for finding work on the autumn **harvest**. The local *ANPE* office sometimes have ideas but really the best approach is to go straight to the villages and ask around. Other passions here are **bullfighting** (Spanish style, to the death) and **rugby**, while in August there's a lively **Feria**.

If you're staying, there's a good scatter of **hotels** around av Gambetta and place Jean-Jaurès – many with cheap rooms – and low-priced foyers at 2 Impasse St-Ursula and on bd de Lattre de Tassigny. *L'Alhambra*, in rue Solferino, and *L'Aristo*, in rue Fourrier, provide dependable **eating** alternatives. The main **PTT** is in av Clémenceau.

NARBONNE

Founded in 600BC and decreed a colony of Rome 700 years later, **NARBONNE** was one of the major French settlements of the Classical world – and a busy seaport through to the Middle Ages when following the expulsion of its Jewish community the town went into quiet decline and the harbour silted up. Today, despite the ominous presence of the Malvesi nuclear power station just 5km out of town, it's a pleasant provincial place: tree-lined walks and esplanades converging on graceful squares, with a well-restored medieval quarter dominated by the giant bulk of the 13–14C **Cathédrale St-Just**.

This, Narbonne's principal attraction, is despite its size only the choir of an unfinished edifice whoe dimensions and style – northern Gothic – were once again to remind the restless local populace who was boss. Certaintly, it's just the sort of building to cow a god-fearing peasant into obedience: staggeringly broad and high inside, with imposing tapestries and stained glass; though if you look around, there are more delicate touches, principally in the sculpture and the beautiful *Chapelle d'Annonciade*, tranquilly symmetrical in pale stone with elegant pillars and vaulting. Through a marble-paved courtyard, the adjacent **Archbishop's Palace** houses **Musées** of archaeology and art; the former, including artefacts from Roman *Narbo* and a bronze of Romulus and Remus given by the city of Rome in 1982 to commemorate 2,100 years since the founding of the colony.

The narrow streets of the old *cité*, around the cathedral, harbour further Roman pieces: a **horreum** on rue Rouget de L'Isle, and beside the Hôtel de Ville, the source Ferriol, a natural spring. In the square here are two medieval towers – Tour de Martin and Donjon Gilles Aycelin, the latter with 162 climbable steps to the top. Southwards, on the far side of the canal, a covered market on bd Ferroud and the Gothic church of **St-Paul** between them reward a short trek, the latter for its stone frog, sat enigmatically in a stone basin in the South aisle – petrified, apparently, for interrupting Mass with his croak.

The **SI** have a summer **annexe** by the canal along Cours de la République, and a more central **office** next to the cathedral on place Roger Salengro. There may still be a cheap hostel next door, but if that's bitten the dust walk down to av Pierre Semard and the SNCF station, where you'll find most of Narbonne's more inexpensive **hotels and restaurants**. **Campsites** appear more frequently the closer you get to the sea. If you've a car or bike (rentable, as usual, from the SNCF station) and want to get **out of town** for an afternoon, head off to **Montagne de la Clape** – strange, moonscape hills, rare in this part of France, with a Saracen castle and sailors' cemetery.

CARCASSONNE

Modern **CARCASSONNE**, prefecture of the Aude, isn't of much interest. But just 2km distant – a steep summer's walk – its **medieval Cité** is one of the sights of Languedoc. Immaculately restored, enclosed by a double bastion of massive walls spiked with turrets and crenallations, it stands complete and still inhabited – though increasingly with gift shops, chintzy cafés and restaurants. It is extremely popular, well too much for its own good, but even so the experience of being surrounded by such a thorough restoration of medievalism isn't something I'd pass over.

The **fortifications**, originally Roman and visigothic; successfully starved off the forces of Charlemagne and later, for a while, Simon de Montfort. They then slowly fell into disrepair and decrepitude until 1844, and the spirited restoration work of Viollet-le-Duc. What you see now is a mix of all periods recreated and 'unified' by his arches and buttresses: a complete vision, but one that's also somewhat less than historically correct, with current restorations 'correcting' the turrets by replacing their slates with tiles, and various other projects.

Coming from the modern city, you enter the *enceinte* through the staunch bastion of Porte d'Aude. If you want a map, a room (see below) or details, the SI run a summer annexe in Porte Narbonne, the other main gateway. There's no charge for entry into the main part of the city, or the grassy *lices* between the two sets of walls – one of its most tranquil enclaves – but admission to the **Château de Comtal**, the principal sight, is heavy. Tours, which you're obliged to take, run throughout the day and last an hour: frankly, if money's tight you can quite safely give it a miss. On the other side of the Cité, much more pleasing, and free, is the **Église St-Nazaire**, a lovely combination of Romanesque nave and 13C Gothic choir, pierced by stained glass generally considered the finest in southern France. Only the tower spoils it, a Viollet-le-Duc reconstruction in Visigoth style totally at odds with the rest of the building.

But, the *lices* apart, much the best way to see the Cité is in aimless wanderings amid its streets and alleyways – a bizarre blend of bars and amusements against purposefully quaint medieval settings. **Accommodation** as you'd expect is pricey apart from a terminally overbooked youth hostel (centrally situated on the main street, rue Trenceval) and hunting around for a cheap room brings little joy. Affordable **restaurants**, too, are thin on the ground, and other than the excellent *L'Ostal des Troubadours*, at 5 rue Viollet le Duc, you'd be better off trekking back to the modern *Ville Basse* for both a meal and a bed. The **SI** here is at 15 bd Camille-Pelletan, and has an additional annexe at the SNCF station beside the Jardin des Plantes. Around the jardin, you'll also find Carcassonne's main concentration of cheap **hotels**. Best is *Bonnefoux*, 40 rue de la Libetre, but if that's either full or too expensive the *Centre International Foyer*, at 91 rue Aime-Ramon has low-priced rooms. The **gare routière** is in bd Sabatier; bike-hire from *Bourrouet,* 12bis rue Auguste Comte; and there's a municipal **campsite** out towards the old Cité, by the stadium on av Sarrail. And once in the Ville Basse **cheap eats** are no problem: there are dozens of restaurants around, many serving the regional speciality, *cassoulet*, a substantial stew of pork, beans and sausage, and, at its best, delicious.

SOUTH AND EAST OF CARCASSONNE: MINERVE AND THE COAST

Inland from Carcassonne the countryside folds south into the wooded hills and pastures of the Aude *département*, dotted with **feudal castles** almost inaccessible on rocky peaks. It was in these sturdy strongholds that the local lords allowed the surrounding population, Cathar or Catholic, to take refuge when threatened with the Albigensian Crusade in the Middle Ages. If you've transport the most impressive are PEYREPERTUSE, QUERIBUS and MONTSEGUR; if not the difficulty of access is likely to defeat you.

Pushing east, the small fortified village of **MINERVE**; besieged by Simon de Montfort in 1210, is now capital of a district producing one of the region's best wines – **Minervois**, a rich heavy red. It's set in curious rocky terrain, terraced with vines or covered in wild garrigue and, beneath the ground, strange rock formations like the two *Ponts Naturels*: eerie natural tunnels winding under the road. In the town, the Romanesque church houses a 5C altar; the museum has a good section devoted to Cathars, whose castle here was left in ruins by the crusaders.

East to the Coast, the stretch between NARBONNE-PLAGE and PORT-LEUCAT, where Roussillon begins, has broad deserted beaches and plenty of sunshine. It sounds great, but the truth is that most of the strands are windy, remote and shadeless, and what settlements there are, dull and run-down. Best bets, if you're determined, are probably **NARBONNE-PLAGE** itself, with several **campsites, cheap hotels** around place des Karentes, and on good long beach, not entirely ruined by the flanking car parks; or **FLEURY D'AUDE**, a new creation with major **naturist amenities.** Two to avoid are GRUISSAN – vast sand flats and a tacky new resort area, and PORT LA NOUVELLE, the last of Languedoc's coastal towns, grouped about a grubby, unappealing harbour. Somewhere in between all these come the old-established resort villages of **LA TAMARISSIÈRE, SERIGNAN-PLAGE** and **VALRAS,** all with reasonable beaches, campsites and easy access from BÉZIERS.

ROUSSILLON

Catalan-speaking **Roussillon** was one of the Spanish territories in the northern Pyrenees ceded to France in 1659, after having long been in rebellion against Madrid. Despite its Catalan identity, there's little support nowadays either for separation from France or reunification with Spain; in fact the local people, especially in the more remote mountain villages, were for a long time oblivious of the change from Spanish to French rule, and not until the outbreak of the First World War did it become common knowledge which country they actually belonged to.

Life in this forgotten corner of the country remains simple and largely agricultural, the land given over to pasture in the mountainous interior, and down on the warm dry coastal plain, and along the fertile valley of the river Tet, to vineyards, orchards and market gardens.

As far as **language** is concerned you'll find most people bilingual in Catalan and French, sometimes in Spanish, too. Catalan names, however, are an initial bar to pronunciation Xs (*sh* sound), CHs (*k*), Us (*oo*) and final Gs (*tch*) abound.

PERPIGNAN

PERPIGNAN is a big city, quite out of character with the rest of its province. Suburbs sprawl to all sides, populated mainly with the refugees of the Spanish civil war – Catalans from the Communist and Anarchist groupings who opposed and fought Franco. It is a place that seems vibrant, and moving out of long poverty. And though not immediately attractive it makes a good base for exploring inland Roussillon and the long sandy beaches of its coast.

At the heart of the city, as ever, is the old **medieval centre**: historically of particular interest, for it was once mainland capital of the kingdom of Majorca, later at Aragon. As such it has a unique closeness to the Islamic world of the Moors. And indeed if you take a close look at the 13C **Palais des Rois de Majorque**, in the vast fortified **Citadelle** (9.30–12 & 2–6; cl. Tues), you can still find the evidence. The Citadelle is partially occupied by the military but you are shown a sumptuous *salle* and also the two palace **chapels**, one on top of the other, facing the courtyard. The lower, echoey chamber is the point of interest, with its worn, painted frieze running around the walls: its design is abstract, and faded now from · recognition, but its language is Arabic and its text the tenet of Islam: 'There is no god but God, and Muhammad is his Messenger.'

North from here – and dominating the busiest area of town – is **La Castillet**, a small 14C riverside fort and city gate, now home to the *Casa Pairal*, a fascinating museum of Roussillon's Catalan culture (10–1 & 3–5, cl. Tues). Behind it, scattered with palm – as well as plane trees, and newly renovated with pedestrianised, marble-paved streets and galleried sidewalks, extends the heart of the old town. Its focus is **place de la Loge**, a small square chequered with coloured marble and fringed with historic buildings. The 14C **Loge de la Mer**, built of unwieldy plain blocks of stone dashed with a little restrained Gothic-Renaissance ornamentation, used to be the maritime exchange – today, rather wonderfully, it's a fast-food joint. Next door, the Hôtel de Ville sits superciliously behind a massive wrought iron gate, and alongside it the 15C Palais de la Députation, embassy of the kings of Aragon. Two or three times a week in summer the square is venue for performances of the *Sardana* – a fervent Catalan folkdance accompanied by music played on pipe and tambourine.

The **Cathédrale St-Jean** – in the square of the same name – is a couple of blocks to the east, clothed in a gaudy herringbone skin and topped with two stone towers and scallop-patterned dome. Inside it is similarly overwhelming – 'curious rather than beautiful' wrote Freda White – and not at all French with its patterned walls and ceilings, and tall, gold-laden side-chapels. And that, save for the **Musée Rigaud's** market gallery of Spanish and Catalan artists (at 16 rue de l'Ange, near place Arago), is about as far as Perpignan sights go.

For details of events – films, exhibitions, concerts – the SI, close by place de la Loge on Quai de Lattre de Tassigny, publish free monthly listings. One of the City's stranger happenings, thoroughly Spanish in spirit, is the Good Friday *Procession de la Sanch* ('blood'), a hooded procession of penitents led by one of the old medieval brotherhoods. Most cheaper **hotels** and **restaurants** are gathered, predictably, around the gare SNCF on av Général de Gaulle. About a kilometre away in the riverside Parc de la Pépinière, there's a **youth hostel** (34.63.32: turn left out of the station and right along av Grand Bretagne), but far preferable is the **Foyer** at 32 rue Maréchal Foch, near the SI (34.39.36). There are two feasible **campsites**: *Catalan* and *Garriole*, both signposted from the centre.

If you arrive – or want to leave – by bus, the main **gare routière** is off av Général Leclerc, by the wholesale *Marché de Gros*, though some buses also leave from the more central tree-lined Promenade des Platanes. **Bikes** can be hired from *Cycles Mercier*, up the road from the gare SNCF on av de Gaulle.

THE ROUSSILLON COAST

Buses run regularly from Perpignan down to the major Roussillon **coastal resorts**, and though few are particularly appealing, and a number worth avoiding, there's still less development here than across the border in Spanish Catalonia, and to the south stretches remain almost deserted.

PORT LEUCATE, the first resort you come to, is set on a narrow strip of land between the sea and a large saltwater *étang*: A modern resort, with a chic new marina and a large naturist colony, a little way north of town, this is probably one to avoid. The kind of place that draws cachet from the likes of Auberon Waugh, son of Evelyn and, to date, only journalist to give the *Rough Guides* a bum review! South of here, past a liner beached to serve as casino and nightclub, is **PORT BARCARÈS** – little more promising, with fifteen campsites, a zoo and a 'family pleasure park'. Heading on, past the excavated ruins of *RUSCINO* (Gallo-Roman capital of the region), you enter sports holiday territory at **CANET-PLAGE** and **ST-CYPRIEN**. Campsites abound at both, and most other facilities, but there's nothing exactly unique to detain you. For action, press on to **ARGELÈS-PLAGE**, better value and packed with bars and discos. For real beach attractions keep going . . .

South of Argelès the coast improves dramatically, the Pyrenees reaching down to the sea in a beautiful series of corniches, with magnificent views and some gorgeously untouched little beaches and coves. This is the **Côte Vermeille** – 'Vermillion coast' – and **COLLIOURE**, the first town of any note that you reach, is its so-called 'pearl'. It is certainly a shift, arranged around two curvy bays separated by a 12C hilltop fortress – the **Château Royal**, ex-seat of the Majorcan king and now flying the Catalan flag. Over the last decades of the last century, and the first of this, Collioure was a major artists' colony – Matisse, Dufy, Braque and Picasso all painted here, and the Fauvist movement was born. You can see posters and drawings signed by many of them, Picasso included, at the *Hôtel-Restaurant Les Templiers*, and out of season you might even stand a chance of a room too (not cheap – but surprisingly reasonable). In summer you'll be competing with sizeable crowds. Best bets are the four nearby **campsites**. If you need a room the **SI** on the corner of the Port de Plaisance will advise, or at least give you phone numbers.

Freda White wrote of Collioure as 'the last of the beautiful villages of France – there is nothing beyond', and certainly everything you come across further south is less remarkable; only the coast road itself continues to impress. **PORT-VENDRES** enjoys a fine scenic setting around a broad natural harbour, **BANYULS** is home to a rich sweet local wine, **CERBÈRE**, wickedly named, guards the border. All have further **campsites**.

INLAND: THE ROAD TO ANDORRA

Inland from Perpignan you hit wild, unbeaten country, the road winding and rising gradually into the foothills of the Pyrenees. There are several buses daily up here from Perpignan and, fun in itself, **Le Petit Train Jaune**, an SNCF train which takes you through some truly spectacular scenery from VILLEFRANCHE-DE-CONFLENT to LA TOUR DE CAROL. At most stations on the line you have to hail the train like a bus; to get off ask the driver.

SNCF buses run as far as VILLEFRANCHE, via **PRADES**, a small sunny town at the foot of the mountains, with a Tuesday market and a summer music festival organised by the Catalan cellist Pablo Cassals, and held 3km out of town in the Abbaye-St-Michel-de-Cuxa. This is a good base for walkers, too, with three one-star hotels and a couple of campsites. Main local goal, 20km distant on the GR36, is the 2,784m Pic du Canigou – easiest approached by way of VERNET-LES-BAINS. Neighbouring **VILLEFRANCHE** is a touristy place, cut in two by the river Cady and flanked above by the tumbling **Gorges de la Tet**.

At **SAILLAGOUSE** road and railway join: a small village with a **youth hostel** (1km from the station; 68.04.71.69). Beyond is the mountain resort of **FONT-ROMEU**, with a **campsite**, walking and skiers' facilities, and some pricey hotels. From either, minor roads run to the curious enclave of **LLIVIA**, a small town that along with the surrounding country-side is officially part of Spain, and has its own (unmanned) border posts. At **ODEILLO**, a short walk from Font-Romeu, is a remarkable **Solar Furnace**, generating 1,000kw by way of mirrors and where you can look in on a fascinating inside exhibition(9–6; free). Three km further on, near TARGASSONNE, a solar power station has been built on a hilltop.

Almost on the border, **LA TOUR DE CAROL** has a gare SNCF on the main Barcelona-Toulouse-Paris line. From **PORTA**, the walkers route GR7 climbs up a river valley into **ANDORRA**, and down the Riu Madriu to the capital **ANDORRA LA VELLA**, after zigzagging through high, bare mountain passes. Andorra, a tiny Catalan nation state, is again good walkers' country, though don't expect any curiosity from its small capital. Taking advantage of duty-free status, this is now little more than a drive-in supermarket and petrol station. And in winter, with unusually cheap skiing, site of one of Europe's most notorious après-ski scenes.

TRAVEL DETAILS

Trains
In summer, overnight sleepers link Languedoc with the Channel ports of Calais and Boulogne. Among other overnight trains is the occasional cheap summer special with a bar and disco on board but no sleeping accommodation: one of these departs Paris at midnight and gets to Port-Bou on the Spanish border at noon.

From Nîmes 5–6 TGVs daily to Paris (4½hr); frequent to Avignon (½hr), Montpellier (½hr), Sète (1hr), Béziers (1½hrs), Narbonne (1hr50), and Perpignan (2½hrs) or Carcassonne (2½hrs); 4 daily to Paris via Alès (40mins) Cévennes villages, Clermont-Ferrand (5hrs), and Vichy (6hrs), including (June-Sept) Le Cevenol, a *train touristique*; more frequent between Nîmes and Alès only. 3–4 daily to Arles (20mins) and Marseille (1hr).
From Montpellier 5–6 TGVs daily to Paris (5hrs); frequent to Lyon via Nîmes (½hr) and Avignon (1hr); and to Sète (½hr), Béziers (1hr), Narbonne (1hr20), and Perpignan (2hrs) or Carcassonne (2hrs); 3–4 daily to Arles (1hr) and Marseille (1hr40).
From Sète frequent to Montpellier (½hr), Nîmes (1hr), Avignon (1½hrs); and to Béziers (½hr), Narbonne (50mins), and Perpignan (1½hrs) or Carcassonne (1½hrs); 3–4 daily to Marseille (2hrs10) via Arles (1½hrs).
From Béziers 4 daily to Bedarieux (40mins), Millau (2hrs), and into Massif Central; 3–4 daily to Marseille (2½hrs) via Sète (½hr), Montpellier (1hr), Nîmes (1½hr), Arles (2hrs); more frequent continuing to Avignon (2hrs) from

Nîmes; frequent to Narbonne (20mins) and Perpignan (1hr) or Carcassonne (1hr).
From Narbonne frequent throughout day to Carcassonne (40mins); 8 daily continue to Toulouse or Bordeaux; several daily to Perpignan (30–40mins), Cerbère (1–1½hrs). Port-Bou (1hr20–1h40) – several continue into Spain; frequent to Béziers (20mins), Sète (50mins), Montpellier (1hr20), Nîmes (1hr50), Avignon (2hr20); 3–4 daily via Nîmes and Arles (2hrs) to Marseille (2hrs40).
From Carcassonne 8 daily to Toulouse (45mins) or Bordeaux (3hrs20); frequent to Narbonne (40mins); several daily to Béziers (1hr), Sète (1½hrs), Montpellier (2hrs), Nîmes (2½hrs), Avignon (3hrs); 3–4 daily via Nîmes to Arles (3hrs20) and Marseille (4hrs).
From Perpignan take SNCF bus out of town to Villefranche-le-Conflent, from where Le Petit Train Jaune goes 4 times daily up through Pyrenees to Le Tour de Carol (2hrs); several daily to Narbonne (30–40mins), Béziers (1hr), Sète (1½hrs), Montpellier (2hrs), Nîmes (2½hrs), Avignon (3hrs); 5 daily to Collioure (20mins), Cerbère (30–50mins) and Port-Bou (50mins–1hr20); some continue into Spain.

Buses
From Montpellier good network radiating out, with about 6 daily on N9 to Gignac (45mins), Lodève (1¼hrs), Millau (2½hrs); 4 or 5 to Clermont l'Hérault (1hr) and Bedarieux (2hrs); 2–5 daily to Pézenas and Béziers; occasional to Sommières and Alès; 6–11 daily to Sète (1hr).

From Bézier 2–5 daily to Montpellier, Agde, Bedarieux, Clermont l'Hérault, Lodève.

From Perpignan frequent to Canet and other coast towns; a few to Collioure; 4–5 SNCF and other buses daily along N116 (up Tet valley).

From Sète 6–11 daily to Montpellier (1hr).

Ferries

From Sète weekly to Morocco, Balearic islands and Alicante (Spain), and Algeria.

Chapter ten

THE MASSIF CENTRAL

One of the loveliest spots on earth . . . a country without roads, without guides, without any facilities for locomotion, where every discovery must be conquered at the price of danger or fatigue . . . a soil cut up with deep ravines, crossed in every way by lofty walls of lava, and furrowed by numerous torrents.

So one of George Sand's characters described the Haute Loire, central *département* of the **Massif Central**, and it's a description that could to a large extent still be applied to the whole region. For, thickly forested, and sliced by numerous rivers and lakes, these mountains are geologically the oldest part of France, and culturally one of the most firmly rooted in the past. Industry and tourism have made few inroads here, and the people remain rural and taciturn (they have a reputation, largely unfounded, for unfriendliness), and with an enduring sense of regional identity. Heart of the region is the **Auvergne**, a hard, inaccessible landscape dotted with *puys*, curious volcanic peaks; very poor, it is startlingly insular and staunchly religious, sheltering Romanesque churches in almost every village, and rigid, black sculptures of the Madonna and child. To the south-east, gentler and forested are the hills of the **Cévennes**, perhaps the most beautiful stretch, and with purpose for walkers in the 'Stevenson route'.

Considering the Massif Central takes up such a huge portion of the rugged centre of France, only a handful of towns stand out. **Le Puy**, spiked with jagged pinnacles of lava and with a majestic cathedral, is the most obviously compelling, but there is appeal, too, in the elegant spa city of **Vichy** and in the capital **Clermont-Ferrand**, the three of which together make a neat axis along which to space your explorations.

NORTH AND EASTERN AUVERGNE

The north and eastern portions of Auvergne make up much the most densely populated part of the Massif Central, taking in Clermont-Ferrand, Vichy and Le Puy, and the industrial (and footballing) centre of St-

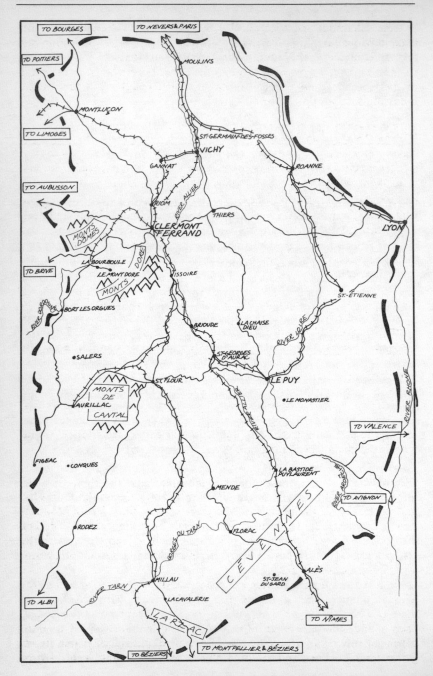

TO BOURGES

TO NEVERS & PARIS

TO POITIERS

MOULINS

MONTLUÇON

TO LIMOGES

ST-GERMAIN-DES-FOSSES

VICHY

GANNAT

ROANNE

TO AUBUSSON

RIOM

RIVER ALLIER

THIERS

CLERMONT-FERRAND

LYON

MONTS DÔMES

LA BOURBOULE

MONTS DORE

TO BRIVE

LE MONT DORE

ISSOIRE

MONTS DORE

BORT LES ORGUES

RIVER DORDOGNE

BRIOUDE

LA CHAISE DIEU

RIVER DORE

ST-ÉTIENNE

SALERS

ST-GEORGES D'AURAC

ST-FLOUR

LE PUY

MONTS DE AURILLAC CANTAL

LE MONASTIER

RIVER RHÔNE

TO VALENCE

FIGEAC

CONQUES

RIVER TRUYÈRE

LA BASTIDE PUYLAURENT

MENDE

RIVER ARDÈCHE

TO AVIGNON

RODEZ

GORGES DU TARN

FLORAC

C É V E N N E S

TO ALBI

RIVER TARN

MILLAU

ALÈS

ST-JEAN DU GARD

LA CAVALERIE

L A R Z A C

TO NÎMES

TO BÉZIERS

TO MONTPELLIER & BÉZIERS

Etienne. **Clermont** and **Vichy** both have good train links with Paris and make obvious jumping off points – not just for points in this section but for much of the vast National Park of the Auvergne, to the west (see p. 322). **Le Puy**, a slow haul through the central mountains, gives access to the Cévennes and Ardèche (both of which you'll again find in the following section, pp. 328–32).

CLERMONT-FERRAND

Geographic and economic centre of the Massif Central, big, industrial **CLERMONT-FERRAND** is an incongruous capital for rustic Auvergne. It is a lively, youthful place, with a major university, and a manufacturing base that (with St-Etienne and Paris) has steadily been depopulating the villages of the province. As a base for this side of the Massif it's ideal, with a wide choice of rooms and some good restaurants and bars. And it has interest in its own right, too – a well preserved historic centre and the nearby spectacle of **Puy de Dôme** and of the **Parc des Volcans** (see p. 322).

Clermont, called 'ville noire' for its houses built in the local black volcanic rock, and neighbouring Montferrand, were united in 1631 to form a single city. Both, despite long (and vaguely illustrious) pasts were by then peacefully obscure. It took the arrival of one Mme Daubrée, niece of Charles Macintosh (of raincoat fame), to change things. She brought all the skills of her uncle to France with her, and made rubber into bouncing balls for her children, an idea taken up by her entrepreneurial husband when he opened a small factory in 1832 dedicated to the making and marketing of rubber goods. His partner's grandsons, Edouard and André **Michelin**, adapted the factory to the demands of the emerging pneumatic tyre industry and so the Michelin empire was forged – and with it the city's (continuing) industrial base.

Clermont

Old Clermont, cluttered remnant of pre-tyre (and guidebook) days is the part of the city you're likely to spend most of your time, Vieux Montferrand – or what little is left of it – stands out on a limb to the east. The 'black', *ville-noire*, aspect of the place is immediately apparent, with the traditional heart of the city heaped untidily around the summit of a worn-away volcanic peak.

Main streets of this quarter are rue des Gras – where you'll find the **Musée Ranquet** (Daily 2–4; Sun & Thurs 10–12, cl. Mon; free), one of the city's best museums with displays on local history back to Roman finds – and, running roughly parallel, rue de la Boucherie, a fragrant bazaar of tiny shops selling all manner of food and spices. These streets gather up to the dark and soaring **Cathédrale Notre Dame**, its black-grey

volcanic stone evocatively and accurately described by Freda White as
'like the darkest shade of a pigeon's wing'. This stone, black lava brought
from nearby Volvic, was first used in the 13C (the cathedral dates from
1248 and until then tools were not strong enough to cut it), and its
uncommon strength permitted a radical change in construction and design
by making it possible to build vaults and pillars of unheard of slenderness
and height. Inside, the building is Gothic at its most movingly inspired,
delicately aspiring heavenwards out of the gloom; despite its heavy 19C
fixtures (the originals, as so often, having been destroyed in the revolution). Off the nave, there is access to the *Tour de la Bayette* (small
charge) with extensive views across the city. From this vantage, too, you
can make out why locals use the cathedral as a short cut — something
the authorities have been trying to stamp out for years, though these days
there at least aren't flocks of animals in tow.

A short step north-east of the cathedral stands Clermont's other great
church, the **Basilique Notre-Dame du Port**: a century older and in almost
total contrast. Not only in style — it is Romanesque — but in substance,
built from softer stone in pre-lava working days, and consequently
corroding badly from exposure to Clermont's polluted air. For all that,
it's a beautiful building, pure Auvergnat Romanesque with a Madonna
and Child over the south door in the strangely stylised local form, both

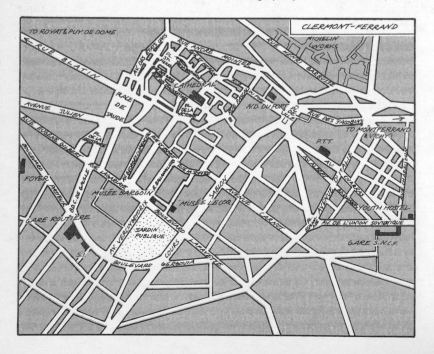

figures stiff and upright, the child more like a dwarf than an infant. Inside, it exudes the broody mysteriousness so often generated by Romanesque; put a franc in the slot and you can light up the intricately carved ensemble of leaves, knights and Biblical figures on the church's pillars and capitals. Outside the church, in **place Delille**, Pope Urban II preached the First Crusade in 1095, to a vast crowd who receiving his speech with the Occitan cry of 'Dios lo Volt' (God wills it), the phrase adopted by the crusaders in justification of all subsequent massacres.

On the edge of old Clermont, the huge and soulless **place de Jaude** is by day the noisome hub of the city centre and its main shopping area; by night a desolate no-man's land of drunks and glue-sniffers. In the centre stands a rousing statue of the Gaulish chieftain Vercingetorix, who in 53BC led his people to a local victory over Julius Caesar. Take a walk up from here to **place St Pierre**, Clermont's principal marketplace, with a morning produce market (Tues-Sat), at its liveliest on Saturday mornings. Nearby, a couple of museums scattered around the busy boulevards that enclose the city centre may be of interest if you've an hour or so to kill: the **Musée Lecoq**, outside a large park of the same name where you can't walk or even lie on the grass, has a fair natural history collection; the **Musée Bargoin**, a short walk west of the centre, forms the other half of the Musée Ranquet (and keeps the same hours) with exhibits of archaeology, religious sculpture and visual arts. Both museums are open the same hours as the Ranquet museum.

Montferrand, Royat and Puy de Dôme

Montferrand once greatly outshone its neighbour and rival but since the cities' union has gradually become enmeshed in suburbia which is a pity – for what remains of the original town is elegant, and recently immaculately restored. For a break from the more frenetic atmosphere of Clermont, you can get out here easily enough on bus 7 from place de Jaude.

The other city suburb, **Royat**, to the west, began as a spa resort in the 19C. Higher and breezier than Clermont, it is again an attractive hour or so's respite. There are few particular sights – the ruins of Roman baths in the park, a fortified Romanesque church – but the centre has a villagey feel about it, leading out to riverside walks.

For a longer and more directed walk, a couple of hours from Royat (or bus from Clermont) will bring you to Puy de Dôme, one of the tallest of the *puys*, with sweeping views back towards the town and over to Parc des Volcans, stretching away amid shreds of cloud. Close to the summit ruins survive of a Roman temple to Mercury, in its time considered one of the marvels of the Empire, fashioned from over fifty different kinds of marble and with an enormous bronze statue of Mercury where a TV antenna now stands.

Walking out to the Puy from Clermont, or Royat, allow a good half day – and take food. The restaurant on the top enjoys a monopoly and makes full use of it.

Some practical details

The main **SI office** in Clermont is at 69 bd Gergovia, with annexes at the railway station (Mon-Sat only), on place de Jaude (June-Sept) and rue de la Rodade in Montferrand (June-Sept). At any of these you should be able pick up a copy of *Le Mois à Clermont*, which details everything that's happening in the city. **Other sources of info** include the *Centre d'Information Jeunesse* (8 place Regensburg) who concentrate on long-term accommodation and jobs; *Service d'Accueil des Étudiants Étrangers* and *CROUS*, both student offices in rue Étienne Dollet, south of the main SI; *Chamina* (Occitan for *cheminer* – to follow a path) at 5 rue Pierre le Vénérable, who give information on footpaths and can reserve overnight accommodation in Massif Central *gîtes*; and an *information bureau* for Parc des Volcans at 28 rue St-Esprit.

Cheap beds aren't hard to find. There's a *youth hostel*, 55 av USSR, conveniently placed just 2mins' walk from the train station; a *Foyer International de Jeunesse*, at 12 place Regensburg, in the midst of a noisy housing estate; and the *Maison St Jean* (Foyer des Jeunes Travailleurs), 17 rue Gaultier de Biauzat, which does good value B & B. **Inexpensive hotels** include *Petit Vitesse*, 63 av USSR, with well-priced full board, *Hôtel Auvergne*, 67 av Charras, and the *Moderne*, 57 av Charras – all a minute or two's walk from the train station. Slightly dearer but good value are the *Bellevue*, 1 av USSR, and *Hôtel Fleury*, at 2 bd Fleury. The *Strasbourg*, next door to the youth hostel, is a relais routier with a restaurant downstairs. **For campers**, ROYAT has one- and four-star sites, and there's a three-star site a little further out in CEYRAT.

Eating, four restaurants should be enough to cover most pockets, tastes and palates: the *Bungalow*, 30 rue Ballainvilliers, serves good fish and vegetarian dishes (the café next door is a popular punk-anarchist hangout); *La Couscousserie*, 20 rue Cadene, just off place de Jaude, is North African, and *Pied de Cochon*, at 4 rue Lamartine, again near place de Jaude, does an amazingly cheap three-course menu. And if all of these still work out too pricey, there's a *self-service restaurant* on rue Cheval-Blanc that costs even less. **Good places to drink** later on are *Le Clown*, 65 rue A France, which has nightly live jazz, and *Le Drop*, at bd Trudaine.

Focal point of the **city transport system** is place de Jaude: you can get just about anywhere in town from here, and there's an information and ticket booth to find out how. You can either buy a single ticket which lasts an hour, or, much cheaper, invest in a book of ten tickets or a daily *Carte de Jour*. There are frequent bus connections between the **gare routière**, next to the SI, and St-Étienne, Volvic, Riom, Le Puy and Vichy, and trains leave regularly for Paris via Riom and Vichy – the **gare SNCF** is on av URSS. *Le Cévenol*, a stopping train **through the mountains to Nîmes**, is one of the most enchanting French rail journeys you can take – so much so that during the summer SNCF run a *train touristique* with entertainment on board.

And, finally, **bike-hire** is an offer at *Mazerat* (5 bd Gergovia) and **Allostop** (hitching service) are at 22 av des Etats Unis (73.36.72.33).

RIOM

Just 15km north of Clermont, Riom is sedate and provincial – one-time capital of entire Auvergne and now, studded with Renaissance architecture, one of the minor gems of the northern Massif. You may not want to stay beyond a morning's wandering, but it provides a worthwhile stopover for lunch if you're on the way up to Vichy. It's an aloof, old-world kind of place, still Auvergne's judicial capital, with a 19C **Palais de Justice** that stands on the site of a grand palace built when the Dukes of Berry controlled this region in the 14C. Of the palace, only the *Ste-Chapelle* survives, incorporated in the new building, with some fine stained glass and tapestries (accompanied visits, Mon-Sat 10–11.30/ 2–5.30). Not far away, in rue de Commerce, the **Eglise Notre Dame du Marthuret** holds Riom's most valued treasures, two statues of the Virgin and Child – one a Black Madonna, the other, the so-called *Vierge à l'Oiseau*, a touchingly realistic piece of carving that portrays the young Christ with a bird fluttering in His hands. A copy stands in the entrance hall of the church (its original site), where you can see it with the advantage of daylight.

Riom's **SI** is also in rue de Commerce and, if you decide to stay over, most of the **hotels** scatter on and around the junction of that street and bd Desaix. Cheapest are *Desaix* and *Hôtel du Square*, which both have their own restaurant with an inexpensive menu. Cheaper still is *Hôtel de Lyon*, a little further out at Faubourg de la Bade.

Trains from Riom run frequently to VICHY (and CLERMONT). Local buses – from the *gare* and various other points – also serve **MOZAC**, on the edge of town, with a 12C **abbey church**, its Romanesque sculpture beautiful as ever, continuing on to the bourgeois spa-resort of **CHÂTEL GUYON** (10–20mins). With thirty different **hot springs**, great views over the surrounding countryside (and *puys*), and a couple of well equipped **campsites**, this is as good a place as any if you want to rest up a night.

VICHY

VICHY is famous for two things: its wartime puppet government under **Marshal Pétain** and its curative **sulphurous springs**, which attract thousands of ageing and ailing visitors – *curistes*, they're called – every year. And while there's nothing left to suggest that Vichy was once capital of a collaborative Nazi state – the building that used to house the Pétain government has been anonymously turned into an office block, and the SI, in the same building, are careful to make no reference at all to what once went on upstairs – the fact that it's one of France's foremost spa resorts colours everything you see here. The population is largely elderly, genteel and rich, and swells severalfold in summer; they come here to drink the water, wallow in it, inhale its steam or be sprayed with it, and the town is almost entirely devoted to catering for them.

All of which should make this a place to avoid. Yet it's hard to dislike. There's a real fin-de-siècle charm about the town, and a curious fascination in its continuing function. Vichy revolves around the **Parc des Sources**, a stately tree-shaded park that takes up most of its centre. At its north end stands the **Palais**, or *Hall*, an enormous iron-framed greenhouse in which people sit around and chat or read newspapers, while from a large tiled stand in the middle the various waters emerge from their spouts. The *curistes* line up to get their prescribed cupful, and for a small fee you can join them. The *Celestin* is the only one of the springs that is bottled and widely drunk – if you're into taste experience, try the remaining five. They are progressively more foul and sulphurous, with the *source de l'Hôpital*, which has its own circular building at the far end of the park, an almost unbelievably nasty creation. Each of the springs is prescribed for a different ailment and the tradition is, conveniently enough for the local hotel and tourist business, that apart from the *Celestin* they must all be drunk on the spot to be efficacious: a dubious but effective way of drawing in the crowds.

Although all the springs technically belong to the nation, and treatment is partially funded by the state, they are in fact run privately for profit by the *Compagnie Fermière*, first created in the 19C to prepare for a trip by the startlingly reactionary Napoleon III. The Compagnie have a monopoly not only on selling the waters; but also run the casino and numerous hotels, including Vichy's grandest, the *Pavillion Sevigné*. Even the chairs conveniently dotted about the Parc des Sources belong to the Compagnie. And Vichy never fails to make money: there are over 200 hotels in town – one reason why it was chosen for the wartime government. Marshal Pétain's own offices were at the *Pavillion*, the Gestapo had their HQ at the *Hôtel Portugal*. There is absolutely nothing to commemorate either.

After the waters, Vichy's curiosities are limited. There is pleasant wooded riverside in parc d'Allier, created again for Napoleon III. And, not far from here, the old town boasts the strange Église de St-Blaise, actually two churches in one, with a 1930s Baroque number built onto the original Romanesque – an effect which sounds hideous but is rather imaginative. Inside, another Auvergne Black Virgin, *Notre-Dame des Malades*, stands surrounded by plaques of grateful cure from those who stacked their odds both with her and the sulphur.

As for nightlife, Vichy, despite the *curistes*, can be surprisingly active. The area to make for, full of cafés and brasseries, is around the junction of rue Clemenceau, rue de Pans, rue Lucas and rue Jean-Jaurès, a corner known locally as *les quatre chemins*. Most of the places here serve cheap meals and snacks (*Vichysoisse*, inevitably, is on offer) and they're the obvious place to drink. If you want to move on from here, *Greenfields* – despite the name – is generally most animated of the discos.

Inexpensive and adequate hotels are to be found, near the **gare SNCF**, along av des Celestins, or there's a **youth hostel** – invariably empty – across the river in rue du Stade. Local buses all stop at the station, the **gare routière** is on the corner of rue Doumier and rue Jardet, by the central place Charles de Gaulle.

SOUTH TO LE PUY

South from Vichy, the N106/D906 makes slow progress through green mountain country. **THIERS**, on the banks of the fast, twisting Durolle river is a pleasant surprise, its steep streets hiding some lovely 15C timbered houses and a couple of interesting Romanesque churches, as well as stupendous views over the surrounding mountains. Thiers is noted, in France at least, for its cutlery, and scores of shops sell fine quality knives and other implements. Should you fancy a stop, **accommodation** is limited, but there's a **campsite** at nearby LE BREUIL.

Climbing higher, the road winds on to **LA CHAISE DIEU**, a hill village dominated by the sturdy square towers of an impressive medieval **abbey church,** one of the finest monastic buildings in the country and home to an eerily unfinished fresco of the *Dance of Death*, which shows the shadowy figures of Death plucking delicately at the coarse plump bodies of the living, who determinedly affect not to notice. 'It is yourself', says the I5C text below – as indeed it might have been in that age of the Black Death and Hundred Years War. Nearby, in place de l'Echo, the **Salle de l'Echo** is another product of the risk of contagion, if not from plague then from leprosy, for in this room, once used to take confession from the sick and dying, two people can turn their backs on each other and stand in opposite corners and have a perfectly audible conversation just by whispering. The **SI** is to the right of the church in the central place de la Mairie, and a couple of **two-star hotels** and a **campsite** form a feasible chance of a bed for the night if there's a possibility of arriving late in Le Puy.

An alternative way down to Le Puy is to take the main N09 and N102 from Clermont-Ferrand, a quicker but much less spectacular route.

ISSOIRE is the only place of any note you pass, a small, rather drab industrial town, clasped into a tight centre within a wide circle of boulevards. A stronghold of Protestantism, it was decimated during the 17C Wars of Religion, and a pillar erected in its place with the simple inscription *Ici fut Issoire* (Here was Issoire). Just about the only thing to survive was the church – **St-Austremont** – Romanesque again, with marvellously carved capitals and a beautiful crypt. Otherwise there's not a great deal to see: Issoire is a popular spot for a stopover, but its hotels are not as cheap as they might be.

ST-ÉTIENNE, over to the east, is another possible approach to Le Puy, and offers one extremely good reason for an (albeit passing) visit in its own right. This is the **Palais des Arts** at 8 place Louis Comte, an unexpected mine of contemporary art, not least a comprehensive group of work by symbolist artists – Meunier and Maurin among them – and a good modern American section, in which Andy Warhol and Frank Stella figure highly. Look out, too, for the creations of Rodin, Matisse, Léger and Ernst, and rooms given over entirely to recent French art, all excitingly and imaginatively laid out.

It would be a shame, though, if you were forced to stay here, *La ville ou l'on fabrique de Tout* (the town that makes everything), St-Etienne is otherwise unrelievedly industrial, a major armaments centre, and enclosed for miles around by grim mineworkings, factory chimneys and warehouses. Only one thing redeems it for a visitor (and probably for most residents too) and that's the football team, *les Verts*, whose stickers you see on car windows all over the country. The centre, if you make your way in, is bland and characterless; the mood one of decline, with the recent closure of coalfields. For the committed, or unfortunate, **bus 10** runs into the centre of town (SI on the corner of place Jean-Jaurès) from the **railway station**. Cheapest **hotel** around is the *Splendid* (16 rue de Théâtre) near place du Peuple.

LE-PUY-EN-VELAY

A strange town in a strange setting, **LE-PUY-EN-VELAY** litters across a broad basin in the mountains, a muddle of red roofs barbed with tall poles of volcanic rock. Capital of the Haute Loire, it isn't easy to get to – from Clermont or Nîmes you have to change trains at St-Georges d'Aurac – but well repays the effort. In medieval times it was the assembly point for **St-Jacques pilgrims*** coming from the east of France and Germany and amid the cobbled streets of the old town are some of the finest endowed **churches** in the land. In addition to which there is the pure weirdness attraction of the countryside hereabout.

---

*The clearly waymarked GR65 follows their route all the way from here to ST-JEAN-PIED-DE-PORT in the Basque country (see p. 259) and over the frontier into Spain.

Arriving by bus or train you'll find yourself on place M. Leclerc, 10mins walk from **place de Breuil**, focus of the new town, and within easy striking distance of some reasonably-priced **hotels**. Most are in the new town: *Hôtel La Verveine*, place Cadelade, has musical plumbing, a good restaurant and the best prices. Other possibilities include *Le Progrès*, in the same square, and *des Cordeliers* – a little more expensive but excellent value, hidden in its own courtyard down rue des Cordeliers, off rue Portail d'Avignon. There are two **campsites**: *Bouthezard* (three-star), 30mins from the station along chemin de Roderie, and *de Causans* (one-star) in bd Pte-Betrand; and there are **student foyers** in Faubourg St-Jean, at rue du Consulat (from place du Martouret: rue Courrerie, rue Pannesac and turn right) and in Roche-Arnaud, 20mins from the *gare* (left out of the station, left again before the park into rue Rousseau, across rue Farigade to rue Lavastre, into rue Reynaud and it's on the left). For information, the **SI** is in a large building between place Breuil and place Michelet, and has a **summer annexe** in rue des Tables near the cathedral.

Focussing the **old town**, and reached over the steep sequence of streets and steps, that terrace the town's *puy* foundation, the **Cathedral** is almost Byzantine in style, striped with alternate layers of light and dark stone and capped with a line of small cupolas. Oddly enough, you enter from below, the nave-level reached by clambering up yet more steps; on the way take a look at the *Fever Stone*, a curative shrine, named through the miracle of a woman's deliverance – restored to health having lain down upon it to die. Patchy gold frescoes pull you inside the church – eye-achingly dark and gloomy through the volcanic rock of which it's built – and towards the city's particular *Black Virgin*, copy of a revered original burnt during the Revolution, and still taken out, dusted down and paraded through the town every 15 August – Assumption day. Other, lesser treasures are displayed, at the back of the church in the sacristy, beyond which is the entrance to the cloister, 12C, disarmingly beautiful, and patterned with the same stripes as the cathedral façade surrounding church buildings here – with some splendid 19C stone mansions – form a small, independent *Ville Sainte*.

The cathedral is simply one of several strange and unique sights in this town, most of them stacked on suitably wearying heights. At the summit of all – visible from any street you might find yourself in – is the giant crimson statue of **Notre-Dame-de-France**, a fabulous monster fashioned from the metal of guns captured in the Crimean war.

Precarious on the summit of the other, even steeper, and pointed *puy*, the Rocher d'Aiguilhe, is the church of **St-Michel-d'Aiguilhe** (9–dusk), an 11C structure that seems to grow out of the rock itself. It's a tough assent but one you should definitely make – a quirky little building decorated with mosaic, arabesques and trefoil arches, its bizarre shape forced to follow that of the available flat ground.

Back down below, lacemakers – a traditional, now phoney industry – do a fine trade, doilies and lace shawls hanging enticingly outside shops for tourists. But it's surface only; deeper into Le Puy's maze of narrow streets the old lanes are uncluttered and wonderful. In the **new part of town**, beyond the squat **Tour Pannesac**, place de Breuil joins place Michelet and forms a sociable hub, with spacious public gardens. Busy bd Maréchal Fayolle runs on into place Cadelade, where lies another of Le Puy's crazier aspects: the extraordinary bulbous tower of the **Pages Verveine distillery**. The *verveine* (verbena) plant is normally used to make *tisane* (herb tea), but in this region produces a powerful digestive liqueur instead. Other local specialities are fat sausages, called *Jésus*, and green lentils, invariably cooked in pork fat or served with pork like most Haute Loire dishes; the *Salad auvergnat*, which features on most menus, is a substantial dish of green lentils cooked in lard, with chunks of ham, egg, potatoes and mayonnaise.

The least expensive **meals** in Le Puy are at the *self-service restaurant* in the same building as the SI. More interesting bars and restaurants are sprinkled around places Breuil and Michelet. *Le Michelet*, a popular piano bar, can be lively, and in the old town, *Le Bistrot*, on place de le Halle, has live music and a connoisseur's choice of beers. Produce **markets** take place on Wednesdays and Saturdays in place du Martouret, with a Saturday **fleamarket** in place du Clauzel.

THE PARC DES VOLCANS AND SOUTHERN MASSIF

Much of Western Auvergne falls within the 1,400 square mile **Parc Naturel Régional des Volcans d'Auvergne** – the Auvergne Volcano park – a wild country of peaks, gorges and lakes serrated by a phenomenal concentration of *puys*, most of them fragments of gigantic primeval volcanoes that have been weathered away. The youngest, 4,000 years old, are the **Monts Dômes** west of Clermont-Ferrand, where there were 112 small volcanoes; the **Monts Dores** slightly to their south had only three centres of volcanic activity but much more intense, leaving hundreds of jagged projections; while further south the **Cantal mountains** contained, geologists say, one titanic volcano 3,000m high and 60km in circumference, which has left a number of high crests. Within all this are scattered very traditional villages, a stylish handful of spa-towns – **Le Mont Dore** and **La Bourboule**, most notably – and a growing number of winter sports resorts. GR footpaths cross some of the most interesting and difficult terrain, for information on them or *gîtes d'étapes* and skiing in the park area, contact the *Centre d'Information* at 28 rue St-Espirt in Clermont-Ferrand.

Further south the cold hard *causses* – plateaux – of the **southern Massif**, the quiet, wild hills of **the Cévennes** and, to the east, the mountainous **Ardèche** are all arguably parts of the southern province of Languedoc, but have an identity shaped by the mountains and quite different from that of the Mediterranean provinces.

WEST FROM CLERMONT: LE MONT DORE AND AROUND

Leaving Clermont to the west, lush pastures is interspersed with abrupt irruptions of *puys*, green hills plunging down to the village of **ORCIVAL**, a pretty but over-touristed little place that harbours a stunning 12C basilica. The church, its Romanesque exterior topped with a spired octagonal tower and fanned with tiny chapels is a treat, but inside it's monstrous – Gregorian musak trying to impose an atmosphere of piety on the day-trippers, and with a choir sectioned off by an electronic alarm system. The alarm is to protect – inevitably – a *Black Virgin*, this time enamelled and gilded, the object of pilgrimage since before the 6C and still carried through the streets on Ascension day. In the Middle Ages she was known as 'Our Lady of Iron and Chains', and was worshipped by former convicts who had survived imprisonment. Ironic that today it is she who is confined in high security.

Built along the banks of the young and shallow Dordogne, here hardly more than a trickle, **LE MONT DORE** is an old-established spa resort in the best tradition – good food and drink, walks in pleasant countryside and a hopefully bearable cure at the baths for some not-too-serious ailment. Altogether a wholesome sort of place with a civilised edge. The **Établissement Thermal** stands right in the town centre, and early every morning *curistes*, easily identifiable by tight-drawn scarves and overcoats, stream into the building, self-proclaimed 'world centre for the treatment of asthma'. Walkers frequent the town too, using it as a base for hikes out to the **Puy de Sancy** – 15km away and, at 1,885m, Auvergne's rooftop.

The town is brimming with *hotels*, so if you're planning on staying, there should be no problem finding a room – try *Le Ruche* or *Le Moulin*. **Campsites**, too, are in good supply – the municipal *Les Crouzets* opposite the railway station is the nearest – and there's a big and comfortable **youth hostel** 3km out on Route de Saucy. Ask at the **SI** on the corner of av Leclerc for a copy of *Le Semaine au Mont Dore*, and also for their pamphlet on walks and drives in the area.

Seven km down the road, an easy hitch, is **LA BOURBOULE**. Known as the sister to Le Mont Dore it is another traditional spa – the 'capital of allergies', this one – but with a more open feel, and, because of its lower altitude, weather a degree or two warmer. The big casino, the domed Grandes Thermes baths, and several other turn-of-the-century buildings which used to house privately-run baths, are ornate, gilded and wonderfully vulgar, and have a certain faded, off-season look to them – as does the whole town.

Behind the townhall, the wooded **Parc Fenestre** turns out to be surprisingly large, a téléphérique taking you right up to **Plateau de Charlannes**, 1,300m, where it's possible to walk in the woods or ski in winter. All in all, it's a cool, tranquil place to unwind: as the SI's leaflet says, 'You will be able to put your vital node to rest in La Bourboule'. The SI (in the town hall on place de la République) also sell a booklet of local walks. Hotels, as at Le Mont Dore, are plentiful but none especially cheap – av Guéneau de Mussy has some likely one-stars – but there's a good selection of **campsites** 4km away, eg. at Murat le Quaire, and along the Le Mont Dore road.

Wintertime, both Le Mont Dore and La Bourboule double as ski-resorts – centres of a **ski-de-fond** area of well-worked-out circular pistes, some over 20km in length. Skiable paths connect La Bourboule to other ski-villages in the locality – SANCY, BESSE, CHASTREIX and PICHER-ANDE – and conventional downhill skiing is possible too, on the nearby Puy de Saucy

SOUTH: AURILLAC AND THE CANTAL

Capital of the Cantal region, **AURILLAC** is a pleasant provincial centre – busy and modern. While not worth a special journey for itself, it forms the best springboard for jaunts into the extraordinarily beautiful mountain country around.

Arrive by train and it's a 15min walk into the centre, the vigorous **place du Square**, where you'll find the **SI** – which book hotel rooms and dispense maps, including the invaluable *IGN Monts du Cantal*. Plenty of hotels have **cheap rooms and meals** – *Hôtel Damiens*, 20 rue des Carmes, *Hôtel du Palais*, 2 rue Beauclaire and *Hôtel de Paris*, next to the station, are three good ones – and there's a municipal **campsite** just outside the town centre on av Veyre. A further option is the *Foyer des Jeunes Travailleurs* on rue Garric. **Bikes** are on hire at *Malgouzou*, 22 rue Guy-de-Veyre, and **buses** leave daily from the main square for villages on the road to St-Flour and Conques.

Aurillac itself you can exhaust fairly quickly, and apart from a couple of small **museums** concealed in the pedestrianised *vieille ville* – and a good one devoted to volcanoes in the Château St-Etienne – there's not a lot to see or do. Wednesdays or Saturdays are the best times to be here, when peasants and farmers flock into town to sell their produce and livestock. The town – and Cantal – is noted for a traditionally rustic cuisine, with dishes like *tripoux*, stuffed sheeps' feet wrapped in pieces of sheeps' stomach, seen on menus from here to St-Flour and down to Chaudee-Aigues on the southern edge of the Cantal. More enticing, perhaps is Cantal cheese – not unlike cheddar, and one of the least expensive and most popular in France.

North and east of Aurillac spread the precipitous tree-clad slopes of **the Cantal**. The Aurillac SI dole out information on the area and can book rooms in hotels and pensions, and the slow but reliable bus and train network provides a way of getting around perfectly in tune with the pace of the region. Forty km north of Aurillac, **SALERS**, prettily walled around a turreted main square but almost impossible to reach without your own wheels, is marred only by its souvenier shops, fleets of tour buses and gangs of wandering visitors. *Hôtel des Ramparts* is a one-star Logis with fairly dear rooms but a cheap three-course menu, and there's a campsite, *Le Mouriol*, open summertime only.

East of here the peak of Puy Mary (1,787m) and the tall cone of Puy Griou (1,694m) rise above the rolling hills. **MURAT**, industrial but attractive nonetheless, 'a clambering little town' Freda White calls it, is one possible base for climbing them; it has a good campsite. Slightly closer in is **LE LIORAN** – a summertime walkers' resort and winter cross-country ski centre – easiest reached by train from Aurillac. Travelling by bus the AURILLAC-ST-FLOUR line takes you through Murat and numerous other mountain villages, most with a modest hotel or two and *camping à la ferme*, and all tempting places to stop over a while. **THIÉZAC**, one of the most enticing, has a **campsite**; and both bus and train go to **VIC-SUR-CÈRE** – towny and unpretentious, with some interesting mansions, good walking up into the nearby hills, a handful of **hotels** and restaurants and again a **campsite**.

Beyond USSEL the *puys* thin out and the country becomes high and flat all the way to **ST-FLOUR**, with an inviting old centre, worth the long haul from the gare SNCF (best catch a bus up to Allée Pompidou, on the old city's western fringe). There are numerous hotels, dormitory **beds** and a youth hostel, **La Sanfloraine**, av de Besserette, and two **campsites**, one in the upper town, one down the hill near the station.

Focal point of the old city is the **place d'Armes**, busied by a market on Saturday mornings and dominated by a severe 14C **Cathedral**, built of dull grey rock, squared-off in shape, and outside at least, extremely plain. At first glance the interior seems equally austere. But it's high and beautifully vaulted with bare stone blocks, with slight traces of frescoes and some elaborate woodcarving – most prominently, a 15C figure of a black Christ on the cross. Behind the cathedral expansive vistas take in the lower town and its two rivers. Back in place d'Armes, you'll find a **museum** of local life and the **SI**.

Pushing **on south**, you reach a district in which the *Maquis* were very active: 15,000 Resistance fighters operated in this immediate locality, often having full-scale shoot-outs with the German army; a **monument** near the junction of the D4 and N9 marks the site of a battle that left a thousand *Maquis* dead. Further on, the road winds below the **Garabit Viaduct,** on an extraordinarily delicate railway bridge of steel girders, completed in 1884 by Eiffel.

LARZAC AND THE *CAUSSES*

High plateaux, bleak, windswept and sparsely populated with primitive villages, the **Causses** of the southern Massif – **Larzac, Noir, Méjean** and **Sauveterre** – are rugged, independent countryside. All four are riddled with strange caves, rock formations, grottoes and underground tunnels, in between deep and narrow gorges: between Larzac and Causse Noir cuts the Vallée de la Dourbie; between the Noir and Méjean tears the Gorges de la Jonte; and gashed between Méjean and Sauveterre lies the most spectacular valley of all, the Gorges du Tarn.

Recently, the **CAUSSE DU LARZAC** hit the headlines over sustained political resistance to the high-profile presence of the French military here. Originally there was a small military camp at a village called **LA CAVALERIE,** long tolerated for the cash its soldiers brought in. But in the early 1970s the army decided to expand the place vastly and use it as a permanent strategic base. The result was explosive. A federation was formed – **Paysans du Larzac** – which gave name (and impetus) to the local **separatist movement**; successful acts of sabotage were committed, and three vast peace festivals held here – in 1981, 1983 and again in 1985. The army has now moved out and Mitterrand, supposedly, has cancelled plans here but you will find Larzac graffiti from here to Lyon, a shorthand for opposition to the army, the state, and Parisian central government, and in favour of self-determination and the independence of the South.

The best way to immerse yourself in the empty, sometimes eery atmosphere of Larzac is to walk – **GRs 7, 71** and **74** cross the plateau – though it's advisable not to attempt it without a topo-guide. I tried it once and got hopelessly lost. The plateau's best-known village, **ROQUEFORT-SUR-SOULZON**, is home to Roquefort cheese, one of the most revered cheeses in France, sharp and creamy, blue-streaked and made from local ewes' milk. Its delicate maturity can only be reached in the caves here, and efforts to reproduce the conditions artifically elsewhere have met with complete failure. The N9 (easy hitching) cuts clear across the plain from here, through LA CAVALERIE to L'HOSPITALET DU LARZAC, a name recalling the days when Larzac was ruled by the Knights Templar and later the Knights Hospitaller. Further on, **LA COUVERTOIRADE** lies 5km off the main road, an unrestored old Templar city within forbidding fortifications, and on the face of things little changed since the Middle Ages – until, that is, you get asked for money just to enter the place. South again is **LE CAYLAR**, a simple town in a wild rocky setting, and the **Pas de l'Escalette** (Ladder Pass), the dramatic twisting descent from Larzac to the Languedoc plain. The name comes from a time when the only way on to Larzac using this route was to climb ladders fixed to the 300m high cliff-face.

At the foot of Causse Noir and Larzac, sharp by the meting of the Tarn and Dourbie, **MILLAU** is beautifully situated no matter how you approach it – a vivacious town, quite large, with broad streets arcaded by the branches of pollarded *platanes*. There's not much to see, apart from the unusual octagonal belfry and fountain in the central square, but it has a good southern feel to it, and makes for a wise overnight stop. The town has loads of **hotels**, though no amazing bargains, and two **campsites** just across the pont de Cureplat. There's an **SI** on the corner of av Merle, and both **bus** and **train station** are a few hundred yards from the town centre on bd de la République.

A narrow difficult road, incongruously jammed with crawling traffic, follows the **Gorges du Tarn** all the way along its course – a dramatic ride, and at its most spectacular between LE ROZIER and **STE-ENIMIE**. The latter is a well-placed, much restored little town, full of cafés and places to rent bikes, or canoes for trips on the river. From here the Tarn road continues to **FLORAC** and the Cévennes, while a minor route scurries up on to the **Causse de Sauveterre**, through the desolate village of SAUVETERRE to MENDE, capital of the Lozère, lounging comfortably in the valley of the Lot.

The old and twisting streets of **MENDE** surround an immense overbearing **Cathedral**, destroyed by Huguenots during the religious wars but conscientiously restored by a bishop of the town in 1600. Inside it is dark and powerful, the air heavy with the lingering odour of incense; when your eyesight adjusts, take a look at the Aubusson tapestries, impressively carved choirstalls and stained glass. Just outside, in the dense network of medieval streets and Renaissance houses, is a **municipal museum**, worth half an hour for its local and pre-history collections. **Foodwise**, Mende is blessed with an unusual number of good *pâtisseries* and *charcuteries*, but there isn't too much cheap **accommodation**. *Hôtel Commerce*, bd Bourzillion, and the two-star *Hôtel Paris*, bd Soubeyran, have a few moderately priced rooms; otherwise fall back on the **campsites**, one on either side of town on the N88. **Buses** leave from place du Foirail for

Cévennes villages, and FLORAC, LE PUY and RODEZ; the **gare SNCF** is on the northern edge of town, across the pont Berlière, and also has connections with villages in the Cévennes.

THE CÉVENNES – STEVENSON'S WALK

South-east brink of the Massif Central, the hills of **the Cévennes** don't achieve the same kind of high altitudes and wild landscapes as the rest of the region. Instead, they're gently forested with chestnut and pine, and green with fields of pasture and scrub, cut through with fast-flowing streams banked by deciduous woods. Historically a Protestant area, the people here had a tough time of it during the religious wars, with some of the country's most notorious Catholic repression – at its worst during the 18C Camisard war.

At the end of a fine September in 1878, the Scottish writer **Robert Louis Stevenson**, then aged 28, set off from Le Monastier, near Le Puy, on a trek into the Cévennes. To carry his enormous amount of luggage he purchased – for 65F and a glass of brandy – a donkey whom he immediately named, because of her modest size, Modestine; and the story of their walk together became his book *Travels with a Donkey*.

It was no accident that Stevenson chose this area for his hike: he had

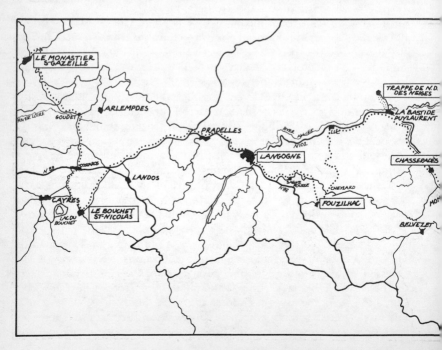

an interest in the Camisards, mystical peasant fighters whom he likened to the Scottish Covenanters, and he began the walk at Le Monastier because Velay, the country around Le Puy, figured so much in the work of George Sand, one of his favourite writers.

At the end of a wet September, a century on, I retraced Stevenson's steps, starting as he did at **LE MONASTIER-SUR-GAZEILLE**, a bright little town in the hills of Haute Loire, with playing fountains, an interesting **abbey church** and a couple of modest **hotels**. In Stevenson's day it had fifty bars; now it has just ten, one of them called *Le Stevenson*. The SI too houses a **Musée Stevenson**, with an odd concoction of items relating to the writer's walk. There's surprising interest in the walk and the book here – and through the region.

The travels began along by the river, Stevenson and Modestine slogging uphill on the far bank to **ST-MARTIN DE FUGÈRES**, where when they passed, the church was full to overflowing. Not enough people live in this farmyard village now even to half-fill it. The road continues beside the deep valley of the young river Loire down to **GOUDET**, pretty with terraced gardens, and a conical, coloured church steeple. The *Café de la Valette*, where Stevenson rested, has recently closed, but there's another café with a quiet garden near the stream.

At **USSEL**, where Modestine ditched her cargo in the dust, much to

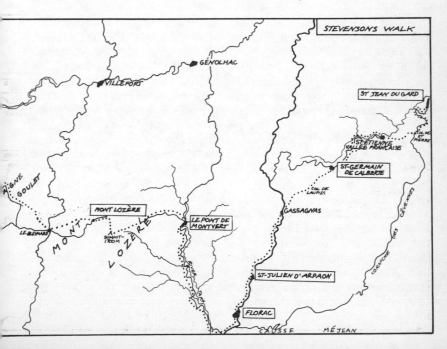

the amusement of the locals, Stevenson sensibly decided to shed some of his fabulously superfluous luggage. Beyond COSTAROS, on the busy N88, is a puzzling tangle of lanes without clear signposting. He got lost here, and you may do, too, trying to follow what are now D49, D311 and D31 towards **LE BOUCHET ST NICHOLAS**, base for the first night. The inn Stevenson used has since closed ('it made no money', I was told), and the only accommodation in Le Bouchet now is a bare room with old mattresses provided for summer walkers. If you don't fancy it, local farmers sometimes let out **rooms** for the night for a small fee – ask around in the village. To PRADELLES (via CHARBONNIER on D53) is a wearisome walk – perhaps best hitched with some 13km of it along the narrow edge of the N88. It was a major highway in Stevenson's day too, but the only traffic he met was on foot. **PRADELLES**, where he wolfed down lunch and was on his way 'before ¾ of an hour', is a medieval town, little modernised, where the road crosses the border between Haute Loire and Lozère – or as they used to be called Velay and Gévaudan – and continues through to **LANGOGNE**, a large modern town where he spent the next night. Gévaudan achieved tremendous notoriety during the 1760s, when the so-called Bête de Gévaudan roamed the area. Thought by some to be a wolf, by others a bear, this mysterious creature attacked, killed and half-devoured over fifty locals, all women and children.

Beyond LANGOGNE, 7km uphill, a tiny left turn leads to SAGNE-ROUSSE, where Stevenson, aiming for **CHEYLARD-L'EVÊQUE**, got lost, found himself in Fouzilhic and then Fouzilhac, and finally camped out in his furlined sleeping bag. Cheylard, 'a few broken ends of village upon a rattling river', hasn't changed much in 100 years, and is still home to an incomprehensible Occitan dialect. A steep track leads up to a cool plateau – bare and bleak in the book, 'like the worst of the Scottish highlands, only worse', but now green and wooded – and after some 10km descends to **LUC** in the Allier valley, where on the hillside gleams a giant white statue of the Madonna, newly erected as Stevenson passed (figures on the railings confirm the date – 1878). In Luc he found a 'clean and large inn', easy enough today in season – though beware that all the hotels close for winter and there are no other lodgings.

Next along, **LA BASTIDE PUYLAURENT** is quite a resort, with two **hotels**, **restaurants**, and a **railway station** with train connections to Paris, Alès and Nîmes. Stevenson stayed at the Trappist monastery of **Notre Dame des Neiges**, 4km away and now a routine tourist drop that has abandoned all vows of silence and is unlikely to offer any accommodation. Stevenson also spent an unpleasant night in a humble inn at CHASSERADÈS, though there's no trace of that now and the existing hotel again closes out of season, the only alternative accommodation is a miserable little *gîte d'étape*, 4km further on.

From here **GR74** climbs a stony track to the summit of **Montagne du Goulet** (1,413m), and down again to **LE BLEYMARD**, a small country town from which an old drove road, now the **GR7**, heads up Mont Lozère. About 7km up, where our hero slept under the stars, there's a hotel (summer only, once more) and basic *gîte d'étape*. The **Parc National des Cévennes**, a huge conservation area, starts here, ancient stone waymarkers, which Stevenson followed, leading across to **PIC DE FINIELS** – at 1,699m the windy zenith of Mont Lozèrre. Here under a clear morning sky the Alpilles are visible to the east, and to the south-east the Mediterranean. A tricky path beside a stream leads down to the tiny hamlet of **FINIELS**, and the slender D20, which follows the pastoral Rieumalet valley, to the genial little town of **PONT DE MONTVERT**, noisy with the foaming Tarn rushing through its centre. A beautiful stone bridge crosses the river to the hotel where Stevenson stopped for lunch: the *Cévennes*, still going strong. At Pont de Montvert the Camisards' holy war against France was sparked by the murder of the tyrannical Abbé du Chayla, local representative of the Catholic authorities, who used to imprison and torture Protestants in the cellars of his riverside house (which can still be seen).

Out of the town the road follows the Tarn, passing the villages of COCURÈS and BÉDOUÈS (Stevenson recalled these in the wrong order) and eventually, after 20km, reaching **FLORAC**, a shady clutch of buildings on the steep river Pecher. The main draw here is an impressive **château**, which houses the information and exhibition centre of the *Parc National des Cévennes*, with details on footpaths, *gîtes*, history and wildlife. Stevenson found a bed in rue Thérond, now the back entrance of the two-star *Grand Hôtel du Parc*, which has a few cheap rooms. The popular *Restaurant des Fleurs* is a good place to eat, and buses connect with Alès, Pont de Montvert, Genolhac and Millau.

ST-JULIEN, another night in the open, is 9km away on the N106, below ruins of a hillside castle. A similar distance beyond is CASSAGNAS, where Stevenson's path left the road, crossing the river and climbing through woods to the **Col de Laupies**. The track is obscure and overgrown now, but still exists. From the top, a rough but clearly-marked Route Forestière descends to **ST-GERMAIN DE CALBERTE**, one of the few Catholic villages in the Cévennes (and burial site of the Abbé du Chayla), where a quiet road runs on to fortified ST-ÉTIENNE and LE MARTINET. From here remnants of an ancient paved highway climb brokenly to the **Col de St-Pierre**, on the Corniche des Cévennes (a popular 'scenic' drive), edging finally down to ST-JEAN DU GARD.

ST-JEAN is a welcoming southern town with ramparts, an old bridge, a Romanesque clock tower, and plenty of low to medium priced **hotels** and **restaurants**. Its motto, in Occitan, is *Al Sourel de la Liberta* – in the sunlight of freedom – and in nearby **MAS SOUBEYRAN**, in the house of a leading Camisard, the **Musée du Desert** gives something of an insight into the Camisards' struggle.

At St-Jean, exhausted, Stevenson ended his walk, sold Modestine for a fraction of her original price, and took a carriage to **ALÈS**, a big, brash place which fancies itself the capital of the Cévennes, though it's not actually in the mountains. It is, however, on the scenic Nîmes-Clermont-Paris train route, and centre of an extensive network of local buses reaching into the Cévennes and north Languedoc.

By stopping here, Stevenson had not crossed the whole of the Cévennes, though he had seen a large chunk of it. West of St-Jean lies the southern part of the range, centred on **Mont Aigoual** (1,567m). If you're planning a hike, useful maps for both areas are IGN 354 – *Parc des Cévennes*, and IGN 265 – *Mont Lozère*.

The Ardèche

Heading east, the gentle hills of the Cévennes steepen into the mountains of **the Ardèche**, a craggy region cloaked with chestnut forests that produce delicious and sought-after marron glacés and purées. It's savagely beautiful here, a popular area for activity holidays, with at its dramatic heart the gorge of the river Ardèche, treacherously fast-flowing at times and which until recently you couldn't see except by canoe, though now a road follows the ravine's rough northern clifftop. Travelling is difficult in the Ardèche – there are few towns or villages and even fewer buses and roads – but if you persevere you'll generally find the rewards more than repay the effort. **Canoes** can be hired at **VALLON-PONT D'ARC**, a favoured tourist centre, though if you decide to do this bear in mind that the river froths with dangerous rapids, surges with an unpredictable current and in autumn rises alarmingly fast (sometimes over 20ft in a few hours).

TRAVEL DETAILS

Trains

From Clermont-Ferrand 4 daily to Paris (4hrs) via Riom (12mins), Vichy (38mins), and St-Germaine des Fosses (46mins); sleeper trains on this line at night; 11 daily just as far as St-Germaine, where can change for Roanne (50mins) and Lyon (2hrs10); 3–6 daily to St-Étienne (2hrs40) via Thiers; some night trains go to Nîmes (6¼hrs); in daytime, 2–3 daily to Nîmes (4hrs50) and Marseille (6hrs), stopping at all stations including St-Georges d'Aurac, where change for Le Puy (2hrs); 4 daily to Royat (6mins), Laqueille (1hr9), La Bour-boule (1hr20), Le Mont Dore (1hr30); 4 others daily just to Laqueille, where connections for trains into the Dordogne; 4–5 daily to Toulouse (6hrs) via Issoire (27mins), Arvant (48mins), Neussargues (1hr33), Le Lioran (1hr57), Vic-sur-Cère (2hrs14), Aurillac (2hrs30); some involve changing at Neussargues; also change there for St Flour, Le Monastier (change for Mende), Millau, and into Languedoc.
From Riom 4 daily to Paris via Vichy (26mins); very frequent to Clermont-Ferrand (12mins).
From Vichy some night trains through

to Nîmes (7hrs); 1 or 2 daytime stopping trains to Nîmes (5½hrs); 4 daily to Paris; frequent to Clermont-Ferrand (38mins).

From Le Puy 3–4 daily to St-Étienne (1¾hrs) and Lyon (3½hrs); sporadic to St-Georges d'Aurac where change for Clermont-Ferrand (2hrs) or Nîmes (4hrs).

From St-Étienne 2 early morning trains daily to St-Germaine des Fosses (3hrs); 3 TGVs daily to Lyon (45mins) and Paris (2hrs50); 3–6 daily to Clermont-Ferrand (2hrs40).

From Aurillac 4–5 daily to Vic-sur-Cère (15mins), Le Lioran (½hr), Neussargues (1hr), Arvant (1¾hrs), Issoire (2hrs), Clermont-Ferrand (2½hrs); 4–5 daily to Toulouse (4½hrs).

From St-Flour 2–3 daily on line to Neussargues, Le Monastier (change for Mende), Millau, and on to Béziers.

Buses (slow!)

From Clermont-Ferrand daily departures to St-Étienne, Volvic, Riom, Chatelguyon, Le Puy, Vichy.

From Le Puy daily SNCF bus to Chaise-Dieu, Thiers, Clermont (estimated 4hrs); daily to local villages, including Le Monastier-sur-Gazeille.

Chapter eleven
BURGUNDY

Peaceful, rural and old-fashioned, **Burgundy** is one of the most prosperous regions of modern France. For centuries its powerful dukes remained independent of the French crown, even siding with the English in the Hundred Years War. Their power at one stage embraced all of Franche-Comté, Alsace and Lorraine, Belgium, Holland, Picardy and Flanders, and it was only in 1477 when Charles the Bold was killed in battle that the French kings were finally able to rid themselves of this potentially mortal threat. Everywhere there is startling evidence of this former wealth and power, both secular and religious: at **Dijon**, the dukes' capital; the vast abbey of **Vézelay**; or the ruins of the monastery of **Cluny**, whose influence once was second only to the Pope's.

Because of these monastic foundations Burgundy became, with Poitou and Provence, one of the three great **church-building** areas in the Middle Ages. Practically every village has its Romanesque church, especially round Cluny and Paray-le-Monial. It is hard not to believe this had something to do with its own illustrious Roman past, evident in the substantial Roman remains at **Autun**.

There is good **walking country** in the **Morvan Regional Park**, the **Côte d'Or** and round **Mâcon**, **Solutré** and **Charolles** in the south of the region. The **Canal du Nivernais** between Auxerre and Clamecy also makes an interesting, level hike.

Serious wine devotees, of course, head straight for the great Burgundy **vineyards** strung out southwards from Dijon to Mâcon and beyond and harbouring some of the country's most expensive produce. If you're into good drinking, but lack the funds go in late August or early September, when they're touting for harvesters.

THE ROAD TO DIJON

The road is the **Route Nationale 6**, the old route from Paris to the Mediterranean. It may not be as fast, but, passing as it does through towns like **Sens**, **Auxerre** and **Avallon** that have been part of the fabric of France's history for 2,000 years, it is a great deal more interesting than the bland curves of the Autoroute du Sud.

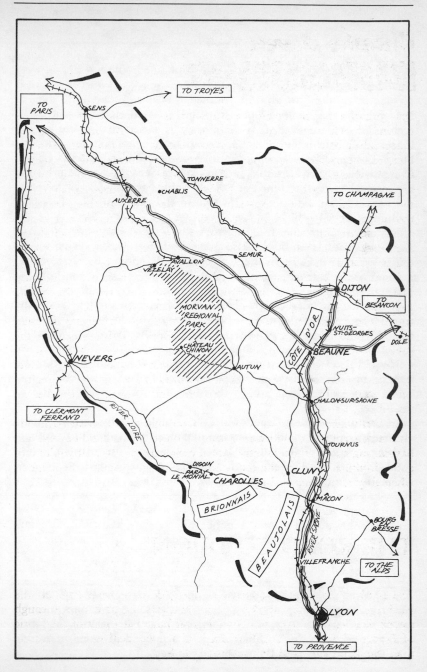

TO PARIS

TO TROYES

SENS

TONNERRE

CHABLIS

AUXERRE

TO CHAMPAGNE

AVALLON

VEZELAY

SEMUR

MORVAN REGIONAL PARK

DIJON

TO BESANCON

NUITS-ST-GEORGES

CÔTE D'OR

DOLE

CHATEAU CHINON

BEAUNE

NEVERS

AUTUN

CHALON-SUR-SAONE

TO CLERMONT FERRAND

RIVER LOIRE

TOURNUS

DIGOIN

PARAY LE MONIAL

CHAROLLES

CLUNY

BRIONNAIS

MÂCON

BOURG EN BRESSE

BEAUJOLAIS

RIVER SAÔNE

VILLEFRANCHE

TO THE ALPS

LYON

TO PROVENCE

SENS

SENS, though never actually part of the Duchy, seems a typically Burgundian town, hard-working and well-fed. Contained within a ring of tree-lined boulevards where the city walls once stood, its ancient centre is dominated by the **Cathedral of St-Étienne**. Begun around 1130 there is still an air of the Romanesque in its solid, squared-off appearance. The architect who completed it, William of Sens, was later asked to rebuild Canterbury Cathedral in England, the link man in this French connection being **Thomas-à-Becket**, who, though ten years under the sod by then, had previously spent several years in exile in Sens. Scenes from his life are represented in the cathedral's oldest **stained glass** (12C) in the north aisle of the choir, and his very own mitre and vestments are on display in the **treasury** (10–12 & 2–5, cl. Tues).

Just to the south is the 13C **Palais Synodal** (guided visits only, 10–12 & 2–5/6; cl. Tues), restored, like so many buildings in this region by the 'purist' Viollet-le-Duc. Its huge vaulted halls, originally designed to accommodate conferences of several hundred priests, now house a museum of religious art.

Facing the cathedral across **place de la République** are fine wood and iron *halles*, where a **market** is held all day Monday and Friday and Saturday mornings. The *place* stands plumb in the centre of town where the main streets, **rue de la République** and **Grande Rue**, intersect. Lined with old houses converted into shops now, they are mainly reserved for pedestrians. There are a couple of particularly fine carved timbered houses on the corner of rue Jean-Cousin, the **Maison d'Abraham** and the **Maison du Pilier**.

At the further end of Grande Rue, the road crosses two broad arms of the **river Yonne**, with houseboats moored at the bank, and leads straight ahead to the **gare SNCF**, about 10mins' walk from the cathedral. *Hôtel de la Gare* and *Hôtel Chemin de Fer*, both with cheap rooms, are opposite the station entrance. *Hôtel le Vauban*, round the corner in av Vauban, is slightly dearer.

For **eating**, there is a cheap self-service, *Brasserie le Senonais*, at 99 rue de la République and a good crêperie, *Aux 4 Vents*, at 3 rue de Brennus. **Bike hire** from Nibel, rue V Guichard. The **SI** is at 3 bd Jean-Jaurès.

AUXERRE

A pretty old town of narrow lanes and handsome squares **AUXERRE** stands on a hill another 50km up the Yonne. It looks its best seen from the riverside with its churches soaring dramatically above the surrounding rooftops. The most interesting of them is the disused church of **St-Germain** at the opposite end of **rue Cauchois** from the Cathedral. It too shows traces of Romanesque origins, though it has been frequently damaged and rebuilt: the fine belfry spire now standing apart from the rest of the builidng (9–12 & 2–6; cl. Tues). What gives it its special value, however, is the **crypt**, one of the very few surviving examples of **Merovingian** (9C and earlier) architecture in the country. In the innermost part are the earliest extant **frescoes** and the tomb of St-Germanus/St-Germain, to whom so many French churches are dedicated.

With its three richly decorated porches (13C) and horizontal bands of carved gables, the **Cathedral** west front is still very attractive despite the loss of one of the flanking towers. Inside, the **choir** is a beautiful specimen of early Gothic. In sunlight the walls are washed with colour filtered through the great rose windows of the transepts. Pigeons and sparrows trapped in the cool interior wing their way about with none of the frantic flapping of creatures caught in a confined space. There has been a church on this site since about 400AD, though nothing visible survives earlier than the five-aisled crypt of the early 11C, again with substantial fragments of fresco still in place.

Rue Fourier leads from the Cathedral square to place **du Marché** and off left to the Hôtel de Ville and the old city gateway known as the **Tour de l'Horloge** with its coloured clock-face (15C).

The **SI** is down by the river at 2 quai de la République by the footbridge. There is a **Bureau d'Informations Jeunesses** at 70 rue du Pont with information on travel and leisure activities. The cheapest accommodation is in *foyers* for women at 16 bd Vaulabelle, men at 16 rue de la Résistance. Among **hotels**, you could try *Hôtel de la Porte de Paris*, 5 rue St-Germain and *Hôtel St-Martin*, 9 rue Germain-Benard. There is a **campsite** on route de Vaux, open from April to October. Finding somewhere to **eat** is easy, as there are numerous reasonably-priced restaurants as well as a self-service, the *Novéco* at 9 place Charles-Surugue.

Around Auxerre

A dozen or so kilometres to the east is the sleepy old town of **CHABLIS** on the banks of the river Serein: the home of the great **white wine** that bears its name. Throughout its meandering back streets discreet notices are pinned to doorways and garages proclaiming the owner a producer, with wine for tasting and buying. If you are on the lookout for a bottle, go for the ones with an *appellation*. *Grand Cru* is the best and *Chablis Premier Cru* the next in line. **Places to stay** are few and pricey and you won't find a bargain restaurant either.

Another 17km bring you to the cheerful but less touristy town of **TONNERRE** on the reedy **Canal de Bourgogne** and the river Armançon. Its oddest scion was the Chevalier d'Eon who spent a mysterious career as a transvestite spy in the 18C. Its most notable building in the 13C **hospital** on the central **rue de l'Hôpital**, a vast and cheerless edifice

founded by Marguerite de Bourgogne, queen of Sicily (10–11.30 &
2–5.30, June-Sept; cl. Tues). Across the square is the **SI**, open only from
April to September (cl. Tues). The *Hôtel du Centre*, also on rue de
l'Hôpital, is the cheapest place to stay – with a reasonable **restaurant**
too. There's a **campsite** between the canal and the river, reached via av
Aristide Briand. **Bike hire** from the **gare SNCF**.

Some 50km further west the **GR2 footpath**, which follows the Seine
all the way from Le Havre, passes through **CHÂTILLON-sur-SEINE** on
its way to the **source** of the river at Baigneux-les-Juifs a little further
south. In Châtillon itself there is a very pretty church at **St-Vorles** from
about 1,000AD with an unusual portico attached to its west front, and
in the small museum are displayed the fabulous **gold finds** from 6C Gallic
tombs at nearby VIX, only discovered in 1953.

AVALLON

AVALLON stands high on a spur above the wooded valley of the little
river Cousin, looking out over the mountainous and sparsely populated
country of the Morvan regional park. It is a small and ancient town of
cobbled streets and plain stone façades, bisected by a sleepy high street,
Grande Rue Aristide Briand. Under the straddling arch of the **Tour de
l'Horloge**, whose spire dominates the town, you come to the church of
St-Lazare, on whose battered Romanesque **façade** (12C) you can still
decipher the elegant carvings of signs of the zodiac, angels and old men
of the Apocalypse. It is dark inside for the nave stands below the level
of the street. Almost opposite, in a house of the 15C, is the SI with an
uninteresting municipal museum behind it. At its further end, **Grand Rue**
passes through the town walls to **Promenade de la Petite Porte**, with
precipitous views across the plunging valley of the Cousin. You can **walk**
from here round the outside of the walls.

Commercial activity today is centred in the 'new' town, with several
broad roads and tree-lined squares. From the **parc des Chaumes** across
the valley (2km by road or a steep climb by path) there's a great **view**
back to the old town, snug within its walls, with cultivated terraces
descending the slope beneath them.

Accommodation in Avallon is generally not cheap, but there are some
simple hotels with inexpensive rooms in **rue de Lyon** and **rue de Paris**.
More comfortable and still with reasonable prices are *Hôtel du Parc*, 3
place de la Gare near the station, and *Au Bon Accueil*, 4 rue de l'Hôpital.
The **Camping Municipal** is 2km out of town along the Route de Lormes,
and there is *camping à la ferme* in the valley of the Cousin. You can **eat**
cheaply and well at *Cheval Blanc*, 55 rue de Lyon and there are other
cheap places in Grande Rue. **Bike hire** from the **gare SNCF**, a few
minutes' walk from the centre, or in rue de Paris by the Renault garage.

If you can get a reliable machine, **cycling** would be the best way of covering the 15km to VÉZELAY (see p. 346) and a bike would also enable you to explore the **Cousin riverside**. A quiet winding road follows the river along the foot of a rocky, wooded escarpment, past watermills-turned-hotel, whose discreet charms cater for the well-heeled bourgeoisie. There is, however, an inexpensive restaurant in the *Hôtel Soleil d'Or* at PONTAUBERT.

East of Avallon **SEMUR-EN-AUXOIS** is an old fortress town on a rocky hill above a loop of the Armançon river. All roads here lead to **place Notre-Dame**, a handsome square, dominated by the large **13C church** of Notre-Dame, another Viollet-le-Duc restoration. Its elaborate west front has had many of its statues removed and the niches left bare. A tall spire crowns the central octagonal tower. Inside, the stained glass of the first side chapel on the left commemorates American soldiers of the First War – a reminder that the battle-fields were not far away.

Down the street in front of the church and off to the left you come to the four sturdy round towers of Semur's once powerful **castle**, dismantled in 1602 because of its usefulness to enemies of the French Crown. The best view is from **Pont Joly** on the river below. The steep steps of **Escalier du Fourneau** lead down to the bank.

Less specifically, the whole town is full of interesting buildings: there's scarcely a street without something to please the eye. One pleasant over-grown **walk** leads round the fortifications encircling the part of town known as Bourg-Notre-Dame. The **SI** is on the small place Gaveau, at the junction of rues de l'Ancienne Comédie, de la Liberté and Buffon, where the medieval **Porte Sauvigny** and **Porte Guillier** combine to form a single, long, covered gateway.

There is a shortage of cafés in Semur, apart from one or two rather expensive *salons de thé*. **Restaurants** are on the gourmet level and pricey too. The two-star *Hôtel de la Côte d'Or*, opposite the SI, has the cheapest **rooms** and a reasonable menu in the restaurant. *Hôtel des Gourmets*, 4 rue Varenne, has an excellent and similarly priced menu, but more expensive rooms. There's a **campsite** 3km away at Lac du Pont.

Not far away, the privately-owned **abbey of FONTENAY** is a beautiful example of the plainest Cistercian Romanesque. You can reach it on the **GR213** from **Montbard**. You are only permitted a 45min tour (9–12 & 2.30–6.30; not cheap), but the country round about is lovely, and Montbard is easily reached by bus or train.

Just down the road towards the village of LES LAUMES, and marked by a huge statue, is the site of the **battle of ALESIA**, where Vercingetorix and his Gauls were finally defeated by the Romans in 52BC. Had they won, the Asterix books might have followed an entirely different course.

DIJON

DIJON was the capital of the Dukes of Burgundy, its fortunes closely reflecting theirs. By the 15C it had become a leading centre of art, religion and politics and continued to be one, even after Burgundy had lost its independence to Louis XI of France.

You sense its former glories more in the substantial town houses of private citizens than in the former seat of the Dukes of Burgundy, the **Palais des Ducs**. Though extensive in area, the Palais is undistinguished from the outside; indeed it has undergone so many changes, especially in the 17–18C, that the Dukes would scarcely recognise it. Its main ceremonial entrance, set back behind a big courtyard, the Cour d'Honneur, opens on to a broad semi-circular 'square', **place de la Libération**, formerly place Royale. With its buildings in honey-coloured stone recently cleaned and restored, it looks very fine. Like the similar place des Victoires in Paris, it was designed by Jules Hardouin-Mansart in the late 17C.

Most of the Palais still has an administrative function as a townhall and the public cannot go inside. That it is known as the Palais des Ducs at all indicates the importance of tourists and their perceptions. Part of it, however, now houses the **Musée des Beaux-Arts** (10–6; cl. Tues) which gives ample opportunity to wander about inside. Most of the rooms, sumptuously decorated in the styles of the 17 and 18C, are taken up with the museum's collections, reckoned among the richest outside Paris. There are **paintings** representing many different schools and periods, from Titian, Rubens and Schongauer to Monet, Manet and other Impressionists; there is a substantial collection of **Flemish** and **Italian** works and quantities of religious artefacts, ivories and tapestries. One of the most interesting exhibits is a small room devoted to the amazingly intricate woodcarving, doorways and furniture of **Hugues Sambin**, the 16C architect and woodcarver. All his work is signed with his two distinctive insignia, a face wearing a loose neckscarf beneath the chin and the curious shape which he called the *choux bourguignon* or Burgundy cabbage – though it resembles no known vegetable. His work is in evidence throughout the city, especially in the massive doors and in the façades of the aristocratic *hôtels*, which he designed with a cabinet-maker's attention to detail.

On the ground floor is the great vaulted palace **kitchen**, a vast room with a magnificent system of chimneys, which had the capacity to prepare banquets for as many as 200 people – though in the heat of the moment the scene must have been truly infernal. On the first floor you can see where these lavish feasts went – a progress through the guts of princes. The **Salle des Gardes**, richly appointed with panelling, tapestries and a minstrels' gallery, was formerly the dining-hall – nowadays though it houses the magnificent 15C **tombs of Philippe le Hardi**, his son **Jean sans Peur** and Jean's wife **Marguerite de Bavière**. Their painted effigies are stretched on marble slabs, attended by winged angels who hold their helmets and heraldic shields, with dormant lions at their feet, while all round the tombs in delicately fretted stonework are represented processions of mourners, representatives of monkish orders and members of the ducal households. Also displayed in the same room is a fine tapestry of the **siege of Dijon** in 1513 and a gilded **retable** of Christ's Passion by the 14C artist Jacques de Baerze. Near the kitchen, too, steps lead up the **Tour de Philippe le Bon** to a terrace with a wide view clear across the city to the hills and valleys beyond (9.30–11.39 & 2.30–5.30 in summer; Wed and Sun pm only, Nov-Easter).

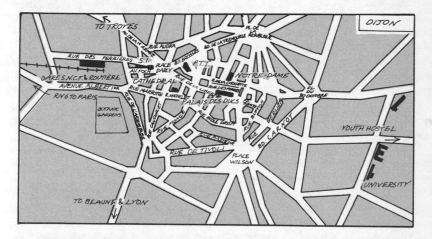

Most of the streets round the Palais des Ducs are for pedestrians only, in particular **rue des Forges** with several handsome old mansions. The **SI** and **Club Alpin** – is housed in **Hôtel Chambellan** at no 34: head through the alley and you find yourself in a beautiful and characteristic courtyard where you can get a proper view of the building (1490). Galleries open on to the courtyard at first and second floor levels, reached by a spiral staircase in one corner of the yard. There's a marvellous piece of stonemason's virtuosity at the top of the stairs: the vaulting of the roof springing from a basket held by the statue of a gardener. At the end of the street you come to the attractive **place François-Rude** with its halftimbered houses and **fountain** with a bronze statue of a grape-harvester. On sunny days it's a favourite hangout, with people crowding the tables of the café-restaurant and sitting on the ground round the fountain.

Close by, **rue de la Chouette** leads through to the very fine church of **Notre Dame**, built in the first half of the 13C and modelled on the Gothic churches of Champagne, which with the Ile de-France led the field in cathedral construction. Set in the north wall of the church is a small carved owl, which people touch for luck in passing and which gave the street its name. Its unusual **west front** consists of two storeys of arcades forming a gallery above the deep triple porches, separated by three bands of richly carved stonework, each adorned with statuettes that serve as gargoyles. Above the façade rises a **Jacquemart clock** with mechanical figures to strike the bells, brought back from Flanders by Duke Philippe le Hardi. The **interior** has some fine glass and one of those odd Black Virgins in a chapel to the right of choir.

Rue de la Chouette leads into **rue de la Musette**, another pedestrian street lined with smart boutiques, ordinary shops and greengrocers with their wares spilling over on to stalls in the street outside. Here too are the large covered *halles*; **market** days are Tuesday, Friday and Saturday until about 1pm.

If you're interested in looking at more of the city's fine **mansions**, the tourist people issue a *dépliant*, or leaflet, entitled *Maisons et Hôtels particuliers du XVe au XVIIIe siècle à Dijon*. One of these hôtels, at 4 rue des Bons-Enfants off place de la Libération, is now the **Musée Magnin**. Still furnished in its original, over-precious manner, it displays a much smaller collection of pictures than the Beaux-Arts: the personal collection of Maurice Magnin, donated to the state in 1938. It includes a number of good paintings by lesser known artists, but above all it's the furniture that makes the museum so intriguing; like being an intruder in a 17C home.

The **Cathédrale de St-Bénigne**, in place St-Bénigne, is another good example of the Burgundian Gothic – of similar date to Notre-Dame. It covers the site of what was considered one of the great buildings of Romanesque Burgundy, along with the abbey of Cluny (also vanished) and St-Philibert at Tournus. Only the circular 11C crypt remains. The roof of the Gothic church is patterned with the coloured glazed tiles that are considered typically Burgundian. Just north of the Cathedral is a good **Archaeological Museum** (9.30–6; cl. Tues), including among its exhibits some interesting pieces of ex-voto and a bronze boat from the source of the Seine at Baigneux-les-Juifs.

Most of Dijon's **town centre** still lies within the area ringed by the old walls. The **Porte Guillaume** arch by **place Darcy** was part of that system of fortifications. Although there are other parks and green areas away from the centre, the **gardens** in place Darcy make a particularly good spot to rest or picnic. And you could do worse than sharpen up your taste buds with a smear of Dijon **mustard** in your sandwiches. Like Norwich in England, Dijon is a world centre of mustard-making. Maille is the best known producer and their **shop** in **rue de la Liberté** sells a range of mustards from the anodyne to cauterising.

If you want to learn something of the Burgundy wines without leaving town, you could go to **La Cour aux Vins**, 3 rue Jeannin, behind the Palais des Ducs. There for about 35F you can taste five top-class wines. There are books on wine in the shop and, two or three times a day, an English-language talk.

In rue de la Liberté, *Librairie de l'Université* and, opposite, *Librairie du Voyageur* are both good bookshops. The former has a few books in English; the latter has a great selection of **local maps and guides.**

Dijon has a good summer **music season**, with classical concerts through June in its *Eté Musical* programme. **L'Estivade**, from 20 June to 15 August, puts on endless music, dance and street theatre performances. **Fête de la Vigne** at the beginning of September is a traditional costume, folklore jamboree, and the **Foire Gastronomique** in the first week of November is a pretext for a disgusting tuck-in to see you through the lean months of winter.

Practicalities

The principal of **SI** office in place Darcy has a **hotel reservation** service and **money-change**. The rue des Forges (no 34) office has more **regional material** and sells a cheap **all-in-one ticket** for the main museums and sights in the Côte d'Or *département*. You can also buy a cheap general **museum ticket** for the city at any one of Dijon's museums.

The **Club Alpin** in the rue des Forges office produces a **booklet** called *Promenez-Vous en Côte d'Or* with all the region's **waymarked paths** in it. **Agence Wasteels** at 20 av Maréchal-Foch, near the station, is a youth-oriented travel agent. **CIJ** has a helpful office at 22 rue Audra on the north side of the Darcy gardens. **Bike hire** from *Rousseau*, 3 place Notre-Dame, only. The **university campus** is at the end of rue de Mirande beyond bd Gabriel. **CROUS**, the student information service, is at 3 rue Maret, near place Darcy.

Finding a **place to stay** is not difficult. There is a cheap **student hostel** in av Maréchal-Leclerc called *Foyer International d'Etudiants* (80.71.51.01). The **youth hostel** proper is part of a modern complex away from the centre of town, called *Centre de Rencontres Internationales* (1 bd Champollion). It's clean, comfortable and equipped with dining-hall and self-service restaurant. There are singles, doubles and dormitories, but the accommodation is often fully booked, so it is wise to ring ahead: 80.71.32.12. There's a travel agent on the premises selling cheap train and plane tickets. It's 4km out, at the end of bus route 5.

As for **hotels**, there is the cheap and tatty *Hôtel de France* near the station at 16 rue des Perrières. *Hôtel Gare et Bossuet* (16 rue Mariotte) is a bargain, but you'll have to put up with a lot of traffic noise. The best bargain is *Hôtel du Theatre* right in the Palais des Ducs quarter at 3 rue des Bons-Enfants — if you can find a place there. *Miroir-Hôtel* in a private alley at 7 rue Bossuet is a bit more expensive.

While it is not difficult to spend a lot of money on food in a town like

Dijon, which calls itself a *ville gastronomique*, you can **eat** perfectly well at reasonable prices too. Even many of the grander hotels and restaurants have one lower-priced menu, though they won't appreciate you in your road dirt. There is a straightforward modern **cafeteria**, *Melodine*, at the corner of av Maréchal-Foch and place Darcy. For a hearty salad lunch, *Relais de la Gare* has several on offer. There's an uninspired **vegetarian** restaurant in rue Pasteur. The best of the cheapies are beyond doubt *La Grande Taverne* – the brasserie-restaurant of the crumbling luxury hotel *Terminus* near the station; *Moulin à Vent* in a 15C house in place François Rude; and the down-home *Étendard*, 4 rue des Perrières off place Darcy.

There is a good **city bus** service, but distances are small enough to make walking easy. If you plan to bus a lot, it's worth getting a **pass** from STRD, in the middle of place Grangier. **Gare routière** for out-of-town journeys is next to **gare SNCF** at the end of av Maréchal-Foch, 5mins from place Darcy. **Hitching** out of town is slow because of the competition from students. For Paris (N5, westbound), go along av Albert 1er and start hitching at the service station near Lac Kir. For Beaune, Lyon, etc. (N74), cross the canal from place 1er Mai and continue down av Jean-Jaurès.

NEVERS

A large thriving city on a hill above the junction of the Loire and Nièvre rivers, **NEVERS** returns François Mitterand as its member of Parliament. The other things it is known for in France are its *nougatine* sweets, and fine **porcelain**, a hallmark since the 17C and well represented in the **municipal museum** in rue St-Genest (10–12 & 2–6, cl. Tues). Movie buffs might also know that Alain Resnais' *Hiroshima, Mon Amour* was made here.

If you arrive at the **station, av Général de Gaulle** takes you due east to the central **place Carnot** by the city **park**, on the north side of which is the convent of St-Gildard, where **Bernadette of Lourdes** ended her days. On the south side of the *place* is the former **Palais Ducal**, with octagonal turrets and an elegant centre tower decorated with sculptures illustrating the family history of François de Clèves, the first Duke in the mid-17C.

Close by, opposite the **Hôtel de Ville**, is the bizarre **Cathédrale de St-Cyr**, looking rather like a deformed spider with representative bits of practically every phase of French architectural history appended to its body. It even manages to have two apses, Romanesque at the west end, Gothic at the east.

Much more interesting and aesthetically satisfying is the church of **St-Étienne** on the east side of the town centre. To get there you go down rue St-Martin at the back of the Palais Ducal, across **place Guy-Coquille** and into **rue St-Étienne**. The church has a very plain exterior, but inside is one of the **prototype pilgrim churches**, with galleries above the aisles, ambulatory and three radiating chapels round the apse. Another exceptional feature for its time – 1097 – was the **direct lighting** of the nave.

If you keep north from place Guy-Coquille up **rue du Commerce**, Nevers' high street, into **rue des Ardilliers** you come to the 18C arch of the **Porte de Paris** straddling the streets. It commemorates one of Europe's major conflicts, the battle of Fontenoy, fought out between Charlemagne's sons in 841AD up towards Auxerre. The stake was Charlemagne's empire, and the outcome the division of his lands east and west of the Rhine, which formed the basis of modern France and Germany.

Down along the **riverbank** by place Mossé and the bridge over the Loire you pass a section of the old town wall and the **Tour Goguin**, part of which is as old as 11C. If you turn in here to the right you come to the square, machicolated tower of **Porte du Croux** with its barbican still intact in front and a small local **archaeology museum** inside. To your right again you get back to the **oldest quarter** of town round the Cathedral – rue Morlon and rue de la Cathédrale, for instance – with its dilapidated half-timbered houses, alleys and stairs extending down to the river.

Av Général de Gaulle is a good place to find inexpensive **restaurants** and **cafés**. Try *Gambrinus*, for example. There are several **hotels** in the area too, though it is a bit noisy. *Hôtel Villa du Parc* at 16 rue de Lourdes near the park is better for two than one. *Hôtel Beauséjour* – very close at 5 rue St-Gildard – is cheaper, as is *Hôtel Thermidor* in rue Tillier (first left in av Général de Gaulle). There is a **Camping Municipal** on the other side of the Loire, just over the bridge.

SI at 31 rue du Rempart near place Carnot. **Bike hire** from Laroche, 28 rue St-Genest. **Gare routière** in rue Chemin de Fer.

THE MORVAN PARK, ABBEYS AND ROMANS

The **Parc Naturel Régional du Morvan** lies right in the middle of Burgundy. It is another of those wild, beautiful, inhospitable regions whose decline into total depopulation the state is trying to arrest by developing it as an outdoor holiday playground. Within the park, **transport** is difficult without your own car, but there are a number of well-known places on the fringes which are well served by public transport. In the south-east **Autun** was one of the principal cities of Roman Gaul, while nearby is **Cluny**, the powerhouse of western Christendon in the Middle Ages. Whether or not the folk memory of Roman buildings in Autun had anything to do with it, this corner of Burgundy produced in **Cluny abbey**, **Autun cathedral** and **Vézelay**, on the northern edge of the park, some of the most influential Romanesque buildings in the country.

THE PARC DU MORVAN

The **monts de Morvan** – the Morvan hills – are thickly wooded with beech and oak, steep in places and around 800m in altitude. It is good **walking** country and the **Maison du Parc** at St-Brisson puts out a booklet describing the routes called *Sentiers Pédestres en Morvan*. The GR13 crosses the park from Vézelay to St-Léger. The centre of the park is CHÂTEAU-CHINON, a quiet country town, with its SI just inside the medieval gate of Porte Notre-Dame. There is a tremendous view of the surrounding countryside if you climb to the top of the hill behind the town. (Daily **bus connection** to Autun, leaving early in the morning and returning in the evening.)

Camping is the most readily available form of cheap accommodation in the park, but there are a number of **gîtes d'étape** as well – full details from the Maison du Parc. SAULIEU on the park's eastern edge, once a military station on the Roman Via Agrippa, has a couple of **cheap hotels** and makes a good base. It has an attractive early **12C church** with a tomb said to be that of **Saint Andoche**, one of the earliest Christian martyrs around 179AD, probably a victim of one of the first clashes between pagan Roman religion and the young and revolutionary Christian movement that was gaining ground in Gaul. It is also well known for its restaurants, though they won't do the budget any good.

VÉZELAY

A hundred years ago the village of **VÉZELAY** on the northern edge of the park was abandoned and collapsing, although its **abbey church**, one of the seminal buildings of the Romanesque period, had already been reconstructed by Viollet-le-Duc in the mid-19C. A great shrine on a hill, clustered about by the picturesque dwellings of a medieval village, close to the mainest of roads – it was inevitable that in modern times it should become a great shrine of tourism. It's an undeniably attractive place nonetheless, inspite of the hotels and restaurants, art galleries and craft shops, with steep lanes climbing through lovingly restored medieval gates to the pale church at the top.

From the **outside** it appears merely large, Romanesque with a nod to Gothic, with flying buttresses, a square tower at either end and a frieze of gargoyles under the eaves. Inside you step first into a vast **narthex**, where triple doors open on to the nave, adorned with quaintly stiff and ill-proportioned figures illustrating the lives of Lazarus, John the Baptist and Mary Magdalene, for whom the church is named **La Madeleine**. The long **nave**, lit by a clerestory standing free above the lower aisles, is roofed with flattened arches constructed of alternating light and darker stone. Fretted mouldings edge the arches and arcades. The supporting piers are crowned with finely cut **capitals** of knights and devils, foliage and fictitious beasts. The choir, built later in the second part of the 12C, is already firmly in the Gothic manner. In the **crypt** a shrine contains relics once thought to be the bones of Mary Magdalene.

It was these bones which put the original Benedictine abbey on the map in the 9C. Their removal here from the church of St-Maximin in Provence immediately established the abbey as a great **centre of pilgrimage**. The wealth that followed soured relations between the arrogant, tyrannical abbots and the local population, who more than once rose against them and set the monastery on fire. **St Bernard**, founder of the reforming and puritanical Cistercian order of monks preached the First Crusade from here, and from here too **Richard-Coeur-de-Lion** set off on the Third Crusade in 1190. But the abbey's heyday ended in 1280 when it was discovered that Mary's bones still lay after all at St-Maximin. To aid decline the Protestants seriously vandalised the buildings in the 16C and the whole establishment was disbanded by the Revolution.

The small **SI** is on the right in rue St-Pierre as you walk up towards the church (open Easter to Sept; cl.) Wed and Sun pm). There's a good **youth hostel** with camping space 1km along the road to L'ETANG. SNCF buses for Sermizelles (on the Avallon-Auxerre line) leave from Garage de la Madeleine in the main square, as does the bus from Avallon (normally one a day in the afternoon).

AUTUN

Red-brown roofs patinaed with lichen, in their midst a Gothic spire as erect as a unicorn's horn – even today **AUTUN** is hardly bigger than the circumference of its medieval walls, and they in turn followed the line of the earlier Roman fortifications.

Autun was once the leading city of **Roman Gaul**. The Emperor Augustus founded it as part of his massive and in the long term highly successful campaign to pacify and Romanise the broody Celts of defeated Vercingetorix. **Augustodunum** – even its name symbolised the marriage of urban Rome and independent, tribal, rural Gaul; '-dunum' meant a fortress, and only a few miles west, on the summit of **Mt Beuvray** at the southern limit of the Morvan, is the site of one of the Gauls' major hilltop forts, **Bibracte**. The draw of the new Augustodunum rapidly eclipsed it despite its importance as a centre of the Gallic metalworking industry with outlets to Marseille and the Mediterranean. Considerable reminders of this Roman past exist in modern Autun.

Two of the city's four gates survive. **Porte St-André** in rue de la Croix Blanche is 20m wide and 14m high with two main arches for traffic flanked by smaller ones for pedestrians. Above is an arcaded gallery supported by Ionic pilasters. It is a fine piece of engineering as well as being in remarkably good condition. **Porte d'Arroux**, close to the river in Faubourg d'Arroux, is similar, slightly taller and more elegant, but not so well preserved. From just the other side of the river, about 1km outside the walls, is the so-called **Temple of Janus**, the remains of a large square tower, which was probably some kind of defensive work. On the eastern side of town in what is now a park off av des 2ème Dragons are the few remains of the largest Roman **theatre** in Gaul – an indication of the town's importance.

There is a good and well-displayed collection of finds from these Roman and Gallic sites in the **Musée Rolin** at 3 rue des Bancs near the Cathedral (very variable times; cl. Tues and the month of Feb). One room is devoted to the Bibracte and its bronze-making.

The **Cathédrale de St-Lazare**, modelled on the vanished abbey of Cluny, is another fine Burgundian church of the mid-12C. Its west front, flanked by square towers, has the characteristic narthex running across its full width, protecting one of the most finely carved and best preserved *Last Judgement tympana* to have come down to us. Most unusually it is signed too, by one Ghislebertus. It was saved from certain disfigurement during the Revolution, ironically because Voltaire had so disparaged the style of its carving that it had been plastered over. The very simple interior has interesting affinities with the town's Roman structures, as is again characteristic of the Cluny school of buildings. In the place of columns, you have fluted pilasters, obviously inspired by those of the Porte d'Arroux. The capitals, though hard to see clearly in the gloom, the central pillar of the door and the flanking colonnettes are all notable for the quality of their carving.

Despite being well frequented by tourists Autun is not very expensive. There are a couple of reasonable **hotels** near the station at the bottom of the main street, av Charles de Gaulle: *Hôtel de France* (a *Logis de France*) and *Commerce et Touring*. If you turn right out of the station and follow the road round to Faubourg St-Andoche (10mins), you come to the cheaper *Hôtel Le Petit Paris*. There is a municipal **campsite** on the banks of the river Ternin. There are good and inexpensive **places to eat** in the vast Champ-de-Mars square and av Charles de Gaulle.

Just south of Autun is the small but important industrial town of **LE CREUSOT**, made famous by the Schneider ironworks – the Ironbridge of France. The first French railway locomotive was made at the Schneider works in 1836, and the 75mm field gun that was the mainstay of the artillery in the First World War. There is an **Ecomusée du Creusot-Montceau-les-Mines** – probably the best of its kind in France – recalling the history of the ironworks and the coalmines of neighbouring Montceau-les-Mines that supplied the fuel for the furnaces. It was created by one joint effort of local unions, workers and kids who can no longer get jobs in the redundancy-hit industry.

CLUNY

The voice of **CLUNY**'s abbot once made monarchs tremble. His power in the Christian world was second only to that of the Pope, his intellectual influence arguably greater.

The monastery was founded in 910 in response to a widely felt revulsion against the corruption of the existing church and a universal longing for some spiritual reassurance at a time of great worldly insecurity at the approach of the first millennium. All it took was a couple of vigorous early abbots to build the power of Cluny into a veritable empire. They established numerous subordinate houses, especially along the pilgrim routes of St-Jacques. Ironically, the growing wealth and secular involvement of the monastery only led to the decline of its spiritual influence, which was superseded by the reforming seal of St-Bernard's Cistercian monks based at Cîteaux close to Dijon. In time Cluny became a royal appointment – a convenient device for dressing the king's temporal machinations up in a little spiritual respectability. Both Richelieu and Mazarin were abbots for a time.

Now practically nothing remains. The Revolution suppressed the monastery and **Hugues of Semur**'s vast and influential **11C church**, once the largest building in Christendom with St Peter's in Rome, was dismantled in 1810. All you can see of it is an octagonal belfry, the south transept, some fragments of the apse and, in the refectory, some of the surviving capitals from its immense columns – disappointing, but nonetheless evocative. From the top of the **Tour de Fromage** (entry inside the **SI**) you can reconstruct it in your imagination. Visits are by guided tour only (10–11.30 & 2–4, Oct-March; cl. Tues and Wed; 9–11.30 & 2–6, April-Sept). The **Musée Ochier** inside the 13C **logis** of the last abbot to be freely elected helps to flesh out the picture with reconstructions and fragments of sculpture.

If you're planning to stay, a municipal **hostel** called *Cluny Accueil* is the cheapest place, just a little dearer than a regular youth hostel. It's in Chemin du Prado, between rue Porte de Paris and the D980 bypass, close to the Pont de la Levée bus stop. There's **camping** on the other side of the Pont; turn right in rue des Griottons and it's on the left. *Hôtel de l'Abbaye, Hôtel des Marroniers* and the *relais routier* in av de la Gare have inexpensive **rooms**. The cheapest place to **eat** is the créperie, *En Cathie Mini*, next to Musée Ochier.

Some 50km to the west across the country of the **Charolais**, whose heavy white bulls are used to father herds of hybrid British cattle, you come to the lovely old town of **PARAY-LE-MONIAL** on the banks of the river Bourbince. Approached from Cluny, its **church** will be interesting for it was built at the same time and in direct imitation of the abbey church. Simple and powerful, it looks particularly good standing amid spacious gardens close to the river. The elegantly-curving ambulatory is supported by slender 'classical' columns. *Notre-Dame* is its proper name, although it is sometimes known as the *Basilique du Sacré-Coeur*, for following the visions of Marguerite-Marie Alacoque, a 17C nun, Paray became the centre of the **cult of the Sacred Heart** in France – second only to Lourdes in the number of pilgrims it attracts. It certainly won't be a Paray hôtelier you hear scoffing at her 1920 canonisation.

For accommodation, the **cheapest rooms** are to be had at *Hôtel Terminus*. Alternatively, try *Hôtel St-Roch*. Both are in av de la Gare. The *Foyer des Jeunes Travailleurs* is good too, if you can get in (rue Michel Anguier). There is **camping** by the river on bd Dauphin-Louis.

The **station** hires out **bikes**, again an excellent way of exploring. The gentle **BRIONNAIS** country to the south of Paray, is peppered with small villages and Romanesque churches, precursors or offspring of Cluny.

THE VINEYARDS

Burgundy farmers have been growing the grape since the 2C AD. And they have never had it so good, which is why they are so reticent about the quirks of soil and climate and tricks of pruning and spraying that make their wines so special. Vines are temperamental things. Frost on the wrong day, sun on the wrong day, too much water, level ground, and they won't come up with the goods. They like a slope, which is why so many wines are called *Côte* something, and the best wine comes from the top of the slope.

Contrary to what you might expect the best Burgundy vineyards are often divided into very small holdings. This is largely a result of the redistribution of the vast Cluny monastery estates among the local peasantry after the Revolution. The monks, as was often the case in the wine trade, had been front-runners here too.

Detailed in this section are the main wine-producing areas of Burgundy: **Côte d'Or, Mâcon, Beaujolais**, along with the smaller **Chalonnais** region. They are all strung out along the main Dijon-Lyon roads: very accessible and much visited. The fifth area, **Chablis,** is included with Auxerre in the north-west corner of Burgundy (see p. 337). Also included here, as they are in the area, are the towns of **Tournus** and **Bourg-en-Bresse.**

BEAUNE AND THE CÔTE D'OR

Burgundy's best wines come from a narrow strip of hillside called the **CÔTE D'OR** that runs south-east from Dijon to Santenay. It is divided into two regions: **Côte de Nuits** from Dijon to Corgoloin and **Côte de Beaune.** With few exceptions the reds of Côte de Nuits are considered the best; they are richer, age better and cost more. Côte de Beaune is known for its whites. On both Côtes it is the oldest vine stock that produces the best wine. The vineyards now extend into the higher hills behind the Côte d'Or and these are known as the *Hautes Côtes de Nuits* and *Hautes Côtes de Beaune.* It is pretty country: narrow wooded stream valleys or *combes* that make great walks.

Along the foot of the Côte d'Or from Dijon to Beaune the N74 runs by a string of villages whose names will sound in the ears of wine-buffs like Pavlov's bell: **Gevrey-Chambertin, Vougeot, Vosne-Romanée, Nuits-St-Georges,** the commercial centre of Côte de Nuits. In some villages you'll see *caves* offering *dégustation,* but this is usually an inducement to buy. Bear in mind that any Côte d'Or wine going at what seem bargain prices is certainly either too old, too young or a bad year.

There is a good-value, one-day pass, called the **Bourgogne Pass,** available from the Dijon tourist office. It entitles you to a round trip from Dijon to Beaune and back. The bus stops at all the villages on or near the N74 and you can get off when and where the spirit moves you.

Many of the wine villages are attractive little places with a campsite or cheap hotel if you want to take your time. **VOUGEOT,** whose Clos-Vougeot vineyards were cultivated by the Cistercian monks of Cîteaux, has a 16C **château** which is open to visitors (9–11.30 & 2–5.30) for half-hour guided tours in which you get to see the Vendangeoire de Cîteaux, **wine-cellar** with its massive 13C wine-presses. The château today is the home of a sort of freemasonry of the wine trade. The **Confrérie des Chevaliers du Tastevin,** which holds highly ritualised meetings known as *chapitres* at intervals throughout the year – in effect, a pretext for a damn great blow-out.* The château at ALOXE-CORTON, where Charlemagne

---

*The major annual **beanfeast** of the wine trade known as the **Trois Glorieuses** takes place on the third weekend in November. The first day meeting or **chapitre** is held at the Château de Clos de Vougeot. On the Sunday there is an **auction** at the covered market in Beaune of the new wines produced by the prestigious Hospices de Beaune – an important occasion for wine-bibers, but also one which sets the prices for most of the rest of the region's wines. The third night is the **Paulée** at Meursault, a big party to which growers bring their own wine. The climax of the evening is the award of a literary prize – one hundred bottles of the very best wine to some lucky author.

had a vineyard, is also visitable. At MEURSAULT, whose white wines, like those of Corton-Charlemagne, are highly regarded, you can visit the premises of several producers.

BEAUNE itself has many charms – set amid vineyards, ringed by ancient walls – but it is wholly devoted to tourism. Chief attraction is the 15C hospital, **Hôtel-Dieu** on the corner of **place de la Halle** opposite the **SI**. It can be visited on a hurried and expensive guided tour (9–11.40 & 2–6 daily). It is built in Flemish style – Flanders belonged to Burgundy at the time – with wooden galleries and dormer windows set into a steep roof patterned with coloured tiles and decorated with gilded weather vanes, though you only see all this once you have penetrated into the inner courtyard. Inside there is an enormous paved room with a painted timber roof, the **Grande Salle des Malades**, which until 1948 continued to serve its original purpose of housing the sick. Last item on the tour is the *polyptych of the Last Judgement*, a splendid 15C altarpiece by Rogier van der Weyden depicting several contemporary dignitaries amid its religious portraits, including Nicolas Rolin, who built the hospital, and his wife, and Duke Philippe le Bon, whose chancellor he was.

It is here that the Hospices de Beaune's wines are auctioned on the third Sunday in November. The considerable profits from this lavish sale go, believe it or not, to charity. The Hospices still exist solely for the care of the sick and aged.

The private residence of the Dukes of Burgundy, in **rue d'Enfer**, now houses the **Musée du Vin** (9–11.30 & 2–5, Oct-April; 10–12 & 2–5.45, May-Sept) with some mammoth presses and an interesting collection of tools used in the trade. Everything looks as if it were made for the use of giants.

At the other end of rue d'Enfer the church of **Notre-Dame** is about the only thing free in town. It has a fine Gothic tower, triple doorway in the Cluniac style and an attractive Romanesque apse with three radiating chapels. Inside are five very fine wool and silk **tapestries** depicting the Life of the Virgin (15C) – on show from April to November.

Most **hotels** in Beaune are expensive and booked up. However, it's worth trying *Hôtel St-Nicolas*, 69 rue du Faubourg St-Nicolas, which has a few cheaper rooms, and *Hôtel Foch*, 24 bd Foch. Both are outside the town walls. The *Foyer des Jeunes Travailleurs* opposite the hospital in rue Guigone de Salins sometimes has room (phone 80.22.21.83 to check). There is a big four-star **campsite**, *Camping les Cent-Vignes*, about 1km from town in rue Dubois off rue du Faubourg St-Nicolas.

The land of snails in *sauce bourguignonne*, Beaune is full of good and expensive restaurants. For **cheaper eating** place Monge, place Carnot and rue Lorraine are the best areas to look. *La Jambe de Bois* is a good self-service snack bar, and there's the Saturday morning **market** in place Carnot for picnic food.

The centre is a longish walk from the **gare SNCF**: up av du 8 Septembre, across the boulevard, up rue du Château, rue des Tonneliers and into place Monge. Alternatively, there is a **bus** – nos 1 or 2 from the stop opposite the station. The station hires out **bikes**, as does M Bouillot in rue du Faubourg St-Nicolas. There is no real bus station; **buses** leave from just outside the walls at the end of rue Maufoux. The **SI** dispalys bus times on its noticeboard, and also has a list of wine *caves* open to the public.

CHALON, MÂCON AND THE BEAUJOLAIS

Beyond SANTENAY the land changes, and so do the grapes, to become the vineyards of the small **Côte Chalonnaise** region. Industrial **CHALON** itself, on the main Dijon-Lyon axis, lacks appeal, with disappointingly few remnants of its long history. Hotels are plentiful but aiming at the business travellers and not cheap. But it's the capital of rolling and pretty countryside, noted for its prestigious, mainly white, wines. The best known of the **wine villages** are RULLY (sparkling white), MERCUREY (framed and highly expensive), GIVRY, BUXY and MONTAGNY. All are peaceful old places. An **SNCF bus** from CHALON to MÂCON takes in some of the area and if you enjoy *Boeuf Bourgignon* you can ponder it in the making through the windows – vineyards right next to fields of Charolais cattle.

MÂCON is a large modern town, a centre of the wine industry, on the road south to Lyon. It is a place you might make an overnight stop at, not one where you would want to stay. Along the N6 as it passes through the town there are a number of two-star **hotels**, adequate but pricey, mostly advertising their soundproofing. The **SI** is at 187 rue Carnot. **Gares SNCF** and **routière** (next to each other) are behind the busy intersection of rues Gambetta, Victor Hugo, and Bigonnet.

The **wine-producing** country – the Mâconnais – lies to the west of the town. Its reds are good, but the best known are the highly priced white from the villages of **Pouilly, Fuissé, Vinzelles** and **Prissé**. A curious phenomenon in the landscape is the 500m **Solutré** rock, which evidently puzzled prehistoric man as it does modern visitors. An incredible quantity of horse, reindeer, bison and mammoth bones have been found here, forming a layer 18 inches to 6ft in depth and covering an area of 4,000 square metres.

Imperceptibly as you go south the Mâconnais becomes the **Beaujolais**, a larger area of terraced hills producing large quantities of light, fruity red wine. The region is divided broadly into three *appellations*: Beaujolais (ordinaire), Beaujolais-Villages (from the bettern northern half) and Beau-jolais-Supérieur (containing more natural alcohol). At the same time some of the old-established vineyards – the *crus* – produce something better than the average. The well-marked **Route de Beaujolais** winds through these villages, though it is possible to sample some of the best wines at **La Maison du Beaujolais** in St-Jean-d'Ardières (8–12, cl. Tues). The name Beaujolais comes from the region's main village, BEAUJEU – not itself a wine-producer. VILLEFRANCHE-SUR-SAÔNE, where the Route ends, is the commercial centre.

TOURNUS AND BOURG-EN-BRESSE

TOURNUS is a small walled town just off the autoroute and N6 between Chalon and Mâcon. As you enter the town from the station through a narrow gateway flanked by medieval towers it all seems a touch too well preserved, especially round the huge abbey church of **St-Philibert**, the finest surviving example of Burgundian Romanesque. Further into the town there are some lovely arcaded shopfronts and substantial hotels and, in **place de l'Hôtel de Ville**, the remains of an arcaded sidewalk. From the **riverside quays**, you look out over the broad sweep of the river Saône and its wide, flat valley beneath huge piling cloudscapes that seem so typically French. If you walk in the riverside woods in spring you'll find big colonies of the rare Snake's Head Fritillary, a beautiful flower whose high-shouldered bells are chequered all over with little squares of rose- or rusty-brown.

St-Philibert is a remarkable construction: three churches piled one on the other. The **crypt** is 9C; the **main church**, which you enter through a low, dark narthex, dates mostly from the early 11C. The massive **nave** has had its original timber roof replaced by barrel vaults at right angles to the axis of the church, like the corrugations in a sheet of galvanised iron, while the aisles are groin-vaulted. **St-Michel**; the castellated upper church, actually stands on top of the narthex of this one, and is said to be – most improbably – younger than its nave.

If you are **planning to stay**, *Hôtel Le Terminus* close to the station in av Gambetta and actually on the N6 is surprisingly good value. its food is good too, and not expensive. In the centre of town, *La Petite Auberge* in place Lacretelle is a popular bar with simple rooms above, while *Hôtel de Bourgogne* has good food but more expensive accommodation. There is a cheap bar-restaurant-hotel on the corner of rue Bessard and rue Fénelon, signposted simply *R Gras*. The *Café de la Poste* on the corner of rue Jean-Jaurès has cheap snacks and meals. **Camping** *Le Pas Fleury* is by the river just south of the town off the N6.

BOURG-EN-BRESSE, a few kilometres east of Mâcon, means two things in France, neither specially flattering to itself: chickens and **BROU**. Poultry-raising is the speciality of the flat farmland that surrounds the town and Brou is an uninteresting suburban village about 1km distant which happens to have a **church** that is arguably the best piece of early 16C architecture in France. Inside it has some marvellous glass, choir stalls as beautifully imagined and carved as those at Auch and St-Bertrand-de-Comminges and stonecarving in the choir screen and tombs as delicate as you'll find anywhere. The tombs belong to Philibert le Beau, Duke of Savoy, his wife Margaret of Austria and his mother Margaret of Bourbon. And hereby hangs the tale. Philibert was killed in a hunting accident two years after his marriage to Margaret. In grief at his loss and fearing it might be divine punishment for his failure to carry out his mother's wish for a monastery to be built at Brou she undertook the work, including his extravagant church to serve as a mausoleum for them both. Margaret died in 1530 before the church was completed. The entwined initials P and M and her strange motto, *Fortune, Infortune, Fort Une* (in good times or in bad one woman is strong) recur throughout the church. The sculptor, Conrad Meyt, and architect, Van Boghen, were both Flemish craftsmen from Dijon.

From Bourg station **bus no 2** goes to the town centre and no 1 to Brou. The **SI** is in Centre Albert Camus, 6 av Alsace-Lorraine. In summer there is an annex by Brou church. Wednesday is **market** day in place Carriat, and on the first and third Wednesdays each month there is a livestock market as well. There are three reasonable **hotels** in av A Baudin, 2mins' walk from the station: *Hôtel de Genève, Paris et Lyon* and *Hôtel des Bains*. The last two both have inexpensive restaurants. Camping Municipal in av des Sports.

TRAVEL DETAILS

Trains

From Sens frequent to Paris (50mins–1½hrs); 7 daily to Dijon (2hrs10), via Laroche-Migennes junction (30mins) and Tonnerre (55mins); 3–5 daily to Auxerre (¾hr) and Avallon (2hrs), a few continue to Autun (4hrs).

From Auxerre 7 or 8 daily to Paris (1¾hr), some changing at Laroche-Migennes; 4–5 daily to Avallon (1hr5) and Autun (about 3hrs).

From Avallon 2 or 3 weekly direct to Paris; 4–5 daily to Auxerre (1hr5); 4–5 daily to Autun (about 2hrs).

From Tonnerre 6 daily on Paris (1¾hrs) – Dijon (1¼hr) line.

From Dijon 9 direct TGVs daily to Paris (1hr40); 6 stopping trains to Paris (3hrs) via Montbard (¾hr), Tonnerre (1¼hrs), Laroche-Migennes (1hr40), Sens (2hrs10); several late at night and early morning only non-stop to Lyon (1hr40); about 14 others daily to Lyon (1¾hrs) stopping variously at Nuits-St-Georges (20mins), Beaune (33mins), Chalon (½–1hr), Tournus (1hr25), Mâcon (1–2hrs), Villefranche (2hrs23) – journey times not always the same.

From Beaune 2 TGVs daily to Paris (2hrs); About 7 daily on Dijon (33mins)–Lyon (2½hrs) line, some stopping everywhere, others only at Chalon and Mâcon.

From Mâcon 5 direct TGVs to Paris daily (1hr40); 4 TGVs daily to Bourg (20mins) and Geneva (1hr50); note TGVs leave from Mâcon-Loché station, 6km out of town; several other trains/SNCF buses daily to Bourg; around 14 daily to Dijon (1hr10) and Lyon (40mins).

From Bourg 4 TGVs daily to Paris (2hrs) via Mâcon (20mins); 4 TGVs daily to Geneva (1½hrs); 2 daily direct to Dijon (1¾–2½hrs); 8 daily to Mâcon (½hr); 14 daily to Lyon (about 1hr).

From Autun 4–5 daily to Auxerre (3hrs), Avallon (2hrs), Sens (4hrs).

From Nevers about 5 daily non-stop to Paris (2hrs); several stopping trains daily to Paris (3hrs); 5 daily to Clermont-Ferrand (1hr50).

Buses

From Sens 4 daily to Auxerre (very slow); 4–5 daily to Troyes (1¾hrs).

From Auxerre 4 daily to Sens; other sporadic village buses, including to Chablis.

From Avallon 1 daily (in early am) to Vézelay (½hr); 1 daily to Dijon (2½–3hrs) via Semur.

From Semur SNCF buses to Les Laumes (on Paris-Dijon line), Saulieu, and Montbard (gare SNCF); 1 daily to Auxerre.

From Dijon daily services through villages to Avallon; Beaune; Nuits and other wine villages; Autun.

From Macon 7 SNCF buses daily to Chalon (2¼hrs) via Cluny (¾hr); 2–5 daily to Paray-le-Monial, Charolles, Cluny, and everywhere on N79.

From Bourg 1 SNCF bus daily to Lyon (1hr40).

From Cluny 7 SNCF buses daily to Chalon (1hr20) and Mâcon (¾hr); 2–5 daily to Charolles and Paray.

From Autun SNCF buses daily to Montchanin (TGV station); 1 daily but to Château-Chinon; 1 daily to Beaune and Dijon.

From Nevers several daily along N6 to La Charité, Cosne, Moulins, Montchanin.

From Paray 2–5 daily to Digoin, Charolles, Cluny, Mâcon.

Chapter twelve

EAST: CHAMPAGNE TO ALSACE

The four regions of this chapter – **Champagne, the Ardennes, Lorraine** and **Alsace** – make up a vast tract of France, and extend along the least defined of its borders. They have been a battleground for a thousand years: disputed through the Middle Ages by independent dukes and bishops whose allegiance was endlessly contested by the kings of France and the princes of the Holy Roman Empire, and scene in this century of some of the worst fighting of both World Wars.

Champagne, physically, is perhaps the least enticing. Sparsely populated, it is dank, northern territory, needing only a few drops of rain for total gloom to descend, and boasting only one town, **Troyes**, with interest enough to shelter and amuse yourself for a day or two. But it is not for such reasons that you'd come here. The name – the wine – is the compulsion: cocaine of French (or any other) alcohol, and here for the tasting at the great *maisons* of Epernay and Reims, or for havesting (relatively lucrative) towards the end of September.

Ardennes, to the west, and **Lorraine**, to the east, seem too at times like The Zone of Thomas Pynchon's *Gravity's Rainbow;* strange, detached regions, scattered with battlesites, where it is possible to go for miles without seeing a soul. And the towns, when they come, seem sombre places, mindful of past struggles (the *maquis* fought heroically in these parts), and neglected by, and contemptuous of, Paris. The most extraordinary of all battlesites is **Verdun**, scarred by the heaviest fighting of all during the 1914–18 war. Relief, if you travel this region, comes in **Nancy**, the provincial capital and as elegant an 18C town as any in France.

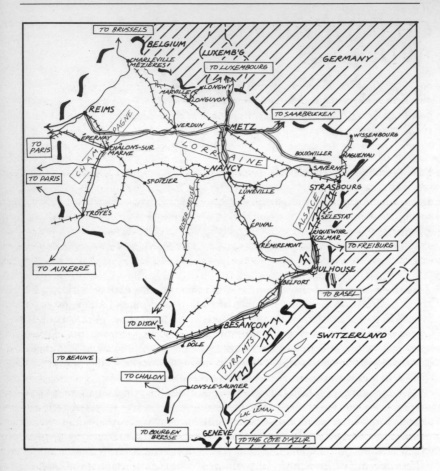

But it is in **Alsace**, in the wet wooded mountains of the **Vosges**, and in the Rhineland cathedral city of **Strasbourg**, that the north-east is at its most distinctive and interesting. With Lorraine, it became part of France only in the late 18C, saw a further period of German rule from 1871–1918, and was temporarily re-annexed again under Hitler. This past, and the German influence, is immediately and everywhere apparent, and its effect on a people who consider themselves thoroughly French is an oddly attractive one. If you are a walker, there is an evident appeal, too, in the **Jura**, foothills to the Alps, between the old watchmakers' town of **Besançon** and the Swiss border.

CHAMPAGNE AND THE ARDENNES

Slothrop's head is a balloon, which rises not vertically but horizontally, constantly across the room, whilst staying in one place. Each brain cell has become a bubble: he's been transmuted to black Epernay grapes, cool shadows, noble cuvées.

Thomas Pynchon, *Gravity's Rainbow*

From summer through to the late September harvest – and afterwards when the leaves turn gold and amber – the **Champagne vines**, seen from a distance in evening sunlight, perhaps under a rainbow or two, have a strong affinity with the future of their fruit. From close to they're rather menacing, planted with the precision of armies, pacing down the slopes.

Nowhere else in France, let alone the rest of the world, are you allowed to make champagne. That is to say, you can blend wines from chalk soil vineyards, double ferment them, turn and tilt the bottles bit by bit to clear the sediment, add some vintage liqueur, store the result for years at the requisite constant temperature and produce a bubbling golden liquid. But you cannot call it champagne – an outrageous monopoly to keep the region's sparkling wines in the luxury class perhaps. The people here will tell you the difference comes from the squid fossils in the chalk, the lie of the land and its critical climate, the evolution of the grapes, the regulated pruning methods, the legally enforced quantity of juice pressed. All of which really is irrelevant: there's no need to argue that champagne is special, though, oddly enough amid the extravagant praises glossily printed by the champagne industry, there is one startling omission. No reference is made to the fact that it's an extremely exhilarating drug, which is after all, why people drink it.

The vineyards are owned either by *maisons* who produce the *grande marque* champagne, or by small cultivators, *vignerons*, who sell the grapes to the *maisons*. The **vignerons** also make their own champagne and will happily offer a glass and sell you a bottle at half the price of a *grande marque* (ask at any Champagne region SI or CIVC for a list of addresses). The difference between the two comes down to capital. The *maisons* can afford to blend grapes from anything up to sixty different vineyards and tie up their investment to mature their champagne for several years longer than the legal minimum. So the wine they produce is undoubtedly superior – and not much cheaper here than in a good UK off-licence.

If you could visit the head offices of Cartiers or Dior, the atmosphere would probably be similar to the champagne **maisons** whose palaces are divided between Épernay and Reims. All the visits are free but some require appointments: don't be put off – they'll speak English and with an appointment visit you're more likely to get *dégustation*. Their audio-visuals and (cold) cellar tours are also informative and don't just plug brand names. Again, you can get a full list of addresses and times from any SI or CIVC.

Though there are **campsites** and **places to stay** in the countryside – a youth hostel in VERZY (14 rue du Bassin; 26.97.90.10), or good *gîte d'étape* in AY (c/o M Brun, 1 Impasse St-Vincent) – the best **bases** are ÉPERNAY, for total champagne dedication, and REIMS with an easy train link between them. If you want to work on the **harvest** contact either the *maisons* direct (see below, or SI lists); the *Agences Nationales pour l'Emploi* (at 11 rue Jean-Moët ÉPERNAY, 26.51.01.33, or 57 rue Talleyrand, REIMS, 26.88.46.76); or try the Verzy youth hostel (where casual workers arc often recruited, or advertised).

ÉPERNAY

Though a pleasant enough town, the only real reason for coming to ÉPERNAY is to visit the champagne maisons, whose tours, should you decide to take them all, could keep you occupied for a full day. Largest, and probably the most famous, is **Moët et Chandon** (20 av de Cham-pagne), who own Mercier, Ruinart and a variety of other concerns, including, incidentally, Dior pérfumes. By its own reckoning, a Moët champagne cork pops somewhere in the world every two seconds. The cellars are adorned with memories of Napoleon, a good friend of the original M Moët, and the vintage is named after the monastic hero of champagne history, Don Perignon. It's open 9.30–12.30 & 2–5.30, weekdays in summer, weekends only in winter; the visit ends with a glass.

Of other *maison* visits, the most rewarding are Mercier (up the road at no 70) and Castellane. **Mercier**'s glamour relic is a giant barrel that held 200,000 bottles worth when M Mercier took it to the Paris Exposition of 1889, with the help of twenty-four oxen – only to be upstaged by the Eiffel Tower. Visits round the cellars here are by electric train, fun, and again climaxing in *dégustation*. Hours are Mon-Sat 9.30–12 & 2–5.30, Suns till 4.30 only. **Castellane**, over by the station at 57 rue de Verdun in a kind of neoclassical signal box, keep similar hours, though only from 15 June-15 Sept. They have a small museum, in addition to visits to the *caves* down below.

Some **cheap hotels** in Épernay are *de la Cloche* (5 place Mendès France) and *du Palais* (51 rue St-Thibault) in the centre and *de la Terrasse* (7 quai de Marne) by the river. The **youth hostel** may have reopened – enquire at the **SI** in place Thiers, a short walk from the gare SNCF, or at the **MJC** (8 rue de Reims), which also has accommodation. The **campsite** is 1½km to the north in the Parc des Sports, on the south bank of the Marne (route de Cumières). **Bikes,** if you feel like roaming around the *vignerons*, can be hired at the station or behind the church near the SI, c/o M Buffet. Full addresses for everything to do with champagne, from the CIVC (5 rue Henri-Martin)

REIMS

Walking the dreary streets of REIMS, the one cheering, or further downheartening, thought is that below your feet are millions upon millions of bottles of bubbly. Above ground the actions of 1914–18 saw the end of all but 200 buildings. It nearly finished off the **Cathedral**, too, though, battered about, this survives – and, with a *maison* visit or two, redeems and justifies at least a half day's visit.

The cathedral's lure is threefold: kaleidoscopic patterns in the stained glass (Marc Chagall designs in the east chapel, Champagne processes glorified in the south transept), a series of unusually lovely tapestries, and a joke, running inexplicably about the mutilated statuary on the west front. Next door, the **Musée Tau** (10–12 & 2–6/5) displays oddments of sculpture at a closer level – more grinning angels, friendly looking gargoyles and a superb Eve, shiftily clutching the monster of sin. And as added narrative, embroidered tapestries of the *Song of Songs* line the walls. The building, the old Bishop's Palace, also preserves, in a state of somewhat absurd veneration, the paraphernalia of reactionary Charles X's coronation – right down to the Dauphin's hatbox.

More tapestries and stonework from the oldest building of Reims, the **Basilique St-Rémi**, are displayed, alongside its remains, in the **Abbaye St-Rémi**, about 1km to the south of the cathedral on rue Simon (10–12 & 2–6, Tues 2–6 only, wkends 10–7 only). And there are remnants too, amid the stuffed treasure house on the Musée St-Denis (10–12 & 2–6, cl. Tues) and the **Hôtel Vergeur** (10–6, cl. Mons), both of which could do well by converting to antique shops. The latter boasts two sets of Dürer engravings – an *Apocalypse* and *Passion of Christ*, though to see them you'll have to pace through a long guided tour to the whole works.

Which, with Champagne around the corner, may not seem a very good use of time. For the serious business, head to **place des Droits des Hommes**, around or nearby which are most of the Reims *maisons*. If you're limiting yourself to one – and there's no need for such a course – I'd recommend the **Maison Veuve Cliquot-Ponsardin** (no 1 in the *place*). In the early growth days of capitalism the widowed Mme Cliquot took over her husband's businesses, and later bequeathed it not to her children but to her business manager – each rather radical breaks with tradition. In keeping with this past, the *maison* is one of the least pompous. Its *caves*, with horror movie fungi, are old Gallo-Roman quarries. Visits are 9–11.15 & 2–5 (wkends 2–5; Nov-April by appointment only).

Pommery, too, at 5 place du Général Gouvard, have excavated Roman quarries for cellars (they claim – in good Champagne one-upmanship – to have been first to do so). And at **Taittingers** (9 place St-Niçaise) there are still more ancient *caves*, with doodles and carvings added in the chalk by more recent workers, and statues of St-Vincent and St-Jean, patron saints respectively of *vignerons* and cellar-hands. Visits are 9–11 & 2–5 at both – Pommery from March-Nov.

Some practical details
The motorway running along the Marne canal and the horrendous dual carriageways around its centre make Reims feel much bigger than it is. Having crossed two of these boulevards just outside the station and bearing to your right you come straight to **place Drouet d'Erlon**, an avenue with bars, restaurants and most of the city's life, such as it is. At the end, the road jinks to the right and becomes rue Dubois then rue des Capucins. The SI, 1 rue Jadart, is just off rue des Capucins after crossing rue Libergier which goes straight up to the cathedral. Some **hotels** to try in the centre are *Thillois*, 17 rue de Thillois, *Bourgeois*, 5 place Léon Bourgeois and *Monopole*, 28 place Drouet d'Erlon. To the north-east on av Jean-Jaurès there's *St-André* (no. 46) and Zodiac (no 155). Near the *maisons* in the south, try *St-Niçaise*, 6–8 place St-Nicaise. **Camping municipal** is about 1½km further out from the *maisons* on av Hoche (bus Z, 4 stops on from place des Droits des Hommes).

TROYES

Away from the vineyards, the **plains of Champagne** are not an inspiring sight. They grow more wheat and cabbages per hectare than any other region of France – but this has obviously brought no great benefits to the villages. Some look so run down you feel the shutters would fall off if you so much as popped a paper bag – and few are much more than hamlets, with grocery vans doing the rounds once a week and not a *boulangerie* in sight. Neither CHALONS, looming in the distance from Reims, nor the smaller towns which follow the Marne to its source, are sufficient inducement to cross the plains. After REIMS and ÉPERNAY, the single – albeit considerable – attraction of the region is the town of TROYES, off to the south.

   The mayor of **TROYES** as housing minister under Giscard introduced measures to curb property developments in old town centres, not to limit speculation but because high-rise eyesores between historic buildings were not acceptable for the most aesthetic nation in the universe. His policies may have failed elsewhere, but the mayor could trot back home and take comfort in the restored and preserved quarters of the ancient capital of Champagne. And there were certainly architectural glories to protect amid the high narrow city streets: an elegant Gothic cathedral, half a dozen superb lesser churches and a couple of fistfuls of Renaissance mansions.

The old town walls, however, are gone – replaced by the usual circuit of boulevards, shaped, as the tourist pamphlets are at pains to point out, like a champagne cork. In fact they're more like a sock – eminently suitable since hosiery and knitted goods have been the most important industry since the end of the Middle Ages. In 1630 Louis XIII decreed that charitable houses had to be self-supporting so the orphanage of the **Hôpital de la Trinité** set their charges to work making knitted stockings. Colbert introduced better machines, thanks to his spies in England, by the time the first generation of child labourers were experienced *bonnetiers*. Today the business accounts for more than half the town's employment. Some of the machines and products can be seen in a **Musée de la Bonneterie** in **Hôtel de Vauluisant** (rue de Vauluisant, open 10–12 & 2–6, cl. Tues). But much more enjoyable is the collection of tools housed in the old orphanage **Hôtel de Mauroy** at 7 rue de la Trinité. The *Hôtel*, beautifully restored, is an example to all 'crafts' museums – visually appealing and unsentimentally respectful of the traditions. It's open daily 9–12 & 2–6.

The other outstanding museum in Troyes is the **Musée d'Art Moderne** housed in the old Bishops' Palace in the cathedral square (11–6, cl. Tues). It shows part of an extraordinary private collection of art from 1850–1950, particularly strong on the Fauvists – Dufy, Van Dongen, Vlaminck and Dérain – and with other works by Degas, Courbet, Gauguin, Matisse (a tapestry and three canvases), Bonnard, Braque, Modigliani, Rodin, Robert Delaunay and Ernst – none of them second bests.

The **Cathédrale St-Pierre et St-Paul** next door is little less gorgeous in colour and light: a pale Gothic nave stroked with reflections from wonderful stained glass windows. It is open 8.30–12 & 2–5. Other Troyes churches also have visiting hours and you're only allowed to peer into the sumptuous **St-Pantaléon**, opposite Hôtel de Vauluisant. In the **Église St-Jean**, now surrounded by a pedestrian precinct, Henry V married Catherine of France after being recognised as heir to the French throne in the 1420 Treaty of Troyes, his only claim to the title being that he had successively ravaged the already divided country – no doubt without a single one of the qualities attributed to Prince Hal by Shakespeare.

Arriving at Troyes you should find yourself a short walk from the centre: the **gares SNCF** and **routière** are side by side, just outside bd Carnot (one of the circuit). Not all buses use the main station, though, and if you're heading for the sticks best check first with the SI around the corner fom the *gares* at 16 bd Carnot. **Places to stay** around the station are plentiful: *de la Gare* (8 bd Canot), *de Paris* and *La Monnaie* (54 and 64 rue Roger Salengro) are inexpensive. Others, more centrally located, include *Le Trianon* (2 rue Pithou), *du Centre* (43 rue Mole) and *Embassy* (51 rue Raymond Poincaré), and outside termtime there may be rooms in the city's foyers – the SI will have details. The **youth hostel** is 6km out of town at 8 rue Jules Ferry, Rosières (bus to the Chartreux terminus then bus 11 to ROSIÈRES, stop *Liberté*). Opposite the sign saying Vielaines a path leads down to the 14C priory – a youth hostel with a difference – where you can stay all year round as well as camp in the grounds. The municipal **campsite** in 2km north-east of Troyes at PONT STE-MARIE (bus 1).

For **eats** there's considerable variety, with plenty of brasseries around the pedestrian precinct. *Le Provençal* at 18 rue Gen Saussier with good, cheap and quick standard fare proves how unnecessary fast food is in France. In the same street there's a very good (though fairly expensive) Lebanese restaurant, *Tou-Feu-Tou-Flam* which stays open late.

CHARLEVILLE AND THE ARDENNES

The people of **the Ardennes** have suffered war after war down the valley of the Meuse – which, once lost, gave invading armies a clear path to Paris. The hilly terrain and deep forests (that frightened even Julius Caesar's legionnaires) gave some advantage to the last war's Resistance fighters when Ardennes was annexed to Germany, but even peacetime living has never been easy. The main employment over the last century is coming to an end – the slateworks have all closed down and the ironworks are following suit. The only offering from Paris has been a nuclear power station in the loop of the Meuse at Chooz. To which one local comment is to be seen etched high on a half-cut cliff of slate just downstream: 'Nuke the Elysée!'.

The only way this rugged and unarable land is going to survive is by encouraging tourism. As yet it's far from developed but that's a major attraction. The usual starting-off point for exploring the north is **CHARLEVILLE-MÉZIÈRES** which spreads across the meandering Meuse before the valley closes in and the forests take over. It's a sombre town that has only one native to honour, the poet Arthur Rimbaud (1854–91). He ran away from Charlesville four times, the last time aged 17; joined Verlaine in Paris; fought in the Commune, and, after twice surviving attempts by the elder poet on his life, gave up poetry for good and fled the country (aged 19). After wandering between Europe and the Far East he became a successful trader in Ethiopia and Aden and only returned to France for surgery, which killed him, in a Marseilles hospital. The **Musée Arthur Rimbaud** in the *Vieux Moulin*, is in the process of being expanded and should contain a lot of pictures of this strange youth and those he hung out with as well as facsimiles and all manner of documentation. It should be open, complete or not, 10–12 & 2–6, cl. Mon.

The central square of Charleville, **place Ducale**, is the result of the 17C local duke's envy of the contemporary place des Vosges in Paris. The **SI** is just off it to the west at 2 rue Mantoue, and can provide information for the whole region. The **gare SNCF** is a 5min bus ride away (take any of the buses going to the right as you come out, and ask someone to tell you when you reach place Nevers, just below place des Vosges): the **gare routière** is a couple of blocks north of place Nevers, between rues du Daga and Noel. Three fairly central **hotels** to try are *L'Auto* (42 av du M Leclerc), *Le Marcassin* (10 rue d'Alsace) and *Meuse* (8 rue de l'Épargne). For the **youth hostel** (3 rue des Tambours), take bus 9, direction *La Brouette* from the station or place Nevers (stop *Auberge de Jeunesse*). The town **campsite** is south of place Ducale, over the river past the Vieux Moulin and to the left.

Northern Ardennes – along the Meuse

George Sand wrote of the Ardennes stretch of the Meuse that 'its high wooded cliffs, strangely solid and compact, are like some inexorable destiny that encloses, pushes and twists the river without permitting it a single whim or any escape'. What all the tourist literature writes about, however, are the legends of macho medieval struggles between Good and Evil whose characters have given names to some of the curious rocks and crests. The grandest of these, where the schist formations have taken the most peculiar turns, is the **Roc de la Tour**, also known as the devil's castle, up a path off the D31 to HAUTES RIVIÈRES, 3½km out of MONTHERMÉ.

The journey through this frontier country should ideally be done on foot, or skis or by **boat**. The alternatives for the latter are good old *bateau-mouches* or live-in pleasure boats – not wildly expensive if you can split the cost four or six ways. If you're interested, contact *Loisirs Accueil en Ardennes*, 18 av G Corneau, Charleville. At the same office you'll also find the Ardennes tourist *comité*, who can provide **walking maps** of the region. The **GR12** is an attractive route, circling the Lac des Vieux Forges (17km east of Charleville – and with canoe hire), then meeting the Meuse at Bogny and crossing over to the even more sinuous Semoy Valley and Hautes Rivières. There are plenty of other tracks too, just watch out for *chasse* signs: French hunting types make even the British look sane, wandering about with their safety catches off. Setting out, **trains** follow the Meuse into Belgium, and a few **buses** run up to MONTHERMÉ and HAUTES RIVIÈRES.

In the **forests**, back from the river, are an astonishing amount (and variety) of mushrooms, along with wild strawberries and bilberries, and, for connoisseurs of water, the faintly lemoned spring water of ST-VLADIMIR; just out of Haybes on the Hargnies road. Wild boars are the main quarry being hunted – and nowhere near as dangerous as the pursuers. The four-hooved beasts would seem to be more intelligent too, rooting about near the crosses of the Resistance memorial near REVIN while hunters stalk the forest at a respectful distance.

Campsites through the region are easily found and there are a few cheap **hotels** along the way: *Micass* in BOGNY-SUR-MEUSE (1 place de la République); *Terminus* in REVIN (44 av Danton); *Lion* in FUMAY (7 rue de la Gare); *Jeanne d'Arc* in HAYBES-SUR-MEUSE (32 Grande Rue); *Univers* (37 av Lartigue); and *Lido* (2 rue du Gen de Gaulle) in GIVET, the last town before the border.

LORRAINE

In the last war, when de Gaulle and the Free French chose as their emblem **Lorraine's** double-barred cross they were making a powerful point. For it is this region, above all others, that the French associate with war. And the battle site at **Verdun**, where in 1916 the French army fought one of the most bloody and protracted encounters of all time, is in all but name a national pilgrimage. The SNCF still lay on extra trains here for the celebration of Armistice Day, though there can be few left alive who knew and mourn the 700,000 dead.

The rest of Lorraine – rolling farmland in the south, ailing smokestack industry in the north – seems to stand in the shadows if you pause at Verdun, or the Second World War **Maginot line** fort of **Fermont**. And in truth there's not a lot to hold you here, except perhaps **Nancy**, the region's capital – an elegant city, lighter in tone than the rest of its province, and with a quietly wonderful museum of Art Nouveau.

VERDUN AND THE MAGINOT LINE

At Verdun even the pretence of rationality failed. The slaughter was so hideous that even a trench system could not survive . . . In the town, tourists inspect the memorials. One monument shows French soldiers forming a human wall of comradeship against the enemy. In another, France is personified as a medieval knight; resting on a sword, he dominates a steep flight of steps built into the old ramparts. There is another view of reality. Near the railway station, Rodin's statue shows a winged Victory as neither calm nor triumphant, but demented by rage and horror. Her legs are tangled in a dead soldier and she shrieks for survival.

Donald Horne, *The Great Museum*

VERDUN is still a town, but that in itself is of little interest. You arrive – the **gares** SNCF and **routière** are side by side, a couple of cheap, clean

hotels nearby — and it is straightaway the events of 1916 that take over. For this place, which the German general, von Falkenhayn, chose 'to bleed the French army to death and strike a devastating blow at the morale of the French people', is, with Dunkerque, Dresden, Stalingrad, Nagasaki, one of the names we have chosen to represent war forever. It is a strange site to pass into tourism, but an instructive one. You don't forget — or regret — seeing it.

The battle opened on the morning of 21 February with a German artillery barrage which lasted 10 hours and expended 2 million shells. It concentrated on the forts of Vaux and Douaumont which the French had built after the 1870 German invasion.* When the battle ended ten months later, its toll was approaching a million, and nine villages had been pounded to nothing — not even their sites are detectable in aerial photos of the time and the land today still follows the curves of shell craters. It is said that the heavy artillery shells ploughed the ground to a depth of 8m, and though much of it is now reafforested there are parts that steadfastly refuse all but the coarsest vegetation.

From 1 May to 15 Sept the **Verdun SI** (across the river from the old tower) run minibus **tours of the battlefield**. They begin at 2pm, last 4 hours, and are expensive. But the guides are interesting and the expense is not one that you are likely to repeat. The tour covers the forts of Vaux and Douaumont, the ossuary of Douaumont and a museum on the site of the vanished village of Fleury.

Douaumont commands the highest point of a ridge. Completed in 1912 it was the strongest of thirty-eight forts built to defend Verdun. But by one of those characteristic aberrations of military top brass, the armament of these forts was greatly reduced in 1915. When the Germans attacked in 1916 twenty men were enough to overrun the garrison of fifty-seven French territorials. The fort is built on three levels, two of them under-ground. Its claustrophobic, dungeon-like galleries are hung with stalactites from the damp. The Germans, who held it for eight months, had 3,000 men housed in its cramped quarters, under siege continuously, with no toilets, the ventilation ducts blocked for protection against gas, infested with vermin, plagued by rats which attacked the sleeping and the dead indiscriminately. In one night, when their ammunition exploded, 1,300 men died in the blast.

When the French retook the fort, it was with Moroccan troops in the Vanguard. General Mangin, revered by officialdom as the heroic victor of the battle, was known to his troops as 'the butcher' for his practice

---

*The 1870 invasion secured Alsace and the greater part of Lorraine for Germany — and they held both fot the next 48 years. The military symbolism of this part of the country is hard to underestimate — nor the 1870 invasion, either, which had seen German troops at the walls of Paris.

of shoving colonial troops into the front line as cannon fodder. As the film shown in the projection room of the museum at Fleury observes, men who had no desire to kill were forced on pain of the firing squad to slaughter their fellow human beings. Official history accords little attention to their spontaneous and scarcely organised mutinies and refusals.

Close to the fort is a cemetery containing the graves of 15,000 men, the Christians commemorated by rows of identical crosses, the Moroccans with gravestones slanted in the direction of Mecca. Nearby a vast mausoleum contains the bones of a further 130,000 unidentified dead, picked from the battlefield by a French priest.

These horrors are all graphically documented in the **museum at Fleury**. There is no attempt to glorify either side. Contemporary newsreels and photos present the stark truth. In the well of the museum, a section of the shell-torn terrain has been reconstructed as the battle left it.

The tour's last call is at the fort of **Vaux**, where after six days' hand-to-hand fighting in the confined, gas-filled galleries, the French garrison, reduced to drinking their urine, were left with no alternative but surrender. On the exterior wall of the fort a plaque commemorates the last messenger pigeon sent to the command post in Verdun vainly asking for reinforcements. Having safely delivered its message, the pigeon expired as a result of flying through the gas-filled air above the battlefield.

The Maginot line

About 50km north of VERDUN, near the small town of LONGUYON, you can see how little was learnt from the battle. For here – open daily 1.30–5/4, wkends only in Oct – you can visit the underground fort of FERMONT, which, with a series of others, and various other defences above ground, formed the **Maginot Line**, first grand failure of the Second World War.

Constructed between 1930 and 1940 **the Line** was the brain-child of the Minister of War André Maginot. It was immensely costly, and, when put to the test in 1940, it proved to be totally useless, for the Germans simply went round the end of it. **FERMONT** was one of the largest forts, with nine fire points, served by 6km of underground tunnels and a garrison of 600. The entrance is hidden in woodland. Nothing shows above ground but the scarcely noticeable domes of the gun turrets. Below, the tunnels are equipped with electric trains, monorails, lifts, power plants and all the other technological paraphernalia necessary to support such a lunatic enterprise. But then, it is hard to scoff in any wisdom: the place has the blinkered feel of a nuclear bunker, and we have allowed them to be built by our own governments.

There are **trains** to LONGUYON from METZ and CONFLANS. From VERDUN you have to change at Conflans. It is possible, though not easy, to hitch across country via DAMVILLERS and Marville. It is 8km from Longuyon to Fermont and you'll probably have to walk it. Coming back the best thing is to hijack a fellow-visitor in the car park. In Longuyon *Hôtel de Lorraine* by the station is an attractive place to stay.

METZ

Very much a northern town, **METZ** seems solid, and confident of hard-headed business values. The **railway station** sets the tone, a vast granite building of 1900 in Rhenish Romanesque, matched by the **post office** opposite. It's not a place to plan on staying in, but there are several **hotels** and **eating** places in front of the station, and a **youth hostel** and **camping** on the banks of the Moselle by Pont Thionville.

To reach the centre take rue Gambetta, rue Harelle (**SI** by the reconstructed Porte Serpenoise) and turn right along av Schuman to **place de la République,** a big square with shops and cafés and the formal gardens of the Esplanade overlooking the Moselle. On the right of the Esplanade is a handsome classical Palais de Justice in yellow stone. To the left a gravel walk leads to **St-Pierre-aux-Nonnains**, not much to look at, but one of the oldest churches in the land – 4C, at least in part. Behind it, on the other side of the École des Beaux Arts, rue de la Citadelle leads to an unusual octagonal chapel built by the Templars (13C) and on to the leafy square Giraud, with the splendidly gabled and creepered Gothic mansion of the Governor of Metz.

From the north side of place de la République, **rue des Clercs** leads through the principal shopping area to the fine classical **place d'Armes** (18C) flanked by a pedimented and colonnaded **Hôtel de Ville**. All rather dwarfed by the short-in-length but very tall **Cathédrale de St-Etienne** (13C), its nave the highest in France after Beauvais and Amiens. The best feature – as at Reims – is the glass, both medieval and modern, and again including windows by Chagall.

NANCY

Only 40mins away by train, **NANCY** capital of Lorraine, is lighter and more southern in feel than Metz. The central area has been little affected by modern redevelopment, and remains much more 18C than 19C. For this city has the last of the independent dukes of Lorraine to thank, Stanislas Leczinski, dethroned king of Poland, father-in-law of Louis XV. During the twenty-odd years of his office in the middle of the 18C he ordered some of the most successful urban redevelopment of the period in all France.

Pride of place goes to **place Stanislas**. From the **railway station**, go under the Doric **Porte Stanislas** and all the way down **rue Stanislas** to the bottom.

The middle of the wide square belongs to the solitary statue of the portly Stanislas himself. The south side is entirely taken up by the **Hôtel de Ville**, its roof line topped with a balustrade ornamented with florid urns and *amorini*. From its walls lozenge-shaped lanterns dangle from the beaks of gilded cocks. The other buildings are similar, though not as big. The entrances to the square are closed by superb wrought iron gates, but the best work of all is in the railings which close the north-eastern and north-western corners, framing gloriously extravagant fountains with lead statues of Neptune and Amphitrite.

The **SI**, **PTT** and **Beaux Arts** are all on the square: the latter (10–12 & 2–6, cl. Mon am/Tues) boasts Dufys and Matisses but nothing very outstanding. Time in museums here is better spent at the **Musée de Zoologie** (rue Ste-Catherine – which leads off Stanislas; 2–6, cl. Tues), upstairs a colossal jumble of stuffed animals and birds, all appallingly displayed and labelled, down a startling aquarium of exotic fish beating even Matisse. Or make your way to the unpromisingly named **Musée de l'École de Nancy** (38 rue Sergent Blandan; 10–12 & 2–6/5; cl. Tues) in a 1909 villa built for the Corbin family, founders of the big Magasins Réunis chain of department stores. Even if you are not into Art Nouveau, this collection is exciting. Although not all the collection belongs to the Corbins the museum is arranged as if it were a private house. The

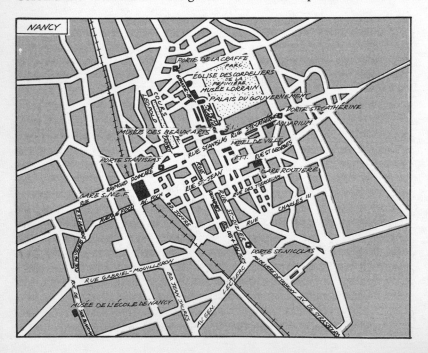

furniture is all outstanding – swirling curvilinear forms, whether the object is mantlepiece or sofa, buffet or piano. And the standards of workmanship are incredibly high. Nancy was the centre of the movement founded by Émile Gallé, manufacturer of glass and ceramics, prominent here, of course. A fourth museum, which does demand prior interest, is devoted to the history of Lorraine, housed in the old palace of the dukes (10–12 & 2–6/5).

There are several cheap **hotels** in the rue Stanislas-rue des Carmes area. Try the *Académie* at 7 rue Michottes or *Choley*, 28 rue Gustave Simon, both off rue Stanislas about half-way down. For food, rue Grande-rue has several possibilities, and a very nice, arty cafe, *Le Concert*; rue des Maréchaux is also good restaurant ground. The **youth hostel** is out at the *Centre d'Accueil*, Château de Rémicourt, VILLERS-LES-NANCY (83.27.73.67) – 15mins by bus: plus 15 on foot (no signposts). To find it take bus no 6 in rue des Carmes, direction *Vandoeuvre*, and get off at the *Mangin* stop, immediately after a left turn by a housing estate called Les Jonquilles; then go back to the main road, turn left and straight across the first major intersection, leaving the École d'Architecture at the edge of a park on your left; take the next left, a small road running uphill beside the park – a gate on the left leads to the château (*Camping de Brabois* is nearby).

Lunéville

Lunéville (20mins by train from Nancy) was renowned for its *faïence* works, set up by Stanislas. There is a collection, and a pretty one, in a dusty museum (9–12, 2–6; cl. Tues) in the immense 18C **château,** but it is too small to merit a detour for anyone not a specialist. The rest of the museum is occupied by cavalry uniforms and weaponry, Lunéville being a garrison town.

What is worth a detour is M Chapleur's private **motorbike museum,** smack opposite the gates of the château, the *Musée de la moto et du vélo* (9–12 & 2–6; cl. Mon). Monsieur Chapleur started collecting in the 1930s when he was a mechanic at Citroen's. He has over 200 models of different nationality on display, all overhauled and in working order when they go into the museum. And they are beauties, works of art in copper, brass, chrome and steel. Some of the push-bikes go back to 1865. The motorbikes are mostly 1900–40. Several of the older bikes are probably unique; one certainly is – a 1906 René Gillet 4½hp belt-driven tandem. Many look like flying bombs and must have been incredibly dangerous to ride: bits of meccano with a couple of hefty cylinders welded on and capable of 100kph in 1900.

To get to the museum – and château – from the station, take rue Carnot (**hotels**), place Léopold, rue Gen Leclerc, rue de la Charité, and turn right in front of the vast red Baroque church of St-Jacques.

ALSACE

There's no denying **Alsace's** attractiveness – old stone and half-timbered towns amid thickly wooded hills – but it's a quaintness that has also firmly been turned into a commodity. **Strasbourg**, the capital, escapes the tweeness of its smaller neighbours – and should definitely be seen. Elsewhere you may want to direct travels around some of the province's unusually good **museums**: Grunewald's amazing **Issenheim altarpiece** at **Colmar, cars, railways** and **cotton** at **Mulhouse**, and the chilling **Resistance museum** at **Besançon**.

SAVERNE AND THE NORTHERN VOSGES

SAVERNE, 50mins from Lunéville, is the first Alsatian town you come to on the Paris-Strasbourg line. It is not as picturesque as some, but has the region's characteristic steep-pitched roofs, dormer windows and window-boxes full of geraniums. It has always been strategically important because it commands the only easy route across the Vosges at a point where the hills are pinched to a narrow waist.

As such, it is a good base for exploring the **Parc Naturel Régional des Vosges du Nord** and for day walks. There is a clean, friendly **youth hostel** in the vast red sandstone château just over the canal bridge in Grand' Rue. A pretty and easy walk (about 2 hours there and back) is to the ruined castle of **Haut Barr**. Take rue Poincaré opposite the château, turn right in rue de Paris and immediately left into rue du Haut-Barr along the canal. Keep on to the end, past leafy suburban villas. A wood begins at the end of the road with a signboard indicating various walks. Take the path waymarked Haut-Barr through woods of chestnut, beech and larch. The castle stands dramatically on a narrow sandstone ridge with fearsome drops either side and views across the wooded hills and eastward over the plain towards Strasbourg. MARMOUTIER – 6km from Saverne and easily walkable – has a fine church with an unusual front. Ask the **SI** (in Hôtel de Ville) for other walking possibilities.

The obvious route on from here is to STRASBOURG, but if you're curious about this pocket of the country, SNCF buses wind through the villages and apple orchards along the German border. **WISSEMBOURG**, at the northern end of the Vosges, is one of the more interesting – and unspoilt, despite its popularity with German weekenders. A considerable section of its walls survives, built like the stonework on the houses in the local red sandstone; the church, 13C, is bordered by a canal; and the village also has a linguistic curiosity – speaking a dialect derived from Frankish, unlike Alsatian which is similar to that spoken on the German bank of the Rhine. If you stay, the best bets are **hotels** *de la Gare* and *de l'Europe* by the railway station; upmarket, but with one very nice inexpensive double, is the *Hôtel du Cygne*, by the townhall on central place de la République.

OBERSEEBACH and HUNSPACH and the CHÂTEAU DE FLECK-ENSTEIN in the woods on the frontier make good local excursions.

STRASBOURG

STRASBOURG is prosperous, beautiful and modern: big enough at a quarter of a million people to have a metropolitan air, but without being overwhelming. It has one of the loveliest – perhaps the loveliest – cathedrals in France; one of the oldest (and still most active) universities; and, ancient commercial crossroads that it is, is current seat of the Council of Europe and, part time, of the European parliament. You are perhaps unlikely to be planning time in France around the east, but travelling through or near the region this is the one city worth special detour.

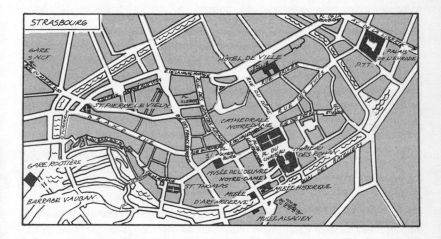

It is not difficult to **find your way around**. The city concentrates its interest in a small island area encircled by the river Ill. There are several two-star **hotels** in the station square, more along the adjoining rue du Maire Kuss (try the *Royale, Victoria, Grillon* or *Colmar*) which leads to Pont Kuss over the Ill. For the **youth hostel**, modern with a bar and excellent canteen, you can get a 3, 13 or 23 bus by the next bridge upstream (on the right) – stop, *Auberge de Jeunesse*. For the city centre, **rue du 22 novembre** takes you to **place Kléber**, the commercial centre, where all the bus routes converge.

A more picturesque approach to the old centre is along **quai Turckheim**, where you see the first of four square towers guarding the so-called **Ponts Couverts** over a series of canals. They are part of the 14C city fortifications. Just upstream is a dam built by Vauban to protect the city from waterborne assault. Known as **La Petite France**, the area is very pretty, all 16C and 17C houses with carved woodwork and decked with flowers, but predictably it is a tourist hot spot, with the horrid little *Petit Train* honking its twee way through the lanes.

Place Gutenberg is named for the printer, pioneer of type, whose statue occupies the middle of the square; he lived in Strasbourg in the early 15C. The west side of the square is taken up by the 16C Hôtel de Commerce (**SI** on ground floor), where the writer Arthur Young, fascinated, watched the night-time destruction of the magistrates' records during the Revolution. But all this is distraction. The one thing you are conscious of is the **Cathédrale de Notre-Dame**, all in pinky-red sandstone, soaring out of the close huddle of medieval houses at its feet, with a spire of such delicate, flaky lightness it seems designed to be eaten. Inside, too, it is magnificent, the high nave a model of proportion and enhanced by a glorious sequence of **glass**. The finest of all, perhaps, are the windows in the south aisle, depicting the life of Christ, and the Creation, next to the door. But they are all beautiful, including the modern glass in the apse, designed in 1956 by Max Ingrand to commemorate the first European institutions in the city.

On the left of the nave the **pulpit**, late 15C, is another masterpiece of intricacy in stone. Nearby, in the south transept, are two of the cathedral's most popular sights. One is the slender triple-tiered column known as the *Pilier des Anges*, 13C Romanesque with some of the most graceful and expressive statuary of its age. The other is an enormous, and enormously complicated, **astrological clock** built by Schwilgué of Strasbourg in 1838 – just the sort of curio that warms the cockles of wonder-seeking tourists and their organisers. They roll up in droves to witness the clock's crowning performance of the day, striking the hour of noon, which it does, with unerring accuracy, at 1231, that being 12 o'clock Strasbourg mean time. Death strikes the chimes. The Apostles parade in front of Christ, who occupies the highest storey of the clock; as each one passes he receives Christ's blessing. As the fourth, eighth and twelfth pass, a cock crows!

It is entertaining, but the chief advantage of paying your 3F is that, since it is the only way of entering the cathedral at this time of day, there are fewer people about than at other times.

South of the cathedral, the treelined **place du Château**, where the ridiculous *Petit Train* starts its journey, is enclosed by the Lycée Fustel and the Château des Rohans, both 18C buildings, the latter designed for the immensely powerful Rohan family who for several generations in a row secured a corner of the market in cardinal's hats. Next door the **Musée de l'oeuvre Notre-Dame** (10–12 & 2–6, cl. Tues & ams Oct–April wkdays) houses original sculptures from the cathedral fronts – damaged in the Revolution and replaced today by copies. Both sets repay attention. And there are other treasures here: glass from the city's original Roman-esque cathedral; the 11C Wissembourg Christ, said to be the oldest representation of a human figure in stained glass; the architect's original drawings for the statuary, done on parchment, in fascinating detail, down to the different expressions on each figure's face.

The **Château des Rohans** itself houses three museums: **Arts Décoratifs**, **Beaux-Arts** and **Archéologique** (same hours as above). The apartments of the château are not especially interesting: vast and opulent, what the French call *tape-à-l'oeil* – hit-you-in-the-eye. Of the collections only the Art Déco stands out – and that as slightly specialist interest, with its 18C *faïence* crafted in the city by Paul Hannong. If you feel museum-orien-tated, though, there's another trio close by, around place du Marché-aux-Cochons-de-Lait (sucking-pig market square). The **Musée Historique**, in the old Grande Boucherie, is mainly concerned with the city (though it also has an oddball collection of mechanical toys upstairs). Opposite, the **Musée d'Art Moderne** has an impressive 'permanent' collection – Monet, Klimt, Ernst, Klee, Jean Arp – though it is frustratingly hidden away whenever they have a temporary exhibition. And last, there is the **Musée Alsacien**: painted furniture and other local artefacts in a traditional house, just across the Pont du Corbeau. All keep similar hours to the Notre-Dame Works Museum.

Upstream is **quai des Bateliers**, part of the old business quarter. Take a look at the 14C **Cour du Courbeau** off place du Corbeau. Two bridges downstream is Pont St-Thomas, leading to the church of **St-Thomas**, with a Romanesque façade and Gothic towers. Since 1549 it has been the principal Protestant church. Strasbourg was a bastion of the Reformation, and one its leaders, Martin Bucer, preached in this church. The amazing piece of sculpture behind the altar is the tomb of the Maréchal de Saxe, by the sculptor Pigalle (18C).

The area east of the cathedral is good for a stroll too, rue des Fréres leading to place St-Etienne and rue des Juifs. **Place du Marché Gayot**, right behind the cathedral, is very pretty with an unpretentious student-type café on one side. From the north side of the cathedral rue du Dôme leads to the 18C **place Broglie** with the Hôtel de Ville and *préfet*'s residence and some imposing 18C bourgeois mansions round about. It was at no 4 place Broglie that Rouget de Lisle first sang the Marseillaise for the mayor of Strasbourg (1712), who had challenged him at dinner the night before to knock out a rousing song for the troops of the army of the Rhine.

Across the river here, **place de la République** is surrounded by vast

German-Gothic edifices, erected during the Imperial Prussian occupation post-1870. The **Post Office**, down av de la Liberté, is one such. If you cross the river Aar by Pont de l'Université (Goethe studied here), and turn left along Allée de la Robertsau, flanked by confident turn-of-the-century bourgeois residences, you come to the **Orangerie park** and, opposite, the **Palais de l'Europe**. It is an imposing and adventurous piece of contemporary architecture (1977), suitably vast, in matt silver, pinky-bronze glass and red concrete, with the contemporary equivalent of a turret jutting from one corner. The interior, or at least the part you can visit, is surprisingly poky and cheaply finished with the exception of the European Parliament's debating chamber.

Some details

Strasbourg usually has a fair amount **going on**. If you're here in termtime check noticeboards at the university. In summer, pick up the *Saison d'Eté* listings leaflet from the SI. Regular events include **free concerts** in the Orangerie and Contades parks, an international **music festival** (mid-June), another, independent European cinema in the autumn and a third, of **mime** and **clowning**, in November.

For **food**, beware the more touristy places and if you're hard up go for Germanic Alsace snacks – *wurst sauerkraut* and the like. The *FEC* **student restaurant** in place St-Etienne has rock-bottom prices and good meals too: ask a student to buy you a ticket.

As for other practicalities, **bikes** can be hired from the SNCF; **buses** leave from place des Halles and place des Anciens Abbatoirs; the *Club Vosgien* (4 rue de la Douane) have **hiking information**; the CIJ are at 7 rue des Ecrivains (88.37.33.33); and there's a **laundrette** in the Grand' Rue.

Hitching out towards the German frontier, take Pont du Corbeau, Pont d'Austerlitz and then Route du Rhin. For *Allostop* call 88.37.13.13 or look in at the office at 5 rue Général Zimmer.

SOUTH ALONG THE RHINE FRONTIER: COLMAR TO MULHOUSE

COLMAR, about 50mins by train south of Strasbourg, has urban-sprawled unattractively both sides of its railway tracks, but its old centre is typically and picturesquely Alsatian, with lots of crooked houses, half-timbered and painted, on crooked lanes. It is very pretty and very touristry. That is the problem with Alsace. Left to its own devices, it stays the right side of Disneyland, but under the impact of tourism and the desire to make money it comes close to caricaturing itself.

Aside from prettiness, Colmar is the proud possessor of some very remarkable paintings, housed in its **Musée d'Unterlinden**, and above all the *Issenheim altarpiece*, painted by Mathias Grünewald at the beginning of the 16C, one of the last and most extraordinary of all medieval Gothic paintings. From the station, go straight ahead and turn left into av de la République (**hotels**: *de l'Europe, La Chaumière, Rhin et Danube;* **PTT** on the left and a **cafeteria**, which, though plastic in décor, sells very good food at good prices). The museum is just beyond the intersection at the end of av de la République in a former Dominican convent (13C) (9–12 & 2–6/5, cl. Tues).

Although displayed 'exploded', the **Issenheim altarpiece** was designed to make a single piece. On the front was the Crucifixion, almost luridly expressive: a tortured Christ with stretched bony rib-cage and outsize hands turned upward with fingers splayed in pain flanked by his pale fainting mother, St John and Mary Magdalene. Then it unfolded, respective to its function on feast days, Sundays and weekdays, to reveal an Annunciation, Resurrection, Virgin and Child, and finally a sculpted panel depicting the saints Anthony, Augustine and Jerome. Completed in 1515, the painting is affected by Renaissance innovations in light and perspective but still rooted in the medieval spirit, with an intense mysticism and shifts of mood in its subject matter. Other works in the Museum are, inevitably, secondary but they'd do credit elsewhere and there's a surprisingly interesting collection of modern paintings in the basement.

A little to the south, reached by rue des Têtes and rue des Boulangers, the **Domican church** (9.30–6.30, small charge) has some fine glass and, above all, a radiantly beautiful altarpiece by Schongauer (who is also represented in the Unterlinden), painted in 1473, known as *The Virgin in a bower of roses*. Down rue des Serruriers you come to the church of **St-Martin** on a square with numerous cafés, and from here, rue des Marchands leads past to the painted **Maison Pfister** and on towards the knowingly picturesque **Quartier de Krutenau**, its houses all backing onto the river.

If you plan to stay in Colmar, there's a reasonable **youth hostel**: from the station turn left, over the railway bridge, along av de la Liberté to the second lights, then right onto rue Albert Schweitzer and it's behind the shops on the left (about 20mins' walk). The local **SI** (by the museum) sell *Club Vosgien* maps and a booklet of day **walks** in the hills behind the town. And **buses**, from the gare SNCF, leave for most towns in these parts, including LE BONHOMME and mountain destinations. The Colmar-Sélestat road enables you to take in the so-called **Route du Vin**. Alsatian wines, dry and white, are definitely worth getting to know.

RIQUEWIHR, 8km south along the SÉLESTAT bus route, is an extra-ordinarily pretty village. Mostly 16C, mostly intact, and prime tourist territory. It has a single cobbled street which runs lengthwise through the village, rising gently to the Dolder, a 13C gate. The vineyards which made, and still make, its prosperity reach to the foot of the walls. Indeed they begin the minute you leave Colmar, flooding over the level plain right up to the first slopes of the Vosges.

MULHOUSE, 20mins down the line from Colmar, is a large sprawling industrial city that got rich around 1800, on printed cotton fabrics and allied trades. Not having much of a centre it is no city for strollers but it does have three unusual museums – devoted to cars, railways and cotton fabrics.

The latter, the **Musée de l'Impression sur étoffes** (10–12 & 2–6, cl. Tues) is very close to the station, just along the canal to the right. It is expensive but excellent, a vast collection of the most beautiful fabrics imaginable – 18C Indian and Persian imports (which revolutionised the European ready-to-wear market), silks from Turkestan, Uzbekistan and others -ans, batiks from Java, Senegalese materials, some superb kimonos from Japan, and a unique display of scarves from France, Britain and the US.

The other two museums are trickier to get to. For the trains, the **Musée Français du Chemin de Fer** (10–5, again pricey), you'll need to take bus no 1 to the end of the line, near the suburb of Dornach, then follow the signs. Rolling stock on display includes Napoleon III's ADCs' drawing-room, decorated by Viollet-le-Duc in 1856, and a luxuriously appointed 1926 diner from the Golden Arrow. There are cranes, stations, signals and other railwayana, but the stars of the show are the big locomotives with their brightly painted boilers, gleaming wheels and pistons and tangles of brass and copper piping. Cold steel they may be, but you could be forgiven for thinking they had life in them. Real craftsmen's work. As, too, are most of the 600 cars on exhibit in the **Musée National de l'Automobile** (10–6, cl. Tues: similarly pricey), which you can reach by taking bus 2 or 7 from place de l'Europe. They range fom the earliest attempts at powered vehicles, like the extraordinary wooden-wheeled Jacquot steam 'car' of 1878, to 1968 Porsche racing cars, and contemporary factory prototypes. The largest group are the locally made Bugattis: dozens of glorious racing cars, coupés and limousines, the pride of them the Bugatti Royale with two of the seven made on show – one Ettore Bugatti's own, with bodywork designed by his son.

Finding a room in Mulhouse can be tricky. There are a couple of reasonable **hotels** by the railway station, but if these are full the **youth hostel** is about your only bet. Again it's a little way out: bus 4 or 6 from place de l'Europe in the city centre to the *Salle des Sports* in rue de l'Illberg.

BESANÇON

BESANÇON, capital of Franche-Comté, is an ancient and attractive town enclosed in a loop of the river Doubs at the northern edge of the Jura mountains, the foothills of the Alps. It was the birthplace of rayonne, in 1890, and a major centre of clock-making in France, until the western Pacific started getting its act together. Wooded hills enclose it tightly. This constriction and the sober grey stone of its façades give it a slightly mournful air.

There is no youth hostel, but the **Centre International de Séjour,** in the new town at 19 rue Martin du Gard (81.50.07.54; bus 8 from the station to L'Épitaphe) have dormitory beds. Alternatively, opposite the station the **hotels** *Alsace-Lorraine* and *Florel* are cheap and slightly down-at-heel, or try also *Regina* at 91 Grande Rue in the old town. **Camping** is at Plage de Chalezuele, 5km out on the Belfort road. The **CAF**, at 14 rue Luc Breton, organise a lot of **hiking** expeditions into the Jura.

To get into the centre from the station, follow av du Maréchal Foch down to the river and keep along the bank to the first or second bridge. The **SI** is by the second bridge. On the other side **rue de la République** leads to the central **place du 8 septembre** in front of the 16C Hôtel de Ville.

The principal street is **Grande Rue,** on the line of the old Roman road, and overlooked by a craggy hill above the river, capped by another of Vauban's prodigious citadels. At its top end (the livelier part with shops and cafés) there is an excellent **Beaux Arts** (9.30–12 & 2–6; cl. Tues) with two magnificent Bonnards, other good representative 19C and 20C works, and a rather wonderful clock collection. Midway down, the **Palais Granvelle,** a fine 16C mansion, houses a local history museum – not very illuminating. Continuing up you pass place Victor Hugo (he was born at no 140) and come to the **Porte Noire**, a 2C Roman triumphal arch spanning the street and partially embedded in the adjoining houses. In the shady little **square archéologique** beside it are the remains of a *nymphaeum*, a small reservoir of water fed by an aqueduct. Beyond the Porte is the 18C cathedral of **St-Jean**, boring and self-congratulatory.

The **Citadelle** (9–6.30/5.30) is about 15 mins walk and houses three highly worthwhile museums (all at 11.30–1.30). The **Musée Agraire** has old farming implements; the **Folklore Comtois**, pottery, furniture, etc: all fascinating stuff. But the main one is the **Musée de la Résistance et de la Déportation** – a superb aid to understanding the post-war French political consciousness, and unbelievably harrowing. Outside the museum building, four stakes mark the spot where the Germans shot local *résistants*. Inside, the first rooms document the rise of Nazism and French fascism with chilling and fascinating photographs, exhibits (a bar of soap stamped *RIF* – pure Jew fat) and quotations; moving on to the Vichy government (there is a telegram of encouragement sent by Marshall Pétain to the French troops of the Legion of Volunteers against Bolshevism, fighting alongside the Germans on the eastern front); and finally, as counterbalance, to the Resistance – much being made of General Leclerc's vow at Koufra in the Libyan desert, whose capture in January 1941 was the first entirely French victory of the war: 'We will not stop until the French flag flies once more over Metz and Strasbourg', a vow which he kept, when he entered the city at the head of a division in November 1944.

TRAVEL DETAILS

Trains
From Reims frequently to Paris-Est (2hrs), Épernay (25mins) and Charleville-Mézières (55mins).
From Troyes frequent service to Paris-Est (1½hrs).
From Verdun 1 to 4 trains daily to Paris-Est (3hrs), changing at Chalons-sur-Marne (1hr20); 1–3 trains to Metz (1¼hrs), changing at Conflans (½hr).
From Metz 2 to Longuyon (1½hrs); 3–4 to Paris-Est (3hrs); 2 or 3 to Strasbourg (2½hrs) – some go on to Colmar and Mulhouse: several to Nancy (1¼hrs).
From Nancy frequent service to Paris-Est (3½hrs); several to Lunéville (40mins); 2 or 3 to Saverne (1hr); 2 to Strasbourg (1hr20).

From Strasbourg frequent to Paris-Est (4hrs); 1 to 3 to Wissembourg (1hr); several to Basel (1½–2hrs), via Colmar (50mins) and Mulhouse (1hr20) – not all stop at Colmar.
From Mulhouse several to Belfort (30–45mins).
From Besançon several to Belfort (1–1½hrs); 5–6 to Paris-Lyon (2½hrs) – more frequent if you change at Dijon.

Buses
From Reims 3 to Troyes (2 hrs10–3hrs).
From Épernay 1 to Troyes, changing at Romilly (3½hrs).
From Colmar regularly to Mulhouse (1hr), Sélestat (1hr) and to destinations in Germany.

Chapter thirteen
THE ALPS

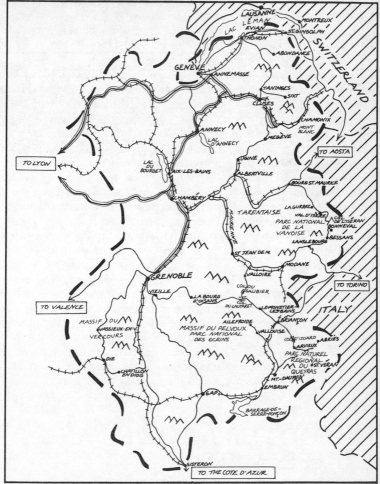

'I need torrents, rocks, pine-trees, dark forests, mountains, rugged paths to go up and down, precipices at my elbow to give me a good fright,' Rousseau wrote in his Confessions. I would add wild flowers (best seen in the first half of July). But, yes, these are the principal joys of **the Alps**. The best, though not the only way to appreciate them is on foot. There are four national or **regional parks** in the area covered by this chapter: Vanoise, Écrins, Queyras and Vercors, all with round-the-park trails, requiring one to two weeks' walking. The **Tour of Mont Blanc** path is of similar length. Then there are two transalpine routes: the **Grande Traversée des Alpes**, which crosses all the major massifs from St-Gingolph on Lake Geneva to Nice, and **Le Balcon des Alpes**, a gentler, village-to-village itinerary through the western foothills.

All these **routes** are clearly waymarked, equipped with refuge huts and *gîtes d'étape*, and described in Topo-guides. The *CIMES* office in Grenoble (see below) will provide detailed information on all GR paths. In addition, local tourist offices often produce detailed maps of walks in their own areas (Chamonix and Sixt, for example). You should not, however, undertake any **high-level, long-distance hikes** unless you are an experienced hill-walker. If you are not, and like the sound of some of these trails, read a specialised hiking book first, before making any plans, or simply limit your sights to more **local targets**. You can find plenty of day-walks to do from a base in or close to any of the parks; and there are some satisfying road routes, too. A tent will give you greatest flexibility, since hotels are seasonal and their prices inflated. The **Vercors**, **Chartreuse**, **Aravis** (east of Annecy), **Faucigny** and **Chablais** (Morzine, Sixt) areas are the gentlest, and quietest, introductions.

The Alps get very crowded in season. Mountain holidays are in vogue, and walking is big business. Unfortunately, you are more or less obliged to go in **season** if you want to walk; apart from unreliable weather, anywhere above 2,000m will be snowbound until the beginning of July. The Chamonix-Mont Blanc area is far the worst for overcrowding – best avoided, unless you are going to get out on the mountain where other people cannot go. I found **Parc du Queyras** the least touristy, and sunniest, of the high parks. Together with parts of **Haute Tarentaise** it still has a few 'genuine' Alpine villages – a species that has become more or less extinct since the Alps have been turned into one great resort. Very beautiful, don't get me wrong, but a resort, nonetheless.

THE FOOTHILL TOWNS AND VERCORS MASSIF

Strung in a line along their western edge, **Grenoble**, **Chambéry** and **Annecy** are the gateways to the highest parts of the French Alps. Of the three Grenoble, with its large university, is the liveliest, but all are interesting enough to merit a short stay. (There is a fourth town, Aix-les-Bains, but it's a dull and elderly spa.) You can't really avoid them anyway, as nearly all Alpine traffic – road and rail – is routed through them.

GRENOBLE AND THE VERCORS

The economic and intellectual capital of the French Alps, **GRENOBLE**, is a lively, thriving, modern city, beautifully situated on the Drac and Isère rivers, surrounded by mountains and home to a university of more than 30,000 students. The city's prosperity was originally founded on glove-making, but in the 19C its economy diversified to include mining, cement, papermills, hydro-electric power (white coal, as they called it) and metallurgy. Today, it is a centre of chemical and electronics industries and nuclear research. The Atomic Energy Commission has big new laboratories on the banks of the Drac. 'It is a city with plenty of brains,' said a builder who gave me a lift. 'There's hardly a worker left.'

The best thing to do first is take the **téléférique** from the riverside quai Stéphane Jay to **Fort de la Bastille** on the steep slopes above the north bank of the Isère. It may be a touristy thing to do, but if you eschew all *téléfériques* in the Alps – there are hundreds of them – you will miss out on a lot of spectacular views. This one, like most of them, is pricey, though you can economise by walking down. The ride is hair-raising, for you are whisked steeply and swiftly into the air in a sort of transparent egg, which allows you to see very clearly how far you would fall in the event of an accident.

Though the fort itself is of little interest, the view is fantastic. At your feet the Isère, milky, grey and swollen with snow-melt, tears at the piles of the old bridges which join the St-Laurent quarter, colonised by Italian immigrants in the 19C, to the nucleus of the medieval town, whose red roofs cluster tightly round the church of St-André. To the east, snowfields gleam in the cwms and gullies of the Belledonne massif (2,978m). Southeast is Taillefer and south-south-east the dip where Route Napoléon passes over the mountains to Sisteron and the Mediterranean. This is the road Napoleon took after his escape from Elba in March 1815 on his way to rally his forces for the campaign that led to his final defeat at Waterloo. To the west are the steep white cliffs of the Vercors massif; the highest peak, dominating the city, is Moucherotte (1,901m). The jagged peaks at your back are the outworks of the Chartreuse massif. North-east on a clear day you can see the white peaks of Mont Blanc up the deep glacial valley of the Isère, known as La Grésivaudan. It was in this valley that the first French hydro-electric scheme went into action in 1869.

Upstream from the *téléférique* station is the 16C **Palais de Justice** (open to the public) with **place St-André** behind and the church of St-André. Built in the 13C and much restored, the church is of little architectural interest, but the narrow streets leading back towards places Grenette, Vaucanson and Verdun take you through the liveliest and most colourful quarter of the city, the focus of life for shoppers and strollers alike. **Place Grenette** is the favourite resort of café loungers.

Nearby at 14 rue J J Rousseau is a small **museum** dedicated to the French Resistance (3–6, Mon & Wed; 3–7, Sat), who were particularly active in the Vercors massif. Stendhal was born in the house, though the city's museum of Stendhaliana is itself in a corner of the public gardens just behind the St-André church. Also close to place Grenette, at 14 rue de la République, are the offices of the **SI** and **CIMES**, the walkers' organisation for the Alpine region.

If you go to the **Musée des Beaux Arts** (1–7; cl. Tues & hols) in the handsome 19C place de Verdun – which you should, as it has an excellent collection of contemporary and representative works by the big names in 20C art – it is worth continuing to **Parc Paul Mistral**. On the corner at the end of rue Haxo is a pretty public garden with some fine trees and the **Natural History Museum**, which has a huge collection of fossils and rocks, animals and birds, including specimens of all the Alpine birds of prey, unfortunately very badly displayed. On the edge of the park stands the modern steel, glass and concrete **Hôtel de Ville**: not an exciting building, all straight lines and square corners, but refreshing in its contemporary attempt. Its central courtyard and interior are adorned with contemporary works of art and in the park behind is an earlier and more frivolous structure, an 87m concrete tower designed by Perret, one of the pioneers of modern French architecture, in 1925. The concrete looks shabby now. You could not call it attractive, but it too is boldly and unapologetically modern.

Apart from the Beaux Arts museum, the most interesting thing to see is the **Musée Dauphinois** (9–12 & 2–6; cl. Tues), occupying the former convent of Ste-Marie-d'en-Haut, up a cobbled path opposite the Isère footbridge by the Palais de Justice. Imaginatively laid out, it is largely devoted to the history and arts and crafts of the province of Dauphiné – this side of the Alps, French since the 14C, unlike neighbouring Savoie, which with Nice was only relinquished by the Italians in 1860. There are exhibits on the life of the mountain people, 'les gens de là-haut', the people from up there, who like most poor mountaineers were obliged to travel the world as peddlers and knife-grinders. Many, too, were involved in smuggling, and there is a fascinating collection of body-hugging flasks used for contraband liquor. The most unusual section is the so-called *Roman des Grenoblois*, the story of the people of Grenoble told in an excellent audio-visual presentation through the lives of various members of a representative selection of families, ranging from immigrant workers to wealthy industrialists. France's first trade union or workers' Provident society was established in Grenoble in 1803 by the glove-makers.

There are numerous **hotels** in the railway station area: *Suisse et Bordeaux*, on the corner of av Viallet; *l'Université*, in rue Denfert-Rochereau; *de la Gare*, at 55 av Alsace-Lorraine. *Bellevue* is much more agreeably situated, as its name suggests, on the corner of quai Stéphane Jay and rue Belgrade near the téléférique, though the nicest of the cheapies I investigated was *Hôtel de la Poste* at 25 rue de la Poste off place Vaucanson – the entrance is grubby and wicked-looking, but the hotel itself is spotless and friendly. Alternatively, there's a modern **youth hostel** (excellent canteen) at ÉCHIROLLES, a 10min bus ride south (no 8 from cours Jean-Jaurès) to stop La Quinzaine, by a large Casino supermarket. The supermarket has an excellent *charcuterie* with takeaway dishes and salads, and a cafeteria serving good, reasonably-priced meals. The hostel is 150m down av Grésivaudan, well placed if you are hitching south: just keep on down cours Jean-Jaurès. There is a large **Camping Municipal** between rue Albert Reynier and av Beaumarchais, which the no 8 bus runs past on its way to the hostel. Beware, however, that buses stop early in Grenoble, around 8pm.

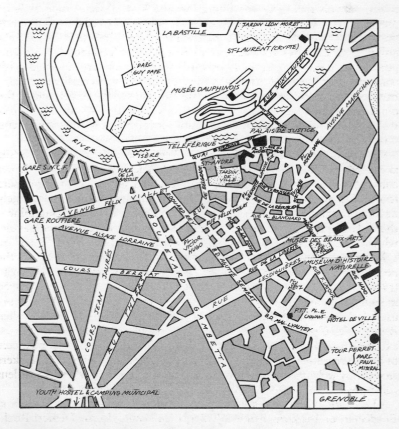

Other **practical details: Allostop** at rue Barginet; **Information Jeunesse,** 1 passage du Palais de Justice; **bike hire** from M Strippoli, 62 quai Perrière or M Rollo, 1 av Jeanne d'arc; **laundrettes** at 65 place St-Bruno (on the way to Pont du Drac) and 27 av Jean Perrot near the park. **Gare routière** is next door to **gare SNCF.** The main **PTT/Poste Restante** is miles away near the park, in bd Lyautey. **Club Alpin Français** at 32 av F Viallet. **CIMES** (Maison du Tourisme, 14 rue de la République, 38027 Grenoble-Cedex) is the place for hiking information.

Around Grenoble: the Vercors and Chartreuse massifs

Both massifs, but particularly Vercors, are very close to Grenoble. They are relatively gentle too, so if you're starting your Alpine ventures here, you can use them to break the feet in. The Grenoble CIMES office publishes route descriptions with extracts from the IGN 1: 25,000 map.

The Vercors massif
Simplest and most accessible of the CIMES walks is no 4: a **4 hour return hike to St-Nizier,** just over the rim of the Vercors mountains. Start by taking bus 5 from place Victor Hugo and get off in SEYSSINET village by the school. For most of the way you follow the·**GR9** with its red and white waymarks. The path starts about 200m uphill from the school on the right. It is not difficult, but the path does cross the D106 a few times, and the continuation is not always obvious after the road sections, so you should get the leaflet. It is about 2½ hours to St-Nizier (return the same way) – a beautiful path through thick woods with long views back over Grenoble to the mountains beyond. The lovely purplish Martagon lily blooms in the woods in early July. ST-NIZIER has **hotels** and a small **campsite.** It is a further 3½ hours (there and back) to the top of **Moucherotte** on the GR91.

Two other good, though more strenuous, walks are described in leaflets 6 and 11. 6 is **from Villard-de-lans** in the Vercors massif down to CLAIX, not far from Grenoble – a descent of 1,700m: about 7 hours. 11 describes a long (9 hours) and a shorter (6½ hours) **circuit of Mont Aiguille,** starting from the railway station in Clelles (1 hour by train south of Grenoble). Both are highly recommended, and by all accounts rightly so, by the CIMES office.

The best way to explore the Vercors would be to **base yourself,** say, in VILLARD-DE-LANS (**camping** and **hotels**) and backpack around.

If you just want **to travel through** – it is very pretty and undeveloped – you will have to hitch, which is perfectly possible. I got from Grenoble down the length of the plateau to Die and back to Grenoble over the Col de Grimone in a day. To get started, take the 11/14 trolley just off place Victor Hugo to SASSENAGE AIR LIQUIDE and get off at LA ROLLANDIÈRE, one stop before the terminus. Start hitching on the road to LANS-EN-VERCORS more or less opposite the stop. The road winds up through a steep wooded gorge to come out in a wide valley full of hay meadows towards LANS and VILLARD. Turn right at Villard on the Pont-en-Royans road into the **Gorges de la Bourne**. The gorge becomes rapidly deeper and narrower, the road cuts right in under the rocks, the river running far below, with tree-hung cliffs almost shutting out the sky above. Take a left fork here and you climb up to a lovely green valley before descending to ST-MARTIN and LA CHAPELLE (*gîtes d'étape, Nouvel Hôtel, Hôtel des Sports*). Thence the road climbs again to the wide dry **plateau of Vassieux** bordered to the east by a rocky ridge rising from thick pine forest and to the west by low hills covered with scrubby, *maquis*-like vegetation.

It was here round the village of **Vassieux** that the fighters of the Vercors *maquis* suffered a bloody and bitter defeat at the hands of the SS in July 1944. From 1942–3 they had been gradually turning the Vercors into a Resistance stronghold, to the annoyance of the Germans who finally, in June 1944, decided to wipe them out. They encircled and attacked the *maquisards* with vastly superior forces and parachuted an SS division on to Vassieux. The French appealed in vain for Allied support and were very bitter about the lack of response. The Germans took vicious reprisals, and despite their attempts to disperse into the woods, 700 *maquisards* and civilians were killed and several villages razed. The Germans' most ferocious act was to murder the wounded with their nurses and doctors in **Grotte de la Liure**, a cave off the La Chapelle-Col de Rousset road, now a sort of national shrine.

Vassieux, a dull little village, now rebuilt (*gîte d'étape*: Mme Chapays) has a memorial cemetery and small **museum** (9–6, 1 April–1 Nov; free) with documents, photos and other memorabilia to do with the *maquis* and the battle. In the field outside are the remains of two gliders used by the German paratroops.

From Vassieux I followed the **Col de Rousset** road through woods of pine and fir and down the steep twisting descent to **DIE,** with terrific views of the white crags and pinnacles of the south-east end of the massif. Die (**Camping Municipal** and **hotels**) is a pretty and hot little place, with section of its 3C ramparts still visible to the north-east: as you go out of town on the Gap road there is a Roman triumphal arch built into the medieval city walls on the left. Its most alluring feature, though, is the bubbly white wine it produces, *Clairette de Die*.

South along the river Drôme you come to the **Pont de Quart** and fork left for Châtillon: not a bad place to wait on a hot day, for you can swim in the river below the bridge. **Châtillon** is a lovely village in a narrowing valley bottom surrounded by apple and peach orchards, vineyards, walnut trees and fields of lavender. It has a distinctly southern feel (two **hotels** and a **Camping Municipal**). From here on, the road enters the narrow sunless trench of the **Gorges des Gas**, winding up between sheer rock walls to **Grimone**, a mountain hamlet on the flanks of a grassy valley with fir trees darkening the higher slopes. The Col de Grimone is visible above the village. If you have to walk it, a path cuts across the valley directly to the col. From the col it must be about 7km down to the main Grenoble road, a tarmac trudge alleviated by the view eastwards to the mountains. If you are fed up with hitching you can get the train back to Grenoble.

Massif de la Chartreuse and Grande Chartreuse monastery

The **Chartreuse massif** stretches north from Grenoble towards Chambéry, and like Vercors it is not easy to visit without your own vehicle. The landscape, however, is spectacular: precipitous limestone peaks, mountain pastures and thick forest. The **Grande Chartreuse monastery**, the main local landmark, lies up the narrow Gorges des Guiers Mort, southeast of ST-LAURENT-DU-PORT. It is not open to visitors, though there is a museum nearby at LA CORRÉRIE illustrating the life of the Carthusian order to which the monastery belongs.

CHAMBÉRY

CHAMBÉRY lies just south of Lac du Bourget in a valley separating the Massif de la Chartreuse from the Bauges mountains: historically, an important strategic position commanding the entrance to the big Alpine valleys that led to the passes into Italy. The earliest settlement was on the rock of Lemenc behind the railway station (the church of St-Pierre-de-Lemenc off bd de Lemenc has a 6C baptistry in its crypt). The present town grew up round the castle built by Count Thomas of Savoie in 1232, when Chambéry became capital of the ancient province, and flourished particularly in the 14C under the three Amadeuses – the last of whom served ten years as anti-Pope. Although superseded by Turin as capital of the Duchy in 1563, it remained an important commercial and cultural centre and the emotional focus of all French Savoyards: 'the winter residence of almost all the nobility of Savoy,' Arthur Young reported in 1789, before its mid-19C incorporation into France.

As usual, the most interesting district is the **old city centre**. To reach it, turn left out of the station down rue Sommeiller to the crossroads at the end, and take another left into the tree-lined bd de la Colonne, where all the **city buses** stop, the SI is on the left. Half-way down the street is the splendidly extravagant **Fontaine des Eléphants**, with the heads and shoulders of four large bronze elephants projecting from a stone pediment supporting a tall column, on top of which stands a statue of Comte de

Boigne, a native son who made a fortune in the French East India Company in the 18C and spent some of it on his home town. Past this, on the right, and you're at the **Musée Savoisien** (10–12 & 2–6; cl. Tues), a Savoyard parallel to the Musée Dauphinois at Grenoble and, like it, recording the lost rural life of the mountain communities. On the first floor are some very lovely paintings by Savoyard primitives and painted wood statues from various churches in the region; up above, unbearably hot, are tools, carts, hay-sledges, old photos, and some very fine furniture from a house in Bessans, including a fascinating kitchen range made of wood and lined with *lauzes* (slabs of Schist). Well worth a visit.

Next to the museum in the hot, enclosed little place Métropole, is the **Cathedral** with a handsome, though much restored, Flamboyant façade. The inside is painted in elaborate 19C *trompe-l'oeil*, imitating the twisting shapes and whorls of the Flamboyant style. During the Revolution it became the seat of the National Assembly of the Allobroges. How pitifully pompous those well-meant titles seem now. A passage leads from the *place* to rue de la Croix d'Or, with numerous restaurants, and to the right, the long rectangular **place St-Léger** with a fountain and cafés, hub of the city's social life (Rousseau and Mme de Warens lived at no 54 in 1735). Street musicians and players perform here on summer evenings. Towards the further end of the *place*, the town's smartest street, **rue de Boigne**, leads back to the Elephant Fountain. Past this intersection, on the left, a narrow medieval lane, rue Basse-du-Château, brings you out beneath the elegant apse of the **Sainte-Chapelle**, the castle chapel (early 15C).

The entrance to the Château itself (guided tours only, 10.30 & 2–5, 15 June – 15 Sept; cl. Sun am) is on your left. I mistimed my visit and didn't get to see the inside. It is a massive and imposing structure, home of the Dukes of Savoie until they transferred to Turin, but I suspect the only bit worth seeing is the Sainte Chapelle, whose lancet windows and star-vaulting look elegant and pleasing from photographs. It was built to house the Holy Shroud, that much-venerated and today highly controversial piece of linen brought back from the Crusades and reputed to be Christ's winding sheet. The Dukes took it with them to Turin where it still lies in the cathedral.

For **hotels**, try *du Château*, rue J-P Veyrat; *Home Savoyard*, 15 place St-Léger; *Perriat*, 20 place St-Léger; *Revard*, place de la Gare; or *Voyageurs*, 3 rue Doppet. The **Maison des Jeunes et de la Culture** at 311 Faubourg Montmélian is a possibility. The nearest **campsites** are at BASSENS and ST-ALBAN: bus *ligne C*, direction Albertville, from the SI. **Bike hire**: *D Brouard*, 28 av de Turin. **Gare routière** is in place de la Gare (SNCF). **PTT** in av Général Leclerc, opposite the station.

ANNECY

Sited at the edge of a turquoise lake, and bounded to the east by the eroded peaks of La Tournette (2,351m) and to the west by the long wooded ridge of Le Semnoz (1,699m), **ANNECY** is very much a transit point for hikers. It offers good access to the Mont Blanc area and on to Lake Geneva and the northern Prealps (see page 407). Historically, it enjoyed a brief flurry of importance in the early 16C, when Geneva opted for the Reformation and the fugitive Catholic bishop decamped here with a train of ecclesiastics and a prosperous, cultivated, bourgeois élite.

The most interesting core of the city lies at the foot of the castle mound. It is a warren of lanes, passages and arcaded houses below and between which flow branches of the **Canal du Thiou**, which drains the lake into the river Fier. The houses, canalside railings and numerous restaurants and cafés are stacked with displays of geraniums and petunias. It is picture-book pretty and, inevitably, full of tourists.

If you are coming from the station, go straight ahead to rue Royale and turn left. Rue Royale becomes the arcaded rue Paquier, with the 17C **Hôtel de Sales** at no 12, once a residence of the kings of Sardinia. Opposite the end of the street is the **Centre Bonlieu**, a modern shopping precinct which also houses the **SI**. Annecy has a particularly friendly and go-ahead director of tourism and the office is very helpful. Ask them, if you are having trouble finding a place to stay, which is more than likely in summertime.

Beyond Bonlieu, the treelined avenue d'Albigny leads west past the lakeside lawns of the Champ de Mars, joined by a bridge to the shady public gardens at the back of the Hôtel de Ville. Opposite is the 15C church of **St-Maurice**, originally built for a Dominican convent. (Numerous Savoyard churches are dedicated to St-Maurice. He was the commander of a Theban legion sent to put down a rebellion in the late 3C. Converted to Christianity, he and his soldiers refused to sacrifice to the pagan gods of Rome and were put to death for their pains.) Inside, the apse, with attractive Flamboyant windows, is badly distorted, the walls leaning outwards to an alarming degree; on the left of the choir is a fine fresco dated 1438, all in tones of grey.

Opposite the church door, rue Grenette leads into **rue Jean-Jacques Rousseau**. Just past the uninteresting Gothic cathedral where Rousseau sang as a chorister is an 18C Bishop's palace, now the police commissariat, built on the site of the house where Mme de Warens, Rousseau's lover, lived. Converted from Protestantism, she was paid by the Catholic authorities to save other erring souls. The 16-year-old Rousseau, on the run from his miserable engraver's apprenticeship in Geneva, came to lodge with her on Palm Sunday 1728. She was 28. Their first meeting took place on the steps of the church, Rousseau recording 'in a moment

I was hers, and certain that a faith preached by such missionaries would not fail to lead to paradise . . .'. His admirers have placed his bust in the courtyard of the commissariat. Continuing across the canal bridge, with a view of the grand old **Palais de l'Isle** (prison, mint, lawcourts in its time), you come to rue de l'Isle and **rue Ste-Claire**, the main street of the old town, with arcaded shops and houses. No 18 is Hôtel Favre, where in 1606 Antoine Favre, an eminent lawyer, and François de Sales founded the literary-intellectual Académie Florimontane 'because the Muses thrive in the mountains of Savoie'. At the end of the street is its original medieval gateway.

From rue de l'Isle the narrow Rampe du Château leads up to the **Castle**, former home of the Counts of Genevois and the Dukes of Nemours, a junior branch of the house of Savoie. There has been a castle on the site from the 11C. The Nemours, finding the old fortress too rough and unpolished for their taste, added living quarters in the 16C, which now house the miscellaneous collections of the **Musée du Château** (10–12 & 2–6; cl. Tues): archaeological finds from Boutae; Bronze and Iron Age metallurgy with comparative photos of similar still-surviving skills like scythe- and axe-making; Savoyard popular art, furniture and wood-carving, and, on the top floor, an excellent display illustrating the geology of the Alps.

Places to stay and other practicalities

The **youth hostel** is a good 45min walk from the old town: cross the main canal bridge along rue des Marquisats, and turn right at the lights into av de Trésum, then left on bd de la Corniche, which loops up into the woods of Le Semnoz, becoming the Route de Semnoz; the hostel stands in a clearing by a small zoo (there is a shortcut through the woods but for the first time at least it is best to stick to the road). **Other good hostel-type accommodation** is available at: *Centre International de Séjour* on rue des Marquisats by the lake (canteen); *Foyer d'Évire*, Montée de Novel, off rue des Martyres de la Déportation (bus no 4 to Évire terminal); and, for women only, the *Maison de la Jeune Fille*, 1 av du Rhône. **Camping Municipal** is off bd de la Corniche – turn right up a lane opposite Chemin du Tillier, it's round on the left past Hôtel du Belvédère. Best value **hotels** are *des Alpes* in rue de la Poste, *Nouvel* in rue Vaugelas and *Rives du Lac* in rue des Marquisats.

As to **other practicalities**, there's **bike hire** from the gare SNCF and *Loca Sport* (37 av de Loverchy), and round-the-lake **boat trips**, at a reasonable price, from *Compagnie des Bateaux* by the mouth of the Thiou canal. The annual **Festival de la Vieille Ville** takes place in the first fortnight of July, with lots of music (pop, rock, classical), mostly free; a festival of **Italian cinema** at the end of September. You'll find a useful **laundrette** in the *Nouvelles Galeries* shopping complex at 25 av du

Parmelan; the **PTT** in rue de la Poste, near the stations (the gares routière and SNCF are side by side). The SI sells a 1:50,000 **map of the Annecy area** with **walking trails** marked. The best and longest hike is the **Tour du Lac**, taking in Le Semnoz and La Tournette (path connects with GR96). There are also loops and shorter bits suitable for day walks.

THE NATIONAL PARKS

The trouble with designating an area as a **national park** is that it draws attention, i.e. loads of people, to it. These parks are beautiful and, luckily, the scale of the mountains is big enough to absorb considerable numbers of visitors. But you won't have the paths to yourself after about 10am in July and August – which are the only **times of year** when hiking is really practicable.

As for **accommodation**, you can **camp** freely on the fringes of the parks, but once inside you are supposed to pitch a tent only in emergency and move on after one night. Gîtes and **refuges** are probably the best solution – saves weight, too. Hotels are out – overpriced and overbooked.

For **guides**, there are the GR Topo-guides and CIMES' *La Grande Traversée des Alpes* in French; The Mountaineers/Cordée *100 Hikes in the Alps* and Cicerone Press's *GR5* by Colin Turner in English.

Access to the **Vanoise** park is easiest from CHAMBÉRY (with frequent trains to MODANE). For **Queyras** and **Écrins** it's best to set out from GRENOBLE: either by bus via LE BOURG-D'OISANS to BRIANÇON (jumping off point for the Écrins), or by train via GAP to MONT-DAUPHIN (for Queyras) and on round beyond to BRIANÇON. If you hitch – not hard if you look a hiker – you could follow any of these routes.

PARC REGIONAL DU QUEYRAS

The **railway from GRENOBLE-GAP** seems an obvious approach to Queyras. The path it follows is the **Route Napoléon**, taken by the Emperor in 1815. It runs through the town of VIZILLE, where there's a vast château, meeting place in 1788 of the Estates of Grenoble, whose demand for liberty for all Frenchmen and the suspension of parliament is often though of as the catalyst for the French Revolution. And then it veers off, climbing steeply, to the village of LAFFREY, where Napoleon, finding his way barred by troops from Grenoble, made his great melo-dramatic gesture of throwing open his coat, challenging: 'Soldiers, I am your Emperor! If anyone among you wishes to kill me, here I am!' The commanding officer ordered his soldiers to fire, but instead of shooting there were cries of 'Vive l'Empéreur!' His own party augmented by these soldiers, Napoleon entered Grenoble in triumph. He wrote in his memoirs: 'As far as Grenoble, I was merely an adventurer. At Grenoble, I became a prince'.

From **GAP** (numerous **hotels** and three **campsites,** and good train links to Paris and Marseilles) the railway and D64 strike east towards **EMBRUN,** the landscape becoming very Mediterranean, low scrub covering the mountainsides, poor shallow soil, and white friable rock. Embrun stands on a rock overlooking the huge man-made lake of **Serre-Ponçon,** which is rapidly being developed as a summer resort with campsites, wind-surfing schools and the like. It has been a fortress town for centuries. Hadrian made it the capital of the Martime Alps and from the 3C to the Revolution it was the seat of an important archbishopric. The **SI**, in a former chapel of the Cordeliers, has a bureau for **mountain guides** (5–7, July-Aug) and **accompagnateurs** who organise a daily programme of walks in the surrounding mountains. Embrun's chief sight is its **Cathedral,** 12C, with a porch in alternating courses of black and white marble in the Italian Lombard style, its roof supported on columns of pink marble resting on lions' backs – an arrangement that inspired numerous imitators throughout the region.

Eighteen km up the road you come to **MONT-DAUPHIN,** where **buses** leave for Ceillac, Ville-Vieille and St-Véran in the Queyras national park. They meet the Paris-Briançon trains: the 7.45 am bus going all the way to ST-VÉRAN (arriving 9.10, every day except Sun throughout the year), others only as far as VILLE-VIEILLE (the 4.55 pm operates only in the summer season). It is, however, easy to get a lift in these parts; there are always climbers and hikers about with transport. Mont-Dauphin itself is just a station, with – opposite – an abandoned but formidably bastioned village – one of many Alpine fortifications designed by Vauban in the 17C commanding the entrance to the valley of the Guil.

The park
The road into the Queyras park follows the river Guil from MONT-DAU-PHIN, through to the village of **GUILLESTRE,** its houses in typical Queyras-style with open granaries on the upper floors, its church with a lion-porch emulating the cathedral at Embrun. You may want to stop here a night: there are several **hotels, campsites** and a **youth hostel.** Beyond the village, in the Combe du Queyras, the river gorge narrows to a claustrophobic crack with walls up to 400m high. Far below the road, the stream, incredibly clear, boils down over red and green rocks. It was only in this century that road-building techniques became sufficiently sophisticated to cope with these narrows. Previously they had to be circumvented by a detour over the adjacent heights. At the upper end of

the Combe the valley broadens briefly and you see ahead the fort of **Château-Queyras** barring the way so completely that there is scarcely room for the road to squeeze round its base. Vauban at work again, though the original fortress was medieval.

Just beyond is **VILLE-VIEILLE**, where the road for ST-VÉRAN branches right over the Guil and up the ravine of the Aigue Blanche torrent. A smaller place than Guillestre, it has only a few old houses still intact, and a church with the square tower and octagonal steeple flanked by four short triangular pinnacles characteristic of this corner of the Alps. A Latin inscription in the porch says the church was destroyed in 1574 by the 'impiety of the Calvinists' and restored by the 'piety' of the Catholics. There is a painted sundial on the tower, which is also characteristic of the region.

Straight on, the road follows the Guil through the villages of AIGUILLES, ABRIÈS, LA MONTA (all with *gîtes d'étape*), to the **Belvédère du Viso**, close to the Italian border and **Monte Viso**, at 3,841m the highest peak in the area. Above the Belvédère is the **Col de la Traversette**, where in 1480 the Marquis of Saluces drove a 70m tunnel through the mountain. It has been reopened at various times through history, but is finally closed now.

East of L'ECHALP a variant of the GR58, which does the circuit of

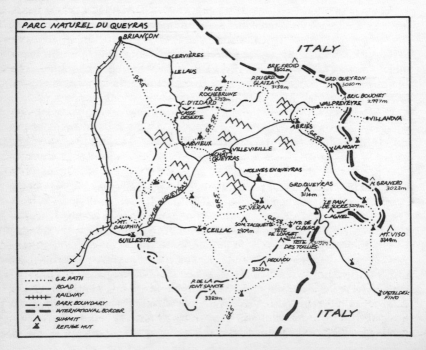

the park, climbs up to the **Col de la Croix**, used in former times by Italian peasants bringing produce to market in Abriès. South of the village the path climbs to the pastures of **Alp de Médille**, where you can see across to Monte Viso, then on past the **lakes** of Egourgéou, Bariche and Foréant to **Col Vieux** and west to the **Refuge Agnel**, whence you can continue on to St-Véran.

At 2,040m **ST-VÉRAN** claims to be the highest permanently inhabited village in Europe. It lies on the east side of the valley of the Aigue Blanche torrent, backed by acres of steep lush mountain pasture. On the opposite side rock walls and slopes of scree rise to snowy ridges. In the valley bottom and on any treeless patch of ground, no matter how steep, you can see the remains of abandoned terraces. They were in use up until the last war, though as with most high Alpine villages, traditional farming activity has practically died out. Only one Provençal shepherd still brings his flocks to the village pastures in summertime. Today the principal economic activity is entertaining day-trippers. Though still pretty, it has lost its soul and looks rather uncared for.

The houses are part-stone, part-timber. The upper storeys, usually timber, consist of long granaries with two or three tiers of rickety wooden balconies tacked on to the front for drying hay or firewood and ripening crops. The roofs are pine planks or huge slabs of schist – *lauzes* – arranged in diamond patterns. There are several refurbished old drinking-fountains, made entirely of wood. The stone church stands prettily on the higher of the two 'streets', its white tower silhouetted against the bare crags across the valley, as a mountain church should. It too has a porch whose columns rest on crudely carved lions, one holding a man in its paws. The interior is surprisingly rich, with Baroque altars and retables.

Just south of the village, past a triple cross adorned with the intruments of Christ's Passion and an inscription adjuring the passer-by to choose between the saintly, conventional or rebellious life ('l'homme révolté qui n'est jamais content'), the **GR58**, waymarked and easy to follow, turns down right to the river, where there are some good places to camp. The path continues up the left bank through woods of pine and larch as far as the chapel of Notre-Dame-de-Clausis. There, above the timberline, it crosses to the right bank of the stream and winds up damp grassy slopes to the **Col de Chamoussière**, about 3½ hours from St-Véran. The ridge to the right of the col marks the frontier with Italy. In the valley below you see the **Refuge Agnel**, about an hour away, with the Pain de Sucre (3,208m) behind it. From there you can continue on to **L'ÉCHALP**. In early July there are glorious flowers in the meadows leading up to the col: violets, potentilla, Black Vanilla Orchids, jovibarb, dianthus, silene acaulis, hypericum, anemones, trollius europaeus, Mountain Buttercup, gentians, soldanella, campanulas.

For a **base in these parts**, you're really best off camping. Rooms are expensive, though there's one reasonable hotel at ST-VÉRAN, the *Coste Belle* at the south end of the upper street, and a *gîte d'étape* by the hairpin bend at the north and, belonging to M Brunet who keeps the *Hôtel Etoile de Neige*. The *Neige* also does meals. If you are feeding yourself, there are only two small shops and they tend to run out of bread, fruit and vegetables.

Hiking down to VILLE-VIEILLE takes about 2½ hours from ST-VÉRAN, all roadwork (save for an initial short cut to MOLINES), but downhill and pretty. MOLINES and its neighbours, LA RUA and PONTGILLARDE, seem to have preserved their traditional rural character better than St-Véran. The houses are better kept, the hay meadows still mown – there is nothing prettier than these little patches of Alpine meadow, always steep and irregular in shape, full of wild flowers and neatly scythed by hand.

Queyras to Briançon

Running over the 2,360m **Col d'Izoard**, the direct route from Queyras to Briançon is a beautiful trip and saves backtracking to MONT-DAUPHIN. There are no buses but it's reasonably promising hitching.

The road turns up right just west of CHÂTEAU-QUEYRAS along a wooded ravine to the village of **ARVIEUX** lying in a high valley surrounded by fields and meadows. A church with the characteristic tower and steeple stands guard at the entrance to the village. The GR5 passes through. *Hôtel Casse Déserte* has dormitory accommodation. Further up the valley at LA CHALP and BRUNISSARD are *gîtes d'étape*.

Going up to **the col**, above the timberline, you cross the **Casse Déserte**, a wild, desolate region with huge screes running down off the peaks and weirdly eroded orangy rocks. From the top you look out over miles and miles of mountain landscape. The road loops down the other side through thick forest to LE LAUS, a cluster of half-a-dozen old stone houses with long, sloping, wooden roofs set in meadows beside the stream, then CERVIÈRES, and west into the deep valley of the Durance at BRIANÇON, dominated by the vast **Massif des Écrins**.

BRIANÇON AND THE PARC NATIONAL DES ÉCRINS

Imposing and fortified, built on a rocky height overlooking the valleys of the Durance and Guisane, **BRIANÇON** guards the road to the Col de Montgenèvre, one of the oldest and most important passes into Italy. Originally a Gallic settlement, the Romans made it an 'oppidum', with the name of Brigantium, to guard their Mons Matrona road from Milan to Vienne. In the Middle Ages it was the capital of the 'république des escartons', a federation of mountain communities grouped together for mutual defence and the preservation of their liberties and privileges.

The **old town**, mainly 18C, is enclosed within another set of Vauban's walls. If you come in by car the best thing is to stop at the **Champ de Mars** at the top of the hill and look around from there; otherwise you will have to struggle up from the unprepossessing modern town that has grown up on the more accessible ground at the foot of the hill. You enter the walls by the **Porte Pignerol**. In front of you the narrow main street tips steeply downhill, known as *grande gargouille* because of the stream running down its middle. To your right is the sturdy, plain church of Notre-Dame, designed by Vauban, again with an eye to defence. The citadel, the highest point of his fortifications, can be visited, but only as part of an organised tour (ask the SI, on the right by Porte Pignerol). In marked contrast to the relatively untouristy Queyras, Briançon and all the other towns and villages on this side of the Écrins park are crawling with people in summer.

At the foot of av de la République, which leads up to the old town from the new, there is a subsidiary **tourist office** with a **mountain guides'** desk, providing information about the Écrins for walkers and climbers. For places to stay, try *Hôtel Aux Trois Chamois* in the Champ de Mars (full board only in July & August); or *de la Paix* at 3 rue Porte Méane to the right of Grande Rue. The best bet in the old town seems to be *Le Rustique* in rue Pont d'Asfeld, to the left of Grande Rue. In the lower town, try *Hôtel de la Chaussée*, in rue Centrale, opposite the SI. **Camping Le Schappe** is to the left after the bridge on the Durance in rue Centrale. There is a *gîte d'étape* at LE FONTENIL 2km along the Montgenèvre road.

Near Briançon, NÉVACHE and the valley of the river Clarée are said to be very beautiful.

Into the park: towards Mont-Pelvoux

The usual **approach to the Parc des Écrins**, with some very serious climbing goals at its end, is from the train station at ARGENTIÈRES-LA-BESSÉE, a scruffy, depressed little place with a recently closed aluminium works, south towards MONT-DAUPHIN. From here a small road cuts into the valley towards VALLOUISE, the ice-capped monster of **Mont-Pelvoux** (3,946m) rearing in front of you all the way.

On the right by the first village you come to, LA BATIE, are the remains of the so-called **Mur des Vaudois**. Despite the name, the origins of the wall are uncertain. It was probably built either to keep out companies of marauding soldiers-turned-bandit or to control the spread of plague in the 14C. These Vaudois (Waldensians in English) are not to be confused with the inhabitants of the Swiss canton of Vaud. They were members of a religious sect, sort of precursors of Protestantism, founded in the late 12C by Pierre Valdo, a merchant from Lyon, who preached against worldly wealth and the corruption of the clergy. Practising as he preached, he gave his wealth to the poor. Excommunicated in 1186 the Vaudois came more and more to deny the authority of the church. Persecuted, they sought refuge in the remote mountain valleys of Pelvoux, especially in the area round Vallouise and Argentières. Their numbers were also probably augmented by refugees from the Inquisition's persecutions of the Cathars in Languedoc.

There was a crop of executions for sorcery in the early 15C, and many of the victims were probably Vaudois, burnt to death in purpose-built wooden cabins. In 1488, Charles VIII launched a full-scale crusade against them. There is a spot west of Ailefroide known as Baume Chapelue where they were smoked out by the military and butchered. They were finally exterminated in the 18C after the revocation of the Edict of Nantes, when 8,000 troops went on the rampage, creating total desolation and 'leaving neither people nor animals'.

On the right beyond La Batie, the village of **LES VIGNEAUX** (with a *gîte d'étape*) shrugs off such a past: a lovely place, surrounded by apple orchards and backed by the fierce crags of Montbrison. The **church** has a fine old door and lock under a vaulted porch. Beside it on the exterior wall of the church are two bands of paintings depicting the Seven Deadly Sins. In the upper band the Sins are naive representations of men and women riding various beasts (lion, hound, monkey) and chained by the neck. A man carrying a leg of mutton and drinking wine from a flask represents gluttony; a woman with rouged cheeks, green stockings and displaying an enticing expanse of thigh, represents lust. In the lower band they are all getting their come-uppance, writhing in the agonies of Hell fire.

VALLOUISE lies under a steep wooded spur at the junction of two valleys, the Gyronde (or Gyr, as it is called upstream of Vallouise) and the Gérendoine. The great glaciered peaks visible up the latter valley are Les Bans, up in front still is Mont-Pelvoux. The nucleus of the old village – narrow lanes between sombre stone chalets – is again its **church**, 15C with characteristic tower and steeple and a 16C porch on pink marble pillars. A fresco of the Adoration of the Magi adorns the tympanum above the door, itself magnificent with carved Gothic panels along the top and an ancient lock and bolt with a chimera's head at one end. Remains of an enormously long-legged figure, partially painted over, cover the end wall of the apse. Inside, as at Les Vigneaux, are more frescoes, including at the back of the church six naive statues on painted wood.

There is a **camp ground, gîte d'étape** and several **hotels** open from Dec-April and July-Sept/Oct. The *Edelweiss* is cheapest, but all rooms in the village are likely to be full in July and August.

The **GR54** which does the circuit of the Écrins park passes through

Vallouise and the stage on from here to LE MONETIER – **Lac de l'Éychauda** is one of the best. Another good walk is to the hamlet of PUY AILLAUD high on the west flank of the Gyr valley. The path starts just to the right of the church and zigzags up the steep slope behind it with almost aerial views of the valley beneath. The Vallouise *Maison du Parc des Écrins* provides **hiking information**. There is a **minibus** service as far as AILEFROIDE in summer, starting from the bar next to the Edelweiss hotel. To walk takes 2 hours or so.

AILEFROIDE, under the last slopes of Pelvoux (three **campsites**), is also a major centre for climbers and walkers. There is a **Bureau des Guides**. A path follows the road on up the valley as far as the so-called **Pré de Madame Carle** by the old *refuge Cézanne* (1½ hours). In fact, it is not a 'pré' or meadow at all, but a jumble of rocks brought down by the torrent from which you can see the **Barre des Écrins** towering above the Glacier Noir. At 4,102m, it is also the highest peak in the massif – and one of the major Alpine climbs. From the bridge another path runs north, up to the **Refuge du Glacier Blanc** on the edge of the glacier at 2,550m (about 2½ hours). Anywhere beyond this on the **Pelvoux massif** is snow and ice – experienced climbers' territory.

From the north: La Grave, Lautaret and Le Casset

Coming in to the mountains from GRENOBLE along the D91, you have various alternative approaches to the **Parc des Écrins** – and the possibility of a substantial two-day circuit between LA GRAVE and LE CASSET. The road itself, though, is grand enough, crossing the 2,058m **Col du Lautaret**. It is kept open all year and served regularly by the GRENOBLE-BRIANÇON bus.

LA GRAVE, midway between LA BOURG and BRIANÇON, faces the majestic glaciers of La Meije (3,983m). It could be a good base for walking. The **GR54** climbs up to Le Chazelet on the slopes north-west of the village and continues to the **Plateau de Paris** and the **Lac Noir**, which numerous walkers recommended to me as providing breathtaking views of La Meije. And it is only 11km on to the Col du Lautaret, with the still higher Col du Galibier just beyond. There is no public transport up Galibier – which is closed by snow from mid-October to mid-June – but in season you should be able to hitch up, and back to LA GRAVE or on to LE CASSET inside a day.

The **Col du Lautaret** has been in use for centuries. The Roman road from Milan to Vienne crossed it. Indeed its name derives from the small temple (*altaretum*) the Romans built to placate the deity of the mountains. They called it '*collis de altareto*'. Round the col is a huge expanse of meadow long known to botanists for its glorious variety of Alpine flowers, seen at their best in mid-July. There is a **Jardin Alpin**, maintained by the University of Grenoble (8–12 & 2–6, 1 July–15 Sept), which includes plants from mountain ranges throughout the world. It is a great spot for picnicking or lounging waiting for a lift, for you look full-face into the glaciers hanging off La Meije and the sight is intoxicating. On a clear sunny day the dazzling luminosity of the ice and the burning intensity of the sky above it is such that you can hardly bear to look.

The **Col du Galibier** is less frequented – a tremendous haul up to 2,556m, utterly bare and wild, with the huge red-veined peak of the Grand Galibier rearing up on the right and a fearsome spiny ridge blocking the horizon beyond. To the north you can see Mont Blanc. The pass used to mark the frontier between France and Savoie. A monument on the south side of the col commemorates Henri Desgranges, founder of the Tour de France cycle race. Crossing the col is one of the most gruelling stages in the race. The long ascent is brutal, and the breakneck speed of descent terrifying. The road loops down in hairpin after hairpin, through VALLOIRE, a sizeable ski resort, whose church is reputedly one of the most richly decorated in Savoie, over the Col du Télégraphe at 1,570m and steeply down into the deep wooded valley of the Arc, known as La Maurienne, with the Massif de la Vanoise rising abruptly behind.

LE CASSET, back on the D28, just before MONETIER-LES-BAINS, is a hamlet of dilapidated old houses clustered round a church with a bulbous dome. The site is superb: streams and meadows all about, reaching to the foot of the larch-covered mountainsides, the Glacier du Casset imminent, white and dazzling above the green of the larches. There is a **campsite** and *gîte d'étape* near the church. But provided you choose a spot where the hay has already been mown it seems you can camp anywhere. There is a café and grocery store in the village, which in season is overcrowded.

The **GR54** goes through the village. A good day walk is to follow it as far as the **Col d'Arsine**, about 3 hours, whence you can either turn back or go on down to **La Grave** on the north side of the park, making an overnight stop at the *Refuge de l'Alpe* below the col.

The path crosses the Guisane near the *gîte* and follows a track through the woods, first on the left, and later on the right bank of the Petit Tabuc stream. From the end of the track you cross some grassy clearings before entering the trees again and climbing up to a milky-looking lakelet, the **Lac de la Douche**, at the foot of the Glacier du Casset. Thence a clear path zigzags up a very steep slope to come out in a long valley leading eventually to the Col d'Arsine. Masses of ground-hugging red rhododendrons grow along the banks of the stream. About half-way up are some tumbledown huts, the **Chalets d'Arsine**, by a series of blue-grey tarns. Up on the left are a whole series of **glaciers**. The biggest is the Glacier d'Arsine, hanging from the walls of the long jagged ridge suspended between the Montagne des Agneaux and the Pic de Neige Cordier to the west. Early in the morning there are colonies of marmots playing above the banks of the stream.

PARC NATIONAL DE LA VANOISE

The park occupies the eastern end of the **Vanoise massif**, the area contained between the upper valleys of the Isère and Arc rivers. It is extremely popular, with over 500km of waymarked paths, crossings of the **GR5**, **GR55** and the **GTA** (Grande Traversée des Alpes), and numerous refuges along the trails. For information on the spot, the SIs in MODANE, VAL D'ISÈRE, BOURG-ST-MAURICE are helpful. The *Maison du Parc* in CHAMBÉRY (135 rue St-Julian) also gives advice and sell maps.

Modane and the Haute-Maurienne

MODANE is a dreary little place, destroyed by Allied bombing in 1943 and now little more than a railway junction. Nonetheless it is a good kicking-off point for walkers on the south side of the park – easily accessible by rail and with a well-sited grassy **Camping Municipal** just up the road to the Fréjus tunnel (which leads to Bardonecchia in Italy). The *Hôtel de l'Europe*, just beyond the Fréjus turning in the street parallel to the main road, is a friendly place if you want a room – and serves good matronly meals designed for the roadweary.

The **GR5** sets out from the northern edge of the transpontine section of Modane and leads up to the **Refuge de l'Orgère**, whence a path joins up with the **GR55** leading north to PRALOGNAN, over the **Col de la Vanoise** and right across the park to Val Claret on the Lac de Tignes – a tremendous walk. The GR5 itself keeps east of La Dent Parrachée, describing a great loop through the Refuge d'Entre-Deux-Eaux before continuing up the north flank of the Arc valley and over the Col de l'Iséran to Val d'Isère.

The **Arc valley**, dark and enclosed below Modane, widens and lightens above it, with meadows and patches of cultivation in the valley bottom and the lighter foliage of larches gracing the mountainsides. Notwithstanding the lessening of gloom, it is hardly a joyous landscape, especially under a stormy sky. Bare crags hang above the steep meadows on the north flanks, glaciers threaten to the south and east. The villages, though attractive to the modern eye, are poor and humble places, the houses squat and built of rough grey stone, the homes of people who have had to struggle to wring a living from harsh weather and unyielding soil. It is at first surprising to find such a wealth of exuberant **Baroque art** in the outwardly simple **churches**. But probably it is precisely because of the harshness and poverty of their lives that these mountain people sought to express their piety with such colourful vitality. Schools of local artists flourished particularly in the 17C and 18C, inspired and influenced by itinerant Italian artists who came and went across the adjacent frontier. *Haute Maurienne Information* in LANSLEBOURG organise tours of the churches in AVRIEUX, BRAMANS (where Horace Walpole's dog Toby was eaten by a wolf while being exercised behind his postchaise), TERMIGNON, LANSLEVILLARD and BESSANS. **LANSLEBOURG** is also the start of the climb to the **Mont Cenis pass** over to Susa in Italy, another ancient trans-Alpine route. Last stop before the perils of the trek, it was once a prosperous and thriving town. Relief at finishing the climb from the French side was tempered by an alarming descent **en ramasse**, a sort of crude sledge, which shot downhill at breakneck speed much to the alarm of travellers. 'So fast you lose all sense and understanding,' a terrified merchant from Douai recounted in 1518.

BESSANS, further up the valley, retains its village character better than most. Its low, squat dwellings are built of rough stone with tiny window openings and roofed with heavy slabs to withstand the long hard winters. Most have south-facing balconies to make the most of the sun and galleries under deep eaves for drying *grebons*, the bricks of cow-dung and straw used locally for fuel. The **church** has a collection of 17C painted wooden statues and a retable signed Clappier. The Clappiers were a local family who produced several generations of artists. On the other side of the small cemetery, where old ladies in black tend the graves, the **chapel of St-Antoine** has exterior murals of the Virtues and Deadly Sins and fine 16C frescoes; ask the priest to unlock the chapel – his house is on the right of the road leading east from the village square. Two km up the road you pass the chapel of Notre-Dame-des-Graces on the right, with another ex-voto by Jean Clappier. On the opposite side of the river the hamlet of LE VILLARON has a **gîte d'étape**.

BONNEVAL-SUR-ARC (1,835m), 10km upstream, lies at the foot of the **Col de l'Iséran** in a rather bleaker setting close to the timberline. At the head of the Arc valley to the east you can see the huge glaciers of the Sources de l'Arc. Better preserved and more obviously picturesque than Bessans, Bonneval stops a lot of tourists on their way to and from the col. It is in danger of becoming twee.

Nonetheless, like all these Haute-Maurienne villages, Bonneval has a highly individual identity – quite different to Bessans. Its houses cluster tightly round the church, with only the narrowest of lanes between them. You feel the need for mutual protection and warmth being even stronger here, and sense how very isolated these places were until only a few years ago, cut off for months by heavy snow, forced in upon their own resources. Life was dangerous too, even for experienced locals. Several graves in the churchyard record deaths by avalanche.

Alternative bases to Modane and Bessans in Haute-Maurienne include the **campsites** at TERMIGNON, LANSLEBOURG and LANSLEVILLARD; *gîtes d'étape* at TERMIGNON, SARDIÈRES, BRAMANS, and LE VILLARON; or the **youth hostel** at LANSLEBOURG. **Hotels** are also numerous, but expensive and hard to find space in summer.

The Col de l'Iséran and Haute Tarentaise

As with all the other high Alpine passes the **Col de l'Iséran** has been used for centuries by local people. Despite the dangers of weather and the arduous climb, it was far the quickest route between the remote **upper valleys** of the **Arc** and **Isère**. The volume of traffic was too small to disturb the nature of the tiny communities that eked out an existence on the approaches. But 20C roads and the development of winter sports have changed all that. VAL D'ISÈRE, for instance, once a tiny mountain village, has become a hideous agglomeration of cafés, supermarkets and apartments for skiers.

From October to June **the pass** is usually blocked by snow. But in summer, being the highest pass in the Alps at 2,770m, it is one of the 'sights' that motorised tourists feel they must do – and usually quite straightforward to hitch. A word of warning, though, if you try. Don't do it in light summer clothing, especially on a cool cloudy day. My lift put me down at the chalet on the col. It had been drizzling in Bonneval. On the col the temperature was 2°, and it was blowing a blizzard – on 18 July!

The road begins above BONNEVAL, offering splendid views of the glaciers at the head of the Arc, and then follows the rocky gully of the Lenta stream (lots of marmots about) through a narrow defile and out into a desolate cirque, where the Lenta rises and masses of anemones bloom in the stony ground. Behind the chalet on the col a path climbs west to the **Pointe des Lessières** (2½ hours return), whence on a clear day you can see the Italian side of Mont Blanc and the whole of the frontier chain of peaks.

VAL D'ISÈRE is a convenient centre for walking (details from the SI), but no place to stay. If you need, or decide, to, there's a campsite just on the edge of the resort at LE LAISINANT. Downstream, **TIGNES** and its artificial lake are equally unattractive: another major resort. But thereafter the valley is lovely, deep and wooded, with villages perched on grassy shoulders high on either flank.

Exploring the valley make for **Les Brevières**. Seven km beyond, a lane turns left **into the valley bottom** to LA SAVINAZ and LA GURRAZ, whose creamy church tower is a landmark for miles around. High above, though looking dangerously close, the green ice cliffs that terminate the Glacier de la Gurraz hang off the edge of Mont Pourri (3,799m). From the turning, **the lane** veers steeply down through trees and hay meadows full of flowers, past ruinous houses, to the river. The climb up the opposite bank is hard going, past impossibly steep fields. You take a right fork for LA GURRAZ across a rickety plank bridge in the jaws of a defile. It is about an hour's walk, once you're on the lane.

And **LA GURRAZ** shouldn't disappoint you. It is tiny and untouched by tourism: a dozen old houses with wide eaves and weathered balconies spread with sweet drying hay, and firewood stacked outside. Only the old people remain, but they keep the traditional agricultural economy ticking over. The houses are all sited in the lee of the knoll for protection against avalanches which come thundering off the glacier above the village, thousands of tons of snow and rock, almost sheer down into a cwm behind. If you are unlucky enough to be out of doors when one occurs, the blast knocks you off your feet, and can even suffocate you.

There are no provisions available, so bring your own. I camped 200m beyond the village overlooking the valley, with a tongue of glacier poised on the brow of a cliff not far above me. Other hamlets on the opposite flank of the valley look just as interesting. The prettiest is LE MONAT, in the mouth of a small hanging valley, also accessible by car from La Thuile further along the Bourg-St-Maurice road.

From La Gurraz a signposted path climbs to **Refuge de la Martin** in 1½ hours. It zigzags up the slope behind LA SAVINAZ, on to a spur by a ruined chalet, where a right-hand path goes up the rocks overhead to the edge of the glacier. The refuge path continues left along the side of a deep gully, whose flanks are thick with the white St Bruno's Lily. It crosses a ferocious torrent by a plank bridge and follows a mule track up to the *alpage* by the refuge, where cows and sheep are turned out to graze. The **Mont Pourri glaciers** are directly above. Opposite is the big **Glacier de la Sassière** and up to your right VAL D'ISÈRE with the Col de l'Iséran behind it.

MONT BLANC AND LAKE GENEVA

Mont Blanc is the biggest tourist draw in the Alps, but so spectacular it's worth turning a blind eye to that. Besides, if you're going to walk in the area, you soon get away from the worst of the crowds.

ANNECY is the easiest place to get to it from, and of the two road routes the one via the old ski resort of MEGÈVE is the most interesting – though, from Ugine onwards, the hardest to hitch. The alternative route goes through CLUSES.

MONT BLANC

The two **approaches** to the 'Blonk' – as English climbers insist on calling the mountain – come together at LE FAYET, where the **tramway du Mont-Blanc** begins its 1¼ hour haul to the **Nid d'Aigle**, a vantage point on the north-west slope. Unless you're doing a full photographic survey I'd say give that a miss. There's much more exciting access from CHAMONIX-MONT BLANC, just 30km further on.

Chamonix-Mont Blanc

If Mont Blanc was anything less than outstanding there would be no point in going to **CHAMONIX**. Its village identity has been submerged in a sprawl of development, it is extremely expensive, and always crawling with tourists. The **Musée Alpin** (2–7, June-Sept) will interest mountain freaks, though it is not as exciting as you would expect; among various bits of equipment, documents and letters, is Jacques Balmat's account of his first ascent of the 'Blonk' written in almost phonetically spelt French. And finding a bed for the night can be a big problem. There's a **youth hostel** at LES PÈLERINS, just west of Chamonix proper (bus to LES HOUCHES and get off at *PÈLERINS ÉCOLE*: the hostel, signposted, is at 103 Montée Jacques-Balmat), and there's other sporadic dormitory accommodation (details from the SI). **Hotels**, unless you phone ahead, are probably out. But **campsites** are numerous, even if there is only room for a small tent. Two convenient ones are *Les Molliases* on the left of the main road going west from Chamonix towards the Mont Blanc tunnel entrance and *Les Arolles* on the opposite side of the road – about 15mins' walk from the station.

There are various touristy things to do that in other circumstances you might baulk at. But if you don't do them there is not much else, unless you are an experienced walker or climber. The first is to take the **rack railway** from the Gare du Montenvers to the vast glacier known as the **Mer de Glace**, a favourite with Victorian travellers. The second, best of all, the very expensive **téléférique to the Aiguille du Midi** (3,842m): if mountains excite you, you won't regret the outlay, and penny-pinching by buying a ticket only as far as the Plan du Midi is a waste of money – you won't see anything. You must, however, go before 9am; first, because the summits usually cloud over towards midday and, second, because any later there will be huge crowds and you may have to wait 2 hours. And take warm clothes: even on a summer day it will be well below zero on the top.

The Aiguille is a terrifying granite pinnacle on which the *téléférique* dock and a restaurant are precariously balanced. The view is incredible. At your feet is the snowy plateau of the **Col du Midi**, with the glaciers of the Vallée Blanche and Géant crawling off left at their millennial pace. To the right a steep snowfield leads to the 'easy' ridge route to the summit with its beetling cap of ice (4,807m).

Away to the front, rank upon rank of snow-and-ice-capped monsters recede into the distance. Most impressive of all, closing the horizon to your left, from east to south, is a mind-blowing cirque of needle-sharp peaks and precipitous couloirs: Aiguille Verte, Triollet, the Jorasses, with the Matterhorn and Monte Rosa visible in the far distance across a glorious landscape of rock, snow and cloud-filled valleys – the lethal testing-ground of all true-crazed climbers. And there are plenty of them still at it, swapping tales in the valley campsites of difficult pitches, rockfalls and other people's accidents, so casually you'd think the whole thing was a picnic.

The mountain was in fact first climbed in 1786 by Dr Paccard and Jacques Balmat, both natives of Chamonix, inspired by de Saussure, a Genevese naturalist's offer of a reward. The first woman to climb the mountain was Marie Paradis, who ran a tea-shop in Chamonix. Alpine exploration and climbing developed apace in the 19C with the English well to the fore. Early technique was primitive and dangerous in the extreme. Even when guides began to use rope at all, they did not bother to rope themselves to their parties. When Edward Whymper, one of the most renowned early Alpinists, made the first successful ascent of the Matterhorn in 1865, his party lost four members because the old worn piece of rope they casually attached themselves to simply snapped.

Chamonix valley: some possible hikes

Opposite Mont Blanc, the north side of Chamonix valley is enclosed by the lower but nonetheless impressive **Aiguilles Rouges**, with another *téléférique* to Le Brévent, the 2,525m peak directly above the town. I didn't visit this side at all, but there are numerous walks along the massif; in particular, the **Grand** and **Petit Balcon Sud** trails give spectacular views of Mont Blanc and present no problems to the walker. A highly recommended **two-day hike** is the GR5 stage north from Le Brévent to the village of SIXT via **Lac d'Anterne**, with a night at the Refuge d'Anterne. The classic **long-distance route** is the two-week **Tour du Mont Blanc** (TMB), described in a *Topo-Guide* and Andrew Harvey's *Tour of Mont Blanc* (Cicerone Press).

For up to the minute **walking and climbing information**, consult the **Office du Tourisme** or Maison de la Montagne, both near the church in Chamonix. The Maison de la Montagne houses the *Bureau des Guides*, *Office de Haute Montagne* and a meteorological service. The Office de Tourisme publishes a large-scale **map of summer walks** in the area. The Guides run rock and ice-climbing schools. If you are keen on bagging Europe's highest summit, a guide will cost you around £180 for the *voie normale*.

NORTHERN PRE-ALPS: THE CIRQUE DU FER-À-CHEVAL

The **Northern pre-Alps**, climbing back from the shore of Lake Geneva, are cooler, softer and greener country. They are less well known than the mightier ranges further south but they're also a lot less frequented. For walkers, there's considerable potential – the only real problem being access off the main routes. To get into the **Giffre valley**, with its **Fer-à-Cheval** hikers' circuit, you need to hitch or bus over to TANINGES from CLUSES, or go down to ANNEMEASSE, right at the frontier with Geneva. Buses run through from ANNEMASSE, via TANINGES, to SAMOËNS and SIXT.

SAMOËNS, at the foot of the Aiguille de Criou and with the tall peak of Le Buet in the distance, is an attractive village with an unusual church – very late Gothic with a doorway of crouching lions like those in the Queyras. It was built in the 16C, well behind times with the Renaissance in full flow elsewhere though a pattern you find (and expect) in these remote Alpine valleys. Traditionally, Samoëns' chief product has been stonemasons. Up to the First War, the men of the village set out each spring, tools on their backs, to seek work in the cities of France and Switzerland. Their guild, *les frahans*, evolved its own brand of rhyming slang, *le mourne*, so they could communicate secretly among themselves.

East of Samoëns the valley narrows into the Gorge des Tines before opening out again at **SIXT**, another pretty village on the confluence of two branches of the Giffre, the Giffre-Haut which comes down from Salvagny and the Giffre-Bas which rises in the Cirque du Fer-à-Cheval.

The Cirque begins about 6km from Sixt – there is a footpath along the left bank of the Giffre-Bas. It is a vast semicircle of rock walls up to 700m in height and 4 or 5km long, blue with haze on a summer's day and striated with long, tumbling chains of white water from the still melting snow. Up to mid-June there are thirty or more of these immense waterfalls. The left end of the cirque is dominated by a huge spike of rock known as the Goat's Horn, *La Corne du Chamois*. At its foot the valley of the Giffre bends sharply north to its source in the glaciers above the Fond de la Combe. The bowl of the cirque is thickly wooded except for a circular meadow in the middle where the road ends.

There is an **SI** and a **park office** here, though nowhere to buy provisions. The park office produce a folder of walks in the region – useful and well illustrated. They recommend in particular the walk to the **Refuge du Lac de la Vogeale** (3½ hours), the **Chalets de Sales** via the spectacular Cascade du Rouget waterfalls on the GR5 and GR96, and the GR5 stage to the **Lac d'Anterne** and on to LE BRÉVENT and CHAMONIX. My 1902 *Baedeker*, which seems to have done every conceivable Alpine route,

describes a 'fatiguing but interesting' 12–13 hour route over the Buet to
CHAMONIX.

SIXT, SAMOËNS and TANINGES are all equipped with **campsites**.
SIXT also has a **gîte d'étape**.

ÉVIAN AND LAKE GENEVA

Much the nicest way to reach ÉVIAN or any of the **lakeside towns** is by
boat from GENEVA (3 hours to Évian). Seventy-two km long, 13km
wide and an amazing 310m deep, the lake – **Lac Léman** to the French –
is fed and drained by the Rhône. It is a real inland sea, subject to violent
storms as Byron and Shelley discovered to their discomfort in 1816. On
a calm day, though, sailing slowly across its silk-smooth surface is a
serene experience. The boat calls first at a series of flower-decked villages
on the Swiss shore with the long level ridge of the Jura mountains in the
background. The first stop on the French side is the walled village of
YVOIRES, its houses packed on a low rise behind the shore, guarded by
a massive 14C castle. Mont Blanc and a host of other peaks appear
shining in the distance. Next you call at THONON-LES-BAINS, flanked,
just outside town, by the 15C **Château de Ripaille** built by Duke Amadeus
VIII and used by him as a retreat before and after his stint as anti-Pope.
'Faire la ripaille' has come to mean 'have a really riotous time' in French,
which is apparently rather unfair to the Duke, who led a much quieter
life than popular imagination wanted to believe. Thonon was also the
place from which St-François de Sales set out on his donkey to reclaim
the erring Protestants of Chablais for Rome.

Why visit ÉVIAN? Well, unless you are a well-heeled invalid or
gambler, there probably isn't much point, except as the end of a pleasant,
leisurely trip on the lake. The famous water is now bottled at Amphion,
but the **Source Cachat** still bubbles away behind the Evian company's
beautiful 19C offices, all wood, coloured glass, cupolas and patterned
tiles – much the best building in town. Anyone can go along and help
themselves to spring water. The waterfront is elegantly laid out with
squares of billiard-table grass, brilliant flowerbeds and rare trees. It is
pretty, restful and not very exciting, like most spa towns. If you stay,
there are several **hotels** that would make a large hole in your budget, and
one or two that would wipe it out altogether. Near the port, at the east
end of rue Nationale, the main shopping street, the hotels *Léman* and
Regina are reasonable. There are numerous **campsites**, some way out of
town. The **SI** and **gare routière** are both on the waterfront by the Casino.

TRAVEL DETAILS

Trains

From Grenoble 2 or 3 to Paris-Lyon (7¼hrs); very frequent to Lyon (1½hrs–1hr45); 2 to Gap (2½hrs) and Briançon (4hrs), changing at Veynes-Dévoluy.

From Annecy about 10 to St-Gervais (1¼–2hrs).

From St-Gervais 7 to Chamonix (35mins).

From Chambéry frequent to Modane (40mins–1hr20); 5 to Bourg-St-Maurice (2hrs); very frequent to Lyon (1½–2½hrs).

From Briançon 3 to Marseille (4½hrs).

From Annemasse very frequent service to Évian (35mins); 4 or 5 to Annecy, changing at La-Roche-sur-Foron (1¼hrs) – 1 through train daily only; 1 through train to Paris-Lyon (8hrs).

From Geneva 4 to Paris-Lyon (3hrs45).

Buses

From Chamonix 3 to Annecy via La-Roche-sur-Foron (3hrs); 1 to Annecy via Megève (3hrs); 1 to Geneva (2½hrs); 1 to Grenoble (3½hrs).

Ferries

From Geneva several daily down the lake.

Chapter fourteen

PROVENCE AND THE RHÔNE VALLEY

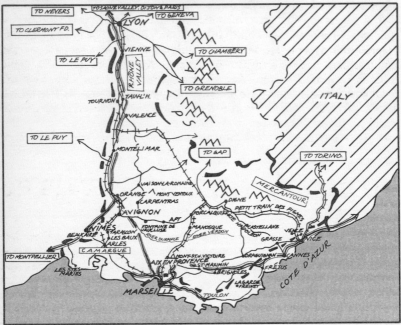

For its cultural and scenic vitality, **Provence** has few rivals in France. With the Alps on one side and the Rhône estuary on the other, it encompasses snow-capped mountains, delta rice plantations, forests of cork and pine, and the gross and gorgeous Côte d'Azur (covered in the following chapter). Fully integrated into the French Republic only in the last century, the region has been ruled – and divided between – Greeks and Romans, Saracens, Popes, foreign dukes, and the royal houses of Holland, Monaco and Sardinia. All have left their mark: Roman baths at **Aix**, theatre at **Orange** and amphitheatre at **Arles**; the Palais des Papes in **Avignon** from the great church schisms of the Dark Ages; and a hundred and one *citadelles* clinging to the sides and summits of hills in remembrance of the constant threat of invasion. And amid these shifting structures of power the people have preserved their local dialects and an easy tolerance of the foreigners who continue to buy and build on their beautiful land.

In the north the peaks of the Massif Central dictate the one and only easy passage from Provence to the centre – the **Rhône Valley**. Here lies **Lyon**, French rather than Provencal, but a city nonetheless with a very distinctive flavour, not to be lightly dismissed. For the rest, the cities cluster down towards the coast – ports to the east, but the majority of the major centres crowding around the great Rhône delta. In the south the appeal lies above all in the overwhelming scents and tinges of Mediterranean vegetation; the heat, the hills, and that extraordinary intensity of light which has played so important a part in 20C art. The best collections of paintings are on the coast, but still around Aix you can see the countryside if not the canvases of **Cézanne** (born there in 1839), while Arles is inseparable from **Van Gogh's** 12-month stay. Nowadays the dominant artistic events are in **theatre** and **classical music** for which there's a summer festival bandwagon following the spectacular annual events at Aix and Avignon.

LYON AND THE RHÔNE VALLEY

The **Rhône valley**, north-south trail of ancient armies, medieval traders and modern rail and road, is nowadays as heavily industrialised as the least attractive parts of the North. Fuming factories, oil refineries and nuclear power stations vie with the vineyards and market gardens, and with the orchards whose trees have been given a permanent tilt by the fearsome Mistral wind. But if the build-up gets too much you can always escape to the Alps or Massif Central to either side, or just close your eyes and wait for Provence. And as compensation there's **Lyon**, everything that big cities get the bright lights for – good food, hundreds of bars, music, movies, and people without provincial chips on their shoulders.

LYON

The extent of **LYON**, its grotesque urban sprawl, rather than the population of the city proper gives it the position of No 1 provincial capital against the claims of Marseilles. Lyon lacks the mystique of its southern rival and its charms are not so obvious, but behind the evident and austere bourgeois stronghold of banking and commerce – hosting international trade fairs and boasting Europe's largest shopping centre – thrive diverse artistic fields. Theatre, classical music, *nouvelle cuisine*, film and furniture design have all had innovators in this city – a fact that not even Parisians can look down on. Then too there's the old Gothic city and

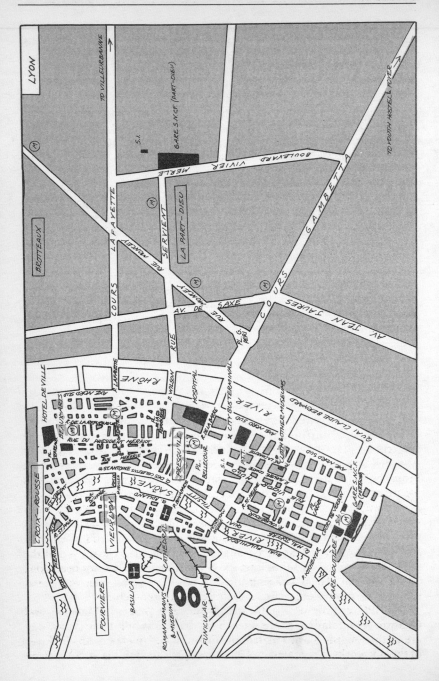

parts of its Roman predecessor, while amongst the museums (most of them free) is a magnificent collection of textiles and silks, the latter long one of Lyon's most important products.

Arriving and getting around town

Smog, exhaust grime, car and chemical plants disfigure the city as you cut through on the main **north-south autoroute**, crossing and re-crossing the Saône before these waters merge with the brown and bubbling Rhône racing the traffic on its banks. But **reaching the hidden centre** is not so difficult – **from the autoroute** take the exit to Perrache. By **train** or **bus**, the Lyon-Perrache stations (and an adjoining SI in Centre Perrache) are within the heart of the city, the *Presqu'île*, formed by the imminent merger of the two rivers. Most trains and SNCF buses also stop at the less central Lyon-Part-Dieu, terminus of the techno-miracle 2-hour **TGV** connection with Paris. Speedy transport all round the city is no problem, with **buses**, **trams** and **métro**, all operating on a single flat fare ticket valid for an hour. You can get a map and two- or three-day passes at any métro station. The city bus terminal is at place Poncet, next door to **place Bellecour**, the vast and characterless central square which has the main SI on the south-east corner. Once here, the district to head for is **Vieux Lyon** on the west back of the Saône, beneath the summit of Fourvière from where the Romans once controlled this strategic confluence of routes across their empire.

Vieux Lyon and Fourvière

If you're into cricking your neck at Gothic and Renaissance façades overshadowing narrow streets, **Vieux Lyon** is a real treat. Wandering into courtyards you'll see beautifully restored stairway-towers and often an opening to a vaulted passage that leads out to a different street: these shortcut alleyways, known as *traboules*, sometimes imitate the corridors of a building, and are a distinctive feature of the older parts of Lyon. From the tranquil **rue St-Jean**, main street of Vieux Lyon, *traboules* lead off from nos 19 and 24, and at **place du Gouvernement**, the door at no 3 opens up a quick route to the *quai*. Keep your eyes open and you'll find dozens more. Place du Gouvernement, like the other small squares, **place du Change** (with its prize medieval edifice at no 2) and **place de la Beleine**, exude the relaxed ease of the ancient monied classes – and the not so badly off now. But at least the restoration work has not been done all for tourism. The architectural riches have preserved their residential use and the *traboules* still assist nifty get-away manoeuvres.

The 19C creator of the theatrical puppets, **Guignol**, **Madelon** and **Gnafron** – as familiar to the French as the less subtle Punch and Judy are to the English – was a native of Vieux Lyon. Guignol is an employee of the silk works, a layabout and bar-room philosopher, his mate Gnafron a drunkard, and his wife Madelon, predictably, quarrelsome and thrifty. You can see them and their successors, along with puppets from all over the world, at the **Musée de la Marionnette** (housed in the same building as the *Musée de Vieux Lyon*: 14 rue Gadagne; 10–12 & 2–6; cl. Tues) and in performance at the Palais du Conservatoire for times and prices inquire at the SI.

Before exhausting the exploration of Vieux Lyon, where almost every street is tempting, you should take a look inside the unprepossessing **Cathédrale St-Jean**. Clocks are always a bit of a surprise in places of worship, but the 14C time-piece here is a sensation. Surrounded by moving figures that pop in and out like cuckoos, and the sun revolving round the earth, the faces accurately tell not only the time, day, date and zodiac of the sun and moon, but also the religious feast days up until the year 2019. The minute hand diminishing and elongating around an oval face is particularly addictive watching. Around the church, some of the medieval windows may entice your attention and you can also visit the choir school (the *Manécanterie*) in which survives a small fragment of cloisters predating the body of the cathedral.

One block south of St-Jean, gare St-Jean is the station for the tunnelled **funicular up to Fourvière**, surfacing at the Basilique de Notre-Dame (6–7/ 6; cl. 12–2 in winter), contemporary with the Sacré-Coeur of Paris but far, far grosser. The interior miasma of multi-coloured marble and mosaic are enough to make you think that the 19C revolutions could have been provoked merely by the bad taste of the bourgeoisie. As a visual antidote make your way to the **belvédère** behind the adjoining Vieux Chapelle, and you'll probably find Lyon and its curving rivers the epitome of beauty by comparison.

A short walk south from the basilica brings you to the site of the **Roman City**, where stand the remains of two theatres which you can wander round for free (8–12 & 2–5; cl. wkends). Better still is the display of prehistoric and Roman remains in the **Musée de la Civilisation Gallo-Romaine**, built into the hillside in several underground levels. Within this clever structure you'll see the bronze inscriptions of rights given to Roman citizens of Gaul by the native born Emperor Claudius, a Gaulish lunar calendar and models showing the technical workings of the theatres.

The modern town

The old silk weavers' quarter of **La Croix Rousse**, ascending from place Terreaux at the northern end of the Presqu'île, is again riddled with *traboules*. During the 19C insurrections here, silk weavers, known locally as *canuts* and then the city's chief source of wealth, rebelled against their industrial slavery on several occasions, under black flags and the slogan 'Live Working or Die Fighting'. On the whole they did the latter, and in their hundreds too, most notably in 1843 when troops were brought in.

La Croix Rousse remains a run-down clothing district today, with sweat shops and grim old factories still in use. The last remnants of the silk industry – 300 or so artisans – run a co-op *atelier* and showhouse at the **Maison des Canuts**, 10 rue d'Ivry (8.30–12 & 2–6.30; cl. Sun) but the line of descent and dissent from the original *canuts* is not very apparent.

Cheap restaurants and bars fringe **place de la Croix Rousse**, centre of the district, while down the slope to the west, at 51 rue du Bon Pasteur, is the *atelier* of **Totem**, a group of post-modernist designers who unleash a madness of colour and imagination on to chairs, tables and interiors. If you don't like that sort of thing, take comfort in the rational, mono-chrome remains of a **Roman amphitheatre** in the Jardin des Plantes three blocks down.

Place Terreaux itself is dominated by an arresting mythical equestrian entourage caught in mid-flight amidst jets. Opposite bulks the Hôtel de Ville, though nothing marks the legendary but real escape from its cellars by the anarchist hero Bakunin after an abortive uprising in 1870. To multiply the conflicting associations, this square was also the site of the guillotine in the days when Robespierre had it in for Lyon in a big way. The southern side is formed by the vast palace containing the **Musée des Beaux Arts** (10.45–6; cl. Tues), room after room of sculpture from the Middle Ages to the 19C on the ground floor; Oriental Art and Lyonnais painting above. Though tempting to dismiss the latter collection as municipal pride, it contains some interesting 19C works of oddly mystical and naturalistic tendencies: *The Poem of the Soul* series by Louis Janmot, *Good and Bad* by Victor Orsel. The canvases and murals by Puvis de Chavannes are also worth a look. The second floor is entirely given over to paintings: Veronese, Tintoretto, Zurbaran, Rembrandt and Rubens dominating the pre-18C contributions, and supplemented by some powerful 19C Romantics: Géricault's *Mad Woman*; *La Maraichère*, attri-buted to David; and Delacroix' *Woman with a Parrot*. Only the modern collection is a disappointment, despite a massive representation of all the top names.

Despite, or because of, the pedestrian streets running from place Terreaux to Perrache station (rues Victor Hugo and de la République) the **Presqu'île** doesn't invite lazy strolling and the *quais* hold charm only for motorists in fast cars. It's good for shops, food and late night bars, with most going on in the area around place Celestins, where at No. 2 you'll find a **women's centre** and feminist bookshop, while down on the *quai* there's a Monday market. But place Terreaux is definitely the more relaxed end and you can get there in no time at all on the métro from the station (to Mᵒ Hôtel de Ville). If you want to walk, take rue de la Charité rather than rue Victor Hugo: the **Musée Histoire des Tissus** at no 34 (10–12 & 2–5.30; cl. Mon) justifies the steep entry charge not by the quality but by the sheer weight of the collecion. The problem is to avoid getting stuck on one period – Byzantine and ancient Greek cloth, for example, or the 16C Persian carpets. Remember the *canuts* as you wander through the displays of Lyon silks, and amongst this century's textiles look out for the abstract colour rhythms of Sonia Delaunay's designs. A completely different way to blow your money will present itself at no 9: *La Truffe Blanche* pâtisserie, no less typical of Lyon excellence than the silks or Totem tables.

The recent development of **La Part Dieu** east of the Rhône – high rise office surplus, radio and TV, vast public amenities, the shopping centre and one of the best auditoriums in France – is part of Lyon's drive to become an international city of commerce. It's also the honeypot to tempt enterprises born in Lyon to bring their Paris HQs back home (the Crédit Lyonnais bank, for example). But the near-on 300kph Paris trains departing from La Part Dieu rather cut the ground from under the feet of such ambitions. None of the 1970s architecture of the ensemble is particularly inspiring, although the **food shops** in Les Halles de la Part Dieu could well claim to have the best selection of food in all France.

Further east you reach the working-class suburb of **Villeurbanne**, in which unlikely as it may seem, is based the **Théâtre Nationale Populaire**, originally an experimental company set up by the Lyonnais director Roger Planchon, now the no. 2 state theatre. The SI have programme details, and you should find that the sensual impact of the productions easily compensates for any language problems. For more straightforward relaxation head north from La Part Dieu to **Brotteaux** where you'll find greenery, and in early summer every colour that roses can grow, in the **Parc de la Tête d'Or**.

Rooms, entertainment and practicalities

Though no **hotels** are wildly cheap, there's a good choice between Perrache station and place Bellecour: *d'Ainay* (14 rue des Ramparts), *de la Marne* (78 rue de la Charité), *des Marroniers* (5 rue des Marroniers) and, just north-west of place Bellecour, the unnamed pension on the first floor of 100 rue de Président Herriot, are all worth a try. The **youth hostel** is 4km out in Venissieux (51 rue Roger Salengro; 876.39.23) on bus 35 from Bellecour to the Georges Levy stop or bus 53 from Perrache to Etats-Unis-Viviani. A second option is close by, the **Centre International de Séjour** (46 rue Commandant Pégoud; 876.14.22) off bd des Etats Unis. And if all else fails, there are **emergency lodgings** at the *Accueil en Gare* in the covered walkway between Centre Perrache and the station. **Camping** is not very practicable unless you've got a car, with all the sites 10km or so outside town: three at the Parc de Loisirs de Miribil-Jonage to the north-east, one at St-Genies-Laval to the south-west and another off the N6 between Dardilly and Limonest, north-west of the city.

The area round Lyon is the **gastronomic** centre of France, where the cream and butter rich cuisine of the north meets the garlic, oil and herbs of the south. The best poultry and pork comes from nearby Bresse, the Rhône valley supplies fruit and vegetables and fish is provided by the mountain lakes. Many of the classics of French cuisine – quenelles, frogs' legs, and numerous sausages – originated here, and it's equally famous now for **nouvelle cuisine**, thanks to Paul Bocuse. This Lyonnais self-publicist and globe-trotting apostle of the art is the most famous chef in France, and his restaurant, just north of Lyon in Collonges-au-Mont-d'Or, one of the most expensive. But Lyon can offer classical meals for perfectly acceptable prices, often in tucked away little places with no name or menu displayed, known locally as *bouchons* or *Chez la Mère*'s. Good areas to look are around place Bellecour (rue des Marroniers especially), in the place des Celestins district, around place Terreaux and in Vieux Lyon.

Local wines, Beaujolais and Côtes du Rhône, aren't at all expensive, even in restaurants. For picnics, the choice of sweet and savoury goodies from the charcuteries and pâtisseries is overwhelming. If you need quick eats, use one of the numerous takeaways and a couple of cafeterias on the Presqu'île pedestrian streets, or grab something at *Le Caveau* café on place Poncet.

Rue Mercier is excellent for **late night bars** with **live music**. Otherwise try *Hot Club* (26 rue Lanterne) for jazz or *Le Jardin* (24 rue Royale). The *Grand Café des Négociants* (place Regaud) is popular day and night; *Damier* (8 rue St-George) is **women-only** and *Epi Bar* (2 rue Bellecorderie) is one of the many **gay** bars. If you want to **bop**, *Cité des Lumières* (15 rue Ferranchat), *Club des Iles* (1 grand rue des Feuillants) and *Eléphant Noir* (22 Imbert Colomes) are all reggae and salsa joints. For punk/hard rock, head for *Why Not* (38 rue de l'Arbre Sec) and *West Side* (159 bd Stalingrad, Villerubanne). The two most popular standard discos are *BC Blues* (25 place Carnot) and *Palladium* (30 bd Deruelle).

The **what's-on listings** to get is *Lyon-Poche*, out every Wednesday and available from newsagents: it details restaurants as well as all the arts and entertainments. 160 **films** are screened a week, many of them foreign and *version originale*. The two movies you might want to see (perhaps when you get back home) are *L'Horloger de St Paul* and *Une Semaine de Vacances* both set in Lyon and directed by the Lyonnais Bernard Tavernier, the one serious French film-maker currently able to achieve commercial success. In September there's a festival of rare films, preceded by an excellent marionette festival and one for the French composer Berlioz. But the major annual art event is the **International Festival of Music and Drama,** with shows in the Roman theatres, from mid-June to mid-July. **Classical** enthusiasts can have a good time all year round with the concerts at La Part Dieu and the Opéra.

To help you get around all this, **bikes** can be hired from *Motobecane François* (139 av Mi de Saxe), while the two agencies for **hitching** are *Allostop* (8 rue de la Bombarde; 842.38.29) and *Lyon-Stop* (29 rue Pasteur; 858.65.29). *Allostop* can also help with cheap bus and train travel, as can numerous **travel agencies** listed by the SI. *CROUS* (59 rue de la Madeleine) and *CIJ* (9 quai des Celestins) may both be useful if you're planning to stay a while.

SOUTH ALONG THE VALLEY

The journey south from Lyon can feel like a compulsive race to get to Provence, with river, rail and road dictating a pace down the river banks that forbids you to stop. The first big town, **VIENNE**, offers no inducement from its riverside aspect to break away and drop in, but if you enjoy classical ruins enough not to wait for the better offerings in Provence, it will repay an afternoon or day's visit. Behind the grim *quais* lies a quiet city scattered with remnants of its once illustrious position as Roman capital of Provençal Gaul. All the sites are well signed and open between April and mid-October (9–12 & 2–6.30) and the SI is on the opposite end of Cours Brillier from the gare SNCF, on the corner with quai Jean-Jaurès south of the second bridge. Beyond the remains, there's little to hang around for, but if you find yourself stuck here you'll find a cheap hotel, *de Provence*, in rue Voltaire off Cours Brillier and a foyer at the *MJC* (rue Laurent Florentin; 53.21.97).

From Vienne, if you have wheels and time, you could cross over the Rhône and explore the **vineyards**. The reds are good, and there are two whites that would be a major extravagance to drink elsewhere – *Condrieu* and, a bit further south, *Château-Grillat*. Wine or no wine, by the time you reach **VALENCE**, the atmosphere is definitely southern. If you want to celebrate your arrival in the *Midi*, as the French call the south, there are plenty of bars and restaurants in the old town around the cathedral and on the main streets av Faure and bd Clerc. The rows of plane trees, low pitched tiled roofs and lounging about café life confirm the proximity of Provence. Which is unfortunate for Valence since it just incites rapid departure for lower latitudes. Even so, you may well decide to spend the night here, and if that happens there are plenty of unpretentious **hotels** between the cafés and restaurants along bd Clerc and av Faure. There is, too, a municipal **campsite** and a large, comfortable **hostel** with accommodation in shared rooms. Getting out is easy; the **SNCF station** is on av Selhard, another good area for hotels; and the **gare routière** in place Gen Leclerc, alongside the main SI.

About 20km downstream, the Drôme river joins the Rhône from the east. For drivers bored with main roads and unconcerned with speed and petrol, there's a wonderful mountain route along the deserted Drôme valley to SISTERON and Eastern Provence. But on the straight Rhône path, it's nonstop down to Orange save for perhaps one quick detour for nougat at MONTÉLIMAR.

WESTERN PROVENCE

Past Valence the pull of the Mediterranean becomes increasingly insistent as the strident colours of the landscape and the hard Provencal light grow ever more vivid. **Western Provence** is a small but disparate region, ranging from the bleak, marshy plains of the **Camargue** and the Rhône delta to the greenish orange hills of the **Vaucluse**, so familiar from Cézanne's paintings, rising gently to the mountains in the east. The Camargue aside, it's a neatly concentrated area, and one where it makes perfect sense to pick one spot as a base and cover the major sights from there in a series of day trips. Of the cities, **Avignon** stands out both historically and culturally, its central location at the end of the Rhône corridor making it an obvious target if you're coming from the north. On the way take a look at **Orange**, worth a stop-off for its Roman remains. **Arles** too, just a short jaunt south of Avignon, clutches a rich nest of classical treasures.

ORANGE, VAISON-LA-ROMAINE AND CARPENTRAS

Visitors don't come to **ORANGE** in their thousands just because it's the first town they reach in Provence. They come to see a monumental wall, blocking the southern side of place des Frères Mounet and described by Louis XIV as the finest in his kingdom, a plain stone construction of inhuman dimensions built as a backdrop for Roman entertainments. Once on the other side, having paid a hefty but unnegotiable sum (daily 9–12 & 2–6/5), all becomes amazingly clear. Amazing because it's the only **Roman theatre** in which the façade still stands: you can make out murals of centaurs on its surface and, in rows of columned niches, the over-sized statue of Augustus Caesar. The seats still encrust the hill of St-Eutrope and the stone supports on the stage could to this day prop an awning roof to protect spectators – to the left of the stage you can walk through to the ruins of a vast stadium and temple. The only thing that's near impossible to visualise is the original performances, and it's now used every July and August for an international festival of choral music – frankly, not the best time to come to Orange.

If you arrived by road from the north, you will already have seen the second great Roman monument of Orange, the **Arc de Triomphe** – a triple-arched entry gloating, predictably, on imperial victories over the

Gauls. As you can see from the oppressive symbols in the sculpted façade, it's another extraordinary preservation job, but of limited interest, and really the most remarkable thing about the arch is that it has survived at all. More Roman stone is on view in the **Musée des Beaux Arts** (opposite the theatre with the same opening hours and ticket) – not the best of museums but a curious one in that its collection includes oddities like the drawings of Frank Brangwyn, an English painter who learnt his craft with William Morris and whose commissioned designs for the London Houses of Parliament were rejected as being better suited to a nightclub. As odd, though at least explicable (Frank Brangwyn never even went to Orange), is the pedigree of places that the name of the town has engendered. Place-names in Holland, the USA and South Africa, and the fanatical Orange order in Ireland, were christened, in Protestant fashion, after the Dutch royal family, who took their name from the tiny Provencal territory they owned for 150 years before Orange become French in 1713.

Should you want to stay, there are cheap **hotels** dotted around place des Herbes in the vieille ville. It's quite a walk from the **gare SNCF** and **bus station** on av F Mistral where you'll also find accommodation. At the top of St-Eutrope, on the site of the former Roman Capitol, is a **campsite** and pleasant park from which to view the town and theatre or in which to take a snooze. The SI is on Cours A Briand, bordering the old town on the west. Every Thursday morning, all the sensual produce of Provence – olives, truffles, garlic, honey and lavender – are laid out in the Cours **market**. It's also one of the best streets for **restaurants**, though you can just as easily fill yourself with *pan bagna* (salad-stuffed sandwiches) in the cafés on place de la République or place des Herbes.

From the **gare routière** on Cours Pourtoles (rather than at the station) you can get buses on to Avignon, Aix and Marseilles. Also, four buses a day make the half-hour run to **VAISON-LA-ROMAINE**, another town very much on the Roman remains circuit, its speciality being the excavations of a rich residential district in which the floor mosaics are still intact. Get yourself to place Sautel in the modern town (linked by a Roman bridge with a medieval citadel on the flank of the hill opposite) and you're near the SI and the entrances to the two **Roman quarters** (daily 9–6/5). The ticket for these also includes a **museum** with marble statuary and a mask from the theatre (Quartier de Puymin; daily 9–6), a guided tour of the villas, and the Romanesque **cathedral and cloisters** of Notre Dame de Nazareth. As in Orange, the theatre, while not so impressive, hosts a summer festival of drama, music and ballet in which Roman taste takes no part. The one drawback to all this is that Vaison-la-Romaine sports few cheap and central **places to stay** – only a one-star Logis (*à l'Escargot d'Or*) on route d'Orange, or a summer **foyer** and **campsite** at the *À Coeur Joie* centre on av César-Geoffray. Your best bet is probably to use the **youth hostel** at SEGURET (36.93.31) 8km back towards Orange.

The hill to which Vaison-la-Romaine's *haute ville* clings is at the foot of **Mont Ventoux**, rising 20km east to nearly 2,000m, the last Alpine outcrop. But you don't need skis or rope to climb it, just wheels and a map to get you on to the D974. On a clear day you can see not only the higher Alps but right across to Languedoc and Roussillon to the west. AVIGNON lies nearer at hand, past the crossroads town of **CARPEN-TRAS**, where yet another performing arts junket competes for summer visitors, and whose only unique features are a medieval synagogue, an undemanding local museum and the production of *berlingots*, op-art caramel sweets.

AVIGNON

Prefecture of the Vaucluse, and in many ways one of the most compelling towns in the whole of southern France, **AVIGNON** has drawn a variety of responses over the years. Petrarch, living nearby in the 14C, called it a sink of vice; Lawrence Durrell was fascinated by its tenebrous monuments and putrescent squares; while James Pope-Hennessey was more positive and wrote of the 'indolent and almost audible excitement' of its streets. Of the three, I prefer the last view, and regard it as the most true. Sure, the city has always been known as something of a decadent place: since the Middle Ages it has been a refuge of criminals, and the squalor and poverty of its narrow streets and squares is apparent even today. But overriding all this is a distinctive pulsing life and youthful exuberance with which few towns in France can compare, and which reaches a crescendo during the summer festival.

Avignon's **battlements** still enclose the city, brownish, sun-burnt and utterly complete since restoration, or in some places reconstruction, by Viollet-le-Duc in the last century. Above rises the **Palais des Papes**, bulky reminder of the city's days as Papal seat when, driven out of Rome by factional in-fighting, the Pope set up house here and remained for almost a century. Quite a time it was too: corruption, greed and venality flourished in the city, and Avignon became notorious as a centre of crime and hedonism; plague, too, grew epidemic and the Pope, Clement V, had fires burning either side of him in his cavernous, draughty palace to keep out the ague. Five popes succeeded him, all French, and chose to remain in Avignon, between them building the palace, purchasing the whole town from Joanna, Queen of Naples and Countess of Provence, for 80,000 ducats (which, incidentally, was never paid) and constructing the walls with their thirty-seven towers and seven gates. The ramparts were higher then, before the moat was filled in, and must have seemed even more imposing, though even now they give the city a potent sense of

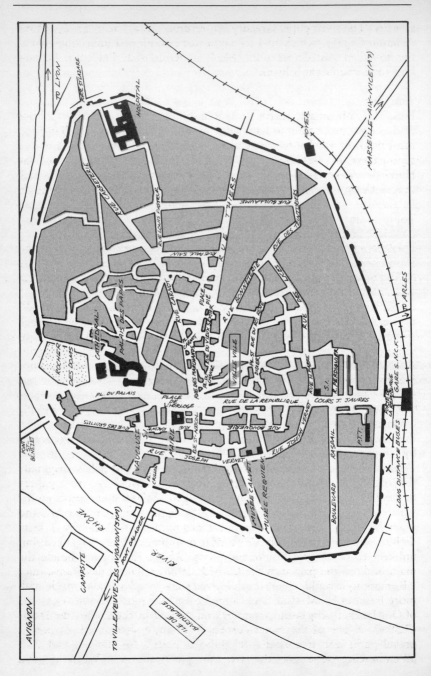

AVIGNON

security. The sixth pope, Gregory XI, returned to Rome in 1376, but the Avignon Papacy, which had its supporters, continued under the rule of the so-called Anti-Popes until 1424, a period that has since become known as the Great Schism.

The city

From the railway station rue de la République forms the busy backbone of the city, opening out at its far end into the vibrant **place de l'Horloge**, focal point of all that happens, cluttered with café tables and scene of a summer evening fleamarket. At its edge lie a florid 19C theatre and the Hôtel de Ville, while beyond, past the stationary police wagons which keep a sharp eye out for illicit drug-dealing, spreads the broad place du Palais with, flanking its right-hand side, the fortress-like **Palais des Papes**. Tours – on the hour in French, at 10.30 and 2.45 in English – are expensive and excruciatingly dull, but as they're the only way of getting inside you may as well join one. Once in, you can always wander off and explore on your own.

The complex is actually two palaces in one, to the right the austere Old Palace of the Cistercian Benedict XII, put up in 1342, and adjoining that a later and more consciously elegant structure built for Clement VI ten years later. The tours start in the older of the two, taking you through a central courtyard (which may be full of scaffolded seats and hard to see if you're here during the festival) and into a grand, soulless interior stripped bare except for some patchy frescoes – some, in the first floor Banqueting Hall, by the Sienese painter Martini – and some large Gobelin tapestries, hung in the ground floor Salle de Consistoire, where the Pope received distinguished guests. Lighter, and more cheerfully embellished with murals of hunting scenes, is Clement VI's bedroom in the new palace; take a look also at the Grand Audience Hall, decorated by Giovanetti, Martini's protégé.

At the far end of the square, the honey-coloured **Petit Palais**, originally the 14C home of one of the Pope's aides, was turned over to a gallery in the 1970s to house the overflow of Avignon School paintings from the Musée Calvert, fragments of sculpture from the town Lapidarium, and a set of Italian primitives that were acquired from Rome by a local dignitary in the last century. It's a neat museum, carefully arranged, but unlikely to detain you for terribly long. Above the square, beside the main body of the palace, is the **Cathédrale Notre Dame des Doms**, once a Romanesque building but much altered since, heavily ornate inside with more frescoes by Martini, and capped by a ludicrously top-heavy statue of Our Lady. Rising steeply from behind the palace, the **Rocher des Doms** (7.30–7) is one of the nicest corners in town, a shady park of ponds, gravel paths and tree-fringed flowerbeds, perfect for lunches and with all-embracing views over the river, the fortifications of Villeneuve and the bloomy Provencal countryside beyond. Down below, and accessible from the town ramparts, the **Pont St-Benezet**, known to schoolkids everywhere from the nursery rhyme ('Sur le pont d'Avignon . . .'), prongs a stunted arm across the water. Benezet was a shepherd boy who, spurred on by divine instructions, built the bridge between 1177 and 1185, bringing prosperity to the town and sanctity to himself; though of his original twenty-two arches only four remain, the rest destroyed by war and the Rhône's frequent flooding.

Back in the heart of the city, place de l'Horloge leads into Avignon's **old quarter** – tiny streets, shuttered houses for the most part – and on the other side of rue de la République, in rue Vernet, the **Musée Calvert** (9–12 & 2–6, cl. Tues), housed in an 18C hotel around an attractive courtyard. It's an elderly, cluttered museum, worth a look as much for its old-world setting as the collection, which in the main is mediocre and coated with dust and grime. Some works, however, do stand out, especially the 19C and 20C items, and notably David's *Barra*, a picture of a youth who was martyred during the Revolution for refusing to recognise the monarchy. Other things to watch out for after you've waded through a host of dross include a small set of works by the expressionist painter Soutine, and some early canvases by Matisse and Dufy. Next door, the **Musée Requien** has an interesting herbarium, and if you're still culture-hungry after that, the Jesuit church on rue de la République holds a small **Lapidarium**, though most of its more interesting pieces have found their way of late to the Petit Palais.

Action and essentials . . .
The main **PTT**, one of the two local **bus terminals** and the **railway station** all lurk outside the ramparts at the Porte de la République. The other **bus terminal** is in the centre of town on place Pie, on the edge of a pedestrian area of narrow streets. Here you'll also find a large covered **market**, *Les Halles*, open every day except Monday and selling a vast array of vegetables, charcuterie, buckets of olives and dozens of strong local cheeses like *Buchette de Banon*, *Tarare Crème, Predaion* and *Baretous*. In the town's better pâtisseries search out *fougasse* – somewhere between a pie, bread and a biscuit – and *papalines d'Avignon*, spherical pink liqueur chocolates made with sixty-two herbs, terribly hard to make but very easy to eat.

For general information on the city (where to stay, eat, dance, etc.) pick up a copy of *Avignon Pratique* from the **SI** on Cous J Jaurès (cl. Sun except during the festival). More specifically, good cheap **places to eat** include *Flunch Cafétéria*, on bd Raspail, *Au Petit Nice* and *Le Ritz* in place de l'Horloge, and the self-service *Cafétéria Les Arts*. For eating on your feet, takeaway crêpes, pizzas and *pan bagna* are available all over town. Cheap **accommodation** isn't hard to find either, though it fills up fast during the festival. The three-star *Hôtel Bristol-Terminus*, on rue de la République, has some low-priced singles, and in rue Agricole Perdiguier, a narrow turning off Cours J Jaurès, there are three inexpensive pensions: *Splendid*, *Parc* and, least enticing but cheapest, *Pacific*. *Hôtel Jacquemart*, in rue Felicien, is also surprisingly reasonable, and there's a **hostel** in the Squash Club, at 32 bd Limbert, and a **foyer** at 33 rue Eisenhower. If you're **camping**, simply cross the Pont Daladier to the Ile de Bathelasse and use *Camping Bagatelle*.

Avignon's huge annual **Festival**, one of Europe's leading drama festivals, takes place in the last three weeks of July and the first week of August, and attracts well over 100,000 people. Every day there's a range of theatre, classical and modern, sometimes by the best known companies in France, sometimes by unknowns; jazz and classical concerts; dance and films; in seventeen different official venues including the Palais des Papes. Then too, there are endless impromptu outdoor performances. But do remember that accommodation is horribly hard to find and the authorities no longer allow people to sleep in the streets or parks. Even without the festival, there are arts events going on all year round; noticeboards in the SI have all the latest details.

THE VAUCLUSE

An aristocratic escape from an overcrowded city, **VILLENEUVE-LÈS-AVIGNON** ('lès' means 'near') grew up during Avignon's Papal period and remains small and unspoiled to this day – and it has an intense concentration of historic sights well worth crossing the river for. After the 14C **Tour Philippe le Bel**, first thing you see arriving from Avignon, the centre-piece of the town is the **Fort St-André**, high above the roofs with classic views over the city across the river that Corot among others was inspired to paint. Inside it's mostly ruins, overgrown with creepers. In better condition is the **Church of Notre Dame**, with a 14C polychrome ivory *Madonna* in its treasury, carved in the curve of the elephant's tusk. Better still is the **Chartreuse du Val de Bénédiction**, founded by Innocent VI in 1356 and the largest charterhouse in France, a village in itself with cobbled streets, houses, cloisters and tiny courtyards. Before you leave, take a few minutes to stick your head around the door of the **Musée Municipal**, just a short walk from the Chartreuse, to see its one outstanding painting, the *Coronation of the Virgin* by local artist Quarton. This 15C work depicts a fiery Hell, Christ on the cross and the Virgin in Heaven, all against a backdrop made up from the buildings of Avignon and aspects of the local landscape. **To get to Villeneuve** from Avignon catch a no 10 bus (marked 'Villeneuve puis Les Angles') and get on place du Marché; once here there's an **SI** on the same square.

The other side of Avignon the N100 heads east, picking off a succession of nondescript small towns. Watery ISLE-SUR-SORGUE comes first, where a turning forks off to **FONTAINE DE VAUCLUSE**, one of the most powerful natural springs in the world, with up to 12,000 cubic metres of water per minute bursting from the foot of a high semi-circle of cliff. The setting is dramatic enough, and in spring it's an astonishing spectacle, but in summer months the water dwindles while the tide of visitors reaches its flood – many, like scores of British 19C travellers who eulogised about this spot, coming not for the Fontaine itself but because this was where Francesco Petrarch lived and wrote his poems for the mysterious Laura, whom he had seen in Avignon and fallen madly in love with. Like all great poets, his love remained unrequited, since it's thought she was a member of the de Sade family and already married. A **youth hostel** (20.31.65), 1km from the village and well signposted, should be able to provide a bed, and a **campsite** space for a tent. There's a **SI** in place de l'Eglise.

ROUSSILLON, a short hike off the main road, sits on a ridge above some dazzling ochre quarries, steep cliffs and tunnels of red and yellow sand that colour your skin and clothes. There's a **campsite** here or you can push on to neighbouring **GORDES**, another curious spot, built into a steep hillside with the houses stacked almost on top of each other. Above broods a fortified **Château**, a lung-wrenching climb but worthwhile for some stirring views, a fine Renaissance fireplace and, if you like his work, rotating studies by Vasarely (10–12 & 2–6, cl. Tues).

SOUTH OF AVIGNON

Continuing south you have a choice of two routes: one tracking the Rhône down to BEAUCAIRE and TARASCON, the second a smaller road crossing flat market garden country until it reaches the jagged peaks of the Alpilles hills. At their foot lies **ST-RÉMY**, where Van Gogh committed himself to a nursing home in 1889 after chopping off part of his ear. The hospital, in the monastery of St-Paul de Mausole, still stands: his room and the gardens where he painted, in that last frenetic year of melancholy and creativity, are open to the public. But little St-Rémy has other claims to fame besides Van Gogh: the 16C astrologer Nostradamus was born here, in rue Hoche, and Gertrude Stein stayed a year in the *Hôtel de la Ville Verte*, the only one that existed in 1922 – though now there are a number of hotels and campsites if you want to stop. A kilometre or so south is the bleak, though archaeologically important site of the Gallo-Roman town **Glanum**, with an archway and mausoleum still standing: a creepy, spooky place after dark – plain dull before.

From St-Rémy the road struggles uphill to the perched village of **LES BAUX**, whose spectacular setting and dramatic history are now totally given over to an artificial community of money-spinning arts and crafts people who thrive off the thousands of tourists packing the narrow streets. In the Middle Ages the seigneurs of Les Baux wielded a surprising amount of influence, winning control over a considerable area of Provence and becoming counts and princes in several of the region's miniature states. Despite the day-trippers, the town tries hard to maintain some semblance of this illustrious past, foremost inside a crumbly medieval stronghold, carved out of the solid rock and now no more than a shell-like remain.

If you had taken the first road out of Avignon, the N570, you'd have come eventually to **TARASCON**, favourite hangout of Good King René (see p. 432) and dominated by its mighty castle, pitched on a rock beside the river. Little restored, yet remarkably complete, it served as a prison for many years after René's death; now it lies empty and open for visits – the perfect medieval citadel with corner turrets, vast echoey halls and a central courtyard. In the town itself the only thing to see is the Gothic church of St-Martha, dedicated to, and holding the relics of – in a 5C sarcophagus in the crypt – the saint who supposedly landed here from the Holy Land after the death of Christ (see p. 430) and subdued a dragon that had been terrorising the town.

Eyeing Tarascon warily from the opposite bank, the fortress at **BEAU-CAIRE** has all but disappeared except for its external walls, which still sit grandly above the tumbling village. This point on the Rhône was for a long time the border between Provence and Languedoc, a sensitive frontier since Languedoc had been annexed to the French kingdom and was ruled from the north, while Provence maintained a fragile and fierce independence. History and the sheer attractiveness of the place apart though, there's little to hold you for long, and by now you may well be yearning for bed and board at Arles, or a trek further south to the windy mystery of the Camargue.

ARLES

The most striking thing about **ARLES** is its history. For over 2,500 years its streets have seen continuous habitation: it was an important trading town in Roman times, capital of Gaul and one of the most urbane centres in the Empire; Constantine had his capital here before he moved it east; and in the early Middle Ages it became a flourishing centre of the Christian faith, the town where in 597 St Augustine was crowned first archbishop of England. All of which has left an indelible stamp on the city today. Signs of Arles' past importance hit you hard as soon as you arrive, not least the massive Roman **Arena** – huge, magnificent, overbearing, and though not quite as well preserved as the one at Nîmes, more or less unscathed by the centuries. Here, as at Nîmes, men were pitted against bulls, wild boar, lions and often each other, usually prisoners of war but sometimes professional gladiators, engaged in a fight to the death. Gladiators had necessarily short careers but could achieve great fame if they survived a number of contests. Around the arena there would have been canopies to protect the delicate audience from the sun, and cauldrons of boiling saffron to mask the stench of blood. The sand was pure white, sometimes speckled with glinting metal shavings or dyed brilliant colours. The towers at each side are not Roman but 12C, a relic of the time when the whole arena was used as a fortified village; in 1826 excavations uncovered some 200 houses and even a church. Now, again like Nîmes, the arena plays summer host to flamboyant, Spanish-style *mis-à-mort* bullfights: gory, gratuitous affairs that go off in a blaze of ceremony.

Arles has a tremendous amount to see if you want to, and most things are conveniently close together. A **global ticket** to all museums and monuments, valid for one year, is the least expensive way even if you don't manage to get around to everything. **Opening times** are fairly uniform, but change from month to month; roughly speaking they're 8.30/9–12/12.30 & 2–4.30/7.

Alongside the arena are remnants of a **Roman theatre** – remnants because it was vandalised by Christians and then used as a quarry for stone to build the city's churches and ramparts. Only a couple of columns remain from the original stage wall (contrast this with the theatre at Nîmes) and just twenty rows of seats, but concerts are still held here nonetheless. From the theatre follow the park down to the wide main street of modern Arles, bd des Lices, and cross to the ancient **Alyscamps cemetery**. Just a few minutes away, and now a graceful avenue lined with poplars and tombs, this was from the Roman era until the Middle Ages one of the grandest and most famous burial grounds in the western world: the best of the tombs were dismantled or destroyed after the 15C.

Of the post-Roman era – and Arles' time as a major early Christian centre – the major surviving relic is the **Cathédrale St-Trophime**, one of the first Romanesque churches in France. It's a good example of the Provencal style, although the west front, with its highly decorative doorway facing on to place de la République, is untypically ornate – the elaborate frieze shows the damned, on the right, descending naked to the eternal fires of Hell, and on the left, the saved proceeding happy and fully-dressed into Abraham's bosom. Inside, the church is lofty and plain, adorned only by dusky tapestries and some dull, sombre paintings. Through the Bishop's Palace, the airy Cloisters are an interesting mix of Gothic and Romanesque styles, with some fine carving on the columns and capitals showing scenes from the Life of Christ, and a sunny upper gallery often given over to temporary exhibitions of variable quality.

Near St-Trophime, cluster several small museums, nearest the **Musée Lapidaire d'Art Païen** (pagan art), housed opposite in the one-time church of St-Anne, with a rich selection of mosaics, Roman sarcophagi and statues rescued from the theatre. The **Musée d'Art Chrétien**, in the old Jesuit college, is similarly good. Here sarcophagi taken mostly from the Alyscamps cemetery show a revealing transition from the styles of the earlier pagan models. Steps lead down to the musty *Cryptoporticus*, built by the Romans as a wheat store under their forum and used as an air-raid shelter during the last war. In a different vein, the **Musée Arleten** displays local folk art, setting out to capture something of 19C Provencal life in a collection brought together by the Provencal poet Mistral, who financed the museum from the proceeds of his Nobel prize for literature. A statue of Mistral stands in place du Forum, unveiled in his own presence in 1909, when he gave a reading and made a speech that reduced the audience of assorted dignitaries to tears of emotion.

Place du Forum doubles with République as the central town square. As its name suggests, this was the site of the ancient Roman forum, and today it's an equally important meeting point for travellers, tourists, tramps and locals. Over looking the square, with a piece of Roman masonry in one wall, is the *Hôtel de Nord-Pinus*, where Stendhal, Merimée and Henry James all stayed (though not at the same time), and in one corner Van Gogh's celebrated *Café at Arles* continue to thrive. The 'Yellow House', where he lived, at 2 place Lamartine near the *gare*, was destroyed in the last war, but the building that replaced it looks strangely similar, and the square itself has the same open, countrified quality that can be seen in the painting. Here Gauguin lived with him for several weeks, a disastrous mismatch which terminated infamously with Van Gogh cutting off part of his ear in a fit of rage and despair and presenting it to a prostitute friend.

A couple of hundred metres north of place du Forum, on the banks of the Rhône, the **Musée Reattu** is housed in the 15C Grand Priory of the Knights of St John of Jerusalem. Its worst features are the paintings by Reattu himself, who should have been content to have the place named after him, but once you've dismissed those, there are some quirky treasures worth catching. Among these is a collection of fifty-seven rough drawings by Picasso – thumbnail sketches really, some of interest more for the hand that did them but a few magnificent in their nonchalance – and a small assortment of photographs by Beaton, Man Ray and other notables, displayed only, alas, in sporadic temporary exhibits.

Festivals, food and the facts of life

From June to September Arles hosts numerous **festivals and fetes**, among them a Festival of Photography in early July and, highlight of the year, a Dance Festival in the last two weeks of that month. The SI is centrally placed on bd des Lices, well worth popping in if only to pick up a copy of their free handbook, which is packed with useful info on the town. **Accommodation** tends to be pricey but **eating** is cheap, and scores of restaurants and brasseries in the town centre offer bargain-priced menus spiced with local specialities. Best area for a moderately-priced room is around place du Forum and place Voltaire, and there's a good **hostel** (96.18.25) in av Maréchal Foch. **Camping**, most accessible of the sites are *Camping City* (the largest, on Route de Crau; bus Crau) and *Pontes de la Camargue* (Route de Tarascon; bus Tarascon).

The **gare SNCF** is in av Paulin Talabot just north of place Lamartine, and you can either **hire a bike** from there or go to *Ets. Montuori*, on rue 4 Sept. Most **buses** leave from offices on bd Clémenceau, with regular services to Montpellier, Avignon, Les Baux, Aix and Marseilles. To cross the Camargue to LES SAINTES MARIES take an SNCF bus from the train station.

THE CAMARGUE

South of Arles the flat land of **the Camargue** spreads across the Rhône delta, a wind-blasted watery region where black bulls, raised for Provencal bullfights and rarely sighted, roam vast ranges, troops of half-wild horses wander free, and in the expanses of still water, herons and pink flamingos stand or fly in their hundreds. The animals are herded by *gardians*, cowboys who work on horseback and wear wide-brimmed black hats, bandanas, and leather boots and leggings. Most of the Camargue has been designated a *Parc Régional*, the heart of which is an extensive enclosed *Réserve Naturelle Zoologique et Botanique*, mainly a sanctuary for rare birds to which access is restricted to permit-holders. The land outside is farmed in the main as rice paddies, or given over to vineyards – scattered with isolated farmhouses and primitive hamlets, low whitewashed buildings seemingly lost and forgotten. You can choose from two main roads: one to lonely SALIN DE GIRAUD, east of the huge **Etang de Vaccarès**, the other to **LES SAINTES MARIES DE LA MER,** on the coast west of the étang close by a long, duney shore of broad sand beaches – though you can forget any notions of sunbathing because it's teeming with giant mosquitoes, horseflies and some of their more unfamiliar relatives. This, together with the wind, also makes it a difficult area for cycling or hitching.

LES SAINTES MARIES DE LA MER is a lovely old town with two claims to fame. The first, that Van Gogh used to come here to paint, is fact; the second is one of the Catholic church's more improbable legends. Following the crucifixion of Christ, his friends and relatives were hounded out of the Holy Land and put to sea together, landing ultimately on the French coast where Les Saintes Maries stands today. The party consisted of Mary Magdalene, the Virgin Mary's sister Mary, the mother of apostles John and James, who was *also* called Mary, their maidservant Sarah and a mixed crowd that included Martha, Lazarus, Maximinus and Sidonius. On arriving here, the group split up, Maximinus and Mary Magdalene going to St-Maximin, where they are buried in the church; Martha heading up to Tarascon to conquer the mythical Tarasque dragon (see p. 427); and the other two Marys and Sarah hanging on here, which has since been named in their honour. Actually, a couple of centuries separate the characters, and details have become hazy over the years, but it's a good enough yarn for the church to have given it full credence and for gypsies to have adopted the maidservant Sarah as their patron saint. Every year on 24 May they arrive here in their thousands for two days of festivities which climax with the reliquary of St Sarah, in the form of a dark, seated statue dressed in white, being carried into the sea at the head of a long procession of tourists, gypsies, *gardians* and people from Arles in their traditional dress. It's a festival that's well worth catching – a good-humoured, sleepless affair in which everyone joins – but if you can't make it, there are smaller pilgrimages here on the second-to-last Sunday in October and the first Sunday in December.

All in all, Les Saintes Maries makes much the best base for exploring the Camargue. The **SI**, on av Van Gogh, has details on **hotels**, though most are over-priced, wildlife information centres, local walks, bike-hire in town, horseback tours and hire of horses. If you can't handle the hotel rates, there's a **youth hostel** (97.91.72) in PIOCH BADET, 9km away on the Arles bus route, or two large **campsites** on the edge of town, the best *La Brise* with 2,000 places and bike-rental. For **eating**, you can't better the freshly-caught fish, served up in most of the central town restaurants.

SOUTH AND EASTERN PROVENCE

East of the Rhône delta spreads the verdant heart of Provence, lifting back from its most discovered fringe, the Côte d'Azur (covered in Chapter 15), in a broad series of corniches up to the hilly backcountry of the coastal massifs – a rough, rocky landscape inscribed by circuitous roads and covered with scrubby holm oak, broom, wild herbs and flowers. Behind rise the foothills of the Alps, dotted with lofty villages and with few major towns: ideal country for walkers, or for slow but wonderfully scenic journeying by bus or train. Only one large town stands out, **Aix-en-Provence**, a lively cultural centre for the west of the region and a good starting-point for your travels. From here you can take the main N7 through the nub of Provence to sun, sea and people in Cannes and around, and then branch north into the mountains which, once free of the ruinous tourist infrastructure of the Côte, are delightfully undisturbed.

AIX-EN-PROVENCE

AIX is the perfect southern city, a great former Provencal capital full of Renaissance mansions in picturesque disrepair, its central tangle of medieval lanes and alleys encircled by broad tree-lined avenues. It was first settled by the Romans, who gave it the name Aquae Sextiae for the hot mineral springs they discovered here: after they left it declined, emerging again in the 15C for its greatest and most famous period of prosperity when, under 'Good King René', Aix became capital of an independent Provençal state and a mushrooming centre of arts and culture. Not really a king at all (except nominally, of far-off Naples), René has passed into legend as the ultimate Renaissance man: an accomplished linguist, mathematician, artist and musician, there seems to have been nothing to which he couldn't turn his hand. It seems clear that, at least, he created the refined cultural centre which Aix remains today – instituting a number of far-sighted economic reforms, encouraging festivals, chivalry and the arts and, perhaps his greatest achievement of all, bringing the Muscat grape to this part of France. René died heirless in 1480, and with him died both the golden age and independence, Aix soon passing to the French crown. But the spirit of his reforms is evident even today, above all in the frequent festivals, exhibitions and dance events. Foremost among these is the *Festival International d'Art Lyrique et de Musique*, from mid-July to early August, with scores of performances in the theatres, on the fringe, around the streets.

Cours Mirabeau, its rows of leafy *platanes* punctuated by ornate fountains (including the *Fontaine du Roi René*, with the old king holding up his Muscat grapes), is the pulsing heart of the modern town, an avenue as beautiful as any in Europe. One side, lined with banks and offices, has a sedate commercial air, while on the other all the life of the town goes on, café tables flooding out along the Cours in a bubble of conversation – meeting place for locals and stage for street entertainers, jugglers and acrobats. At the far end lies place de la Libération, fountained fulcrum of the town, leading on to the **Casino** and **Etablissement Thermal** in Cours Sextius, where people still drink the waters which made the town famous – though they have strangely subsided of late – and continue to swear to their medical efficacy.

The oldest part of town, **Vieil Aix**, lies east of here, a peaceful mesh of narrow lanes opening unexpectedly into elegant squares ringed by grand balconied town houses. In a 17C hotel on rue Gaston a small **museum** gives a rundown on local history, its best exhibits being a collection of eighty or so tiny figures, *santons*, once used in Christmas cribs and really deliberate portrayals of typical Provençal types. At the centre of the old quarter is the calmly handsome place Hôtel de Ville, the **town hall** containing a library with some 300,000 volumes and,

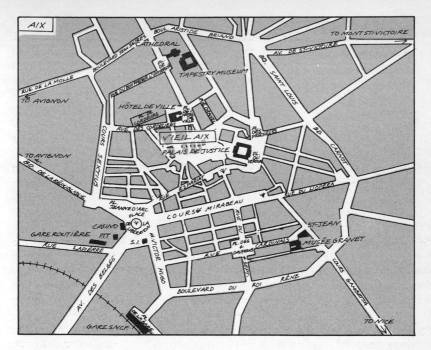

north of here, the **Cathédrale St-Sauveur**. This is a strange muddle of
architectural styles, ranging from a 4C or 5C baptistry to the flowery
16C Gothic tower and façade, and taking in some exquisite Romanesque
cloisters. In the nave hangs Nicolas Froment's triptych of the *Burning
Bush*, painted for King René in 1476. It represents the Virgin and Child
in flames appearing to Moses, a scene which in the Middle Ages came to
symbolise the virginity of Mary; the left panel shows the donor, René,
with his Queen Jeanne kneeling in prayer. Also worth examination is a
series of Brussels tapestries, woven for Canterbury Cathedral in 1511 but
sold to the French for a miserly sum under Cromwell. The **Archbishop's
Palace**, next door, holds further tapestries, including some early 18C
works from Beauvais which illustrate scenes from the life of Don Quixote
(10–12 & 2–6/5; cl. Tues; expensive).

Head south from here, back to and beyond Cours Mirabeau, and you
reach the 13C church of **St-Jean de Malte**, a former temple of the Knights
of St John of Malta, next to which is an old priory which houses the
extensive **Musée Granet** (10–12 & 2–6; cl. Tues). As well as pre-Roman
finds from *Entremont*, the hilltop town 3km away which the Romans
first subdued before colonising Aquae Sextiae, and a Book of Hours once
believed illuminated by King René himself, the museum has a good array
of 19C French paintings, among them an Ingres portrait of the local artist

after whom the museum was named, and some oil studies by David and Géricault. Glance, too, at the Dutch and Flemish sections, which include a rare portrait by Carel Fabritius, works by Rubens and Jorcaens, and a neat Rembrandt self-portrait. What was missing until recently were any works at all by Aix's most famous native, Paul Cézanne, an artist who was never appreciated here while he was alive. This was righted in 1984, though only by eight minor works, two of which he did while still at art school.

Cézanne was born at 28 rue de l'Opéra and later lived at 23 rue Boulegar. He was able to live without a regular job thanks to the legacy left him by his businessman father. An outcast in his lifetime (neighbourhood urchins used to throw pebbles at him in the street), he's now widely regarded as one of the greatest of all modern artists. His atelier, in the avenue named after him on the northern edge of town, has been laid open to the public (daily 10–12/2–5/6, cl. Tues) and filled with reproductions of his better known works, personal effects and even imitative displays of his more famous still-life arrangements – though to be honest it's a rather stagnant and unimaginative show.

Fondation Vasarely, on av Marcel Pagnol, pays homage to another, though rather less respected, modern painter, the Hungarian-born op-artist Vasarely. This, in a building designed by the artist himself – and, ironically enough, set in the old Cézanne family estate – is a showcase for something like 800 of his carefully geometric abstractions. If you're into his stuff, be sure to check out the exhibit in the château at GORDES, a little way east of Avignon, or buy something at the Co-op and keep the bag – another of Vasarely's designs.

Living in – and getting out of – Aix

Distances are small in Aix, so it's an easy town to explore on foot; and although it has little in the way of industry or commerce it supports a large number of art galleries, dozens of pricey *confiseurs* selling the local almond speciality, *calissons*, and a thriving university, which in turn lends quite a lively night-scene. For **eating**, Cours Mirabeau is, not surprisingly, over-priced, but there are cheaper places down side turnings. *La Vesuve*, on rue Clémenceau, for example, is an inexpensive Italian; and there's a vegetarian eatery, *Le Blé en Herbe*, at 7 rue Mignet. **Reasonably-priced hotels**, however, are rare. Only *Hôtel du Casino*, rue Leydet, is anything like cheap, and you may well be best off at the good and clean **youth hostel** (42–20.15.99), a well-signposted 2km walk from the train station at Quartier du Jas de Bouffan, av Marcel Pagnol – alternatively take bus 8 to Estienne d'Orves, or bus 12 to Vasarely. The **gare routière** is in rue Lapidaire, behind the main **PTT** on av des Belges, and the **gare SNCF**, from where you can hire a **bike**, is at the end of av Victor Hugo, a short walk from place de la Libération.

If you want to **escape from town** altogether, head east for artist country. Here, where Cézanne wrote that 'Light is spiritualised', he found the inspiration for many of his most renowned landscapes. **Mont St-Victoire**, a wild wedge of rock about 10km from the centre of Aix, was a constant theme – particularly its aspect from nearby Bellevue – and the D17 which skirts its southern edge has since been dubbed the 'Route de Cézanne'. On the mountain's north side lies VAUVENARGUES, a small village overlooked by a 17C château which was home for **Pablo Picasso** for fifteen years until his death in 1973: he lies buried in the grounds.

THE ROUTE TO CANNES AND THE CÔTE

Leaving Aix, you can take a bus east along the old *Via Aurelia*, in its day one of the most important Roman highways, connecting Rome and Arles, now the N7 which divides the rural but densely populated Var *département* in two, cutting behind the coastal massifs and the marauding sun-worshippers of the Côte d'Azur to skirt a tranquil region of terraced hills, vineyards, pine and olive groves, spotted with fields of brilliant lavender. South of the main road, the **Massif de la St-Baume** looms over the stretch of coast between Marseilles and Toulon, rising to well over 1,000m in places and criss-crossed by footpaths, notably GR9 and GR99, with GR98 running along the crest.

On its northern side, and the first town you reach following the N7 lies **ST-MAXIMIN-LA-SAINTE-BAUME**, a warren of medieval streets and fetid alleys climbing from a fine shady esplanade to the Gothic **Basilica of St-Maximin**. It was here, according to the legend, that Mary Magdalene and St Maximinus settled and finally died, after being banished from the Holy Land (see p. 430); the present church was built to house their relics, only 'discovered' in 1279 by Charles of Anjou. It's a rough-hewn building, coarse exterior doors giving way to an interior blotched with once-rich frescoes, and studded with a mass of artwork from a range of periods. 17C stucco and indifferent Renaissance additions mingle with more inspiring medieval items, most memorably a painted wooden statue of John the Baptist, and a large 16C gilded retable depicting a wan Jesus crucified with naturalistic goriness against a background that includes Avignon's Papal Palace. Downstairs in the crypt, actually part of a 5C Roman villa, lie the reasons why St-Maximin has long been a place of pilgrimage, the bodies of the two saints: Mary Magdalene's skull, set into a gilded statue and viewable through a metal gate (press a button to get 5mins of light), makes a stark and unsettling contrast to the artifice of its surroundings.

If you're staying in St-Maximin, the best place to look for **a room and a meal** is in av Albert (the Aix road) or the main place Malherbe; there's a **campsite** out on the route de Mazaugues.

Further down the N7, the **Massif des Maures**, its name derived from an Occitan word meaning 'dark forest', reaches down to ST-TROPEZ. Long deserted, the Massif has few villages of any size – only **LA GARDE FREINET** deserving any kind of detour. This was the last stronghold in France of the Saracens, and their fortress survives in ruins 1km south of town on the GR9. A simple **youth hostel** and **campsite** (43.60.05) make it a viable place to stop before the money-grabbing hoteliers of St-Tropez.

The last coastal massif, the **Massif de l'Esterelle**, shielding the shoreline behind Fréjus and Cannes, was until recently a notorious haunt of highwaymen and escaped convicts, its wild mimosa forests and few roads providing a plethora of inaccessible hideouts. Even now it's tough going for even the most intrepid hikers and walkers, and only some sheer and difficult 'fire roads' (forest fires are common here) provide access to the interior of the region.

THE PROVENÇAL ALPS

East of Cannes the Alps plunge straight down to the sea, a rugged mountainous area only sporadically interspered with villages perched on slender peaks, fortified to deter attacks by pirates, bandits and the innumerable armies which have passed this way en route to richer pickings to the east and west. You'd expect these *villages perchés* to be relatively tourist-free, but proximity to the Côte d'Azur and their classically medieval appearance have been drawing hordes of visitors for some time now. If you join them, the best axis for taking in the region is the N85, delving back deep into the mountains from Cannes. It's an old Alpine highway, known as **Route Napoléon** since Napoleon Bonaparte, having escaped from exile on Elba, travelled this way in 1815 trying to re-establish himself as ruler of France. Equipped with a band of armed supporters, he met only nominal resistance on the way, and arrived eventually in Grenoble as a hero to cheering crowds and bedecked streets. The sign of an eagle, seen along the road today, recalls Napoleon's ambitious declaration: 'The eagle will fly from steeple to steeple as far as the towers of Notre Dame.' A daily bus will take you all the way from Golfe Juan, where Napoleon made his initial landings, to Grenoble: around 8 hours for the whole trip.

Towards Digne: along the Route Napoléon

High technology and defence industries are the most immediately striking aspects of **GRASSE**, first town the bus reaches, easily superceding the much-vaunted perfume industry of the town, for which it remains world capital (three out of four bottles use Grasse essences). If you decide to jump off here you'll find little to keep you for very long. Tours of the perfume factories are possible, if expensive (Fragonard, Molinard and Galimard are all open to the public); you see the huge mounds of petals needed to make just a few drops of perfume and there's a perfume museum next door to the Fragonard plant. More interesting is the Museum of Provencal Art on rue Mirabeau. Once the home of the painter Fragonard, a native of Grasse even though he spent most of his life currying favour with the aristocracy in Paris, it has disappointingly few original examples of his lusty work. You have to be content with a youthful self-portrait and a copy of his *Pursuit of Love* series, now in the Frick Collection in New York, painted for and rejected by Mme du Barry in 1770 because they were considered old-fashioned at a time when a new, more classical and sober style was beginning to creep in.

Other than that, some awesome views south, and the old town's vibrant Arab quarter, there's nothing much to lure you off the bus. *Hôtel Napoléon* is your cheapest chance of a **bed** if you stay, and bd Jeu de Ballon the most likely street for a **cheap meal**. There's an SI in place de la Foux.

In many ways the high altitude village of **CASTELLANE** is no more enticing than Grasse, clogged with cars either doing the Napoleon road or branching off for the **Gorges du Verdon**, but at least this latter is justification enough for a detour. The so-called 'Grand Canyon of Europe', 13 miles long and at its sheerest points well over 2,000ft deep, the gorge is inland Provence's greatest natural attraction – to the extent that in 1947 the *Corniche Sublime* road was carved out of the solid rock to provide access to some of its finest vistas. It's a must if you have a car; Castellane is a great deal more missable, but difficult to avoid if you want to see the canyon, for which it's the obvious base. The SI, in the Mairie at the junction of rue Nationale and rue St-Michel, will advise you on how to visit if you don't have wheels; GR4 is the most rewarding walk, and though demanding, not at all dangerous. **Accommodation** can be difficult, however, and even if you can find a non rip-off hotel it's quite likely to be full. A better bet is the **youth hostel**, 12 hitchable km from Castellane at PALUD-SUR-VERDON (74.68.72), or around a dozen **campsites** spaced along the routes de Digne and Gorges du Verdon, four of them within a couple of kilometres of town.

Next major stop on the N85, airy **DIGNE-LES-BAINS** continues to attract visitors to its mineral springs, giving the town a healthful, prosperous feel and a genteel nightlife of spectacles, *soirées* and open-air summer events. Near the town centre the **Great Fountain** gives some indication of the mineral content of the local water, built in 1829 and already entirely furred up with calcium deposits. The waters aside, though, there's little that's all that distinctive about Digne: only an unusual preponderance of outdoor modern sculpture and, south of the town on the Castellane road, the **Alexandra David Neel Foundation** (3–5pm only), a Tibetan centre in her old home, which attracts colonies of Tibetan monks to the town annually. Food and rooms tend to be uniformly good, but correspondingly priced, with only a couple of inexpensive hotels – *Le Petit St Jean* in Cours des Ares, and *Hotel Julia* in place Pied de Ville – with good value menus. There's a **campsite** in av du Camping, north of town, and a **SI** at the junction of av Demontzey and bd Gassendi (the main street). The **gare routière** is just behind here; note that SNCF buses use the gare routière too. As well as the **SNCF station**, inconveniently placed over on the south side of the river Bléone, towards the main N85 highway.

SNCF share the gare with **Chemins de Fer de la Provence** (CFP), an old private railway company which operates a narrow gauge service through the mountains between Digne and Nice. Leaving the Gare du Sud in Nice four times a day, their train climbs the valleys of the Var and the Vaire to THORAME-HAUTE, and by a succession of mountain stations reaches Digne. In summer this service forms part of the Alpazur holiday train between Grenoble and Nice; SNCF tickets are not valid on CFP trains except for the France Vacances pass or when they specify Alpazur. Locally it's known as *Le Petit Train des Pignes.*

Sisteron

From Digne the road follows the river Bléone to its confluence with the Durance, a river popularly known as one of the 'three scourges of Provence' because of its irritating unpredictability, either dwindling away to no more than a trickle or swamping the entire area in floods (the other two scourges are the mistral and, in years gone by, the *parlement* of Aix). Though under control now, and helping to irrigate the Provencal countryside, the Durance is still enormous, complicated and full of islands. There's a meeting of roads here too, the N96 heading south towards the small, attractive town of MANOSQUE and FORCALQUIER, while the Route Napoléon continues north tracking the Durance up to SISTERON.

High up in a magnificent rocky setting, where the mountains suddenly close in on the Durance, Sisteron, once known as the key to Provence, stands dramatic sentry on the Dauphine border, five robust towers remaining of its ancient ramparts and the **citadelle** towering proudly on a peak above town. Originally built in the 13C, the citadelle (open 9–7.30) was reconstructed in the 16C by the military engineer Jean Erard, and then destroyed again by completely unnecessary American bombing in 1944. Work continues still on its second rebuilding, but it's a tremendous sight for all that, hollow façade though the frame of angular walls may be. The few hundred yards up make a surprisingly steep walk, and for those who can't manage it a 'train' provides an expensive shuttle service from place de la République.

Sisteron's old centre affords at least a morning of aimless wandering, a net of curious covered alleyways, here called *androne*, opening out into tiny squares with fountains. If you prefer something slightly more ordered, follow the SI's signposted route around town, starting at the Église Notre-Dame, a simple, unsophisticated building both outside and in, and taking in the odd 19C clocktower and, at the far end of rue de la Saunière, a great panorama of the Durance and the massive rock-slabs through which it passes. Sisteron also makes much the cheapest base for the region: most of its many **hotels** work out very reasonably – especially *Hôtel de la Poste* on rue Droite; the *Hostellerie Provençal*, on the corner of av J Moulin and rue des Combes is even cheaper; and there's a riverside **campsite** on the far side of the Durance. *Hôtel des Androne* is a good place to eat, and there's a multitude of others beside. *Mejy*, on route de Marseilles, hire **bikes**; **buses** stop in av Paul Arene, opposite the **PTT**, and the **SNCF station** is in av de la Libération.

ST-PAUL-DE-VENCE, VENCE AND THE PARC DE MERCANTOUR

First stop up the road from Cannes, **ST-PAUL-DE-VENCE**, a fortified jumble of houses heaping up out of the cypress groves that surround it, has been positively and irredeemably spoilt by visitors from the Côte – exploited for its location, its appearance, and most of all for the fact that just about every modern French artist hung out here at one time or another. Its tiny centre is a shameless combination of money-hungry souvenir shops and restaurants thronged by camera-hung tourists having a day off from the beach. Nevertheless there are two things which make it worth coming here, both a result of the town's time as an artistic centre. First, the private art collection of the plush **Hôtel Colombe d'Or**, made up of canvases astutely accepted in lieu of cash from artists – Modigliani, Bonnard, Dufy, Utrillo – who stayed here when it wasn't quite so sumptuous. Once upon a time you were allowed to wander in and view the paintings for free; now it'll cost you the price of a meal or a room – roughly equivalent in St-Paul to an arm and a leg. Second, and though not a great deal cheaper worth every centime, is the **Fondation Maeght** (10–12.30 & 3–7). A carefully signposted walk from town, the foundation was set up in 1964 not just as an art gallery but as a centre for all kinds of modern creative activity, with a library, bookshop, ceramics studio and a hall for concerts of ballet and classical music. José Luis Sert, the Catalan architect, designed the building, and commissioned people like Miro to embellish the terraces and Georges Braque to work on the pool and stained glass. Best in the collection of paintings are works by Kandinsky and modern French artists including Braque, Matisse, Léger and Chagall, but only a fraction are on permanent display; come here at any time and the only thing you can be sure of seeing is a group of

Giacometti bronzes and the pictures of Kandinsky and Chagall – the rest of the gallery space is usually turned over to temporary exhibits.

For eating and sleeping push on to **VENCE**, 5km up the road, where the tourist trade has not yet penetrated to quite such a degree and you should be able to find something a touch more affordable, if not exactly cheap. Vence, too, has artistic connections. D H Lawrence died here of TB in 1930, and lay in the little village cemetery for five years until he was disinterred, cremated and his ashes sent to a more spiritual rest in New Mexico. And Matisse lived on the outskirts of the town just a couple of decades later, having retired here after a severe illness to decorate his **Chapelle de la Rosaire**, which he called 'despite its imperfections . . . my masterpiece'. The chapel, 1½km from the centre of town on av Matisse, is free and open Tuesdays and Thursdays 10–11.30 & 2.30–5.30. Matisse was in his late 70s when he started work, undertaking the task as a gift to the order of Dominican nuns who had nursed him during his illness. From the outside it's a simple white house, the blue and white tiled roof topped with a wrought iron cross. The interior, too, is deceptively plain, stark white walls covered with black line drawings of the *Stations of the Cross* and *Dominican monks*, only the dazzle of the stained glass windows bringing colour to bear. But every detail is from the hand of Matisse, from the fittings and fixtures inside the chapel right down to the vestments worn by the priests – all designed with a caring and moving devotion that is only marred these days by the amount of people crowding into the place.

East of Vence, beyond a string of over-restored, over-prettified hill villages, get yourself to **TENDE**, which is much the best point from which to explore the high altitudes of the **Parc National de Mercantour** and its centre, between Mont Bego (2,872m) and Cime du Disable (2,685m), the **Vallée des Merveilles**, home to over 100,000 Bronze Age engravings cut into its rock faces. To stay in Tende, best use the **youth hostel** (04.62.74), up the steps beside the church at the end of rue Ste-Cathérine, both for its prices and some unequalled views over the town: the houses mounting the sharp slope on which the town is built; the thin sliver of wall that remains from the local château; and, unexpectedly gaudy among the trees, the pink and orange belfry of Tende's idiosyncratic parish church. The **railway station** is at the top of town, off the main street, and connects with points as far as Nice. The **SI**, in rue A Vassalo near the station, have details on **footpaths** (GRs 5, 52 and 4) and *gîtes d'étape* in the Mercantour region – real hiking country, where trails can be tricky and the weather dangerously changeable outside July to September. Inside the National Park area, camping and fires are not allowed, but there are basic refuges and gîtes at manageable intervals. For more on the park, contact Parc National de Mercantour, 23 rue d'Italie, 06000 Nice.

TRAVEL DETAILS

Trains and SNCF buses

TGV from Lyon 11–21 daily from Lyon-Perrache to Lyon-Part-Dieu (10mins) and Paris (2hrs10); 3 daily from Lyon-Part-Dieu to Lyon-Perrache (10mins) and St-Etienne (47mins); 2 or 3 daily from Lyon-Part-Dieu to Grenoble (1¼hrs).

From Avignon 5–8 daily to Nîmes (30mins) and Montpellier (55mins); 10–13 daily to Valence (55mins) and Paris (3¾–4hrs); 9–11 daily to Marseille (55–60mins), 2 continuing to Toulon (1hr40).

Other trains heading north from Lyon lots of sleepers late in the evening; 3 or 4 trains daily stopping at most stations on the way to Dijon (2hrs) and Paris (5hrs); 6 or 7 daily to Mâcon (40mins), Chalon (1hr10), Dijon (1hr44).

East and West from Lyon frequent to Roanne (1½hr) and St-Etienne (approx. 1hr); 8 – 10 daily to Grenoble (1¼–1¾hrs); 5–6 daily to Bourg-en-Bresse (1hr50).

Rhône valley Numerous trains go up and down this line day and night – they don't all stop at every one of these places, but most do. Many others only cover part of the route. Journey times approx. from Lyon to Vienne (20mins), Valence (55mins), Montélimar (1hr20–2hrs), Orange (1hr50–2½hrs), Avignon (2–3hrs), continue from Avignon to Arles (20–30mins) and Marseille (about 1hr), about 6 daily.

From Digne 8 SNCF buses daily to St-Auban (about 35mins), continue by SNCF bus or train to Veynes-Devoluy (another 1–1¼hrs), and change at Veynes for train to Valence (2hrs), or Grenoble (2hrs); *Chemins de Fer de Provence*, a private railway company, goes from Digne station via 15 small stations to Nice (3hrs20), 4 daily, SNCF tickets not valid except France Vacances, or where Alpazur specified; Alpazur is a *train touristique* (1 July–9 Sept only) running from Lyon via Grenoble to Digne, where change on to CFP to continue to Nice; daily dep. Lyon 12.23, arr. Nice 20.53; dep. Nice 9.00, arr. Lyon 18.14; St-Auban (SNCF bus, 35 mins); continuing by train to Manosque (25mins from St-Auban); Aix-en-Provence (1hr10); Marseille (1hr45), 6 daily.

Eastern Provence. From Nice via many small villages to Breuil-sur-Roya (1hr10), 6 daily, and Tende (2hrs), 3 daily.

Buses

There's a good town-to-town service along the **N7** all the way from Lyon to the Côte d'Azur. Two buses daily go all the way from Grenoble to Nice and back along the N85, stopping at Grasse (2hrs from Nice, via Cannes), Castellane (3hrs, midday bus stops here 1hr for lunch break), Digne (1¼hrs from Castellane), Sisteron (40mins from Digne). Several buses between Grasse and Cannes only (45mins). Avignon is the focus of a network of local and long-distance buses.

Chapter fifteen
THE CÔTE D'AZUR

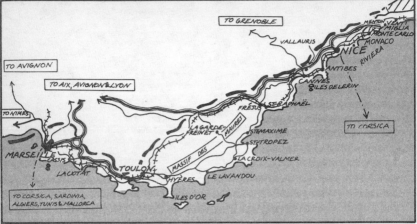

The **Côte d'Azur** has to be the most built-up, overpopulated, over-eulogised and expensive stretch of coast anywhere in the world. There are only two industries to speak of – tourism and building, plus related services of estate agents, yacht traffic wardens and rolls royce valeting. Le Pen posters go undefaced and construction companies pick their labourers from queues of North African immigrants as galley owners on the same coast used to choose their slaves. Meanwhile a hotel serves tender meat morsels to its clients' pets in a restaurant for dogs.

On the other hand, in every gap between the monstrous habitations – in the **Esterel**, the **St-Tropez** peninsula, the **islands** off Cannes and Hyères, the **Massif des Maures** – the remarkable beauty of the hills and land's edge, the scent of the plant life, the February mimosa blossom and the strange synthesis of the Mediterranean pollutants that makes the water so translucent, devastate the senses. Seeing the works of innumerable **artists** seduced by the land and light is another justification: **Cocteau** in Menton and Villefranche, **Matisse** and **Chagall** in Nice, **Picasso** in Antibes and Vallauris and collections of **Fauvists** and **Impressionists** at St-Tropez, Nice and Hauts-de-Cagne. And it must be said that places like **Monaco** and **Cannes**, the star excrescences of the coast, have a twisted entertainment value.

The **months to avoid** definitely are July and August when the overflowing campsites become health hazards, all hotels are booked up, the people overworked and the vegetation at its most barren.

NICE AND THE RIVIERA

Between Nice and the Italian border, the **Riviera** mountains brake their fall for just a few precious metres levelling off to the shore. Before foreign aristocrats took a fancy to this coast – a phenomenon of the last century – there were just medieval hilltop villages and fishing ports. Now it is nonstop conurbation or resort, excessively upmarket. Only **Nice** has real substance – a major city far enough away from Paris to preserve a distinctive character.

NICE

The capital of the Riviera and fifth largest town of France should be a loathsome place. It's twin-towned with Cape Town, South Africa, and it's been run for decades by a right-wing clique, recently accused by Graham Greene of outright corruption. Living off inflated property values and fat business accounts, **NICE**'s ruling class has not evolved much from the 18C Russian and English aristocrats who first built their mansions here. The *rentiers* and retired of select nationalities now reside here with their pensions and incomes ensuring the startlingly high inverse ratio of individual income to economic activity. There are more vandalised phone boxes in Nice than in any other French town and it can't even boast a sand beach. And yet it is delightful. The sun, sea and affable Niçois cover a multitude of sins. And the city makes the best base for visiting the 30km of the Riviera coast to the border and west as far as Cannes.

Orientation and a room

It doesn't take long to get a feel for the **layout** of Nice. Shadowed by mountains that curve down to the sea east of its port, it still breaks up more or less into old and new. The **Vieille Ville** groups about the hill of Le Château, its limits, once signalled by the river Paillon, now **bd Jean-Jaurès**, built along its course. Along the seafront, the **promenade des Anglais** runs a cool 5km, until forced to curve inland to make way for the sea-projecting runways of the airport. The central square, **place Massena**, is at the bottom of the main street, av Jean Médecin, – the name of the present mayor though in fact named after his father, the previous incumbent. Off to the north is the exclusive hillside suburb of **Cimiez**.

Arriving, the main **gare SNCF** (*Nice Ville*) is a relatively short step from all this, off a couple of blocks to the left from the top of av Jean Médecin. The **gare routière** for once is closer in, on the corner of bd Jean-Jaurès and Traverse Emile Zola, in the shadow of the old town.

In season, at least, the **SI's hotel reservation service** at the train station is worth taking advantage of. There are lots of cheap hotels close at hand but it's not a very pleasant area. More centrally, **in the Vieille Ville**, the liveliest quarter day and night, you might try *Taverne St-Antoine* (4 rue Central), *de Tende* (7 place St-François), *Le Touristique* (7 rue Alexandre Mari) and *Opéra* (15 rue de la Préfecture). Or **across the Paillon**, there's *Chauvin* and *Grand Hôtel de la Poste* (8 and 16 rue Chauvin) and *Elite* (40 bd Victor Hugo).

The **youth hostel** is quite a way out of town and, for two people, more expensive than a hotel. It's on route Forestière on the slopes of Mont Alban (bus 14 from place Massena, direction *Mont Boron*, stop *L'Auberge*); open 7–10 & 6–11 only; 89.23.64. Slightly cheaper but equally distant and with a 10.30 curfew is *Clairvallon Relais International de la Jeunesse* on av Scudéri north of Cimiez (bus 15 and 22); open all day; 93.81.27.63. Much closer to the centre there's the *Résidence Les Collinettes*, 3 av R Schuman (bus 7a and 17), open July and August, 4–10; 93.37.24.30. The only **campsite** anywhere near Nice is the very small *Camping Terry*, route de Grenoble, Lingostière, 6½km north of the airport on the N202 and not on any bus route.

There's an **SI** near the seafront at 5 av Gustav V as well as at the airport and the station.

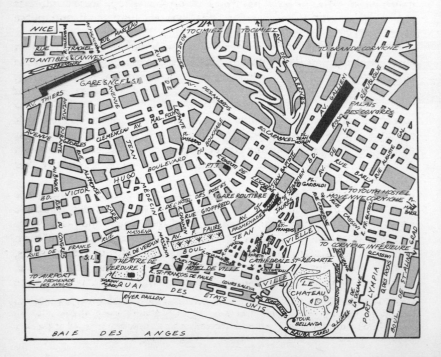

The Vieille Ville

According to the ex-pats and police, the **old town** is an area of drug-pushing, dark-skinned muggers with neat sidelines in car locks and window catches. Which is another way of saying that it hasn't yet been gentrified and enjoys a virtual monopoly on the city's charm and character. It's a poor area – and the dangerous image and heroin trade aren't altogether fiction – but people who live there say they feel perfectly safe. If you look very obviously a tourist – standard victims everywhere on this coast – you may at times feel otherwise. But short of not carrying all your money round the street it's not a place you need feel any great caution about. And in a few years nothing of this will probably remain valid: already people are being moved out, temporarily they are told, while their houses are renovated and the rents soar beyond their means, and the old well-knit community is dispersed into high concrete boxes circling the city.

The central and largest space is **place Rosetti**, where the soft coloured Baroque **Cathédrale de St-Réparate** just manages to be visible in the concatenation of eight narrow, crammed streets. Most wanders around the quarter will inevitably surface here and shaded or sunlit terraced cafés await; just around the corner, too, at 3 rue Benoît Bunico, is the friendly leftist haven of *Le Papier Mâché*, a co-op bookshop, restaurant, arts centre and meeting place for feminist, ecology, anti-racist and peace groups.

Rue Rosetti or the stepped rue du Château bring you from here to an entrance to the **Parc du Château** (or you can take the lift from the eastern end of rue des Ponchettes), decked out in mock Grecian style – harking back to the 4C BC and the original Greek settlement of *Nikea*. The point of the climb, apart from the very pleasant perfumed greenery, is the view stretching westwards and, nearer at hand, the muddle of the Vieille Ville's rooftops with the Niçois speciality of mosaiced green, red and yellow glazed tiles gleaming from the cathedral clock tower. Right at the top a viewing table points you in the useful direction of St Petersburg and other, actual, places.

Below rue de la Préfecture, although still Vieux Nice, the atmosphere changes abruptly with wider streets meeting at right angles alongside grandiloquent governmental buildings. The **Cours Saleya** and **place Pierre Gautier**, once wholesale flower* and vegetable markets, have been revamped, ignoring local opposition, to smaller groups of general stalls, and still some flowers along with bric-à-brac (on Mons) and arts and crafts (Suns and Weds), stylish backdrops though for the best daytime

---

* The wholesale flower market has been moved miles away to bd Georges Pompidou in St-Augustin, near the airport (bus 9 or 10, stop *Marché* gare). If you want an unparalleled seduction of two senses in the early hours of the morning – 8 at the very latest – a smallish sum paid to the guards at the gate will let you in.

eating and drinking. Over in place St-François, north from place Rosetti, the Vieille Ville's fish market is more firmly entrenched, its colours persisting till late at night when all the old streets are hosed down with enough water to paddle in.

Cimiez and elsewhere

Cimiez has always been a posh place. Its principal streets – av des Arènes de Cimiez and bd de Cimiez – rise between plush, high-walled villas to what was the social centre of the town's elite some seventeen centuries ago, when the city was capital of the Roman province of *Alps-Maritimae*. Excavations of **Roman baths** have revealed enough detail to distinguish the sumptuous and elaborate facilities for the top tax official and his cronies, the plainer public baths and a separate complex for women. The accompanying archaeological finds take up the ground floor of the **Villa des Arènes** (free admission, 10–12 & 2.30/2–6.30/5; cl. Mon) over-looking the baths. The next floor takes you worlds away from the military ancients into the joyous lines and light of **Matisse**, displayed in the same light as their creation, for it was in Nice that he spent most of his life. The collection covers every period and includes the studies for *La Dance*, the huge blue and pink mural in the Palais de Chaillot in Paris, models for the chapel he designed in Vence, and a near complete set of the bronze sculptures. Among the paintings are the 1905 *portrait of Madame Matisse, A Tempest in Nice* (1919–20), and the 1947 *Still Life with Pomegranites*.

At the foot of the hill, just off bd Cimiez on av du Docteur Menard, **Chagall's Biblical Message** is housed in a perfect museum build specially for the work and opened by the artist in 1972. The rooms are light and white and cool, with windows allowing you to see the greenery of the garden beyond the indescribable shades between pink and red of the *Song of Songs* canvases. The seventeen paintings are all based on the Old Testament and complemented with etchings and engravings. To the building itself, Chagall contributed a mosaic and stained glass windows. It's open 10–7 July-September; otherwise 10–12 & 2–5; cl. Tues and free on Wed.

Bus 15 from the centre of Nice (place Massena) runs past the Chagall museum and up to bd Arènes. Alternatives for Cimiez, but not for the Chagall, are buses 17, 20 and 22.

Other **Nice museums** have more limited appeal. For paintings the **Beaux Arts** (33 av des Baumettes, 10–12 & 3–6; cl. Mons; bus routes 38/40, stop *Cheret*) can't compare with the Matisses and Chagalls, and has too many whimsical canvases by Jules Cheret, who died in Nice in 1932, and far too much of GA Mossa, a recently deceased Nice establish-ment figure, whose lurid symbolist paintings retch of women hating. But there are modern works that come as unexpected delights, a Rodin bust of Victor Hugo, a whole room full of Dufy and some very amusing Van Dongens such as the *Archangel's Tango*. Monet, Sisley and Degas also grace the walls. **Temporary exhibitions** of contemporary art are also shown in the Acropolis and at 59 and 77 quai des Etats Unis (10.30–12 & 2–6 except Mons and Sun am). The **Russian Orthodox Cathedral** off bd de Tsarevitch at the end of av Nicholas II (bus 14 or 17, stop *Tsarevitch*) is not a museum though you do pay to get in.

Elsewhere in Nice there's interest – and occasional astonishment – in the general **architecture of money**: 18–19C Italian Baroque and neoclassical, florid belle-époque, exotic aristo fantasy. And of course there's the **beach**, lively enough amid the shingles, once you're past the fiendish dual carriageway of the **promenade des Anglais** (which originally was just that – for the English residents of the last century). Or if you're into the other side of Nice life there's the **promenade de Paillon**, above the gare routière, mainly the preserve of heroin junkies and male prostitutes.

Food, fun and practicalities

The old town stays up the latest and is full of **restaurants** from the very cheap to the well over-priced. On Cours Saleya, *Le Safari* (at no 1) serves good Niçois cuisine not too expensively, and there are takeaways (*not* fast food) for the Niçois tuna and salad-stuffed *pan beignat*. The port is another scenic spot for stuffing yourself, particularly on just one course of very filling fish soup which can be cheaper and more satisfying than a *menu fixe*. Or for real cheapies try rue Trachel, north of the station; *Chez Nino* and *Le Kentia* (nos 50 and 32) have excellent low priced menus. Gourmet vegetarians should hit *Les Contes du Gourmand* (40 rue de la Buffa). The pedestrian precinct around rue Massena is very touristy with rip-off restaurants, fast food, sex shops and so forth but places tend to stay open on Sundays unlike the rest of Nice. *Le Bistingo*, the restaurant at 2 rue Massena, stays open all night.

At 1 rue de la Loge, in the old town, *Le Tube* has live reggae Thursday to Saturday nights and French piano and *chansons* the rest of the week (ring to enter, no admission charge, one-price drinks). For jazz piano and rather more expensive drinks, there's *L'Ascot* on the descente Crolti. And in summer you may well find rock concerts – often British bands – on at the *Théâtre Verdure* tent in the Jardin Albert I; hear them for free, or pay if you want to look in, too.

As well as *Le Papier Mâché* (see Vieille Ville), *Utopie* (3 rue Joseph Cadei) combines a feminist café-restaurant with a bookshop and art gallery. Among **gay** venues, *Le Bentleys* (rue de la Tour, cl. Sun), is women only; *Blue Boy* (69 rue Spinete; wkends only, from 11) is exclusively male.

Nice **festivals** include Italian films in December, Jazz in July, dance in August, and the unspeakably commercialised carnival in February. For information on official culture, you can get a broadsheet from the municipal office at 2 place Masséna. For alternative culture, *Le Papier Mâché*.

And lastly, since Nice is the centre of the Riviera, a few **practical listings**:

Bike hire from *Loca 2 Roues* (29 rue Gounod) or *Moto Rent* (3 rue Barralis).

Books *English Bookshop* (10 rue Blacas).

24-hr chemist at 7 rue Massena.

Doctor phone 83.01.01 for emergencies; *Hôpital de St-Roch*, 5 rue Pierre Devoluy.

Films *La Semeuse* (21 rue St-Joseph) has occasional good movies; or there's an arts *cinémathèque* in the Acropolis Palais de Congrès.

Laundrette *Taxi-Lav* (7am–8pm) at 24 av St-Augustine or 22 rue Pertinax.

Poste Restante PTT, place Wilson, 06000 Nice.

Showers at the station.

Tobacco *Le Cassini* (30 rue Cassini) is an all-night *tabac*.

Youth information *CIJ*, Esplanade des Victoires.

THE CORNICHES

The **corniche roads** – three of them – run east from NICE to MONACO and MENTON, the last town of the French Riviera. They are each classic routes, switchbacking above the sea, and each covered by **bus**. In addition, the **train** line follows the lower road, the *Corniche Inférieure*. If you want **to stay** in the hills here the only real choice is between the **campsite** at LES ROMARINS (above ÈZE on the *Grande Corniche*) and the *Hôtel Cesarée*, fairly modestly priced, at LA TURBIE. But it makes more sense to base yourself in Nice and treat these routes as pleasure-rides to a glimpse of the bizarre phenomenon of MONACO.

Of the three, the **Moyenne Corniche** is the most filmic, a real cliff-hanging car chase road. Eleven km from Nice, the medieval village of ÈZE clings to its rock just below the corniche, infested with antique dealers, pseudo artisans and other caterers to the touristic rich. As with the even more picturesque citadel of **ROQUEBRUNE**, above the Grande Corniche near Menton, it's hard to recall that the labyrinth of tiny vaulted passages and stairways was designed not for charm but from fear of attack. The ultimate defence, the castle, no longer exists in Èze itself: a cacti garden takes its place, the only escape from the commerce below and with views of the far horizon from whence the invaders used to appear. From Èze you can reach the shore through open countryside, via **sentier Frédéric Nietzsche***, which descends from place du Centenaire at the foot of the rock to the Corniche Inférieure at the eastern limit of ÈZE-SUR-MER (signposted to *La Village*).

The characteristic **Côte d'Azur mansions** representing unrestrained fantasies of the original owners and the stylistic incompatability of same, parade along the **Corniche Inférieure** or lurk screened from view on the promontories of Cap Ferrat and Cap Martin with gardens full of man-eating cacti and piranha ponds – if the plethora of '*Défense d'entrer-Danger de Mort*' signs are anything to go by. A few have become museums such as the **Ville Kerylos** on rue Eiffel, just east of the casino in BEAULIEU (open 2–6 & 3–7; cl. Mon & Sept). The man responsible for this near perfect reproduction of an ancient Greek villa used to eat, dress and behave as an Athenian citizen, taking social baths with his male friends and assigning separate suites to women. It's a visual knockout, however perverse.

VILLEFRANCHE-SUR-MER, the resort closest to Nice on the lower corniche, has been spared architectural eyesores only to be marred by lurking US and French warships attracted by the deep waters of the bay. But as long as your visit doesn't coincide with shore leave the old town on the waterfront feels almost like the genuine article – an illusion which the price of the quayside restaurants should quickly dispell. But the small fishing port does still operate, and it is overlooked by the medieval **chapelle de St-Pierre** (9.30–12 & 2–6; cl. Fri) which **Jean Cocteau** decorated in 1957. Above the altar St Peter walks on water supported by an angel to the outrage of the fishes and the amusements of Christ. The fishermen's eyes are drawn as fishes; the ceramic eyes on either side of the door are the flames of the apocalypse and other eyes with no lids to blink appear amidst the symmetric doodle patterns on the pillars and arches.

And lastly, if you return from Monaco and want no vision but the sea, there is the **Grande Corniche**, on the crest of the mountains. You pass through LA TURBIE en route, close by which is the **Trophie des Alpes** – a monumental plinth left here to commemorate Augustus Caesar's path in the 6C, and his total subjugation of the local peoples. The sight of it from the road should be enough, though like everything in these parts it has been fenced and (perhaps less like most things) has admission hours for viewing – 9–12 & 2–5.30.

MONACO

Monstrosities are common on the Côte d'Azur, but nowhere, not even Cannes, can outdo **MONACO**. This tiny independent principality has lived off gambling and class for a century and is one of the greatest property speculation sites in the world – Manhattan-on-sea without the saving aesthetic grace of the skyscrapers rising from a single level. Finding

---

* The philosopher is said to have conceived part of *Thus Spoke Zarathustra*, his shaggy dog story against believing answers to ultimate questions, on this path – which is not quite as hard going as the book.

out about the workings of the regime is not easy but it is clear that Prince Rainier is the one autocratic ruler left in Europe. A copy of every French law is automatically sent to Monaco, reworded and put to the prince. If he likes the law it is passed, if not, not. There is a parliament of limited function elected by *Monagesque* nationals – about 16 per cent of the population – and no opposition to the royal family. What the citizens and residents like so much is that they pay no income tax and their riches are protected by rigorous security forces.

The 3km long state consists of the old town of **Monaco** around the palace on a high promontory to the west, **La Condamine** behind the harbour, **Larvotto**, the bathing resort with artificial beaches of imported sand to the east, and **Monte Carlo** in the middle. The **gares SNCF** and **routière** are at place d'Armes below the palace rock in La Condamine. If you must stay more than one day in Monaco this is the best area for **hotels**. But they're expensive. You could try *de France* and *Cosmopolite*, 6 and 4 rue de la Turbie; *de la Poste* and *l'Etoile*, 3 and 4 rue des Oliviers. La Condamine and the old town are also the places to look for **restaurants** but good food and reasonable prices don't match. Italian cuisine is likely to be the best value for money: try *Polpetta*, 2 rue Paradis north of Monte Carlo one block away from France. There's no campsite, Caravans are illegal in the state – as are bathing costumes, bare feet and chests once you step off the beach. There are no border formalities, French currency is valid, and bus and museum charges are considerably higher. The one good free public service are the lifts, (marked on the SI map), incredibly clean, un-graffitied and efficient, for north-south journeys. **Bikes** can be hired from *Auto-Motos* garage, 7 rue de la Colle, to the left off av Prince from place d'Armes. Buses 1 and 2, direction Jardin Exotique or St-Roman, take you to the *Casino-Tourism* stop with the SI at 2a bd des Moulins and place du Casino just to the south.

The **Casino** must be seen if nothing else. Entrance is restricted to those over 21 and you may have to show your passport. Shorts and teeshirts are frowned upon and for the more interesting sections, skirts, jackets, ties and so forth are more or less obligatory; any coats or large bags will involve you in cloakroom fees.

In the first gambling hall, the *American Room*, slot machines surround the American roulette, craps and blackjack tables, the managers are Las Vegas trained, the lights low and the air oppressively smokey. Above this slice of Nevada, however, the walls and ceilings are turn-of-the-century rococo extravagance and in the adjoining *Pink Salon bar* female nudes smoking cigarettes adorn the ceilings. But the heart of the place is the *European Gaming Rooms*, through the American Room and Salles Touzet. You have to pay to get in (the same price as a museum) and you must look like a gambler not a tourist (no cameras, for example). More richly decorated than the American Room and much bigger, the atmosphere, early afternoon or out of season, is that of a cathedral. No flashing lights or clinking coins, just quiet voiced croupiers and sliding chips. Elderly gamblers pace silently, fingering 500F notes (the maximum unnegotiated stake here is 500,000F), close circuit TV cameras above the chandeliers watch the gamblers watching the tables and no one drinks. On mid-summer evenings the place is packed out and the vice loses its sacred and exclusive touch.

Around the Casino are more casinos and the city's palace-hotels and grands cafés – all held by the same monopoly. The *American bar* of the **Hôtel de Paris** is, according to its publicity, the place where 'the world's most elite society' meets. As long as you dress up and are ready to be outraged (in English) if asked why you haven't ordered a 15 quid drink, you can entertain yourself, free of charge, watching tedious humans with fascinating bank accounts against the background of belle-époque decadence.

Other amusements such as the glacé icing **old town**, where every other shop sells Prince Rainier mugs and other assorted junk, toy **palace** and assorted **museums** are less rewarding, with the possible exception of the aquarium in the basement of the **Musée Océanographique** (9.30–9/7; bus 1/2, *Monaco-Ville*) where the fishy beings outdo the wierdest Kandinsky, Hieronymous Bosch or Zandra Rhodes creations.

One particular **time to avoid** Monaco is around the start of June (Ascension Day to the following Sunday) when racing cars burn round the port and Casino for the Formula 1 **Grand Prix**, and every space in sight of the circuit is inaccessible without a ticket.

MENTON

MENTON, the easternmost town on the French coast, is even more of a rich retirement haven than Nice. No trace here now of its revolutionary 1848 days when with Roquebrune, it broke away from Monaco to be an independent republic before Paris sucked it in twelve years later. The pride and joy of this town is its lemon crop which it celebrates in a citrus fruit extravaganza every February. But a *citron pressé* (pure lemon juice) served in a Menton bar still costs far more than an imported Belgian beer. Its real speciality should be weddings, for this is the place to come were you ever to need a French registry marriage. The **Salles des Marriages** in the **Hôtel de Ville** (on central place Ardoiono) was decorated by Jean Cocteau in his inimitable style and can be visited without matrimonial intentions by asking the receptionist by the main door (Mon-Sat 8.30–12.30 & 1.30–5). On the wall above the official desk a couple face each other with strange topological connections between the sun, her *Mentonaise* head-dress and his fisherman's cap. A Saracen wedding party on the right hand wall reveals a disapproving bride's mum, the spurned girlfriend of the groom and her armed revengeful brother amongst the cheerful guests. On the left hand wall is the story of Orpheus and Euridice at the doomed moment when Orpheus has just looked back. Meanwhile on the ceiling Poetry rides Pegasus, tattered Science juggles with the planets and Love, open-eyed, waits with bow and arrow at the ready. For further confusion the carpet is mock pantherskin and lamps of bronze eucalyptus leaves line the hall.

There are other **Cocteau works** in the **museum** he set up himself in the little orange brick bastion by quai Napoléon III south of the old port. Open from Wed-Sun 10–12 & 2–6, it contains more *Mentonaise* lovers in the *Inamorati* series, a collection of delightful *Animaux Fantastiques* and the powerful tapestry of *Judith and Holopherne* simultaneously telling the sequence of seduction, assassination and escape. There are also photographs, poems, a portrait by his friend, Picasso, and ceramics.

As the *quai* bends round the western end of the Baie de Garavan from the Cocteau museum a long flight of black and white pebbled steps leads to the **Parvis St-Michel** and the perfect pink and yellow proportions of St Michael's church. With more steps up to another square, a chapel of apricot and white marble, pastel campanales and disappearing stairways between long lived houses, this is the Italianate and beautiful façade of the **Vieille Ville**. Just to the south the winding steps, tunnelled alleys and overhanging houses are the poorest part of town and certain, soon, to face the speculators' gaze.

East of the old town overlooking the bay are the exclusive gardened villas. To the west is the modern town arranged around three main streets parallel to the promenade. The **gare SNCF** is on the top one, bd Albert I, from which a short walk to the left as you come out brings you to the north-south avenues divided by gardens, de Verdun and Boyer. The SI is at 8 av Boyer and the *gare routière* between the continuation of the two avenues north of the railway line on the Esplanade de Carei. Some **hotels** worth trying are *Claridges*, 39 av de Verdun; further west, the *Parisien*, 27 av Cernuschi; the *Auberge Provençale*, 11 rue Trenca, near the old town, or around the station. For the overpriced **youth hostel** on Plateau St-Michel, take bus 6, direction *Ciappes de Castellar* and get off at *Camping St-Michel*. As well as the **campsite** here there are two more on the route de Gorbio to the west (at nos 49 and 67), and one on the sea front, av du Banastron, between Menton and Cap Martin. **Vegetarians** have the best eating treat in Menton at the *Artisan Gourmand*, 25 rue Marin, off rue St-Michel, the main street between the old and modern town, one block from the promenade which becomes av Felix Faure. But if you want to eat **fish**, try *Chez Gemaine*, 46 promenade Maréchal Leclerc near the gare routière, and if you don't want to spend much, browse through the menus on rue St-Michel.

ALONG THE BAIE DES ANGES: RENOIR, LÉGER AND PICASSO

West of Nice airport the **baie des Anges** laps at 20C resorts with two fine examples of concrete corpulence, the giant petrified sails with viciously pointed corners of the Villeneuve-Loubet-Plage marina, and an apartment complex 1km long and sixteen storeys high barricading the shingle beach. The old towns and softer visual stimulation lie inland.

At **CAGNES-SUR-MER** the house where **Renoir** spent the last sixteen years of his life, **Les Collettes**, has become a memorial museum – his painting materials and studio left as they were, displayed with a few of his works. It's open 2–7 in summer, till 5 in winter, cl. Tues and mid-Oct–mid-Nov. From here, the Montée de la Bougade leads up to HAUTS-DE-CAGNES, the oldest of this three-tier village, where the medieval castle has a museum dedicated to the olive tree and the **Musée d'Art Moderne Méditerranéen** (10–12 & 2.30/2–7/6; again cl. Tues & mid-Oct–mid-Nov) dedicated to the painters who have worked on the coast in the last 100 years.

Fernand Léger spent many years in **BIOT**, half way to Antibes, where a brilliant collection of his works can be seen in and on the **Musée Fernand Léger**, just south-east of the village (10–12 & 2.30/2 – 6.30/5, cl. Tues; bus from Antibes).

His fellow pioneer of cubism, **Pablo Picasso**, was offered, when he returned to the Mediterranean after the war, the dusty museum in **ANTIBES** castle as a studio. He spent an extremely prolific few months there and when he moved to Vallauris left his output to what is now the **Musée Picasso** (10–12 & 3–7/5; again cl. Tues & Nov) adding other works later on. There are numerous ceramics; still lifes of sea urchins; the wonderful *Ulysses at ses Sirènes* – a great round head against a mast which the ship, sea and sirens labyrinth around; goats and fauns in cubist undisguise; and a whole room full of drawings. Picasso is also the subject here of other painters and photographers, including Man Ray and Bill Brandt and there are works by contemporaries, among them Léger's tapestry, in best revolutionary cubist style, of construction workers.

Picasso stayed ten years in **VALLAURIS**, where he first turned his hands to clay, thereby reviving one of the traditional crafts of this little town in the hills above Golfe Juan. Today the main street, av George Clemenceau, sells nothing but pottery – much of it the garishly glazed bowls and figurines that could feature in souvenir shops anywhere. The **Madoura** pottery, where Picasso worked, is off rue 19 mars 1962, to the right as you come down av Clemenceau. It has the sole rights on reproducing his designs, which are for sale, at a price, in the shop (cl. wkends). At the top of the main street Picasso's bronze *Man with a Sheep* stands in the market place, opposite the castle courtyard, where an early medieval **chapel** with the architectural simplicity of an air raid shelter was painted by the artist as **La Guerre et la Paix** in 1952. At first glance it's easy to be unimpressed (as many critics still are). It looks mucky and slapdash with paint runs on the unyielding plywood panel surface. But stay a while and the passion of this violently drawn pacifism slowly emerges: a music score trampled by hooves and about to be engulfed in flames, a fighter's lance holding the scales of justice and a shield – symbol of peace. Recent 'just wars' and 'peace operations' come to mind. The chapel is open daily (except Tues) 10–12 & 2–6. Buses from CANNES and GOLFE JUAN SNCF arrive close to the castle.

At only 20mins' train ride from NICE it is not worth hunting for rooms in **ANTIBES** (SI in the central place Général de Gaulle if you need details) nor at **JUAN-LES-PINS**, a summer St-Moritz where the rich or famed retreat to their well-screened cages on the **CAP D'ANTIBES**.

CENTRAL RESORTS AND ISLANDS

In which the **Côte d'Azur myth** – **St-Tropez** – turns out to be for real. Other resorts, with honourable exceptions to **Hyères**, to the west, and the **islands**, fare less well . . .

CANNES AND THE LÉRIN ISLANDS

Fishing village turned millionaires' residence, **CANNES'** main source of income is business junketing – in an ever multiplying calendar of festivals, conferences, tournaments and trade shows. The spin-offs of entertaining, pampering and putting up the jetloads of hacks, stars and celebrities, is sewn up by the same few people who organise the shows in the first place. The main venue is the **Palais des Festivals**, an orange concrete mega-bunker, on the prime seaside spot beside the old port, that cries out for an inverse neutron bomb. The seafront promenade, **La Croisette**, and the **Vieux Port** are the main focus of Cannes life forms. The fine sand **beach** looks like an industrial production line for parasols with neat rows extending the length of the shore, changing colour with each change of concession for this privately exploited strand. The 1km length of La Croisette is magnified, to little aesthetic effect, by the size of the apartment blocks and by the 19C palace–hotels like the *Carlton* and *Majestic*, survivors of a fast-disappearing breed. Half-way along is the tacky **Palais Croisette**, home of the Film Festival – which is a strictly credentials only event.

As nowhere else along the *Côte*, save St-Tropez, the millionaires here choose to eat their meals served by white frocked crew on their yacht decks, feigning oblivion of landborne spectators a crumb's throw away. Behind this dubious entertainment of watching *langoustines* disappear down overfed mouths, you can buy your own food in the **covered market** two blocks back from the Mairie, and wander through the day's flower shipments along from the Allées de la Liberté opposite the port. The old town, **Le Suquet,** on the steep hill overlooking the bay, masks its miserable passageways, on which those who don't benefit from the town's economy live, with twee cosmetic streets. Beyond Le Suquet there's more beach and better chance of not having to pay for it.

If you're compelled to stay in Cannes, the best concentration of **hotels** is in the centre, between the gare SNCF and La Croisette, around the main street of rue Antibes/Felix Fauré. Possibilities include the *Bougogne* and *Cybelle-Bec Fin* (13 and 12 rue de 24 Août); *des Pyrénnés* (8 rue Châteauneuf); *Régence* (13 rue St-Honoré) or Chalet de l'Isère (42 av de Grasse), just into the northern expansion of the town across the *Voie Rapide*. Inevitably there's no youth hostel and not much in the way of reasonably priced camping either. There are **SIs** at the gare SNCF and in the Palais des Festivals. Le Suquet is full of **restaurants**, which get cheaper as you reach the top. Two good ones in the centre are *Au Bec Fin* at the hotel Cybelle-Bec Fin and *La Croisette* (15 rue du Commandant André). The **gare routière** is at the **gare SNCF**, except for the coastal bus and all seven of the town buses (which leave from the Mairie). A minibus shuttles along the seafront from square Frédérick Mistral, west of Le Suquet, to Palm Beach Casino on Pointe Croisette at the other end of the bay, via the Mairie. You can **hire bikes** from *Cycles Corot* (47 rue G Clémenceau) in Le Suquet.

Îles de Lérins

The **LÉRINS ISLANDS** would be lovely anywhere, but at 15mins' ferry ride from Cannes, they're not far short of paradise facing purgatory. **Boats** leave from the *gare maritime* in the old port, 7.30–3.30 in summer (nine crossings daily, reduced to five – last at 2.45 – out of season). Last boats back leave St-Honorat at 4.45 and Ste-Marguerite at 6 or 7 (summer times). Taking a picnic is a good idea as the handful of restaurants have a lucrative monopoly.

ST-HONORAT, the smaller southern island, has been owned by monks almost continuously since its namesake and patron founded a monastery here in 410AD. It was a famous bishop seminary – St Patrick trained seven years have before setting out for Ireland. The present **abbey** buildings are 19C, with older cloisters which only men can visit, but behind them, on the sea's edge, stands an earlier fortified version – the only building on the whole coast that both looks and is really old (11C). There are no cars or shops or bars or hotels on St-Honorat: just vines, lavender and olives cultivated by the monks, and pine and eucalyptus trees shading the path beside the white rock shore and mixing with the scent of rosemary, thyme and wild honeysuckle.

STE-MARGUERITE is a bit of a let down in comparison. The water is sludgy round the port, the pond at the western end is stagnant and the aleppo pines and evergreen oak woods are so thick that most of the paths are in semi-darkness. The western end is the most accessible, and the best points to swim are the rocky inlets across the island from the port.

Fort Ste-Marguerite – the site – was built by the Spanish when they occupied both islands. Later Vauban rounded, or rather starred, it off, presumably for Louis XIV's *gloire* since the strategic value of an immense fort facing your own mainland is zero. There are cells to see and a *Musée de la Mer* (9.30/10.30–12 & 2 till the last boat) of local finds, mostly Roman but including remnants of a 10C Arab ship. But you may find it just as rewarding to laze about (for free) on the grassy ramparts of this vast construction.

DOWN THE COAST TO ST-RAPHAËL AND FRÉJUS

Down the coast from Cannes an arc of brilliant red volcanic rock tumbles down to the sea from harsh crags, and from the Corniche (the N98) minor roads lead up into the wild terrain of the Massif Esterel. The shoreline, a mass of little **beaches**, cut by rocky promontories, is the least inhabited stretch of the Côte. Some of the beaches are shingle, some sand, and if you're after relatively uncrowded swimming they're a good choice for a couple of days. The Cannes-St-Raphaël **train** follows the coast almost all the way and there are **buses** too. Best bets for **accommodation** are LE TRAYAS (with a **youth hostel** – *Villa Solange*, rte de la Veronses, 94.44.14.34, and **hotels** *de la Poste* and *Les Terraces*) and LE DRAMONT (*Hôtel du Débarquement*, 87 rue du Débarquement). Or there are **campsites** at BOULOURIS, LE DRAMONT and AGAY. In summer, pick up lists and phone numbers from any of the Côte SIs and try to reserve in advance (both for beds or camping space).

The familiar Côte scene of yachts and long parasoled beaches reasserts itself, after 40km or so, at ST-RAPHAËL, now more or less one conurbation with the town of FRÉJUS, 3km inland and linked with it by fast and frequent trains.

Both were established by the Romans – Fréjus as a naval base under Octavius, St-Raphaël as a resort for its veterans – and various remnants of this past lie scattered about the towns. Most of any significance are at Fréjus, whose population was far larger in Roman times. They include an **amphitheatre** (rue Henri Vardon), used in its damaged state for bullfights and rock concerts, a **theatre** (av du XV Corps d'Armés), also pressed into service for shows, and, to its east, a few arches of the old

aqueduct. Perhaps more interesting, though, are the legacies of medieval Fréjus and of the early 20C. For the former, make for the **cathedral close** on place Formige, with superb 12C Romanesque cloisters and a late medieval fantasy ceiling, and a small museum with a complete Roman mosaic of a leopard; guided tours only, daily except Tues, 9.30–12 & 2–6/4. The more recent past comes in the shape of a **Vietnamese pagoda** and an abandoned **Sudanese mosque** – both built by French Colonial troops. The pagoda, still maintained as a Buddhist temple, is on the crossroads of the RN7 to Cannes and the D100, about 2km out of Fréjus; it is open daily 3–6. You may have to hitch to the mosque which is on the left off the D4 to Bagnols, in the middle of an army camp 2km from the RN7 junction. A strange, guava-coloured and fort-like building, it is decorated inside with fading murals of desert journeys gracefully sketched in white on the dark pink walls.

Two possible **hotels** in FRÉJUS are *Les Glycines* (22 bd Sévérin Décuers, south of the centre) and *La Riviera* (90 rue Grisolle, close to the station), or there's a **youth hostel** (94.52.18.75) and **campsite** near the Pagoda at the end of the chemin de Counillier in DOMAINE DE BELLEVUE. More campsites further down the Cannes road. **SI** on central place Calvini.

ST-RAPHAËL has a better choice of **hotels**: try *des Templiers* (place de la République) and *Suisse* (av de Valescure) in the old town north of the station; or *Le Yacht* (av de Cdt Guilbaud), overlooking the port, and, one block behind, *Le Grand Levant* (rue Thiers). The **SI** is opposite the **gares SNCF** and **routière**. **Bikes** can be hired at 56 av Gallieni (and in Fréjus at 85 rue E Poupé).

THE CÔTE DE MAURES AND ST-TROPEZ PENINSULA

Where the Esterel gives out, the **Massif des Maures** takes over – providing a backdrop of cork, pine and chestnut-covered hills dropping into bowls of cultivated fields and vineyards alongside villages of medieval confinement. The tangle of resorts from the Golfe de Fréjus are all – with the single, spectacular exception of ST-TROPEZ – smaller or lesser clones of a single resort, STE-MAXIME.

STE-MAXIME is the perfect Côte stereotype: palmed corniche and pleasure boat harbour, casino, golden beaches with well-heeled windsurfers and waterskiers, and an outnumbering of travel agents by estate agents by something like ten to one. It is beginning to sprawl a little too much, like many of its neighbours, but the seduction of the water's edge, and the roads designed for topless speeding in convertibles, is hard to deny.

The problem, inevitably, is one of money and space. All resorts between

ST-RAPHAËL and HYÈRES are expensive and summer sees their **hotels and campsites** (which are spaced at intervals the whole way) severely overstretched. Before setting out it's essential to pick up full SI lists for the region and phone around. The only *youth hostel* is at LA GARDE FREINET (just inland of St-Tropez, to which it's connected by bus via GRIMAUD; open mid-March to Sept; 94.43.60.05), a one time Saracen stronghold and now favoured retirement home of Oxbridge professors. If you've wheels, **camping at farms** can be a good fallback: again ask the SI for lists and numbers.

Travel along this strip of the Côte is done by car: either your own or someone else's. There are no longer trains, while buses, except for the direct route between ST-RAPHAËL-STE-MAXIME-HYÈRES, are infrequent.

The St-Tropez peninsula

ST-TROPEZ stands quite apart from its neighbours: a little village, gathered around a port founded by the ancient Greeks and which until recently was only easily accessible by boat. Admittedly the road from LE FOUX now has summer traffic jams as bad as Nice or Marseille – but the look of the place doesn't reflect this. In fact it still looks pretty much as it did in the – perhaps one should say *its* – movies. An enduring and in some ways rather wonderful fantasy.

Its emergence to present chic and financial cachet modelled the development of those other Mediterranean clichés – Ibiza, Mykonos, Hammammet. In the late 19C, when only fishing boats moored here and strangers were virtually unknown, the painter **Paul Signac** turned up and stayed, soon followed by, among others, **Matisse, Bonnard** and **Marquet** – Bohemians hanging out in the sun away from the respectable convalescents of Cannes or Nice. And then in 1956 Roger Vadim arrived, with crew, to film **Brigitte Bardot** in *Et Dieu Créa La Femme*. The cult took off, the 1960s took place, and the resort is now big money mainstream. Bardot still owns a house here but the yachts – bigger than anywhere else in Europe in their restricted harbour space – are owned more often these days by Manhattan or City of London banks.

The road into St-Tropez from LE FOUX splits in two as it enters the village, with the *gare routière* between them and, a short distance beyond in rue de la Nouvelle Poste, the **Musée de l'Annonciade** (10–12 & 3/2– 7/6; cl. Tues & Nov), a reason, if you have no other, for coming here. Within are representative works by Matisse and most of the other artists who worked here: grey, grim, northern scenes of Paris, Boulogne and Westminster, and then local, brilliantly sunlit scenes by the same brush. A delight, it is arguably the best collection of 1890–1940 French art outside Paris.

Keep going, beyond the museum, and you will hit the **Vieux Port**. And here you have it, the St-Trop experience of the 1980s: the quayside café clientele *face à face* with the yacht deck martini sippers, the latest fashion looks parading in between, defining the French word *frimer* (derived from sham) which means exactly this – to stroll vanitously in places like St-Tropez.

Beyond, if you walk up rue de la Mairie from the quai Jean-Jaurès and past the townhall, a street to the left leads to the rocky **Baie de la Glaye**. Further up, along rue de la Ponche, you reach the **fishing port** with a tiny beach. Both these spots are miraculously free from commercialisation. Beyond the fishing port, roads lead up to the 16C **Citadelle**. Its maritime museum is not very interesting but the walk round the ramparts on an overgrown path has the best views of the gulf and the back of the town – views that have not changed since their translations in oil on to canvas.

The shops and restaurants of St-Tropez would be equally at home, serving the same clientele, in Bond Street, Madison Avenue or Paris's own rue du Faubourg St-Honoré. Absolutely nothing is cheap in this town. Of **hotels**, the only one vaguely affordable is *Les Lauriers* (rue du Temple). **Camping** on the peninsula can be pricey (try the three on the plan below). As for **eating**, forget the quayside and if you're prepared to spend just twice the normal price for a decent meal, try *La Ponche* on place du Révelin by the fishing port, or *L'Amandier* (26 rue de la

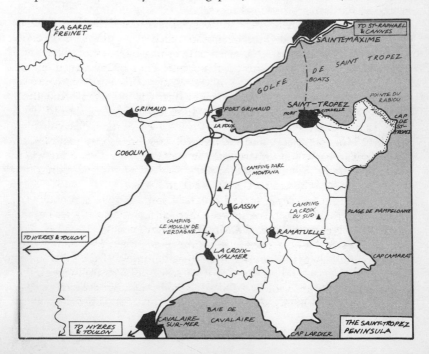

Citadelle). *Sénéquier*, one of the quayside cafés, is renowned for its superb nougat which you can buy from their shop at the rear at extortionate rates. The SI is on the corner of the quay and rue de la Citadelle. **Bikes** can be hired at *Vespa* (5 rue Quaranta).

The southern bay of **the St-Tropez peninsula** – CAVALAIRE – has long stretches of sheltered sandy beaches and slopes above sprouting second residences like a cabbage patch gone to seed. Around St-Tropez and east to the POINTE DE RABIOU, the same reproduction goes on, only with more luxurious villas and wider spaces between them. And then, amazingly, or rather because of government intervention and complex ownerships, the land in between is almost uninhabited.

The best view of this richly green and flowering countryside is from the hilltop village of **GASSIN**, its lower neighbour RAMATUELLE, or the tiny road between them, where three ruined windmills could once catch the wind from every direction. Gassin is the shape and size of a small ship perched on a summit, once a Moorish stronghold now, of course, highly chic. It's an excellent place for a blow-out dinner, sitting outside by the village wall with a spectacular panorama east over the peninsula. Of the handful of restaurants, *Le Pescadou* serves delicious food for unoutrageous prices.

PAMPELONNE is the most famous of the beaches and credited with the first French topless bathing. Four km long, shallow for 50m or so and exposed to the wind, it's sometimes scourged by dried sea vegetation but spotless glitter comes from the unending line of beach bars and restaurants with patios and sofas serving cocktails and gluttonous icecreams.

At the head of the Golfe de St-Tropez, **PORT GRIMAUD** is the ultimate Côte d'Azur property development and should, as such, unquestionably be visited. This is not just another private estate but a private lake-built pleasure city with waterways for roads and yachts parked at the bottom of every garden. Built in the 1960s, all the houses are in exquisitely tasteful old Provençal style, and living space goes for 14,000F per square metre. That non-owners are let in at all is interesting – but presumably deliberate, to keep generating enough envy to justify the prices.

HYÈRES AND THE ÎLES D'OR

Walled and medieval, old **HYÈRES** lies on the slopes of the Casteou hill, 5km from the sea with a ruined **castle** on the summit. From the top of the keep and the ivy clad towers that outreach the oak and lotus trees, you can see the modern expansion of the town with its proliferation of palm trees and, beyond, the peculiar Presqu'île de Giens, leashed to the mainland by a narrow isthmus and parallel sand bar enclosing salt marshes in between. Out to sea, east of Giens, the three Îles d'Or (or Îles d'Hyères) are visible.

Lacking a central seafront, Hyères lost out on the snob front when the Côte clientele switched from winter convalescents to quayside strutters. Consequently it's very appealing: the casino is used for cinema and youth clubs, the old town is neither a tourist trap nor a slum, and the land around is covered with strawberry fields, vines and peach orchards rather than holiday shelving units. The only blight on all this is the presence of a French Air Force base just north of the main port, from which test pilots play with the latest fiendish multi-million franc exports up and down the coast.

The **gare SNCF** is 1½ km south-west of the centre at the end of av Edith Cavell, with frequent buses to the **gare routière** on place Clemenceau from which a medieval gatehouse opens into rue Maissillon and the **Vieille Ville**. *Central* (17 av J Clotis), *Globe* (10 cours Strasbourg) and *Marius* (1 place du Marché) are the cheapest of the nearby **hotels**. There's no youth hostel but plenty of **camping** sites on the coast: in LES SALINS, due east of Hyères and at L'AYGUADE and LE CEINTURON further south where the beach gets rather stony and the air base too close (bus 66S). Or, on the isthmus there's a municipal camping at LA CAPTE (bus 66), several on GIENS and one at L'ALMANARRE west of the town. The **SI** is in the rotunda off av de Belgique, two blocks south of place Clemenceau, and **bikes** which you may well need, can be hired at 59 av Alphonse Denis or 33 av Gambetta.

For eating and drinking, there are the terraced **cafés** and **morning market** in the spacious lounging about square at the top of rue Maissillon; takeaway **food stalls** on rue Portalet sloping seawards from the square; **restaurants** all around this corner of the Vieille Ville as well as east along the street that divides the old and the new towns, as it becomes rue Alphonse Denis. For a scenic wander walk up from the tower on the square and head through the oldest parts of the Vieille Ville to Parc St-Bernard. After these gardens, full of nearly every Mediterranean flower, you can continue up to the castle.

The Îles d'Or

A haven from tempests in ancient times, then peaceful habitat of monks and farmers, the **ÎLES D'OR** became a base for coastal attacks by an endless succession of assorted aggressors (including of course the Brits). They are covered in forts, half-destroyed, rebuilt, abandoned, from the 16C when François I started a trend of underfunded fort building, to the 20C when the German gun positions on Port Cros and Levant were put out of action by the Americans. Porquerolles and Levant are still not free of garrisons thanks to the knack of the French armed forces for getting prime beauty sites for bases.

PORQUEROLLES, the largest island and easiest accessible, has a proper village around the port with a market, *boules* playing and plenty of cafés; there are also a few **hotels** and restaurants, though none of them particularly cheap. This is the only cultivated island and it has its own wine, *appellation Côtes des Îles*. The landscapes are beautiful and it's big enough to find yourself alone, and get lost. The southern shoreline is all cliffs with scary paths meandering close to the edge through heather and exuberant Provençal growth. The sandy beaches are on either side of the village and the *terrain militaire* is on the northern tip. If you want to hire a **bike**, try at the top of the main square just to the left.

The dense vegetation and mini mountains make **PORT CROS** harder going though it's less than half the size of Porquerolles. It takes a couple of hours to walk from the port to the nearest beach, **plage de la Palu**; a similar amount to cross the island via **Vallon de la Solitude** or **Vallon de la Fausse Monnaie**. There are only thirty human inhabitants but a lot of wildlife: the Port Cros birds, reptiles, rats and rabbits, fauna and flora are all protected by **National Park** status – you're not allowed to light a cigarette away from the port, nor to camp or pick any flowers. In fact, unless you're an obsessive botanist it's not the most interesting of islands.

The tiny bit of the **ÎLE DE LEVANT** spared by the military is a **nudist colony**, set up in the village of **Heliopolis** in the early 1930s. About sixty people live here all the year round, joined by thousands who come just for the summer, and tens of thousands of day trippers. The residents' preferred street dress is '*les plus petits costumes en Europe*', on sale as you get off the boat, and they are a lot more friendly to people who stay, even a few days, than to the voyeuristic 2-hour visitors. They also get on well with the soldiers from the base and don't lead soap opera lives. In this ecological haven, almost always humid and sunny, however, plant life does go wild. Giant geraniums and nasturtiums climb 3m hedges overhung by gigantic eucalyptus trees.

To **get to the islands**, the closest ports are LA TOUR FONDUE on the south-east tip of the Presqu'île de Giens, from where the company *Le Hyèroise* operates round trips to all three, HYÈRES port (TVL company) and LE LAVENDOU, 15 quai Gabriel-Péri.

NOT THE CÔTE: TOWARDS MARSEILLE

From the squalid naval base of **Toulon** to the vast and rather wonderful seediness of **Marseille**, this stretch of the Mediterranean is definitely not the Côte d'Azur. There is no continuous corniche, no villas in the Grand Style, and work is geared to an annual rather than summer cycle. **Cassis** is the exception, but Marseille the overriding attraction – a city that couldn't be confused with any other, no matter where you were dropped in it.

TOULON TO MARSEILLE

Half of **Toulon** was destroyed in the last war and the rebuilt whole is dominated by the French Mediterranean Fleet and its arsenal. It's big, dense, ugly and joyless. If you get stuck here for a few hours, the one good thing to do is to take the **funicular** up to **Mont Faron**, away from the city. Views from here will increase desire to move out. If for some reason you need a room, the **SI**, down below at 8 av Colbert, can advise; they're open 8.30–12 & 2–6, July–Aug 8–8 plus Suns 9–12.

The shipbuilding town of **LA CIOTAT**, half-way between Toulon and Marseille is a more inspiring prospect. It is the only small working-class town left on the coast – and one of the few places the Left gets more votes than Le Pen – but in evident decline, with massive lay-offs threatened. If you want to stop before Marseille, however, it does have a string of nearby **campsites**; some good **cheap hotels** (try the central *Ciotat Plage*, 3 av de Provence, *Beau Rivage*, 1 av Beau Rivage, or *La Marine*, 1 av F Gassion); an excellent **beach** and **boat trips** to the Île Verte and nearby *calanques*, the creeks which tear much of this part of the coastline. The strangest sight in La Ciotat itself are the rock formations of the promontory beyond the shipyards in the **Parc National du Mugel** (7–8/6, free). A path leads up from the entrance past scooped vertical hollows to a narrow terrace overlooking the sea. The cliff face looks like the habitat of some gravity-defying, burrowing beast – all the erosions by wind and sea on this chalk free matter. To get into the centre from the **gare SNCF** you'll need to take the bus (which leaves outside). If you're into **silent movies**, the *Eden Cinema*, where some of the earliest screenings in France took place, hosts a festival in July.

CASSIS, its old fishing port hemmed in by cliffs, with toytown development behind, could probably apply for a transfer to the Côte des Maures and fetch a good price. It's a cutesy place, knowingly so, and with solid Côte prices (not a cheap room to be had – and no nearby campsight). It is dominated, as with all good southern resorts, by a medieval castle – though this one is not a sight to be visited, but the refitted residence of M. Michelin, authoritarian boss of the family tyres and guides firm.

Portside posing and drinking aside, the favoured tourist pastimes are **boat trips** to the **calanques** – at their most spectacular hereabouts. Several companies operate from the port but check if they let you off or just tour in and out and be prepared for quite rough seas. Or, if you're feeling energetic, you can take the well signed footpath from the route des Calanques behind the western beach. It's about 1½ hours' walk to the furthest and best, **En Vau**, where you can climb down rocks to reach the shore. Intrepid pines find root holds and sunbathers find ledges on the chaotic white gnawed cliffs. And swimming in the deep water of the creeks beneath these heights is pretty tasty.

MARSEILLE

The most renowned and populated city after Paris, **MARSEILLE** over the centuries has, like the capital, prospered and been ransacked, lost its privileges to French kings and foreign armies, refound its fortunes, suffered plagues, religious bigotry, republican and royalist terror and had its own Commune and Bastille storming. The national anthem is named after *Marseillaise* revolutionaries and in the current state of the *Patrie*, Marseille has twice the national average unemployment.

With this, of course, it has an unrivalled reputation as the city of heroin, the mafia and prostitution – all well earned. But lawlessness never seems to take over, one explanation being that the rackets are so well meshed into corruption at the townhall. Gaston Defferre, the mayor of Marseille for the last thirty years and now Minister for the Interior as well, always comes out clean. He runs the city as if it was his private property (to quote John Ardagh's *France in the 1980s*, see p. 506) and owns two of the city's newspapers. The dominating fear and violence in the city is racial. With the worst housing, lowest paid jobs or no jobs at all, the Arabs, mostly Algerian, have to live with racist attacks and abuse, particularly from the police, as constants in their daily lives. Le Pen has a huge grassroot following here and gets more votes than the PS.

You might not choose to live in Marseille but it's a wonderful place to visit – a real port city in the old traditions, full of people arriving and departing with the ships. It's as cosmopolitan as Paris, with the considerable advantage of being nearly 800km further south.

Orientation and accommodation

Unless you arrive by boat, Marseille has to be approached from the surrounding protective heights of three mountain ranges. The views as you descend all encompass the barricade of high rise concrete on the

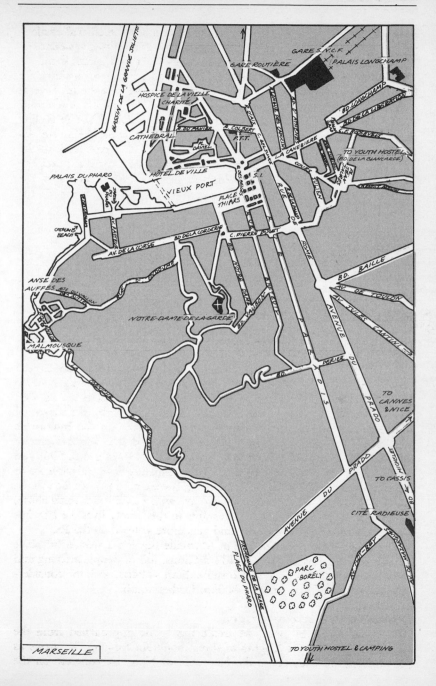

MARSEILLE

lower slopes, the vast roadstead with docks stretching miles north from the original **Vieux Port** and, just to the south of the old port, Marseille's classic landmark, the **Basilique de Notre Dame de la Garde**. Perched on a high rock and crowned by a monumental gold Virgin that gleams to ships far out to sea, the church itself is a neo-Byzantine riot, but for close-up city-scape it can't be beaten (bus 60 from the Vieux Port).

The city divides into sixteen *arrondissements*, which spiral out from the town centre at the head of the old port, and have good transport links by both bus and métro. The **gare routière** round the corner from the **gare SNCF: St-Charles**, on place Victor Hugo, is in the 1er. The monumental stairway from the station down to bd d'Athènes was built in 1923 with art deco railings and lamps, and steps wide enough for people to sit and chat, play cards and lie dead drunk without being an obstacle. From bd d'Athènes you reach the main east-west artery running down to the Vieux Port, the **Canebière**, full of banks, airline offices, cinemas and night-time paranoia. The main SI is along this at no 4, with an annexe at St-Charles.

Cheap hotels are plentiful though many are permanently filled by lodgers. In the 1er there's *Biarritz* (24 rue Curiol), the *Brager* and *Athénée* (83 and 63 rue de la Palud), *Caravelle* (5 rue Guy Moquet) and *de Nice* (11 rue Sénac). Another option is to stay in a classified building on bd Michelet, the seventeen-storey **Cité Radieuse** completed by Le Corbusier in 1952 and hailed as a landmark in 20C architecture. The hotel is on the third floor and not a lot more expensive than the others listed. You can get there on buses 21 or 22 from the Canebière to *Cité Le Corbusier*. There are also two **youth hostels**, both 4km from the centre: *Bois Luzy* (76 av de Bois Luzy, 12e; 91.49.06.18; bus 8 direction *St-Julien* from Centre Bourse, stop *Bois Luzy*) and *Bonneveine* (47 av J Vidal, impasse Dr Bonfils, 8e; 91.73.21.81; bus 44 direction *Roy d'Espagne* from the Canebière, stop *Sablier Cité Borély*) in one of the most desirable districts of the city – and close by the Prado beach. Three stops back from it on the 44 bus route is *Camping de Bonneveine* (187 av Clot Bey). Another **campsite** in the same area is *Les Vagues* (52 av de Bonneveine) for which you need to take métro 1 to Castellane then bus 19, direction *Madrague-de-Montredon* to *Les Gâtons Plage*.

Free **bus and métro plans** are available from the SI or RTM, the transport office at 7 rue Reine Elizabeth. The last métro is at 12.30 and you can combine bus and métro to any distance on one standard ticket.

The city

The cafés around the end of the **Vieux Port** indulge the sedentary pleasures of observing street life, despite the fumes of traffic and fish – the latter straight off the boats on the quai des Belges – and the lack of any quay front claim to beauty. The clientele of Cannes and St-Tropez and, no doubt, the ancient Greeks who built the port in the first place, would find it all unbearably downmarket. But then Marseille is a real town.

For a few hour's purposefulness, **boats** leave fairly regularly from Quai des Belges for the evil island fortress of the **Château d'If**, for which the required reading is Dumas' great adventure story, *The Count of Monte Cristo*. Apart from this hero, no one ever escaped. The guide shows you cells of a man who wore his hat in the presence of Louis XIV, a sailor who punched an officer, revolutionaries and religious prisoners, all of whom went insane or died (and usually both) in this securest of state prisons.

Up until 1943 a mass of narrow streets twisted their way up to rue Caisserie from the northern quay, providing hideouts for the Resistance. But the population was deported, and then, taking care to preserve the 17C townhall, the old Palais de Justice and other superior buildings, the Germans dynamited the rest of the quartier du Vieux Port out of existence. After the war, archaeologists derived some benefit from this destruction by finding remains of the Greco-Roman docks equipped with vast storage jars for food stuffs which can be seen in situ at the **Musée des Docks Romains** on place Vivaux (10–12 & 2–6.30; cl. Tues & Weds am). Along rue Caisserie there are steps leading up into the surviving remnants of the old town, known as **Le Panier**. On the top of the hill, almost hidden by the high tenement buildings around it, stands the **Hospice de la Vieille Charité**, a 17C workhouse with a gorgeous Baroque chapel surrounded by columned arcades in pink stone, all recently restored. Only the tiny grilled windows on the exterior speak of its original use. It's now a culture house and perhaps the prettiest building in Marseille. But people in the local cafés will tell you that it was '*beaucoup plus jolie*' when a hundred local families, all with at least ten children, lived in the Hospice before it was dolled up. They scoff at the idea of Le Panier being gentrified and crack jokes about how the bourgeois are going to get to the concerts and exhibitions without passing through this 80 per cent Arab quarter. There's little tension here between the working-class French and the immigrants, and none of them want to be moved out to high-rise HLM council estates on the city's perimeter.

The Canebière is the real *cordon sanitaire* between the Algerians, and the committedly bourgeois. According to the latter, they are being driven further south, to the most salubrious areas of town. The area between St-Charles, the Canebière and west to bd d'Aix and cours Belsunce, is the first place the French will cite as the Algerian frontline. This triangle is a highly active and unofficial trading ground for Arabs in Europe and from the Arab world. Hi-fis, suits and jeans from France and Germany are traded with spices, cloth and metalware from across the Mediterranean on flattened cardboard boxes on the streets. No French middlemen are involved, hence the horror. For more regulated shopping, the main streets are rue de Rome and rue de Paradis south of the Canebière. On both sides, the pavements are lined day and night with prostitutes who must be unique in their friendliness to other women.

At the top of bd Longchamps, the **Palais Longchamp**, like the steps of St-Charles, is typical of Marseille's grandiose municipal structures. It was built to celebrate the completion of an aqueduct in 1869, though the triumphant scale probably has more to do with another opening that year, of much more significance to the city's prosperity, the Suez canal. The palace's left wing is the city's **Beaux Arts**, hot, a little stuffy, but with a fair share of goodies – most notably three beautiful paintings by Françoise Duparc (1726–76), whose first name has consistently found itself masculinised in catalogues both French and British, and a room of political cartoons by the 19C satirist from Marseille, Daumier. The museum is open along with the **Musée d'Histoire Naturelle** in the other wing, from 10–12 & 2–6.30 (again cl. Tues & Wed am) and accessible via buses 80 and 41 or métro Cinq Avenues-Lonchamp. Marseille's main collection of contemporary art with occasional exhibitions of 20C greats is the **Musée Cantini** (19 rue Grignan) – same hours.

The **Palais de Pharo** and its surrounding park, a prime rock venue amongst other things, overlook the length of the Vieux Port. To the west, the military monopolises the coast until the overcrowded and small **Les Catalans beach**. From there the long-winded **Promenade de la Corniche du Président J F Kennedy** follows the cliffs past the dramatic statue and arch that frames the setting sun of the **Monument aux Morts d'Orient**, to the heavily landscaped **Plage du Prado**, best of the local strands – and with remarkably clean water due to recent anti-pollution schemes.

Just south of the monument steps lead down to an inlet, the **Anse des Auffes**, which is the nearest Marseille gets to being picturesque. Small fishing boats are beached on the rocks, the dominant sound is the sea and narrow stairways and lanes lead nowhere. Back from here the route du Vallon des Auffes circuitously links up with a network of tiny streets high above the Anse, the quartier of **Endoume**. South, where the corniche cuts inland, **Malmousque** is another tranquil labyrinth. The end of the promontory is *terrain militaire* but a public path follows the coast eastwards with steps down to tiny bays and beaches which are perfect for swimming when the Mistral wind is not inciting the waves. You can see along the coast as far as Cap Croisette and, out to sea, the abandoned monastery on the Îles d'Endoume and the Château d'If.

For **buses along the corniche** from the old port, take 83 to av du Prado, 19 to MADRAGUE-DE-MONTREDON or 20 to CAP CROISETTE.

Food and action

Marseille is **gastronomically** significant – home base for the sea fish speciality *bouillabaisse*, a saffron and garlic flavoured fish stock with bits of fish, croutons and rouille to throw in and unresolved theories about which fish and where and how they must be caught. But one thing's certain – if it's less than 100F it's not the real thing. It's a meal in itself and known to be good at **restaurants** *La Samaritaine* (43 quai du Port) or, more expensively, *Michel* (63 rue des Catalans) and *Calypso* opposite. South of the port, place Thiars has a better choice of eating places than the *quais* and in **Le Panier**, the restaurant at 43 rue Lorette, with no written menu and full of noisy parties and large families, has fun, excellent food and isn't expensive. The **Anse des Auffes** restaurants are very tempting but not cheap. At *Chez Alex* (43 rue Curiol) you can eat Italian without fear of the bill. In the same area, around place Jean-Jaurès, there's a feminist-run restaurant, *Perlimpinpin*, and *La Garga*, owned by the gay collective *La Boulangerie Gay*, at 7 and 17 rue André Poggioli, both mixed.

For other action, the **SI** publish a three-monthly round-up of sports and entertainment and the PCF daily, *La Marseillaise* has listings on page 4. Several **cinemas** screen v.o.'s, and there are interesting shows (sometimes in English) put on at the *Théâtre du Merlan* (av Raimu, 14e), part of a cultural centre in one of the worst concrete suburbs – with a police commissariat on the ground floor.

The city's **Women's Movement** is based at 95 rue Benoît Malon (5e) with people around on Tuesdays and Thursdays 6.30–10.30; on the same days between 12–6 the library and information centre is open at 81 rue Senac. *La Douce Amère*, a lesbian group, can be contacted c/o *La Boulangerie Gay* (48 rue de Bruys). This mixed **gay** collective is a campaigning organisation and arranges, every other year, a July *Université d'Eté Homosexuelle*. The bar is open every evening with Thursday reserved for women.

A place for anyone and everyone to go and **drink** is *Le Veve* (rue Sainte) which has games, occasional live local music and cheap beer. And if you don't mind going out of town for a **bop**, the *Stardust* (av Alexandre Delabre, Les Goudes – near Cap Croissette) is hetero and doesn't cost much.

Other **relevant addresses:**

Air Terminal for the *Aéroport de Marignane* at gare St-Charles.
Bike hire from Ulysses, av du Parc Borely; very expensive.
Consulates UK and Canada, 24 av Prado; USA, 9 rue Armeny.
Hospital Hôtel Dieu, 6 place Daviel (91.91.61).
Poste Restante La Poste Colbert, 1 rue Henri Barbusse, 13001 Marseille.
Youth Information *CIJ*, Stade Vallier, 4 rue de la Visitation.

TRAVEL DETAILS

Trains

The **Ventimiglia line** follows the coast more or less the whole way from Marseille to Menton, running inland only over the stretch between Fréjus and Toulon. Major stops are at Monaco, Nice, Antibes, Cannes, St-Raphaël and Toulon. The full journey takes between 2¾–3½hrs.

From Nice 8 daily to Menton (35–40mins); 6 daily to St Raphaël (1hr–1hr25); 20 daily to Marseille (2¼–2½hrs) and 7 daily to Paris-Gare de Lyon (10hrs40–12hrs).

Cannes to Menton 18 daily (1hr25).

From Marseille 15 daily to Cassis (25–30mins); 18 daily to La Ciotat (30–40mins); 2 daily to Hyères (1hr15); 9 daily to Paris-Gare de Lyon (5hrs–7hrs40).

From St-Raphaël 7 daily to Paris-Gare de Lyon (9–9½hrs).

Buses

For most journeys along the Côte, buses are much slower, more expensive and less frequent than trains.

Hyères to Toulon SNCF 10 daily (½hr); 5 daily to La Foux (1¼–1½hrs).

Boats

From Marseille (Bassin de la Joliette) to Corsica, Sardinia, Algiers, Tunis and Majorca.

From Nice to Corsica (summer day excursions operated by *SNCM*, 3 av Gustav V, depart quai de la Commerce; also car ferry service).

From St-Raphaël to St-Tropez, Port Grimaud, Îles de Lérins (summer excursions again operated by MMG, quai Nomy).

From St-Tropez to Ste-Maxime (MMG, quai Jean-Jaurès).

From Juan-les-les Pins to the Îles de Lérins (embarcadère Coubet).

Part three
CONTEXTS

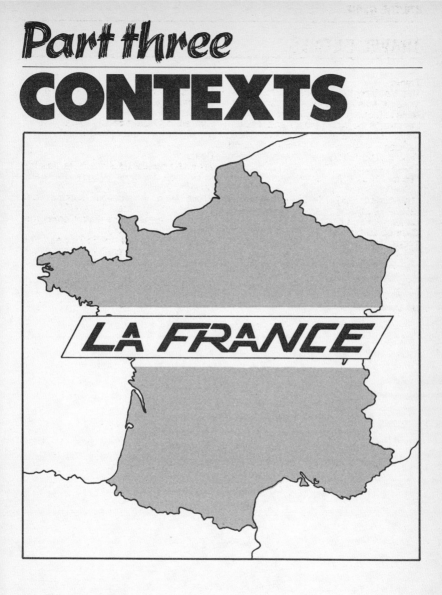

HISTORICAL FRAMEWORK

Early civilisations

Traces of human existence are rare in France before about 50,000BC. Thereafter, beginning with the **Mousterian civilisation**, they become more and more numerous, with a particularly heavy concentration of continuously occupied sites in the **Périgord** region of the Dordogne. It was here, near the village of Les Eyzies, that the Late Stone Age Cro-Magnon man was discovered, who flourished from around 25,000BC. They were hunters and cave-dwellers who developed a remarkably sophisticated culture, the evidence of which is visible in the beautiful paintings and engravings preserved on the walls of the region's caves.

By 10,000BC human communities had spread out widely across the whole of France. The ice cap receded; the climate became warmer and wetter, and by about 7,000BC farming and pastoral communities had begun to develop. By 4,500BC the first **dolmens** appear in **Brittany**; around 2,000BC copper made its appearance; and by 1,800BC the **Bronze Age** has arrived, particularly strong in the east and south-east of the country, and there is evidence of trade with Spain, central Europe and Wessex in Britain. Around 1,200BC the **Champs d'Urnes people**, who buried their dead in sunken urns, began to make incursions from the east. By 900BC the **Halstatt people** brought iron – their settlements concentrated in Burgundy. Alsace and Franche-Comté near the principal deposits of iron ore – joined around 450BC by **Celts**.

Pre-Roman Gaul

There were about 15 million people living in **Gaul**, as the Romans called what we call France (and parts of Belgium), when Julius Caesar arrived in 58BC to complete the Roman conquest. The southern part – modern **Provence** mostly – had been a colony since 118BC and exposed to the civilising influences of Italy and Greece for much longer. Greek colonists had founded Marseilles/Massilia as far back as 600BC. But even the inhabitants of the rest of the country, what the Romans called 'long-haired Gaul', were far from shaggy barbarians. Though the economy was basically rural, they had established large **hilltop towns** by 100BC, notably at Bibracte near Autun, where archaeologists have identified separate merchants' quarters, metalworkers' quarters and so on. They had invented the barrel and soap, and were skilful manufacturers. By 500BC they were capable of making metal-wheeled carts, as was proved by the 6C 'chariot tombs' of **Vix**, where a young woman was found buried seated in a cart with its wheels ranged against the wall. She was wearing rich gold jewellery and lying beside Greek vases and Black Figure pottery, dating the burial at around 500BC and revealing the extent of commercial relations. Interestingly, too, the Gauls' money was based on the gold *staters* minted by Philip of Macedon, father of Alexander the Great.

Conquest and Romanisation

Gallic **tribal rivalries** made the Romans' job very much easier. And even when at last they were able to unite under Vercingetorix in 52BC, the occasion was their total and final defeat by **Julius Caesar** at the battle of Alesia. Although a long time ago, this was one of the major turning points in the history of the country. **Roman victory** fixed the frontier between Gaul and the Germanic peoples at the Rhine. It saved Gaul from disintegrating because of internal dissension and made it a Latin province. During the five centuries of peace that followed, the Gauls farmed, manufactured and traded, became urbanised, embourgeoised and educated – and learnt Latin. In other words, Roman victory at Alesia laid the foundations of modern French culture, and laid them firmly enough to survive the centuries of chaos and destruction that followed the collapse of Roman power.

Augustus and **Claudius** were the emperors who set the process of **Romanisation** going. Lyon/Lugdunum was founded as the capital of Roman Gaul as early as 43BC. Augustus initiated numerous others, like Autun, Limoges and Bayeux, built roads, settled Roman colonists on the land, and reorganised the entire administration. Gauls were incorporated into the Roman army and given citizenship; Claudius made it possible for them to hold high office and become members of the Roman Senate, blurring the distinction and resentment between coloniser and colonised. Vespasian secured the frontiers beyond the Rhine, thus assuring a couple of hundred years of peace and economic expansion.

Serious **disruptions** of the pax Romana only began in the 3C. Oppressive aristocratic rule and economic crisis turned the destitute peasantry into gangs of marauding brigands – precursors of the medieval *jacquerie*. But most devastating of all, there began a series of incursions across the Rhine frontier by various restless **Germanic tribes**, the Alemanni and Franks first, who pushed down as far as Spain, ravaging farmland and destroying towns.

In the 4C the reforms of the emperor **Diocletian** secured some decades of respite from both internal and external pressures. Towns were rebuilt and fortified, an interesting development that foreshadowed feudalism and the independent power of the nobles since, due to the uncertainty of the times, big landed estates or *villae* tended to become more and more self-sufficient – economically, administratively and militarily. By the 5C the Germanic invaders were back, **Alans**, **Vandals** and **Suevi**, with **Franks** and **Burgundians** in their wake. While the Roman administration assimiliated them as far as possible, granting them land in return for military duties, many Gauls, by now thoroughly Latinised, entered the service of the Burgundian court of Lyon or the Visigoth kings of Toulouse as skilled administrators and advisers.

The Franks and Charlemagne

By 500 the **Franks**, who gave their name to modern France, had become the dominant invading power. Their most celebrated king, **Clovis**, consolidated his hold on northern France and drove the Visigoths out of the south-west into Spain. In 507 he made the till-then insignificant little trading town of Paris his capital and became a Christian, which inevitably hastened the **Christianisation** of the most influential elements in Frankish society. Under succeeding **Merovingian** – as the dynasty was called – rulers, the kingdom began to disintegrate until in the 8C the Pepin family, who were the Merovin-

gians' chancellors, began to take effective control. In 732 one of their most dynamic scions, **Charles Martel**, reunited the kingdom and saved western Christendom from the northward expansion of Islam by defeating the Spanish Moors at the **battle of Poitiers**. In 754 Charles's son, Pepin, had himself crowned king by the Pope, thus inaugurating the **Carolingian dynasty** and establishing for the first time the principle of the divine right of kings. His son was **Charlemagne**, who extended Frankish control over the whole of what had been Roman Gaul and far beyond. On Christmas Day 800 he was crowned emperor of the Holy Roman Empire, though again, following his death, the kingdom fell apart in his grandsons' squabbles over who was to inherit the bits of his empire. At the Treaty of Verdun in 843 they agreed on a division of territory which corresponded roughly with the extent of contemporary France and Germany.

Charlemagne's administrative system had involved the royal appointment of counts and bishops to govern the various provinces of the empire. Under the destabilising attacks of the Norman/Norsemen/Vikings during the 9C, Carolingian kings were obliged to delegate more power and autonomy to these **provincial governors**, whose lands, like **Aquitaine** and **Burgundy**, already had separate regional identities as a result of earlier invasions – the Visigoths in Aquitaine, the Burgundians in Burgundy, for example. Gradually the power of these princes overshadowed that of the king, whose lands were confined to the Ile-de-France. When the last Carolingian died in 987, it was only natural that they should elect one of their own number to take his place. This was Hugues Capet, founder of a dynasty that lasted until 1328.

The rise of the French kings

From 1,000 to 1,500AD you see the gradual extension and consolidation of the power of the **French kings**, accompanied by the growth of a centralised administrative system and bureaucracy. These objectives also determined their foreign policy, which was chiefly concerned with restricting Papal interference in French affairs and the long struggle to check the English kings' involvement in French territory. While progress towards these goals was remarkably steady and single-minded, there were setbacks, principally in the seesawing fortunes of the conflict with the English.

Surrounded by vassals much stronger than themselves, **Hugues Capet** and his successors remained weak throughout the 11C, though they made the most of their feudal rights. As Dukes of the French, Counts of Paris and anointed kings, they enjoyed a prestige that their vassals dared not offend – not least because that would have set a dangerous precedent of disobedience for their own lesser vassals.

At the beginning of the 12C, having successfully tamed his own vassals in the Ile-de-France, Louis VI had a stroke of luck. **Eleanor**, daughter of the powerful Duke of Aquitaine, was left in his care on her father's death, so he promptly married her to his son, the future Louis VII. Unfortunately, the marriage ended in divorce and Eleanor immediately – in 1152 – remarried, to Henry of Normandy, shortly to become **Henry II** of England. Thus the English gained control of a huge chunk of French territory, stretching from the Channel to the Pyrenees. Though their fortunes fluctuated over the ensuing 300 years, they remained a perpetual thorn in the side for the French kings and a dangerous source of alliances for any rebellious French vassals.

Philippe Auguste (1180–1223) made considerable headway in undermining English rule by exploiting the bitter relations between Henry II and his three sons, one of whom was Richard Coeur-de-Lion. But he fell out with Richard when they took part in the Third Crusade together. Luckily Richard died before he was able to claw back Philippe's gains and by the end of his reign, Philippe had recovered all of Normandy and the English possessions north of the Loire. For the first time, the royal lands were greater than those of any other French lord. The foundations of a systematic administration and civil service had been established in **Paris**, and Philippe had firmly and quietly marked his independence from the Papacy by refusing to take any interest in the crusade against the heretic Cathars of Languedoc. When Languedoc and Poitou came under royal control in the reign of his son, Louis VIII, France was

by far the greatest power in western Europe.

The Hundred Years War

In 1328 the Capetian monarchy had its first succession problems, which led directly to the ruinous **Hundred Years War** with the English. Charles IV, last of the line, had only daughters, and when it was decided that France could not be ruled by a queen, the English king, **Edward III**, whose mother was Charles's sister, claimed the throne of France for himself. The French chose **Philippe, Count of Valois**, instead, and Edward acquiesced for a time. But when Philippe began whittling away at his possessions in Aquitaine, he renewed his claim and embarked on war. Though, with its population of about 12 million, France was a far richer and more powerful country, its army was no match for the superior organisation and tactics of the English. Edward won a total victory at **Crécy** in 1346 and seized the port of Calais as a permanent bridgehead. Ten years later, his son, the Black Prince, actually took the French king, Jean le Bon, prisoner at the battle of Poitiers.

Although by 1375 French military fortunes had improved to the point where the English had been forced back on Calais and the Gascon coast, the strains of war, administrative abuses and the madness of Charles VI caused other kinds of damage. In 1358 there were **insurrections** among the Picardy peasantry (the *Jacquerie*), and the townsmen of Paris under the leadership of Etienne Marcel – both brutally repressed, as were subsequent risings in Paris in 1382 and 1412.

The consequences of the king's madness led to the formation of two rival factions in the aftermath of the murder of the king's brother, the Duke of Orleans, by the Duke of Burgundy. The **Armagnacs** gathered round the young Orleans, and the other faction round the **Burgundys**. Both called in the English.

In 1415 Henry V of England inflicted another crushing defeat on the French army at **Agincourt**. The Burgundians seized Paris, took the royal family prisoner and recognised Henry as heir to the French throne. When Charles VI died in 1422, Henry's brother, the Duke of Bedford, took over the government of the whole of France north of the Loire, while the young king Charles VII rather ineffectually governed the south from his refugee capital at Bourges.

At this point **Joan of Arc** arrived on the scene. In 1429 she raised the English siege of the crucial town of Orleans and had Charles properly crowned at Rheims. Although she fell into the hands of the Burgundians who sold her to the English, and was tried and burnt as a heretic, her dynamism and martyrdom raised French morale and tipped the scales against the English. Except for a toehold at Calais they were finally driven from France altogether in 1453.

By the end of the century, **Dauphiné**, **Burgundy**, **Franche-Comté** and **Provence** were under royal control, and an effective standing army had been created. The taxation system had been overhauled, and France had emerged from the Middle Ages a rich, powerful state, firmly under the centralised authority of an absolute monarch.

The Wars of Religion

After half a century of self-confident but inconclusive seeking after military *gloire* in Italy, brought to an end by the Treaty of Cateau-Cambresis in 1559, France was plunged into another period of devastating internal conflict. The **Protestant** ideas of Luther and Calvin had gained widespread adherence among the poor, artisan, bourgeois and noble classes of society, despite spasmodically brutal attempts by François I and Henri II to stamp them out. When Catherine de Médicis, acting as Regent for Henri III, implemented a more tolerant policy, she provoked violent reaction from the ultra-Catholic faction led by the Guise family. Their massacre of a Protestant congregation coming out of church in March 1562 began a civil **war of religions** that, interspersed with ineffective truces and accords, lasted for the next thirty years. Well-organised and well-led by the Prince de Condé and Admiral Coligny the **Huguenots**, as the French Protestants are called, kept their end up very successfully, until Condé was killed at the battle of Jarnac, near Cognac, in 1569. 1572 saw one of the blackest events in the memory of French Protestants, even today: the **massacre of St Bartholomew's Day**. Coligny and 3,000 Protestants gathered in Paris for the wedding of Marguerite, the king's sister, to the Protestant Henri of Navarre,

were slaughtered at the instigation of the Guises – a bloodbath which was copied across France, especially in the south and west where the Protestants were strongest.

In 1584 the king's son died, leaving his brother-in-law **Henri of Navarre** heir to the throne, to the fury of the Guises and their Catholic league who seized Paris and drove out the king. In retaliation Henri III murdered the Duc de Guise, and found himself forced into alliance with Henri of Navarre, whom the Pope had excommunicated. In 1589 Henri III was himself assassinated, leaving Henri of Navarre to become Henri IV of France. But it took another four years of fighting and the abjuration of his faith for the new king to be recognised. 'Paris is worth a Mass,' he is reputed to have said.

Once on the throne Henri IV set about reconstruction and reconciliation. By the **Edict of Nantes** of 1598 the Huguenots were accorded freedom of conscience, freedom of worship in certain places, the right to attend the same schools and hold the same offices as Catholics, their own courts, and the possession of a number of fortresses as a guarantee against renewed attack, the most important being La Rochelle and Montpellier.

Kings, cardinals and absolute power

The main themes of the 17C, when France was ruled by just two kings, **Louis XIII** (1610–43) and **Louis XIV** (1643–1715), are, on the domestic front, the strengthening of the centralised state embodied in the person of the king; and in external affairs, the securing of frontiers in the Pyrenees, on the Rhine and in the north, coupled with the attempt to prevent the unification of the territories of the Habsburg kings of Spain and Austria. Both kings had the good fortune to be served by capable, hard-working ministers dedicated to these objectives. Louis XIII had **Cardinal Richelieu** and Louis XIV, **Cardinals Mazarin** and **Colbert**. Both reigns were perturbed in their early years by the inevitable aristocratic attempts at a coup d'état.

Having crushed revolts by Louis XIII's brother, Gaston Duke of Orleans, **Richelieu's** commitment to extending royal absolutism brought him into renewed conflict with the Protestants. Believing that their retention of separate fortresses within the kingdom was a threat to security, he attacked and took La Rochelle in 1627. Although he was unable to extirpate Protestantism altogether, they were never again to present a military threat.

The other important facet of his domestic policy was the promotion of economic self-sufficiency – **mercantilism**. To this end, he encouraged the growth of the luxury craft industries, especially textiles, that France was to excel at right up to the Revolution. He built up the navy and granted privileges to companies involved in establishing colonies in North America, Africa and the West Indies.

In pursuing his foreign policy objectives he adroitly kept France out of actual military involvement by paying substantial sums of money to the great Swedish king and general, Gustavus Adolphus, to encourage him to continue his wars against the Habsburgs in Germany. When in 1635 he was finally obliged to commit French troops they made significant gains against the Spanish in the Netherlands, Alsace and Lorraine and won Roussillon for France. He died just a few months before Louis XIII in 1642.

As Louis XIV was still an infant, his mother, Anne of Austria, acted as Regent, served by Richelieu's protégé, **Cardinal Mazarin**, who was hated quite as much as his predecessor by the traditional aristocracy and the *parlements**, jealous of their privileges and angry that an upstart should receive such preferment over themselves. Spurred by these grievances, which were in any case exacerbated by the ruinous cost of the Spanish wars, various groups in French society combined in a series of revolts, known as the **Frondes**.

The first was the Fronde of 1648, led by the *parlement* of Paris, which took up the cause of the hereditary provincial tax-collecting officials who resented the supervisory role of the *intendants*, appointed directly by the central royal bureaucracy to keep an eye on them. Paris rose in revolt but capitulated at the advance of royal troops. This was quickly followed by an aristocratic Fronde, supported by various peasant risings around the country. These revolts

* The French *parlements* were unelected bodies, with the function of high courts and administrative councils.

were suppressed easily enough, and should not be seen as proper revolutionary movements. They were rather the attempts of various reactionary groups to preserve their privileges in the face of growing state power.

Financial pressure was relieved when in 1659 Mazarin successfully brought the Spanish wars to an end with the **Treaty of the Pyrenees**, cemented by the marriage of Louis XIV and the daughter of Philip IV of Spain. On reaching the age of majority in 1661 **Louis** declared that he was going to be his own man and do without a first minister like Mazarin. He proceeded to appoint a number of able ministers of his own, with whose aid he embarked on a long struggle to modernise the administration in the teeth of opposition from a thoroughly reactionary society.

Le Tellier and his son Louvois provided him with a well-equipped and well-trained professional army that could muster some 400,000 men by 1670. But the principal reforms were carried out by **Colbert,** who set about streamlining the state's finances and tackling bureaucratic corruption. Although he was never able wholly to overcome the opposition of the provincial *parlements* and nobility, he did manage to produce a surplus in state revenue. Attempting to compensate for deficiences in the taxation system by stimulating trade, he set up a free trade area in northern and central France, continued Richelieu's mercantilist economic policies, established the French East India Company and built up the navy and merchant fleets with a view to challenging the world commercial supremacy of the Dutch.

These were all policies which the hard-working king was involved in and approved of. But in addition to his love of an extravagant court life at Versailles, which earned him the title of **the Sun King,** he had another obsession more ruinous to the state – the love of a prestigious military victory. There were sound political reasons for the **campaigns** he embarked on, but they did not help balance the budget.

Using his wife's Spanish connection he demanded the cession of certain Spanish provinces in the Low Countries, then embarked on a war against the Dutch in 1672. Forced to make peace at the **Treaty of Nijmegen** in 1678 by his arch-enemy, the Protestant William of

Orange (later king of England), he nonetheless came out of the war with the addition of Franche-Comté to French territory, plus a number of northern towns. In 1681 he simply grabbed Strasbourg, and got away with it.

In 1685, under the influence of his very Catholic mistress, Madame de Maintenon, he removed all privileges from the Huguenots by revoking the Edict of Nantes. This incensed the Protestant powers who formed the League of Augsburg against him. Another long and exhausting war followed, ending, most unfavourably to the French, in the **Peace of Rijswik** (1697). No sooner was this concluded when Louis became embroiled in the question of who was to succeed the moribund Charles II of Spain.

Both Louis and Leopold Habsburg, Holy Roman Emperor, had married sisters of Charles. The prospect of Leopold acquiring the Spanish Habsburgs' possessions in addition to his own vast lands was not welcome to Louis or any other European power. When Charles died and it was discovered that he had named Louis' grandson, Philippe, as his heir, here again was a shift in the balance of power that the English, Dutch and Austrians were not prepared to tolerate. William of Orange, now king of England as well as ruler of the United Provinces, organised a Grand Alliance against Louis. The so-called **War of the Spanish Succession** broke out and it went badly for the French, largely thanks to the brilliant generalship of the Duke of Marlborough. A severe winter in 1709 compounded the hardships with famine and bread riots at home, causing Louis to seek negotiations. The terms were too harsh for him and the war dragged on until 1713, leaving the country totally impoverished. The Sun King went out with scarcely a whimper.

Louis XV to the Revolution

While France remained in many ways a prosperous and powerful state, largely thanks to colonial trade, the tensions between central government and traditional vested interests proved too great to be reconciled. As the *parlement* of Paris became more and more the focus of opposition to the royal will, bringing the country to a state of virtual ungovernability in the rein of **Louis XVI,**

so the diversity of mutually irreconcilable interests sheltering behind that parliamentary umbrella came more and more to the fore, bringing the country to a climax of tension which could only be resolved in the turmoil of **Revolution.**

Louis XV was two when his great-grandfather died. During the Regency, the traditional aristocracy and the *parlements*, who for different reasons hated Louis XIV's advisers, scrabbled – successfully – to recover a lot of their lost power and prestige. An experiment with government by aristocratic councils failed, and attempts to absorb the immense national debt by selling shares in an overseas trading company ended in a collapse like the English South Sea Bubble. When the prudent and reasonable Cardinal Fleury came to prominence on the Regent's death in 1726, the nation's lot began to improve. The Atlantic seaboard towns grew rich on trade with the American and Caribbean colonies, though industrial production did not improve much and the disparity in wealth between countryside and the growing towns continued to enlarge.

In the mid-century there followed more disastrous military ventures, the **War of Austrian Succession** and the **Seven Years War,** both of which were in effect contests with England for control of the colonial territories in America and India, contests which France lost. The need to finance the war led to the introduction of a new tax, the Twentieth, which was to be levied on everyone. The *parlement*, which had successfully opposed earlier taxation, fought the Crown over its religious policies and resisted John Law's 'South Sea Bubble' scheme, dug its toes in again. This led to renewed conflict over Louis' pro-Jesuit religious policy. The *parlement* staged a strike, was exiled from Paris, then inevitably reinstated. Disputes about its role continued until the *parlement* of Paris was actually abolished in 1771, to the outrage of the privileged groups in society which considered it the defender of their special interests.

The division between the **parlements** and the king and his ministers continued to sharpen during the reign of Louis XVI, which began in 1774. Attempts by the enlightened finance minister Turgot to cooperate with the *parlements* and introduce reforms to alleviate the tax burden on the poor produced only short-term results. The national debt trebled between 1774 and 1787. Ironically the one radical attempt to introduce an effective and equitable tax system led directly to the Revolution. Calonne, finance minister in 1786, tried to get his proposed tax approved by an **Assembly of Notables,** a device that had not been employed for more than a hundred years. His purpose was to bypass the parlement, which could be relied on to oppose any radical proposal. The attempt backfired. He lost his post, and the *parlement* ended up demanding a meeting of the **Estates-General,** representing the nobles, the clergy and the bourgeoisie, as being the only body competent to discuss such matters. The Crown responded by exiling and then recalling the *parlement* of Paris several times. As law and order began to break down, it gave in and agreed to summon the Estates-General on 17 May 1789.

Revolution
Against a background of deepening economic crisis and general misery exacerbated by the catastrophic harvest of 1788, controversy focussed on how the **Estates-General** should be constituted. Should they meet separately as on the last occasion – in 1614. This was the solution favoured by the *parlement* of Paris, a measure of its reactionary nature: for separate meetings would make it easy for the privileged, i.e. the clergy and nobility, to outvote the Third Estate, the bourgeoisie. The king ruled that they should hold a joint meeting with the Third Estate represented by as many deputies as the other two Estates combined, but no decisions were made about the order of voting.

On 17 June 1789 the **Third Estate** seized the initiative and declared itself the National Assembly. Some of the lower clergy and liberal nobility joined them. The king appeared to accept the situation, and on 9 July the Assembly declared itself the National Constituent Assembly. The king then tried to intimidate it by calling in troops, which unleashed the anger of the people of Paris, the sans-culottes. On 14 July they stormed the fortress of **the Bastille,** symbol of the oppressive nature of the *ancien régime.* Similar insurrections occurred throughout the country, accompanied by widespread peasant attacks on landowners' châteaux, the destruction of records of debt and other symbols of their oppression. On the night of 4 August the Assembly abolished the feudal rights and privileges of the nobility – a momentous shift of gear in the **revolutionary process,** although in reality it did little to alter the situation. Later that month they adopted the Declaration of the **Rights of Man.** In December church lands were nationalised, and the Pope retaliated by declaring the principles of the Revolution impious.

Bourgeois elements in the Assembly tried to bring about a compromise with the nobility with a view to establishing a constitutional monarchy, but these overtures were rebuffed. Emigré aristocrats were already working to bring about foreign invasion to overthrow the Revolution. In June 1791 the king was arrested trying to escape from Paris. The Assembly, following an initiative of the wealthier bourgeois **Girondin** faction, decided to go to war to protect the Revolution. But the ill-prepared Revolutionary army met with numerous setbacks.

On 10 August 1792 the sans-culottes set up a **revolutionary Commune** in Paris and imprisoned the king. The Revolution was taking a radical turn. A new National Convention was elected and met on the day the Revolutionary armies finally halted the Prussian invasion at Valmy. A major rift developed between the **Girondins** and the **Jacobins** and sans-culottes over the abolition of the monarchy. The radicals carried the day. In January 1793 Louis XVI was executed. By June the Girondins had been ousted.

Counter-revolutionary forces were gathering in the provinces and abroad. A Committee of Public Safety was set up as chief organ of the government. Left-wing popular pressure brought laws on general conscription and price controls, and a deliberate policy of de-Christianisation. Robespierre was co-opted on to the Committee as the best man to contain the pressure from the streets.

The Terror began. In addition to the hated Marie-Antoinette, Robespierre felt strong enough to guillotine his opponents to both right and left. But the effect of so many rolling heads was to cool people's faith in the Revolution. By mid-1794 Robespierre himself was arrested and executed, and his fall marked the end of radicalism. More conservative forces gained control of the government, de-controlled the economy, repressed popular risings, limited the suffrage and established a five-man executive Directory (1795).

The rise of Napoleon

In 1799 a **General Bonaparte,** who had made a name as commander of the Revolutionary armies in Italy and Egypt, returned to France and took power in a coup d'état. He was appointed First Consul with power to choose officials, initiate legislation, etc. He redesigned the tax system and created the Bank of France, replaced the power of local institutions by a corps of *prefets* answerable to himself, made judges into state functionaries – in short, laid the foundations of the modern French administrative system.

Though he upheld the fundamental reforms of the Revolution, the retrograde nature of his regime became more and more apparent with the proscription of the Jacobins, amnesty of the émigrés and restoration of their unsold property, re-introduction of slavery in the colonies, recognition of the church and so on. Although alarmingly revolutionary in the eyes of the rest of Europe, his Civil Code worked essentially to the advantage of the bourgeoisie.

In 1804 he had himself crowned **Emperor** in the presence of the Pope. After 1808 the revolt of Spain, aided by the British, signalled a turning of the tide in the long series of dazzling military successes. The nation began to grow weary of the burden of unceasing war. In 1812 Napoleon threw himself into the **Russian campaign,** hoping to complete his European conquests. He reached Moscow but the long retreat in terrible winter conditions annihilated his veteran *Grande Armée*. By 1814 he was forced to abdicate by a coalition of European powers, who installed Louis XVIII, brother of the decapitated Louis XVI, as king. In a last effort to recapture power, Napoleon escaped from exile in Elba, reorganised his armies, only to meet final defeat at **Waterloo** on 18 June 1815. Louis XVIII was restored to power.

Restoration of monarchy and the 1830 revolution

The years following Napoleon's downfall were marked by a determined campaign, including a **White Terror,** on the part of those reactionary elements who wanted to wipe out all trace of the Revolution and restore the ancien regime. **Louis XVIII** resisted these moves and was able to appoint a moderate royalist minister. Decazes, under whose leadership the liberal faction who wished to preserve the Revolutionary reforms made steady gains. This process was wrecked by the assassination of the Duc de Berry in an attempt to wipe out the Bourbon family. In response to reactionary outrage the king dismissed Decazes. An attempted liberal insurrection was crushed and the Four Sergeants of La Rochelle were shot by firing squad. Censorship became more rigid and education was once more subjected to the authority of the church.

In 1824 Louis was succeeded by the thoroughly reactionary **Charles X,** who pushed through a law indemnifying émigré aristocrats for property lost during the Revolution. When the growing opposition won a majority in the elections of 1830, the king dissolved the Chamber and restricted the already narrow suffrage.

Barricades went up in the streets of Paris. Charles X abdicated and parliament was persuaded to accept **Louis-Philippe,** Duc d'Orléans, as king. On the face of it, divine right had been superseded by popular sovereignty as the basis of political legitimacy. The **1814 Charter,** which upheld Revolutionary and Napoleonic reforms, was retained, censorship abolished, the tricolour restored as the national flag and the suffrage widened.

The **Citizen King,** as he was called, however, had rather more abolutist notions about being a monarch. In the 1830s his regime survived repeated challenges both from attempted coups by reactionaries and some serious labour unrest in Lyon and Paris. The 1840s were calmer, under the ministry of Guizot, the first Protestant to hold high office in the state. It was at this time that Algeria was first colonised.

Guizot, however, was not popular. He resisted attempts to extend the vote to include the middle ranks of the bourgeoisie. In 1846 economic crisis brought bankruptcies, unemployment and food shortages. Conditions were appalling for the growing urban working class, whose hopes of a juster future received a more and more convincing theoretical basis in the **socialist writings** and activities of Blanqui, Fourier, Louis Blanc and Proudhon amonst others.

When the government banned an opposition 'banquet', the only permissible form of political meeting, in February 1848, workers and students took to the streets. When the army fired on a demonstration and killed forty people, civil war appeared imminent. The Citizen King fled to England.

1848 and the Second Republic

A provisional government was set up, incorporating four radical Republican leaders, including the Socialist Louis Blanc and one Parisian worker. A **republic** was proclaimed. The government issued a right-to-work declaration and set up national workshops to absorb unemployment. The vote was extended to all adult males – an unprecedented move for its time. By the time elections were held in April a new tax designed to ameliorate the financial crisis had antagonised the conservative countryside. A massive conservative majority was returned, to the dismay of the radicals. Three days of bloody streetfighting at the barricades followed, when General Cavaignac, who had distinguished himself in the suppression of Algerian resistance, turned the artillery on the workers. More than 1,500 were killed and 12,000 arrested and exiled.

A reasonably democratic constitution was drawn up and elections called to choose a president. To everyone's surprise, Louis-Napoleon, nephew of the Emperor, romped home. In spite of his liberal reputation, he restricted the vote again, censored the press and pandered to the Catholic church. In 1852, following a coup and further street-fighting, he had himself proclaimed Emperor Napoleon III.

Second Empire: 1852–70

Through the 1850s **Napoleon III** ran an authoritarian regime whose most notable achievement was a rapid growth in industrial and economic power. Foreign trade trebled, the railway system grew enormously, the first investment banks were established and so on. In 1858, in the aftermath of an attempt on

his life by an Italian patriot, the Emperor suddenly embarked on a policy of **liberalisation**, first the economy, which alienated much of the business class. Additional reforms included the right to form trade unions and to strike, an extension of public education, lifting of censorship and the granting of ministerial 'responsibility' under a government headed by the liberal opposition.

Disaster, however, was approaching on the diplomatic front. Involved in a conflict with Bismarck and the rising power of Germany, Napoleon declared war. The French army was quickly defeated and the Emperor himself taken prisoner in 1870. The result at home was a universal demand for the proclamation of a republic. The German armistice agreement insisted on the election of a national assembly to negotiate a proper peace treaty. France lost Alsace and Lorraine, and was obliged to pay hefty war reparations.

Outraged by the monarchist majority returned to the new Assembly and by its chief minister, Thiers', attempt to disarm the National Guard, the people of Paris created their own municipal government, known as **the Commune** (see p. 62).

The Third Republic and the rise of Socialism

Ironically, although **Thiers'** ruthless repression of the Commune decapitated the working-class movement for several years to come, it also strengthened support for the Republic, by reassuring the conservative countryside that Republicanism did not mean subversion. By 1875, having eluded various attempts to restore the monarchy, the Republic began to look as if it were there to stay. The conservative forces predominated through the 1870s. One of their premiers, Jules Ferry, was responsible for creating a free, secular, compulsory public education system and – less laudably – the basis of the French colonial empire in south-east Asia, Tunisia and Madagascar.

In 1889 the collapse of a company set up to build the Panama Canal tainted several members of the government with corruption, which was one factor in the dramatic **Socialist gains** in the elections of 1893. More importantly, the urban working class were becoming more class-conscious under the influence of the ideas of Karl Marx. The strength of the movement, however, was undermined by divisions, the chief one being Jules Guesde's Marxian Party. Among the independent Socialists was **Jean Jaurès**, who joined with Guesde in 1905 to found the **Parti Socialiste**, Section Française de l'Internationale Ouvrière (SFIO). The trade union movement, unified in 1895 as the **Confédération Générale du Travail** (CGT), remained aloof in its anarcho-syndicalist preference for direct action.

The Dreyfus affair

In 1894 **Captain Dreyfus**, a Jewish army officer, was convicted by court-martial of spying for the Germans and shipped off to the penal colony of Devil's Island for life. It soon became clear that he had been framed — by the army itself, yet they refused to reconsider his case. The affair immediately became an issue between the Catholic right-wing and the Republican left, with Jaurès, Emile Zola and Clémenceau coming out in favour of Dreyfus. Charles Maurras, founder of the racist and fascist *Action Française* – precursor of Europe's Blackshirts and Le Pen's National Front – took the part of the army. Though Dreyfus was officially rehabilitated in 1904 (his health ruined by penal servitude in the tropics), the issue is still considered sufficiently sensitive in the traditionalist, aristocratic ranks of the officer class for the Mitterand government to have changed its plans to site a specially commissioned statue.

In the wake of the affair the more radical element in the Republican movement dominated the administration, bringing the army under closer civilian control and dissolving most of the religious orders.

Although the country enjoyed a period of renewed prosperity in the run-up to the First World War, there remained serious unresolved conflicts in the political fabric of French society. On the right, Maurras' lunatic fringe with its strong-arm *Camelots du Roi* and, on the left, the far bigger constituency of the working class was simply not represented in government. Although most workers now voted for it, the Socialist Party was not permitted to participate in bourgeois governments under the constitution of the Second

International, to which it belonged. Anyway, the government had given clear signs of its unwillingness to accommodate working-class interests in the brutal repression of several major strikes.

The First World War

When the time came the hitherto anti-militarist trade union and Socialist leaders (Jaurès was assassinated in 1914) rallied to the flag. The cost of **the war** was even greater for France than for the other participants because it was fought out on French soil. Over a quarter of the 8 million men called up were either killed or crippled. And industrial production fell to 60 per cent of the pre-war level. Combined with memories of the Prussian war of 1870, this was the reason why the French were more aggressive than either the British or the Americans in seeking war damages from the Germans.

In the **post-war struggle for recovery** the interests of the urban working class were again passed over, with the exception of Clémenceau's 8-hour day legislation in 1919. An attempted general strike in 1920 came to nothing, and the workers' strength was again weakened by the formation of new Catholic and Communist unions, and most of all by the irredeemable split in the Socialist Party at the 1920 Congress of Tours. The pro-Lenin majority formed the **French Communist Party**, while the minority faction, under the leadership of Léon Blum, retained the old SFIO title. The bitterness caused by this split has bedevilled the French Left ever since. Both parties resolutely stayed away from government.

As **Depression** deepened in the 1930s and Nazi power across the Rhine became more menacing, fascist thuggery and anti-parliamentary activity increased in France, culminating in a pitched battle outside the Chamber of Deputies in February 1934. (Léon Blum was only saved from being lynched by a funeral cortege through the intervention of some building workers who happened to notice what was going on in the street below.) The effect of this fascist activism was to unite the Left, including the Communists led by the Stalinist Maurice Thorez, in the **Popular Front**. When they won the 1936 elections with a handsome majority in the Chamber, there followed a wave of strikes and factory sit-ins – a spontaneous expression of working-class determination to get their just desserts after a century and a half of frustration. Frightened by the apparently revolutionary situation, the major employers signed the Matignon Agreement with Blum, which provided for wage increases, nationalisation of the armaments industry and partial nationalisation of the Bank of France, a 40-hour week, paid annual leave and collective bargaining on wages. These **reforms** were pushed through parliament, but when Blum tried to introduce exchange controls to check the flight of capital, the Senate threw the proposal out and he resigned. The Left returned to Opposition, where it remained with the exception of coalition governments until 1981. Most of the Popular Fronts reforms were promptly undone.

The Second World War

The agonies of the Second World War were compounded for France by the additional traumas of occupation, collaboration, and Resistance – in effect, a covert civil war. After the 1940 defeat of the Anglo-French forces, Marshal Pétain, a cautious and conservative veteran of the First World War, emerged from retirement to sign an armistice with Hitler and head the collaborationist **Vichy government**, which ostensibly governed the southern part of the country, while the Germans occupied the strategic north and the Atlantic coast. His Prime Minister, Laval, believed it his duty to adapt France to the new authoritarian age heralded by the Nazi conquest of Europe.

There has been endless controversy over who collaborated, how much and how far it was necessary in order to save France from even worse sufferings. One thing at least is clear: Nazi occupation provided a splendid opportunity for the Maurras breed of out-and-out French fascist to go on the rampage, tracking down Communists, Jews, Resistance fighters, Freemasons, indeed all those who, in their demonology, were considered 'alien' bodies in French society.

While some Communists were involved in **the Resistance** right from the start, Hitler's attack on the Soviet Union in 1941 freed the remainder from ideological inhibitions and brought them into the movement on a large scale. Resistance numbers were further increased by young men taking to the hills to escape conscription as labour in Nazi industry. Général de Gaulle's radio appeal from London on 18 June 1940 rallied Frenchmen opposed to right-wing defeatism, and resulted in the *Conseil National de la Résistance*, unifying the different Resistance groups in May 1943. The man to whom this task had been entrusted was Jean Moulin, shortly to be captured by the Gestapo and tortured to death by Klaus Barbie, awaiting trial for war crimes in Lyon jail at the time of writing.

Although British and American governments found him irksome, **de Gaulle** was able to impose himself as the unchallenged spokesman of the Free French, leader of a government in exile, and to insist that the voice of France be heard as an equal in the Allied councils of war. Even the Communists accepted his leadership, though he was far from representing the kind of political interests they could sympathise with.

Thanks, however, to his persistence, representatives of his provisional government moved into liberated areas of France behind the Allied advance after D-day, thereby saving the country from what would certainly have been at least localised outbreaks of civil war. It was also thanks to his insistence that Free French units, notably General Leclerc's 2nd Armoured Division, were allowed to perform the psychologically vital role of being the first Allied troops to enter Paris, Strasbourg and other emotionally important towns in France. Symbolic acts, perhaps, nonetheless important for that, despite the sometimes disdainful attitude of Anglo-Saxons.

The aftermath of war

France emerged from the war demoralised, bankrupt and bombwrecked. The only possible provisional government in the circumstances was de Gaulle's **Free French** and the *Conseil National de la Résistance* which meant a coalition of left and right. In order to deal with the shambles coalmines, air transport and Renault cars were nationalised as an opening move. But a new constitution was required and **elections**, in which French women voted for the first time, returned a large left majority for the new Constituent Assembly, which, however, soon fell to squabbling over the form of the new constitution. De Gaulle resigned in disgust. If he was hoping for a wave of popular sympathy, he didn't get it and retired to the country to sulk.

The constitution finally agreed on, with little enthusiasm in the country, was not much different from the discredited Third Republic. And the new **Fourth Republic** appropriately began its life with a series of short-lived coalitions. In the early days the foundation for welfare were laid, banks nationalised and trade union rights extended. With the exclusion of the Communists from government in 1947, however, thanks to the Cold War and the carrot of American aid under the Marshall Plan, France found itself once more dominated by the right.

If the post-Liberation desire for political reform was quickly frustrated, the spirit that inspired it did bear fruit in other spheres. From being still a rather backward and largely agricultural economy pre-war, France in the 1950s achieved enormous industrial **modernisation and expansion**, its growth rate even rivalling that of West Germany at times. In foreign policy it opted to remain in the US fold, at the same time as taking the initiative in promoting closer **European integration**, first through the European Coal and Steel Community and then, in 1957, through membership of the EEC.

In its **colonial policy**, on the other hand, the Fourth Republic seemed firmly stuck in antiquated imperialist attitudes. The vaguely cosmetic reform of renaming the Empire the French Union brought little result. In 1945, on the surrender of Japan to the Allies, the northern half of the French **Indochina** colony came under the control of Ho Chi Minh and his Communist Vietmin. Attempts to negotiate were bungled and there began an eight-year armed struggle which ended with French defeat at Dien Bien Phu and partition of the country at the Geneva Conference in 1954. At which point the Americans took over in the south with well known consequences.

1954 was also the year in which the government decided to create an **independent nuclear arsenal** and got embroiled in the horrendous **Algerian war of liberation**. If you want to take a charitable view, you can say that the situation was complicated from the

French viewpoint by the legal fiction that Algeria was a *département*, an integral part of France; there were a million or so settlers or *pieds noirs* claiming to be French – and there was oil in the south. But by 1958 half a million troops, most of them conscripts, had been committed to the war, with all the attendant horrors of torture, massacre of civilian populations and so forth. When it began to appear in 1958 that the government would take a more liberal line, the hardline rightists among the settlers and in the army staged a putsch on 13 May and threatened to declare war on France. Général de Gaulle, waiting in the wings to resume his mission to save France, let it be known that in its hour of need and with certain conditions – i.e. stronger powers for the President – the country might call upon his help. Thus, on 1 June 1958, the National Assembly voted him full powers for six months and the Fourth Republic came to an end.

De Gaulle for President

As Prime Minister, then President, of the **Fifth Republic** – with powers much strengthened as he had wished – **de Gaulle** wheeled and dealed with the *pieds noirs* and Algerian rebels, while the war continued. In 1961 a General Salan staged a military revolt and set up the OAS (secret army) organisation to prevent a settlement. When his coup failed, his organisation made several attempts on de Gaulle's life – thereby strengthening the feeling on the mainland that it was time to be shot of Algeria. Eventually in 1962 a referendum gave an overwhelming yes to Algerian independence and pieds noirs refugees flooded into France to provide a rich recruiting source for every brand of fascist or racist activity. Most of the rest of the French colonial empire had achieved independence by this time also.

De Gaulle's style of leadership was haughty and autocratic, more concerned with gloire and grandeur than the everyday problems of ordinary lives. His quirky strutting on the world stage irritated the hell out of France's partners. He blocked British entry to the EEC, cultivated the friendship of the Germans, rebuked the US for its imperialist policies in Vietnam, withdrew from NATO, refused to sign a nuclear test ban treaty and called for a 'free Quebec'. If this projection of French influence was pleasing to some, the very narrowly won presidential election of 1965 (in which Mitterrand was the other contender) showed that a good half of French voters would not be sorry to see the back of the General.

But notwithstanding a certain domestic discontent, the sudden explosion of **May 1968** took everyone by surprise. Beginning with protests against the paternalistic nature of the education system by students at the University of Nanterre, the movement of revolt rapidly spread to the Sorbonne and out into factories and offices. On the night of 10 May barricades went up in the streets of the Quartier Latin in Paris and the CRS responded by wading into everyone, including bystanders and Red Cross volunteers with unbelievable ferocity. A general strike followed, and within a week more than a million people were out, with numerous factory occupations and professionals joining in with journalists striking for freedom of expression, doctors setting up new radically organised practices and so forth. Autogestion – workers' participation – was the dominant slogan. More than specific demands for reform, there was a general feeling that the whole of French institutions needed overhauling: they were too rigid, too hierarchical, too elitist.

De Gaulle seemed to lose his nerve and on 27 May he vanished from the scene. It turned out he had gone to assure himself of the support of the commander of the French army of the Rhine. On his return he appealed to the nation to elect him as the only effective barrier against left-wing dictatorship and dissolved parliament. The frightened silent majority voted massively Gaullist.

Although there were few short-term radical changes (except in education), the shockwaves of May 1968 continue to be felt. Women's Liberation, ecology groups, a gradual relaxing of the formality of French society, a lessening of authoritarianism – all these can be traced to the heady days of May.

Having petulantly staked his presidency on the outcome of yet another referendum on a couple of constitutional amendments and lost, de Gaulle once more took himself sulkily off to his country estate, and retirement.

After de Gaulle

De Gaulle was succeeded as President by his business-oriented ex-Prime Minister, **Pompidou,** who reckoned that wealth, property and competition would solve all the ills of society. In 1972 the much dreamed of and never credible Union de la Gauche came into being – a radical joint manifesto by Communists and Socialists. But Mitterrand did not use it for the Presidential election of 1974 after Pompidou's sudden death, and lost by a narrow margin to Pompidou's finance minister **Valéry Giscard d'Estaing.**

Having announced that his aim was to make France 'an advanced liberal society', Giscard opened his term of office with some spectacular media coups, like inviting Parisian dustmen to breakfast and visiting prisons in Lyon. But apart from reducing the voting age to 18 and liberalising divorce, the advanced liberal society did not make a lot of progress. In the wake of the 1974 oil crisis the government introduced economic austerity measures. Giscard fell out with his ambitious Prime Minister, **Jacques Chirac,** who set out to challenge the leadership with his own RPR party. And in addition to his superior, monarchical style, Giscard further compromised his popularity by accepting diamonds from the child-eating emperor of Central Africa, Bokassa, and by involvement in various other scandals.

The left seemed well placed to win the coming 1978 elections, when the fragile Union cracked, as the Communists began to fear that the Socialists' rising popularity would turn them into the coalitition's junior partners. The result was another right-wing victory, with Giscard able to form a new government, albeit with the grudging support of the RPR. Law and Order and immigrant controls were the dominant features of Giscard's second term. At last in 1981, the seemingly impossible happened. **Mitterrand** was elected President and in the ensuing general election, for the first time in a quarter of a century, the Socialists were returned with a comfortable majority and much rejoicing.

With four Communists in minor ministerial posts to forestall outflanking on the left, they embarked on a programme of nationalisations, increases in social security benefits and the minimum wage, some measures of decentralisation in favour of the regions, the abolition of the death penalty and the imposition of a surtax on higher incomes, backed by talk of a wealth tax. In foreign policy the came out heavily in favour of NATO and Euromissiles. By 1982, feeling the pinch of recession, the government had begun to backtrack, with wage freezes and other austerity measures to reassure business confidence. In 1984 Laurent Fabius, a centrist Mitterrand protégé, replaced the old Socialist mayor of Lille, Pierre Mauroy, as Prime Minister and the Communists promptly withdrew from the government.

Today, with some 2 million unemployed, the government is playing it safe and traditional on the domestic economic front, while continuing to make the right ideological noises about the support for the Sandinistas and sanctions against South Africa. There is, however, no sign of relenting on the continuation of the French independent nuclear deterrent and little sympathy was shown to demands for independence in the Pacific dependence of Nouvelle Calédonie.

Feeling in the country is running high against the Socialists and they seem well set to lose the national Assembly elections in 1986, with Le Pen's fascist National Front picking up support from every conceivable breed of reactionary discontent in the meantime.

ART AND ARCHITECTURE

These are necessarily the briefest of introductions to the subjects, intended as working references to the country's innumerable galleries, collections and monuments.

Painting

From the Middle Ages to the 20C, France has held – with occasional gaps – a leading position in the history of European painting, with Paris, above all, attracting artists from the whole continent. The story of French painting is one of richness and complexity, partly due to this influx of foreign painters and partly due to the capital's stability as an artistic centre.

Beginnings

In the late Middle Ages, the itinerant life of the nobles led them to prefer small and transportable works of art; splendidly **illuminated manuscripts** were much praised and the best painters, usually trained in Paris, continued to work on a small scale until the 15C. In spite of the size of the illuminated image, painters made startling steps towards a realistic interpretation of the world, and in the exploration of new subject matters. Many of these illuminators were also panel painters, foremost of whom was **Jean Fouquet** (c. 1420–c. 1481), born in Tours in the Loire valley, and the central artistic personality of 15C France. Court-painter to Charles VIII, Fouquet drew from both Flemish and Italian sources, utilising the new, fluid oil technique that had been perfected in Flanders, and concerning himself with the problem of representing space convincingly, much like his Italian contemporaries. Through this he moulded a distinct personal style, combining richness of surface with broad, generalised forms, and in his feeling for volume and ordered, geometric shapes, laying down principles which became intrinsic to French art for centuries to come, from Poussin to Seurat and Cézanne.

Two other 15C French artists deserve brief mention here, principally for the broad range of artistic expression they embody. **Enguerrand Quarton** (c. 1410–c. 1466) was the most famous Provençal painter of the time, and his art, profoundly religious in subject as well as feeling, shows already the impact of the Mediterranean sun in the strong light which pervaded his paintings. His *Pietà* in the Louvre is both stark and intensely poignant, while the *Coronation of the Virgin* that hangs at Villeneuve-les-Avignon is a vast panoramic vision not only of heaven but also of a very real earth, in what ranks as one of the first city/landscapes in the history of French painting: Avignon itself is faithfully depicted and the Mont Ste-Victoire, later to be made famous by Cézanne, is clearly recognisable in the distance. The **Master of Moulins**, active in the 1480s and 1490s, was noticeably more northern in temperament, painting both religious altarpieces and portraits commissioned by members of the royal family or the fast-increasing bourgeoisie.

Mannerism and the influence of Italy

At the end of the 15C and the beginning of the 16C, the French invasion of Italy brought both artists and patrons into closer contact with the Italian Renaissance. Some artists were lured to France, not always successfully, the most famous of them, **Leonardo da Vinci**, spending the last three years of his life (1516–19) at the court of François I. From the Loire valley, which until then had been his favourite residence, the French king moved nearer to Paris, where he had several palaces decorated. Italian artists were once again called upon and two of them, **Rosso** and **Primaticcio**, who arrived in France in 1530 and 1532, were to shape the artistic scene in France for the rest of the 16C. Both artists introduced to France the latest Italian style, **Mannerism**, a sometimes anarchic derivation of the High Renaissance of Michelangelo and Raphael. Mannerism, with its emphasis on the fantastic, the luxurious and the large-scale decorative was eminently compatible with the taste of the court, and it was first put to the test in the revamping of the old castle of Fountainebleau. There, a hoard of French painters headed by the two

Italians came to form what was subsequently called the **School of Fontainebleau**. Most French artists worked at Fontainebleau at some point in their career, or were influenced by its homogenous style, but none stand out as personalities of any stature, and for the most part the painting of the time was dull and fanciful in the extreme. **Antoine Caron** (c. 1520–c. 1600), who often worked for Catherine de Médicis, the widow of Henry II, contrived complicated allegorical paintings in which elongated figures are disposed within wide theatre-like scenery packed with ancient monuments and Roman statues. Even the Wars of Religion, raging in the 1550s and 1560s, failed to rouse French artists' sense of drama, and representations of the many massacres then going on were detached and fussy in tone.

Portraiture tended to be more inventive. The portraits of **Jean Clouet** (c. 1485–1541) and his son **François** (c. 1510–72), both official painters to François I, combined sensitivity in the rendering of the sitter's features with a keen sense of abstract design in the arrangement of the figure, conveying with great clarity social status and giving clues to their profession. Though influenced by 16C Italian and Flemish portraits, their work remains nonetheless very French in its general sobriety.

The 17C

In the 17C Italy continued to be a source of inspiration for French artists, most of whom were drawn to Rome, then the most exciting artistic centre in Europe. There, two Italian artists especially dominated the scene in the first decade of the century: Michelangelo Merisi da Caravaggio and Annibale Carracci. **Caravaggio** (d. 1610) often chose low-life subjects and treated them with remarkable realism, a realism which he extended to traditional religious subject matter and which he enhanced by using a strong, harsh lighting technique. Although he had to flee Rome in great haste under sentence of murder in 1606, Caravaggio's art had a profound effect both in terms of subjects and its uncompromising realism. Some French painters like **Moise Valentin** (c. 1594–1632) worked in Rome and were directly influenced by Caravaggio; others, such as the great painter from Lorraine, **Georges de la Tour** (1593–1652),

benefited from his innovations at second hand, gaining inspiration from the Utrecht Caravaggisti who were active at the time in Holland. Starting with a descriptive realism in which naturalistic detail made for a varied painted surface, La Tour gradually simplified both forms and surfaces, producing deeply felt religious paintings in which figures appear as carved out of the surrounding gloom by the magical light of a candle. Sadly, his output was very small – just some forty or so works in all. Low-life subjects and attention to naturalistic detail were also important aspects of the work of the **Le Nain Brothers**, especially **Louis** (1593–1648), who depicted with great sympathy, but never with sentimentality, the condition of the peasantry. He chose moments of inactivity or repose within the lives of the peasants and his paintings achieve timelessness and monumentality by their very stillness.

The other Italian artist of influence, the Bolognese **Annibale Carracci** (d. 1609), impressed French painters not only with his skill as a decorator but, more tellingly, with his ordered, balanced landscapes, which were to prove of prime importance for the development of the classical landscape in general and in particular for those by **Claude Lorrain** (1600–82). Claude, who started life as a pastry cook, was born in Lorraine, near Nancy. He left France for Italy to practise his trade and worked in the household of a landscape painter in Rome, somehow persuading his master, who painted landscapes in the classical manner of Carracci, to let him abandon pastry for painting. Later he travelled to Naples, where the beauty of the harbour and bay made a lasting impression on him, the golden light of the southern port, and of Rome and its surrounding countryside, providing him with endless subjects of study which he drew, sketched and painted for the rest of his life. Claude's landscapes are airy compositions in which religious or mythological figures are lost within an idealised, Arcadian nature, bathed in a luminous, transparent light which, golden or silvery, lends a tranquil mood.

Landscapes, harsher and even more ordered, but also recalling the Arcadian mood of antiquity, were painted by the other French painter who elected to make Rome his home, **Nicolas Poussin**

(1593–1665). Like Claude, Poussin selected his themes from the rich sources of Greek, Roman and Christian myths and stories, but unlike Claude, his figures are not subdued by nature but rather dominate it, in the tradition of the masters of the High Renaissance, like Raphael and Titian, whom he greatly admired. During the working out of a painting Poussin would make small models, arrange them on an improvised stage and then sketch the puppet scene – something which may explain why his figures often have a still, frozen quality. Poussin only briefly returned to Paris, called by the king, Louis XIII, to undertake some large decorative works quite unsuited to his style or character. Back in Rome he refined a style which became increasingly classical and severe. Many other artists visited Italy but most returned to France, the luckiest to be employed at the court to boost the royal images of Louis XIII and XIV and the egos of their respective ministers, Richelieu and Colbert. **Simon Vouet** (1590–1649), **Charles Le Brun** (1619–90) and **Pierre Mignard** (1612–95) all performed that task with skill, often using ancient history and mythology to suggest flattering comparisons with the reigning monarch. The official aspect of their works was paralleled by the creation of the new **Academy of Painting and Sculpture** in 1648, an institution which dominated the arts in France for the next few hundred years, if only by the way artists reacted against it. Only **Philippe de Champaigne** (1602–74), a painter of Flemish origin, stands out at the time as remotely different, removed from the intrigues and pleasures of the court and instead strongly influenced by the teaching and moral code of Jansenism, a purist and severe form of the Catholic faith. The apparent simplicity and starkness of his portraits hides an unusually perceptive understanding of his sitters' personalities. But it was the more courtly, fun-loving portraits and paintings by artists like Mignard which were to influence most of the art of the following century.

The early 18C
The semi-official art encouraged by the foundation of the Academy became more frivolous and lighthearted in the 18C. The court at Versailles lost its attractions and many patrons now were to be found in the hedonistic bourgeoisie and aristocracy living in Paris. History painting, as opposed to genre scenes or portraiture, retained its position of prestige, but at the same time the various categories began to merge and many artists tried their hands at landscape, genre, history or decorative works, bringing aspects of one type into another. **Salons**, at which painters exhibited their works, were held with increasing frequency, and bred a new, and some would say dangerous, phenomenon in the art world, the art critic. The philosopher **Diderot** was one of the first of these arbiters of taste, doers and undoers of reputations.

Possibly the most complex personality of the 18C was **Jean-Antoine Watteau** (1684–1721). Primarily a superb draughtsman, Watteau's use of soft and yet rich, light colours showed how much he was struck by the great 17C Flemish painter, Rubens. The open air scenes of flirtatious love painted by Rubens and by the 16C Venetian Giorgione provided Watteau with precedents for his own subtle depictions of dreamy couples (sometimes derived from characters from the Italian Comedy) strolling in delicate, fairy landscapes. In some of these *Fêtes Galantes* and in pictures of solitary musicians or actors (*Gilles*), Watteau conveyed a mood of melancholy, loneliness and poignancy which was quite lacking in the works of his many imitators and followers (Nicolas Lancret, J B Pater). The work of **François Boucher** (1703–70) was probably more representative of the 18C: the pleasure-seeking court of Louis XV found the lightness of morals and colours in his paintings immensely congenial. Boucher's virtuosity is seen at its best when painting women, always rosy, young, delectable and dreamily erotic. **Jean-Honoré Fragonard** (1732–1806) continued this exploration of licentious themes but with an exuberance, a richness of colour and a vitality (*The Swing*) which was a feast for the eyes and raised the subject to a glorification of love. Far more restrained were the paintings of **Jean-Baptiste-Siméon Chardin** (1699–1779), who specialised in homely genre scenes and still-lives, painted with a simplicity which belied a complex use of colours, shapes and space to promote a mood of stillness and tranquillity. **Jean-Baptiste Greuze**

(1725–1805) chose stories which anticipated a reaction against the laxity of the times; the moral and sometimes sentimental character of his paintings was all-pervasive, reinforced by a stage-like composition well suited to cautionary tales.

Neoclassicism

This new seriousness became more severe with the rise of **Neoclassicism**, a movement for which purity and simplicity were essential components of the systematic depiction of edifying stories from the classical authors. Roman history and legends were the most popular subjects, and though **Jacques-Louis David** (1748–1825), a pupil of an earlier exponent of Neoclassicism, J M Vien, fell in with that to a certain extent, he was different in that he was also keenly sensitive to the changing mood and philosophies of his time, and to the reaction against frivolity and self-indulgence. Many of his paintings are reflections of Republican ideals and of contemporary history, from the *Death of Marat* to events from the life of Napoleon who patronised him. For the Emperor and his family David painted some of his most successful portraits – *Madame Recamier* is not only an exquisite example of David's controlled use of shapes and space and his debt to antique Rome, but can also be seen as a paradigm of Neoclassicism. Two painters, **Jean-Antoine Gros** (1771–1835) and **Baron Gérard** (1770–1837), followed David closely, in style and in themes (portraits, Napoleonic history and legend) but often with a touch of softness and heroic poetry which pointed the way to Romanticism.

Jean-August-Dominique Ingres (1780–1867) was a pupil of David; he also studied in Rome before coming back to Paris to develop the purity of line that was the essential and characteristic element of his art. The effective use he made of it, to build up forms and bind compositions, can be admired in conjunction with his recurrent theme of female nudes bathing, or in his magnificent and stately portraits which depict with subtle accuracy the nuances of social status.

Romanticism

Completely opposed to the stress on drawing advocated by Ingres, two artists created, through their emphasis on colours, forms and compositions, pictures which look forward to the later part of the 19C and the Impressionists. **Theodore Gericault** (1791–1824), whose short life was still dominated by the heroic vision of the Napoleonic era, explored with feeling dramatic themes of human suffering in paintings like *The Raft of Medusa*, while his close contemporary, **Eugène Delacroix** (1798–1863), epitomised the **Romantic movement**, its search for emotions and its love of nature, power and change. Delacroix was deeply aware of tradition, and his art was influenced, visually and conceptually, by the great masters of the Renaissance and the 17C and 18C. In many ways he may be regarded as the last great religious and decorative French painter, but through his technical virtuosity, freedom of brushwork and richness of colours, he can, too, be seen as the essential forerunner to the Impressionists. For Delacroix there was no conflict between colour and design: David and Ingres saw these elements as separate aspects of creation, but Delacroix used colours as the basis and structure of his designs. His technical freedom was partly due to his admiration for two English painters, John Constable and his close friend, Richard Parkes Bonington, with whom he shared a studio for a few months; Bonington especially had a freshness of approach to colour and a free handling of paint which had a strong impact on Delacroix. His themes were numerous, and ranged from intimate female nudes, often with mysterious and erotic Middle Eastern overtones, to studies of animals and hunting scenes. Ancient and contemporary history supplied him with some of his most harrowing and dramatic paintings: *The Massacre at Chios*, was based on an event which took place during the Greek wars of independence from the Turks, and *Liberty guiding the People* was painted to commemorate the revolution of 1830. Both paintings were his personal response to contemporary events and the human tragedies they entailed. Other painters working in the romantic tradition were still haunted by the Napoleonic legends, by North Africa (Algeria) and the Middle East, which had become better known to artists and patrons alike during the Napoleonic wars. These were the subjects of many paintings by **Horace Vernet** (1789–1863) and **Jean-Louis-Ernest Meissonier** (1815–91) and **Théodore Chassériau** (1819–56). Among their contemporaries was **Honoré Daumier** (1808–79): very much an isolated figure, influenced by the boldness of approach of caricaturists, he was content to depict everyday subjects such as a laundress or a third class railway carriage – caustic commentaries on professions and politics that work as brilliant observations of the times.

The 19C: landscape and realism

But some painters of the first part of the 19C were fascinated by other themes. Nature, in its true state, unadorned by conventions, became a subject for study, and, running parallel to this, was the realisation that painting could be the visual externalisation of the artist's own emotions and feelings. These two aspects, which had until then only been very tentatively touched upon, were now more fully explored and led directly to the innovations of the Impressionists and later painters. **Jean-Baptiste-Camille Corot** (1796–1875) started to paint landscapes that were fresh, direct and influenced as much by the unpretentious and realistic country scenes of 17C Holland as the balanced compositions of Claude. His loving and attentive studies of nature were much admired by later artists, including Monet.

At the same time a whole group of painters developed similar attitudes to landscape and nature. Helped greatly by the practical improvement of being able to buy oil paint in tubes, rather than as unmixed pigments, they – known as the **Barbizon School** after the village on the outskirts of Paris around which they painted – soon discovered the joy and excitement of *plein-air* (open air) painting. **Theodore Rousseau** (1812–67) was their nominal leader, his paintings of forest undergrowth and forest clearings displaying an intimacy that came from the immediacy of the image. **Charles-François Daubigny** (1817–78), like Rousseau, often infused a sense of drama into his landscapes. **Jean-François Millet** is perhaps the best known associate of the Barbizon group, though he was more interested in the human figure than simple nature. Landscapes, however, were essential settings for his figures; indeed, his most

famous pictures are those exploring the place of Man in Nature and his struggle to survive. *The Sower*, for instance, was a typical Millet theme, suggesting the heroic working life of the peasant. As is so often the case for painters touching on new themes or on ideas which are uncomfortable to the rich and powerful, Millet enjoyed little success during his lifetime, and his art was only widely recognised after his death.

The moralistic and romantic undertone in Millet's work was something which **Gustave Courbet** (1819–77) strove to avoid. Courbet was a socialist, and his frank, outspoken attitude led to his being accused of taking part in the destruction of the column in the place Vendôme after the outbreak of the Commune and, eventually, to his exile. After an initial resounding success in the Salon exhibition of 1849, he endured constant criticism from the academic world and patrons alike: scenes of ordinary life, like the *Funeral at Orneans*, which he often chose to depict, were regarded as unsavoury and deliberately ugly. But Courbet had a deep admiration for the old masters, especially for Rembrandt and the Spanish painters of the 17C and 18C, and his link with tradition was probably one of the underlying themes of his large masterpiece, *The Studio*, which was emphatically rejected by the jury of the 1855 Exposition Universelle, and in which Courbet portrayed himself, surrounded by his model, his friends, colleagues and admirers, among them the poet Baudelaire. Courbet subsequently decided to hold a private exhibition of some forty of his works, writing at the same time a manifesto explaining his intentions of being true to his vision of the world and of creating 'living art'. By writing the word **Realism** in large letters on the door leading to the exhibition he stated his intentions and gave a label to his art.

Impressionism

Like Courbet, **Edouard Manet** (1832–83) was strongly influenced by Spanish painters, whose works had become more easily available to artists when a large collection belonging to the Orleans family was confiscated by the state in 1848. Unlike Courbet, though, he never saw himself as a socialist or indeed as a rebel or avant-garde painter, yet his technique and interpretation of themes was quite new and shocked as many people as it inspired. Manet used bold contrasts of light and very dark colours, giving his paintings a forcefulness which critics often took for lack of sophistication. And his detractors saw much to decry in his reworking of an old subject originally treated by the 16C Venetian painter Giorgione, *Le Déjeuner sur l'Herbe*. Manet's version was shocking because he placed naked and dressed figures together, and because the men were dressed in the costume of the day, implying a pleasure party too specifically contemporary to be 'respectable'. Manet was not interested in painting moral lessons, however, and some of his most successful pictures are reflections of ordinary life in bars and public places, where respectability, as understood by the late 19C bourgeoisie, was certainly lacking. To Manet, painting was to be enjoyed for its own sake and not as a tool for moral instruction – in itself an outlook on the role of art that was quite new, not to say revolutionary, and marked a definite break with the paintings of the past. With Manet the basis of our present expectation and understanding of modern art was laid down.

Although it is doubtful whether Manet either wanted or expected to assume the role of leader, **Claude Monet** (1840–1926) looked to the older artist as the painter in whose works the principles of **Impressionism** were first formulated. Born in Le Havre, Monet came in contact with **Eugène Boudin** (1824–98) whose colourful beach scenes anticipated the way Impressionists approached colours. He then went to Paris to study under Charles Gleyre, a respected teacher in whose studio he met many of the men with whom he formulated his ideas. Monet soon discovered that, for him, light and the way in which it builds up forms and creates an infinity of colours was the element which governed all representations. Under the impact of Manet's bright hues and his unconventional attitude, 'art for art's sake', Monet soon began using pure colours side by side, blending together to create areas of brightness and shade.

In 1874, a group of some thirty artists exhibited together for the first time. Among them were some of the best known names of this period of French art: Dégas, Monet, Renoir, Pissarro. One of Monet's paintings was entitled *Impression: Sun Rising*, a title which was singled out by the critics to ridicule the colourful, loose and non-academic style of these young artists. Overnight they became derisively, the 'Impressionists'. **Camille Pissarro** (1830–1903) was slightly older than most of them and seems to have played the part of an encouraging father-figure, always keenly aware of any new development or new talent. Not a great innovator himself, Pissarro was a very gifted artist whose use of Impressionist technique was supplemented by a lyrical feeling for nature and its seasonal changes. But it was really with **Monet** that Impressionist theory ran its full course, in the way he studied endlessly the impact of light on objects and the way it reveals colours. To understand this phenomenon better, Monet painted the same motif again and again under different conditions of light, at different times of the day and in different seasons, producing whole series of paintings like *Hay Stacks*, *Poplars* and, much later, his *Waterlilies*. In the late 1870s and the early 1880s many other artists helped formulate the new style, but few remained true to its principles for very long. **Auguste Renoir** (1841–1919), who started life as a painter of porcelain, was swept away by Monet's ideas for a while, but soon felt the need to look again at the old masters and to emphasise the importance of drawing to the detriment of colour. Renoir regarded the representation of the female nude as the most taxing and rewarding subject that an artist could tackle. Like Boucher in the 18C, Renoir's nudes are luscious, but they are rarely, if ever, erotic. They have a healthy uncomplicated quality that was, in his later paintings, to become cloyingly, almost overpoweringly, sickly and sweet. Better were his portraits of women fully clothed, both for their obvious and innate sympathy, and their keen sense of design.

Edgar Degas (1834–1917) was yet another artist who, although he exhibited with the Impressionists, did not follow their precepts very closely. The son of a rich banker, he was trained in the tradition of Ingres: design and drawing were an integral part of his art, and whereas Monet was fascinated mainly by light, Degas wanted to express movement in all its forms. His pictures are vivid expressions of the body in action, usually straining under fairly exacting circumstances – dancers and circus artistes were among his favourite subjects, as well as more mundane depictions of laundresses and working women. Like so many artists of the day, Degas's imagination was fired by the discovery of **Japanese prints**, which could for the first time be seen in quantity and provided him with new ideas of composition, not least in their asymmetry of design and the use of large areas of unbroken colour. **Photography**, too, had an impact on artists, if only because it liberated them finally from the task of producing accurate, exacting descriptions of the world.

Degas's extraordinary gift as a draughtsman was matched only by that of the Provençal aristocrat **Henri de Toulouse-Lautrec** (1864–1901). Toulouse-Lautrec, who had broken both his legs as a child, was unusually small, a physical deformity which made him particularly sensitive to free and vivacious movements. A great admirer of Degas, he chose similar themes: people in cafés and theatres, working women and variety dancers all figured large in his work. But unlike Degas, Toulouse-Lautrec looked at more than the body, and his work is scattered with social comment, sometimes sardonic and bitter. In his portrayal of Paris prostitutes, there is sympathy and kindness, and to study them better he lived in a brothel for some time, revealing in his paintings the weariness and sometimes gentleness of these women rather than the squalor which might have been expected.

Post-Impressionism

Though a rather vague term, since it's difficult to date exactly when the backlash against Impressionism took place, **Post-Impressionism** represents in many ways a return to more formal concepts of painting – in composition, in attitudes to subject and in drawing. **Paul Cézanne** (1839–1906), for one, associated only very briefly with the Impressionists and spent most of his working life in relative isolation, obsessed with rendering, as objectively as possible, the essence of form. He saw objects as basic shapes – cylinders, cones, etc. – and tried to give the painting a unity of texture which would

force the spectator to view it, not so much as a representation of the world but rather as an entity in its own right, as an object as real and dense as the objects surrounding it. It was this striving for pictorial unity that led him to cover the entire surface of the picture with small, equal brushstrokes which made no distinction of texture between a tree, a house or the sky. The detached, unemotional way in which Cézanne painted was not unlike that of the 17C artist Poussin, and he found a contemporary parallel in the work of **Georges Seurat.** Seurat (1859–91) was fascinated by current theories on light and colour, and he attempted to apply them in a systematic way, creating different shades and tones by placing tiny spots of pure colour side by side, which the eye could in turn fuse together to see the colours mixed out of their various components. This **pointillist** technique also had the effect of giving monumentality to everyday scenes of contemporary life.

While Cézanne, Seurat and, come to that, the Impressionists, sought to represent the outside world objectively, several other artists – the **Symbolists** – were seeking a different kind of truth, through the subjective experience of fantasy and dreams. **Gustave Moreau** (1826–98) represented, in complex paintings, the intricate worlds of the romantic fairy tale, his visions expressed in a wealth of naturalistic details. The style of **Puvis de Chavannes** (1824–98) was more restrained and more obviously concerned with design and the decorative. And a third artist, **Odilon Redon** (1840–1916) produced some weird and visionary graphic work which intrigued Symbolist writers especially; his less frequent works in colour belong to the later part of his life.

The subjectivity of the Symbolists was of great importance to the art of **Paul Gauguin** (1843–1903). He started life as a stockbroker who collected Impressionist paintings, a Sunday artist who gave up his job in 1883 to dedicate himself to painting. During his stay in Pont-Aven in Brittany, he worked with a number of artists who called themselves the **Nabis, Paul Serusier** and **Emile Bernard** among them, exploring ways of expressing concepts and emotions by means of large areas of colour and powerful forms, and developing a unique style that was heavily indebted to his knowledge of Japanese prints and of the tapestries and stained glass of medieval art. His search for the primitive expression of primitive emotions took him eventually to the South Sea islands and Tahiti, where he found some of his most inspiring subjects and painted some of his best known canvases. A similar derivation from Symbolist art and a wish to exteriorise emotions and ideas by means of strong colours, lines and shapes underlies the work of **Vincent Van Gogh** (1853–1890), a Dutch painter who came to live in France. Like Gauguin, with whom he had an admiring but stormy friendship, Van Gogh started painting relatively late in life, lightening his palette in Paris under the influence of the Impressionists, and then heading south to Arles where, struck by the harshness of the Mediterranean light, he turned out frantic expressionist pieces like *The Reaper* and *Wheatfield with Crows*. In all his later pictures the paint is thickly laid on in increasingly abstract patterns that follow the shapes and tortuous paths of his deep, inner melancholy.

Both Gauguin and Van Gogh saw objects and colours as means of representing ideas and subjective feeling. **Edouard Vuillard** (1868–1940) and **Pierre Bonnard** (1867–1947) combined this with Cézanne's insistence on unifying the surface and texture of the picture. The result was, in both cases, paintings of often intimate scenes in which figures and objects are blended together in a series of complicated patterns. In some of Vuillard's works especially, people dressed in chequered material, for example, seem to merge into the flowered wallpaper behind them; and in the paintings of Bonnard, the glowing design of the canvas itself is as important as what it's trying to represent.

The 20C: Fauvism, Cubism, Dada and Surrealism

The 20C kicked off to a colourful start with the **Fauvist** exhibition of 1905, an appropriately anarchic beginning to a century which, in France more than anywhere, was to see radical changes in attitudes towards painting. The painters who took part in the exhibition included, most influentially, **Henri Matisse** (1869–1954), and **André Derain**

(1880–1954), **Georges Rouault** (1871–1958) and **Albert Marquet** (1975–1947), and they were quickly nicknamed the Fauves (the Wild Beasts) for their use of bright, wild colours that often bore no relation whatsoever to the reality of the object depicted. Skies were just as likely green as blue since, for the Fauves, colour was a way of composing, of structuring a picture, and not necessarily a reflection of real life.

But Fauvism was just the beginning: the first decades of the 20C were in Paris times of intense excitement and artistic activity, and painters and sculptors from all over Europe flocked to the capital to take part in the liberation from conventional art which individuals and groups were gradually instigating. **Pablo Picasso** (1881–1973) was one of the first, arriving here in 1900 from Spain, and shortly after starting work on his first *Blue Period* paintings, which describe the sad and squalid life of itinerant actors in tones of blue. Later, while Matisse was experimenting with colours and their decorative potential, Piccaso came under the sway of Cézanne and his organisation of forms into geometrical shapes. He also learned from primitive, and especially African, sculpture and out of these studies came a painting which heralded a definite new direction, not only for Picasso's own style, but for the whole of modern art – Les Demoiselles d'Avignon. Executed in 1907, this painting combined Cézanne's analysis of forms with the visual impact of African masks, and it was from this semi-abstract picture that Picasso went on to develop the theory of **Cubism,** inspiring artists like **Georges Braque** (1882–1963) and **Juan Gris** (1887–1927), another Spaniard, and formulating a whole new movement. The Cubists' aim was to depict objects not so much as they saw them but rather as they knew them to be: a bottle, a guitar were shown from the front, from the side and from the back as if the eye could take in all at once every facet and plane of the object. Braque and Picasso first analysed forms into these facets (analytical Cubism), then gradually reduced them to series of colours and shapes (synthetic Cubism), among which a few recognisable symbols such as letters, fragments of newspaper and numbers appeared. The complexity of different planes overlapping one another made the deciphering of Cubist paintings sometimes difficult, and the very last phase of Cubism tended increasingly towards abstraction.

Spin-offs of Cubism were many: movements like **Orphism,** headed by **Robert Delaunay** (1885–1941), who experimented not with objects but with the colours of the spectrum; and **Futurism,** which evolved first in Italy, then in Paris, and explored movement and the bright new technology of the industrial age. **Fernand Leger** (1881–1955), too, one of the main exponents of the so-called School of Paris, had become acquainted with modern machinery during the First World War, and he exploited his fascination for its smoothness and power to create geometric and monumental compositions of technical imagery which were indebted to both Cézanne and Cubism. The war meanwhile had affected many artists: in Switzerland, **Dada** was born out of the scorn artists felt for the petty bourgeois and nationalistic values that had led to the bloodshed, a nihilistic movement that sought to knock down all traditionally accepted ideas. It was best exemplified in the work of the Frenchman **Marcel Duchamp** (1887–1968), who selected ready-made objects of everyday usage and elevated them, without modification, to the rank of works of art by pulling them out of their ordinary context, or defaced sacred cows like the Mona Lisa by decorating her with a moustache and an obscene caption.

Dada was also a literary movement, which through one of its main poets, André Breton, led to the setting out of **Surrealism** as a new conceptual and artistic movement. It was the unconscious and its dark uncharted territories which interested the Surrealists: they derived much of their imagery from Freud and even experimented in words and images with free-association techniques. Strangely enough, most of the 'French' Surrealists were foreigners, primarily the German **Max Ernst** (1891–1976) and the Spaniards **Yves Tanguy** (1900–55) and **Salvador Dali** (b. 1904). Mournful landscapes of weird, often terrifying images evoked our worst nightmares in often very precise details, and with an anguish that went on to influence artists for years to come. Picasso, for instance, shocked by the massacre of the Spanish town of *Guernica* in 1936, drew greatly from Surrealism to produce the disquieting figures of his painting of the same name.

The **Second World War** put an end to the prominence of Paris as the artistic melting pot of Europe. Painters had rushed there at the beginning of the 20C and after the First World War, contributing by their individuality, originality and different nationality to the richness and constant renewal of artistic endeavour, but at the beginning of the Second World War they emigrated to the United States. And although many have since drifted back, artistic leadership has remained in New York, but desertion of Paris should not obscure the fact that over a span of some six centuries, French painters or painters trained or domiciled in France produced some of the most significant monuments of European painting.

ANNE ROOK

Architecture

In common with all former provinces of Rome, it is to that model of organised authority that the official architecture of France has returned most readily. A number of substantial **Roman building works** survive. In Nîmes – the *Maison Carrée* and the *Temple of Diana*, one of four vaulted Roman temples in Europe. *Gateways* remain at Autun and Rheims and *Amphitheatres* can be seen at Nîmes and Arles. The *Pont du Gard* aqueduct at Nîmes is still a magnificent and ageless monument of civil engineering.

The **Carolingian** dynasty of Charlemagne attempted a revival of the symbols of civilised authority by recourse to Roman or 'Romanesque' models. Of this era, practically nothing remains visible, though the motifs of arch and vault are carried on in their simplest forms; and the semicircular apse and the basilican plan of nave and aisles persists as the basis of the succeeding phases of Christian architecture. An interesting anomaly is the plan of the church of *St-Front* at Périgueux, a copy of St Mark's in Venice, brought by trading influence west along the Garonne in the early 12C.

Elsewhere development may be

divided roughly north-south of the Loire. Southern **Romanesque** is naturally more Roman, with stone barrel vaults, aisleless naves, and domes. *St-Trophime* at Arles (1150) has a porch directly derived from Roman models and, with the church at St-Gilles nearby, exhibits a delight in carved ornament peculiar to the south at this time. The *cathedral at Angoulême* typifies the use of all these elements.

The South, too, was the readiest route for the introduction of new cultural developments, and it is here that the pointed arch and vault first appear – from Saracen sources – in churches such as *Notre-Dame* at Avignon, *Autun cathedral* and *Ste-Madeleine* at Vézelay (1089–1206), which contains the earliest pointed cross vault in France.

In the northern region the nave with aisles is more usual, together with the development of twin western towers to mask the end of the aisles. The *Abbaye-aux-Hommes* at Caen (1066–77) is typical. It contains the elements later developed as 'Gothic', in piers, pillars, buttresses, arcades, ribbed vaults and spires. The best examples may be found in Normandy, and it is from here with the introduction of the pointed arch from the south that the Gothic style developed.

The reasons behind the development of the **Gothic style** lie in the pursuit of sensations of the sublime; to achieve great height without apparently great weight would seem to imitate religious ambition. Its development in the north is partly due to the availability of good building stone and soft stone for carving, but perhaps more to the growth of royal aspiration and power based in the Ile de France, which in alliance with the Papacy stimulated the building of the great cathedrals of *Paris, Bourges, Chartres, Laon, Le Mans, Rheims* and *Amiens* in the late 12C and 13C. The Gothic phase can be said to begin with the building of the choir of the *abbey of St-Denis* near Paris in 1140 and to run through to the end of the 15C. Architecturally, it encompasses the development of wider, traceried windows of coloured glass, filling the wall spaces liberated by the refinement of vertical structure; the 'rose' or wheel is an early and especially French feature in window tracery. The glass at Chartres shows better than anywhere the concerted architectural effect of these developments. Another distinctive element is the flying buttress outside the walls to resist the outward push of the vaulting.

In the south, as at Albi and Angers, the great churches are generally broader and simpler in plan and external appearance, with aisles often almost as high as the nave. Many secular buildings survive – some of the most notable the work of Viollet-le-Duc, the pre-eminent 19C restorer – and even whole towns, as at *Carcassonne* and *Aigues Mortes*; Avignon has the *bridge* and the *Papal palace/prison*. Castles, of necessity, lent themselves less to the disappearing walls of the Gothic style. The *Château de Pierrefonds*, as restored by Viollet, may be taken as typical. The walls of many others disappeared by force, not fancy, as gunpowder made them obsolete and a more settled and subjugated order led to the development of château-palaces, such as *Châteaudun* (1441) and *Blois*. The *Château de Josselin* in Brittany, is a marvellous example of the smaller fortresses that became common towards the end of the Gothic period. A series of colonial settlements, the *bastides* of the English occupation, remain in the Dordogne region and are a refreshing antidote to triumphal French bombast.

Quite early in the 16C the influence of the new style of the Italian Renaissance began to appear. Coupled with the persistence of Gothic traditions and the necessity of steep roofs and tall chimneys in a French climate, it appears immediately 'Frenchified' rather than pure importation. The châteaux of kings and courtiers around Paris and in the Loire valley, such as *Blois, Chambord, Chenonceau* and *Fontainebleau* exemplify this style. There is a wholly un-Italian concentration of interest on the skyline and an elaboration of detail in the façades at the expense of the clear modelling of form. With the passing of time, however, the style became more purely classical.

The Louvre in Paris and the Château de Blois are notable examples of the developing **classicism**. The wing of the *Château de Blois*, containing the famous staircase designed for François I in 1515, shows the beginning of an emphasis on horizontal lines and an overlay of Italian motifs on a basically Gothic form. The elevations, designed by Mansart in 1635, though distinctively

French, are just as typically classical.

The *Louvre* even more embodies the whole history of the classical style in France, having been worked over by all the grand names of French architecture from Lescot in the early 16C, via François Mansart and Claude Perrault in the 17C, to the later years of the 19C. A recent turning point appears to be the controversial commission to I M Pei to break the bonds of Rome with the power of his pyramid extension.

It is unfortunate that the Renaissance style in France is chiefly seen in structures like the Louvre and Versailles, which on account of their scale can scarcely be experienced as buildings. That this is the case is largely due to the developing despotism and concentration of power under Louis XIII and XIV. But there was a lighter side to this. François Mansart, at *Blois* and *Maisons Lafitte* (1640), shows a certain suavity and elegance which appears again in the 18C in the town houses of the Rococo period, whose generally reticent exteriors bely the vivacity and charm of the private life within.

Claude Perrault on the other hand (1613–88), who designed the great colonnaded east front of the Louvre, gives an austere face to the official architecture of despotism, magnificent but far too imperial to be much enjoyed by common mortals. The high-pitched roofs which had been almost universal until then, are replaced here by the classical balustrade and pediment, the style grand, but cold and supremely secular. Art and architecture were at the time organised by boards and academies, and in the latter style and employment were strictly controlled by royal direction. Between 1643 and 1774 France was governed by two monarchs, who both ruled by the same maxim – absolute power. With such a limitation of ideas at the source of patronage, it is hardly surprising that there was a certain dullness to the era, at least in the acknowledged monuments of French architecture.

Likewise the churches of the **17C and 18C** have a coldness quite different from the German and Flemish Baroque or the Italian. When the Renaissance style first appeared in the early 16C there was no great need for new church building, the country being so well endowed from the Gothic centuries. *St-Etienne-du-Mont*

(1517–1620) and *St-Eustache* (1532–89), both in Paris, show how old forms persisted with only an overlay of the new style. It is with the Jesuits in the 17C that the church embraced the new style to combat the forces of rational disbelief. In Paris the churches of the *Sorbonne* (1653) and *Val-de-Grâce* (1645) exemplify this, and a good number of other grandiose churches in the **Baroque** style, through *Les Invalides* at the end of the 17C to the *Panthéon* of the late 18C. Here is the church triumphant rather than the state, but no more beguiling.

The architect of Les Invalides was Jules Hardouin Mansart, a product of the academy, who also greatly extended the palace of *Versailles* and so created the cinemascope view of France with that seemingly endless horizon of royalty. As an antidote to this pomposity, the *Petit Trianon* at Versailles is as refreshing now as it was to Louis XV, who built it in 1762 as a place of escape for his mistress. And even more so this is true of that other pearl formed of the grit of boredom in the enclosed world of Versailles – *La Petite Ferme*, where Marie-Antoinette played at milkmaids, which epitomises the Arcadian and 'picturesque' fantasy of the painters Boucher and Fragonard.

The lightness and charm that was undermining official grandeur with Arcadian fancies and Rococo decoration was, however, snuffed out by the Revolution. There is no real Revolutionary architecture, as the necessity of order and authority soon asserted itself and an autocracy every bit as absolute returned with Napoleon, drawing on the old grand manner but with a stronger trace of the stern old Roman. One architect, Claude Ledoux, was highly original and influential, both in England and Germany. And the visionary millennialist Boullée could also be said to be a child of revolutionary times, though it is likely that such men were inspired as much by the rediscovered plainness of the Greek Doric order as by radical politics. In Paris it was not the democratic Doric, but the imperial Corinthian order, which re-emerged triumphant in the church of *the Madeleine* (1806) and, with the *Arc de Triomphe* like some colossal paperweight, reimposed the authority of academic architecture, in contrast to the fancy dress architecture of contemporary Regency England.

The restoration of legitimate monarchy after the **fall of Napoleon** stimulated a revival of interest in older Gothic and early Renaissance styles, which offered a symbol of dynastic reassurance not only to the state but also to the newly rich. So in the private and commercial architecture of the 19C these earlier styles predominate – in mine-owners' villas and bankers' headquarters. By the time we arrive at the mid-19C a neo-Baroque strain had established itself, a style exemplified by Charles Garnier's *Opéra* in Paris (1861–74), which under the heading of Second Empire and with its associations of voluptuous good living and seductive painting and general 'ooh la la' provides probably the most persistent image of France among the non-French – though you should avoid being blinded by Puritan distaste to the splendid spatial and decorative sensations that the style can arouse. It is probably as true in France today as it is in Britain that 19C buildings are due for a reassessment and keener appreciation.

Parallel to correct, official classicism and robust, exuberant, commercial Baroque, there is a third strand running through the 19C which was ultimately more fruitful. The rational engineering approach, embodied in the official **School of Roads and Bridges** and invigorated by the teaching of Viollet-le-Duc who reinterpreted the Gothic style as pure structure, led to the development of new structural techniques out of which 'modern' architectural style was born. Iron was the first significant new material, often used in imitation of Gothic forms and destined to be developed as an individual architectural style in America. In the *Eiffel Tower* (1889) France set up a potent symbol of things to come.

A more significantly French develop-ment was in the use of reinforced concrete towards the end of the century, most notably by Auguste Perret whose 1903 apartment house at 25 rue Franklin, Paris 16e turns the concrete structure into a visible virtue and breaks with conventional façades. Changes in the patterns of work and travel were making the need for new urban planning very acute in cities like Paris. Perret and other modernists were all for high rise towers which would better the haphazard lay-outs in America by a rational integration

to new street systems. Some of their designs for gigantic skyscraper avenues and suburban rings look now like totali-tarian horror movie sets. But it was tradition not charity that blocked their projects at the time.

The greatest proponent of the super New York scale, who also had genuine, if mistaken, concern for how people lived, was **Le Corbusier**, the most famous 20C French architect. His stature may now appear diminished by the ascendency of a blander style in concrete boxing, as well as in the significant technical and social failures of his buildings and his total disregard for historic streets and monuments. But while his manifesto '*Vers une architecture moderne*' sounds like a call to arms for a new and revolu-tionary movement, Le Corbusier would be perhaps more fairly assessed as the original, inimitable and highly individual artist he undoubtedly was. You should try to see some of his work – there's the *Cité Radieuse* in Marseilles and plenty in Paris – to make your own mind up about the man largely responsible for changing the face and form of buildings throughout the world.

One respect in which Paris at the turn of the century lagged far behind London, Glasgow, Chicago and New York, was in **underground transport**. First proposed in the 1870s, it took twenty years of furious debate before the *Paris métro* was finally realised in 1900. The design of the entrances was as contro-versial as every other aspect of the system, but the first commission went to Hector Guimard, renowned for his vari-ations on the then current fashion in style. The whirling metal railings, Art Nouveau lettering and bizarre antennae like orange lamps were his creation. But conservatives were not amused when it came to sites such as the Opéra: Charles Garnier, architect of that edifice, demanded classical marble and bronze porticoes for every station, and his line was followed, on a less grandiose scale, wherever the métro steps surfaced by a major monument. Thus Guimard was out of a job. Some of the early ones remain (*Place des Abbesses* is one), as do some of the white tiled interiors, replaced after the Second World War in central stations by bright paint with matching seats and display cases.

Art Nouveau designs also found their way on to buildings – the early department stores in Paris are the best example – but the new materials and simple geometry of the modern or International Style, favoured the Art Deco look – again you're most likely to come across them in the capital.

Skipping the miserable cheap packaging of most 1950s and 1960s buildings everywhere, France again becomes one of the most exciting patrons of international architecture in **present times**. The *Centre Beaubourg*, by Renzo Piano and Richard Rogers, derided, adored and visited by millions, maximises space by putting on the outside the service elements usually concealed in walls and floors. The visible ducts, cables and pipes are painted following the colour code of architectural plans. You might think the whole thing is a professional joke. But it is one of the great contemporary buildings in western Europe – for its originality, popularity and fitness for its use.

In **housing**, new styles and forms are to be seen in city suburbs and holiday resorts, much of it disastrous and visually disgusting but interesting to look at when you don't have to live there. The latest state-funded projects confirm French seriousness about innovative design – in Paris, the pyramid in the Louvre and the *Porte de la Villette* complex. The latter also exemplifies a new move away from demolition to clever restoration, in this case 19C market halls. Throughout the country you'll see far older period streets, medieval and Renaissance, that look as if they've never been touched. More often than not, the restoration has been carried out by the *Maisons de Compagnonage*. These are the old crafts guilds who have maintained traditional building skills, handing them down still from master to apprentice (and never to women), as well as taking on new industrial skills.

Above all, though, bear in mind the extent and variety of architecture in France and don't feel intimidated by the established sights. If the empty grandeur of the Loire châteaux is oppressive, there are numerous smaller country houses open to the public and municipal buildings such as the *Hôtel de Ville*, that even in the smallest town has some charm or amusement to it. It is also possible in France to experience whole towns as consistent places of architecture, not only Carcassonne and Aigues Mortes, Dinan and Nancy, but villages off the main roads in which time seems to have stopped way back. And, besides, from any hotel bedroom, you can simply take your delight in what Le Corbusier called 'the magnificent play of forms seen in light' in the view of morning sunlight over ordinary provincial tiles and chimneys.

ROBIN SALMON

CONTEMPORARY ISSUES

In recent years the greatest political and public passions have been aroused over education, agricultural policy, decentralisation and changes in the constitution. Racism, sexism and nuclear weapons – the most fundamental aspects of French society and state – have not engaged the same debates and protests.

Racism: France and its immigrants

If nothing else cracks the image of France as a civilised nation, its treatment of immigrants should. Which is not to say that French racism is any worse than in neighbouring countries, notably Britain, but it's never had the same high profile. No token Arabs chair commissions, no music culture joins French youth, and the guardians of the intellect atone old war guilt by exclusive concern with anti-semitism.

A seemingly vast reservoir of racial hatred is tapped with ease by the main fascist party, the **Front National** (FN). According to some calculations a quarter of the Socialist voters in 1981 switched to Le Pen, the FN leader, for the European elections in 1985. Le Pen's record manifests very well the contradiction of nationalism in the country that first proclaimed *Liberté, Fraternité et Egalité*: he fought in the Resistance throughout the German occupation but later supported torture of Arabs in the Algerian war of independence.

French ideology still clings to the Napoleonic claim of the civilising mission – to bring up the world to the ideals of the 1789 Revolution. When the **colonised countries** demanded their own freedom, fraternity and equality, imperialist logic could not cope. You are French, parliament would scream at its overseas *députés*, you cannot be nationalist. But the **Algerians** fought their war and won. For this they are hated – and all other Arabs by association, more than any other race. Obscenities – 'they're a dirty people' the most classic – are commonplace, casual and pass unchallenged. White people will not live near Arabs, work with Arabs nor speak to Arabs and they do their best to 'protect' their daughters likewise with myths of rape and robbery. There's no question of whose side the law is on when racial abuse ends in a fight. In Marseille recently an Algerian kid was shot while having his papers checked

and the police officer got off with a slippery trigger. Another officer prosecuted for torturing an Arab teenager in custody did have to resign.

Assaults committed by individuals without a uniform are less discriminatory. The standard spraypaint message when a house, a synagogue or a black sports hall has been done over is 'Jews to the oven. Vive Le Pen. France for the French. A good Arab is a dead Arab'. **Jewish communities** have been the victims of horrendous attacks in recent years, many of them 'signed' by the FN. The older generation remembers only too well the assistance given by the Vichy government to the SS. Trust can be hard but aside from the current neo-fascist activities, practical discrimination rarely occurs except in the quirky higher echelons of business and state.

Black Africans are much less numerous than Arabs in France and being for the most part middle class and university educated, are held in less contempt. Those without such benefits, and lacking the support of a common community, are likely to suffer more than anyone in getting housing, social security and jobs. **Corsicans** get the treatment the British give the Irish; the **South East Asians** benefit from the racism that approves distance and separatism. As for the half million or so foreigners hired as domestic servants – often **Spanish** or **Portuguese** (the largest immigrant group) – their isolation in the toxic nexus of class and racial superiority puts them, perhaps, in the worst boat of all. While on the varying attitudes to different peoples, Anglo-French enmity deserves a mention. If you're white and **English** (Scots, Irish and Welsh doesn't apply) you may experience in France an inkling of what it's like to be discriminated against for your race.

Law and government policy have kept the **immigrant population** downtrodden ever since they were first encouraged to come as vital cheap labour for the post-war recovery. They were denied citizens' rights – no vote, no automatic permit renewal, forbidden to form their own organisations and threatened with deportation at the slightest provocation. Treated like scum by entry officials, foremen, French fellow workers, union and party reps, they were housed in hostels run by ex-colonial officers with curfews in force and visitors restricted. Later, when families were allowed to join the workers, shantytowns replaced hostels, then 'transit cities' and then council-run HLM estates which the French themselves would immediately move out of. Children born in France had their parents' nationality stamped on their passport. Many of them left school illiterate since no provision was made for language and culture problems.

In 1976 **Giscard** used the spectre of unemployment to ban all new work permits and offered derisory lump sums to immigrants to return home. Few French men or women would do the low paid filthy jobs thus vacated, but that was not the prime concern. Worries were being expressed about the dilution of French civilisation by 4 million foreigners.

Hope for change appeared with the **Socialist victory** of 1981. The manifesto even spoke of voting rights. An amnesty was granted to all illegal immigrants, the ban on organising was lifted, permits would be automatically renewed and no more information would be passed to intelligence services back home. Taking advantage of their new rights, years of grievance were confronted in strikes against racism in several car factories. The following year industrial action was against lay-offs and the racist selection of who was to go. The Communist union soon backed off. The CFDT fought a little longer then stepped down and Mitterrand started muttering about Shi'ites and Fundamentalists. Illegal immigrants were again hounded; reaction was back. As for the other parties, the **PCF** (Communist party) had harassed blacks in the twisted tactics of getting the votes of the French poor, while the **right**, losing votes to Le Pen, have desperately tried to out-trump FN policies. Law and order is persistently linked to immigration by the Opposition. And the **Gaullist** Chirac's latest promise is a ban on abortion to raise 'French' numbers in the face of the invading hordes from south of the Mediterranean.

Liberal organisations, with a humanist or Christian bias, have existed for years, doing their small bit for individual victims of discrimination. But the strongest **anti-racist** groups now are those formed by immigrant workers since 1981. On the national level, *SOS Racisme* (19 rue Martell, Paris 10e; 246.53.52) has recently been set up to raise public consciousness and combat racism wherever it occurs. Young and idealistic with no real political programme, it is at least doing something and showing that there is broad-based concern somewhere amongst the French population.

The Women's Movement

Does the French **Women's Movement** still exist? According to the media it died a silent death in 1982. There are no more Women's Day marches, no more major demonstrations, no direct action. Just over a decade since the first feminist meetings during *May 1968*, bookshops and cafés have started closing, publications reach their last number, girls leaving school deny problems with boys and talk of kids and marriage, and women won't be mobilised. Meanwhile Yvette Roudy, the minister for women's rights, doles out money and trots equal pay and opportunity laws through parliament, the Elysée palace invites 400 women for an official celebration of Women's Day; in law, education and work the sexes are equal; abortion is legal; rape gets long sentences; and women run businesses and read the television news.

The **MLF** (*Mouvement de Libération des Femmes*) is not, however, dead nor is France a paragon of parity. Feminists are still at work – running battered women's homes and rape crisis centres, campaigning in their unions or parties, gathering information in the first women's news agency, writing, making films and, as ever, theorising along divergent lines. Their movement may be fragmented but it's certainly not in pieces. And entrenched attitudes are still deadly, laws don't get applied, domestic relations stick to old forms and abortion is far from a free choice. If the MLF is currently in low profile, that has partly to do with the gear switching needed from the May 1968 decade to 1980s austerity, and partly to do with the Socialists in power. To enshrine change in laws is easy now – the doors to the ministry are always open. Meanwhile, 'outside the women's sphere' the Socialist government becomes steadily more reformist and then reactionary as the economy worsens. Cuts in public spending and presidential encouragement send women back to their homes and hungry husbands.

It was as late as 1944 that French women got the vote (and promptly filled more seats in the Assemblée Nationale than they've ever managed since). *Députés* or not, they were still inferior to their husbands or fathers in the eyes of the law. In 1949, dismissing all that had been written on feminism in the 19C as 'voluminous nonsense', **Simone de Beauvoir** published *The Second Sex* – the first modern analysis of women's oppression. But it was not until the 1960s that divorce and marriage laws changed and contraception became legal.

The contemporary **liberation movement** achieved its first public recognition in 1970 at the Arc de Triomphe in Paris when women laid a wreath to the wife of the Unknown Soldier. The following year the group *Féministes Révolutionnaires* organised over 300 prominent public signatures of women who had had abortions. The campaign for reform started and with the unified backing of left-wing feminists and mixed groups, abortion became legal in 1974. The inevitable differences between Communist and Socialist women on the one hand and radical feminists on the other was no more of a problem here than it was in any other country. But the convulsive intellectual culture of Paris spawned another women's group with the ponderous title of *Psychanalyse et Politique*, referred to as **Pysche et Po**. The leader of this elitist and well funded sect was hailed by initiates as the first coming of a new female being. The messianic Antoinette Fouque owed her contorted vision of anti-capitalist yet capitalist, female yet anti-feminist revolution to nothing masculine save the entire language and practice of her ex-psycho-analyst and famous theoretician Jacques Lacan. Without studying his writings the talk in *Psyche et Po* meetings was incomprehensible and women who managed to extricate themselves described the experience as akin to the subjugation and thought denial of far right religious groups. Outside the Paris intellectual milieu Antoinette and her acolytes might not have mattered but they were not just abstract theorists. Since 1972 *Psyche et Po* has been out to dominate the Women's Movement. While deriding all feminist practice they would appear at marches at the last moment with crackshot 'troops' in uniform (red jumpsuits on one 8 March) and fight to get their banners to the front. Their limitless funds never went to general campaigns. Instead the money found its way to lawyers for prosecution of non *Psyche et Po* bookshops, presses and individuals, and to the media for publicity campaigns propagating the group's exclusive claim to the movement. In 1979 they registered themselves as a limited company entitled *Mouvement de la Libération des Femmes* thus patenting the name MLF. Thereafter the entire mainstream of the movement from the *Féministes Révolutionnaires* to the Marxist *Lutte des Classes* were termed by the media the 'dissident MLF'. Yet they had been responsible for every progressive change in the position of women since 1968 while coping with their own considerable political differences and fighting off *Psyche et Po*. It is not surprising that exhaustion should have hit and the movement needs a breather before further battles.

In the **mid-1980s**, France still has a long way to go. Women's rights may be institutionalised but machismo has hardly been dented. Working-class women, who have always been approached from above by the feminists (whether Communist or Separatist) while organising their own strikes, factory occupations and other protests, are still trapped with all the cooking, cleaning and childcare even when they work full time. The educated, middle-class activists may have provided shelters from male violence but men and marriage have never been confronted to the extent they have in other countries. The appearance of women whether in public or on posters is male controlled. Without make-up, chic clothes and a recent hair-do, you cannot be taken seriously. Conforming to that and holding a position of power, male colleagues will still say you're too pretty for politics, business or whatever. The advertising image is whimpering and weak or suspendered and pouting, usually nude and always immaculate. And the manipulators of the trade say this honours feminine beauty. In 1983 **Yvette Roudy**, the women's rights minister, introduced a bill to outlaw degrading, discriminating and violence-inciting images of women. She foresaw little opposition since a similar anti-racist law had recently been passed. Outrage, hysteria and the amassed fury of male intellectuals, journalists and, of course, advertisers, slaughtered the bill before it could even be debated. And Yvette Roudy now finds her party isn't giving her a safe seat for the next elections.

Feminists should not have been surprised by the reaction to the bill. The problem is not complacency. The need for other urgent measures – like abolishing the restrictions on abortion – are recognised full well, as is the fact that the Pro-Life forces can outmobilise them with ease in the present climate. Chirac, the Gaullist leader, threatens to repeal the legislation altogether when he comes to power and that looks set to happen. But if or when the Socialists go, it seems likely that the Women's Movement will surge back into action, strengthened by the experience of a sympathetic but still sexist government.

The fledgling peace movement

They can't be drowned like unwanted puppies – François Mitterrand on nuclear weapons, 1969

Since **de Gaulle**, France has had its own independent nuclear deterrent, the **force de frappe** (striking force) or *force de dissuasion* as Giscard tactfully renamed it while preserving a potential first strike strategy. De Gaulle withdrew from NATO on the military level whilst remaining in the alliance, with the result that the US had to give up its French bases. So, for a start, the issue of foreign weapons placed on national soil does not arise in contrast to Britain and its NATO neighbours. **Independence** from American defence policy has always been a source of French pride, as too have the exclusively made-in-France weapon systems which have developed so happily hand in hand with the nuclear power programmes and the conventional arms trade in which France is the world leader after the US and USSR. No problem either with **testing grounds** – France has its own Pacific islands, and no qualms about dissuading, even killing, objectors such as Greenpeace.

Of the four main **political parties**, not one is committed, even on a scrap of paper, to dismantling the independent deterrent – they know it would be electoral suicide. There was a moment, in 1972 while the Right were ensconced in power like hereditary juntas, when the Socialist and Communist parties signed a joint manifesto for total disarmament and the dissolution of NATO and the Warsaw Pact. Admittedly Mitterrand removed the Communist clause to destroy existing stocks, thinking no doubt of how they would squeal. But, in any case, within five years both parties have done about-turns in their separate acrobatics.

So the Socialist – and left-wing – victory in **1981** held no illusions. Tests would continue, the neutron bomb would go ahead and a leading member of the Socialist party in power was heard to say that 'any self-respecting country must have nuclear weapons'. Perhaps in his view it was charitable to support the siting of Cruise and Pershing in countries who didn't have their own. Others argued with the loosest of logic that America musn't be vexed by noises against Euromissiles if socialist changes to France were to be made. And those who didn't agree kept quiet for the sake of party unity. So the line of the President – he whose awesome finger alone, without foreign consultation, can press the button – prevailed, and Reagan declared Mitterrand his favoured ally. The PCF opposed the US weapons of course – they don't like nukes unless they're French or Soviet. And the right-wing loves nukes like law and order. With such a **consensus** across the political spectrum, debate has hardly had a chance.

The **media** are silent. When the subject does come up, it is for the same knee-jerk response that de Gaulle fostered so effectively: the bomb makes us safe, the bomb saves our soldiers, the bomb belongs to us and the bomb keeps our world power status. In the first TV programme devoted solely to the issue (in 1985), the film star Yves Montand presented a mocked up film of a Soviet land invasion occupying Paris, and Resistance kids with skates and walkmans shot while leafleting the métro adding the modern touch. The question posed was not disarmament but European nukes versus NATO nukes and the response given the following morning to the righteously outraged Russian ambassador goes unrecorded. For most viewers the scenario was credible – that's the way invading armies always get to France. But films like *The War Game* or *The Day After* about nuclear blow-outs would never reach the screen – the horror has yet to grip the public imagination. Likewise the arguments for disarmament. On opinion polls the *force de frappe* gets majority backing for the grandeur it gives to the country, though very few 'would like it used'. The position of the church is more or less the same.

The greatest psychological block to developing a French peace consciousness is in the associations of the word 'pacifist'. It's a dirty word, conjuring up appeasers, collaborators and Communists. Ever since 1948 the peace movement that has existed has been inspired by the **PCF**. Huge rallies have been held and condemned by the Socialist and right-wing press for the taint of Czechoslovakia, Poland or Afghanistan. The complexities of the PCF position and their relation in and out of government with the Socialists have obliged the politics of peace to be so vague as to hardly exist. Another broader based campaigning group, the **Appel des Cents**, again initiated by the PCF, has forced the media to confess that it's not just a bunch of commies who are concerned. But the slogans have never got further than 'I love peace', and east block peace groups, SS20s and the *force de frappe* remain unnamed.

However, outside the political parties, in the cracks of this streamlined state, activist life does exist. The **Larzac movement** of pacifists and ecologists took their name from the plateau in the Massif Central, site of a major army base. Their campaign against an enlargement of the military grounds had the style and ideals of *May 1968*. Yet they won – Mitterrand cancelled the plans within his first year of office. And in 1982 Larzac joined other assorted left-wing, Christian and alternative groups, to set up an umbrella organisation for the non-aligned French peace movement. **CODENE** (*Comité pour le désarmement nucléaire en Europe*), the result, aimed to develop a political programme and provide the in-depth analyses lacking elsewhere. It has established links with the other European peace movements and in the eyes of the media it is now the French representative of peace, even though the two Communist backed organisations can always mobilise more people on the streets. CODENE's politics are similar to END's (European Nuclear Disarmament) but it cannot call for unilateral French disarmament until the public are better informed.

The tortuous old board game of party divisions, and media party links, makes unified action between the three main peace groups impossible. From the French point of view the alliances embraced by British CND are totally amazing. But in their separate ways the *Mouvement de la Paix*, the *Appel des Cents* and *CODENE* are getting through to people that nukes are not like Concorde or garlic. If the Socialists fall from power in 1986, numbers will hopefully build, with PS members liberated from the dominant party (and Mitterrand) line. The French peace movement has arrived, and, for the moment, doesn't look like going away. It will, however, be a while before the link that's been missing in European peace campaigns is in any real degree fixed.

The **addresses** are: **CODENE**, 23 rue Notre-Dame-de-la-Lorette, 75009 Paris. **Mouvement de la Paix**, 35 rue de Clichy, 45009 Paris. **Apel des Cents**, 67 rue de l'Aqueduc, 750101 Paris.

We are indebted for the information in this piece to the *END Journal* and in particular to its contributors Patricia Chilton and Jolyon Howorth.

BOOKS

Travel

Donald Horne *The Great Museum: the Representation of History* (Pluto, £5.50). Original, stimulating analysis of the role of tourism, how it reflects history and ideology, and how we're affected by it. Not the most obvious book to carry around France but if you take it you'll read it: for the comments on Romanesque architecture, Verdun and the battlefield sites, Revolutionary mementos . . . and 101 other insights.

Edwin Mullins *The Pilgrimage to Santiago* (1974, o/p). The main medieval pilgrim route to the shrine of St James (Santiago) began in Paris on the rue St-Jacques. Mullins retraces the *Chemin* in this book, details the bizarre pilgrim-industry that peaked in the 12C–15C, and points you to the churches along the way. Fascinating stuff, treating architecture (properly) as social history.

Freda White *Three Rivers of France* (Faber, £4.95), *West of the Rhone* (o/p), *Ways of Aquitaine* (o/p). Freda White spent a great deal of time in France in the 1950s – before tourism came along to the backwater communities that were her interest. These are all evocative books, slipping in the history and culture painlessly, if not always too accurately.

Rodney Gallop *A Book of the Basques* (1930, o/p). Still the classic study of Basque life, before the 20C destroyed its particularity, by an English clergyman who learnt Basque and adopted the country as his own.

Eric Newby *On the Shores of the Mediterranean* (Picador, £3.95). Not Newby's best, and not greatly about France, but with a short and wonderful chapter on dinner at the *Negresco* in Nice. Compulsive and vicarious pleasures.

Robert Louis Stevenson *Travels with a Donkey* (Dent, £2.95). Mile by mile account of Stevenson's twelve-day trek in the Haute Loire and Cévennes uplands with a donkey – Modestine – on heat. One of the more readable 'travel classics' on France, and a journey interestingly reworked by Robert Holmes (in *Granta 10: Travel Writing*, Penguin, £3.95, and his forthcoming book *In Stevenson's Footpaths*). Persistent devotees of Stevenson's footpaths – and

there are a surprising amount of both in France – might be interested in his first book, *Inland Voyage*, on the waterways of the north (included in the Dent edition of *Travels*) and *The Cévennes Journal* (Mainstream Press, £5.95).

Laurence Sterne *A Sentimental Journey Through France and Italy* (Penguin, £1.50). Part of Tristam Shandy – the first bit of intentionally mad British novel-writing – who despite the title never gets further south than Versailles.

Henry James *A Little Tour in France* (OUP, £3.30). **Tobias Smollett** *Travels through France and Italy* (OUP, £3.95). **Hilaire Belloc** *The Pyrenees* (o/p). **Stendhal** *Travels in the South of France* (Calder & Boyars). The big names. And not a lot more than that.

History

MIDDLE AGES (AND BEFORE)

Emmanuel Le Roy Ladurie *Montaillou* (Penguin, £4.95). Village gossip of who's sleeping with whom, tales of trips to Spain and details of work, all extracted by the Inquisition from Cathar peasants of the eastern Pyrenees in the 14C, and stored away till the last decade in the Vatican archives. Though academic and heavygoing in places, most of this book reads like an early novel.

Barbara Tuchman *Distant Mirror* (Penguin, £3.50). Tells the history of the 14C – plagues, wars, peasant uprisings and crusades – by following the life of a sympathetic French noblemen whose career takes him through England, Italy and Byzantium and finally ends in a Turkish prison.

J. W. Huizinga *The Waning of the Middle Ages* (Pelican, £3.95). Primarily a study of the culture of the Burgundian and French courts – but a masterpiece that goes far beyond this, building up meticulous detail to recreate the whole life and the mentality of the 14C and 15C.

Uderzo and Goscinny *Asterix and the Gauls* (Hodder Dargaud, 95p a comic). Take it as present day French attitudes to their history, or as accurate portrayal of the Roman conquest – either way it's great reading.

REVOLUTION

Christopher Hibbert *The French*

Revolution (Penguin, £4.95). Good concise popular history of the period and events.

Thomas Paine *The Rights of Man* (Penguin, £2.75). Written in 1791 in response to English conservatives' views on the situation in France, this reasoned and passionate tract expresses the ideas of both the American and French revolutions. It was immediately banned on publication, and its author charged with treason, but enough copies had crossed the Channel and been translated for Paine to be elected to the Convention by the people of Calais.

Gustav Flaubert *A Sentimental Education* (Penguin, £2.25). The novel that gives the best idea of what it was like to live in Paris through the 1848 revolution.

Karl Marx *Surveys from Exile* (Penguin, £3.95). *On the Paris Commune* (Lawrence & Wishart, U.S.). 'Survey's includes Marx's speeches and articles at the time of the 1848 revolution and after, including an analysis, riddled with jokes, of Napoleon III's rise to power. 'Paris Commune', more rousing prose, has a history of the commune by Engels.

Alfred Cobban *A History of Modern France* (3 vols: 1715–99, 1799–1871 and 1871–1962; Penguin, £2.25 to £2.75). Complete and very readable account of the main political, social and economic strands in French history from the death of Louis XIV to mid-de Gaulle.

19C AND 20C

Theodore Zeldin *France 1845–1945* (OUP, five vols, £5.95). Five thematic volumes on all matters French. All good reads.

David Thomson *Democracy in France since 1870* (OUP, o/p). An inquiry, sympathetic to the left, into why a country with such a strong socialist tradition should have had so many reactionary governments.

Alexander Worth *France 1940–55* (Beacon Press, Boston). Extremely good and emotionally engaged portrayal of the most taboo period in French history – the Occupation, followed by the Cold War and colonial struggle years in which the same political tensions and heart-searchings were at play.

Max Bloch *Strange Defeat* (Norton & Co, New York). Moving personal study of the reasons for France's defeat and subsequent caving-in to fascism. Found amongst the papers of this Sorbonne historian after his death at the hands of the Gestapo in 1942.

Society and politics

John Ardagh *France in the 1980s* (Penguin, £5.50). Comprehensive overview up to 1982 – covering food, film, education and holidays as well as politics and economics – from a social democrat and journalistic position. Very useful on details, lousy on feminism, and not a bad book to take to the seaside.

Theodore Zeldin *The French* (Fontana, £4.95). A coffee-table book without the pictures, based on the author's extensive conversations with an extremely wide variety of people about money, sex, phobias, parents and everything else.

D L Hanley, A P Kerr and N H Waites *Contemporary France* (Routledge & Kegan Paul, £6.95). Well written and accurate academic textbook if you want to fathom the practicalities of power in France – the constitution, parties, trade unions, new policies, etc. It also has an excellent opening chapter on the period since the war.

Simone de Beauvoir *The Second Sex* (Penguin, £4.50). One of the prime texts of western feminism, written in 1949, covering women's inferior status in history, literature, mythology, psychoanalysis, philosophy and everyday life. The style is dry and intellectual but the subject matter easily compensates.

Claire Duchen *Feminism in France: from May '68 to Mitterrand* (RKP, £6.95). Charts the evolution of the women's movement through to its present crisis (see p. 501), clarifying the divergent political stances and feminist theory which informs the various groups, and placing them in the wider French political context.

Jolyon Howorth *The Politics of Peace* (END/Merlin Press, £1.95). Short, to the point and utterly readable analysis of why the French peace movement is so behind its European neighbours.

Graham Greene *J'Accuse* (private edn, Nice). Greene's blistering attack on current corruptions in Nice, for which, he says, he now has to sleep with a gun under his pillow.

Roland Barthes *Mythologies* (Paladin, £2.50). Completely brilliant description of how the ideas, prejudices and contradictions of French thought and behaviour manifest themselves – in food, wine, cars, travel guides and other cultural offerings.

The New State of the World Atlas (Pluto, £6.96). One of the best reference books going, not just for France but for any country whose vital statistics you want to know: how much they pollute the earth; their wealth; their exploitation of women; their record on human rights; and just about every other depressing detail.

Art, architecture and photographs

Edward Lucie-Smith A Concise History of French Painting (Thames & Hudson, £5.95). If you're after an art reference book, this will do as well as any . . . though there are of course hundreds of other books on particular French art movements (Thames & Hudson do useful introductions to Impressionism, Expressionism, Symbolism, etc.) and individual painters.

John Berger Ways of Seeing (Penguin, £2.75). A book that can change the way you look at paintings without making you feel ignorant or insensitive to the art – much of it, here, French.

Anthony Blunt Art and Architecture in France, 1500–1700 (Penguin, £9.95). Incredibly tedious art history by the well-known, late, Establishment spy.

Kenneth John Conat Carolingian and Romanesque Architecture, 800–1200 (Penguin, £2.95). Good European study with concentration on Cluny and the Saint Jacques pilgrim route.

Norma Evenson Paris: A Century of Change, 1878–1978 (Yale, £0.00). The other end of the scale: a large illustrated volume which makes the development of urban planning and the fabric of Paris an enthralling subject – mainly because the author's ultimate concern is always with people not panoramas.

Jacques-Henri Lartigue Diary of a Century (Penguin, o/p). Book of pictures by a great photographer, from the day he was given a camera in 1901, through to the 1970s. Contains wonderful scenes of aristocratic leisure – on Normandy and Côte d'Azur beaches and racecourses – plus his own diary commentary.

Brassai Le Paris Secret des Années 30 (Gallimard, Paris). Extraordinary photos of the capital's nightlife in the 1930s – brothels, music halls, street cleaners, transvestites and the underworld – each one a work of art and a familiar world (now long since gone) to Brassai and his

mate Henry Miller who accompanied him on his night-time expeditions.

French fiction: A Top 20
CLASSICS
1. **Gustave Flaubert** Madame Bovary (Penguin, £1.95).
2. **Emile Zola** Germinal (Penguin, £2.95).
3. **Emile Zola** La Bête Humaine (Penguin, £2.50).
4. **Victor Hugo** Les Misérables (Penguin, £4.95).
5. **Marcel Proust** In Remembrance of Things Past (3 vols; Penguin, £6.96 each).
6. **Honoré de Balzac** Old Goriot (Penguin, £2.50).
7. **Honoré de Balzac** The Chouans (Penguin, £2.95).
8. **Alexandre Dumas** The Count of Monte Cristo (Bantam, £1.50).
9. **Lautreamont** Maldoror.
10. **Stendhal** Scarlet and Black (Penguin, £1.95).
MODERNS
1. **Jean Genet** Thief's Journal (Penguin, £3.50).
2. **Henri Michaux** Selected Writings (New Directions, US).
3. **Marguerite Yourcenar** Memoirs of Hadrian (Penguin, £2.75).
4. **Jean-Paul Sartre** Iron in the Soul (Penguin, £2.95).
5. **Simenon** Maigret at the Crossroads (Penguin Omnibus, £3.50).
6. **Simone de Beauvoir** The Mandarins (Flamingo, £3.95).
7. **André Gide** The Immoralist (Penguin, £1.95).
8. **Alain Robbe-Grillett.** The Eraser (Calder, o/p).
9. **Boris Vian** The Ants.
10. **Albert Camus** The Plague (Penguin, £1.95).

France in fiction

George Orwell Down and Out in Paris and London (Penguin, £1.95). Breadline living in the 1930s – Orwell at his best.

Anaïs Nin The Journals 1931–74 (7 vols, Quarter, £2.50–3.95 each), Journal of a Wife, 1923–27 (Peter Owen, £6.95). Not fiction, but a detailed literary narrative of French and US fiction makers from the first half of this century (not least in herself) in Paris and elsewhere. The more famous Erotica (Quarter, £2.95) was also, of course written in Paris – for Parisian porno connoiseurs. And if this is all you've read, get hold of *A Spy in the House of Love* (Penguin, £1.95), finest of her excellent novels.

Henry Miller *Quiet Days in Clichy* (o/p), *Tropic of Cancer* (Granada, £2.95), *Tropic of Capricorn* (Granada, £1.95). Nin's best Parisian mate, erratic, but with occasional flights of genius in describing 1930s, semen-stained Paris.

Lawrence Durrell *The Avignon Quintet: Monsieur, Livia, Constance, Sebastian, Quinx* (Faber, about £3.95 each). Miller's best mate, less prone to flights of genius but good on decaying grandeur in this evocation of the Nazi occupation of Avignon and surrounding countryside.

Jack Kerouac *Sartori in Paris* (Quartet, £2.50). . . . and in Brittany, too. Uniquely inconsequential Kerouac experiences. Recommended.

John Berger *Pig Earth* (Chatto, £3.95). Best of Berger's trilogy drawn from the French peasant village in which he lives.

Specific guides

Rob Hunter *Walking in France* (Hamlyn, £6.95), *Cycle Touring in France* (F Muller, £4.95). Good accounts of the regional walking and cycling possibilities – with useful addresses. Worthwhile acquisitions if you're looking for new places to go.

Kev Reynolds *Walks and Climbs in the Pyrenees* (Cicerone Press, £4.95); **Andrew Harper** *The Tour of Mont Blanc* (Cicerone Press, £4.95). Reliable and detailed route descriptions – for all levels

of difficulty except serious climbers. *Pyrenees West, Pyrenees East, Pyrenees Central* (West Col, £6.96–8.95). These are more serious guides than the Cicerone ventures – but good stuff if you're committed. They again cover both hiking and climbing.

Topo-Guides des Sentiers de Grande Randonnée (CNSGR, Paris). A series of route descriptions (in French, but not hard to follow) of all the major GR paths. Available in map shops in the UK.

George Veron *Haute Randonnée Pyrénées* (CAF, Paris). East to west description of the High Level route across the Pyrenees. Again in easy French.

W. Lippert *Fleurs des Montagnes, Alpages et Forêts* (Miniguide Nathan Tout Terrain). Best palm-sized, colour illustrated guide if you want something to pack away with your gear in the mountains.

Gai Guide (Gai Pied, Paris). Dependable listings of gay clubs, saunas, restaurants, music venues and pick-up spots throughout France. Lesbian addresses are included though the photos are all male erotica.

Gault et Millau: France (Gault et Millau, £9.95). Now appearing in English, this is *the* French run-down on food and restaurants, as serious as a religious tract and an annual enticement to avarice, greed and (if you haven't got the readies) theft.

ONWARDS FROM FRANCE

The choice of travel onwards from France is enormous, not just for the number of common borders but because Paris is a major junction for **continental train routes**. You could hop on the East-West Express at the Gare du Nord and stop in **Warsaw** or ride on to **Moscow**. Direct trains link Paris with all the East European capitals, as well as **Istanbul**, **Athens**, **Algeciras** on the southern tip of Spain and the Italian ports of **Naples** and **Brindisi**. And there are daily rail and boat connections with **London**, **Oslo** and **Stockholm**.

Visas can be obtained in Paris for all these destinations and for others where representation is rarer (or lacking) elsewhere: Madagascar, Benin, Central African Republic, Niger, Congo, Mauritania, Guinea, Equatorial Guinea, Djibouti and Comoros, all have their major **diplomatic offices** here. For **EEC members**, the only border that makes the most of its formalities is Switzerland, who are also keen on slapping supplements on trains passing through their territory. Travelling north, it's easy not to notice crossing the border into Belgium where the main practical difference is cheaper booze and petrol.

For cheap air travel Paris is no match for London or Athens. But since world flight patterns still reflect old empires you'll find regular flights to certain **central** and **west African countries**, to **Algeria** and **Morocco**, and to **Vietnam** and **south-east Asia**. Long distance 'internal flights' to current **colonies*** are available should you feel extravagant impulses to land on a Caribbean or Pacific island. But don't choose Mururoa – it's the French nuclear testing site, nor Nouvelle Calédonie (close to New Zealand), which may soon come off Air France lists if all goes well with the independence struggle.

*Guadeloupe and Martinique in the Caribbean, Réunion (Indian Ocean), St Pierre and Miquelon (off Newfoundland) and French Guiana (South America) are not officially colonies but extensions of the mainland. As *départements* they send *députés* to the Assemblée Nationale, have the same law, the same police forces and nothing like the same standard of living. The other islands, the Overseas Territories, are ruled by governors, and otherwise unrepresented.

More realistically, **Italy** and **Spain** are close at hand for hotter latitudes and less expensive Latin lifestyles. The updated *Rough Guide to Spain* should tell you all you need to know and various *Rough Guides* to Italian cities and regions are in the making.

For crossing the Mediterranean to **Tunisia** or **Morocco** – both again covered by *Rough Guides* – your best bet is to go via Naples or Algeciras. You can then make your way overland to **Algeria**. There are French ferries to Tangiers from Sète and to Algiers and Tunis from Marseilles but they're booked up years (literally) in advance. Marseilles also serves **Majorca**, **Sardinia** and **Corsica**.

In terms of holidays, and perhaps, at some future point, in terms of nationhood, **CORSICA** is a country in itself with a completely separate feel from the mainland. It's not therefore included in this guide but here are some details of the easily accessible, beautiful and notorious French island.

Arrival Ferries are expensive with a car though wheels are a great advantage on the island. On foot and specially out of season, prices are very reasonable. They run from Marseilles, Nice and Toulon to Bastia, the capital Ajaccio, Calvi, Ile Rousse and Propriano. You'll find SIs in all the 50 port towns though the main office for the whole island is in Ajaccio. Despite the French organisation, officialdom and prices, a difference in culture is very apparent and the staple food is not *cuisine française*.

Trains The SNCF network is pretty minimal, with rarely more than one train a day. One line connects Ajaccio and Bastia via the central Corte and Ponte-Leccia. The other runs from Ponte-Leccia to Ile Rousse and Calvi. A tramway serves the beaches between these two ports.

Buses and hitching are both difficult. An infrequent bus follows the coast around the island and another does the main cross route Ajaccio-Bastia. Cycling and walking in this mountainous terrain are ardous but that's what most people opt for.

Highlights The mountains, particularly the wild Castaguiccia region between

Ponte-Leccia and the eastern coast; from snowcaps to palm trees around the Golfe de Porto; Napoleon's home town – Ajaccio; and the fervently separatist town of Corte.

Sleeping Campsites won't be a problem but for rooms in July and August be prepared to hunt around.

Politics Corsica is *a département* of France, though the Socialist government have given it greater local powers with a new Regional Assembly. The main separatist and outlawed party is the FNLC (Front Nationale pour la Libération de Corse). You needn't fear their well publicised bombs – tourists are the last people they want to hit.

LANGUAGE

French is a far from easy language, despite the number of shared words with English but the bare essentials are not difficult and make all the difference. Even just saying 'Bonjour Madame/Monsieur' when you go in a shop and then pointing will usually get you a smile and helpful service. People working in hotels, restaurants, etc. almost always speak English and tend to use it even if you're trying in French – be grateful not insulted.

Differentiating words is the initial problem in **understanding spoken French** – it's very hard to get people to slow down. In the last resort of getting them to write it down you'll probably find you know half the words anyway. Regional accents may complicate things in the south and east but they're nowhere near as marked as in English.

Pronunciation

One easy rule to remember is that consonants at the ends of words are usually silent. *Pas plus tard* (not later), for example, is pronunced pa plu tarr. But when the following word begins with a vowel, you run the two together, thus: *pas après* (not after) becomes pazapre.

Vowels are the hardest sounds to get right. Roughly:

a	as in h**a**t
e	as in g**e**t
é	between g**e**t and g**a**te
è	between g**e**t and g**u**t
eu	like the u in h**u**rt
i	as in mach**i**ne
o	as in h**o**t
ô, au	as in **o**ver
ou	as in f**oo**d
u	as in a pursed-lip version of **u**se

More awkward are the combinations in/im, en/em, an/am, on/om, un/um at the ends of words or followed by consonants other than n or m. Again, roughly:

in/im	like the **an** in **an**xious
an/am, en/em	like the **don** in **Don**caster when said by a Brummie or someone with a nasal accent
on/om	like the **don** in **Don**caster said by someone with a heavy cold or thirty years of good port and cigars under the belt
un/um	like the **u** in understand

Consonants are much as in English, except that: ch is always sh, ç is s, h is silent, th is the same as t, ll is like the y in yes, w is v and r is growled.

Questions and requests

The simplest way of asking a question is to start with *s'il vous plaît* (please), then name the thing you want in an interrogative tone of voice. For example,

Where is there a bakery?	S'il vous plaît, la boulangerie?
Can you show me the road to Lyon?	S'il vous plaît, la route pour Lyon?

Similarly with requests:

We'd like a room for two.	S'il vous plaît, une chambre pour deux.
Can I have a kilo of oranges?	S'il vous plaît, un kilo d'oranges.

Question words

where	où
how	comment
how many/how much	combien
when	quand
why	pourquoi

at what time	à quelle heure
what is/which is	quel est

Some basic words and phrases

French nouns are divided into masculine and feminine. This causes difficulties with adjectives, whose endings have to change to suit the gender of the nouns they are attached to. If you know some grammar, you will know what to do. If not, stick to the masculine form, which is the simplest – it's what we have done in this glossary.

today	aujourd'hui
yesterday	hier
tomorrow	demain
in the morning	le matin
in the afternoon	l'après-midi
in the evening	le soir
now	maintenant
later	plus tard
at one o'clock	à une heure
at three o'clock	à trois heures
at ten-thirty	à dix heures et demie
at midday	à midi
man	un homme
woman	une femme
here	ici
there	là
this one	ceci
that one	celà
open	ouvert
closed	fermé
big	grand
small	petit
more	plus
less	moins
a little	un peu
a lot	beaucoup
cheap	bon marché
expensive	cher
good	bon
bad	mauvais
hot	chaud
cold	froid
with	avec
without	sans

Talking to people

When addressing people you always use *Monsieur* for a man, *Madame* for a woman, *Mademoiselle* for a girl. Plain *bonjour* by itself is not enough. This isn't as formal as it seems, and you'll find it has its uses when you've forgotten someone's name or want to attract someone's attention.

Excuse me, do you speak English?	Pardon, Madame. Vous parlez anglais?
How do you say it in French?	Comment ça se dit en français?
What's your name?	Comment vous appelez-vous?
My name is . . .	Je m'appelle . . .
I'm English/Irish/Scottish Welsh/American/Australian/ Canadian/Dutch/a New Zealander	Je suis anglais/irlandais/écossais/ gallois/américain/australien/ canadien/hollandais/néo-zélandais
yes	oui
no	non
I understand	Je comprends
I don't understand	Je ne comprends pas
Can you speak slower, please?	S'il vous plaît, parlez moins vite.

OK/agreed	d'accord
please	s'il vous plaît
thank you	merci
hello	bonjour
goodbye	au revoir
good morning/afternoon	bonjour
good evening	bonsoir
good night	bonne nuit
How are you?	Comment allez-vous?/ Ça va?
Fine, thanks	Très bien, merci
I don't know	Je ne sais pas
Let's go	Allons-y
See you tomorrow	À demain
See you soon	À bientôt
Sorry/Excuse me	Pardon, Monsieur/ Je m'excuse
Leave me alone (aggressive):	Fichez-moi la paix!
Please help me	Aidez-moi, s'il vous plaît

Accommodation

a room for one/two/three people	une chambre pour une/deux/trois personnes
a double bed	un lit double
a room with a shower	une chambre avec douche
a room with a bath	une chambre avec salle de bain
Can I see it?	Je peux la voir?
for one, two, three nights	pour une/deux/trois nuits
Can we camp here?	On peut camper ici?
campsite	un camping/terrain de camping
tent	une tente
tent space	un emplacement
hot water	eau chaude
cold water	eau froide
youth hostel	auberge de jeunesse
international membership card	la carte internationale

Finding the way

bus/car/train/taxi/ferry	autobus, bus, car/voiture/train/taxi/ferry
boat/plane	bâteau/avion
bus station	gare routière
bus stop	arrêt
railway station	gare
platform	quai
What time does it leave?	Il part à quelle heure?
What time does it arrive?	Il arrive à quelle heure?
hitch-hiking	autostop
on foot	à pied
how many km	combien de kilometres
how many hours	combien d'heures
Where are you going?	Vous allez où?
I'm going to . . .	Je vais à
I want to get off at . . .	Je voudrais descendre à . . .
the road to	la route pour
near	près/pas loin
far	loin
a ticket to	un billet pour
single ticket	aller simple
return ticket	aller retour
left	à gauche
right	à droite
straight on	tout droit

Other needs

bakery	boulangerie
food shop	alimentation
supermarket	supermarché
to eat	manger
to drink	boire
camping gas	camping gaz
tobacconist	tabac
Post Office	la Poste
stamps	timbres
chemist's	pharmacie
petrol station	poste d'essence
bank	banque
money	argent
toilet	toilettes
police	police
doctor	médecin
telephone	téléphone
hospital	hôpital

Numbers and days

1	un	21	vingt-et-un
2	deux	22	vingt-deux
3	trois	30	trente
4	quatre	40	quarante
5	cinq	50	cinquante
6	six	60	soixante
7	sept	70	soixante-dix
8	huit	75	soixante-quinze
9	neuf	80	quatre-vingts
10	dix	90	quatre-vingt-dix
11	onze	95	quatre-vingt-quinze
12	douze	100	cent
13	treize	101	cent-et-un
14	quatorze	200	deux cents
15	quinze	300	trois cents
16	seize	500	cinq cents
17	dix-sept	1,000	mille
18	dix-huit	2,000	deux milles
19	dix-neuf	1,000,000	un million
20	vingt		

1986	dix-neuf cent-quatre-vingt-six

Days of the week and dates

Sunday	dimanche
Monday	lundi
Tuesday	mardi
Wednesday	mercredi
Thursday	jeudi
Friday	vendredi
Saturday	samedi

September 1st	le premier septembre
March 2nd	le deux mars
July 14th	le quatorze juillet

There are any number of French **phrasebooks** around, most of them adequate: *French Travelmate* (Drew, £1.25) is particularly well put together and easy to refer to.

Among **dictionaries**, Harraps is the standard school dictionary, otherwise pick according to size and price. The *Dictionary of Modern Colloquial French* by Hérail and Lovatt (RKP) is a bit large to carry out, and expensive (£15.00), but it makes great reading – as much for the English expressions as the French. It's French to English only and includes the language of sex, crime, drugs – indeed all the words you ever wanted to understand.

INDEX

HELP US UPDATE
We've done our best to ensure that this, the first edition of **The Rough Guide to France**, is thoroughly up to date and accurate. However, things do change and if you feel we've missed something out, got something wrong, or that more should be said about a particular place, please let us know. We'll be revising the book before long and would find it useful to hear from other travellers. For the best letters we'll send a copy of the new edition, or any other Rough Guide you prefer. Write to us at Rough Guides, RKP, 14 Leicester Square, London WC2H 7PH.

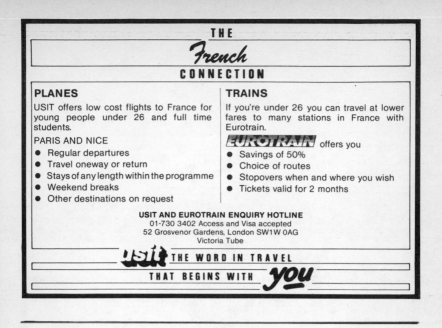

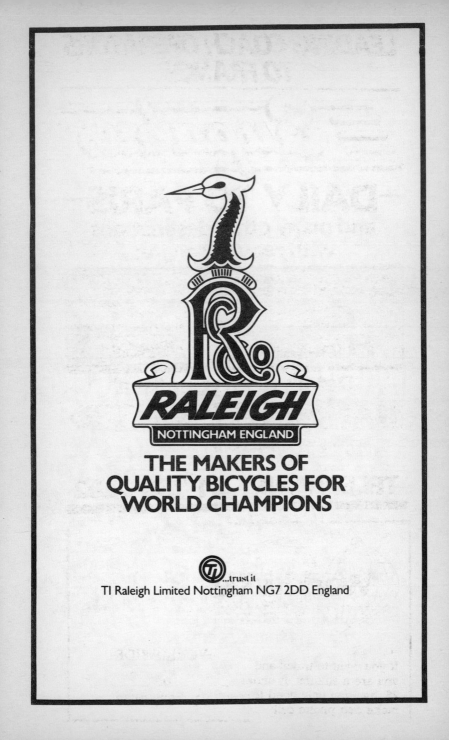

THE MAKERS OF QUALITY BICYCLES FOR WORLD CHAMPIONS